Windows® NT®/2000 Thin Client Solutions: Implementing Terminal Services and Citrix® MetaFrame™

Todd W. Mathers

New Riders

Windows® NT®/2000 Thin Client Solutions: Implementing Terminal Services and Citrix® MetaFrame™

By Todd W. Mathers

Published by:
New Riders
201 West 103rd Street
Indianapolis, IN 46290 USA

FIRST EDITION

International Standard Book Number: 1-57870-239-9

Printed in the United States of America 1 2 3 4 5 6 7 8 9 0

Library of Congress Cataloging-in-Publication Number: 00-100407

03 02 01 7 6 5 4 3 2

Interpretation of the printing code: The rightmost double-digit number is the year of the book's printing; the rightmost single-digit number is the number of the book's printing. For example, the printing code 00-1 shows that the first printing of the book occurred in 2000.

Composed in Sabon and MCPdigital by New Riders Publishing

Printed in the United States of America

Trademark Acknowledgments

Warning and Disclaimer

Publisher
David Dwyer

Executive Editor
Al Valvano

Product Marketing Manager
Stephanie Layton

Managing Editor
Gina Brown

Publicity Manager
Susan Nixon

Acquisitions Editors
Karen Wachs
Leah Williams

Development Editor
Robin Drake

Editors
Jake McFarland
Gayle Johnson

Indexer
Angie Bess

Manufacturing Coordinator
Christine Moos
Jim Conway

Book Designer
Louisa Klucznik

Cover Designer
Aren Howell

Composition
Amy Parker

Proofreader
Debbie Williams

Contents at a Glance

Contents

About the Author

Todd W. Mathers is a thin-client technology consultant and software developer who specializes in the planning and deployment of Microsoft Terminal Server and Citrix MetaFrame. An architect of Citrix implementations since 1996, Todd continues to be involved in enterprise-scale projects for major corporations throughout North America. He is also the founder of the Noisy River Software Corporation, which implements thin client solutions and develops software specifically for Terminal Server and MetaFrame. Todd holds an Honours Bachelor of Mathematics degree in computer science from the University of Waterloo.

Todd is also the author of the best-selling book, *Windows NT Thin Client Solutions: Implementing Terminal Server and Citrix MetaFrame* (MTP, 1998).

About the Technical Reviewers

These reviewers contributed their considerable practical, hands-on expertise to the entire development process for *Windows NT/2000 Thin Client Solutions*. As the book was being written, these dedicated professionals reviewed all the material for technical content, organization, and flow. Their feedback was critical to ensuring that *Windows NT/2000 Thin Client Solutions* fits our readers' need for the highest quality technical information.

John Blackman, MCSE, is a senior technical engineer for Wells Fargo & Co. and has been in the IT industry for more than 15 years. He holds an MCSE accreditation and has an extensive hardware and software background. John started out with the Air Force and moved to Wang Laboratories, where he supported mini-frame systems as well as Banyan Vines networks. He has been an independent consultant for Fortune 500 and small businesses in the Midwest. Currently, he is the lead architect for designing and deploying Terminal Server and MetaFrame to over 25,000 users spread over all 50 states. John lives in the Twin Cities area with his wife and four children; in his spare time (ha ha), he enjoys working on his Jeep and playing with his high-tech toys.

Mark Edwards, MCSE, CCA, is a computer consultant from Surrey, England, specializing in Windows NT implementations and support. He has implemented several large-scale Citrix MetaFrame solutions for global financial institutions. Mark holds a Bachelor of Engineering degree (Honours), MCSE certification, and is a Citrix Certified Administrator (CCA). He is 32, married, and considered by some to be devilishly handsome.

Sanjiv Raja has more than seven years of experience in the IT industry designing leading-edge Microsoft BackOffice, Citrix, Novell, and HP solutions. He started his career designing NetWare-based systems before moving to Microsoft NT and related BackOffice products, and has professional qualifications in Citrix, Novell, and Microsoft products. Sanjiv is currently on assignment designing an NT-based distributed infrastructure deploying Windows NT, Microsoft Exchange, Microsoft Terminal Server/MetaFrame, and HP systems management for a specialist finance company in England. In his spare time he enjoys golf, skiing, the gym, and good theatre.

Acknowledgments

Once again, I must extend an enormous "thank you" to everyone at MTP and New Riders Publishing for all of their incredible work. To the dynamic duo of Karen Wachs and Leah Williams, who time and time again exhibited superhuman patience: You both provided a wonderful mix of humor and professionalism that made this book a definite pleasure to work on. Of course, I still hear the words "work faster" every once in a while, but I'm sure that will eventually subside. To Robin Drake, Jake McFarland, and Gayle Johnson, who had to put up with my insatiable desire to continually add new material: Your attention to detail was invaluable. And finally, my thanks for the excellent work of technical editors John Blackman, Mark Edwards, and Sanjiv Raja, who provided outstanding insight, suggestions, and corrections.

I also want to acknowledge the assistance of Rick Dehlinger, who went out of his way to provide information and assistance regarding his experiences with MetaFrame. Thanks also to the hardware and software vendors who provided me with demos and assistance: Paul Machado from Hummingbird Communications; Tanice Lincoln from NetManage; Alan Frydman and Ruta Wells from NCD; Jeff McNaught, Roger Fortier, and Julie Rose from Wyse Technology; and a big thanks (as always) to Sandra Burns from NetIQ. I must also thank Richard Foote and Shawn Genoway, whose efforts in the first "Thin Client Solutions" helped pave the way for this book.

And to my friends and colleagues who wondered why their name wasn't in the first book and whether it would be in this one, here you go: Petra Bowman, Glen Byam, Gayle Gordon, Mark Gowanny, Linda Hechtl, Mike Manning, Peter McKenzie-Sanders, Bojan Mihajlovski, Mykel Millar, Marius Mocanu, Gord Mummary, J.P. Muscat, Nikolay Nedkov, Patricia Neilson, Dave Petruk (and his cottage of rejuvenation), Rodney Rock, Dawn Skinner, Rob Stewart, Martin Viellette, Steve Walker, Chris Walter, and Beata Ziecina.

And of course, thanks to my family, who once again had to deal with my rejection of any social interaction whatsoever. At least I won't be inside all summer.

Happy reading!

Todd W. Mathers

Tell Us What You Think

As the reader of this book, you are the most important critic and commentator. We value your opinion and want to know what we're doing right, what we could do better, what areas you'd like to see us publish in, and any other words of wisdom you're willing to pass our way.

As the Executive Editor for the Networking team at New Riders Publishing, I welcome your comments. You can fax, email, or write me directly to let me know what you did or didn't like about this book—as well as what we can do to make our books stronger.

Please note that I cannot help you with technical problems related to the topic of this book, and that due to the high volume of mail I receive, I might not be able to reply to every message.

When you write, please be sure to include this book's title and author as well as your name and phone or fax number. I will carefully review your comments and share them with the author and editors who worked on the book.

Fax: 317-581-4663
Email: nrfeedback@newriders.com
Mail: Al Valvano
         Executive Editor
         New Riders Publishing
         201 West 103rd Street
         Indianapolis, IN 46290 USA

Introduction

Welcome to "Windows NT/2000 Thin Client Solutions: Implementing Terminal Services and Citrix MetaFrame." This is a complete update of my first book, "Windows NT Thin Client Solutions," and now includes the latest information on both the Microsoft (Windows NT 4.0 and Windows 2000) and Citrix (MetaFrame 1.8) thin-client products. Please see the "What's New" section for more information on the new and changed material in this edition.

This book is intended to assist you in analyzing, testing, and implementing scalable thin-client solutions using Microsoft Windows 2000 Terminal Services or Windows NT Server 4.0–Terminal Server Edition and Citrix's MetaFrame extensions to these products. Whether you'll be deploying a single server for a small business or multiple server farms connected worldwide for a large corporation, this book provides information that will help to make your implementation a success.

With Terminal Services, the processing of one or more applications is moved completely off a user's desktop and onto a centralized server. Only screen, mouse, and keyboard information is passed between the client and the server. This allows a user running on almost any type of hardware to have access to the latest Windows 32-bit applications (as well as legacy 16-bit and DOS applications).

While the concept of multiuser access to an application is very straightforward, the implementation of Terminal Services brings with it a whole new set of requirements that can easily trip up the unwary Windows veteran. This book provides you with a clear understanding of what thin-client computing is and valuable information on avoiding many of the common traps encountered during a Terminal Services implementation.

The thin-client market has continued to gain tremendous support since Microsoft's initial release of Terminal Server in 1998. More and more companies are looking at how thin-client computing can be used to help them meet their business requirements—not only in the corporate environment but also in the emerging market of application service providers, many of which are using Terminal Services to provide their customers with access to specific applications (such as Microsoft Office) via the Internet.

I'm confident that you'll find this book to be an invaluable resource in helping you to deliver robust, scalable, and stable thin-client solutions.

> **Tip**
>
> *For the latest information regarding this book, including additional tips, comments, and examples, be sure to visit our Web site at* `http://www. newriders.com/1578702399`.

What's New?

The following list provides a summary of some of the new and updated material in this edition:

- Complete coverage of installing, configuring, and supporting a Windows 2000 Terminal Services environment.
- Updated information on tuning and configuring NT 4.0 Terminal Servers.
- The latest Citrix MetaFrame 1.8 information, including Citrix Server Farms, Program Neighborhood, and NFuse.
- Completely updated and expanded application integration information.
- Expanded information on planning and implementing Terminal Server. Detailed discussion on server, network and client planning including server sizing information and availability considerations.
- Updated information of how to access applications available on a Terminal Server via the Internet using Citrix's MetaFrame.

The Contents

This book is divided into three parts. Part I begins by looking at the benefits of thin-client technology, and goes on to describe in detail the main features and functionality available in both versions of Terminal Server and MetaFrame. Part II covers the planning considerations of a Terminal Services implementation, including network, client and server requirements.

Part III provides a detailed look at how to implement and support Terminal Services and MetaFrame. Some of the areas covered include server performance tuning, standardizing client configurations, user management, Internet access, and application installation.

Part I: An Overview of Terminal Services and MetaFrame

Chapter 1, "Going Thin with Terminal Server," introduces you to the key benefits of thin client technology and how they apply to Terminal Server and MetaFrame. Areas such as centralized manageability, improved scalability, and a reduction of the total cost of ownership in an organization are discussed.

Chapter 2, "Microsoft Windows Terminal Server" provides detailed information on the functionality and features of both NT 4.0 and Windows 2000 Terminal Server. Terminal Server client options are also discussed in this chapter.

Chapter 3, "Citrix MetaFrame," focuses on the MetaFrame extensions to Terminal Server and the enhanced functionality that they provide. I begin by looking at the foundation of MetaFrame, the Independent Computing Architecture (ICA) protocol from Citrix, and the added functionality that it provides to Terminal Server.

Part II: Planning a Terminal Server Implementation

Chapter 4, "Project Management Considerations," provides the project manager of a Terminal Server implementation with an introduction to many of the important tasks that need to be managed before and during the early stages of the project, including implementation requirements, business process management, and policies and procedures.

Chapter 5, "Network Planning," examines the importance of the network in your Terminal Server implementation. The RDP and ICA protocols are examined along with some sample utilization results. Printing considerations as well as Internet and dial-up access are also discussed.

Chapter 6, "Client Planning," looks at the importance of proper client planning for a successful Terminal Server project. The various supported RDP and ICA clients are examined in different deployment scenarios.

Chapter 7, "Server Hardware Planning," discusses the two main considerations when planning the hardware requirements of a Terminal Server environment—the capacity-planning requirements and the appropriate hardware sizing to meet those requirements.

Chapter 8, "Server Management Planning," examines the importance of developing a sound technical management plan in order to maximize the scalability and stability of your Terminal Server environment.

Chapter 9, "Software Planning," looks at strategies for categorizing and planning the deployment of the desired software onto Terminal Server.

Part III: Implementing Terminal Server and MetaFrame

Chapter 10, "Terminal Server Installation," details the steps involved in the installation of both Windows NT 4.0 Terminal Server Edition and Windows 2000 Terminal Services.

Chapter 11, "MetaFrame Installation," details the steps involved in the installation of Citrix MetaFrame 1.8 onto a TSE 4.0 or TS 2000 server.

Chapter 12, "Terminal Server Configuration and Tuning," provides a detailed walkthrough of configuring and tuning your Terminal Server for optimal operation. Performance, stability, and security considerations are all discussed, as well as features such as ICA browser tuning and server cloning techniques.

Chapter 13, "RDP Client Installation and Configuration," looks at the steps for installation of the RDP client, and provides more detailed examples of how you would configure the client in each of the implementation categories discussed in Chapter 6.

Chapter 14, "ICA Client Installation and Configuration," looks at the installation steps required for the Citrix ICA client. Configuration details on features such as Program Neighborhood and custom installations are also examined.

Chapter 15, "Web Computing with MetaFrame," discusses the process of Web-enabling an application using the robust toolset available as part of MetaFrame, including their new NFuse product.

Chapter 16, "Group and System Policy Configuration," examines the use of the policy features available in Windows 2000 and NT 4.0 to establish a more controlled and consistent Terminal Server environment. The use of the Windows 2000 Group Policy component of Active Directory as well as NT 4.0 Policy Editor are reviewed in detail.

Chapter 17, "User Profile and Account Configuration," provides information on the role of the user profile in a Terminal Server environment and how to create and manage the profiles in your environment.

Chapter 18, "Server Operations and Support," looks at the shift in responsibility from implementation to operations and the tools that can be used to ensure the availability of the production environment to the end user. Server and user session management are discussed, and I provide examples of some of the available health monitoring tools, both commercial and those included with Terminal Server.

Chapter 19, "Application Integration," provides a detailed discussion of the special application-support features available in Terminal Server, the tools and techniques that will assist you, the process that I typically follow when installing an application, and finally a step-by-step walkthrough of how to install and configure some of the most common applications on Terminal Server.

Part IV: Appendixes

Appendix A, "Terminal Server/MetaFrame Command Reference," contains a complete list and explanation of the new commands available with Terminal Server and MetaFrame.

Appendix B, "Network Primer," provides an introduction to basic computer networking theory and practice.

Appendix C, "File and Folder Security Primer," looks at Windows NTFS security, including the new features available in NTFS 5, which ships with Windows 2000.

Appendix D, "Terminal Server System and Application Volume Security Permissions" provides suggested file security settings for a Terminal Server, including CACLS scripts for both TSE 4.0 and TS 2000.

Appendix E, "Registry Security Primer," looks at the security of the Windows registry, including the available security attributes and the privileges they grant.

Appendix F, "Terminal Server Registry Security Permissions," provides suggested security modifications to the Windows registry that you can implement to improve the security of your Terminal Server.

Conventions Used in this Book

The following conventions are used in this book:

Tip

Tips provide helpful ways of completing a task. ◆

Troubleshooting Tip

Troubleshooting tips resolve problems you may encounter during deployment. ◆

Warning

Warnings provide information you need to know to avoid damage to data, hardware, or software, and to avoid error messages that tell you that you're unable to complete a task. ◆

Author's Note

These areas relate personal experiences I've encountered that give you a real-life understanding of a topic. ◆

Convention	Usage
italic	New terms being defined.
boldface	Text that you are instructed to type, such as a domain name.
`monospace text`	Commands, syntax lines, and so on, as well as Internet addresses such as `www.microsoft.com`.
[	]	Optional elements in syntax lines, such as [drive	directory] in `aclset` [drive	directory]. The vertical bar or pipe (|) separates literal elements, of which you can use either element (but not both) in the command. In this example, the command would be `aclset` (with no parameters), `aclset drive`, or `aclset directory`.
➥	Code-continuation characters are inserted into code when a line shouldn't be broken, but we simply ran out of room on the page.

Naming Conventions

Throughout this book I use the following naming conventions when discussing the Microsoft or Citrix products:

- *Terminal Server* or *Terminal Services* refers to both Windows 2000 Terminal Services and Windows NT 4.0 Terminal Server Edition unless otherwise stated.
- *TSE 4.0* refers to Windows NT 4.0 Terminal Server Edition.
- *TS 2000* refers to Windows 2000 Terminal Services.
- *MF 1.8* refers to MetaFrame 1.8.

General Conventions

Occasionally in the book, I refer to mouse usage: clicking, double-clicking, right-clicking, and so on. Of course, pointing devices other than mice are available, and Terminal Server addresses those as well. Assume that the use of *mouse* is generic for mice, trackballs, and so on, and adjust according to the specific pointing device in use. The same principle applies to the use of "keyboard"; if you use some other type of input device, please make appropriate mental adjustments to refer to your device when reading keyboard instructions.

Warning

Throughout the book I make suggestions regarding changes that can be made in the registry of a Terminal Server. If used incorrectly, this tool can cause system-wide problems that may require you to reinstall Terminal Server. Please exercise caution whenever making changes to the registry. ◆

Part I

An Overview of Terminal Server and MetaFrame

Going Thin with Terminal Server

In this chapter:

- **The Total Cost of Ownership**
  The idea of reducing the Total Cost of Ownership (TCO) is a simple one: Maximize the company's return on investment in technology while minimizing the cost involved in doing so. Terminal Server provides the ability to reduce the TCO of supporting users and their local workstations.

- **Implementation Flexibility**
  Moving the application processing completely off the user's desktop provides much greater flexibility in the implementation process than you would have with a standard desktop deployment.

- **Reusing Existing Technology**
  Although a business may be interested in standardizing on the latest Windows-based applications, the heterogeneous computing environment of most companies doesn't allow for this change without replacing or upgrading the existing hardware. Terminal Server and MetaFrame provide the mechanism to deliver these new applications while at the same time extending the life of existing desktop hardware.

- **Centralized System Management**
  Terminal Server centralizes the management of three components that traditionally exist on the user's desktop: application support and maintenance, maintenance of the operating system, and storage management.

- **Scalability**
  An important requirement for implementing Terminal Server and MetaFrame is the ability to scale to meet the changing needs of a business.

- **Enhancing Security**
  In addition to the standard Windows NT/2000 Security, Terminal
  Server includes features that enable you to establish a secure environ-
  ment in which your user will operate.

The Total Cost of Ownership

Whenever someone mentions the words "thin client," he or she usually follows it with a discussion of how it can do things such as reduce the cost of
end-user support, improve administrative controls for information technology (IT) managers, and provide a means of true rapid application deployment. All these benefits fall collectively under what is termed *Total Cost of
Ownership (TCO)*. The idea of TCO is simple: Maximize the company's
return on investment (ROI) in technology while minimizing the cost
involved in doing so. The costs you're attempting to minimize can be broken down into two categories: hard costs and soft costs. *Hard costs* include
all capital costs, such as hardware or software, and are usually easily quan-
tifiable. *Soft costs* are most often associated with support issues at the
end-user's desktop, but can also include server-side support as it pertains to
the user. Recovering accidentally deleted data is a common example. In
most situations the majority of the soft costs are incurred at the end-user's
desktop. The soft costs are usually much more difficult to measure before-
hand and are very often based on historical data.

Hard Costs

Calculating the hard costs for a project is usually fairly straightforward.
You determine the hardware and software required and then total their
cost. The total amount of hard cost savings in a Terminal Server implementation will vary depending on the type and scope of the project and what
other implementation options are available.

Because Terminal Server and MetaFrame allow both Windows and non-
Windows systems (UNIX, Macintosh, Java) to access the latest 32-bit software (as well as many older 16-bit and DOS applications), under most
circumstances they can reduce or eliminate the need to purchase new client
hardware. This can result in a reduction in the hard costs associated with
the project and hence lower the TCO. Unfortunately, this leads many people
to believe that TCO is related *only* to the hard costs. This is *not* the correct
way to evaluate the total cost of ownership.

Consider this example. Company C has 200 employees, 125 of whom have Pentium systems running Windows 95, while the other 75 have Pentium II systems running Windows NT Workstation 4.0. Company C wants to upgrade all employees to run Windows 2000 Professional, Office 2000, and a new 32-bit application being developed. In addition to this, the users need to be able to continue using any other business-related applications that they're using today. The company is trying to decide on one of two options:

- Update all Pentium computers to support Windows 2000 Professional.
- Provide access from the existing desktops to this new environment using Windows 2000 Terminal Services.

Assuming that the desktop computers cost $1,500 each to replace, Company C is looking at over $185,000 just in hardware to upgrade the 125 Pentium workstations.

On the other hand, out of the 200 employees, the maximum number of concurrent users at any one time is only 100. Based on this fact, Company C determines that they could purchase two servers at approximately $25,000 per server, each of which would be able to support approximately 125 users. These two servers would be used to provide load balancing and completely support the environment if one failed.

Author's Note

Chapter 7, "Server Hardware Planning," talks about hardware considerations for Terminal Server. ◆

Based on the hardware costs alone, the traditional desktop upgrade would cost $135,000 *more* than the Terminal Server solution.

Now consider this slightly different example. Once again we look at Company C, but this time all the computers are already capable of running Windows 2000 Professional, so no hardware upgrades are required. In this scenario, the Terminal Server implementation would incur an additional $50,000 in hardware costs.

When looking at these two examples, you might be tempted to say that Terminal Server is appropriate in the first scenario, but not the second. Unfortunately, hard costs are very rarely the only factor that can be taken into consideration when making this decision. You also need to consider these factors:

- How frequently will the custom and packaged applications require updating? Will this need to be done manually, or is there some automated way of ensuring that everyone has the correct versions? Customized applications can be particularly troublesome because changes are usually directly related to changes in the business, and must be available to everyone at the same time.

- Are the users located geographically close to each other, or are they distributed over a wide area? If the users are spread out, both the initial implementation and future support can be difficult, particularly with the introduction of a new operating system and/or application.

- What other applications do the users run that may cause issues with support or deployment?

These are just a few examples of what are known as soft costs, and these very often have a much greater and longer-lasting impact on TCO.

Soft Costs

Although hard costs may or may not provide an initial reduction in TCO, the long-term and more permanent savings come from the reduction in the overall support costs for the environment. Soft costs are so named because they don't provide a definitive way of being calculated. This doesn't mean that they can't be calculated, but the costs aren't as clear cut as hard costs.

Soft costs fall into three general categories:

- **Hardware maintenance.** The costs of servicing the user's local hardware, including computer upgrades, monitor servicing, and so on.

- **Application support.** The costs associated directly with the applications that a user will run. This mainly has to do with application installations and upgrades.

- **End-user support.** The costs associated with supporting the user. Providing assistance in using an application, configuring printers, scanning and removing viruses, and fixing desktop configurations that have been changed by the user are only a few examples.

Hardware Maintenance Support Costs

When Terminal Server is used to provide users with a complete desktop replacement, it provides definite savings on hardware maintenance by allowing a user's desktop computer to be treated as a "disposable" unit. (*Disposable* in this sense means that the user maintains no local applications or data and the computer can be physically swapped for a different computer with no loss of productivity.)

Author's Note

The term desktop replacement describes the situation where a user's entire computing environment is run off of the Terminal Server. See Chapter 6, "Client Planning," for a detailed explanation of this setup. ◆

Terminal Server can provide savings in hardware maintenance costs by reducing the user's downtime while waiting for a PC to be repaired. A technician can simply bring a replacement PC, swap it for the faulty one, and take away the faulty machine for analysis and repair without further affecting the user's ability to work. Because no applications or data are maintained locally, the user is in no way tied to a specific machine.

In fact, if vacant workstations are available, the user with the troublesome machine isn't even required to wait for the technician before continuing his or her work. The user simply moves to another workstation, logs back on to Terminal Server (in the process receiving the same desktop configuration as always), and continues working. Even if the substitute workstation has completely different software applications, as long as the Terminal Server client is available the user can use the computer.

This consistent desktop is provided using the same roaming profile technique that has been available with Windows NT for quite some time. The computer desktop is no longer tied to the physical workstation. No matter where the user logs on to Terminal Server, he or she receives his or her standard profile information, with access to all the required applications.

Author's Note

Although NT and 2000 today provide the capacity to use roaming profiles, the biggest problem has always been that even though the desktop remains consistent, there's no guarantee that the necessary applications will be available at the substitute computer. Unless the company also imposes a complete standardization on the applications, including exactly where they're installed, there's no guarantee that by moving to another workstation, the user will actually be able to access the applications displayed on his or her desktop.

continues ▶

▶ *continued*

Terminal Server provides the missing component that adds true value to the roaming profile. By ensuring that the user is logging onto a consistent environment (both the visual desktop and the application configuration), regardless of where he or she is physically located, the user is ensured of having access to all the applications on his or her Terminal Server desktop. ◆

Application Support Cost Savings

The centralized management of Terminal Server allows for much greater control over the installation, testing, deployment, and support of applications in production. The cost savings for application support are broken down into the following areas:

- **Application deployment.** The costs of application deployment can be greatly reduced when applications are made available to users via Terminal Server. An application can be made available to your production users in a fraction of the time a traditional desktop deployment would take. Application fixes and updates can also be deployed more quickly when required. Chapter 9 "Software Planning," discusses the change management steps involved in testing and deploying applications into a Terminal Server environment.

- **Application support.** In the desktop environment, there was always the need to either reinstall or reconfigure an application on a user's desktop that had either been installed incorrectly or modified by the end user. Both scenarios are virtually eliminated with Terminal Server, as all users on a Terminal Server run the same version of the application, and (when configured properly) no users have the ability to modify its configuration.

Author's Note

In all of the properly configured installations of Terminal Server that I have worked with, a typical application can be tested and deployed into production within one or two weeks, depending on whether it's a new application or an upgrade. This timeframe includes piloting the application with a test user group to ensure that everything is working properly. When the application works for a few users, it will work for all users. In one case, an application was updated once a month for 2,000 users. One person did the actual software deployment, and it took her a total of 15 minutes to complete. ◆

End-User Support Cost Savings

Terminal Server can substantially reduce the end-user support costs both directly and indirectly. By moving the application software off the user's desktop and onto the Terminal Server, where it's installed and configured, you reduce the requirement for a support person to visit a user's desktop. As mentioned previously, because the software is configured the same way for all users, you no longer have intermittent problems with an improperly configured application for a few users, which a support technician must troubleshoot and resolve.

The biggest "problem" is that the latest Windows operating systems have empowered users with added features, functionality, and ease of use. Although these features make Windows easier to use, they also make it easier for users to modify the configuration of an application or the system itself—something that makes any support person uneasy. There's a very good chance that, in modifying this configuration, a user will render the application or system inoperable. One of the key goals in reducing end-user support costs is to minimize the number of inexperienced users making these types of modifications. With the applications safely installed on a Terminal Server, where they're protected from user modifications by system security, the ability of the user to modify these applications is virtually eliminated.

What the user is left with is a streamlined local desktop, with only the minimum number of components to support. In the ideal scenario, the end user has only a Windows-based terminal, with no components that are configurable by the user. Chapter 6 looks at the various client devices available for use with Terminal Server.

Author's Note

Microsoft has recognized the problems that can result from users having too much access to their desktops and has created a foundation of procedures that spell out how users' workstations can be locked down to prevent them from altering a functional environment. These procedures are collectively known as Microsoft Zero Administration for Windows (ZAW). ZAW works most effectively with Windows NT and 2000 Professional because the integrated security in these products allows for the following items to be implemented:

- *User policies that hide components of the desktop and prevent certain actions from being performed.*

- *File-level security that can be used to control what access a user has to specific files. This can be used to grant a user access to only designated portions of the local hard drive, preventing the user from modifying or deleting system files.*

continues ▶

▶ *continued*

Neither Windows 95 nor 98 has been developed as a secure operating system; as a result, they can't be locked down as tightly.

The biggest drawback to ZAW is that it still must be delivered and managed at the local desktop. If you have 2,000 PCs in an organization, coordinating and managing the control at each desktop can be an enormous task. Microsoft provides the Change and Configuration Management tool with Windows 2000 to ease the implementation of ZAW, but this tool supports only Windows 2000 Professional desktops.

After you have ZAW in place, applications still need to be deployed to the user's desktop and then tracked and updated when required—a nontrivial task in an organization with users spread out around the city, the country, or even the world. Various systems, such as Microsoft Systems Management Server (SMS), can be implemented to make this task easier, but all such tools introduce additional management complexity themselves and most require some user education to ensure that the process functions properly. Changes can be issued from the management system, but updates are neither instantaneous nor guaranteed.

Microsoft has developed a Zero Administration Kit (ZAK) for TSE 4.0 that's available from the Microsoft Web site. ◆

A valuable support tool available with Windows 2000 Terminal Services or MetaFrame is the ability to *shadow* (remotely control) another user's session. Shadowing allows someone to establish a connection with a user's Terminal Server session, seeing exactly what that user is seeing and being able to manipulate the mouse and keyboard for that session as if he or she were sitting at that user's desk. This is a powerful tool that can greatly reduce the support costs for the end user. While remote control options exist today for standard desktop support (such as Microsoft SMS), because Terminal Server already provides high-speed transfer of the screen information from the client to the server, shadowing another user's session results in performance as fast as if the person was logged on locally. Shadowing provides a reliable and stable way of supporting remote users.

When a user calls in with a problem, the support technician can immediately connect and see what the user sees, and either resolve the problem or escalate to a Terminal Server administrator. A visit to the desktop is no longer required to assist the user. The technician can also demonstrate the problem resolution to the user, helping to educate him or her and reduce the chances of a repeat call. By helping to resolve a user's problems more quickly, you're helping to increase his or her productivity. This also allows you to provide support from anywhere that you can connect to your Terminal Server environment.

Windows NT Server 4.0, Terminal Server Edition

To have shadowing with Windows NT Server 4.0, Terminal Server Edition, you need the Citrix MetaFrame product. ✦

Implementation Flexibility

Moving the application processing completely off the user's desktop provides much greater flexibility than a standard desktop deployment in the implementation process. With Terminal Server, you can effectively divide the implementation into two phases: the server configuration and testing phase, and the desktop configuration phase. The two phases can be developed independently of each other and only need to be brought together in the final stages of the project. This allows you to build and test the server without affecting how the user currently works. In many cases this extends even to the piloting phase, where you can provide the user with the ability to work in the Terminal Server environment, but return to working on the local desktop if issues arise with Terminal Server.

Author's Note

A company was looking to implement Terminal Server to deliver Microsoft Office plus three custom applications to their call center. The call center was currently running these applications locally on Pentium-class computers with Windows NT 4.0 Workstation. Slow desktop performance plus their desire to move to Office 2000 in the future was the driving factor for moving to Terminal Server. The plan was to reinstall NT Workstation on each client with no local applications, and then have them access Terminal Server through the Terminal Server client. The company didn't want to replace the desktops until they were sure that users could work properly within the new environment.

After the servers had been built and tested, the company provided users with the Terminal Server client on their existing desktops and allowed them to run against these Terminal Servers prior to rebuilding their desktops. This way, they could validate that everything was working properly before rebuilding the PC. If the user had any issues with the Terminal Server, he or she simply logged out and returned to working on the local desktop until the problem was resolved. ✦

Reusing Existing Technology

The reason that most upgrades are required at the desktop is to accommodate new software or operating system requirements. Implementing Terminal Server can eliminate these requirements and greatly extend the life of a company's existing desktop hardware, in some cases eliminating the need to upgrade or replace until the computer physically breaks down.

The ability to reuse the existing client hardware not only introduces a cost reduction, but more importantly eliminates the need to individually upgrade and configure the workstations. Local ports on client hardware can still be accessed through the client session, allowing the continued use of client peripherals. Although Terminal Server alone can support local printers through COM, USB, and LPT ports, MetaFrame is required to access local client drives or other serial devices connected to a client's local COM port. With Terminal Server, only a simple client installation is required for an existing desktop. This greatly reduces the risk of a client having a new desktop that doesn't function properly (or at all). This reduced risk on the desktop is very important to many companies, especially in departments such as call centers, where an employee who is unable to work has a direct impact on the business or its customers.

The reuse of existing hardware isn't limited to Windows-based computers. With the MetaFrame extensions to Terminal Server, the available client list is increased to include clients such as DOS, Windows 3.1, UNIX (including Linux), Macintosh, OS/2, and Java.

Author's Note

Terminal Server alone provides access only to clients running Windows for Workgroups 3.11, Windows 95/98, Windows NT (3.51, 4.0), Windows 2000, or Windows CE-based terminals and handheld devices. A non–Microsoft RDP Java client (JDK 1.1) does exist from a company called HOB Electronics. For more information and a downloadable client for testing, go to `http://www.hob.de/www_us.` ✦

Centralized System Management

Implementing Terminal Server centralizes the management of three components that traditionally require support at the user's desktop:

- **Application support and maintenance.** As mentioned in the earlier section "Soft Costs," application installations and upgrades are performed only on the Terminal Server and not on client desktops. Corporate-wide deployments can now happen in minutes instead of days or weeks. Application testing also has more validity in a Terminal Server environment, because the testing environment can be configured identically to the production environment. When done in this fashion, piloting results will much more accurately represent the entire community of users who will run that application.

- **Maintenance of the operating system.** As long as the client is running an operating system for which a Terminal Server/MetaFrame client exists, little is required in the way of support for that client OS. Operating system upgrades are centralized to the servers themselves, and when upgraded will automatically be available to all users.

- **Storage management.** The second most common problem with a client computer after insufficient processor speed is usually disk capacity. With the increased power and functionality of applications also come increased disk space requirements for both the application and the data. What's considered adequate today will quickly become inadequate tomorrow. By moving the application onto Terminal Server and the associated data onto a file server you essentially eliminate these concerns. When applications are centralized on a Terminal Server, their storage requirements become much more manageable. If additional disk capacity is required, it needs to be added only once to the appropriate server (Terminal Server or file server). And because a single application installation on a server will service all clients connected to it, much less overall disk capacity is required. If the application requires 20MB, it will take up only 20MB on a Terminal Server, regardless of the number of users who access it. On the desktop, it would take up 20MB on each PC on which it was installed. One thing to note is that application data is rarely stored directly on a Terminal Server, but instead is maintained on a central file server. This allows consistent access to data regardless of how many Terminal Servers are in the environment.

Windows 2000 Terminal Services

Because Terminal Services are an integrated part of Windows 2000 Server, you now have the ability to enable these services in "Remote Administrator" mode. This mode allows any Windows 2000 Server (domain controller, SQL Server, SNA Server, and so on) to be remotely accessed using the Terminal Server client. Previous versions of Windows NT Server required a third-party add-on such as SMS to provide this functionality. Chapter 2, "Microsoft Windows Terminal Server," discusses the different operating modes of Windows 2000 Terminal Services in more detail. ◆

Scalability

One of the key requirements for any computing system is the ability to scale to meet the changing needs of a business. Terminal Server is no exception. For a system to scale well, it should meet the following criteria:

- Scales with minimal impact (ideally no impact) to the existing user community.
- Minimizes the increase in both administrative and user support complexity.
- Can be implemented in a timely fashion.

Unless a Terminal Server implementation can meet all these criteria, any reductions in TCO that its other benefits provide will quickly be lost when the time comes to upgrade or augment the environment.

Luckily, Terminal Server and MetaFrame provide a suite of tools and functionality that can be used to provide maximum scalability for your thin-client environment. A properly deployed Terminal Server/MetaFrame environment with two servers can quickly be scaled to 10 servers with no impact to the current user community and only a small increase in administrative complexity.

Chapter 2, "Microsoft Windows Terminal Server" and Chapter 3, "Citrix MetaFrame," examine the product functionality that's available to meet these scalability criteria.

Enhancing Security

Built on Windows Server technology, Terminal Server provides all the standard security measures found in NT/2000. Enhanced security features provided with both Terminal Server and MetaFrame enable you to establish a secure Terminal Server environment. Because Terminal Server users are running a session that's local to the server, the requirements for file-level security as well as auditing are far greater than what you would normally find on most Windows servers. These security features, along with the centralized management of Terminal Server, help you to establish a more controlled and secure computing environment in which these users will operate. Many of the security controls that are very difficult to manage effectively on a user's desktop (such as file security or system auditing) can be centrally managed and controlled from within your Terminal Server environment. Following are some of the areas of security that can benefit from Terminal Server:

- **Computer virus security.** Moving the execution of applications off the user's desktop can help in reducing the chances of a computer virus affecting your business. The establishment of virus scanning and removal software on your Terminal Servers can further ensure that files are protected from infection. Although completely eliminating the possibility of viruses is a nearly impossible task, the centralized nature of Terminal Server can help reduce the frequency of virus infections and the extent to which they will spread.

- **Application security.** Terminal Server allows for centralized security management of applications and can eliminate a user's ability to access unauthorized applications. A user may have access to run an application, but have no way of copying or modifying the application files. Unauthorized users would have no way of accessing the application without logging onto the Terminal Server environment, where they would require the proper security permissions to access the application files.

- **Data security.** Many users in an organization work with sensitive data that the company doesn't want to make publicly available or doesn't want to have accidentally destroyed. Even if a user is saving data on a protected file server, the information must be brought to the local computer to be manipulated by the application. Applications may create backup or temporary files containing information that continues to exist even when the user is finished working with the file. You can improve the security of this information by forcing users to access the data only through Terminal Server. Further restrictions, such as preventing the mapping of client drives, can help to ensure that the data cannot be downloaded to the client's desktop.

Chapter 8, "Server Management Planning," provides an overview of security planning in Terminal Server, and Chapter 12, "Terminal Server Configuration and Tuning," looks at the implementation details around securing the environment.

2

Microsoft Windows Terminal Server

In this chapter:

- **What is Windows Terminal Server?**
  Terminal Server allows multiple clients to access applications that run 100% on the Terminal Server, with only the screen and keyboard/mouse information being transmitted between the client and the server.

- **Application Servers Versus BackOffice Servers**
  Although a Terminal Server (also called an *application server*) and a standard BackOffice server look to be the same, there's a clear distinction between their functions in the enterprise.

- **Remote Desktop Protocol (RDP)**
  Remote Desktop Protocol (RDP) is Microsoft's distributed presentation services protocol, which controls the transmission of display and user input between the client and the Terminal Server.

- **Scalability**
  Several products, such as *Network Load Balancing* (NLB), *Windows Load Balancing Service* (WLBS), and *NCP ThinPath Load Balancing*, provide scalability to an RDP Terminal Server implementation.

- **Terminal Server Management Tools**
  In addition to the standard administrative tools found on a Windows server, Terminal Server provides tools for supporting the multiuser environment.

- **Terminal Server Clients**
  Windows 2000 ships with the latest version of Microsoft's RDP clients, which allow the use of the new features available with RDP 5.0.

- **Terminal Server Licensing Requirements**
  In addition to the standard client access licenses required for Windows, a Terminal Server client access license is also required for each client that will access the Terminal Server.

What Is Windows Terminal Server?

Both Windows 2000 Terminal Services and NT 4.0 Terminal Server Edition provide multiuser capabilities to their respective operating systems and they're based on the same underlying architecture. This chapter takes a closer look at this architecture, including its history and how it integrates into both the server and the client.

Conceptually, the idea behind Terminal Server is very simple, and will be familiar to anyone who has experience accessing graphical environments such as X Windows, where the application processing happens on a remote server, and only the visual input and output is handled on the client device.

Terminal Server brings this same functionality to the Windows environment, allowing multiple clients to access applications that run 100% on the Terminal Server. Figure 2.1 shows an example of this process, where a user is accessing a Windows 2000 desktop from within the local Windows NT desktop.

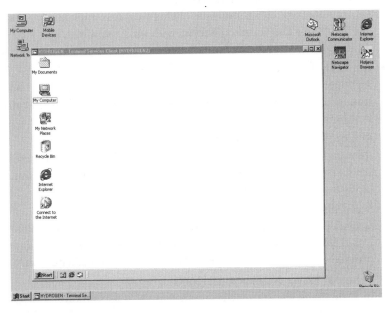

Figure 2.1 *Client access to Windows 2000 Terminal Services.*

Each user session on the Terminal Server is managed completely independently of the others. Memory and other resources allocated to one session are not accessible by any other session. The presentation information (graphics, user input) is passed between the Terminal Server and the client using *RDP* (discussed in the "Remote Desktop Protocol (RDP)" section of this chapter). Access to Terminal Server using RDP is available for the following Windows-based clients:

- Windows 2000
- Windows 95/98
- Windows NT (3.51, 4.0)
- Windows for Workgroups 3.11
- Windows CE-based terminals and handheld devices

Windows NT Server 4.0, Terminal Server Edition

The RDP clients that ship with Windows NT Server 4.0, Terminal Server Edition can be used to access a Windows 2000 Terminal Server, although the new client features available in Windows 2000 aren't accessible. See the later section "Remote Desktop Protocol (RDP)" for more information on these new features and which client version is required. ◆

Support for non–Windows clients such as DOS, UNIX, Macintosh, or Java are available with the Citrix MetaFrame add-in to Terminal Server. See Chapter 3, "Citrix MetaFrame," for a detailed discussion of this topic.

Tip

A non–Microsoft RDP Java client (JDK 1.1) is available from a company called HOB Electronics. For more information and a downloadable client for testing, go to http://www.hob.de/www_us. ◆

The History of Terminal Server

Let's begin by taking a look at the history behind Terminal Server. Although Terminal Server has only been in existence since 1998, the technology behind it isn't new. The Citrix MultiWin technology incorporated into Terminal Server was first conceived in the late 1980s by Ed Iacobucci, who today is the chairman, founder, and chief technical officer of Citrix Systems. Iacobucci worked for IBM from 1978 to 1989, spending most of that time in the personal computer division, designing and architecting operating systems. When Microsoft and IBM set out to develop OS/2, Iacobucci was head of the joint design team. During this time, Iacobucci envisioned a way to allow different types of computers on a network to run OS/2 even though they weren't built to do so. The idea of MultiWin was born.

Neither IBM nor Microsoft was interested in Iacobucci's idea, so he left to form Citrix Systems in 1989. Citrix developed the proposed technology (known as *MultiView*), and it worked. The problem with Citrix's new product was that it was based on OS/2, and the future of OS/2 was looking very dim. In the fall of 1991, with Citrix on the verge of going under, Iacobucci turned to Microsoft. He was interested in rebuilding Citrix's technology based on Windows NT.

At the time, Windows NT's penetration into the market was very small, and Microsoft was confident that if Citrix could deliver this proposed product, it would help to expand NT's market. Microsoft was interested enough not only to grant Citrix license to the NT source code required to make this work, but also to acquire a 6% stake in the company. In August 1995, Citrix shipped *WinFrame*, the first multiuser version of Windows NT.

Author's Note

Many of the most popular features of Citrix MetaFrame today, including server load balancing and application publishing, were originally developed for the WinFrame product. ◆

In 1996, Citrix began working on WinFrame 2.0, which was to be the next major upgrade, based on the Windows NT 4.0 architecture. By early 1997, Citrix had WinFrame 2.0 well into beta. At that time, with NT sales booming, and fearing the possible fragmentation of NT into a UNIX-type operating system, Microsoft decided that it was time to reclaim sole ownership of Windows NT. In February 1997, Microsoft informed Citrix that it was considering developing its own multiuser version of Windows NT. Shortly thereafter, Citrix made a public announcement explaining Microsoft's new position. The day after this announcement, Citrix's stock value lost 60%, closing at $10 5/8 per share, down from $26 1/2.

Over the next several months, during a time of intense negotiations between the two companies, the future of WinFrame remained uncertain until May, when Microsoft and Citrix came to an agreement. Much of the reasoning behind the agreement was Microsoft's desire to become a player in the thin client industry quickly, something that it had very little chance of achieving if required to develop a new product from scratch. (The same day as the announcement, Citrix's stock rose to close at $32 5/8.)

Through this deal, Microsoft licensed the MultiWin technology from Citrix to incorporate into future versions of Windows. Citrix will continue to develop WinFrame 1.x independently in addition to providing the MetaFrame extensions to Terminal Server, both of which are based on Citrix's Independent Computing Architecture (ICA) protocol. (MetaFrame and ICA are discussed in Chapter 3.)

In July 1998, Microsoft shipped Windows NT Server 4.0, Terminal Server Edition, its first thin client operating system. This is a special version of Windows NT Server 4.0, with the multiuser changes incorporated. While it looks exactly like regular NT 4.0, it's architecturally different and is shipped and marketed as a completely independent product with its own hot fixes and service packs. Regular NT 4.0 fixes and service packs don't work with this version of the operating system, and very often the Terminal Server fixes are a few weeks behind in shipping compared to the regular NT fixes.

With the release of Windows 2000 in February 2000, Microsoft has consolidated the multiuser features of Terminal Server into its core server operating system, making these features available as services that can be installed on any Windows 2000 Server product. By merging this functionality, Microsoft has made a huge leap forward in simplifying both the maintenance and availability of its thin client product.

Application Servers Versus BackOffice Servers

For Windows 2000, Microsoft uses the term *application server* to describe the use of Terminal Services to provide remote application support to users. I use this term to describe thin client servers (Terminal Server, WinFrame, and so on) in general, because their main function is to provide users with remote access to applications.

Tip

In the past, a standard Windows file server was sometimes called an application server if it contained application files that users accessed from across the network. This differs from a Terminal Server in that the client still runs the application locally; only the application files are located on the central server. In this book, I use application server to refer to a thin client server only. ◆

The direct opposite of an application server is the standard Windows server. Microsoft uses the name *BackOffice* to describe its suite of server-based products that run on Windows NT/2000 servers. I generalize the term *BackOffice server* to describe a standard Windows server that can run server-based products such as these:

- Web servers (Internet Information Server, Apache)
- File and print servers
- Database management systems (Microsoft SQL Server, Sybase)

There is a clear distinction between an application server and a BackOffice server. On an application server, you would find applications such as these:

- Microsoft Office
- Netscape Communicator
- Lotus Notes

The fact that an application server and a BackOffice server are visually almost identical can have both a positive and a negative impact on your implementation and production management. On the plus side, the similarities allow a skilled Windows administrator to get up to speed quickly on how to install and maintain many of the Terminal Server components. This commonality can also have a negative side, however, as these skilled (and sometimes not so skilled) administrators may make assumptions about the configuration or operation of Terminal Server that are perfectly correct for a BackOffice server, but not for a Terminal Server.

Warning

The upgrade options available with Terminal Server are somewhat restricted in comparison with a regular Windows upgrade. Upgrades from Windows NT Server 3.5x or 4.0 to NT Server 4.0, Terminal Server Edition are not supported, and attempting to do so will result in a warning during installation.

Upgrades to Windows 2000 (with Terminal Services) from NT Server 3.51 or 4.0 are supported when Terminal Services are set up in remote administration mode. Configuring Terminal Services in application mode won't automatically make any existing applications available to multiple user sessions. Existing applications need to be reinstalled. It's suggested that an upgraded NT Server be set up with Terminal Services only in remote administration mode.

You can upgrade from Citrix WinFrame 1.6 or 1.7 to NT Server 4.0, Terminal Server Edition, but a direct upgrade from WinFrame to Windows 2000 is not supported.

Upgrades from Terminal Server Edition to Windows 2000 Server are fully supported. ◆

BackOffice servers and application servers differ in the following key areas:

- Multiuser support
- Hardware requirements

The following sections discuss these areas in more detail.

Multiuser Support

The most obvious difference between a BackOffice server and an application server is the multiuser support. Until Terminal Server access came along, logging onto a Windows server meant one of three things:

- Logging on at the local console.

- Accessing a resource on that server such as a file or printer, the server's registry, or a BackOffice-type application running on that server.

- Accessing the console remotely using a tool such as the SMS Remote Control feature. In this case, you're either the only person logged on to the console (albeit remotely), or you're controlling the session of the person who is physically logged on at that console.

While multiple users can access a resource simultaneously, a BackOffice server can have only one person with an interactive console logon at a time (as shown in Fig. 2.2). This has been the standard operating behavior not only on Windows servers, but also on Windows desktop systems and other PC-based operating systems such as MacOS and OS/2.

Terminal Server ends the restriction that the console user is the only user with an interactive logon. Now there can be 2, 10, 50, or more users logged on concurrently in addition to the console user (see Figure 2.3).

Tip

Windows 2000 Server allows you to install Terminal Services in one of two modes. The first is application server mode, which provides the true Terminal Services feature discussed in this book. The other is a special management mode known as remote administration. As the name implies, remote administration is designed to allow an administrator to access a Windows 2000 BackOffice server through a Terminal Services client strictly for administrative purposes. Only two concurrent logons are supported, and the feature is treated as a remote console logon (similar to SMS remote control). See the later section "Remote Administration Mode" for more information. ◆

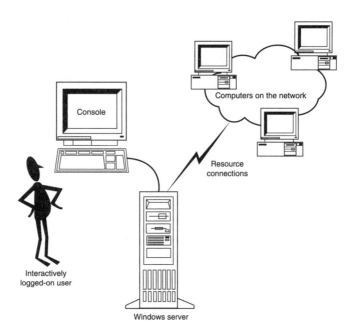

Figure 2.2   *A traditional logon to a Windows server.*

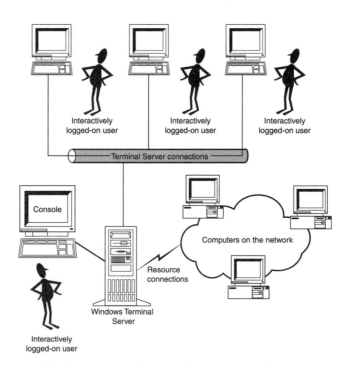

Figure 2.3   *Multiple interactive clients working concurrently on a Terminal Server.*

For Windows to support multiple concurrent interactive sessions, changes had to be made to a number of the underlying Windows operating system components to be able to manage each connected user's session. This is why the Terminal Server Edition of NT 4.0 was developed and maintained separately from the standard NT Server 4.0. Fortunately, these changes have now been incorporated into the base Windows 2000 Server operating system and are present whether or not Terminal Services have been installed. Let's take a brief look at the following major areas of change:

- Multiple user desktops
- Object management
- Process and thread management
- Virtual memory management
- Multiuser application support

Multiple User Desktops

Probably the most obvious area of change is how the server handles each user session's graphical interface. With multiple interactive users, the Terminal Server needs to be able to differentiate the graphics data for each user session. The local (or console) session on a Terminal Server is exactly the same as on a regular Windows server. It contains the two standard windowstation objects (winsta0, Service-0x0-3e7$) and the standard desktop objects (default and winlogon) associated with winsta0.

The interactive windowstation (winsta0) contains a Clipboard, a group of desktop objects, the keyboard, mouse, and display device. This windowstation handles input from the user. The special windowstation Service-0x0-3e7$ is a noninteractive windowstation and is associated with the noninteractive services that use the LocalSystem account. One or more desktop objects are contained within a windowstation. A desktop object has a display area that contains windows, menus, and other user interface components. Only one desktop at a time can be active for a windowstation.

Remote Terminal Server sessions contain only the winsta0 windowstation and *three* desktop objects: default, winlogon, and Disconnect. *Disconnect* is a special desktop that's made active when a user disconnects his or her Terminal Server session (disconnecting is discussed in more detail in the later section "Logoff, Disconnect, and Shutdown"). Remote sessions don't require the Service-0x0-3e7$ windowstation, because all system services run under the local console context.

Object Management

All operating system resources in Windows NT/2000 are represented by objects. The Object Manager, located in the NT Executive, is responsible for creating, modifying, and deleting these objects. Objects exist within what's called an *object namespace*. On a Windows NT Server, there exists only one namespace, since only one interactive session is supported. On Terminal Server, each interactive user session is assigned its own private object namespace, known as a user's *local namespace*. This allows multiple instances of the same application running on a server to create named objects that won't conflict with each other. Objects in one user's namespace are differentiated from the objects in another namespace by the unique name they are given. When creating a named object for a specific session, the Object Manager will append the user's unique session ID to the object name. An application cannot see objects in another user's namespace.

In addition to multiple user namespaces, there is also the *System Global namespace*. This namespace is visible to all sessions on the Terminal Server. In Windows 2000, all services and any applications running on the console execute within the System Global namespace. In Windows NT 4.0, Terminal Server edition, only services that run with the SYSTEM security context execute in the System Global namespace. All console applications and services running with named accounts run in the console User Global namespace. Figure 2.4 depicts the multiple namespaces that exist on both a Windows 2000 and NT 4.0 Terminal Server. The only difference is in how the console namespace is handled.

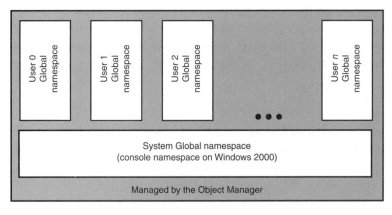

Figure 2.4   *Object namespaces in Windows 2000 and Windows NT 4.0 Terminal Server.*

Tip

The context (user or system global) within an application or one of its components can be controlled using the REGISTER command. For a complete description of this command, see Appendix A, "Terminal Server/MetaFrame Command Reference." ♦

Process and Thread Management

Just as with other components of Terminal Server, the Process Manager has been modified to recognize process and thread objects on a per-session basis. In addition, Microsoft has modified how Terminal Server handles task scheduling and prioritization as compared to a BackOffice server. On a BackOffice server, the process scheduler allocates longer time slices to better support the background applications that typically run on a Windows server. These applications usually have very low user interaction on the console. On a Terminal Server, process scheduling is more like Windows 2000 Professional in that user interaction and foreground tasks are more responsive. The time slices on a Terminal Server are much shorter than those on a BackOffice server. Thread priorities have been modified to maximize user responsiveness. Normally, new processes on Windows NT/2000 are assigned a lower priority than foreground tasks, but because multiple foreground processes exist on a Terminal Server, all starting processes have the same priority as foreground tasks. These changes in process priority and scheduling are what make Terminal Server a poor BackOffice server when compared to regular NT/2000 Servers. BackOffice applications such as SQL Server don't run as well because of these time-slice and priority changes. For this reason, Microsoft doesn't recommend using a Terminal Server to perform any domain controller functions.

Author's Note

When a server is running in remote administration mode, the server remains in the traditional Windows NT/2000 process scheduling configuration and is optimized for running BackOffice applications or acting as a domain controller. ♦

Virtual Memory Management

Every process on a regular Windows server is assigned a virtual address space that's divided between the kernel and user address space. The kernel space is shared between all processes, and each process receives its own user space. User mode threads can access only the user space; kernel mode threads can access both the user and the kernel space. Within the kernel address space are the Windows subsystem and associated drivers. When multiple interactive Terminal Server sessions try to access this single kernel space, it introduces kernel-sharing issues. To resolve this problem, Terminal Server has introduced a new type of address space called the *session address space*. The session address space contains a private copy of the kernel space that's used by all processes within a session. This allows each session to have its own Win32 kernel (also known as *WIN32K.SYS*, which contains the Window Manager and Graphics Device Interface(GDI)), display, and printer drivers.

Multiuser Application Support

In addition to the architectural changes just discussed, modifications to some of the standard Win32 API calls had to be made in order to more easily handle multiple interactive users accessing an application. Traditionally, Windows applications have been developed with the assumption that only one user was running the application interactively on a computer at a time. Many of these programs make improper use of configuration files in the Windows system root or in the system registry. Multiple users simultaneously accessing this information from a single location very often introduce application conflicts.

Terminal Server attempts to deal with this problem by introducing a special method of registry and INI file monitoring so that changes made during an application installation can be properly recorded and reproduced for each user who may run the application. Installing an application using the Add/Remove Programs tool found in the Control Panel activates this special monitoring feature. When applications are installed on a Terminal Server in this fashion, the server is placed into *install mode*, so that it can properly monitor and record system changes. If the application is not installed in this fashion, the server remains in what is known as *user mode*, and any system changes made during the installation will only be properly configured for the person who installed the application. Figure 2.5 shows the Add/Remove Programs tool for Windows 2000.

> *Tip*
>
> *A server can also be switched between install and execute mode from a command prompt using the CHANGE USER command. Details on this command are available in Appendix A and a complete discussion of application installation and configuration is given in Chapter 19.* ✦

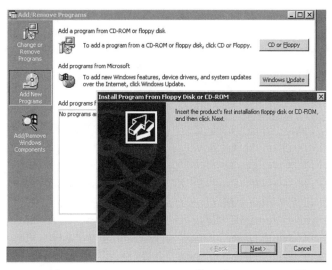

Figure 2.5   *Use Add/Remove Programs to install applications on a Terminal Server.*

Hardware Requirements

To support multiple interactive user sessions, a Terminal Server will usually have more substantial hardware requirements than the equivalent BackOffice server would need to support the same number of users through the traditional client/server scenario (file and print, SQL Server or Web server, for example).

One thing that all NT administrators learn is a standard set of guidelines for various Windows server hardware configurations. Many of the common server setups, such as a file and print server or a Web server, have minimum recommendations for a certain number of users. Table 2.1 shows a sample configuration for a Windows file server, an Internet Information Server (IIS) with Site Server and an Exchange 5.5 server, all sized to handle 200 or more concurrent users.

Table 2.1   *Standard Configuration for Common Windows BackOffice Servers*

	Server Types		
Component	**File**	**Exchange 5.5**	**IIS**
Processor	Pentium	Dual Pentium II	Dual Pentium II
	133 MHz	400 MHz	400 MHz
RAM	128MB	256MB	512MB
Disk capacity	18+ GB SCSI	36+ GB SCSI	18+ GB SCSI

Also common to these servers are hardware redundancy and other fault-tolerance features to maximize the availability of the server.

For BackOffice servers, resources are sized based on the average (or better yet, the maximum) number of concurrent user requests that the server will need to process. Print, mailbox access, and Web page access requests are all examples. The user makes the request and then waits for the server to return the required information.

The hardware sizing for Terminal Server differs greatly from this scenario. Because all users are accessing the server through interactive sessions, the server must be able to provide immediate feedback to any applications that the users are currently running. This requires greater processor and RAM resources than those required by a standard Windows server. Table 2.2 shows a typical Terminal Server configuration to support 100+ *average* concurrent users. An average user is typically someone who runs 3–6 applications simultaneously. These usually consist of a mail program, a word processor, and one or more line-of-business applications such as a host emulator or a client/server application. One or more applications may be 16-bit or DOS apps.

Table 2.2   Typical Terminal Server Configuration for 100+ Average Users

Component	Terminal Server (Supporting 100+ Average Users)
Processor	Quad Pentium II 400 MHz
RAM	2GB
Disk size	6–8 GB SCSI

Tip

For a complete discussion of hardware requirements for Terminal Server, see Chapter 7, "Server Hardware Planning." ◆

Compare this configuration to that of the BackOffice servers in Table 2.1; none of those setups even come close to the necessary requirements for 100+ concurrent Terminal Server users. Based on the memory configurations alone from Table 2.1, the file server hardware would support 3–5 users, the Exchange server hardware 6–7, and the IIS server hardware 20–25.

Tip

The main limiting factor for concurrent users is the amount of physical memory in a Terminal Server. ◆

Remote Administration Mode

As mentioned earlier in the chapter, Windows 2000 Server supports a special configuration of Terminal Services known as *Remote Administration mode*. This allows remote console access to the server but doesn't require any of the special licensing requirements of a full Terminal Server installation. The special tuning changes made to support Terminal Server are not performed when the remote administration feature is installed.

Remember that remote administration will allow anyone with the RDP client to reach the console logon for the server. You should ensure that good password practices are being enforced in your organization to prevent someone from guessing a password that would allow them access to the server.

Remote Desktop Protocol (RDP)

Remote Desktop Protocol (RDP) is Microsoft's distributed presentation services protocol, which controls the transmission of display and user input between the client and the Terminal Server. RDP has been adapted from the T.120 set of standards to meet the specific needs of the Terminal Server environment, and continues to be updated with new features to improve the user's thin client computing experience. The following sections discuss the features available with RDP 4.0, the original release of this protocol with NT 4.0 Terminal Server, and RDP 5.0, which ships with Windows 2000 Terminal Server. I'll begin by outlining the overall behavior of the RDP protocol.

RDP Basics

The transfer of RDP information between the server and the client can be broken down into two main components:

- Graphical data transmission
- Mouse/keyboard data transmission

Graphical Data Transmission

All graphical information that would normally be displayed on the console needs to be encoded and transmitted to the Terminal Server client so that it can be displayed on the user's local desktop. As described in the earlier section "Virtual Memory Management," each user session has its own session address space that contains its own Win32 kernel and display and printer drivers. Each of these sessions uses a special RDP display driver that's responsible for receiving display commands from the GDI (just as a normal driver would) and passing this information to the kernel-mode Terminal Server device driver (termdd.sys). This driver encodes the input as RDP data and passes it on to the transport layer to be sent to the client. On reception at the client, the RDP data is decoded and the display updated accordingly. Figure 2.6 illustrates the flow of graphical data between the server and the client.

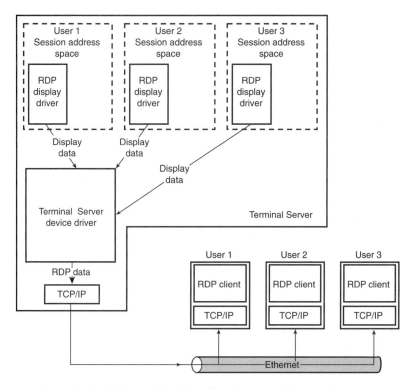

Figure 2.6   *RDP graphical data flow between client and server.*

Mouse/Keyboard Transmission

Every time a user generates an input message (keyboard or mouse), the information is captured by the RDP client, encoded as RDP data, and sent to the server. When input data is received by the Terminal Server device driver on the server, it's decoded and the actual mouse and keyboard input is sent to the Win32 kernel in the user's session address space, where it's processed as normal input. Figure 2.7 shows the flow of input data between the client and the server.

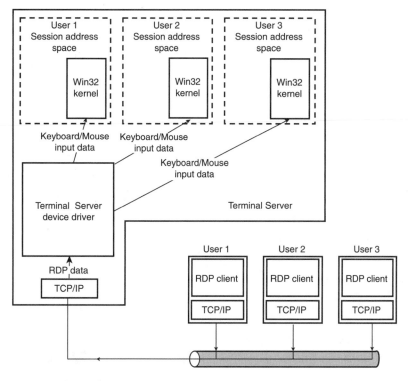

Figure 2.7 *RDP mouse/keyboard data flow between client and server.*

RDP Encryption

To ensure that data is transmitted securely between the client and the server, three encryption levels are available, from which you can choose based on your security requirements. All levels are encrypted using the RC4 encryption algorithm.

- **Low security.** Only data sent from the client to the server is encrypted; data from the server to the client is not encrypted. If the RDP client is Windows 2000, the encryption key is 56-bit. For an older client, the key is 40-bit.

- **Medium security.** Uses the same encryption level (40- or 56-bit) as the low security option, except that data is now encrypted in both directions, from the server to the client and from the client to the server.

- **High security.** Within the United States and Canada, the high security option encrypts data in both directions, using a 128-bit encryption key.

RDP Client Features

RDP version 4.0, which ships with TSE 4.0, provides only the bare requirements for a presentation protocol by delivering the remote desktop to the client. With TS 2000, RDP 5.0 supports a number of new features that enhance the interactions of a Terminal Server session with a user's local desktop. Table 2.3 lists the features available with RDP 5.0 (none of these are available with RDP 4.0), and which version of the RDP client is required in order to utilize these features.

Table 2.3   RDP 5.0 Features and Required Client Versions

Feature	Requires Windows 2000 Terminal Server Client
Local/remote Clipboard integration	Yes
Client printer mapping	Yes
Session remote control	No
Persistent bitmap cache	Yes

The configuration and use of each of these options is discussed in detail in Chapter 13, "RDP Client Installation and Configuration."

Author's Note

Citrix's ICA protocol, which comes as part of MetaFrame, has supported all of the listed RPD 5.0 features in addition to other ICA-only features since WinFrame 1.6. Chapter 3, "Citrix MetaFrame," looks at these ICA features in more detail. Chapter 6, provides a comparison of the features and functionality of ICA and RDP. ♦

Local/Remote Clipboard Integration

One of the new features available with RDP 5.0 is local/remote Clipboard integration. This feature allows Clipboard contents to be cut and pasted seamlessly back and forth between the active Terminal Server session and the user's local desktop. For example, text copied to the Clipboard from Notepad running on the local desktop could immediately be pasted into Microsoft Word running on the user's Terminal Server session. Only graphics and text can be transferred back and forth between the client and the server. The integrated Clipboard feature is optional and can be enabled or disabled at the connection level using Terminal Services Configuration (discussed later in this chapter).

Client Printer Mapping

Another client integration feature available with RDP 5.0 is client printer mapping. This allows printers that are configured on a Windows 2000 32-bit RDP client to be available automatically from within the user's Terminal Server session. The default printer on the local desktop can also be set automatically as the default printer from within Terminal Server. This feature allows a more seamless integration of the Terminal Server client with the local desktop. It also means that, in most circumstances, a user won't have to define printers in both environments. There are some restrictions on the behavior of the client printer mapping, however:

- Client printers are automatically mapped only when using the 32-bit Windows 2000 client. 16-bit clients or Windows-based terminals must have their local printers configured manually.
- The client's printer driver must already exist on the Terminal Server for automatic mapping to take place. If the driver doesn't exist, the printer won't be mapped. A message will be generated in the server's event log.
- Bidirectional printing is not supported.

Any printers that are automatically mapped for a client are visible only to that client. No other user on that server will be able to use those printer connections. Automatic client printer mapping is also optional and can be managed at both the connection level and the user level. At the connection level, you can allow individual user account settings to take effect, or override these and enable or disable printer mappings for all users.

In Chapter 12, "Terminal Server Configuration and Tuning," printer driver requirements for a Terminal Server are discussed.

Remote Control

One of the most exciting new RDP features introduced with RDP 5.0 (and the only one that doesn't require the Windows 2000 client) is the capacity for one person to remotely control another user's active session. With Remote Control, a user with sufficient security privileges can either passively view another person's session or interact with the session using the mouse and keyboard. This feature provides a tremendous benefit to administrators and support staff who may need to interact with another user's session in either a support or training capacity.

Remote Control has the following characteristics:

- A remote control session can't be initiated directly from the console. The console also can't be remotely controlled.

- To remotely control another user's session, your session must be operating in the same or higher video mode (resolution and color depth) as the desired target session.

- You must have the Remote Control privilege in order to remotely control another user's session. This privilege is managed at the connection level through Terminal Services Configuration.

- Users can be configured to receive a confirmation prompt prior to the remote control initiating (this is the default), or the remote control can start without any user notification. This is manageable at both the connection and the individual user level.

- Only one-to-one remote control is currently supported. You can't have multiple people all controlling the same user (many-to-one). You also can't have one person remotely controlling multiple people simultaneously (one-to-many).

- You must be logged onto the same Terminal Server as the user whose system you want to control. You can't remotely control a user located on a different Terminal Server.

Persistent Bitmap Caching

Windows 2000 Terminal Server clients can take advantage of the addition of a *persistent bitmap cache*. RDP 4.0 clients have a bitmap cache, but this is in RAM only and is lost when the client connection to the server is terminated. The persistent bitmap cache is stored on disk so that it can be reused the next time a session is started. This helps to prevent the retransmission of bitmap data that has been sent in a prior session.

When a connection is made to the Terminal Server, the client transmits to the server a list of bitmap keys corresponding to its current cache contents. The server then knows that it's not required to transmit the bitmap contents the first time it wants the client to display those graphics. It can immediately start sending the bitmap key. The persistent cache uses 10MB of disk space; this size can't be modified. Checking the Cache Bitmaps to Disk option in the Terminal Services Client enables caching.

Scalability

Currently, several products are available that can be used to provide scalability to an RDP Terminal Server implementation. Microsoft provides scalability through *Network Load Balancing (NLB)*, which is available with Windows 2000 (Advanced Server or DataCenter Server). If you're implementing NT 4.0 Terminal Server, you can use *Windows Load Balancing Service (WLBS)*. Network Computing Devices (NCD) provides its own load-balancing product for Terminal Server called *NCD ThinPATH Load Balancing*.

The following sections describe NLB and NCD ThinPATH Load Balancing.

Network Load Balancing (NLB)

Microsoft's NLB is a component of Windows Clustering that allows for multiple servers to provide TCP/IP-based services to users through one or more IP addresses (cluster IP addresses). This setup improves both the availability and scalability of a particular service by allowing multiple servers to be grouped together and to operate conceptually as a single entity. The primary use for NLB is to provide redundancy for Web-based services such as Web or FTP servers, but it can also be used to provide Terminal Server scalability.

NLB runs as a network driver on the server and is completely transparent to the TCP/IP networking stack. Each Terminal Server that will participate in the NLB cluster is configured through the Local Area Connection properties found under Network and Dial-Up Connections. The maximum size of a single NLB environment is currently 32 servers, and they must all be located within the same subnet. Figure 2.8 shows the property sheet for NLB.

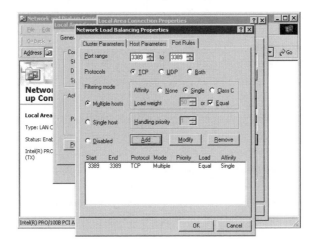

Figure 2.8 *Network Load Balancing properties.*

All servers in an NLB environment monitor the specified ports and virtual IP addresses for the cluster. The distribution algorithm for NLB determines which cluster host will respond to a given client request; on reception, all cluster hosts simultaneously perform this mapping and the appropriate host then handles the packet.

Periodically, all hosts within a cluster exchange status information, allowing for the detection of new or failed hosts and appropriate response. When a host is added, removed, or fails, the cluster enters a state known as *convergence*, where it redistributes the connection load accordingly. During convergence, all cluster connections for the available hosts are serviced, but any requests destined for a failed host continue to fail until convergence is complete and an alternate host has been selected to handle those requests.

Author's Note

A user's Terminal Server session information is not maintained across multiple servers, as the term cluster suggests. If a user is on a server that fails, his or her session and any information currently open within that session will be lost, and the user will have to logon again, to an alternate server in the cluster. ♦

By default, all connections from the same client are directed to the same host server in the cluster. This is known as *single client affinity*. If a client machine has been assigned a static IP address, this means that the user will always connect to the same Terminal Server until the next time a convergence occurs, at which point the user may be assigned to another host server. If a session is currently open when convergence occurs, the user continues to be connected to the current server, but the next time the user connects the host server may be different. Users with a DHCP-assigned address continue to access the same server until they receive a different IP lease (or convergence occurs).

Tip

Client affinity can be disabled, allowing a user to possibly connect to a different Terminal Server every time he or she establishes a new client session, regardless of the IP address. Under these circumstances, if the user leaves a session in a disconnected state on a Terminal Server, it's very likely that the next time that user logs onto Terminal Server, he or she will not reconnect to that session but instead will connect to a new session on a different Terminal Server. If you're going to use NLB with Terminal Server, I recommend that you enable client affinity and set disconnect timeouts. Timeout settings are discussed in the later section "Terminal Services Configuration." ♦

NLB allows for some rudimentary configuration of the load distribution within the cluster. A load weight parameter is available that allows you to specify the percentage of network traffic each host within the cluster will handle. Most often, the default option (Equal) is used, which evenly divides the load among all available hosts in the cluster. Network load balancing is based solely on *network connections* and not on heuristic calculations derived from processor utilization, memory utilization, or any other system factor. This can mean that if a server within the cluster is running in a degraded state, it may continue to attempt to process new client connections, even though another server in the cluster may have the capacity available to better handle the client.

Chapter 8, "Server Management Planning," talks more about load-balancing implementation considerations.

NCD ThinPATH Load Balancing

NCD provides load-balancing functionality for both RDP and ICA implementations of Terminal Server through its *ThinPATH Load Balancing* (*TPLB*) product. TPLB consists of two main components:

- **TPLB Client Services software.** This is installed on the Terminal Server as a service that provides the load-balancing features.
- **Load Balancing Client.** Client software for any Windows 32-bit operating system (Win95, Win98, Windows NT, and Windows 2000) or NCD ThinSTAR Windows-based terminal.

NCD Client Services

The client services component of TPLB must be installed on every Terminal Server that will participate in ThinPATH load balancing, and is managed through the *NCD ThinPATH Client Services* utility shown in Figure 2.9.

This utility provides a simple interface from which all TPLB information is managed. Using this utility, you can perform the following tasks:

- Create "manageable" or "other known" load-balance groups. A group is considered manageable when the servers that it contains are within the same subnet and NT domain. An "other known" group is a load-balanced group that exists on a different subnet or in a different NT domain. Users can still connect to these groups, but the load-balancing information isn't updated automatically for servers in the current subnet and/or domain. The load-balance group is what appears in the client software as an option to connect to.

- Add and remove servers from a load-balance group. When a server belongs to a load-balance group, it's participating in load balancing and is accessible through the NCD client. For example, the group ThinFarm in Figure 2.9 will be visible to clients running the NCD software. If a user connects to that server group, then he or she may be connected to either the CSA or the CSS Terminal Server.

- Add published applications to a group. In addition to connecting to a group by name, you can connect to any published application within a load-balance group. When connecting to a published application, only that specific application is started, not the full Terminal Server desktop session. Published application names appear in the client software as well. Any of the servers within the group can be selected to run the published application based on their current server load, so you must ensure that the software is available on all of the group member servers.

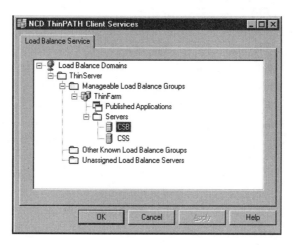

Figure 2.9   *The NCD Client Services utility.*

Tip

TPLB communicates on TCP port 2683. This port option cannot be modified. ◆

NCD Client Services uses a heuristic calculation to determine the current load of a server, which it then shares with all other load-balanced Terminal Servers. When a client connects to a load-balance group, it's connected to the server with the lowest load factor within that group. You can view the current load factor for a server by right-clicking on it and selecting the Properties menu option.

The load factor is based on a number of server conditions, including the number of users on the server and the number of processes in the run queue that are currently being executed. All of these server load factors can be monitored using Performance Monitor. A special Performance Monitor object, *NCD Client Services*, is available for monitoring after you have installed NCD Client Services. The factors used in calculating the current server load cannot be modified.

Author's Note

ThinPATH Client Services are available for both TSE 4.0 and TS 2000. You can find the latest information on the ThinPath toolset on NCD's Web site at http://www.ncd.com. ◆

Load-Balancing Client

On each client that you want to have utilize TPLB, you must install the load-balancing client software as well as the RDP or ICA client. NCD's client software launches the appropriate client with the proper connection information once it has determined what load-balanced server you should be connecting to. Figure 2.10 shows the *NCD Load Balance Connection Manager* application with a defined load-balance connection.

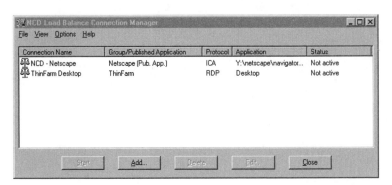

Figure 2.10   *The NCD Load Balance Connection Manager.*

To create connection entries, the Connection Manager must be able to locate a TPLB server so it can retrieve the information on available load-balance groups and published applications. Normally this is done by issuing a TCP/IP broadcast on the client's subnet to port 2683. You can configure the client to perform the broadcast on an alternate subnet, or you can specify a list of servers for the client to query. The server that provides the client with the group and published application information doesn't have to be a server participating in load balancing, but it must have TPLB installed.

Figure 2.11 shows the Connection Wizard used to create new TPLB connections. After selecting which load-balancing group or published application will be used, select the appropriate client (RDP or ICA). Depending on the client selected, certain configuration options are presented, such as color depth, compression support, and sound. Be aware that when creating a published application connect, the client displays the complete path information for the application, both during the connection creation and once the connection has been added (refer to Figure 2.10).

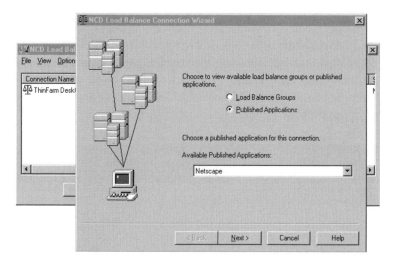

Figure 2.11   *The NCD Load Balance Connection Wizard.*

Scalability Criteria

Let's now look briefly at how these two scalability options for Terminal Server measure up to the three scalability requirements outlined in Chapter 1, "Going Thin with Terminal Server." To review, these requirements are as follows:

- Scales with minimal impact (ideally no impact) to the existing user community.

- Minimizes the increase in both administrative and user support complexity.

- Can be implemented in a timely fashion.

User Impact

Both solutions meet the key requirement for scalability, which is to mini-mize the impact on the end user. For either solution, once the client has been configured to connect to the load-balanced environment, the back-end servers can be manipulated without affecting the end user. Of course, care must still be taken to ensure that a server is not shut down if users are connected to it.

The NCD load-balancing solution introduces the requirement of an additional client, so if you want to introduce load balancing to an existing Terminal Server environment, a means of distributing and configuring this software must also be planned, possibly affecting the user during implemen-tation if it can't be done during off hours. With Microsoft's NLB, you only need to update an existing RDP client to point at the virtual IP address (or name) of the NLB cluster.

Administration and User Support Complexity

On the server side, both solutions provide the ability to centrally manage the load-balanced environment, although NCD's simple console is generally easier to use than the NLB interface. NLB provides more configuration options, but the lack of heuristic balancing based on actual server loading introduces the possibility of skewed client distribution when compared to NCD—particularly if you have servers that differ in processing power. NLB also has a published maximum of 32 load-balanced servers.

On the client side, end-user support staff will need to be trained in how to manage and configure the NCD load-balancing client. The additional steps required to create a load-balancing connection are fairly intuitive, but unless the broadcast destination has been set properly the client won't be able to find the available load-balance groups or published applications. Shortcuts can be created for the NCD entries so the users won't be required to run the NCD Connection Manager.

To configure NLB on the client, you simply create an RDP connection with the IP address (or name) of the NLB cluster. No additional support training is required.

Time to Implement

The higher complexity of NLB generally increases its implementation time and has a sharper learning curve when compared to NCD's solution, although once the standard configuration has been worked out, the installa-tion and deployment on the server side can happen fairly quickly—unless of course there are any hardware additions such as a second NIC for NLB.

NCD's client deployment may significantly increase the time for deploy-ment over the NLB solution, which requires only the creation of the RDP connection.

Terminal Server Management Tools

In addition to the standard administrative tools found on a Windows server, Terminal Server provides additional tools for supporting the multiuser environment. The tool sets differ slightly between Windows 2000 and NT 4.0, Terminal Server Edition. Table 2.4 lists the tools available for each environment, with a brief description of the function of each tool.

Table 2.4   Terminal Server Management Tools

Windows 2000 Tool	Windows 4.0, TSE Tool	Description
Terminal Services Configuration	Terminal Server Connection Configuration	Manage Terminal Server connection types, their transports, and their properties.
Terminal Services Manager	Terminal Server Administration	Manage all active Terminal Servers, users, sessions, and processes.
Active Directory Users and Computers	Not applicable	Manage Terminal Server user accounts in a Windows 2000 domain.
User Manager for Domains	User Manager for Domains	Manage Terminal Server user accounts in a Windows NT 4.0 or 3.51 domain.
Computer Management	User Manager for Domains	Manage local user accounts or groups.
Terminal Services Licensing	Terminal Server License Manager	Manage Terminal Server licensing.
Available Only with. the Windows 2000 Server Resource Kit	Application Security	Restricts all users to only the specified applications.

The following sections look briefly at each tool.

Terminal Services Configuration

Before a user can connect to a Terminal Server, the connections must be defined and configured on the server. This is done using the *Terminal Services Configuration* tool (TSCC)—called *Terminal Server Connection Configuration* on TSE 4.0—where you create the desired connection types and their associated network transport. Figure 2.12 shows the Windows

2000 Terminal Services Configuration application with the RDP connection type and the TCP transport. Currently Terminal Server supports only two connection types, Microsoft RDP and Citrix ICA.

Author's Note

See the earlier section "Remote Desktop Protocol (RDP)" for more information on Microsoft RDP. ✦

TSCC is the starting point for configuring Terminal Server clients. Properties such as access security, minimum encryption level, connection timeout options, or remote control options can be set for a connection type and will affect all users who access the server through that connection type. Figure 2.13 shows the remote control options on the RDP property sheet.

Figure 2.12   *Windows 2000 Terminal Services Configuration.*

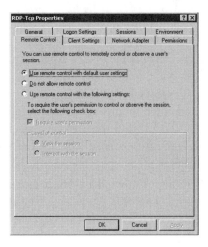

Figure 2.13   *Remote control options for the RDP connection.*

Terminal Services Manager

The *Terminal Services Manager* (*TSAdmin*) tool—called *Terminal Server Administration* on TSE 4.0—is used to manage users, sessions, and processes on each Terminal Server from a single management console. Figure 2.14 shows a typical Terminal Services Manager session. Tasks such as remote control are initiated from within TSAdmin.

The management window is divided into two panels. The left panel contains a list of domains, Terminal Servers, and Terminal Server sessions on the network. The right panel contains a number of tabs with information pertaining to the object currently selected in the left panel. Notice the two idle RDP sessions in the left panel. The server initializes these sessions so that they're available immediately when a user connects to the server. This helps to speed up the client connection process.

Figure 2.14   *Windows 2000 Terminal Services Manager.*

Windows 2000 Active Directory Users and Computers

Users can access a Terminal Server using either a local user account on that Terminal Server or a Windows 2000 domain account on the network. In either case, the user account contains additional information specific to Terminal Server. Figure 2.15 shows the property sheet for a Windows 2000 domain user. The following four tabs all contain user configuration information for Terminal Server:

- **Environment.** Configures how client devices (printers and drives) are handled and whether a specific application is automatically loaded when the user logs onto a Terminal Server. These settings can be overridden on the Terminal Server.

- **Sessions.** Manages the timeout and reconnect settings for the user's Terminal Server session. These settings can be overridden on the Terminal Server.

- **Remote Control.** Enables you to configure how the user can be remotely controlled, *not* how the user can remotely control others. For more information on remote control, see the earlier section "Remote Control."

- **Terminal Services Profile.** Specifies an alternate user profile and home directory that are accessed only when the user logs onto a Terminal Server. These properties are not used when the person logs onto a regular Windows server or Windows 2000 Professional machine. If these fields are left blank, the regular Profile tab values are used.

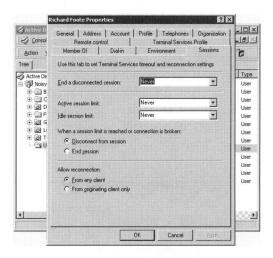

Figure 2.15   *Windows 2000 Terminal Services domain user account.*

Windows 2000 Computer Management

When editing local user accounts or groups on a TS 2000 server, the *Computer Management* utility is used. The properties available are a subset of those available when using the Active Directory Users and Computers utility discussed earlier.

Windows NT 4.0/2000 Terminal Server User Manager for Domains

When operating in an NT 4.0 or 3.51 domain environment, you need to run the special version of User Manager for Domains that ships with Terminal Server in order to "see" the Terminal Server domain user features. The standard User Manager that ships with NT 4.0/3.51 server is not capable of seeing these features.

Author's Note

*Although not explicitly documented, you can have Windows 2000 member servers with Terminal Services running in an NT 4.0 domain. User Manager for Domains is provided with Windows 2000 so that you can configure domain users with the special Terminal Services features. Although no icon is available under Administrative Tools to access it, you can start User Manager for Domains by typing **usrmgr.exe** from the Start, Run menu or from a command prompt. This version of User Manager is functionally identical to the one that ships with NT 4.0, Terminal Server Edition.* ◆

When you start the Terminal Server version of User Manager for Domains, it looks identical to the one available on a standard NT 4.0 server except for the Config button (TS Config in Windows 2000) under User Properties. This accesses the Terminal Server connection options for the user, as shown in Figure 2.16. In addition to the standard NT profile information, you'll also find the Terminal Server profile and home directory options under the Profile button. Chapter 17 discusses in more detail the additional options available through User Manager for Domains.

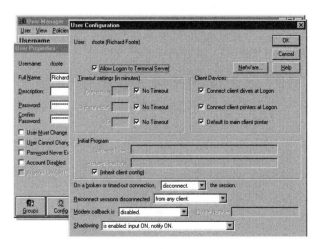

Figure 2.16   *User Manager for Domains Config options.*

> ### Tip
>
> *In an NT 4.0 domain, you should get all of your account administrators in the habit of using the User Manager that ships with Terminal Server to administer all accounts in your domain. This will ensure that created or modified user accounts that require access to the Terminal Server environment will have the proper information available.*
>
> *The Terminal Server version of User Manager can be used on any NT server or workstation. Just copy usrmgr.exe, usrmgr.hlp, regapi.dll, utill.dll, winsta.dll, and wtsapi32.dll from %systemroot%\system32 to the NT system you want to use.* ♦

> ### Warning
>
> *The Terminal Server-specific information for a user account will increase the size of the space required in the SAM to store that information. The size of a standard NT user account is between 1KB and 4KB, depending on the options selected. A user account with Terminal Server options selected can consume between 1KB and 8KB of space, and as a result can cause the SAM to grow very quickly. Even non–Terminal Server accounts that are administered with Terminal Server's User Manager for Domains will be slightly larger than normal. Be aware that the Microsoft recommendation of a maximum SAM size of 60MB for a single domain still applies, so special considerations may be required in order to accommodate Terminal Server domain accounts within your organization.* ♦

Terminal Services Licensing

The Windows 2000 *Terminal Services Licensing* application is used to manage Windows 2000 license servers. To run Terminal Services in application mode, you must have a Windows 2000 license server in your environment. One or more license servers manage the licenses that are issued to clients when they connect to a Terminal Server. A client must have a valid license to log onto a Windows 2000 Terminal Server. Figure 2.17 shows the Terminal Services Licensing application.

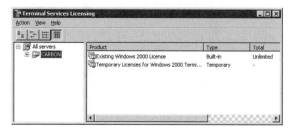

Figure 2.17   *Terminal Services Licensing application.*

If you have a Windows 2000 domain, your license server *must* exist on a domain controller. If you have an NT 4.0 domain, the license server can exist on any Windows 2000 server. Chapter 12 talks in detail about configuring the Windows 2000 license server. See the later section "Terminal Server Licensing Requirements" in this chapter for specifics on Microsoft licensing for Terminal Server.

Author's Note

While NT 4.0, Terminal Server Edition also has a License Manager application, it reports on Terminal Server licenses but does nothing to enforce them. ◆

Application Security Registration

The *Application Security Registration (AppSec)* tool ships with TSE 4.0, but for TS 2000 is available separately with the Windows 2000 Server Resource Kit. If you want to use this tool with TS 2000, you must purchase the resource kit. This utility enables an administrator to restrict user execution access to only those applications listed with ASR. When enabled, any attempt by a user to execute an application not on the list will display an error message. This tool doesn't restrict administrators' access to any application—only non-administrator users. Figure 2.18 shows the AppSec dialog box with the list of default applications. Clicking the Enabled option button immediately enables application security.

Any application that you want to list in the tool must reside on the local hard drive of the server; it can't be located on a network drive. This means that only applications residing on the Terminal Server can be run when AppSec is enabled.

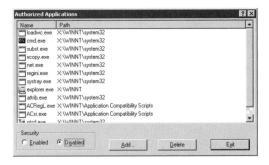

Figure 2.18   *The Application Security Registration utility.*

Terminal Server Clients

Windows 2000 ships with an updated version of the RDP clients that are available in NT 4.0 Terminal Server. Currently three installations of the RDP client are available:

- 32-bit client for Windows 95/98/2000 and NT.

- 16-bit client for Windows for Workgroups 3.11.

- Alpha client for Windows NT running on the Alpha platform. This client is only available with TSE 4.0 and is not included with TS 2000.

If the client hardware can support the appropriate operating system, it will run the corresponding RDP client. Network or dial-up access must be available for the client to connect to the Terminal Server. Two different RDP clients are available: the *Terminal Services Client* and the *Client Connection Manager*.

Terminal Services Client Application

The Terminal Services Client is a simple tool that can be used to establish a Terminal Server session or to run shortcuts created through the Client Connection Manager (discussed next). The Terminal Services Client consists of a single dialog box where you choose the server to connect to and the screen resolution at which you want to connect (see Figure 2.19). You then press Enter to establish the connection. The only visible difference between the Windows 2000 Terminal Server client and the NT 4.0 Terminal Server client is the addition of the Cache Bitmaps to Disk option, which enables or disables persistent bitmap caching (discussed in the earlier section "Persistent Bitmap Caching").

Figure 2.19   *The Terminal Services Client.*

Author's Note

The Terminal Services Client is not really a suitable tool for deployment to the end user, since the user would be required to specify the server and connection resolution. The Client Connection Manager is the recommended tool for developing shortcuts to be distributed to the user. Client installation techniques are discussed further in Chapter 13 "RDP Client Installation and Configuration," and Chapter 14, "ICA Client Installation and Configuration." ◆

Client Connection Manager

The Client Connection Manager (CCM) is used to create and manage connection shortcuts to Terminal Servers. CCM also allows you to configure a connection to launch a specific application immediately, instead of displaying a full desktop. Figure 2.20 shows the properties for an existing connection definition in CCM. The Connection Options tab is arranged slightly differently in the Windows 2000 Terminal Server client than in the NT 4.0 Terminal Server client. The bitmap caching option is now available and the Low Speed Connection option has been renamed to Enable Data Compression. Otherwise, the functionality has remained the same.

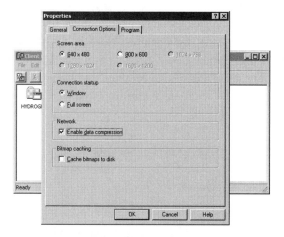

Figure 2.20   *Connection properties in the Client Connection Manager.*

Tip

Use CCM to create shortcuts to specific servers or applications and then place these shortcuts on the user's desktop. Remove CCM and Terminal Services client from the Start menu so that the users are not using these to connect. A user simply double-clicks the shortcut on the desktop to launch an application or session on a Terminal Server. This keeps the interface for the user as simple as possible. ◆

Terminal Server Session Versus the Local Desktop

The following sections talk briefly about some of the functional differences between a Terminal Server session and a local Windows desktop.

Keyboard Shortcuts

Probably the most difficult thing that a new Terminal Server user has to deal with is trying to understand how the client behaves, and becoming used to having a desktop within a desktop. Users may often become confused as to where they're actually running an application—on the desktop or on a Terminal Server. The problems usually manifest themselves when a user attempts to use one of the familiar keyboard shortcuts to perform a certain task. The user issues the keyboard command and suddenly a function of the local desktop is initiated instead of within the desired Terminal Server session function. Table 2.5 lists the common local keyboard shortcuts and the corresponding shortcuts for a Terminal Server session. Currently these keyboard settings cannot be modified. On the console, the standard keyboard shortcuts function properly. The standard keyboard shortcuts will function properly from the console or from a Windows-based terminal.

Table 2.5   The Common Terminal Server Session Shortcut Keys

Desired Function	Local Desktop Shortcut Key	Terminal Server Session Shortcut Key
Move forward between active programs.	Alt+Tab	Alt+Page Up
Move backward between active programs.	Alt+Shift+Tab	Alt+Page Down
Cycle through programs in their start order.	Alt+Esc	Alt+Insert
Display the Start menu.	Ctrl+Esc	Alt+Home
Display the Windows security dialog (Windows Professional/Workstation only).	Ctrl+Alt+Delete	Ctrl+Alt+End
Display the active window's Control menu.	Alt+Spacebar	Alt+Delete
Toggle the client between a window and a full screen session.	Not applicable	Ctrl+Alt+Break

Logoff, Disconnect, and Shutdown

In a Terminal Server session, the Start menu contents differ slightly between Windows 2000 and NT 4.0. For NT 4.0 Terminal Server, the Shutdown option has been completely replaced with a Logoff and Disconnect option.

Shutdown is still available from the NT Security dialog box, but the user must have administrative privileges in order to perform a shutdown of the server.

For Windows 2000, the Shutdown option is available on the Start menu, and when selected opens the Shut Down Windows dialog box (see Figure 2.21). The options available in the drop-down list depend on the security level of the user. Regular users get only the Logoff and Disconnect options. Administrators get the additional Shutdown and Restart options.

Figure 2.21   *Windows 2000 Terminal Server Shut Down Windows dialog box.*

Warning

The right to shutdown/restart a server must be very closely managed in a Terminal Server environment. At one company, a large number of domain administrators also had administrative access to the Terminal Server environment, even though many of them had no idea what Terminal Server was. A number of these users were electing to shut down rather than log off when terminating a session, causing the server to reboot and kicking all the other production users off the system. Once this was pointed out, the administrative user list was quickly reduced. Chapter 8 discusses the security management requirements of Terminal Server in more detail, including restrictions on administrative privileges. ◆

The Disconnect option is a new feature that's available only when Terminal Services have been installed. It enables a user to terminate his or her connection with a Terminal Server while still allowing the actual session to remain active on the server, until one of the following events occurs:

- The user logs back onto the same Terminal Server, at which point he or she is automatically reconnected to the previously disconnected session.
- The idle timeout period for disconnected sessions is reached, at which point the server automatically terminates the session. (For a discussion of timeout period settings, refer to the earlier section "Windows 2000 Active Directory Users and Computers.")
- An administrator manually terminates the session.

The Disconnect option can be useful if you're performing a long process on a Terminal Server, especially over a dial-up connection. As long as the idle timeout options are configured to support it, you can initiate your process on the Terminal Server , disconnect your session, and return later to examine the results. You aren't required to remain connected to the server to ensure that the process finished successfully.

Tip

One downside to the Disconnect feature is that many users don't understand the difference between a logoff and a disconnect. Many of them end up using Disconnect instead of Logoff. If the idle timeout properties aren't set properly, what you may have is a Terminal Server with a large number of disconnected sessions consuming resources that could be used instead by active users.

You should always ensure that a timeout period has been specified for eliminating orphaned disconnect sessions. ✦

Local C: Drive Access

The earlier section "Client Printer Mapping" discussed Terminal Server's capacity to automatically map locally configured client printers. This ability enables users to have access to the same printers whether on the local desktop or a Terminal Server session. Unfortunately, RDP doesn't support the same feature for client drives. When a user is logged onto Terminal Server, he or she won't automatically have access to the local drives; in fact, drive C: will most often equate to the Terminal Server system drive, which can further confuse the user. If the user goes looking for a particular file on drive C: within Terminal Server, it's not likely to be found. If the user attempts to save something to C:, the operation will fail unless the user has administrative privileges to the server. Even though the local client drive could be shared and then mapped from within the Terminal Server session, it most likely won't have the familiar C: drive name.

The only way to adequately address this issue is to educate users on saving data to a common network location that's consistent for both the local desktop and the Terminal Server session.

Tip

The Citrix ICA protocol provides a more robust list of client device mappings than RDP. This includes both client printer and client drive mappings. With ICA, you can provide seamless access to the user's local C: drive. See Chapter 3 for more information on this topic. ✦

Terminal Server Licensing Requirements

In order to implement Windows Terminal Server (4.0 or 2000), you need the following standard Windows server licenses:

- **Windows server license.** This is included with the base operating system.

- **Server client access licenses (CAL).** These are the licenses required to access network resources such as file and print shares. Each client device that will connect to a Terminal Server requires this license. Server CALs must be per-seat for Terminal Server. The per-server option is not valid. If you have 200 users, for example, but only 25 concurrent users are connected to the Terminal Server, you must still purchase the 200 Server CALs. You can't purchase only 25.

In addition to these licenses, you also need a Terminal Server CAL for each client that will access the Terminal Server. The following TS CALs are available, depending on how users will be accessing the server:

- **Internet Connector license.** This is a special client license available to companies that will make their Terminal Server accessible via the Internet. The license allows a maximum of 200 concurrent anonymous users to connect to the Terminal Server. The users must be non-employees of the company that makes the server available. For employees, individual CALs must be purchased.

- **Work at Home CAL.** This special CAL is available to companies that want to give employees access to Terminal Servers both from work *and* from home. To purchase this license, you must also purchase a standard TS CAL (described shortly). A Work at Home CAL combines a standard server CAL and a Terminal Server CAL into one license that's discounted over purchasing these licenses separately. You can't purchase a Work at Home CAL without purchasing a standard TS CAL as well.

- **Standard TS CAL.** This is the Terminal Server CAL required for all situations except for those just described. One license is required for every client that will connect to a Terminal Server.

- **Windows NT Workstation/Windows 2000 Professional CAL.** If the client has a Workstation/Professional license, then he or she is permitted to use this license to access a Terminal Server. A TS CAL is not required.

Windows NT 4.0 Terminal Server provides the Terminal Server License Manager application, which allows you to record the number of valid licenses that you have in your Terminal Server environment, but doesn't provide a mechanism to enforce these licenses.

Windows 2000 provides a completely new license management process for Terminal Server. A new service called *Terminal Services Licensing* records the available Terminal Server client licenses and manages the distribution of these licenses to client devices.

> **Tip**
>
> *Terminal Services Licensing only manages Terminal Server licenses. It does not work with or replace other standard Windows licensing products.* ◆

The licensing service isn't required on each Terminal Server , but must exist on a Windows domain controller in a Windows 2000 domain, or on any Windows 2000 server in an NT 4.0 domain. A server that has the Terminal Services Licensing service running is commonly called a *license server*. One or more license servers can service multiple Windows 2000 Terminal Servers. A Terminal Server must be able to find a valid license server before it can issue licenses to connecting clients.

License servers must be activated before they can begin servicing license requests from Terminal Servers. License servers are activated by going through the Microsoft Clearinghouse, where a digital certificate is issued that can then be applied to the license server to activate it. Once activated, client licenses can be installed on the server so that they can be issued to Terminal Server clients. Until it has been activated, a license server will be able to issue only temporary client licenses that are valid for 90 days. Figure 2.22 shows how a Terminal Server issues a client license to the connecting client. The steps are as follows:

1. The client establishes a connection to a Windows 2000 Terminal Server.

2. The server sends a request for the client license.

3. The client either returns an existing license that it has cached or requests a new license from the server. If the license is valid, the connection is completed.

4. If the license is invalid or the client has requested a new license, the Terminal Server attempts to contact a license server and request a new license.

5. When the Terminal Server receives the license from the license server, it passes the license back to the client so that the license can be cached, and the connection is completed.

Tip

The username and the machine name are both used by the license server to track issued licenses. ◆

Chapter 12 talks more about configuring license servers.

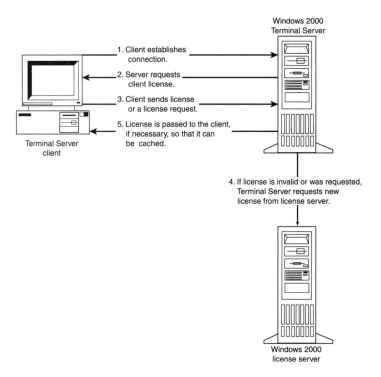

Figure 2.22   *Windows 2000 Terminal Server license issuing process.*

Warning

A common tuning tip for Terminal Server 4.0 is to disable the Terminal Server License service, since it doesn't provide any type of license validation and consumes unnecessary resources. This service is required on a Windows 2000 Terminal Server for clients to be able to connect. ◆

3

Citrix MetaFrame

In this chapter:

- **What is MetaFrame?**
  Citrix MetaFrame is an extension to Terminal Server that provides robust application server support for enterprise implementations of Terminal Server.

- **Independent Computing Architecture (ICA)**
  Citrix's Independent Computing Architecture (ICA) is the distributed presentation services protocol on which all of MetaFrame's functionality is built.

- **Scalability**
  Unlike RDP, which must rely on the Network Load Balancing feature or other third-party tools to provide scalability, Citrix has developed its own load balancing product that integrates with ICA to provide robust support for scaling a MetaFrame environment to meet the needs of any size user environment.

- **Citrix Server Farms**
  A Citrix server farm is a logical grouping of MetaFrame servers that centralizes the management of published applications, and more importantly, their deployment to the end user.

- **MetaFrame Management Tools**
  MetaFrame comes with its own set of tools for managing the various components of the ICA environment.

- **The ICA Client**
  In addition to the standard ICA clients for the Windows operating systems, ICA clients are available for a wide variety of operating systems and environments, such as DOS, Macintosh, and UNIX.

- **MetaFrame Licensing**
  MetaFrame licensing differs from the standard Terminal Server licensing in that you're purchasing concurrent or server-based user licenses instead of client-based licenses.

What Is MetaFrame?

Citrix MetaFrame is an extension to Terminal Server that provides robust application server support for enterprise implementations of Terminal Server. The core technology behind MetaFrame is Citrix's own remote presentation protocol, known as *Independent Computing Architecture (ICA)*. ICA is completely independent of Microsoft's Remote Desktop Protocol discussed in Chapter 2, "Microsoft Windows Terminal Server", and often is implemented in place of RDP, although both can function on a Terminal Server at the same time. A number of the RDP 5.0 features are based on functionality that was previously available only with MetaFrame. These are some of the enterprise features available with MetaFrame:

- Full client device mappings (printers, drives, stereo audio, COM ports)
- Cross-server, one-to-many and many-to-one session shadowing (also known as *remote control*)
- ICA-aware load balancing
- Extensive client support, including DOS, Macintosh, and UNIX
- Support for TCP/IP, IPX, SPX, and NetBEUI

Advantages of MetaFrame

Although Terminal Server with RDP provides a rich set of features and tools, some deficiencies become apparent when looking at a large-scale deployment of the product. MetaFrame overcomes these deficiencies at both the server and client. MetaFrame provides the following main benefits over RDP:

- Enterprise scalability
- Support for heterogeneous computing environments
- Expanded management and configuration tools

Enterprise Scalability

Chapter 2 discusses the scalability characteristics of Terminal Server with RDP and how it measures up to the criteria for scalability outlined in Chapter 1, "Going Thin with Terminal Server." Following are the four main limitations of Microsoft's Network Load Balancing (NLB) when used to scale a Terminal Server/RDP environment as discussed in Chapter 2:

- **Not RDP-aware.** NLB works only at the TCP/IP level, and is unable to take advantage of any RDP-specific features when performing load balancing. Because of this limitation, features such as the ability to reconnect to a disconnected session will be dependent on a number of factors, including the affinity settings for NLB, whether the users remain at the same client device or roam to different machines, and whether they have statically assigned or DHCP IP addresses.

- **Doesn't balance based on processor or memory load.** NLB was developed primarily as a load-balancing tool for Web or FTP servers, and balances between the servers in the cluster based on a percentage of network traffic, not on heuristic calculations based on processor or memory utilization.

- **Requires a large amount of administrative work to establish and maintain the load-balanced environment.** As the number of servers in the cluster increases, so does the work required in maintaining the environment.

- **Limited to a maximum of 32 servers in the load-balancing cluster.**

MetaFrame overcomes all these limitations and provides true enterprise scalability using the Citrix Load Balancing component. Citrix's load balancing is completely integrated using the ICA protocol, and easily managed through the graphical tool *Load Balancing Manager*. The later section "Independent Computing Architecture (ICA)" talks in detail about the scalability features of ICA and MetaFrame.

Support for Heterogeneous Computing Environments

Scalability isn't the only issue that needs to be addressed when looking at implementing Terminal Server in an enterprise environment. The issue of how to deal with a heterogeneous computing environment is, in many ways, the main obstacle to overcome during implementation. Many organizations aren't completely standardized on the Windows operating system with TCP/IP, and few have the resources or desire to move in this direction. In scenarios such as this, Terminal Server could be used to deliver Windows-based applications without modification to an existing non–Windows desktop. While this isn't currently possible with RDP, MetaFrame and ICA fill this need by providing robust support for heterogeneous computing environments.

MetaFrame provides support for heterogeneous computing environments in three ways:

- **Multiple-transport protocol support.** MetaFrame supports TCP/IP, IPX, SPX, and NetBEUI.

- **Robust connection support.** In addition to LAN, WAN, and standard RAS dial-up, MetaFrame also supports direct dial-up, direct asynchronous serial connections, and multiple-console adapters.

- **A wide variety of available clients are supported.**

MetaFrame boasts an extensive list of supported clients that's continually being updated and expanded. Following are some of the most common clients:

- Windows 2000, NT, 95/98, Windows for Workgroups 3.11, Windows 3.1, Windows CE
- DOS (16-bit and 32-bit), Macintosh, Linux (Red Hat, Slackware, Caldera, SuSE)
- UNIX (Solaris, SunOS, SCO, SGI, HP/UX, Compaq Tru64, IBM)
- Java (JDK 1.0, 1.1)
- Web browsers (Internet Explorer, Netscape)

Chapter 6, "Client Planning," looks in detail at the specific features that are available with the different versions of both the RDP and ICA clients.

> **Tip**
>
> *For the most up-to-date list of supported clients for MetaFrame, consult the Citrix Web site (`http://www.citrix.com`). All clients are downloadable free of charge from Citrix.* ◆

Expanded Management and Configuration Tools

MetaFrame provides additional management and configuration tools that are designed for assisting in the administration of large-scale implementations of Terminal Server with MetaFrame. A list of some of these tools is shown here, and each is discussed in more detail later in this chapter:

- **ICA Client Update.** Manages the automatic client update database.
- **Shadow Taskbar.** Allows shadowing of multiple user sessions.
- **Published Application Manager.** Manages published applications and Citrix server farms.
- **Load Balancing Administration.** Used to configure the load balancing parameters on any load-balancing–enabled MetaFrame server.
- **Program Neighborhood.** A client application that allows for single sign-on to a Citrix server farm and the published applications it contains. This feature is new with MetaFrame 1.8.
- **Application Launching and Embedding (ALE).** Allows published applications to be accessed through a Web page on an intranet or the Internet.

Independent Computing Architecture (ICA)

Even after Microsoft and Citrix agreed that Microsoft would license MultiWin for use in developing future versions of multiuser Windows, Citrix still retained ownership of its key technology, the ICA protocol. When first developing its thin-client solution for Windows NT, Citrix created two components: One was the modified Windows operating system that would support multiple interactive user sessions (MultiWin); the other was the presentation protocol to provide the remote computing capabilities. In addition to the standard graphical and keyboard/mouse support that's expected of a presentation protocol, all of the enterprise scalability and management features discussed earlier are based on ICA.

> **Tip**
>
> *The basic behavior of the transfer of ICA graphical and mouse/keyboard data between the server and the client is almost identical to that of the RDP protocol discussed in Chapter 2.* ✦

ICA Browser Service

In addition to the drivers required to handle basic presentation features, every MetaFrame server also runs the ICA Browser service. This service is responsible for maintaining and communicating status information about the server on which it's running to a MetaFrame server that has been elected to maintain a central repository of this information for all other servers on that subnet.

This central repository server is known as the *ICA master browser*. One MetaFrame server is elected as the master browser for each network transport protocol that's in use. For example, if you have both TCP/IP and IPX connections, a separate master browser will handle server information for each protocol. Very often the same MetaFrame server will be the master browser for multiple protocols, but this isn't a requirement. If a server isn't a master browser, it's known as a *member browser*.

A master browser tracks the following information:

- A list of all "known" Citrix servers.
- A list of all published applications.
- A list of all disconnected user sessions and the servers on which they reside.
- The pooled license count.
- Load calculations for all servers that have the Citrix Load Balancing option installed.
- Information on the currently selected backup master browsers (described shortly).

All member browsers on the network periodically send update information about themselves to the master browser. All member browsers are "aware" of which server is currently the master browser.

> ### Tip
>
> *The frequency at which updates are sent from a member browser to a master browser can be tuned to work best within your environment. Chapter 12, "Terminal Server Configuration and Tuning," provides more details about tuning the ICA browser service.* ◆

Figure 3.1 shows two networks separated by a router, each containing MetaFrame servers. The MetaFrame servers in Network A support both TCP/IP and IPX, so each has a master browser. On Network B, only TCP/IP is supported, so there's only one master browser.

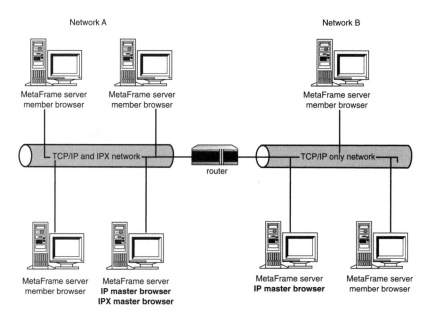

Figure 3.1 *ICA master browsers on two networks.*

Because a master browser election is performed using broadcasts, unless a router is configured to allow these broadcasts to pass through onto the other network (which is rarely the case), the servers on Network A will know nothing about Network B, and vice versa. This is why the two networks need separate master browsers, rather than one master browser for both.

> **Tip**
>
> *To determine which server is currently the master browser, use the command-line utility* QUERY SERVER *(or* QSERVER *for short).* QSERVER *lists all Citrix servers, along with status information such as current connections as well as which are the master and backup browsers. The* M *character on the far right of the server info signals that the server is the current master browser. Likewise,* B *signals a backup master browser. For more information on the* QUERY SERVER *command, see Appendix A, "Terminal Server/MetaFrame Command Reference."* ◆

Master Browser Elections

A master browser election is initiated when one of the following events occurs:

- A MetaFrame server is started or the ICA browser service is stopped and restarted on a server.
- The current master browser doesn't respond to the request of a member browser.
- The current master browser doesn't respond to an ICA client request.
- Two or more master browsers are detected on the same network (for the same transport protocol).

When a master browser election occurs, the master browser is selected based on the following criteria, listed from highest to lowest precedence:

1. The ICA browser has the highest version number.
2. The MetaFrame server has been explicitly configured to run as a master browser.
3. The server is also a Windows domain controller.
4. The ICA browser service has been running longer on this server than on any other server.
5. The name of the MetaFrame server is alphabetically lower than all others.

> **Tip**
>
> *The election criteria differs in MetaFrame 1.8 versus 1.0. The ICA browser version now takes precedence over a server that has been explicitly configured as a master browser. This means that if a MetaFrame 1.0 server has been configured to be the master browser and a 1.8 server is added to the environment, the 1.8 server will win the browser election. This change was made to ensure that the most recent version of the ICA browser service was acting as the master, to support new features such as server farms and Program Neighborhood.* ◆

When an election is initiated, the initiating browser broadcasts its complete set of election criteria. If another browser has higher criteria, it broadcasts its own. When no higher criteria can be broadcast, the last browser to send its information is elected the master browser.

> **Tip**
>
> *The ICA browser service uses UDP port 1604 for inbound requests and sends responses to a random port above 1023. The UDP listening port cannot be modified.* ◆

Consider this example. There are three MetaFrame servers (MF1, MF2, and MF3) and one WinFrame server (WF1) in a small environment. Table 3.1 shows the election criteria for each server.

Table 3.1   Election Criteria for Four Citrix Servers

Criteria	MF1	MF2	MF3	WF1
Configured as a master browser?	No	No	No	Yes
ICA browser version number	1.8	1.8	1.8	1.7
Domain controller?	No	No	No	No
Uptime	21	23	7	0

The three MetaFrame servers are already running, with MF2 currently the master browser when the WinFrame server WF1 is started. The following actions would occur:

1. WF1 broadcasts its election criteria immediately after starting up.

2. After examining the criteria sent from WF1, all three MetaFrame servers immediately broadcast their criteria information because all three have a higher browser version number than the WinFrame server.

3. The next two actions are concurrent:

   3a. After receiving the broadcast information from M2, neither M1 nor M3 attempts to re-send its information, since the M2 uptime is greater than theirs.

   3b. M2 receives the broadcast information from M1 and M3 and once again issues its election criteria because it has a higher uptime.

4. No other server has any criteria with greater precedence than M2; after the allotted wait time, M2 declares itself to be the master browser and all other servers become member browsers.

Author's Note

If the three MetaFrame servers had been version 1.0 instead of 1.8, the old election criteria would have been used and the WinFrame server would have become the master browser because it had been explicitly configured to do so. To set a server to become a master browser automatically, use the Citrix Server Administration utility discussed in the later section "Citrix Server Administration." ♦

Tip

An election can be manually forced by issuing the command QSERVER /election from a command prompt. See Appendix A for a complete description of the QSERVER command. ♦

ICA Clients and the Master Browser

In addition to maintaining information on the MetaFrame servers in the environment, the master browser also plays an integral part in providing connectivity to the ICA client. The ICA client communicates with the master browser to retrieve the list of available servers and published applications, as well as information on defined application sets for the user.

The client can locate a master browser in one of two ways:

- By issuing a broadcast on the network and querying the first MetaFrame server that responds to determine which server is the master browser.

- By contacting a set of servers explicitly listed on the client to determine which server is the master browser.

Figure 3.2 shows the Custom ICA Connections Properties dialog box, where you define the list of MetaFrame servers that the client would query in order to find the master browser. The client attempts to contact all listed servers simultaneously; the first one to respond is used to find the master browser. If the address list is set to [Auto-Locate], the master browser is found by using the broadcast method. If no Citrix servers are located on the client's subnet, the server location information *must* be provided for the client to be able to contact the master browser.

For each of the protocols supported by ICA, you can define up to three server groups (one primary and two backups), each containing a maximum of five servers. The corresponding server location group is used, depending on what protocol the user is using to connect to the environment. Chapter 14, "ICA Client Installation and Configuration," discusses in detail the configuration of the ICA client.

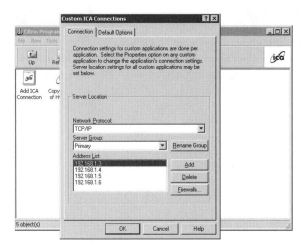

Figure 3.2 *ICA server location properties.*

Depending on your network configuration, it may be possible for you to use an IP broadcast address as an entry in the server location for TCP/IP instead of explicitly listing MetaFrame servers. For example, if your primary set of Terminal Servers is located on the class C network 192.168.1.0, you could provide the entry 192.168.1.255 as an entry in the server location. When the client queries for the master browser, it would send a broadcast message to all hosts on that network. If the servers are on the class B network 128.66.0.0, the server location entry would be 128.66.255.255. You could also define alternate broadcast addresses under the two backup server groups.

The drawback to this strategy, of course, is that now you're allowing broadcasts within the specified subnet, but the added redundancy that this provides may justify the configuration. ✦

ICA Gateways

One of the drawbacks in the design of the ICA browser is the fact that a master browser exists only in the context of a single network. In Figure 3.3, the networks are separated by a router; each has its own master browser instead of a single master browser that's aware of both subnets.

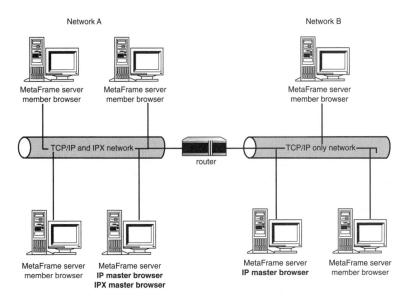

Figure 3.3 *ICA master browsers on two networks.*

This becomes an issue when you have a user who wants to access published applications from both networks. Consider the scenario in Figure 3.4. Again we have two networks, A and B, but this time a client in Network B wants to access Microsoft Word (published on a MetaFrame server in Network A) and Lotus Notes (published on a MetaFrame server in Network B).

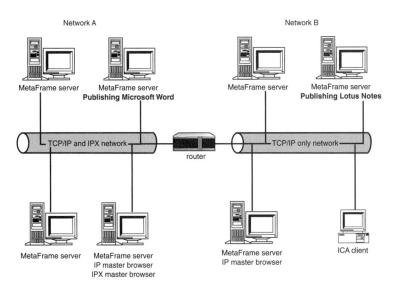

Figure 3.4 *Published applications available on two networks.*

By specifying a server location of [Auto-Locate] in the ICA client, as mentioned earlier, the client could find the master browser in Network B simply by doing a broadcast. Unfortunately, this would only provide the list of published applications for Network B, not Network A. If the server location on the client is populated with a server from Network A, we have the opposite problem. The client would see the applications in Network A, but not in Network B.

Luckily, Citrix provides a solution to this problem using what's known as an *ICA gateway*. An ICA gateway is established between two or more networks to allow the master browsers in each environment to share information with each other. The master browser in each environment will then maintain a list of all servers and published applications for both its own network and the one that's connected via the gateway.

Tip

When an ICA gateway is established, the master browsers exchange information using directed packets. Because of this, ICA gateways work only with routable protocols such as TCP/IP or IPX. For ICA gateways to function properly, the network router must pass ICA Browser traffic between the networks as follows:

Network Protocol	Routed Traffic
TCP/IP	UDP datagrams (port 1604)
IPX	Raw IPX packets ◆

To establish an ICA gateway, at least two MetaFrame servers must be involved. The *local server* is responsible for contacting the *remote server* to establish the ICA gateway and initiate communications between the master browsers in each network. Note the following issues about ICA gateways:

- The terms *local* and *remote* are relative. The local server could be defined in either Network A or B and the same gateway would be established.

- The local and remote servers don't have to be the master browsers. They'll contact their respective master browsers to initiate the gateway communications.

- Multiple local and remote servers can be defined to store redundant gateway information and increase reliability.

- If you want to pool licenses across a gateway, you must define a local/remote pair in both environments. Otherwise, you need only define one local and remote server to set up the two-way gateway between the networks.

- ICA gateways are not transitive. If a gateway exists between Networks A and B, and another between B and C, the gateway A to C is *not* automatically created.

With an ICA gateway in place, the ICA client in Figure 3.4 would be able to specify [Auto-Locate] the server location and see a complete list of published applications available on both networks. Chapter 12 provides a complete description of configuring an ICA gateway.

> ## Tip
>
> *If you're implementing Program Neighborhood and server farms as part of your MetaFrame deployment, there's an alternate solution to ICA gateways for accessing published applications on multiple networks.*
>
> *With Program Neighborhood, users can have access to multiple application sets that can be located in different server farms on different networks. For each application set you want to connect to, you can define a server location list that's unique to that application set. This allows you to create one application set for network A and another set for network B. Application sets are added by simply selecting Find New Application Set from within Program Neighborhood. Figure 3.5 shows the server location option that's available when finding a new application set. Server farms and Program Neighborhood are discussed in more detail later in this chapter.*

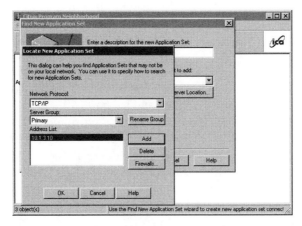

Figure 3.5 *Defining server locations for multiple application sets.* ◆

ICA Encryption

Unlike Terminal Server, which provides full encryption support for RDP in the base installation, MetaFrame ships with only minimal encryption for its ICA connections. With MetaFrame alone, you have only the option of using basic encryption—or none at all. Basic encryption employs a simple exportable algorithm that uses an encryption key less than 40 bits in size. Figure 3.6 shows the encryption settings for an ICA connection.

Warning

Citrix's basic encryption should not be considered secure. If you require secure ICA connectivity, you need the SecureICA option pack. ◆

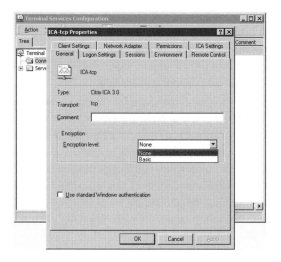

Figure 3.6   *Standard ICA encryption levels.*

SecureICA

If you're concerned about security for your ICA connections, you need to purchase the SecureICA option pack for MetaFrame. SecureICA employs the RSA RC5 encryption algorithm and supports 40-, 56-, or 128-bit keys.

When using SecureICA, the authentication portion of the Terminal Server logon always uses 128-bit encryption, and the remainder of the session data can be encrypted using 40-, 56-, or 128-bit encryption.

Tip

RC5 was developed by RSA Data Security Inc. For more information on RC5 and RC4 (used by RDP), see the RSA Web site at http://www.rsa.com. ◆

Due to changes in the export restrictions on strong encryption by the Bureau of Export Administration in the U.S. Department of Commerce, a single version of SecurICA is now available worldwide (excluding specifically restricted countries). This version employs 128-bit encryption for the authentication and 40-, 56-, or 128-bit levels for session security.

ICA Client Features

The ICA client includes an impressive assortment of desktop integration features that work together to blur the user's perception of local and remote computing. Some of these features are now also available with RDP 5.0, which ships with Windows 2000. See the section "Remote Desktop Protocol (RDP)" in Chapter 2 for more information on the RDP features.

The following list shows a number of the features available with the Citrix ICA clients that ship with MetaFrame. Not all listed features are available with all ICA clients. For a complete list of the features available for each client, see the "ICA Clients" section of Chapter 6.

- Local/remote Clipboard integration
- Client device mapping (printers, disk drives, COM ports, and audio)
- Seamless windows
- Program Neighborhood
- Application Launching and Embedding (ALE)
- Session shadowing
- Business Recovery Client
- Persistent bitmap cache

Local/Remote Clipboard Integration

MetaFrame provides a seamless integration of the Terminal Server session's Clipboard and the local desktop Clipboard. Using the standard cut-and-paste functions (menu commands and hotkeys), you can move data between the two environments as if you were moving it between local applications.

For example, text copied to the Clipboard from Notepad running on the local desktop could be pasted immediately into Microsoft Word running on the user's Terminal Server session. Only graphics and text can be transferred back and forth between the client and the server. The integrated Clipboard feature is optional and can be enabled or disabled at the ICA connection level using Terminal Services Configuration (discussed in Chapter 2) or Citrix Connection Configuration (discussed later in this chapter).

Warning

The synchronization of large Clipboard contents between the client and the server can have a significant impact on performance over a low-bandwidth connection. In this situation, it may be desirable to turn the Clipboard mapping feature off. ✦

Client Disk Drive Mapping

To further integrate the ICA client into your standard desktop, MetaFrame provides client disk drive mapping functionality. This allows for easy transfer of data between the client device and the Terminal Server session. When enabled, local client disk drives are automatically mapped and made available within the Terminal Server session. Local network drive connections are not mapped automatically, but can be mapped manually using either the NET USE command or by selecting the Map Network Drive feature. Figure 3.7 shows My Computer for an ICA Windows 2000 session. Drives A: through G: are mapped back to the equivalent client drive letter. X:, Y:, and Z: (CD-ROM drive) are local *server* drives; and W: is a network drive connection that was established within the Terminal Server session. The Map Network Drive dialog box is also open to show the special client network that's available when browsing for connections. The client network is created by the ICA session and lists all available client drives (both local and network).

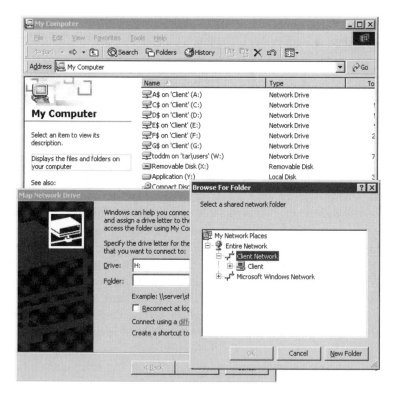

Figure 3.7   *Client drive mappings with the ICA client.*

Notice in Figure 3.7 that the client drives are mapped to their corresponding local drive letter on the server. For example, C: on the Terminal Server session maps to the local C: drive. This one-to-one mapping works only if the local drives on the Terminal Server have been remapped from their standard C:, D:, and so on to drive letters such as X:, Y:, and so on. This remapping is normally done during the MetaFrame installation. See Chapter 11, "MetaFrame Installation," for more information on this topic.

If the server drives haven't been reassigned, client drives will be mapped to server drive letters starting with V: and working backward through all available letters. For example, if my server drives had remained as C:, D:, and E:, my client drives would have mapped as shown in Table 3.2.

Table 3.2   Client Drive Mappings When System Drives are not Reassigned

Local Client Drive Letter	Mapped Server Drive Letter
C:	V:
D:	U:
E:	T:
F:	S:
G:	R:

If any of the drives between R: and V: were in use, they simply would have been skipped and the next available drive letter used. It's clear from this setup that having client drives map to alternate drive letters can certainly be confusing to the end user, particularly when the user searches drive C: within the Terminal Server session and it contains the server's system files and not the user's local C: drive as expected.

Tip

I recommend that your MetaFrame OS and data drives be reassigned to the higher drive letters, such as X:, Y:, or Z:, so that client drives map to their corresponding local drives. This helps to eliminate confusion and is much more intuitive for end users. ◆

The automatic mapping of client drives can be turned on or off at either the connection level or on a per-user basis.

Warning

Although automatic mapping of client drives can be turned off, clients are still able to manually map to their local drives unless additional steps are taken. Chapter 12 discusses client drive mappings and security. ◆

Client Printer Mapping

Printer mappings are very similar to client drive mappings, allowing a user to connect to a MetaFrame server and automatically have the locally configured printers available for printing. This includes both locally attached printers and network printers. In addition to mapping client printers, the local client default printer can also be set automatically as the default in the Terminal Server session.

Figure 3.8 shows the Printers folder for a Terminal Server session with a client-mapped printer. All ICA client printers appear with the name Client*clientname#\\printername*. The `clientname` is assigned in the ICA client, usually during the client installation, and is most often set to be the same as the machine's computer name. To ensure that client printer mapping functions properly, the client name should be unique.

When a user logs off Terminal Server, his or her ICA client printers are automatically deleted unless they still contain active print jobs. If a print job is active on the printer, both the printer and the job will be retained even after the user logs out. An administrator can delete any of these retained printers by using the `CHANGE CLIENT` command-line tool.

Chapter 12 gives more details about configuring and managing client printer mappings and printer driver support.

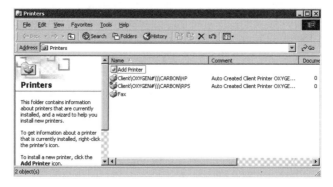

Figure 3.8 *Client printer mappings with the ICA client.*

Any printers that are mapped for an ICA client are visible only to that client and to any administrator logged onto the server. Non-administrators can see only their own printer mappings.

Client printer mappings are optional and can be managed at both the connection level and the user level. At the connection level, you can allow individual user account settings to take effect or override them and enable or disable printer mappings for all users.

Citrix also provides the ICA Client Printer Configuration application, which allows a user to manage client printer connections easily (see Figure 3.9).

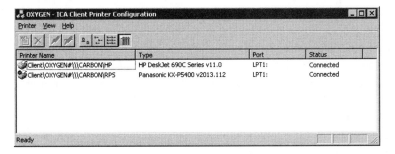

Figure 3.9   *ICA Client Printer Configuration application.*

Warning

In an enterprise environment with a large number of users, it's usually more band-width-efficient to have the user's printers configured on the server and not through local client printer mappings. Printers can be configured on the server in one of three ways:

- *Users map their own printers manually. This is done by selecting Add Printer from the Printers folder.*

- *Through user profiles. Users are assigned Windows profiles that already contain their printer configurations.*

- *Through logon scripts. Windows logon scripts are run when the user logs on to map printers.*

When printers are mapped on the Terminal Server, it allows the print jobs to be spooled on the server and then sent across the network to the printer. When print-ers are accessed through client mappings, the print job is sent from the MetaFrame server to the client, where it's spooled and then sent across the network again to the printer. This essentially causes the print job to make an extra trip on the net-works, which can cause unnecessary bandwidth utilization. This is also discussed in more detail in Chapter 5, "Network Planning." ♦

Client COM Port Mapping

ICA also supports client COM port mapping. This allows devices attached to a local client's COM port, such as serial printers or card reader devices, to be accessible during a MetaFrame session. Unlike printers or disk drives, COM ports are *not* mapped automatically during a user's logon. Client COM ports can be mapped using the NET USE or CHANGE CLIENT command. Client COM ports would be referenced as \\Client\COM*x*:, where *x* is the COM port number. For more information on the CHANGE CLIENT command, see Appendix A.

Client Audio Support

MetaFrame also supports client audio. Like the other mapping functions, it can be disabled in the Terminal Server Connection configuration utility, as well as being turned on or off from within the connection properties of the ICA client.

Tip

Unless sound is a true necessity, I recommend not using it because of the added network bandwidth. ◆

Seamless Windows

One of the most impressive integration features available with the ICA client is the *seamless window connection*. The seamless window is available only for the 32-bit Windows ICA client. Seamless windows allow you to run multiple published applications on your client, each displaying its application window directly on the local desktop. Each window is completely resizable and behaves like a local application, appearing on the taskbar and responding to the Alt+Tab application-switching key combination.

Figure 3.10 shows two seamless window applications open on the desktop (Notepad and Calculator), along with ICA Connection Center. The Connection Center lists all the servers to which the user is currently connected and the applications running on each.

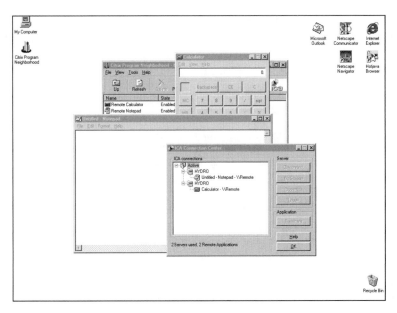

Figure 3.10   *Seamless window applications and the ICA Connection Center.*

Tip

If pooled licenses have been configured in the MetaFrame environment, only one pooled Citrix license will be used, regardless of the number of seamless windows you have open. If pooled licenses have not been configured, one license will be taken for each MetaFrame server to which the user is connected. ◆

Program Neighborhood

Program Neighborhood is available with the Win32 and Java clients as well as directly through a Web browser when used in combination with Citrix NFuse. Program Neighborhood provides single sign-on access to published applications within a Citrix server farm. After the user has been authenticated, his or her credentials are used to automatically connect the user to whichever MetaFrame server is hosting the published application that the user is attempting to access. Program Neighborhood is discussed in the later section "The ICA Client."

Application Launching and Embedding (ALE)

The use of the Web browser as a tool to access information on the Internet and internal corporate intranets is becoming more common each day. The *Application Launching and Embedding (ALE)* feature of MetaFrame provides the tool for integrating Windows-based applications and Web computing. With ALE, a user can access a published application through a Web site.

A published application is accessed by simply clicking the hyperlink on a Web page. The application will either be launched in a separate window or run embedded within the boundaries of the Web page. Figure 3.11 shows the published Calculator application embedded in a Web page. Table 3.3 shows which of the major browsers support launching and/or embedding of published applications within a Web page.

Table 3.3   Launching and Embedding Support by Web Browser Type

Browser	ICA Support	Launching	Embedding
Internet Explorer 3.x or higher	ICA ActiveX control	Yes	Yes
Netscape Navigator 2.20 or higher	ICA Netscape plug-in	Yes	Yes
Netscape Communicator 4.x or higher	ICA Netscape plug-in	Yes	Yes
Windows-based Web browser that supports configurable MIME types	WFica32.exe for 32-bit Windows OS or Wfica16.exe for 16-bit Windows OS	Yes	No
Web browser that supports Java Development Kit (JDK) 1.1	ICA Java client	No	Yes

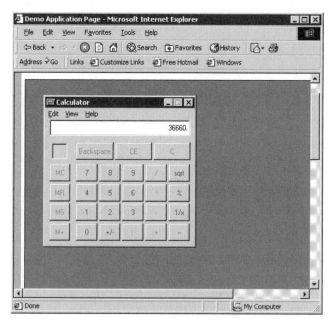

Figure 3.11   *The published Calculator application embedded in a Web page.*

Author's Note

Chapter 15, "Web Computing with MetaFrames," discusses Application Launching and Embedding in detail. ◆

Session Shadowing

One of the features that has been available with ICA (and now available with RDP 5.0) for a while is the ability for one person to be able to shadow (remotely control) another user's session. With sufficient security privileges, a user can view another user's session, either passively or with full control of the mouse and keyboard.

Session shadowing has the following characteristics:

- A user logged on at the console can't be shadowed, but can shadow other users by using the Shadow Taskbar application.

- To shadow another user's session, your session must be operating in the same or higher video mode as the desired target session. For example, if you're logged on with a desktop resolution of 800 × 600 with 16 colors, you can't shadow any session that's operating at a higher resolution than 800 × 600, *or* has greater than 16 colors.

- You must have the Shadow or Remote Control privilege for ICA connections to remotely control another user's session. This privilege is managed through either Terminal Services Configuration or Citrix Connection Configuration.

- Users can be configured to receive a confirmation prompt prior to the shadow being initiated (the default), or the shadow can be started without any user notification. This is manageable at both the connection and the individual user level.

- Unlike RDP, which only supports one-to-one remote control, ICA allows you to shadow one-to-one, one-to-many, or many-to-one. One-to-many is accomplished using the Shadow Taskbar application. Many-to-one allows multiple users to simultaneously shadow another user's session. This can be particularly useful when two or more support staff members want to view the behavior of a user's Terminal Server session.

- ICA shadowing can be done across servers by using the Shadow Taskbar application. You don't need to be logged onto the same server as the user to shadow that user.

- You *can* shadow users running published applications. The user's applications will appear to you inside an empty window while you're shadowing.

- An RDP client can't shadow an ICA client, and vice versa. You must be logged on with the same presentation protocol as the user you want to shadow.

Figure 3.12 shows the Citrix Server Administration utility with the Shadow option selected for a user. On a Windows 2000 Terminal Server, you can initiate shadowing using either the Citrix Server Administration utility or the Terminal Services Manager program.

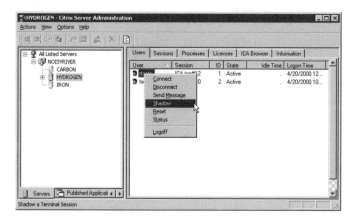

Figure 3.12   *Shadowing through the Citrix Server Administration utility.*

Business Recovery Client

The earlier section "ICA Clients and the Master Browser" explained that the ICA client supports multiple server sites (primary and two backups) through the server location property. This feature allows for improved application availability and redundancy in case of a primary site's failure. Each server group can have up to five servers defined. If none of the five servers is available in the primary group, the five in the first backup group are checked. Figure 3.13 shows the three server location groups.

Persistent Bitmap Caching

Just as with the RDP client, the Citrix ICA client supports a persistent bitmap cache. The persistent bitmap cache is stored on disk so it can be reused the next time a session is started. This helps to prevent the retransmission of bitmap data that has already been sent in a prior session. When a connection is made to the Terminal Server, the client transmits to the server a list of bitmap keys corresponding to its current cache contents. The server then knows that it's not required to transmit the bitmap contents the first time it wants the client to display those graphics. It can start sending the bitmap key immediately.

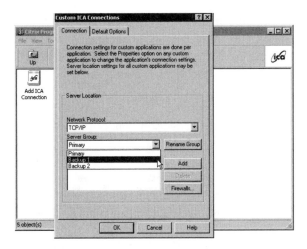

Figure 3.13 *Primary and backup server locations
provide published application redundancy.*

The ICA client's persistent cache is much more configurable than the RDP client's cache. Figure 3.14 shows the bitmap cache settings for the ICA client. The configurable features are as follows:

- **Size of cache.** The persistent cache size is defined as a percentage of the total disk space available.

- **Cache location.** The cache directory can be located anywhere on the client's desktop. By default, it's located under the user's profile directory.

- **Minimum bitmap size to cache.** The default bitmap size is 8KB. The minimum size can be set anywhere between 2KB and 64KB.

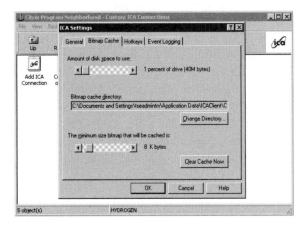

Figure 3.14 *The ICA client's persistent bitmap cache settings.*

Anonymous User Accounts

In some situations, providing a user with an explicit logon to a Terminal Server is both difficult and impractical. The prime example is when dealing with users connecting via the Internet. With potentially thousands of users accessing your application via the Web, it would be impossible to create the appropriate user IDs and passwords. Creating a generic account with a well-known password is a possible solution, but this strategy can introduce security and administrative problems.

Citrix provides a solution to this problem, which is to take the idea of the anonymous user that's common with FTP sites on the Internet and apply it to MetaFrame servers. Citrix anonymous users allow people to access published applications without requiring an explicit logon. The benefit is that this setup provides a way of enforcing restricted access without providing the person with a logon prompt. By forcing all users to access your environment using an anonymous account, what you lose in auditing abilities, you gain in restricted access. By not presenting a logon window to an Internet user, you deny potential hackers an easy means of attempting unauthorized access to your environment.

Anonymous user accounts are local accounts, created on the MetaFrame server, that belong to the local server's Guests and Anonymous user groups by default. For security reasons, these accounts shouldn't be granted any additional permissions, or made a member of any other group. As an added security (and privacy) feature, any desktop settings, user-specific files, or other resources owned by that anonymous user are discarded at the end of that user's session as the cached profile is deleted.

Author's Note

If a MetaFrame server has been created as a domain controller, anonymous accounts can't be created on that server. ◆

When a person starts an application as an anonymous user, the MetaFrame server selects a user ID from the pool of anonymous accounts that aren't currently logged on. During the installation of the MetaFrame software, an anonymous account is created for each user license that exists. The accounts are named Anon000, Anon001, Anon002, and so on, as shown in Figure 3.15. If additional licenses are added later, no additional anonymous accounts are created, and you'll need to add them manually using Computer Management (or User Manager).

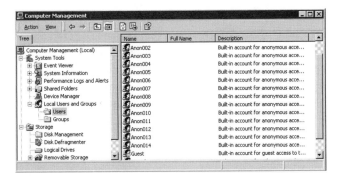

Figure 3.15 *Anonymous user accounts on a MetaFrame server.*

Tip

The easiest (and safest) way to create new anonymous user accounts is simply to copy one that already exists. Make sure that the account you're copying doesn't have any extra permissions assigned. After the accounts have been created, they won't be usable by the MetaFrame server until it has been rebooted. ◆

The following restrictions are also set on anonymous accounts by default:

- **Ten-minute idle timeout.** After 10 minutes of inactivity, the account is disconnected.

- **On a broken or timed-out connection, log off.** This must be enforced to ensure that anonymous sessions aren't tied up by users who are no longer connected. Typically, a broken or timed-out connection will occur when a person exits the browser without properly exiting the published application he or she is accessing.

- **Users can't change the password.** This restriction guards against denial-of-service attacks, in which someone could change the password on an anonymous connection and in so doing render it unavailable for anonymous logons.

Warning

If you change the permissions on an anonymous account, be sure to make the same change for all of them. Users have no control over which anonymous account is assigned when they connect, so there's no way to enable certain permissions for some anonymous accounts but not others. You have no way of controlling access to logon by using one of these accounts.

Never make a security change on an anonymous account unless you're 100% certain that it won't expose your environment to any unnecessary risk. ◆

Scalability

Unlike RDP, which relies on the Network Load Balancing (NLB) feature of Windows 2000 Advanced Server to provide scalability, Citrix has developed its own load balancing product that's tightly integrated with the ICA protocol. Citrix Load Balancing provides robust support for scaling a MetaFrame environment to meet the needs of any size of user environment.

Citrix Load Balancing

The Citrix Load Balancing (CLB) feature is an add-on to MetaFrame that allows a published application to be made available on any number of servers and accessed by a user without any knowledge of which server the application is actually running on. As discussed in the earlier section "ICA Gateways," a user accesses a published application simply by application name, not by server name. Figure 3.16 demonstrates the steps involved for the ICA client to connect to a published application (in this case, Microsoft Word).

1. After locating the master browser, the ICA client contacts the browser with the request for the published application "MS Word."

2. The master browser examines its internal data to find out which server is actually publishing "MS Word" and returns this information to the client.

3. The client then connects to the MetaFrame server provided by the master browser and launches "MS Word."

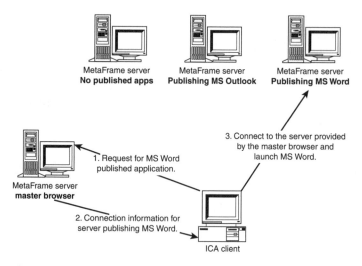

Figure 3.16 *Steps in accessing a standard published application.*

Citrix Load Balancing extends the standard published application process by allowing multiple servers to publish the same application. These servers then send periodic load information about themselves to the master browser. This load information is used to determine which server will actually service a client's request to run a published application. Figure 3.17 demonstrates how load balancing seamlessly integrates into the standard process of accessing a published application. This is the process:

1. All MetaFrame servers with load balancing services installed periodically send their current load information to the master browser.

2. After locating the master browser, the ICA client contacts the browser with the request for the published application.

3. The master browser examines its list of disconnected sessions to determine whether the user already has a disconnected session currently active. If so, the server with that session is returned to the user. Otherwise, the master browser examines which servers are publishing the requested application, selects the one with the least load on it, and returns that server name to the client.

4. The client connects to the MetaFrame server provided by the master browser and launches the desired published application.

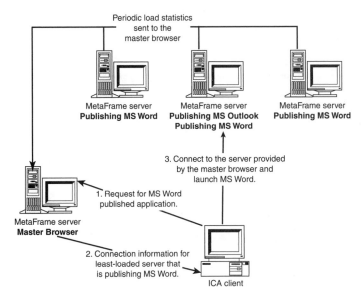

Figure 3.17   *Steps in accessing a load-balanced published application.*

Citrix Load Balancing has the following requirements:

- A Citrix Load Balancing license must be installed on each server that will participate in load balancing published applications. It's not required on a master browser server unless it will also be publishing applications.

- For an application to be load balanced across several servers, it must be installed on each server.

Tip

Citrix Installation Management Services (IMS) is an ICA option pack that enables you to install an application automatically onto a MetaFrame server from which you want to publish the application. See Chapter 19, "Application Integration," for complete information on IMS. ◆

Applications are configured for load balancing using the Published Application Manager. Figure 3.18 shows the selection screen on which you select the servers that will run the published application. Simply by including them to run the published app, you're automatically setting them up to load balance that app. The load balancing calculations for each server can be tuned using the Load Balancing Administration tool. Both the Load Balancing Administration and the Published Application Manager are discussed in more detail later in this chapter.

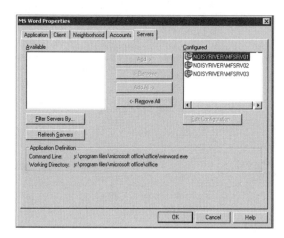

Figure 3.18 *Selecting multiple servers to publish Microsoft Word.*

Scalability Criteria

As Chapter 2 does with RDP, the following sections look briefly at how Citrix Load Balancing meets the scalability criteria discussed in Chapter 1. To review, the criteria are as follows:

- Scales with minimal impact (ideally no impact) to the existing user community.
- Minimizes the increase in both administrative and user support complexity.
- Can be implemented in a timely fashion.

User Impact

When an ICA client has been configured to access a MetaFrame environment using published applications, the introduction of Citrix Load Balancing will have no impact on the user. He or she will continue to access the same published applications, but be transparently directed to one of a number of servers that are publishing the apps. Servers can be added and removed from the environment dynamically without any impact to the user.

> **Author's Note**
>
> *It's common practice to have a MetaFrame environment in which servers can be added and removed as required without affecting the user environment. A load-balanced published application can be removed from a server without affecting any of the users currently on that server, but new users can't log on. After the last user has logged off the server, it can then be taken offline or simply rebooted without any user issues. Built-in redundancy in the load-balanced environment allows servers to be removed without degrading the overall performance or availability of the MetaFrame environment.* ◆

Administration and User Support Complexity

Very little administration is required to support Citrix Load Balancing. On the client side, the user is simply directed to the desired published application. Nothing else is required. On the server side, the application needs to be properly installed and the CLB license installed on each of the load balancing servers. Once this is done, the application is simply published on each of the servers using the Published Application Manager. The default configuration for Citrix Load Balancing is sufficient in most situations so the administrator rarely has to even run Load Balancing Administration tool. This is almost the exact opposite of what's required for setting up Windows 2000's Network Load Balancing.

Author's Note

Here is an example of how well Citrix Load Balancing integrates into a Citrix environment and how little maintenance is required. I have a client with an implementation of approximately 50 load-balanced servers at two different sites (100 servers in total), each managed by only two server administrators. ◆

Time to Implement

Because Citrix Load Balancing is completely integrated into the management of ICA published applications, the implementation time required for CLB is very low. To install CLB, you simply activate the appropriate license code on the server and then configure the published applications as desired. No additional software or hardware is required, and all load balancing management is done completely from within the graphical MetaFrame tools.

Author's Note

I have been able to install Citrix Load Balancing services on two MetaFrame servers and load balance Microsoft Word on them in under 15 minutes. This includes the time required to activate the load balancing licenses through Citrix. Word had already been installed on both of these machines prior to installing load balancing. ◆

Citrix Server Farms

With MetaFrame version 1.8, Citrix introduces the concept of a *server farm*. A Citrix server farm is a logical grouping of MetaFrame servers that centralizes the management of published applications, and more importantly, their deployment to the end user.

Server farms overcome the two main issues that existed with the previous version of MetaFrame when attempting to deliver published applications across a large number of servers:

- **No single sign-on.** Unless anonymous accounts were being used, whenever a user connected to a server for the first time to access a published application, the user was required to enter his or her user ID and password. The need to repeatedly provide logon information was one of the most common complaints from the user community in this situation.

- **Configuration on the client.** For a user to access a published application, the necessary connection information still needed to be configured on the client's device. The introduction of a new application to a user required updating the client (either manually or by some other means) to make the application accessible.

Single Sign-On

Server farms provide the ability to use *single sign-on* to access any published application defined in the server farm. If a user is running the Program Neighborhood client application, he or she will be prompted to enter Windows domain credentials when first launching the program (see Figure 3.19). The credentials are validated, then cached and used to automatically authenticate the user on any server that may be required in order to access the desired published application. The user is no longer prompted when connecting to any MetaFrame server within the server farm. This feature greatly increases the seamless integration of published applications into the user's local desktop environment.

Figure 3.19   *Program Neighborhood's single sign-on dialog box.*

Published Application "Push"

Once the user logs into Program Neighborhood, any applications that the user is authorized to access within that server farm will automatically be made available within Program Neighborhood (see Figure 3.20). Shortcuts to launching the published application can also be configured to appear on the local desktop and/or in the local Start menu. This grouping of applications is known as an *application set*. The ability to "push" applications greatly simplifies both the administrator's and the end-user support person's responsibilities for maintaining the client. Applications are added and removed from a user's application set simply by adding or removing the user's access to that application.

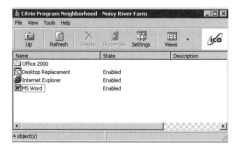

Figure 3.20   *An application set made available to the user within the server farm.*

Server Farm User Authentication

For a server farm to function, it must have access to a user account base that's available to all MetaFrame servers in the farm. This account base is used to assign user access to published applications and for authentication by Program Neighborhood. The user account base depends on the Windows domain structure in the environment. The important consideration is that all domains containing MetaFrame servers participating in the server farm trust the domain containing the user accounts. Figure 3.21 shows the dialog box within the Published Application Manager where the desired user account domain for authentication is selected.

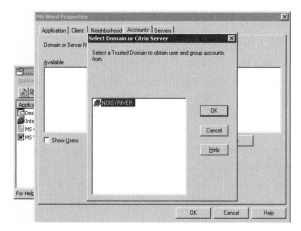

Figure 3.21   *Selecting the user account domain for published application security.*

The simplest example is the *single domain model* that contains both servers and user accounts. All MetaFrame servers in the domain can participate in a server farm and all user accounts in that domain can be configured to access applications in that farm.

In a multiple-domain environment, the proper Windows trust relationships must be in place. Figure 3.22 shows MetaFrame servers in two resource domains that are part of a single server farm. User accounts are maintained in the account domain, which is trusted by both resource domains. This is typically known as the *master domain model*. A user can access a published application within the server farm, regardless of which server the application is actually configured on.

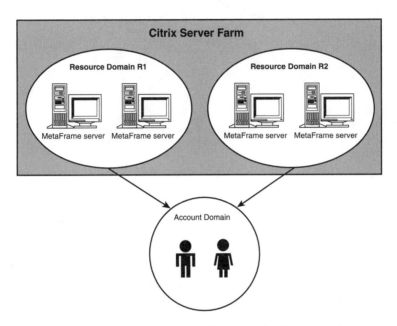

Figure 3.22   *Sample Citrix server farm configuration for the master domain model.*

Many large corporations have what's known as a *multiple master domain model*, which contains multiple account domains and multiple resource domains. Figure 3.23 shows an example of this type of setup, with three resource domains and two account domains. In this example, only R1 and R2 are participating in a server farm. Because R1 and R2 both trust A1, this will be the common user account base. Users in A2 can't participate in this farm unless R1 is set up to trust A2. MetaFrame servers in R3 can't belong to this farm because R3 doesn't trust A1.

Author's Note

Remember that trust relationships under Windows NT are not transitive. That is, even though R1 trusts A1 and A1 trusts A2, this doesn't automatically imply that R1 trusts A2. In a Windows 2000 domain, trust relationships are transitive. So in this case, R1 would automatically trust A2. ◆

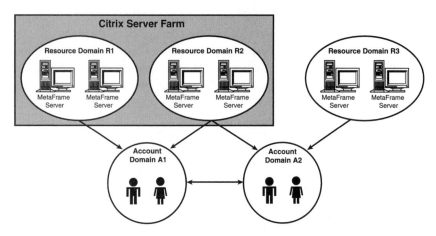

Figure 3.23   *Sample Citrix server farm configuration*
for the multiple master domain model.

Tip

Citrix released at least two hotfixes for MetaFrame 1.8 (prior to service pack 1) to resolve problems with accessing trusted domains. Check the Citrix Web site (http://www.citrix.com) for the latest hotfixes prior to implementing a server farm. Chapter 12 discusses managing MetaFrame hotfixes. ◆

A server farm can contain MetaFrame servers located on different networks only if an ICA gateway has been defined between the networks. This is required so that the master browsers can share the necessary published application information. In the server farm setups shown in Figures 3.22 and 3.23, an ICA gateway would have to exist between the R1 and R2 resource domains if they resided on different networks. See the earlier section "ICA Gateway" for more information on this topic.

Tip

If a MetaFrame server belongs to a workgroup instead of a domain, it can participate in a server farm only if it's the only server in that farm. Multiple workgroup servers can't exist within a single farm because they share no common user account base. Local server accounts on one server can't be used to authenticate on another. If you want to have multiple servers in a server farm, they must all be members of a Windows domain. ◆

Managing a Server Farm

Servers in a server farm are managed using the Published Application Manager tool. Currently, this tool doesn't provide an interface for adding all desired servers to a farm. To add a server to a farm, you must manage each server individually, making the necessary changes to the Server farm properties as shown in Figure 3.24.

Figure 3.24   *Configuring server farm properties for a Citrix server.*

To get a list of all existing server farms and the member servers, you must use the QUERY SERVER command-line tool with the /SERVERFARM parameter.

After a server belongs to a server farm, no other management is necessary aside from configuring any required published applications on the member servers.

Multiple Server Farms

There's no restriction on the number of server farms you can create, although limitations on their interoperability do exist:

- Server farms are managed completely independently of each other. Any published applications within one farm are not manageable from another.

- A user authenticated on one farm cannot transparently access another farm, even if both farms share a common user account base.

- A MetaFrame server can belong to only one server farm at a time.

Maintaining multiple server farms is rarely a requirement when all users exist in a common account base. Multiple server farms are most often used when a MetaFrame environment is distributed over a large geographical area or divided between two or more networks where an ICA gateway cannot be established for one reason or another. In this case, it's usually easier to maintain the environments separately instead of coordinating management between the two sites. Multiple farms are also required if Windows domains exist and trust relationships can't be implemented between them.

Author's Note

Proper planning is very important when implementing a server farm. I discuss this issue further in Chapter 8. ◆

MetaFrame Management Tools

MetaFrame comes with its own set of tools for managing the ICA environment effectively. The tool set described here is for version 1.8 of MetaFrame and is essentially the same for both the NT 4.0 and the Windows 2000 versions of the product. I'll note any differences between the operating systems when talking about each tool. Table 3.4 lists the MetaFrame tools available.

Table 3.4   MetaFrame Management Tools

MetaFrame Tool	Description
Activation Wizard	Performs an online activation of any Citrix product license.
Citrix Connection Configuration	Manages Terminal Server connection types (ICA and RDP), their transports, and their properties.
Citrix Server Administration	Manages all active MetaFrame servers, Terminal Servers, users, sessions, and processes.
Citrix Licensing	Used to install and enable all product licenses on a MetaFrame server.
ICA Client Update Utility	Manages the automatic client update database.
Load Balancing Administration	Configures the load balancing parameters on any load-balancing-enabled MetaFrame server.
Published Application Manager	Manages published applications and Citrix server farms.
Shadow Taskbar	Allows the simultaneous shadowing of multiple user sessions, even from the console.

The following sections look briefly at each tool.

Activation Wizard

All Citrix software works with an activation code licensing system. Every product has an associated license number that must be activated with an activation code (obtained from Citrix) that will then allow you to use the software. Most products have a grace period of approximately 30 days, during which time you can test the product to ensure that it's working properly before you activate it. SecureICA is one exception to this rule, requiring immediate activation for it to work.

One way in which you can obtain an activation code is to use the *Activation Wizard* (known as the *Citrix Licensing Activation Wizard* in NT 4.0). Double-clicking on the wizard icon provides you with two options. The first is activation over the Internet using ICA and TCP/IP to connect to a published application running on a Citrix server at the Citrix office. The second is to activate the licenses through Citrix's Self-Service Web site. The Web site can also be accessed at the URL http://www.citrix.com/activate. Figure 3.25 shows the Citrix Activation Web site.

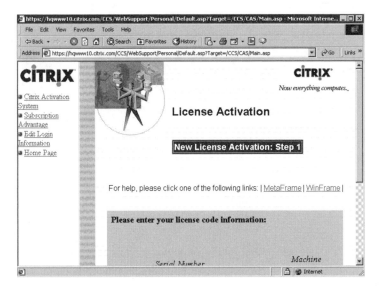

Figure 3.25 *Connecting to the Citrix License Activation Web site.*

Author's Note

Chapter 12 goes step by step through the process of activating a Citrix license. ◆

Citrix Connection Configuration

Citrix Connection Configuration (CCC) provides the same connection configuration features found in the Terminal Services Configuration utility that comes with Terminal Server. When MetaFrame is installed, additional connection features become available, such as setting up connections for different network transports, including asynchronous ICA connections through an attached modem or other multiple-port serial device. Terminal Services Configuration can be used to manage both ICA and RDP connections.

Citrix Server Administration

In addition to supporting all the standard features provided by Terminal Services Manager (Terminal Server Administration on NT 4.0), *Citrix Server Administration* (CSA) supports additional ICA functionality such as viewing server farms, managing published applications, and ICA video connections. Figure 3.26 shows the published applications within the Noisy River Farm server farm. By expanding an application you can see what servers are currently publishing that application.

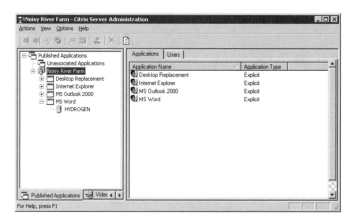

Figure 3.26   *Published applications in a server farm visible through Citrix Server Administration.*

CSA is used for managing member/master ICA browser settings as well as ICA gateway configuration and management. For each existing Citrix server, the properties of the ICA browser service on that server can be managed. Figure 3.27 shows the ICA browser settings for a MetaFrame server. When the All Servers icon is selected in the left pane, the properties for ICA gateways can be configured.

Author's Note

For more information on ICA gateways, see the earlier section "ICA Gateways."
For more information on master and member ICA browsers, see the earlier section
"ICA Browser Service." ◆

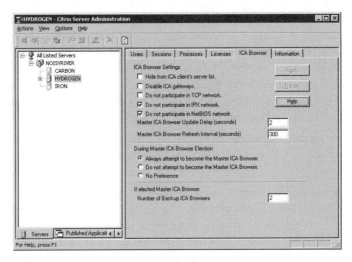

Figure 3.27   *The ICA browser settings for a typical MetaFrame server.*

The settings for the browser service are divided into three general sections:

- **ICA Browser Settings.** These settings affect the general behavior of a member browser, including whether it's visible in the server lists for ICA clients and how often update information is transferred to a master browser.

- **During Master ICA Browser Election.** These settings control whether the member browser will ever attempt to become a master browser.

- **If Elected Master ICA Browser.** These settings apply only when the member browser has been elected as a master browser.

Author's Note

For a detailed explanation of each of these features, see the "Additional
MetaFrame Configuration Options" section in Chapter 12. ◆

Citrix Licensing

In conjunction with the Activation Wizard, the Citrix Licensing tool is used to perform the following:

- **Add and remove Citrix licenses.** Licenses are added by simply entering the serial number for the Citrix product. Once added, it will automatically show the proper license description, and default to showing Activated as being No. Once a license has been added, a separate step must be performed in order to activate it. A license is typically valid without activation for 30 days. After 30 days, the license will expire and the feature set will no longer be available. If an activated license is deleted, you will have to go through the entire activation process again if the license is later reapplied.

- **Activate any of the installed licenses.** The activation code obtained from the Activation Wizard is used by this tool to actually activate the license.

- **Manage pooled user licenses.** User licenses from multiple Citrix servers can be pooled together so that the licenses can be shared between the servers. This also allows licenses to be applied to a couple of servers and shared instead of manually divided and installed across a number of servers. By the same token, licenses can be excluded from the pool and set to be applicable to only a specific server.

Figure 3.28 shows the Citrix Licensing application with four activated licenses: the base user license for the server and a load balancing license.

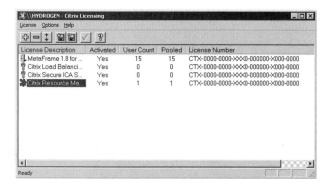

Figure 3.28   *The Citrix Licensing application.*

Tip

A common practice is to exclude a small number of server-based licenses (2-3) from the pool for administrativeconnections, so that the server is remotely accessible regardless of the contion of the license pool. ◆

ICA Client Update Configuration

Within an enterprise environment, upgrading the ICA client can be a major project in itself and can have a direct impact on two of the benefits of Terminal Server—centralized management and reduced maintenance costs. MetaFrame's solution to this problem is the ICA Client Update Configuration tool and the automatic client update feature of ICA.

Author's Note

Automatic client updating is supported with version 4.20.581 or higher of the ICA client. Older ICA client versions such as those that shipped with WinFrame 1.6 must be manually upgraded to at least 581 before they can take advantage of auto-updating. ◆

This utility provides the ability to automatically update the Citrix ICA client on a user's desktop when he or she logs on to a MetaFrame server, pulling the latest client files from a centrally managed database. The administrator can schedule the automatic download and installation of the client software to the user's device when that user next logs onto the MetaFrame server. This provides a simple solution to the issue of keeping the version of the ICA client up to date and configured properly. The Client Update Configuration enables you to fully configure how various ICA clients are updated, including whether the update is visible or transparent to the user, and whether only older clients are updated, or all clients. Figure 3.29 shows the properties for the Win32 client update object.

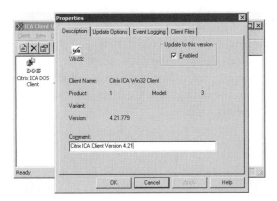

Figure 3.29   *Win32 client update options.*

Client installations can be preconfigured with all the necessary client settings, such as server locations and published application or server lists. This is also known as the *ReadyConnect Client*.

Author's Note

Chapter 14 walks through the process of configuring and using the Client Update Configuration utility. ◆

Load Balancing Administration

Load Balancing Administration (LBA) is used to configure the parameters on any load-balanced MetaFrame server. Figure 3.30 shows the LBA application window.

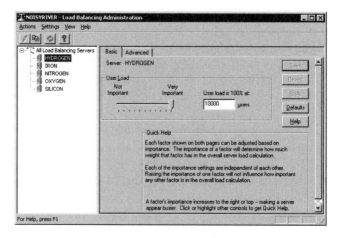

Figure 3.30   *Load Balancing Administration window.*

Citrix Load Balancing calculations are based on six factors, whose importance is controlled by LBA:

- **User load.** This is the basic calculation, and the only one that's normally used when determining the load of the server. The other five factors are usually set to Not Important, which means that they're excluded from the load-balancing calculations. User load is the ratio of one of the following:

  Current users to (total # of local plus pooled licenses)

  or

  Current users to (total # of users that the system can support)

The ratio used is the one that contains the fewer of licenses or supported users. For example, if current users is 37, total licenses is 50, and the total users the system can support is 45, the ratio 37:45 is used. By default, the total number of users a system can support is set to *10,000*. This value should be modified to reflect your own server's maximum capacity.

- **Pagefile usage.** The pagefile usage is the ratio of the current pagefile size to defined minimum allowed free space left in the pagefile.

- **Swap activity.** The swap activity is simply the number of times per second that the pagefile is being accessed.

- **Processor usage.** This is the percentage of time that the combined system processors are being utilized.

- **Memory load.** Memory load is the ratio of available memory to total memory.

- **Sessions.** Session usage is the ratio of configured ICA connections to available (free) ICA connections.

An overall adjustment can be made to these calculations, which is used to "artificially" raise or lower the calculated load on the server. By default, no adjustment is made.

Tip

Once the desired load-balancing parameters have been set, the information can be copied to similar servers in the server farm by simply selecting Copy from the Settings menu. ◆

Warning

RDP connections to a MetaFrame server will not be included in load-balancing calculations. The only way to capture their usage is to employ advanced load-balancing calculations that would include such things as pagefile usage, processor usage, and memory load. ◆

Figure 3.31 shows both the basic and advanced settings for Citrix Load Balancing Administration.

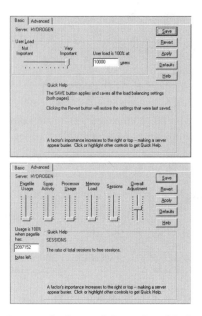

Figure 3.31   *Basic and advanced Citrix Load Balancing settings.*

Published Application Manager

Published Application Manager is the central tool for managing published applications. As a result, it's also responsible for the following functions:

- **Managing Citrix server farms.** Server farms allow servers and applications to be grouped together and automatically made available to users without any configuration on the client's local device. See the earlier section "Citrix Server Farms" for details.

- **Managing load-balanced published apps.** A load-balanced application is handled in the same way as a regular application except that it's made available on multiple servers.

- **Creating ICA and HTML files for making published applications available on a Web page.** ICA files contain the necessary information for the appropriate ICA Web client to launch the desired published application. Chapter 15 explains in detail how to make applications available on the Web.

Published Application Manager uses a simple wizard interface for performing almost all its functions. Figure 3.32 shows Microsoft Word being published to a Citrix server. Application publishing is covered in Chapter 19.

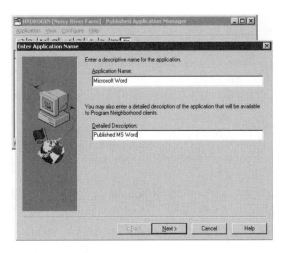

Figure 3.32   *Publishing Microsoft Word using Published Application Manager.*

Shadow Taskbar

The Shadow Taskbar is a simple management tool that enables you to shadow
multiple ICA connections. The Shadow Taskbar also works from a MetaFrame
server console, although you can't shadow the console itself. When running
Shadow Taskbar, a simple taskbar appears with a button representing all users
you're currently shadowing. You can move between them by simply clicking
on the appropriate button. Clicking on the Shadow button on the taskbar
brings up the Shadow Session dialog box (see Figure 3.33), from which you
can select one or more users to start or stop shadowing.

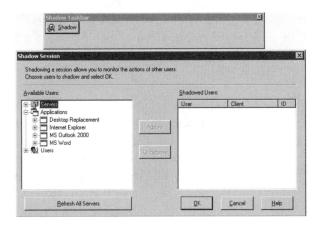

Figure 3.33   *The Shadow Session dialog box for the Shadow Taskbar.*

> ### Tip
>
> *The Shadow Taskbar also provides the ability to enable logging of the application's usage by Terminal Server users. This information goes to a log file that you specify and not to the Event Log.* ◆

The ICA Client

In addition to the standard Windows clients, ICA clients are available for a wide variety of operating systems and environments. These are some of the most common clients:

- Windows 2000, NT, 95/98, Windows for Workgroups 3.11, Windows 3.1, Windows CE
- DOS, Macintosh, Linux (Red Hat, Slackware, Caldera, SuSE)
- UNIX (Solaris, SunOS, SCO, SGI, HP/UX, Compaq Tru64, IBM)
- Java (JDK 1.0, 1.1)
- Web-based (Internet Explorer, Netscape)

> ### Tip
>
> *For the most up-to-date list of supported clients for MetaFrame, consult the Citrix Web site (*http://www.citrix.com*). All clients are downloadable free of charge from the Citrix site.* ◆

Depending on the client, one of two ICA client applications will be used. The *Remote Application Manager* is available for all clients except Java and Web, which have their own special clients. The other client application, *Program Neighborhood*, is available for Win32 ICA clients (Windows 2000, NT, and 95/98) and Java client. It is also available through a Web browser when used in conjunction with Citrix NFuse. NFuse will be discussed in more detail in Chapter 15.

Remote Application Manager

Remote Application Manager is the original ICA client application; it has been around since the original versions of WinFrame were released. It has undergone a number of improvements since that time, but the basic functionality remains the same. Figure 3.34 shows the main Remote Application Manager interface with the properties for an ICA connection. Both server and published application selections can be created within the Remote

Application Manager. Server locations can also be configured to allow access to servers and published apps located on a different network than the client (see the earlier section "ICA Browser Service"). Chapter 14 describes how to configure the Remote Application Manager.

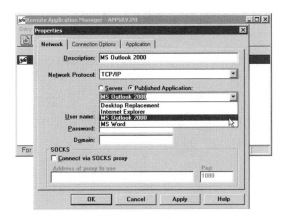

Figure 3.34   *ICA connection properties within the Remote Application Manager.*

Program Neighborhood

A user accessing multiple published applications on different MetaFrame servers using the Remote Application Manager is required to authenticate on each server. This is a major issue in distributing published applications across a large server environment.

With MetaFrame 1.8, Citrix provides a solution to this problem for Win32 and Web/Java ICA clients with Program Neighborhood. One of Program Neighborhood's functions is to provide a single sign-on for all published applications that a user can run within a Citrix server farm. After the user has entered his or her account information into Program Neighborhood, this information is used to connect the user to whatever Terminal Server is required to access the desired published application.

Program Neighborhood also automatically retrieves the proper application set(s) for the user. An *application set* is a group of applications defined within a server farm by a MetaFrame administrator as being accessible by that user. With the Win32 client, the application set icons can be configured to appear automatically on the Start menu and/or the user's local desktop. With NFuse, the accessible applications are displayed on a Web page built dynamically based on the contents of the application set. Chapter 15 talks in detail about ICA Web clients and NFuse.

In addition to predefined application sets, a user can also create custom ICA connections. This provides the same functionality originally available in the Remote Application Manager. Figure 3.35 shows the property dialog box for a custom ICA connection.

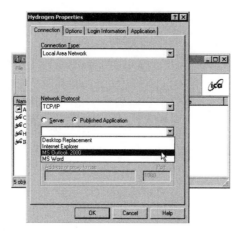

Figure 3.35 *Custom ICA connection properties within Program Neighborhood.*

Web and Java Clients

The Web and Java ICA clients are an exception to the standard client applications that are usually run. Both of these clients establish a connection to a MetaFrame server by reading the connection information from an ICA file. The ICA file is a plain-text file that can be manually created by an administrator or generated from within the Published Application Manager. A sample ICA file to access a Microsoft Word published application is shown below. Chapter 15 looks more closely at both of these clients.

```
[WFClient]
Version=2
TcpBrowserAddress=192.168.55.122
[ApplicationServers]
MS Word=
[MS Word]
Address=MS Word
InitialProgram=#MS Word
DesiredHRES=640
DesiredVRES=480
DesiredColor=2
TransportDriver=TCP/IP
WinStationDriver=ICA 3.0
```

MetaFrame Licensing

MetaFrame licensing differs from the standard Terminal Server licensing in that you purchase concurrent or server-based user licenses instead of client-based licenses. When you install 25 Citrix user licenses on a MetaFrame server, for example, it allows up to 25 concurrent ICA connections at any one time. They don't have to be the same 25 users every time. You could install the ICA client on 100 desktops and any 25 out of those 100 would be able to log on at any given time.

Warning

MetaFrame licenses are not a replacement for the required Microsoft licenses. You're still required to purchase all necessary Terminal Server client access licenses as described in Chapter 2. ◆

Citrix also allows you to carry these licenses across multiple MetaFrame servers, using what's known as *license pooling*. With license pooling, you can purchase 300 licenses for 5 MetaFrame servers, which then allows any combination of 300 users to log on to the available MetaFrame servers. License pooling allows you to implement redundancy into your environment by not having to tie licenses to each of your MetaFrame servers, and then losing access to those licenses if the server goes down for any reason.

Author's Note

The ICA Master browser is responsible for maintaining the pooled license count. ◆

Licenses can be pooled between MetaFrame and WinFrame 1.7 or higher servers. This allows any existing WinFrame licenses to be available in a MetaFrame environment. You're still required to purchase the base MetaFrame product.

Part II

Planning a Terminal Server Implementation

4

Project Management Considerations

In this chapter:

- **Implementation Requirements**
  Without clearly defining why Terminal Server is being used, who will use it, and how it will be implemented, it's likely that the end product won't function as you or the business expected.

- **Business Process Management**
  An important part of managing a Terminal Server project is being able to effectively manage the migration of the business processes from the existing "as is" model to the future "to be" model.

- **Policies and Procedures**
  An important part of developing your "to-be" model is creating or modifying policies and procedures for both your clients and your servers.

Implementation Requirements

Although the material in this chapter is targeted mainly toward the project manager of a Terminal Server implementation, I feel that it's worthwhile for anyone involved in the project to have a clear understanding of the implementation requirements—not only what they are, but also why they're needed. Many technical people I've met feel that this is really nothing more than "fluff" and has little impact on the "real" work they're required to do in order to drive the project to completion. While the technology is certainly important (or you wouldn't be reading this), without clearly outlining why it's being used, who will use it, and how it will be implemented, it's very likely that the end product won't function as you or the business expected.

Some of the most common problems that befall many projects include the following:

- **Significantly over budget.** Poor planning and unforeseen difficulties require additional human and financial resources.

- **Late delivery.** A lack of thorough project planning affects delivery dates.

- **Reduction in scope.** Either portions of the project that were originally in scope are omitted, or functionality that was originally planned has to be deferred or dropped completely.

- **Negative impact to the business.** This includes situations where the implementation introduces some major obstacles that require repeated rollbacks and redeployments to correct, not only affecting delivery dates and the project budget, but also the user's confidence in the product.

- **Failure to manage end users' and management's expectations.** Quite often people will read the hype surrounding Terminal Server and feel it can deliver everything for nothing. This is not the case, and failure to manage their expectations from the start will have negative repercussions throughout the project.

- **Project cancellation.** The entire project is terminated because of any of the problems described in this list, usually a combination of all of them.

While it can be argued that these difficulties happen more often than not, I have yet to see a Terminal Server implementation encounter any of them when proper implementation planning and project management had occurred.

Author's Note

Very often when I hear people complain about issues they have had with a Terminal Server implementation, the problems could easily have been avoided if the proper implementation planning had been performed. ◆

One factor in minimizing potential problems arising during implementation is to understand what I consider the five key implementation requirements:

- Documentation
- Leveraging desktop deployment flexibility
- Defining the scope of Terminal Server in your business
- Enlisting executive sponsors
- Not promising what you can't deliver

Documentation

The root problem with documentation has traditionally been that it was inconvenient. There was no easy way to store documentation so that it could be easily located, searched, or modified. Document management systems exist, but many organizations don't have the money to implement or resources to manage such an environment.

The growth of the Internet as a business tool has greatly accelerated the development of products for authoring and managing Web-based information. The ease of use and availability of these tools, coupled with corporate intranets and extranets, has had an extremely positive impact on document management. Documentation can now be stored on an intranet Web site, easily accessible to anyone who's interested. Considering that Windows ships with both Web server and Web browser software, and that word processing tools such as Microsoft Word can easily create HTML files, there's no excuse for not having current, accessible documentation for your Terminal Server project.

Certainly, accessibility alone doesn't guarantee that documentation will actually be created. Time and resources must be available to ensure that the necessary documentation is written. Even if you're not responsible for managing the implementation, don't fool yourself into believing that you're saving time by not writing documentation. In fact, you're doing the opposite. Documentation is very much like insurance, whose inherent worth becomes apparent only when it's needed. Documentation is the foundation for training, upgrades, and even disaster recovery of your Terminal Server environment. When your applications or systems are running smoothly, you don't think about documentation, but if disaster strikes, documentation can provide valuable information that might otherwise be forgotten.

Author's Note

I can't even count how many times I've heard the statement that documentation will be written after the project is completed. Very rarely has this ever happened. By the end of the project, resources such as time and/or money have run out (because of a lack of documentation and planning, perhaps?) and another project is usually waiting to take its place.

Writing documentation makes you think about what you're doing and why you're doing it. It will help you uncover problems or deficiencies in your plan before they have the opportunity to affect your project. ◆

As the project progresses through the implementation, documentation provides a clear footprint of where you've been and where you're going. This allows people who are new to the project to be brought up to speed quickly, without misinterpreting the project's purpose, scope, and direction.

Leveraging Desktop Deployment Flexibility

A Terminal Server implementation is a unique combination of client and server interaction that's unlike a traditional Windows server deployment. Although changes will be made to the client desktop, removing some or possibly all applications from the user's local control, the driving factor of the implementation is not the desktop. The desktop is simply the tool that you will use to deliver Terminal Server access to the user.

Terminal Server provides you with additional flexibility in your deployment that you wouldn't normally have in a traditional desktop upgrade project. Leveraging this flexibility will greatly reduce the impact on end users during the rollout. The goal is to introduce Terminal Server to them with minimal disruption to their work productivity.

Some areas of flexibility are

- **Piloting.** Imagine being able to provide the user with two computers during a pilot. One contains the desktop that the user is piloting, and the other the user's original desktop. As soon as the user encounters a problem with the pilot computer, he or she simply returns to the original desktop until the problem is resolved. The Terminal Server client provides this same functionality. During piloting, the user can run in his or her new Terminal Server environment, returning to the local desktop if problems arise.

- **Testing validation.** One problem that continually arises when performing a desktop upgrade is that differences in client hardware and software can pose compatibility issues for the applications you're deploying. What works fine on one desktop refuses to run on another. The centralized nature of Terminal Server overcomes this problem and provides true validation for your piloting. Testing with a small group of users has greater value in a Terminal Server deployment because once the application is working properly for them, it will work for all users. Testing that Terminal Server is working properly doesn't require that you deploy it to a large number of users. By keeping the initial test groups small, you eliminate many problems early on while being able to quickly respond to user's issues as they arise. If Terminal Server isn't working for 5 users, it won't work for 50. Large-scale pilots add no value until you have validated the small test group. Don't fall into the trap of trying to do too much too quickly.

- **Training.** Terminal Server provides you with the ability to train a user on his or her Terminal Server session from any location, on any client device. Traditional training would involve sending users to a room to train on a generic computer with a configuration that usually didn't accurately reflect the user's personal computer setup. Terminal Server allows users to see a familiar session, regardless of where they're physically located. Training is more consistent with how they'll actually be working. I've been involved in a couple of implementations in which a training room was established with Terminal Server accessible both to demonstrate the new environment and also to train administrative and support staff *prior* to initiating user testing.

- **Application migration.** It's very likely that not all users will have all their local applications moved to Terminal Server. This is an advantage of Terminal Server that isn't always apparent, and in many cases is actually played down. Many references to Terminal Server imply that an implementation requires moving all local applications to the server. I feel that this thinking is tied too much to the traditional desktop upgrade, where all applications are moved to the new computer or reinstalled on the new operating system. Terminal Server provides the unique advantage of moving specific applications into the thin client environment, while leaving other applications, such as those requiring special hardware, on the local computer. Too often I see issues arise in an implementation where a single application that's required by only a few users is holding up an entire deployment. (See the next section for more details.)

Defining the Scope of Terminal Server in Your Business

Human and financial resources and the types of applications in your current user environment will determine the scope of Terminal Server in your business. One of the decisions that will be made very early on in the planning stage of your deployment is determining what the target user community will be. As mentioned in the preceding section, a common problem with many implementations is the misconception that *all* of the user's applications must be moved off the desktop and onto the Terminal Server if any benefit is to be seen in Total Cost of Ownership (TCO). This isn't true. In fact, even moving only a subset of a user's applications can reduce TCO. The key is choosing the right software to move:

- Moving applications that have few support costs or are updated infrequently will show only a small reduction in TCO. Usually the benefits in this situation are not seen until the next major upgrade is required.

- Some prime targets to move are those applications that currently have large support or deployment costs. In most circumstances, the resulting move and standardization of the running environment to Terminal Server will help reduce many of the application issues and costs.

Terminal Server isn't an all-or-nothing solution, and application migrations don't need to all be planned to happen at once. Applications that don't fit within the scope of the project should be left to run on the user's desktop until a later date. If you want to have a successful deployment, clearly define the scope of the project from the beginning and deviate from it as little as possible. The two areas where I have most often seen a change in the scope of Terminal Server are as follows:

- **Client scope.** Partway into the project, a decision is made to expand the client scope to include another user group that appears to be similar to the currently targeted users. Very often this includes adding applications required by these new users. In almost every situation where this has happened, hardware capacity or application issues have caused unexpected problems and delays in the implementation. Whenever possible, avoid modifying the client scope once you have moved beyond planning into piloting or the actual deployment. I discuss determining client scope in the later section "Developing the 'To-Be' Model."

- **Application scope.** Although you're very likely to add and remove applications during the planning, testing, and even the pilot stage of your project, the deployment stage is not the time to be making application additions or modifications. Almost every project will encounter a situation in which an application will be discovered during deployment that would be a good candidate for inclusion in the project. *Don't* add these applications to your environment unless absolutely necessary. I would suggest instead that the information be inventoried so that it can be reviewed and prioritized at a later time. Any unplanned modifications will almost always have a negative impact on the production environment, particularly if they haven't been part of any previous testing or piloting.

Enlisting Executive Sponsors

Every project must have three things in order to succeed:

- Leadership
- Money
- Human resources

To ensure that these elements are available for the duration of your project, you must enlist the support of one or more *executive sponsors*. An executive sponsor is a senior person within your business who can ensure that the changes you want to introduce are accepted and endorsed by the company from the top down. Top-down knowledge of the project ensures alignment with the company's strategic direction and is your only weapon in dealing with users and management who introduce resistance to your project for political or personal reasons. If you attempt to work in isolation without this top-down support, you will repeatedly have to justify your intentions and run the risk of losing access to one or more of the listed elements.

Author's Note

I was called in once to consult for a company that was having issues with a Terminal Server implementation. They had deployed the product to approximately 200 users and application problems were affecting the users' ability to work. After speaking with a couple of users, I found out that neither they nor their manager had received any prior notification that this change was even being made. Inadequate piloting and training had resulted in an unacceptable release situation. Within a week the project was terminated, and all users were rolled back to their original desktops. The decision to deploy Terminal Server had come from the server support department without the official support of the end users' management. Even though the decision to deploy Terminal Server made sense both technically and from a business perspective, because the proper people had not endorsed it, the project was not allowed to proceed. ◆

Don't Promise What You Can't Deliver

While it sounds quite simple, delivering on promises is very often the issue that causes the most problems. I don't know how many times I have heard someone promise things such as increased performance or greater stability without having any clear idea whether they can deliver this. If an application is slow or buggy on the local desktop, there's no guarantee that moving it to Terminal Server will eliminate either of these problems. It depends on whether the issues are due to the client desktop or the application itself. An application that leaks memory when run on the desktop will continue to leak memory when run on Terminal Server.

Make sure that you set realistic expectations for users. If you end up delivering more, all the better—but don't promise things that you later can't deliver.

Business Process Management

An important part of managing a Terminal Server project is being able to manage the migration of the business processes effectively from the existing "as-is" model to the future "to-be" model. This migration is often called *business process reengineering (BPR)*. When planning the BPR, there are two things you're trying to achieve:

- Minimizing the change in how users must perform their work. You want to integrate Terminal Server into their environment with as little disruption as possible.

- Optimizing the process of managing the end user. By implementing Terminal Server, you're looking to reduce the support requirements of the user and optimize the support that must still be performed. This includes support at the server as well as at the client.

You need to consider the changes that you're introducing to the way in which these jobs have traditionally been done. For example, the existing activities required for maintaining a single desktop will be reduced or eliminated. Application support, hardware support, software upgrades, and training will all be affected. To maximize the benefits of your Terminal Server implementation, you must communicate these changes as effectively as possible. A clearly documented change in business processes will also minimize the uncertainly and misunderstanding around what exactly Terminal Server is bringing to your organization.

> **Tip**
>
> *One common area with a large amount of uncertainty is in the end-user support department. One of the key factors for introducing Terminal Server is the reduction in desktop support costs and hence a reduction in TCO. Most desktop support staff members equate the introduction of Terminal Server with the elimination of their jobs. While this is very rarely the case, Terminal Server will affect how end-user support staff perform their jobs. By involving these support people early and making it clear what their support role will be once the implementation is complete, you'll have a much easier time with enlisting their cooperation to support you during the project.* ◆

To develop an effective BPR plan, you need to have an understanding of how the processes exist today and how they will work after the implementation. These are known as the "as-is" and "to-be" business process models, and together they form the roadmap for your Terminal Server implementation.

Developing the "As-Is" Model

The starting point for developing your BPR plan is determining what your business processes are today. This is commonly known as your *"as-is" model*. In an ideal world, a company would have an "as-is" model available with all the necessary information. In most cases, some form of a model will need to be developed. In forming this model, you need to concentrate on four areas:

- **Users and user support.** Look at how the users work today—which applications they commonly use and which they don't. Before you begin, you should already have an idea as to what groups you will be targeting for the Terminal Server deployment. When preparing the "as-is" model, be sure to look for such things as one-off applications or other exceptions that will need to be flagged and accounted for when planning the implementation. Note what additional hardware users might use or access, particularly such things as file or print servers, scanners, modems, or even proprietary "dongles" required by certain applications. Document concerns, issues, and suggestions that users may have about the existing environment. This will help in determining hardware requirements, pilot user groups, initial implementation groups, special needs users, and exceptions that may need to be excluded from your Terminal Server deployment. Often, you'll be able to establish a group of users during this time that will be used to pilot and test the initial Terminal Server environment.

  Another valuable user consideration is the establishment of measures for such factors as logon times, application speed, time to access network resources, and time required for switching between applications. You shouldn't spend a lot of time attempting to gather large amounts of detailed quantitative data, but some average times can be useful in determining where Terminal Server can save time or boost performance of existing hardware. Remember; don't promise performance gains with Terminal Server until you're sure you can deliver them.

- **Network and network support.** The inclusion of the most accurate network infrastructure information available is a critical component of your "as-is" model. A network diagram should be available that includes all relevant client and server networks that will interact with your Terminal Servers. The types of networks and the supported protocols should also be included. A key piece of information is why servers have been placed in certain locations and if there are any issues with moving them. This is important when looking at where the Terminal Servers will be situated on the network. You'll need to co-locate them with whatever other servers users will need to access through their

Terminal Server sessions. Knowing which servers can be moved and which can't will help in developing an accurate "to-be" model. A network support contact will be required not only to assist with any network issues that may arise but also as a resource for accurate information on network capacity and future direction.

- **Servers and server support.** You need to inventory which server hardware and associated operating systems are currently in production. Of particular interest will be those systems utilized by the end user, such as file and print servers. A Windows domain diagram with the appropriate trust relationships should be included if anything other than a simple domain is in effect. WINS, DHCP, DNS, and other network servers should also be noted, depending on the network protocols being used.

  Determine what domain the Terminal Servers will reside in, and what users are responsible for administering the appropriate resource and account domains. Terminal Server will require the creation of customized administrative groups in the appropriate account domain to support the environment, so including the administrators in the planning process is critical. Don't expect to have anyone's full cooperation if you spring your Terminal Server requirements on him or her at the last minute. A clear understanding of how Terminal Server will fit into the infrastructure is another key requirement to a smooth implementation.

- **Software.** Determine the current software standards within the organization and any exceptions that should exist. Knowing the number of licenses that exist for software is important in determining how the software will be made available on a Terminal Server and whether access restrictions may be required. It's not uncommon to publish applications and manage their licensing by restricting access to members of a specific Windows security group.

Developing the "To-Be" Model

I've always looked on the development of the *"to-be" model* as the creation of the answer to the question, "What are you trying to achieve?" The simple answer is that you're deploying Terminal Server and moving software off the local desktop to run on the server, but the complete answer is much more than that. Your "to-be" model will provide answers to the following questions:

- Who will be using Terminal Server?
- How were these people chosen?
- What software are you going to deploy?

- Which users will use what software?
- What deployment method will you use (desktop replacement, application replacement, etc.)?
- Where will the servers be located and who will be responsible for supporting them?

The most common way to develop the "to-be" model is to work from the "as-is" model to determine the end state in each documented situation. For example, in your "as-is" model you will have noted existing user configurations along with the processes in place to support them. In your "to-be" model, you document how these setups would change to reflect the Terminal Server environment. The information doesn't necessarily need to be extensive, but does need to clearly point out the changes that will be occurring. The changes in how support staff handle client hardware issues might go something like this:

"If a user is having any hardware-related issue, then the desktop support person shouldn't attempt to repair the computer at the user's desk. The user should be directed to sit at an alternate desk and connect to Terminal Server through that machine until this one has been repaired. If no alternate desk is available, a Windows terminal should be provided temporarily, to allow the user to have Terminal Server access until a replacement machine can be delivered. Under no circumstances should the client hardware be disassembled or repaired while the user waits. Getting the user up and working again should be your first priority."

Some other examples might include

- **Updating the network diagram to show the position of the Terminal Servers and any other new or moved hardware within the infrastructure.** A visual representation of your implementation is an excellent way to describe what's happening.
- **Developing Terminal Server-specific support procedures for your help desk so that they can efficiently handle calls from your new users.** This would include training on how to use the remote control features.

To ensure that your "to-be" model is what's required by the business, take the time to describe the implementation clearly and note where you anticipate possible issues. Work closely with the appropriate contacts within the business to ensure that your goals are in line with both their requirements and yours. Afterward, you'll have a plan for implementing Terminal Server that's both clearly understood and accepted by the business.

Policies and Procedures

An important part of developing your "to-be" model is creating or modifying policies and procedures (POPs) for both your clients and your servers. These POPs will be used not only for managing and constructing the environment during implementation, but for continued management once in production. Create POPs that will add value and lead to a more manageable environment—don't create them simply because you *can*. Before putting any POP in place, ask yourself these questions:

- Does the POP you want to introduce resolve or control an issue that exists today or is anticipated to exist in the near future? An example might be setting disk quotas on personal file areas.

- Is this POP easy to communicate? Will it be understood easily by others?

- Is the POP simple enough that the people who are supposed to abide by it (users, developers, and administrators) will do so, or will they seek ways to circumvent it?

- What are the possible ramifications if this POP is not implemented?

Selecting Policies to Implement

Your company most likely already has a number of POPs in place. They are most often implemented to protect the business from legal recourse, lost revenue, or tarnishing of its public image. Some common examples include

- A ban on the use of non-corporate or pirated software from home or the Internet. Being caught with pirated software during an audit can be damaging to both the finances and the reputation of an organization.

- A ban on the viewing or possession of pornographic and other material that may be offensive to others. The downloading of computer files of any kind can also place a large burden on a company's Internet or storage resources.

- Rules concerning the storage of personal data such as personal taxes or children's projects on corporate computers.

- Rules against storing company information on a local PC instead of in an environment (such as a network) where the information is more secure, both from theft and from loss through accidental or purposeful destruction.

- Taking suitable measures to protect against the theft or destruction of company property, including corporate "secrets."

Although each of these issues is important, all are behavioral policies and none of them are specific to the Terminal Server environment. The policies can exist without requiring Terminal Server, and Terminal Server can exist without these policies.

Terminal Server can be used to make the enforcement of these policies easier. For example, using Terminal Server as a complete desktop replacement and providing the user with only a diskless Windows-based terminal would completely remove the need to enforce a policy concerning running pirated software or the local storage of company information for these users.

When developing Terminal Server POPs, concentrate on those that directly relate to its creation, its administration, or its support.

Many POPs for Terminal Server are identical to those designed for the regular desktop environment. The key difference is in the amount of effort expended in enforcement. The enforcement of POPs is inherently difficult when it must be taken out to each user's desktop. The most obvious reason is that it's nearly impossible to monitor or control what users are doing without a very high level of maintenance.

Microsoft has attempted to address this problem by introducing their guidelines for *Zero Administration for Windows (ZAW)*, a set of POPs describing how to reduce the maintenance costs of the end user's desktop. The downside to ZAW is the level of maintenance required to support it.

> **Warning**
>
> *Microsoft's Zero Administration Kit (ZAK) for Windows NT Server, Terminal Server Edition, version 4.0 is intended to aid Terminal Server administrators in creating a more controlled and secure environment and is a supplement to the existing ZAK for Windows NT Workstation documentation. ZAK for Terminal Server is discussed in more detail in Chapter 8, "Server Management Planning."* ◆

These are some of the common areas where you may want to develop POPs for Terminal Server:

- **Terminal Server system installation, configuration, and disaster recovery.** By developing a standard procedure for the creation of your Terminal Servers, you ensure that additional machines can be built at any time to augment the current environment, or possibly recover in a disaster situation.

- **Commercial software selection, installation, upgrades, and back-out plans.** A POP on how software that runs on Terminal Server is managed is very important. It allows you to determine quickly whether a piece of software is suitable for running in the environment, along with the guidelines for testing and implementing into production.

- **Software developer guidelines.** This includes such things as documenting the software installation requirements for the applications in your environment. This is probably the most difficult policy to put into place in a large corporation. Because in-house developers move around frequently and new projects are born quickly, it can be difficult to communicate and enforce in a timely fashion. Very often you'll encounter an application that needs to be deployed on Terminal Server, but wasn't tested in such an environment throughout the development process.

Author's Note

Remember that most developers and their managers will know very little about Terminal Server and will most often completely ignore it until their application is complete. At this point, it can be difficult for them to make code changes if necessary to get their application to run in Terminal Server. This can mean that either the program will end up on the user's desktop, or you'll need to perform some workaround in Terminal Server to get the program to work. Easy accessibility to the necessary Terminal Server policies is key to ensuring that they're followed. ◆

- **In-house and custom-developed software management.** This includes unit testing, acceptance testing, piloting, production promotion, and "emergency" fixes due to software bugs. The proper process for moving these applications into production goes hand in hand with the need to ensure that applications are developed to run in Terminal Server.

Specific policies and procedures for clients, servers, networks, and applications are discussed in the next few chapters, which talk in more detail about implementation planning for each component.

The centralized manageability and homogenous environment introduced by Terminal Server makes it very suitable for defining policies and procedures that can be enforced effectively. Terminal Server brings the user's desktop logically closer to the administrators of the environment, while still providing the required functionality to the user.

5

Network Planning

In this chapter:

- **Terminal Server and Your Network**
  By design, Terminal Server relies heavily on the network infrastructure of an organization to function effectively. The perceived stability of Terminal Server depends on the underlying stability and design of the network.

- **RDP and ICA**
  Both RDP and ICA have network requirements that must be taken into consideration when performing network planning.

- **Printing Considerations**
  With Terminal Server, you need to pay particular attention to both the location of printers and how clients will access them.

- **Dial-up Access**
  The low bandwidth requirements of Terminal Server make it well suited for providing remote users with access to applications and data within the environment.

- **Internet Access**
  Many organizations are looking to use Terminal Server to provide access to corporate applications and resources via the Internet.

Terminal Server and Your Network

By design, Terminal Server relies heavily on the network infrastructure of an organization to function effectively. The perceived stability of Terminal Server depends on the underlying stability and design of the network. A solid understanding of how to configure and deploy Terminal Server is only part of the criteria required for a successful implementation. If users are unable to maintain a reliable connection to the Terminal Server, the environment is unusable from the perspective of both the users and the business.

Author's Note

If you're unfamiliar with the general concepts of networking, see Appendix B, "Network Primer," where I provide an introduction to network communications protocols and physical and logical networks. ♦

If you wanted to perform a traditional application deployment into your company's existing infrastructure, you would need to consider such things as the application's traffic patterns to ensure that the network was designed to meet the application's needs (or vice versa).

In general, applications fall into two broad categories:

- Bandwidth efficient
- Bandwidth inefficient

Bandwidth-inefficient applications waste available network resources, whereas bandwidth-efficient applications make the best use of the existing network resources. An example is the traditional client/server database application. When a bandwidth-inefficient application makes a call to the database server, it asks the server to return a large portion or possibly all of the data in the database to the client for local manipulation. By contrast, a bandwidth-efficient application has the database server perform the required computations, returning only the formulated result to the client.

Consider Figure 5.1, which represents the historical network design concept known as the *80/20 rule*. In this design, the majority (80%) of the communications for local clients is handled by the local file server and never traverses other network segments. Most (if not all) local services would be lost in the event of a local file server failure. Twenty percent of the traffic would still be destined for other network segments. This traffic would most likely include email or access to other shared resources or services.

The increased network demands of many of today's applications, along with changes in how corporations have traditionally worked, are pushing network engineers to develop new networks (in many cases, redesigning existing networks) that can handle these requirements. Cross-functional teams not physically co-located, support issues, server clusters, application-specific file servers, the introduction of new internetworking devices such as multi-technology layer 3, and traditional switches have all contributed to this need. Figure 5.2 shows the shift in design theory and the migration to flat networks, in which the main function of the router now becomes that of isolation, rather than the interconnection of network segments.

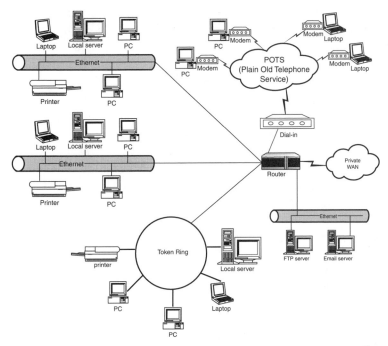

Figure 5.1   *The 80/20 rule: 80% local traffic versus 20% remote traffic.*

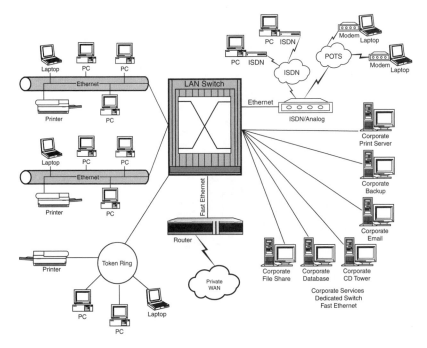

Figure 5.2   *The migration to flat networks: any-to-any corporate communications.*

One common mistake when planning a Terminal Server implementation is to assume that the network requirements are the same as for a traditional application deployment. Most network engineers won't intuitively know the differences between Terminal Server and a regular application deployment, and may plan network infrastructure changes that aren't required, particularly if the existing environment is based around the 80/20 rule.

The way in which Terminal Server operates can allow for a continued return on investment (ROI) for these types of networks. Unlike the traditional client/server relationships in which the desktop client is communicating directly with the database server, Terminal Server creates an indirect communication path from the client to the Terminal Server and then from there to the destination database server. This is demonstrated in Figure 5.3, which depicts the data flow between the client, the Terminal Server, and the back end database or file servers.

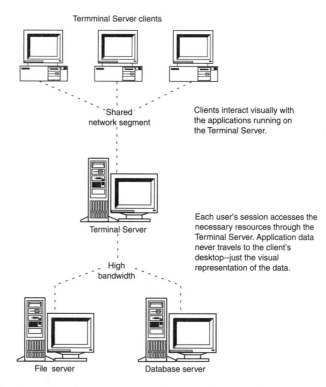

Figure 5.3   *Data flow between Terminal Server clients and back end servers.*

As the figure shows, the database or file server is no longer in direct communication with the client. Instead, the communications occur between the client's Terminal Server session and the appropriate back end server. This creates a situation where the high-bandwidth requirements exist only between the Terminal Server and the data or file server.

Understanding the data flow patterns and required resources for the applications that you'll be putting on Terminal Server will help determine the deployment strategies for your implementation. You need to ensure that bandwidth has been maximized between the Terminal Server(s) and the database/file server(s) that the applications will utilize. Very often, this involves co-locating these servers onto a high-speed backbone to provide dedicated bandwidth, reduce latency, and improve scalability and fault tolerance.

Author's Note

To sum up, good Terminal Server design dictates that Terminal Servers and back end servers should occupy the same LAN segment whenever possible. ◆

Terminal Server Placement in Your LAN

With the lower bandwidth requirements between the client and the Terminal Server (discussed later in this chapter), local area networks (LANs) based on the 80/20 rule or the flat network model can often be used with a Terminal Server implementation without the costly requirements of an infrastructure change. Figure 5.4 illustrates how the network from Figure 5.1 might look after a Terminal Server implementation. The previously distributed servers have now been centralized on the same network as the Terminal Servers. This setup allows for fast local access to the required resources through Terminal Server. The existing client networks now only have to support the desired presentation protocol (ICA or RDP) traffic.

Figure 5.5 shows a similar configuration with a flat network implementation with Terminal Server. In most situations the centralized servers are connected via full-duplex Fast Ethernet, with shared client segments connected to a backbone router or switch.

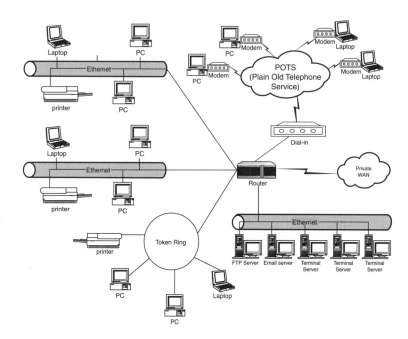

Figure 5.4   *An 80/20 network after a Terminal Server implementation.*

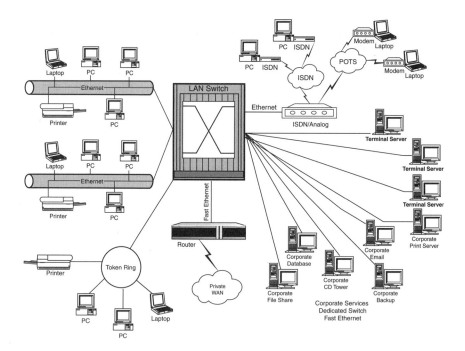

Figure 5.5   *A flat network after a Terminal Server implementation.*

WAN Considerations

The concepts discussed to this point with regard to Terminal Server and the LAN can be extended to include the wide area network (WAN). Today, the very costly WAN lines are under siege from the amount of traffic that's being forced over them. Situations in which clients are accessing network resources located in a separate building—or sometimes even miles away in a separate city—are becoming more common. As a result, companies are forced to keep up by acquiring higher bandwidth connections through leases or other means.

Through the proper deployment of Terminal Server in a WAN configuration, Remote Desktop Protocol (RDP) or Independent Computing Architecture (ICA) can help to greatly reduce the bandwidth requirements of the existing WAN and extend its ROI. To do this successfully, it's important to have a clear idea of the existing bandwidth available, possible latency issues, and the data flow requirements of the clients and their applications.

Figure 5.6 illustrates a common mistake made when wide area deployments of Terminal Server are being planned. The mistake is in co-locating the Terminal Servers with the clients instead of with the data servers. By placing the server local to the client, you're forcing the Terminal Server to cross a WAN connection in order to access the required resources, resulting in the same bandwidth requirements that existed prior to Terminal Server. On further inspection, it's clear that this isn't the optimal solution.

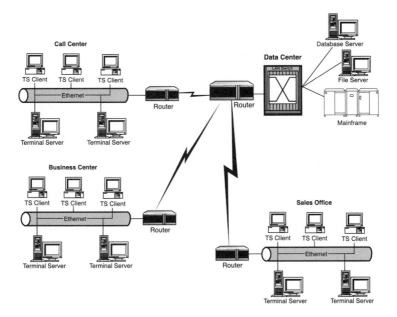

Figure 5.6 *An incorrect deployment of Terminal Servers.*

Figure 5.7 depicts resource allocation and deployment providing the best use of wide area bandwidth. Using this deployment strategy, only the RDP and ICA traffic will traverse the wide area connections. All the bandwidth-intensive processing requirements are at the same physical location as the high-speed switched backbone.

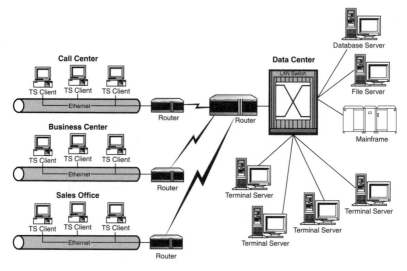

Figure 5.7   *A correct deployment of Terminal Servers.*

Figure 5.7 demonstrates what I consider an ideal scenario for implementing Terminal Server over a WAN. Most often you won't have the luxury of migrating all resources into one location, whether for resource or business reasons. In this situation you need to carefully review what resources can and can't be moved, and position the Terminal Servers accordingly. You may also want to investigate dividing your Terminal Server environment between two or more locations. MetaFrame's server farm feature spans physical networks, allowing for a divided server environment with very little increase in administrative complexity.

Figure 5.8 shows an example of Terminal Servers divided between two locations. One set of Terminal Servers resides at the corporate head office, running a client/server application that accesses a database server, which is also at that location. These Terminal Servers are used solely by the sales office that's also on the same network (Sales Office #2). The data center contains the remainder of the Terminal Servers that make up the environment. Two MetaFrame farm configurations are possible in this environment:

- A single farm, containing published applications from both sites. This strategy would require an ICA gateway. ICA gateways are discussed in Chapter 3, "Citrix MetaFrame."

- Two separate server farms, one in each location. The user would access the appropriate farm based on the desired application.

In either situation, for the ICA information to pass between the two networks and the appropriate clients, the network routers would have to be configured to allow UDP traffic to pass through them. I discuss the ICA and RDP protocol requirements a little later in this chapter.

You could also use RDP in this scenario, but the user would be required to maintain two separate desktops (one for each location), or would have to run the applications within RDP session windows.

Author's Note

Client configurations are discussed in Chapter 6, "Client Planning." ◆

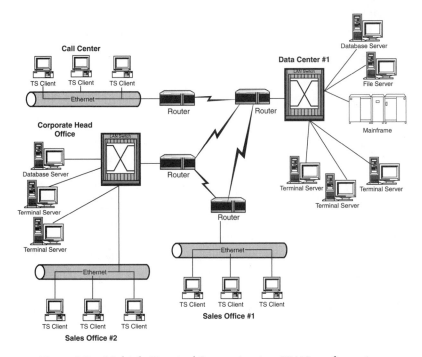

Figure 5.8   *Multiple Terminal Server sites in a WAN configuration.*

Single Points of Failure

One issue that becomes immediately apparent with the centralization of the environment to support Terminal Server is the creation of single points of failure. Look again at Figure 5.8 in the preceding section. If the WAN link to the corporate office goes down, Sales Office #1 will not be able to access any published applications from that location. There are two ways that you can attempt to deal with this problem:

- Develop redundancy in the network to eliminate the single points of network failure. The addition of a WAN link directly from Sales Office #1 to the head office would provide a redundant link to protect against failure.

- Maintain a duplicate Terminal Server environment in a different location that's also accessible. If one site is lost, the other is still available to support user requests. By placing a set of Terminal Servers plus the database server at Sales Office #1, you would protect against all WAN failures.

In almost every situation, the first of these solutions is the preferred method, from both cost and logistics standpoints. Duplicating the Terminal Server environment would probably also require a means of replicating the information between the two database servers, which in turn would result in increased bandwidth requirements. The creation of a low-bandwidth redundant WAN link directly between the two sites would be much more cost effective and much easier to manage.

You should carefully evaluate the requirements for redundancy in your WAN and what risks are associated with each possible failure point. By highlighting the critical interconnections, you can then look to position the Terminal Servers so as to best minimize these redundancy requirements.

Latency and Network Utilization on Client Performance

Although one of the highly touted features of Terminal Server is its ability to function well over low-bandwidth connections, it's still critical that reliable, sustained communication channels exist between the client and the Terminal Server. One of the most important network requirements for Terminal Server is minimizing the latency in the client connection to the server. Latency is critical because of the impact it can have on the user's perceived server or application performance. Latency manifests itself to the user as sluggish screen updates or unresponsive keyboard or mouse input.

Author's Note

When latency is an issue in the environment, users encounter situations in which they can move the mouse pointer around the desktop but can't click on anything or provide keyboard input to the Terminal Server session. This is because the local mouse tracking is handled by the client independently of data being sent to or received from the server. ♦

High latency can also result in client disconnects from the Terminal Server. For optimal user interaction with the Terminal Server, latency should be kept under 100ms. At 150ms users experience a decline in responsiveness, and anything over 300ms will usually result in severe client performance issues. Keeping the average utilization in a network segment to less than 30% will help to minimize latency on that segment.

Tip

A simple latency test is to use ping *to gather average round-trip times between a computer on the client network and one on the server network. For example, on a Windows system the following command would ping the server PMT 100 times with packets 1KB in size and pipe the output to a text file called out.txt:*

```
ping -t -n 100 -l 1000 PMT > out.txt
```

You can then average the round-trip times to get an idea as to the average latency in your network. While not exact, the results will certainly give you an idea as to whether potential latency problems may exist. ♦

Both RDP and ICA have similar utilization requirements, with an average of about 20Kbps per connected user session. The exact value depends on a number of factors, including compression, bitmap caching, and client device mapping features such as Clipboard or print mapping. In many situations, 20Kbps is *above* the average requirement, but is adequate for performing some initial estimates on network requirements—particularly over lower-bandwidth connections, such as 56K frame relay or ISDN.

A more accurate utilization assessment will require performing some analysis in a test environment running the applications that you intend to deploy. The applications that will be used have an impact on the overall utilization of the client. Highly graphical applications have higher require-ments than simple word processing applications. Table 5.1 shows an exam-ple of the average utilization for both ICA and RDP in different connection configurations. The results were collected over a half-hour timeframe while running a WinBatch script that executed various Microsoft Word and Microsoft Excel functions. A script was used so that a repeatable client ses-sion could be run to gather comparable information. Performance Monitor was run on the Terminal Server and collected data on the session object.

Author's Note

*Citrix's Supercache feature was not enabled during these tests. For more informa-
tion on this option, see the "Terminal Server Performance Tuning" section of
Chapter 12, "Terminal Server Configuration and Tuning." ◆*

Warning

*The results demonstrated here are simply an example of how average values can
be gathered. This information should not be construed as the absolute truth on
how the RDP or ICA protocols will perform under different circumstances. ◆*

Table 5.1   Sample of ICA 3.0, RDP 4.0, and RDP 5.0 Protocol Utilizations

Protocol	Options	Maximum Kbps	Minimum Kbps	Average Kbps	Time(s)
ICA 3.0	None	43.49	0.36	7.58	1879
ICA 3.0	Compression	16.60	0.04	2.44	1879
ICA 3.0	Compression + bitmap caching	38.68	0.04	2.74	1879
RDP 4.0	None	87.85	0.12	16.24	1879
RDP 4.0	Compression	35.09	0.11	6.94	1879
RDP 4.0	Compression + bitmap caching	31.74	0.11	6.65	1879
RDP 5.0	None	75.57	0.00	9.89	1900
RDP 5.0	Compression	57.26	0.00	4.49	1900
RDP 5.0	Compression + bitmap caching	53.13	0.00	4.53	1900

Figure 5.9 shows the graphed data for the three different ICA sessions;
Figure 5.10 shows the corresponding results for the RDP 5.0 sessions. In
both cases, notice that both the "compression" and "compression with
bitmap caching" graphs are practically identical. In my tests, there was very
little graphical data being displayed, mostly text entry and data manipulation in Microsoft Excel and Microsoft Word. Although the results are very
specific to the described configuration, they demonstrate how some average
numbers can be obtained quickly for a given setup. Of course, longer sampling times with multiple users would provide more accurate estimates on
the bandwidth requirements for each protocol with the selected options.

ICA with no compression or bitmap caching (ICA-tcp#14)
Performance Monitor
ICA with compression only (ICA-tcp#15)
ICA with compression and bitmap caching (ICA-tcp#16)

Figure 5.9 *Graphed results for the ICA user sessions.*

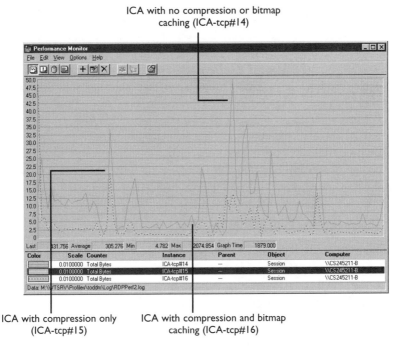

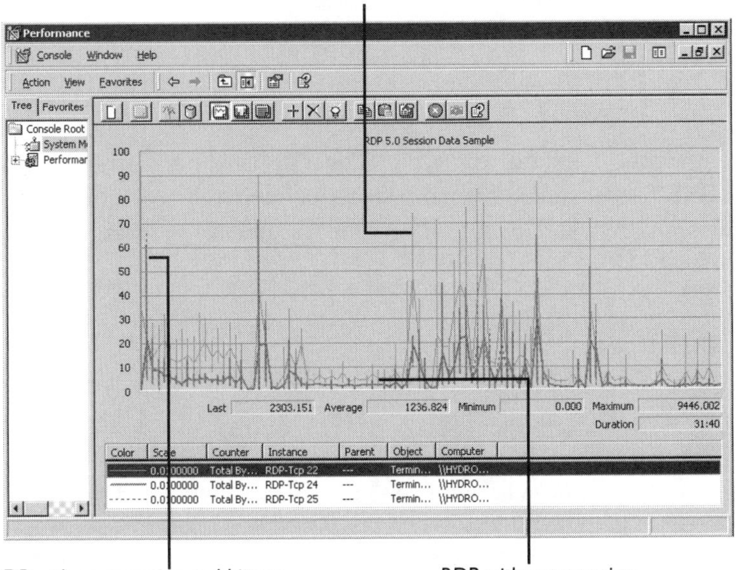

RDP with no compression or bitmap caching (RDP-tcp#22)
Performance
RDP 5.0 Session Data Sample
RDP with compression and bitmap caching (RDP-tcp#25)
RDP with compression only (RDP-tcp#24)

Figure 5.10 *Graphed results for the RDP 5.0 user sessions.*

Author's Note

Terminal Server provides special counters for Performance Monitor that can be used for monitoring user sessions, including the number of input and output bytes per session. On Windows NT 4.0, Terminal Server Edition, the object labeled Session contains the appropriate counters, while on Windows 2000 Terminal Services, the object is labeled Terminal Services Session. For both, all currently available sessions are listed for monitoring. ◆

Let's assume that after some vigorous testing, it's determined that 12Kbps is the average utilization per client. If this was the *only* traffic on a 10Mbps shared Ethernet segment, theoretically it could support approximately 250 clients without exceeding the 30% utilization cap discussed earlier. The formula to derive this is the following:

```
C = (B/A) × P
```

where

C = Number of client nodes.

B = Total bandwidth available in Kbps.

A = Average utilization per node in Kbps/client.

P = Percentage utilization cap.

So, with an average utilization per node of 12Kbps, a total bandwidth of 10Mbps (10000Kbps), and a utilization percentage cap of 30% (0.3) would give you the following:

```
C = (10000Kbps / 12Kbps/client) × 0.3

  = 833.33 clients × 0.3

  = 250 clients
```

Of course, the commonly taught practical upper limit is around 75 nodes on a single Ethernet shared segment, so it's unlikely that any organization has a node count anywhere near 250. A typical segment today has between 12 and 48 hosts.

RDP and ICA

For the TCP/IP protocol, RDP and ICA use the following well-known ports:

Protocol	Function	Port Number
RDP	Listening port for client connections	TCP:3389
	Load balancing (using Microsoft Network Load Balancing)	UDP:2504
ICA	Listening port for client connections	TCP:1494
	ICA Browser (includes Load Balancing)	UDP:1604

The ICA listening port can be modified by using the ICAPORT command. (See its description in Appendix A, "Terminal Server/MetaFrame Command Reference," for more information on this command, or simply type **ICAPORT** from a command prompt to find the usage information.) After the listening port has changed, any ICA clients that want to connect to this server will have to be modified to connect to this different port. The ICA browser and RDP ports can't be modified.

Client-Generated Server Lists

Both ICA and RDP clients can query for a list of all available MetaFrame/Terminal Servers. An RDP client generates a list of Terminal Servers by querying the master (or backup) Microsoft network browser for a list of servers with the Terminal Server server type. For an RDP client to be able to view a list of Terminal Servers located on a different network from the client, the appropriate name services (DNS/WINS) must be configured in the environment. Regardless of whether a user can generate a complete server list, a server connection can be established as long as the address or hostname is known.

Author's Note

For readers who are familiar with the Microsoft network browser system, the Terminal Server type is SV_TYPE_TERMINALSERVER with the hexadecimal code 0x02000000. If you were to use the browstat *command on a Windows 2000/NT4 workstation, a Windows 2000 Terminal Server entry would look something like this:*

```
\\TSE01   NT  05.00 (W,S,NT,SS,BBR,02000000)
```

Note that, in addition to the standard types such as workstation (W) and server (S), it also shows the type 02000000, *flagging it as a Terminal Server.* ◆

Server browsing from an ICA client doesn't use Microsoft's network browsing, but instead uses the ICA browser service running on an elected MetaFrame server master browser. The client communicates with the master browser in order to acquire both the server list and the published application list. Communication with the server is established using directed datagrams to UDP port 1604. This same port is used in all communications between MetaFrame servers, including load balancing and server farm information. For users to get a list of servers located on a different network, the router must pass this UDP data. Just as with RDP, an ICA client can still connect to a MetaFrame server, even if it doesn't show up on the server list, as long as the network address or computer name is known and a network path to that server is available.

Author's Note

ICA browsers are discussed in more detail in Chapter 3. ♦

Multihomed Terminal Servers

Special consideration must be given to configuring a Terminal Server as a *multihomed* host. One requirement is that Service Pack 4 or higher be applied to Windows NT 4.0 Terminal Server. A number of issues dealing specifically with multihoming have been corrected by this service pack, including possible access violations and a security hole in disabling source routing that would allow packets containing incorrect data in the route pointer field to be routed through the multihomed host.

Tip

The term multihomed is commonly used to describe a host computer that has multiple IP addresses assigned to it. The host is usually physically connected to multiple networks.

The IPX protocol is not supported in mulithomed computers due to a Microsoft Winsock limitation. ♦

When a MetaFrame server has been set up as a multihomed host, it's possible that the server would be elected as the master ICA browser for both networks. Under these circumstances, two distinct browser data sets are maintained, completely independent of each other.

When a request for the ICA master browser is sent by a client to this machine, the ICA browser checks the routing table on the server and attempts to provide the IP address of the network interface card (NIC) that's accessible by the client. If the client is located on a network to which the server is directly connected, the routing table immediately resolves to the proper interface and the correct information is sent to the client.

A problem arises if the client is located on a network that isn't directly accessible by any of the interfaces on the Terminal Server, as shown in Figure 5.11. Because only one default gateway is active (the gateway associated with the first bound NIC) on a multihomed server, it's possible that the current default gateway won't produce a valid route to the client's network (Client C in the figure). There are two options available to address this issue:

- Install Microsoft Routing and Remote Access Services (RRAS) and use one of the provided routing protocols. See the online documentation provided with RRAS for complete information on configuration and use.

- Define static routes in the server's routing table. Static routes are created using the ROUTE ADD command from a command prompt. Type ROUTE from a Terminal Server command prompt for more information on this command.

Tip

When configuring the TCP/IP properties for your NICs, make sure that you define only one default gateway. ◆

A multihomed configuration is typically considered a way to distribute the load on a Terminal Server between two network cards. One is configured to manage Terminal Server client connections; the other is used for file or database server connections. While it technically makes sense, in all implementations that I've worked with, I have yet to see the scenario where network load on a properly configured Terminal Server environment had any impact on its operation, unless the network itself was suffering from high utilization—at which point, other systems aside from Terminal Server would also be affected.

From the standpoint of Terminal Server connections, it isn't too difficult to multimome a Terminal Server because you can define the network card to which you want to bind the ICA or RDP listening ports (see the "Connection Configuration" section of Chapter 12 for the details on how to create client connections).

But you should be aware that, when running MetaFrame, you can't control which NIC the ICA Browser service will bind to. By default, it will be available on all NICs for each of the installed protocols. This means that under normal ICA browser election conditions, the ICA browser on either interface may become the master browser. You should configure a multihomed MetaFrame server to *not* participate in ICA master browser elections.

If you're planning to have multihomed MetaFrame servers, you'll need to ensure that this is a documented part of the implementation plan for the servers.

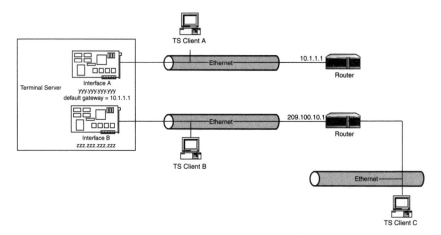

Figure 5.11 *Client accessibility from a multihomed MetaFrame server.*

Tip

Another common problem that arises with a multihomed MetaFrame server is when the QSERVER *command (also known as* QUERY SERVER*) is used to list the master browser data. By default, this command will list information for the first bound interface only. To view the browser information from the second interface, you must explicitly specify the IP address of the interface to be queried. For example, issuing this command:*

```
qserver /tcpserver:192.168.10.5
```

would list the information from the ICA master browser on that subnet. For a complete description of the QSERVER *command, see Appendix A, "Terminal Server/MetaFrame Command Reference." For more information on the ICA master browser, see Chapter 3.* ◆

Supported Protocols

As mentioned in Chapters 1 and 2, the following network protocols are supported by the RDP and ICA presentation protocols:

- RDP currently only runs on top of TCP/IP.
- ICA runs on top of TCP/IP, IPX, SPX, or NetBEUI.

Regardless of which client or protocol is used to connect to a Terminal Server, once the user session has been established on the server, that user can access any available network resources using any of the network protocols installed on the Terminal Server.

For example, a user could use the RDP client to connect (via TCP/IP) to a Terminal Server that's running both TCP/IP and the NWLink IPX/SPX protocol. Once connected, the user could use IPX to connect to any valid NetWare file server. The user session would communicate with the NetWare server using IPX, while Terminal Server and the client session communicate using TCP/IP.

Printing Considerations

An important requirement for almost any user is the ability to print. With Terminal Server, you need to pay particular attention to both the location of printers and how clients will access them. Figure 5.12 shows a typical WAN scenario with printers situated locally on each client network.

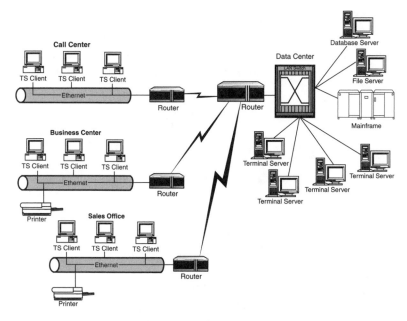

Figure 5.12 *Typical WAN configuration with network printers.*

When a user in this scenario wants to print to a local printer from the Terminal Server session, the print job has to traverse the WAN to reach the desired printer.

All printing requires additional network bandwidth. The exact amount depends on how often users are printing and what they're printing. The larger or more complex the print job, the more bandwidth required. One thing that you can do is to distribute clients, Terminal Servers, print servers, and printers in such a way as to minimize the amount of network travel required to get the print job to the printer. There are three common scenarios for providing a client access to printers from within Terminal Server:

- Remote WAN printing
- Remote LAN printing
- Client printing

The following sections look at each of these scenarios in more detail.

Remote WAN Printing

In this configuration, a print server is located on the same network as the *user*. When the user prints from within Terminal Server, the server sends the print job directly to the print server. I usually refer to this configuration as *remote WAN printing*, because the print server is located across a WAN link from the Terminal Server, as shown in Figure 5.13. This is a common configuration for an existing Windows implementation, since the print server is most often located on the same network as the printers it's supporting.

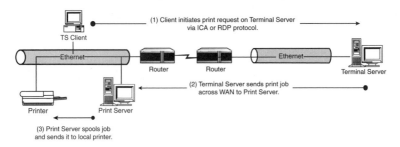

Figure 5.13   *Remote WAN printing.*

When a print job is initiated on the Terminal Server, the data is normally *not* spooled on the Terminal Server, but instead passes immediately to the remote print server where it's spooled for printing to the appropriate printing device.

Remote WAN printing is the preferred configuration method if users on the remote network will need access to print from their local desktops. For example, if you're making Office 2000 available through Terminal Server, but users will continue to run AutoCAD locally, they still need to be able to print from AutoCAD to their printer. This configuration ensures that local printer traffic isn't unnecessarily crossing the WAN. Remember, print jobs that are initiated from within Terminal Server are only crossing the WAN once, on their way from the Terminal Server to the print server.

If users need to run completely from within Terminal Server with no local printing requirements, consider the next scenario, remote LAN printing.

Remote LAN Printing

In this configuration, the print server is located on the same network as the Terminal Server (see Figure 5.14). Print jobs are sent from the Terminal Server to the print server, where they're spooled and then sent to the physical printer located either on the LAN or across a WAN link. I refer to this as *remote LAN printing* because the print server is located on the same network as the Terminal Server.

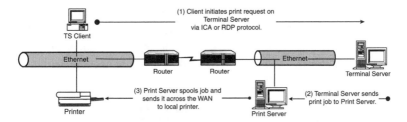

Figure 5.14   *Remote LAN printing.*

Remote LAN printing is the standard configuration when both clients and servers are situated within a single flat network, such as the one shown earlier in Figure 5.2, or possibly an 80/20 LAN configuration as shown in Figure 5.1, since no WAN links exist.

When clients are separated from the Terminal Servers by a WAN link, this scenario is only valid if all remote clients are performing *all* processing from within Terminal Server and don't require the ability to print directly from their local client device. If local printing is required, the user's print job would traverse the WAN twice to print: first from the client to the print server, and then back again from the print server to the physical printer.

Redirected Client Printing

The third scenario involves users printing directly to a printer configured on the local client device. There are two ways that this can be done:

- Use regular Microsoft Networking to create a network printer share on the client device so that it can then be reached from within a Terminal Server session. Of course, this is only valid for Windows-based clients (excluding most Windows terminals).

- Use the automatic client printer mapping feature available with both the RDP and ICA clients. Client printer mapping allows any printer that has been configured on the local client to automatically be configured and available from within the user's Terminal Server session.

Tip

RDP client printing is only supported with Windows 2000 Terminal Services. If you want to use automatic client printing with NT 4.0 Terminal Server, you'll need to use MetaFrame and the ICA client. ♦

The ICA client supports printers that are physically connected to the client as well as network printers to which the client is connected. The RDP client only supports printers that are directly connected to the client device. Figure 5.15 demonstrates the print job flow in the client printer scenario.

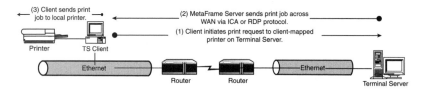

Figure 5.15   *Client printing.*

While the specifics differ on how ICA and RDP handle client printer mappings, the general job flow is similar. The print job is processed on the Terminal Server and directed to the client, which then performs one of the following:

- If the printer is locally attached, the job is spooled on the client and sent to the printer.

- If the printer is a network printer, the job is redirected to the appropriate print server, where it's spooled and printed. This network printer option is only available with the ICA client.

Redirected client printing is most useful in two situations:

- **When clients have printers that are directly connected to their computers.** Client printer mappings provide a seamless way to access a locally attached printer without the user having to create a network share.

- **When used in conjunction with one or more published applications running in a seamless window.** When an application is in a seamless window, it appears to the user to be running locally. Client printer mapping enables the user to consistently access the same printer configuration regardless of whether the application is locally installed or accessed through a MetaFrame server. Seamless window functionality is discussed in Chapter 3.

Client printing is almost always used in combination with remote WAN printing (discussed earlier) when network printers are accessed by using the ICA client. Instead of the Terminal Server directly accessing the print server, it communicates with the client, which in turn contacts the print server. Because of this, the print server should be on the same network as the client to minimize unnecessary network utilization.

Dial-up Access

The low bandwidth requirements of Terminal Server make it well suited to providing remote users with access to applications and data within your environment. This can have great appeal to many organizations because the data itself never has to leave the internal network—only the visual representation is sent to the client.

Citrix's WinFrame product, the first multiuser-based version of Windows NT, was originally developed and marketed as a dial-up solution, allowing dial-up users to have LAN-like access to Windows applications such as Microsoft Mail. While the latest generation of this product contains many new features and enhancements, the basic advantages of accessing the product over a dial-up connection still exist. Many "fat" applications that exhibit extremely poor performance over a dial-up connection run at near-LAN speed when accessed through Terminal Server. Referring once again to Figure 5.1 or 5.2, notice the typical dial-up configuration in an environment with Terminal Server.

From a networking planning standpoint, very little needs to be done to provide dial-up access to a Terminal Server environment. As long as a dial-up user can establish a presence on your network, he or she will be able to use either the RDP or ICA client to access Terminal Server. If you'll be deploying the RDP client, remember that users will require TCP/IP dial-up networking.

Direct dial-in can be configured for the Terminal Server if you install Remote Access Services (RAS) or use the client dial-in option with MetaFrame. I recommend these strategies only for very small Terminal Server implementations, as they don't provide the same robust network support that dedicated dial-up products can provide and place extra resource requirements on the Terminal Server itself. The installation of MetaFrame dial-up support is discussed in Chapter 11, "MetaFrame Installation"; the ICA client dial-up support is covered in Chapter 14, "ICA Client Installation and Configuration."

Internet Access

Today, many organizations are leveraging the availability of the Internet to provide connectivity between remote offices or mobile users and corporate data centers. This is particularly appealing for small to medium sized corporations that don't have the resources to acquire dedicated WAN links between remote offices. In Chapter 15, "Web Computing with MetaFrame," I talk in detail about implementing the Web features available with MetaFrame.

As a result, many organizations are now using Terminal Server to provide access to corporate applications and resources via the Internet. The increased popularity of the Internet coupled with the availability of Web-based ICA clients has spawned the creation of a new service industry known as the *application service provider (ASP)*.

Author's Note

As the name suggests, an ASP provides its customers with access to a set of applications through a thin client solution. Instead of the client purchasing the software and installing it on the local computer, the client leases or rents access to the applications and disk space to store data. This allows organizations such as law or accounting firms to have access to the latest software without the requirements of an in-house information technology (IT) department. A low monthly fixed cost, usually bundled with support, is one of the key selling points of an ASP. You can find out more about ASPs by visiting the Citrix Web site at http://www.citrix.com *or ASP island at* www.aspisland.com ✦

Providing connectivity to Terminal Server via the Internet has its own set of challenges that must be considered carefully. The two areas of focus are security and connectivity.

Security

The number one issue with providing access to your Terminal Server environment over the Internet is security. Simply stated, your goal is to allow only authorized users access to your environment. The type and extent of security that you implement will depend on the size of your organization, what services you want to provide through Terminal Server, and the money that you have available to spend. There are three main configurations that you can implement to provide access to Terminal Server:

- Placing Terminal Server within a demilitarized zone (DMZ).
- Accessing Terminal Server over a virtual private network (VPN).
- Accessing Terminal Server directly using high encryption.

Most other Internet configurations are simply a variation on one of these configurations. I suggest if you're not familiar with firewalls and Internet security that you enlist the assistance of someone who is. There's very little room for error when establishing a secure presence on the Internet.

The Demilitarized Zone

Figure 5.16 shows a typical topology for implementing Internet security. In addition to the obligatory firewall there is also what's called a *demilitarized zone (DMZ)*. A DMZ is a network that's either sandwiched between two firewalls, as shown here, or in some situations sits out in the open directly off the router. In either situation, the DMZ exists as a location where resources that need to be accessed by clients on the Internet can be placed. Access to an external resource doesn't automatically grant them access to the internal network. This way, if a malicious attack compromises the security of an external resource in the DMZ, it doesn't mean that your internal security has been compromised. Without a DMZ, your internal network would be at risk.

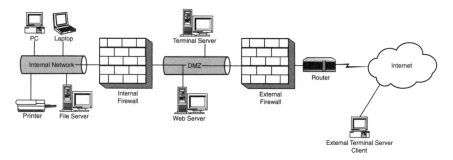

Figure 5.16   *Terminal Server access through a DMZ.*

If you have only a few machines that service the Internet, the DMZ is an optimal configuration, since the inbound connections are limited to a set number of machines that can be administered easily.

The drawback to a DMZ is that there usually are very few (if any) access points open from the DMZ into the internal network, so a resource placed in the DMZ has no access to internal resources such as file servers. This can be a problem, particularly if you want to implement Terminal Server as a means of remote connectivity into the internal network.

Virtual Private Networks

One alternative to placing Terminal Servers into a DMZ is to implement a *virtual private network* (VPN) solution. VPNs have become increasingly popular as the technology has become more stable and secure on the Microsoft platform. A VPN can be thought of as a special case of dial-up access through the Internet. A client on the network establishes a connection to a corporate VPN server visible on the Internet. The VPN encapsulates all data sent between the two points within encrypted packets that hide the actual communications going on between the client and the server. Figure 5.17 shows a VPN between a client on the Internet and a Terminal Server located within the internal network.

VPNs are also used to create extranets. An *extranet* is two or more private networks connected through an unsecured (public) network such as the Internet. A VPN connection exists between the private networks, allowing them to talk securely with each other.

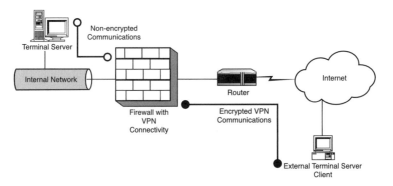

Figure 5.17   *Terminal Server access through a VPN.*

Author's Note

Today, many firewall technologies also provide VPN services. An excellent example of this is Check Point's Firewall-1.

Many ISPs will also provide VPN solutions at their end, completely removing the requirement for you to manage the configuration. ◆

Direct Terminal Server Access

Although I use the term *direct*, in a direct Terminal Server access setup the Terminal Servers themselves are not directly connected to the Internet, but are accessed through a firewall that has the required ports open only to the specific Terminal Server IP addresses. Figure 5.18 shows this configuration, which is very similar in appearance to the VPN example in the preceding section. The one difference is that the security is enforced through the high encryption (either RDP or ICA) of the Terminal Server connection and not through the VPN.

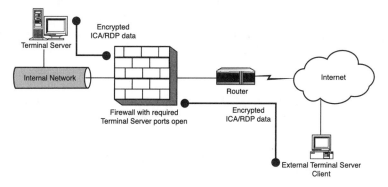

Figure 5.18   *Terminal Server access through a high-encryption client.*

The biggest weakness in this configuration is the passwords used by the users. Unless strong passwords are enforced, a hacker who has the necessary ICA or RDP client has only to guess an account password to gain access to your environment. Additional policies and restrictions on the firewall can help to reduce an unauthorized person's ability to reach the logon prompt only if clients are coming from a static location or using additional client-side firewall security.

Author's Note

Chapter 15 explains how to configure "direct" access to MetaFrame through a firewall, including an example configuration using CheckPoint FireWall-1. ◆

I would consider the direct Terminal Server connection to be an alternative to a VPN solution if you want to provide remote users with access to your Terminal Server environment. If you want to provide anonymous access to your environment—to demonstrate an application, for example—consider placing the Terminal Server in a DMZ configuration.

Connection Availability

An important point to remember whenever utilizing a public network such as the Internet is that you're not in control of latency, bandwidth, or overall stability. If you want to establish an extranet configuration between two branch offices, you may be able to establish a VPN setup with your ISP that includes a quality of service (QoS) minimum that would guarantee a certain level of bandwidth. This solution will not help roaming users who can establish a session from anywhere over the Internet.

Usually, if your clients are establishing an Internet presence through the same ISP as your business is using, the connectivity is more reliable than if the user is connecting through a different ISP. Terminal Server is much less forgiving about changes in bandwidth than some other Internet applications such as FTP or a Web browser.

TCP/UDP Ports

As mentioned earlier, for ICA or RDP packets to pass through a firewall or router the following TCP and UDP ports must be open:

Presentation Protocol	Direction	Port	Notes
ICA	Inbound	TCP:1494	Used to establish the ICA session. An alternate port can be defined on the server, but must also be defined on the client.
ICA	Inbound	UDP:1604	Used for querying for server and application lists and connecting to a load-balanced published application. If users are connecting directly to a server, this port isn't required.
RDP	Inbound	TCP:3389	Used for establishing the RDP session.
Both	Outbound	TCP/UDP: high ports 1023 to 65535	

The rules for establishing an ICA or RDP connection are conceptually the same as for FTP or Telnet sessions. As mentioned earlier, Chapter 15 provides an example configuration using CheckPoint FireWall-1 to allow ICA connectivity.

6

Client Planning

In this chapter:

- **The Thin Client**
  No matter how powerful and robust your server is, or how well you have architected your environment, in the end the success of the project will be measured by the usability of the client.

- **RDP Client Support**
  When looking for a Terminal Server–only client, you're looking for computing devices that support the Microsoft Remote Desktop Protocol (RDP).

- **ICA Client Support**
  The MetaFrame additions extend the reach of the Terminal Server client beyond those supported by RDP to include those devices that support the Citrix Independent Computing Architecture (ICA) protocol.

- **Windows-Based Terminals**
  As with other traditional terminals (3270, VT220, and so on), the goal of the Windows-based terminal is to provide a fast, low-cost, and reliable way to access a Windows Terminal Server environment.

- **Deployment Scenarios with RDP and ICA**
  The presentation protocol that you want to use can influence your decision on what deployment scenario to implement.

- **Client Deployment and Support Planning**
  When planning and developing your Terminal Server implementation, it's easy to get caught up in the technical details and forget or trivialize the planning requirements for both your users and your support staff.

The Thin Client

No matter how powerful and robust your server is, or how well you have architected your environment, in the end the success of the project will be measured by the usability of the client. If users can't work productively in their new environment, you haven't succeeded in your implementation. An understanding of what will be most important and most noticeable to your users will go a long way in helping your deployment.

A Terminal Server client deployment can be classified in one of three broad categories:

- Desktop replacement
- Desktop integration
- Application replacement

The exact features and functionality available within each category will depend on the client that's implemented. Before discussing the pros and cons of specific clients in more detail, I'll begin by looking at the differences between desktop replacement and application replacement.

Desktop Replacement

As the name suggests, *desktop replacement* involves moving all the applications that a user is running on his or her local desktop to run completely from within a Terminal Server session. No applications are running on the client's local device except for the Terminal Server client. When people talk about Terminal Server and thin clients in general, the desktop-replacement scenario is the configuration that usually springs to mind. Figure 6.1 shows a simple example of this scenario: a Windows 2000 desktop session running on a local Windows NT 4.0 desktop.

Two main types of client devices are used to deliver desktop replacement to the end user:

- **Windows-based terminal.** This is the preferred device when a desktop-replacement project is being considered because of its Total Cost of Ownership (TCO) advantages. A *Windows-based terminal* (*WBT*) is conceptually the same as an X Windows or 3270 terminal. Very little local processing or storage is normally provided. Most WBTs have a very small footprint, providing only a monitor, mouse, and keyboard for the user. Additional support such as sound is available, depending on the terminal manufacturer. WBTs are discussed in more detail in the later section "Windows-Based Terminals."

- **Stripped-down personal computer.** In this scenario the PC is functioning as a terminal by providing access to the user's Terminal Server session only, without maintaining local storage or applications. The PC will most often contain only the required network services so that it can establish the session connection, and usually has local security policies to prevent the end user from modifying the PC configuration. Many companies that use PCs to deliver desktop replacement do so in order to reduce their TCO by reusing existing hardware that would otherwise have to be replaced. PCs can have a higher TCO than WBTs, particularly if policies are not in place to prevent users from manipulating the PC's configuration or maintaining local applications or data. Older desktop hardware such as Pentium or 486 class machines make ideal PC terminals, as they typically have sufficient power to support a 32-bit operating system (Windows 95 or 98) and the RDP or ICA client.

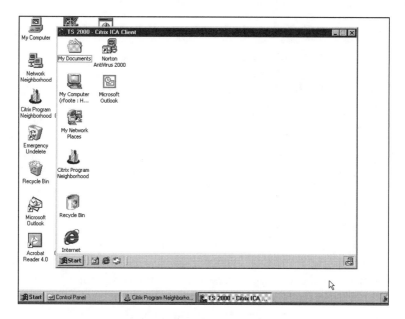

Figure 6.1 *Desktop replacement.*

Desktop replacement is most often targeted at the type of user known as a *task-based worker*. The task-based worker is someone who performs a very specific job function with a common set of applications. A customer service call center is an excellent example of a group of task-based workers. The key to their productivity is access to the required applications. Desktop replacement allows a consistent environment to be available to such users at any time and from any client device.

While desktop replacement is not restricted to task-based workers, I've found that these users are much easier to migrate into a desktop-replacement scenario because of their common application usage and specific job roles. More diversified user groups such as technical support or development staff use a much broader range of applications, and as a result can be much more difficult to move completely to a desktop-replacement environment. For these types of users, an application-replacement scenario usually works best. Application replacement is discussed shortly.

> **Author's Note**
>
> *Any kind of Windows-based terminal deployment usually involves a desktop-replacement scenario. An exception to this rule would be the use of terminals that provide an embedded client operating system that delivers a local desktop. The Netier NetXpress Windows-based terminal is an example, providing an embedded version of Windows NT Workstation that runs on the client device. This terminal even allows applications to be installed locally. In this situation, either desktop or application replacement is a viable option. Of course, cost and performance would be two major considerations when looking at something like this versus a stripped-down PC. ◆*

Desktop Integration

Desktop integration is very similar to desktop replacement, except that instead of the client running solely within the remote desktop, Terminal Server provides the user with access to a Windows desktop in addition to the user's local non–Windows client. For example, a user who has a Macintosh or UNIX X Windows workstation may use Terminal Server to gain access to a Windows desktop. This setup allows an organization to standardize on Windows-based applications without requiring the users to either switch to a Windows desktop or acquire an additional Windows computer to go with their non–Windows machine.

This scenario is most common with users who require very specific client hardware to perform their main job function but also need to run one or more Windows applications. An example might be engineers or architects who use UNIX-based graphical workstations, or desktop publishers who use Macintosh computers. Figure 6.2 demonstrates a Windows 2000 desktop accessed from within a Linux client.

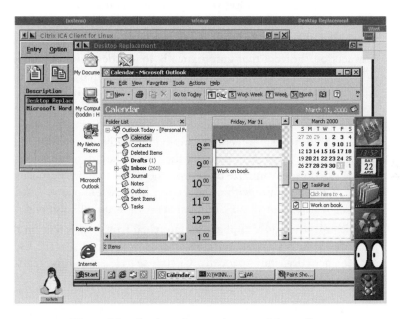

Figure 6.2   *Desktop integration on a Linux client.*

Application Replacement

While desktop replacement is very often the ideal solution for a Terminal Server implementation, it's rarely the most practical. A much more common implementation scenario is *application replacement*. The idea behind application replacement is simply to remove the application from the user's local desktop and make it available from Terminal Server, while leaving other applications in the user's local control. Application replacement allows for a much broader user base to be included in a Terminal Server implementation, since the only requirement is that users need to access the application that will be served by Terminal Server. The affected users are no longer restricted to a particular department or functional group. Application replacement is typically delivered in one of three ways:

- **Terminal Server desktop containing the common applications.** This configuration requires the user to work in two desktops simultaneously (the local desktop and the Terminal Server desktop) and usually should be avoided unless working with power users. Most regular users have a lot of conceptual difficulty working simultaneously in two different desktops. This is equivalent to the Windows desktop integration on non–Windows clients solution discussed earlier.

- **Connection shortcut that automatically loads the desired application.** When loaded, the application runs within a Terminal Server client window that's sized appropriately. Figure 6.3 shows Microsoft Word running in this configuration using the RDP client. Notice that the program contains two title bars: one for the Terminal Server session, and the other for Word itself. Some user training would be required to educate the user on the differences between the two. I should mention that if the user clicks on the Minimize button on the Word title bar in this example, Word would minimize within the session window boundary. Also, as soon as Word is exited, the Terminal Server session will also end.

- **ICA seamless window application launched from a shortcut on the local desktop.** A seamless window application appears to the user as if it's actually running locally. Citrix's seamless windows feature is discussed in detail in Chapter 3, "Citrix MetaFrame."

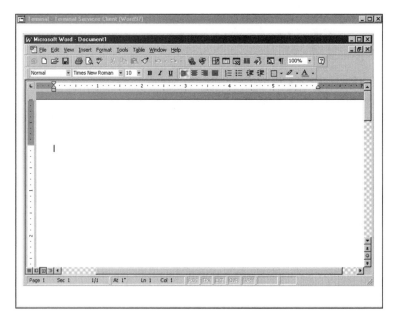

Figure 6.3   *Microsoft Word launched from an RDP client shortcut.*

Because application replacement involves a combination of programs run-ning both locally and from Terminal Server, the Windows-based terminal is not a practical solution unless you're using a device that contains an embed-ded operating system that supports locally installed applications. It's more likely that you'll want to allow users to continue using their existing hard-ware and operating system(s), while providing support for these remote applications. I describe application-replacement options specific to RDP and ICA later in this chapter.

RDP Client Support

As mentioned in Chapter 2, "Microsoft Windows Terminal Server," RDP clients are currently available for the following operating systems:

- Windows 2000
- Windows 95/98
- Windows NT (3.51, 4.0)
- Windows for Workgroups 3.11
- Windows CE–based terminals and handheld devices

Regardless of the operating system, RDP is currently supported over the TCP/IP network transport protocol only. The features of RDP are discussed in more detail in Chapter 2.

Table 6.1 provides a summary of the minimum hardware requirements for each of the Windows operating systems supported by the RDP client (except for the WinCE client, which I discuss later in this chapter). In a desktop-replacement scenario, the minimum recommended hardware for the particular operating system (OS) is more than sufficient, since the only client-side software is the Terminal Server client itself. If the client will be used in an application-replacement role, additional client resources may be required above the recommended minimum, depending on the local applica-tions that will be used. In most application-replacement projects, the clients keep their existing OS and have the Terminal Server client added to their local computer.

Table 6.1   Minimum Windows Client Hardware Requirements

Client OS	Client Type	Minimum RAM	Minimum CPU
Windows 2000 Professional	32-bit	64MB	Pentium 133 or equivalent
Windows NT Workstation 3.51/4.0	32-bit	32MB	Pentium 90 or equivalent
Windows 98	32-bit	24MB	Intel 486/66 or equivalent
Windows 95	32-bit	12MB	Intel 486/33 or equivalent
Windows for Workgroups 3.11	16-bit	4-8MB	Intel 386 or equivalent

Typically your decision on what client operating system to use will depend on the hardware that's currently available or designated for your Terminal Server users. One of the reasons for implementing a thin-client solution is to reduce your total cost of ownership. Extending the return on investment for your existing hardware is certainly one way to accomplish this. Unfortunately, it's not always as simple as picking the client to match your existing hardware.

The key is being able to find the right balance of hardware cost savings and client operating-system support costs. Ideally, you'll maximize your hardware savings while minimizing your support costs. Achieving this 100% is rarely possible, however, so when trying to determine in which direction you should go, minimizing support costs will always deliver greater benefits in the long run.

A simple example of this principle is a comparison between the support costs of Windows for Workgroups (WfW) 3.11 and Windows 98. When comparing the availability of device drivers and the plug-and-play (PnP) features of Win98 with the manual configuration required with WfW, it's quickly apparent that Win98 would be the preferred choice for reducing client support costs. Of course, configuration is not the only thing to consider. The stability of the 32-bit operating system and features such as support for standardized client profiles also help in reducing support costs and increasing manageability.

Author's Note

I have certainly seen exceptions to this rule. I visited one Terminal Server installation where a department was running the WfW clients on identical hardware (Compaq 486 PCs) in a desktop-replacement scenario. The machines were constructed using a hardware drive-duplication product and then delivered to the client. Once the initial WfW machine had been configured to function properly, it was simply a matter of delivering the working image to the users. This is an example of how client support and deployment have been streamlined to minimize the costs of supporting the client, while at the same time reducing hardware costs by reusing existing hardware. ✦

The most common client OS decision is simply to keep using the OS that currently exists on the user's desktop. If the clients are running Windows 95 today, then they're usually left running that client OS after they have been migrated to Terminal Server.

Another consideration is the client licensing costs for using Terminal Server. Because the Windows NT Workstation/2000 Professional license is required for each Terminal Server *client*, it may be worthwhile to consider upgrading clients to run one of these client operating systems in conjunction with the desktop-replacement implementation. This solution has particular appeal for users who are currently running Windows 95 or 98 on newer hardware. The most common configuration for these desktops is a Pentium class machine or higher with a minimum of 32MB of RAM. This configuration would support Workstation/Professional in a desktop-replacement scenario. You would then benefit from the additional desktop security and lockdown features that are available with these operating systems.

Win32 Client

The 32-bit RDP client provides identical client support on all 32-bit Windows operating systems. This includes the following new features that are available with Windows 2000 Terminal Server and RDP 5.0:

- Local/remote Clipboard integration
- Client printer mapping
- Session remote control
- Persistent bitmap cache

Your decision on what 32-bit client OS to implement will usually depend on what your users are running today and whether you're performing a desktop-replacement or application-replacement implementation.

Win16 Client

The 16-bit RDP client provides the same client options as the 32-bit client. The one difference is that the 16-bit client is single-threaded, while the 32-bit client is multi-threaded. This single thread must handle the processing of user interface information as well as the sending and receiving of data. This can result in reduced responsiveness in comparison with the 32-bit client.

As with all 16-bit applications, the client is susceptible to other 16-bit applications "misbehaving" and possibly causing the session to crash. When possible, the 32-bit client should be chosen over the 16-bit client.

Non–Windows Clients

While Microsoft RDP clients are officially supported only on computers running a Windows-based operating system, it's possible to run an RDP client within a Windows emulation system on non–Windows systems such as OS/2 or UNIX. Performance and reliability are questionable in such a configuration, and deployment into production should not be considered without thorough testing.

> **Tip**
>
> *Non-Microsoft RDP clients are available. The Santa Cruz Operation's (SCO) Thin-client middleware product Tarantella supports accessing Windows-based applications running on a Terminal Server via a Web browser. Tarantella sits as a middleware component between the Web browser and the terminal Server. See the Tarantella Web site for more information (*http://www.tarantella.com*).*
>
> *A non–Microsoft RDP Java client (JDK 1.1) is available from HOB Electronics. For more information and a downloadable client for testing, see* http://www.hob.de/www_us. ◆

ICA Client Support

ICA clients are currently available for the following operating systems and computing environments:

- Windows 2000, Windows NT 3.51 and Windows 4.0, 95/98, Windows for Workgroups 3.11, Windows 3.1, Windows CE
- DOS, Macintosh, Linux (Red Hat, Slackware, Caldera, SuSE)
- UNIX (Solaris, SunOS, SCO, SGI, HP/UX, Compaq Tru64, IBM)
- Java (JDK 1.0, 1.1)
- Web browsers (Internet Explorer, Netscape)

ICA is supported on TCP/IP, IPX, SPX, and NetBEUI when supported by the operating system.

> **Tip**
>
> *When implementing a Terminal Server solution, particularly a large-scale enterprise deployment, I recommend that you give the ICA client very serious consideration. The features of ICA are discussed in more detail in Chapter 3. ◆*

Just as with the RDP client, your decision on what client operating system to use for an ICA client will depend on the hardware that's currently available or designated for your users. One of a number of advantages of ICA over RDP is the robust support for heterogeneous computing environments. This allows for much more flexibility in what client will be used, particularly in application-replacement scenarios. In many situations, the ICA client can be introduced with little or no change to the user's existing client OS.

> **Tip**
>
> *Even though you may be using the ICA client instead of the RDP client, you're still required to purchase a client access license for each user who will be connecting to the Terminal Server. This means that if it's practical you may want to consider upgrading the client operating system to NT Workstation/2000 Professional to gain the management features these operating systems provide.* ♦

Table 6.2 summarizes the features available with the different ICA clients. An *X* in a particular cell of the table means that the corresponding feature is supported by that client.

> **Tip**
>
> *I recommend visiting Citrix's Web site at* `http://www.citrix.com` *for the latest information on the supported ICA clients and their feature sets.* ♦

Table 6.2   ICA Client Feature Summary

	Client								
Feature	Win32	Win16	WinCE	DOS	Mac	Linux	UNIX	Java	Web
Program Neighborhood	X							X	X[8]
Published applications	X	X	X	X	X	X	X	X	X
Seamless windows	X								
Client device mapping	X	X	X	X[1]	X[1]	X	X[6]	X[5]	X[2]
Sound support	X	X	X	X	X	X[7]	X[7]		
Encryption	X	X		X	X[3]	X[3]	X[3]	X[3]	X
Client auto update	X	X	X	X	X[4]	X	X		
Clipboard mapping	X	X	X		X	X	X		X

continues ▶

Table 6.2   coninued

| | Client | | | | | | | | |
Feature	Win32	Win16	WinCE	DOS	Mac	Linux	UNIX	Java	Web
Business recovery	X	X	X		X	X	X		
Video	X								
TAPI modems	X								
Asynchronous ICA dial-up connections	X	X	X	X					

1 *Client printers for the DOS and Macintosh clients are not automatically mapped but instead must be mapped manually.*
2 *Client COM port mapping is not supported with the Web clients.*
3 *Macintosh, Java, and UNIX/Linux clients support only basic ICA encryption.*
4 *Future versions of the Macintosh client will be updateable using the automatic client update feature.*
5 *Only client printer mapping is supported with the Java client.*
6 *COM port device mapping is available only with Intel-based Linux workstations.*
7 *Client audio is supported only on Linux, HP, IBM AIX, and Sun SPARC workstations.*
8 *Program Neighborhood support is available within a Web browser when used with Citrix NFuse.*

Win32 Client

The Win32 ICA client provides the most robust support for all of the latest ICA features, such as Program Neighborhood and seamless windows, both of which are key integration components for application replacement in a MetaFrame environment. Just as I mentioned earlier when talking about the 32-bit RDP client, your decision on what 32-bit client OS to use depends on what your users are running today and whether you're performing a desktop-replacement or application-replacement implementation.

In an application-replacement scenario, you may consider upgrading your clients to a 32-bit Windows OS to gain the advantages of Program Neighborhood and seamless windows integration. The main factors in this decision are how many applications will remain on the local desktop and how much work will be required to migrate them from the old OS to the new one.

Win16 Client

The Win16 ICA client is supported on both Windows 3.1 and WfW 3.11. It provides most of the features of the Win32 client, except for Program Neighborhood and seamless windows. The Win16 client is well suited for those environments that may still be running one of these 16-bit operating systems because of hardware cost constraints but that want to move to a 32-bit OS. I would suggest using this client in a desktop-replacement scenario where you already have the 16-bit Windows within your infrastructure and the existing hardware won't support an upgrade to Windows NT/2000 Professional.

As with all 16-bit apps, this client is single-threaded and as a result doesn't deliver the same performance or stability as the 32-bit client.

WinCE Client

The WinCE client is available to run on handheld devices running the Windows CE operating system that meet the following requirements:

- The device must support a color depth of 16 colors or greater, either color or grayscale.
- TCP/IP networking or dial-up access (PPP or SLIP) to the Terminal Server environment.
- One of the supported processors, which currently are SH3, SH4, X86, MIPS, PowerPC, and ARM.

WinCE implementations of Terminal Server are best suited for custom application deployments designed to run specifically within a "CE-sized" environment. The limited viewing area of the handheld devices makes them impractical for running traditional desktop applications such as Word or Excel. While Citrix provides a feature known as *virtual screen panning*, which allows you to access the larger Terminal Server desktop from a handheld device, it would be impractical to ask a user to navigate sessions in this fashion without specific design considerations for these types of users.

Tip

For the most current list of supported handheld devices, see the Citrix CE Web page at http://www.citrix.com/wince.htm. ◆

DOS Client

Two variations of the DOS client exist—a 16-bit and a 32-bit version. The differences are briefly summarized in Table 6.3.

Table 6.3   16-Bit/32-Bit DOS Client Features

Feature	16-Bit DOS	32-Bit DOS
Conventional memory	Approximately 550KB	Approximately 200KB
Extended memory	Not available	As required
Processor support	80286 or higher	80386 or higher
DOS version	MS-DOS 3.3 or higher	MS-DOS 4.0 or higher

Citrix is positioning the 32-bit DOS client as its standard DOS client on a go-forward basis and will be introducing additional functionality that won't be available in the 16-bit client. The 16-bit client is being maintained to provide support for 80286-based clients, which don't support extended DOS functionality. The use of extended memory tends to make the 32-bit DOS client more stable because there's more conventional memory available for other required drivers, such as audio and network drivers.

While the DOS client does provide a good selection of ICA features on legacy hardware, one thing to keep in mind is that it's still a DOS-based client; care must be taken when configuring these clients in order to optimize their performance. Additional DOS components such as SMARTDRV should also be loaded when booting a DOS client, and the persistent caching feature of the ICA client should only be used over low bandwidth (< 56Kb) connections. Chapter 14, "ICA Client Installation and Configuration" talks more about the ICA client installation.

Author's Note

I have heard of situations in which the ICA DOS client has performed extremely poorly in a WAN infrastructure, particularly when coupled with printing. If you're considering such a scenario, I recommend that you also investigate possible alternatives in the event that you encounter similar problems. ◆

If you choose to deploy the DOS client, you'll need to ensure that your support staff is proficient in DOS so that the client can be supported properly.

Macintosh Client

This client provides Mac users with support for the most common ICA client features. To use this client, the following minimum requirements must be met:

- Motorola 68030, 68040, or PowerPC processor
- System 7.1 or later OS version with Thread Manager
- 16-color or 256-color display
- TCP/IP
- Network card or dial-up with PPP connection to the MetaFrame environment

Once configured, the Mac client provides stable access to a MetaFrame environment. The most common configuration for the Mac client is to provide access to a full MetaFrame desktop, which is then used in conjunction with any of the standard Macintosh applications that may be running locally. Because the Mac doesn't operate with a two-button mouse and has a different keyboard layout than standard Windows-based machines, special keyboard combinations have been created to mimic Windows functionality, as shown in Table 6.4. If you'll be deploying the Mac client, make sure that all users have this information so that they can operate in their MetaFrame session effectively.

Table 6.4   *Macintosh ICA Client Shortcut Keys*

MetaFrame Session Key	Macintosh ICA Key Substitute
Alt key	Command/Apple key
Right-click	Minus (–) key on numeric keypad or Option key + mouse click
Insert key	Zero (0) on numeric keypad with the Num Lock turned off

UNIX/Linux Client

Citrix provides a UNIX ICA client for a number of different UNIX platforms. The following UNIX variants are currently supported:

- Sun Solaris—1.0, 2.5.1, or higher on SPARC systems, 2.6 or higher on Intel systems
- Sun SunOS—4.1.4, 5.5.1, or higher on SPARC systems, 5.6 or higher on Intel systems
- Compaq Tru64 (formerly Digital)—3.2 or higher
- HP/UX—10.20 or higher
- IBM AIX—4.1.4 or higher
- SGI IRIX—6.3 or higher
- SCO—OpenServer 5, UnixWare 2.1 or 7
- Linux—RedHat 5.0 or higher, Slackware 3.5 or higher, Caldera 1.3 or higher, SuSE 5.3 or higher

Tip

If you're running a version of UNIX for which an ICA client is not currently available, you have three additional options:

- *Use the ICA Java client through a Java Virtual Machine (JVM) on the workstation.*

- *Access the MetaFrame servers using native X Windows through a special proxy known as an ICA to X proxy. This type of proxy requires a UNIX workstation that supports one of the existing UNIX clients. It's then configured to send and receive X information and convert it to and from ICA so that it can be processed by the MetaFrame environment. Information on how to configure the ICA to X proxy can be found in the UNIX Client Administrator's Guide for the desired client at* `http://download.citrix.com`.

- *Implement Citrix UNIX Integration Services. This allows native X11 connectivity to the MetaFrame server. With these services, any X11 device or PC running X11 display software can connect to the MetaFrame server. ICA client software is not required.* ♦

Other than the COM port mapping and client audio support, all variants of the ICA UNIX client support the same features. The ICA UNIX client is ideal for those environments where the main client machine is a UNIX-based workstation and you want to deliver one or more Windows-based applications to the user. In the past, Windows emulators that ran on UNIX (such as WINE) would have to be used in order to allow access to a very limited set of Windows applications from within UNIX. The ICA client provides much more robust access to native 32-bit Windows applications. When deploying the UNIX client, it's common to provide a Terminal Server desktop from which the required Windows applications are accessed.

Web Client

Some of the most exciting ICA clients available are the Web clients. Using ICA Web clients, users can access and run applications on a Terminal Server from their Web browsers. This provides you with the ability to publish Windows desktop applications for use on a Web page without any code modifications to the applications.

With Citrix NFuse, you can provide Program Neighborhood support directly through the Web browser. NFuse performs the necessary user authentication against a domain and then automatically generates a Web page for the user that contains a link for each application within the user's application set (see Figure 6.4). When the user clicks on a link, the application is launched using the standard ICA Web client that's available to the user. Chapter 15, "Web Computing with MetaFrame," provides details about configuring NFuse to provide Web-based access to application sets.

Figure 6.4 *An NFuse-generated application set in a Web page.*

ICA Web clients enable you to access applications on a Terminal Server in two ways, depending on the specific browser that's being used and the client operating system. The access methods are collectively known as *Application Launching and Embedding (ALE)*, and are described in the following sections.

Application Launching
Application launching is when an ICA hyperlink is clicked on a Web page and the associated application is launched in a separate window on the local Windows desktop. After the application is started, it can be accessed and run like a normal published application. Figure 6.5 shows Microsoft Word launched from a hyperlink on a Web page, using the Sun HotJava Web browser for Windows.

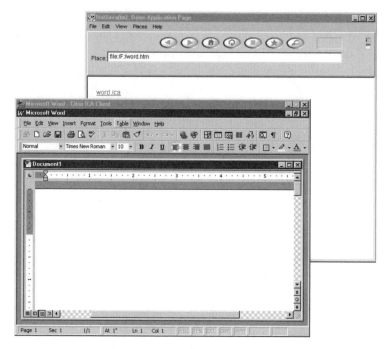

Figure 6.5   *Application launching.*

Application launching is supported by any Windows-based Web browser that supports configurable MIME types. The MIME helpers are WFICA16.exe for 16-bit Windows Web browsers and WFICA32.exe for 32-bit Windows Web browsers.

Application Embedding
Application embedding allows an application to be embedded within the confines of a Web page, appearing to be a component of the page. Figure 6.6 shows Microsoft Excel as an embedded application on a Web page.

Application embedding is available on any Web browser that supports at least one of the following ICA Web client types:

- Netscape Navigator plug-ins
- Microsoft ActiveX Controls
- Java applets

Chapter 15 discusses configuring and using all of the available ICA Web clients.

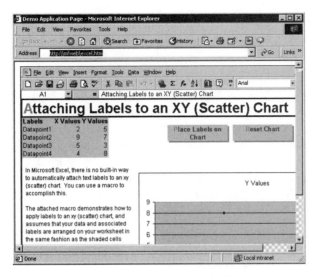

Figure 6.6   *Application embedding.*

Java Client

As mentioned earlier, an ICA Java client is available that allows Web browsers supporting Java applets to access embedded applications within a Web page. In addition to accessing applications in applet mode, the ICA Java client can also allow MetaFrame access in what's known as *application mode*. In application mode, the Java client is executed on any computer that has a JVM supporting Java Development Kit (JDK) 1.1. Once started, the session will appear in its own window on the client's desktop. Configuring and using the Java client in applet mode and application mode is discussed in Chapter 15.

> *Tip*
>
> *One interesting thing to point out is that the ICA Java Client does support accessing Program Neighborhood and viewing available application sets for the user. Program Neighborhood and the Java client are also discussed in Chapter 15.* ◆

Windows-Based Terminals

As with other traditional terminals (3270, VT220, etc.), the goal of the Windows-based terminal (WBT) is to provide a fast, low-cost, and reliable way to access a Windows Terminal Server environment. WBTs have been around since the early days of Citrix WinFrame, and just as the server operating system has matured and grown in popularity, so has the Windows-based terminal.

WBTs fall into three main categories:

- **Windows CE devices.** These terminals run the Windows CE operating system and most often support both the ICA and RDP protocols.

- **Proprietary OS devices.** Any non-CE device is usually considered to be a proprietary WBT. Most of the early WBT manufacturers, such as Wyse, developed their products around these types of terminals, and have now expanded their product lines to include both CE (Wyse 3000–class) terminals and non-CE (Wyse 2000–class) terminals. Some non-CE devices have been developed using versions of DOS, Windows 3.1, and even Linux. Until now most non-CE devices have supported only ICA, but many are now providing RDP and other protocol support, such as X.11.

- **Embedded operating system devices.** Some manufacturers, such as Netier or NCD, provide WBTs containing embedded operating systems that run either on solid-state flash storage or standard hard drives. These terminals also allow limited installation of local applications and can be thought of more as limited personal computers or network computer devices. Netier provides terminals using either an embedded version of Windows 3.1 or Windows NT, and that provide support for both RDP and ICA.

A large number of WBT manufacturers exist today; determining whether you should use WBTs in your implementation, and if so what vendor to choose, can be a major undertaking in itself. Each vendor touts its product as being the fastest and most robust WBT solution, but you should evaluate *at least* three different vendors' products to decide for yourself which product best suits your requirements. *Never* make your decision based solely on marketing information or even suggestions from your peers. You won't know for certain which terminal will meet your needs until you've had the opportunity to use one.

When evaluating Windows-based terminals, look for the following features and capabilities:

- **Performance.** This is something that can vary greatly from one terminal to another. Screen updates, mouse and keyboard response, and printing in particular are all areas where a WBT may not meet the needs of the end user.

- **Centralized management.** For the terminal to be truly cost-effective, it must be manageable from a central location after it has been deployed to the user's desktop. Flash upgrades, asset tracking, or configuration changes should not require physical access to the unit. Multiple units should be configurable with a single command, and shouldn't require management on a unit-by-unit basis. If you have 2,000 terminals deployed in your organization, you want to be able to deliver changes to all of them simultaneously instead of individually.

- **Administration security.** Coupled with centralized management should be security features to protect against unauthorized changes being made to the terminal units, either by the end user or by someone with access to the remote management software. At the very least, an administrative password should be required to implement any changes.

- **RDP and ICA support.** Even if you only require RDP access today, it's a worthwhile investment to have a terminal that also includes ICA support or that allows for a flash upgrade to add this support in the future, if necessary.

- **Support for advanced ICA features.** Beyond supporting standard ICA connections to a MetaFrame server, an ICA WBT must also support the load-balancing and published-application features of MetaFrame. Without this support, you're limited to providing users with access to specific MetaFrame servers, which is of little value in a multiple-server enterprise environment. Terminal manufactures don't yet provide explicit support for Citrix server farms or Program Neighborhood, although embedded NT systems such as Netier's product allow Program Neighborhood to be installed on the client.

- **Encryption support.** The terminal device you choose should support the required encryption levels of the protocol you'll be using. For example, the Wyse WinTerm supports both RDP and ICA encryption (including the SecureICA option pack).

- **Point-to-Point Protocol (PPP) dial-up support.** Many companies have looked to WBTs as an alternative to providing employees with note-book computers simply for remote access from home. Many terminals now support PPP dial up so that users can connect directly into a company's network or dial up their local ISP and connect to a Terminal Server over the Internet. If you want to use terminals within your company, the ability to support PPP could provide further cost savings in areas such as telecommuting. I'll discuss this in more detail shortly.

- **Screen resolution and color depth.** One of the most common complaints about WBTs when they first came onto the market was their relatively low screen resolution, color support, and refresh rates. Today, most terminals provide resolution and color capabilities that exceed the current limits of both the RDP and ICA protocols. Currently the ICA protocol supports a maximum resolution of 1280×1024 with 256 colors. The RDP protocol supports 1024×768 with 256 colors.

- **Additional terminal or browser support.** In addition to ICA and RDP support, many terminals today also support additional terminal emulation modes such as 3270, VT100, X.11, Java, and Web browsing. The ability to use your WBT as a multi-access terminal device may be a valuable option, particularly if the business requires redundant access to certain critical business functions or you want to maintain certain applications, such as Web browsers, outside of your Terminal Server environment. As you might expect, the cost of one of these multipurpose units is usually higher than the equivalent terminal without this support, so unless there's a business need to include these features you could save some money by omitting them.

Table 6.5 lists some of the Windows-based terminal vendors with a sample of their products and the protocols and operating systems they support. For the most up-to-date list of terminal vendors, consult both the Microsoft (www.microsoft.com) and Citrix (www.citrix.com) Web sites.

Table 6.5   Some Windows-Based Terminal Vendors

Vendor	Web Site	Model	Terminal OS	Supported Protocols	
				RDP	ICA
Boundless	www.boundless.com	Capio II 320	Windows CE	Yes	Yes
NCD	www.ncd.com	ThinSTAR 200	ThinSTAR OS (Windows CE core)	Yes	Yes
Neoware	www.neoware.com	2200P	NetOS for WinTerminals	No	Yes
		2300P	Windows CE	Yes	Yes
Netier	www.netier.com	NetXpress SL1000	Embedded Windows 3.1 or NT 4.0 Workstation OS	Yes	Yes
TeleVideo	www.televideo.com	TeleCLIENT TC7000	Windows CE	Yes	Yes
Wyse	www.wyse.com	Winterm 2315SE	Winterm OS	No	Yes
		Winterm 3320SE	Windows CE	Yes	Yes
		5355SE	Linux	No	Yes

Author's Note

One market where WBTs have garnered a lot of attention is as a replacement to the mainframe dumb terminal sector (affectionately known as the green screen). This includes both true green-screen terminals and PCs used primarily as dumb terminal emulators. For many companies, the cost of switching from these terminals to a Windows environment is quite prohibitive, yet they are forced into making these changes simply to remain competitive. WBTs are a cost-effective alternative to the PC as a dumb terminal replacement. The company can maintain the centralized manageability and reduced maintenance costs of dumb terminals and, at the same time, provide users access to the latest Windows software.

Such an environment could be built and tested without any impact to the users. In fact, the multiple-terminal support of many WBTs (such as the Wyse 3320SE) may allow you to swap out your terminals with WBTs, such as 3270 or VT-420, that could continue to provide terminal support until the Terminal Server environment is ready to implement, at which time you could begin to use these terminals as true Windows-based terminals. ◆

Deployment Scenarios with RDP and ICA

Now that you have had the opportunity to review the various client types available for both RDP and ICA, let's return to the discussion of deployment scenarios and examine the features provided by each client.

Desktop Replacement

The RDP client is configured for desktop replacement simply by defining the appropriate server or load-balanced cluster name, as shown in Figure 6.7. A shortcut can then be created on the desktop or added to the Startup folder.

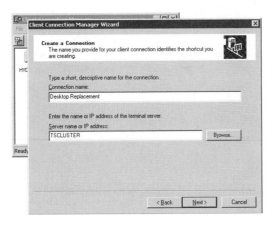

Figure 6.7   *Preparing an RDP client to launch a Terminal Server desktop.*

When configuring the client options, I recommend specifying a "full screen" display. This will hide the local OS desktop from the user. Unfortunately, some of the shortcuts and hotkeys to which many users have grown accustomed with their local desktops won't function the same within a Terminal Server desktop. For example, key combinations have been replaced within Terminal Server, such as Alt+Tab being replaced with Alt+PageUp. This is an important consideration when planning user training. A complete list of shortcut-key substitutes appears in the "Keyboard Shortcuts" section in Chapter 2.

Tip

If users are accessing Terminal Server from a Windows-based terminal, shortcut keys such as Alt+Tab will function normally. ♦

The ICA client configuration for desktop replacement is nearly identical to that for RDP, with the exception of different hotkey definitions. When configuring access to a desktop, you can either explicitly define a MetaFrame server or select a published desktop, as shown in Figure 6.8. Accessing a published desktop instead of an explicit server name is the preferred method, as it hides server details from the user and allows for servers to be added or removed from load balancing without requiring any client configuration changes.

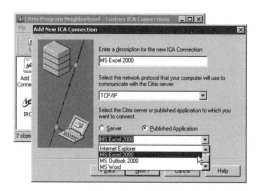

Figure 6.8   *Preparing an ICA client to launch a published Terminal Server desktop.*

Tip

Program Neighborhood is not usually required when performing a desktop replacement with the ICA client. This is because users will rarely have more than one desktop session open at a time and normally will be required to explicitly log onto a server when they first connect to it, instead of relying on Program Neighborhood's auto-authentication feature. ✦

Application Replacement

An RDP client is configured to use specific applications by populating the Program tab, as shown in Figure 6.9. This screenshot shows an RDP client being configured to launch Microsoft Word from drive Y: of the specified Terminal Server. (Refer to Figure 6.3 to see how the RDP client would launch the Word application within the confines of the RDP session window.)

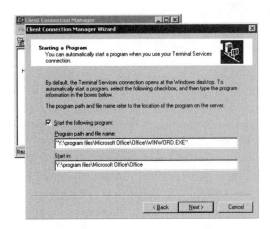

Figure 6.9   *Preparing an RDP client to launch Microsoft Word.*

Although it's technically possible to use the RDP client to deliver application replacement, the limitations on how these connections are configured and how they appear to the end user, in my opinion, make it a poor choice for anything other than the desktop-replacement scenario. Because the application is forced to run within the confines of the RDP session boundary defined by the connection settings, any other applications that are opened by the primary app, such as a Web browser, would also be contained in that window. Figure 6.10 demonstrates this behavior. This is certainly not what the end user would expect and can be extremely difficult to work with, particularly if the user wants to work with the second application alongside the first.

Figure 6.10   *Multiple applications within a single RDP session boundary.*

The ICA client has two modes of operation with regard to the application replacement. The first is identical to that supported by RDP, in which the desired application runs within the confines of a Terminal Server session window. The other is the seamless windows mode available with the 32-bit ICA client. This is the preferred method for any application-replacement implementation on a Windows 32-bit operating system. With seamless windows, the published application on a MetaFrame server appears on the user's local desktop as if it were running locally. There is no Terminal Server session boundary around the application. Also, if an associated application is launched, such as a Web browser, it will appear as its own independent application. Figure 6.11 shows the same applications demonstrated with the RDP protocol in Figure 6.10. Notice that both Microsoft Word and Internet Explorer appear to the user to be independent applications running on the local desktop. They're not contained within the single session window as they were with the RDP client.

Figure 6.11   *Multiple applications launched through ICA's seamless windows.*

For additional applications to be launched, as shown in this example with Word and IE, both apps must be installed on the same Terminal Server. For example, if you're publishing Microsoft Word and want users to be able to launch Microsoft Excel, Excel must be installed on the same server as Word. It *doesn't* have to be published, but must be accessible. By *accessible* I mean that file-level security won't prevent the user from accessing the required executable.

There are also certain limitations on how the seamless windows application can interact with the local desktop. Features such as drag and drop are not supported between the local desktop and a seamless windows session. There is also no support available for a local application to communicate with an application running within a Terminal Server session (using OLE, for example).

Desktop Integration

As mentioned earlier, RDP support of non–Windows operating systems is limited to Windows emulation software or third-party products such as HOB's RDP Java client or SCO's Tarantella. On the other hand, the ICA protocol's robust client support allows for the integration of Windows applications into non–Windows environments. The availability of native clients for Macintosh, UNIX, and Java allow for Terminal Server access on the majority of non–Windows computing systems available today. Because all ICA clients support published applications, the interface for configuring a client connection is nearly identical for all clients with the exception of the Java and Web clients. Figure 6.12 demonstrates configuring access to a published Terminal Server desktop using the Linux client. Through the use of NFuse, you can deliver Program Neighborhood support to any operating system that has a supported Citrix client. For example, through a Web browser, you could access an application set from a Macintosh computer. The NFuse server-side product performs the authentication and generates the Web page with the application links. When the user clicks on a link, the Macintosh client is responsible for establishing the connection and launching the published application. NFuse is discussed in Chapter 15.

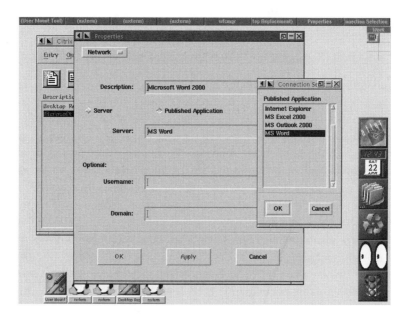

Figure 6.12   *Configuring access to a published Terminal Server desktop using the Linux ICA client.*

Client Deployment and Support Planning

When planning and developing your Terminal Server implementation, it's easy to get caught up in the technical details of servers and clients, while forgetting or trivializing the planning requirements of users and support staff. Through proper client deployment and support planning, you can prepare both users and support staff for the changes you'll be making, and at the same time avoid the trap of attempting to serve every user's individual needs.

When preparing your client deployment and support plan, you need to concentrate on six areas other than what Terminal Server client you intend to use. By addressing each of these areas, you can ensure that you have adequately prepared all parties involved for the changes that you'll be introducing:

- Managing Terminal Server expectations
- User deployment considerations
- Client testing
- Benchmarking
- Deployment strategies
- Training

The following sections discuss each of these areas in more detail.

Managing Terminal Server Expectations

If you've been involved with other implementation projects for software or hardware, you've probably heard someone use the catchall phrase "It will improve performance" when trying to explain to users the benefits they'll see as a result of the implementation. Just as common is the user's reaction, "I thought it was supposed to make it faster," when the user begins to work with the new environment.

Unfortunately, this is an easy trap to fall into, and I've seen it on a number of Terminal Server projects. The most common reason is that the expectations for *both* users and administrators have not been clearly defined and/or not communicated. Communication is an extremely important part of any project, and the information needs to flow to the appropriate people in a timely fashion.

> **Tip**
>
> *When expectations have not been clearly defined and communicated, you may be regularly called upon to defend your reasons for choosing Terminal Server and the proposed environment configuration. It's during these times that the "improves performance" statement most commonly arises. It's easy to promise and almost seems to be something that people want to hear you say. Don't make statements or promises that you can't deliver. ◆*

In most situations, you won't be able to deliver clear expectations until you've had the opportunity to perform some testing and piloting with users to determine the exact changes in performance and stability that are to be expected. Chapter 4, "project Management Considerations," discusses the creation of the "as-is" and "to-be" models. These are valuable guides in helping you to determine areas where performance or stability gains would prove most beneficial. They also provide you with information on users to target for testing and validation.

Until you've had the opportunity to perform testing, concentrate on the benefits that you *know* Terminal Server will bring. Early on, you *can* set expectations that deal with the administration and support of the environment. None of these deal directly with statements about the stability or performance of the applications or the personal experience that users should expect when they utilize the environment. Following are some of the expectations that are truthful, valid, and deliverable from the beginning of the project:

- The applications will be standardized on a single hardware and OS platform. This will allow application developers to detect, correct, and deliver fixes or enhancements to the environment in a more timely fashion. Errors can be more easily detected and diagnosed in comparison to the existing desktop configuration.

- Application *deployment* will be much faster and more reliable, because it's going into a consistent, centrally managed environment.

- Acceptance and user testing will be much more reliable in eliminating problems before they're introduced into production.

- Support staff will no longer have to troubleshoot misconfigured application installations, because all users run from a centrally configured installation that's protected from modification by the end user. Support staff will be able to concentrate on supporting the user's hardware or application usage issues.

- Help desk support staff will be able to take a more active role in resolving user issues *before* they're escalated to a desktop support or network administration person. This can significantly reduce the time required to resolve an issue and can help in meeting any service-level agreements that may exist.

After performing the proper testing, you can consider adding in other expectations such as stability or performance. In general, I tend not to mention expected performance gains at all unless they're definitely noticeable during testing and piloting. Because performance from a user's perspective is relative, what one user considers to be fast will appear slow to another.

One final point on this subject has to do with expectations outside of your control that can surface during the project. It's very likely that support or development staff who have worked with end users in the past may convey their own personal opinions (positive or negative) about Terminal Server. In many situations, these opinions will have a bigger influence on your users' attitudes and expectations than anything that you might tell them. As I mentioned earlier, the only way to manage this effectively is to deliver clear, consistent information to everyone involved in your project, not just to the end users or their managers.

User Deployment Considerations

The extent and type of user deployment considerations that you need to address will depend largely on the implementation scenario that you've chosen (desktop replacement or application replacement, desktop integration). Regardless of the scenario, center your deployment planning around these four specific groups:

- **End users.** These are the people who will actually be operating within the Terminal Server environment.

- **Application developers.** If you're migrating any client/server applications into your Terminal Server environment, you need to ensure that the appropriate application developers are involved in the project.

- **Support staff.** Any help desk or end-user support staff who will be directly responsible for supporting Terminal Server users should be included very early on in deployment planning.

- **Server administrators.** The administrators who traditionally only deal with server issues now need to realize the added responsibilities that come with managing a Terminal Server environment.

End Users

As you would expect, the majority of deployment considerations deal directly with end users. The following considerations are common to all deployment scenarios:

- **Minimizing impacts to productivity.** During piloting and deployment, you need to minimize the impact on the user's ability to work productively. Although this may be difficult at times, it's extremely important to the overall success of the implementation. Both users and management will expect impacts on productivity and will most certainly be vocal if these effects occur. One of the keys to minimizing the impact to the user is to *move slowly*. Don't rush any of the implementation steps, particularly when you're trying to establish the initial pilot. You'll invariably encounter problems early on in piloting, so start out with only one or two users. This way, when problems arise, it's very easy to communicate with the user and work through the problem. If the pilot group is 30 users, you're guaranteed to generate an impact on both their productivity *and* yours, because you'll be spending your time supporting the pilot users instead of building the environment.

- **Local data management.** In the traditional desktop configuration, the typical user maintains a large amount of data on his or her local computer that's critical to day-to-day functions. With the introduction of Terminal Server you will most likely be changing the requirements of how the user is to access this data. If an application is being migrated from the desktop to Terminal Server, you need to ensure that the associated data is also moved to an appropriate location on the network so that it's accessible through Terminal Server. You will *not* want users to continue accessing this data locally. Doing so goes against the whole idea of reducing the dependency on and support requirements for the local desktop. Centralizing data also helps to improve security and allow regular backups to protect against data loss or corruption. Unfortunately, depending on the number of users and the amount of data, ensuring that any local data has been moved to the appropriate network location can be quite labor-intensive.

- **Automated or manual client software updates.** When deploying the RDP or ICA client, one of your decisions will be whether the client is manually installed by a group of desktop support staff, or automatically deployed using a tool such as Microsoft's Systems Management Server—or, in a pure Windows 2000 environment, Windows Installer and Active Directory. Citrix also provides the ability to update an ICA client automatically through a configuration setup on a MetaFrame server. This requires the ICA client on the local desktop, so it's installed initially by desktop support staff or through an automated process. After that point, the client auto update feature can be used. Chapters 13 and 14 discuss the deployment options available, depending on the client in use.

Tip

Refer to Table 6.2, earlier in this chapter, to see which ICA clients support auto client updating. ◆

When performing a desktop replacement, you also need to address the following end-user considerations:

- **Clearly define all users involved in the deployment.** In most desktop-replacement scenarios, you'll provide the user with either a Windows-based terminal or a stripped-down desktop. If the user's current desktop is being replaced or rebuilt, you need to be 100% certain that people who aren't involved in the project don't accidentally receive a new client device. While this sounds obvious, it's worth pointing out. On more than one occasion, I've seen support staff frantically trying to recover the desktop of a user who was migrated to Terminal Server when he or she should not have been. The user's proximity to other users who were being migrated was the reason for the accidental conversion. This is the kind of perceived incompetence you won't want to deal with, particularly since most users don't have backups of their local data and would most likely suffer a huge loss in productivity as a result of such a mistake.

- **Ensure that all applications and data are accounted for.** Make sure that all users who are targeted for deployment have all the necessary applications and data available from within Terminal Server. Data can be very difficult to manage on a user-by-user basis. When possible, the responsibility should be placed on the user to ensure that all required data has been migrated to a file server on the network, so that it will be available after the user has moved to Terminal Server. If applications or data are encountered that weren't accounted for, the user should be treated as an *exception*. Deployment exceptions are discussed in more detail shortly.

  When looking at user data, be sure to consider "personalized" data that assists users in their job functions. Macros, Web favorites, custom dictionaries, or keyboard layouts (particularly with terminal-emulation programs) should all be considered. If these settings won't be migrated to the new environment, someone should inform users prior to the migration so that they don't receive a nasty surprise the first time they launch applications from within their new Terminal Server session.

- **Desktop or Windows-based terminal.** One of the big decisions when looking at desktop replacement is whether to go with the stripped-down desktop or a Windows-based terminal. The decision on what to use will come down to a combination of price, functionality, and manageability:

  - **Price.** If users already have a number of 486 or better computers, recycling these as stripped-down clients will usually cost less than purchasing all new terminals.

- **Functionality.** There's little difference between a PC and a terminal in functionality. One area where a terminal has an advantage is in how much it "feels" like a local desktop, particularly in keyboard shortcuts such as Alt+Tab or Ctrl+Alt+Del. On a regular PC, these shortcuts would process on the local computer and not within the Terminal Server session. PCs have an advantage over *some* terminals in that you can maintain local applications such as terminal emulators as a backup in case the Terminal Server environment is unavailable. Even this advantage has dwindled, however, since many Windows-based terminals today support multiple terminal emulators and even Web browsers in addition to the regular Windows-based terminal support.

- **Manageability.** Windows-based terminals have a definite advantage over PCs in manageability. Even if you're using an OS such as NT or Windows 2000 where you can implement local policies to lock down the desktop, a terminal has very little that can be configured locally and these administrative features can be protected easily by administrative passwords. No local storage means that users can't add applications, one of the leading causes of client desktop issues.

Author's Note

If the business and your users can function with Windows-based terminals, I would recommend them over a stripped-down PC. The ease in manageability and the low failure rate makes terminals ideal for minimizing desktop support. This solution is particularly appealing to companies with remote offices that must access a centralized corporate data center. Many regional offices have very limited IT staff, and terminals are an excellent way to minimize the on-site support in these locations.

Of course these factors will all be weighed in with cost, functionality, and usability. Low-maintenance WBTs are not much good if they're too slow for the users to use productively. ◆

- **Client device requirements.** You should determine what client device mappings, such as printers or drives, will be required by the end user. A good rule is to provide no client mappings unless users explicitly require them. In a desktop-replacement scenario, the only required device mapping is usually for locally attached printers. Drive and Clipboard support are rarely required. All client device mappings use additional bandwidth, so eliminating that requirement—particularly in WAN configurations—helps to minimize the bandwidth required by the client. Unless absolutely required, digital sound support (ICA clients only) should not be enabled. Sound can consume a large amount of network bandwidth, and very rarely is actually required.

Unlike desktop replacement, application replacement has only two special deployment considerations in addition to the common deployment issues listed earlier:

- **Ensure that all application data is accounted for.** Introducing a new application won't be an issue, but when migrating an application from the local desktop to Terminal Server, you need to ensure that the necessary application data has also been moved. Application replacement gives you more flexibility in this area, since you'll rarely provide a user with a completely new desktop, but instead will add the Terminal Server application to the existing computer. You will most likely want to move any of this application data to a location on the network (if it's not there already) so that it's more readily accessible to the application than on the user's local desktop.

- **Client device requirements.** When performing application replacement, you most likely will want to use all device-mapping options that are available to you, with the exception of sound and COM port mappings. Because the application is usually being integrated into the user's existing desktop, you need to provide the most seamless integration between the local and remote applications.

With Windows desktop integration, the goal is to provide access to one or more Windows applications from within a non–Windows client environment. Desktop integration is usually treated as a special case of application replacement because the user won't lose access to local applications (that would be considered a desktop replacement).

Application Developers

When migrating internally developed client/server applications into a Terminal Server environment, you need to ensure that the appropriate development team is both aware of your plans and involved in the implementation. Their involvement is critical to ensuring a smooth implementation of the application. If compatibility problems arise when trying to execute the program in the Terminal Server environment, you'll need the developers' immediate attention to help resolve the problem. If the developers and their manager(s) are unaware of the change, you'll have much greater difficulty in getting their timely support.

Developers also need to be aware that the target environment for their application has changed. Without this knowledge, it's very likely that at some point they'll make an assumption about the environment that's invalid in a multiuser environment. A simple example would be the use of the computer name in maintaining session information for the user. On a desktop this would be valid, since only one person is on a machine at a time, but multiple users may run the application on a single Terminal Server, and as a result, all would share the same computer name. Unless the developers are aware of the multiuser capabilities of Terminal Server, they won't take it into consideration during development.

Tip

Chapter 19, "Application Integration," talks in detail about the installation of applications in a Terminal Server environment. ◆

A requirement for any Terminal Server implementation is the creation of a development/test server where developers can test versions of their application prior to releasing it into production. A test environment is essential; otherwise you run the risk of affecting users if an application is released directly into production without previous Terminal Server testing or is tested on a production server alongside active user sessions.

Usually, the application itself is not developed directly on a Terminal Server, but instead coded and unit-tested on the developer's local workstation. It's then *promoted* to the test Terminal Server, where it's system-tested. The idea of application promotion allows for the creation of clearly defined boundaries where developers do and don't have access to directly influence the operating environment. When an application has been successfully promoted and tested in the test environment, it can then be promoted in a pilot or production environment in exactly the same way. Terminal Server allows for the establishment of well-defined release management processes—something that rarely exists in the traditional PC desktop environment.

Tip

The application development and testing process for Terminal Server is discussed in Chapter 9, "Software Planning."

The reason that developers rarely develop applications directly on Terminal Server is not that it can't be done, but more specifically because of the security permissions required to develop applications effectively. Most developers require administrative access to their local desktop to effectively run most of the development suites available today, including having access to application debuggers.

Although you can have a Terminal Server on which multiple developers have administrative access, unless the developers are completely familiar with the Terminal Server configuration, what usually happens is that one developer installs an additional tool or modifies an existing one that immediately causes the tool to stop functioning for everyone else. Service packs or version upgrades for application-development environments are good examples of tools that are commonly installed in such a scenario. ◆

I've seen both sides of the coin when developers work directly on a Terminal Server. In one situation, eight developers had administrative privileges to a server so that they could run and develop an application. Within a week the server was unusable because of the number of tools and system modifications that had been made. One developer had even installed a service pack without informing anyone else.

On the other hand, I was involved with a project in which three developers worked off a single Terminal Server that they accessed across the Internet to develop a custom Visual Basic application for a customer. This customer also had access to the Terminal Server in order to test the progress of the application immediately after the latest compiled version was available. This allowed developers physically located miles apart to be able to work productively on an application without having to upload/download code or be located on the same LAN/WAN. Visual SourceSafe was used to ensure that one developer's changes didn't clobber another's. ◆

Support Staff

Your support staff is the first contact point for all user issues, and for them to be able to effectively support end users once Terminal Server is deployed, they must be involved early in the project and trained in how to work within the Terminal Server environment. I'll discuss some of the key training points for support staff later in this chapter.

Administrators

Administrators who traditionally deal only with server issues will now need to realize the added responsibilities that come with managing a Terminal Server environment. Not only will they have to ensure that users can function properly within the environment, but they'll also be responsible for any new application releases that may go into production. The administrative role will also take on an application support role, particularly early on, while the bugs are being flushed out of the system.

I have yet to meet an administrator who is very receptive to the idea of having to manage application releases in addition to other support responsibilities, but unfortunately there are few alternatives. Terminal Server is not like a file and print server. With the centralization of management also comes an added responsibility. To maintain the integrity of the system, the number of people with administrative access to the Terminal Servers must be kept to a minimum; as a result, only those select few individuals have sufficient privileges to perform an application installation. Chapter 9 discusses the application release process in more detail, providing a better idea as to where an administrator's responsibilities lie in this process. ◆

Deployment Exceptions

Until you have actually begun your implementation, it's nearly impossible to detect users who will need to be treated as exceptions to the standard Terminal Server implementation. Certainly, you will try to address these issues prior to the release, during the planning and information-gathering portions of the project, but invariably someone is missed who, due to his or her configuration, is a poor candidate for the implementation. The chances of this problem occurring increase as the number of new installations increase.

It's extremely important that you have a process in place to handle exceptions before they occur. The best way to deal with these users is to omit them from the initial implementation and revisit them afterward so that their setups can be dealt with in more detail. *Do not* allow exceptions to delay or change the scope of the implementation; this is one of the primary reasons that a project becomes delayed. What happens most often is that the user has an application that wasn't anticipated by the Terminal Server team; in their haste to include the user in the project, they agree to add this application to the Terminal Server environment. Without the proper testing and piloting, this strategy can be particularly dangerous during the implementation phase. If you have properly planned the deployment, you'll encounter few exceptions and there will be no problems in deferring them until a later date.

Client Testing

During your planning and evaluation, make sure that you have adequately tested the client configuration that you will implement. This client testing is independent of any application testing that you'll perform and is done to ensure that the client functionality that you want to implement is working properly. Features such as client drive or printer mappings or Program Neighborhood should all be tested. These tests don't need to be extensive but should be rigorous enough to help you discover any obvious issues that may arise. It can also help to pinpoint problems before any additional complexity has been introduced.

Client testing is usually scheduled to occur once you have performed the initial Terminal Server installation but prior to any applications being installed on the server. If possible, connectivity testing should be performed from the planned client location, which will help to give an indication of any possible network issues. As part of this testing, you should look at client responsiveness with regard to the keyboard and the mouse. When accessing the Terminal Server from the client location, do the keyboard and mouse respond as expected, or are there delays or lag periods where you can type but the session can't keep up? Mouse clicks that don't respond immediately are another indication. You *must* address any of these issues as soon as possible, because they'll definitely become the number one complaint of the users.

Author's Note

A process that I have used works as follows. I begin by building a base configuration Terminal/MetaFrame Server with the necessary service packs and hotfixes but without any additional configuration changes such as security or user profiles. If I'm running MetaFrame, I publish one or two applications such as WordPad or the full Terminal Server desktop. A server farm is created, if necessary, and assigned the name "Test Farm." After the server is on the network and functioning, I'm ready to test my client configurations.

If only RDP clients will be used, I simply establish a connection to the Terminal Server. If it's an ICA client, I make sure that I can see both servers and published applications in the appropriate client lists and that the Program Neighborhood logon comes up (when appropriate). After the appropriate connection has been established, I can perform client testing, such as application and session response, and features, such as client drive and printer access. ◆

The client testing doesn't have to be "overkill," but should be detailed enough to provide you with a comfort level about whether the thin-client connectivity is functioning properly or not. Issues of periodic connection loss or significant latency delays can usually be uncovered at this time, allowing you the opportunity to correct the problem before going live with all of the users.

User Training

The amount of training required for a Terminal Server implementation depends mainly on the amount of change that's noticeable to the user. Unless you're introducing new applications in conjunction with Terminal Server, the only training will be in how the users work in their new environment. With some planning, you can keep this training to a minimum while providing the users with the information they need to work. Table 6.6 shows a summary of when I've found training to be most beneficial and when minimum guidance is acceptable. An X in a cell means that a user with the associated row-and-column combination should probably have some form of training.

Of course, Table 6.6 is by no means complete, but it demonstrates the areas in which training is usually necessary. For example, a user who has previous experience with a 32-bit Windows OS such as Windows 95 would require no training if presented with a Windows-based terminal as part of a desktop replacement. To the user, the one noticeable difference would be the lack of a local computer with a disk drive. Otherwise, the environment should function very similarly to what the user previously had, including keyboard shortcuts such as Alt+Tab.

Contrast this with a Windows 3.1 user receiving a desktop replacement through a client installed on the user's local desktop. Not only is this user moving to a completely new GUI desktop metaphor (Windows 32-bit), but he or she is also being asked to learn how to navigate within the Terminal Server environment. Again I mention the standard keyboard shortcuts such as Alt+Tab, which in this situation correspond to the local desktop and not the Terminal Server desktop. This user would require more formal training than the previous user.

Table 6.6   Example Training Requirements Based on Desktop Configuration

	Terminal Server Implementation Scenario		
	Desktop Replacement or Integration		
Previous Desktop Configuration	WBT	Existing Desktop	Application Replacement
Windows 32-bit	—	X	—
Windows 16-bit	X	X	X
Non–Windows	X	X	—[1]

1 Application replacement on a non–Windows desktop applies only to operating systems other than DOS.

It's best if the areas that will require training are targeted as early in the project as possible. Training doesn't need to be planned immediately, but the requirements for training should be known. This will help in coordinating the deployment and also in developing the most effective means of training. When you begin to think about training, don't immediately jump to the conclusion that you'll need one or more training rooms full of computers. Although this may be valid in some situations, it's not the only option available to you. Here are some other training possibilities:

- In situations where minimal training is required, consider providing the users with "quick tip" or "frequently asked question" sheets. This usually works best when several support people are available to assist users who are having real difficulties, and the migrated users are seated in the same general vicinity.

- Create "mobile" training areas situated near the users to be migrated. Terminal Server provides increased location independence, so if space permits, consider setting up a group of workstations where you can bring in users to go over any required training. The proximity to their desks will make it easier to pull the users away, and may even allow them to perform their regular job functions for an extended period at that location. This way, you can assist these users with any issues they may have, while allowing them to continue working. You'll also be able to resolve many issues such as improperly configured profiles or logon scripts immediately, without the users having to phone someone and then wait for assistance.

The idea is to take the time to develop the training strategies that are best for both you and your users.

Author's Note

I was involved in a deployment where we were required to replace the users' old Windows 3.1 computers with similar hardware updated with Windows 95 in a complete desktop replacement scenario. In addition to replacing the computers, we were told to minimize the time during which these users couldn't work.

Because the users were coming from a Windows 3.1 environment, we couldn't simply update their desktops the night before and leave the users to fend for themselves. The users had to be productive almost immediately after being migrated.

To achieve this objective, we did the following:

1. *We set up four trainee computers in a meeting room on the same floor as the users. Four was the maximum number of users who could be taken away from their job at one time.*

2. *We pre-built a number of Windows 95 computers from extra hardware. These machines would be swapped with the user's existing hardware, and then that hardware would be rebuilt and redistributed to the next set of users. The machines were built using a hardware disk-imaging tool.*

3. *To deploy the new desktop and provide the users with training, we developed an assembly-line approach. The four users were taken to the training room, where they were guided through the startup and logon of a computer that was identical to the configuration they would be getting. They were then given approximately 20–30 minutes of training on the environment. During this time, each of the existing computers was swapped for one of the other computers and verified to work properly. Extra machines were always on hand in case of problems. Instead of trying to fix the problems, we simply tried another machine until we found one that worked.*

Although this method was by no means the most rapid implementation, the requirements of the business were satisfied in that users were taken away from their jobs for a minimal amount of time and upon returning were immediately back working properly. Their hardware, logon IDs, passwords, and profiles had already been validated during their training session. ◆

Support Staff Training

The training required for the user is relatively minor; the majority of the training that you'll need to coordinate will be for the computer support staff in your organization. As I've mentioned before, it's extremely important to have these groups involved early in the project. A vast wealth of experience and knowledge about your company's environment lies within these groups. They can help to identify pitfalls, application nuances, user or department requirements, and support statistics. These statistics can be important in targeting trouble areas in applications and helping to implement more stable versions in Terminal Server, or in educating the support staff on how to deal with these issues now that the application will reside in Terminal Server.

Your help desk staff will need to be trained to do the following:

- Identify whether an application resides on a Terminal Server or on the user's local desktop.

- Use the support tools of Terminal Server/MetaFrame such as *remote control* to visually assist the user in resolving the problem. In many situations, simply being able to see what a person is attempting to describe will dramatically increase the chances of resolving the problem over the phone instead of requiring a visit from a support person.

Author's Note

Session remote control is a powerful tool that your help desk can employ in the support of Terminal Server users to greatly reduce the number of calls that must be escalated to a desktop support person to resolve. All of your support staff should be given training ahead of time on how to employ remote control as part of the standard support process. This can easily be simulated in a test or training lab where pre-scripted scenarios can be played out involving a client and the support staff. Not only will such a session educate the support team on how to use the tools, but it will get them involved in the project in a positive way. ◆

- Identify when a support issue requires the assistance of a Terminal Server administrator or an end-user support person. Calling on other support departments when not required causes an unnecessary increase in the time to get the user's issue resolved. Certainly, you shouldn't expect this distinction to happen immediately. Most help desk personnel have been trained to delegate problems to the end-user support staff as quickly as possible. It will take time to educate these people about the added support capabilities of Terminal Server.

At the same time, you'll also need to train your end-user support staff to do the following:

- Install and configure the client software as required for the environment.

- Understand what client device-mappings are and which ones have been implemented and are supported by which client types in your environment.

- Identify when a person is having an issue with a Terminal Server application or a local application, and determine whether performance or accessibility problems are a result of Terminal Server or some other connectivity device, such as a SQL Server or the network itself.

- Identify when a user can simply have his or her PC replaced with a new one instead of attempting to resolve the issue at the user's desk. This sounds like a simple enough thing to do, but remember that the support staff has always worked in the opposite frame of mind. They have always attempted to resolve issues at the desktop while the user waits. It needs to be made very clear that this is not a requirement in most situations.

Author's Note

Just as I suggested with session remote control, this support process can quite easily be simulated in a lab or test environment with client machines. I have found that a visual example of simply swapping faulty devices seems to have more of a lasting impact on the support person than simply telling them what to do. ◆

- Know when to call on the services of a Terminal Server administrator to assist in resolving a problem.

You must not exclude these support groups or provide them with only minimal information. They may perceive this as an indication that their services are either no longer necessary or inadequate for the tasks at hand. This can make it extremely difficult to get their assistance at any time later in the project. You're guaranteed to require the services of the support staff at some point, and they'll prove to be a valuable component of your project.

User Profile, Policy, and Account Planning

As part of the client planning phase, you should begin to look at the configuration and rights for your users' accounts. Typically, this will involve deciding on the profiles, policies, and account-configuration settings that you will be implementing. The information can be broken down into the following four areas:

- **User rights.** These special security permissions control a user's access to perform certain base operations on a server. Being able to execute a shutdown or manage security logs are just two examples of the features that are available within the user rights. See Chapter 12, "Terminal Server Configuration and Tuning."

- **User profiles.** Every user of a Windows NT/2000 computer has what's known as a *user profile*. A user profile contains a combination of the user's desktop settings (such as icons, screen colors, or window positions) as well as user-specific information (such as network or printer connections). A profile also contains a copy of the contents of the HKEY_CURRENT_USER registry information, which is automatically loaded when the user logs on. This contains application information specific to that user.

  Some of the decisions that you need to make involve determining where the user profiles will reside and whether they'll be stored on a user-by-user basis, or if you'll create one or more mandatory profiles and force your users to use those. Chapter 17, "User Profile and Account Configuration," discusses the details of how to create and manage each of the profile types.

- **Group and system policies.** Policies provide a mechanism by which you can control the features available within a user's profile. In general, a policy configures a number of registry components in order to enforce any restrictions or changes that you have requested. Some examples of policies include removing the Run command from the Start menu or preventing temporary Internet files from being stored within the user's profile (which is usually the default). Windows 2000 introduces a new set of policies known as *group policies*, which can be centrally managed through the Active Directory. In Chapter 16, "Group and System Policy Configuration," I discuss how to implement policies within your environment.

- **Account security and auditing.** Account security deals with the configuration of settings such as password expiration and minimum length. Auditing allows you to monitor the security activities occurring within your environment. Typically, you'll audit occurrences such as logons and attempts to access restricted tools or data. Chapter 12 discusses some of the default auditing and security settings that you should use.

7

Server Hardware Planning

In this chapter:

- **The Assessment Process**
  Four requirements need to be considered when assessing the hardware configuration that will be used in your Terminal Server implementation: user capacity requirements, application requirements, system availability, and risk tolerance.

- **Determining the Requirements**
  To properly size your Terminal Server environment, you first need to understand exactly what will be required and expected by both the users and the business.

- **Hardware Sizing**
  Once you have an idea as to the number of servers and concurrent users per server in your environment, the next step is to determine the hardware requirements that will support this environment.

- **Load Testing**
  After gathering and analyzing your requirements and developing a sizing estimate for your server hardware, the next step is to perform some baseline testing on this configuration with your applications.

- **Determining the Number of Required Servers**
  Once all of the sizing and load testing is finally complete, you should be able to predict the number of users that a server in your environment will be able to support. Now you're ready to look at the number of servers that will be required in the environment.

The Assessment Process

These are two of the most common questions that I receive from people interested in implementing Terminal Server:

- How many users can I expect to run on a single server?
- What are the server requirements in order to support *x* number of users?

Unfortunately, there's no easy answer to either question—for a number of reasons. Following are just a few of those reasons:

- **Your server requirements will be influenced heavily by the applications that you plan to implement.** The server requirements for running Microsoft Word by itself are very different from those required for concurrently running Word, Excel, Great Plains, and SAPGUI. Different applications will stress a server in different ways. One application may have high memory requirements, for example, while another has high processor requirements.

- **Users with different skill levels and job functions utilize server resources in different ways.** For example, data entry workers introduce a smaller load on a server than a power user who's performing advanced Excel calculations.

- **Even users within the same job classification will actually work within the Terminal Server environment in different ways.** One user may open all of his or her applications immediately after logging on, and then switch between them as necessary throughout the day. Another user may open and close the applications only as required.

So how do you go about sizing a Terminal Server environment? To properly size the hardware requirements for your implementation, you have to take the time to work iteratively through a process of estimating and then fine-tuning to meet the expectations of the project. Don't expect to come up with a sizing solution simply by estimating user and memory requirements, performing some calculations, and then extrapolating the results. To properly size your environment, you need to develop a proposed sizing, perform some real user testing with the applications against that estimated size, and from the results, determine what's a reasonable expectation for the number of servers and the user load per server.

Figure 7.1 shows the process that I typically follow when sizing the requirements for an implementation. While the steps themselves seem quite trivial, the actual work performed during each step varies, depending largely on the implementation requirements determined in step 1.

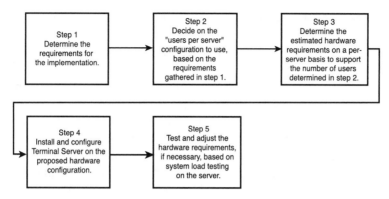

Figure 7.1 *The server-sizing life cycle.*

The remainder of this chapter works through the steps involved in the process illustrated in Figure 7.1.

Determining the Requirements

To properly size your Terminal Server environment you first need to understand exactly what will be required and expected by both the users and the business. These requirements must be taken into consideration when making your sizing decisions. In general, there are four areas to consider when determining environmental requirements:

- User capacity requirements
- Application requirements
- System availability
- Risk tolerance

The following sections describe in detail the considerations for each of these areas.

User Capacity Requirements

There are two things to consider when looking at user capacity requirements. The first is the maximum number of *concurrent* user sessions in the environment, as well as the total user base that will be receiving the ICA or RDP client. An accurate determination of this number is very important. I typically add 10–15% to this estimate as a buffer. For example, say I'm sizing an environment that will need to support 400 concurrent user sessions in a desktop-replacement scenario, with a total client deployment of 600. So, even though I have 400 concurrent connections, theoretically there could be 600 if all users decided to connect at the same time. To the 400 concurrent user sessions, I add my 15% buffer to get a total of 460.

Notice that I'm referring to user "sessions" instead of simply looking at "users." I prefer to use this generalization to take into consideration the situation where you might be distributing published applications instead of a complete desktop.

The exact number of concurrent sessions that you'll have in an application-deployment scenario depends on how you distribute applications between servers. As I mentioned in Chapter 6, "Client Planning," if any applications are dependent on each other (for example, Internet Explorer and Microsoft Word), you need to make them available on the same server.

With this in mind, let's say for example that you want to publish two applications, AppA and AppB. Looking at them individually, you determine that AppA will have 300 concurrent sessions and AppB will have 400 concurrent sessions. If the applications are completely independent, you have the option of publishing them on the same server or on different servers. If they are handled independently, you can size the hardware separately for each application (simply following the steps in Figure 7.1 for each app).

If you're going to combine these apps on the same server, you need to size the hardware to accommodate an environment with somewhere between 400 and 700 user sessions. The total session count depends on whether the same user runs both applications (using only one connection), or different users run each application (taking one session connection per application).

In addition to sizing the number of concurrent user sessions, you also need to categorize the computing requirements of each user. Table 7.1 lists how users are typically divided, depending on whether it's an application-replacement or desktop-replacement scenario.

Table 7.1   Common Terminal Server User Types

User Type	Desktop Replacement	Application Replacement
Light user	Usually runs two or three applications—a line-of-business app plus host access or email.	Typically performs consistent and repetitive operations such as data entry. Processing is typically light and server downtime has little impact on the user's productivity.
Medium user	Runs between three and six applications, consisting of two or more client/server apps in addition to office or business productivity tools such as Word or Microsoft Project.	Usually performs a specific task or job function as part of a business workflow. Overall processing requirements are higher than those of a light user, plus they're typically more dependent on the availability of the environment. If the Terminal Server is down, their jobs are affected. A call center employee typically fits into this category.

User Type	Desktop Replacement	Application Replacement
Heavy user	Runs more than six applications and utilizes advanced functionality such as charting, graphics, or numerical calculations.	When the published application is extremely process-intensive and/or memory-intensive, users are grouped into this category. Job productivity is affected if the Terminal Server is down.

Ideally you'd like to be able to determine the number of user sessions in each category that will make up the total concurrent user load, but rarely is this calculation easily achievable; even if it was, it's typically of little value in determining your final hardware configuration.

If you're going to be publishing individual applications, I recommend that you group users into the medium user category (unless the application is memory-intensive and/or processor-intensive). If you're implementing a desktop-replacement scenario, group users into the heavy category. You can never go wrong overestimating your server hardware requirements, because any additional capacity will provide room for such things as fail-over or environment growth.

If you prefer to perform a more detailed breakdown of the user sessions, I suggest that you look at the total user base instead of concurrent connections and establish a percentage of the users who fall into each category.

For example, I might have the following breakdown of my 600 total users:

- 25 light users (4%)
- 250 medium users (42%)
- 325 heavy users (54%)

Using these percentages, I can divide my 460 concurrent users as follows:

- 18 light users (460 × 4%)
- 194 medium users (460 × 42%)
- 248 heavy users (460 × 54%)

Application Requirements

Now that you have an estimate as to the number and types of users who will access your environment, the next step is to categorize the types of applications you'll be serving and whether they're 32-bit, 16-bit, or DOS. It's particularly important to flag any 16-bit or DOS applications, because they introduce additional resource requirements (sometimes substantial). Chapter 9, "Software Planning," talks in more detail about application considerations.

In general, all applications of the same type can be grouped together when performing the sizing calculations, so calculations based on an application-by-application basis are usually unnecessary. What this means is that you can classify Word 2000, PowerPoint 2000, and IE5 as 32-bit apps instead of looking at them individually.

Based on the information that you gather, you should create a listing similar to the one shown in Table 7.2. Here I've listed each of the user categories and estimated how many instances of each application type would be running for a given user type. For example, a light user in my environment will typically run two 32-bit applications and one 16-bit application.

So at any given time, I could expect 36 instances of a 32-bit application and 18 instances of a 16-bit application to be running in my Terminal Server environment for each concurrent light user . Remember that this is for my entire Terminal Server environment, however I end up sizing it, not necessarily for a single server.

As I mentioned previously, it's usually easier to simply base your estimates on medium or heavy users instead of dividing the applications into individual user categories. When doing this, you can usually base your calculations on the applications that would be run by the majority of the users or the applications run by your heavy users, whichever is greater. In my example, I could simply look at my 460 concurrent heavy users running six 32-bit applications and one 16-bit app. This would give a total of 2,760 instances of a 32-bit application and 460 instances of a 16-bit application running in my Terminal Server environment.

Table 7.2   Application Distribution Based on User Types

User Category	32-bit Apps	16-bit Apps	DOS Apps
Light Users	2	1	0
Medium Users	4	0	0
Heavy Users	6	1	0

Remember, if you're publishing applications on independent servers, you'll need to prepare separate instance totals for each application. Looking again at my earlier example of applications AppA and AppB (both 32-bit), my instance totals would be as shown in Table 7.3. As I've said, I typically use the medium user type with published applications.

Table 7.3   Sample Published Application Distribution

User Category	32-Bit Applications
Medium Users	300 (AppA)
Medium Users	400 (AppB)

If published applications are grouped on a single server, you'll need to determine the total concurrent user sessions, because multiple published applications that are run by a single user from the same server use only one connection. This means that if you combined the 700 total application instances for AppA and AppB, you could actually have fewer total concurrent sessions if some users run both applications. Worst-case scenario, you would base your sizing on the 700 total application instances.

System Availability

Another area of consideration that's very often completely overlooked during Terminal Server sizing is the business requirement for system availability. Does your environment need to be accessible 24x7, or only during local business hours? The expected time of availability for your Terminal Server environment will have a large bearing on your final sizing considerations. Be sure to provide sufficient capacity so that you can take servers offline for maintenance or upgrade while minimizing the impacts on system availability.

For my sizing example, I'll assume that my environment needs to be available 24x7, with the peak concurrent user load occurring between 8 a.m. and 6 p.m. Between 6 p.m. and 8 a.m. the concurrent user load drops from 400 down to 150. Using my 15% rule, I size this off peak-load at approximately 175. Table 7.4 summarizes this information.

Table 7.4   *Estimated Concurrent Usage Based on System Availability Requirements*

	Concurrent User Load	
Hours of Operation	Estimated	Plus 15% Overhead
8 a.m. to 6 p.m.	400	460
6 p.m. to 8 a.m.	150	175

I'll take this information into consideration during my system sizing and plan an environment in such a way that I can take certain servers offline after 6 p.m. while keeping others online to support the 175 concurrent-user load for the second shift.

Author's Note

As you might expect, because the concurrent load is lower during the off-peak hours in this example, it will be easier to accommodate taking servers offline than it would be if the load was consistent (400) during all hours. ◆

Risk Tolerance

The final area of consideration is the level of risk tolerance that your business has for downtime. While you would ideally like to never have a Terminal Server go down, the reality is that you'll have an unexpected server failure at some point. Your goal in designing and implementing your environment is to minimize these outages and their impact on users.

Your company's level of risk tolerance will have a significant bearing on your final decision as to the number of users that you'll have per server. The reason is actually quite simple. The more users that you have running on a single Terminal Server, the more users who are affected if the server goes down. The amount of risk tolerance is very often dependent on the types of applications that will be running in the Terminal Server environment, and how critical they are to the business. A mission-critical application has a much lower tolerance level than office productivity tools such as word processors or mail readers.

Of course, given the choice, most organizations would like to minimize their risk as much as possible, but realistically the costs of doing this make it impractical. A compromise must be reached between risk and cost when determining the user-per-server ratio.

The easiest way to do this is to provide a simple table containing different percentages of the total concurrent user count (not including the 10–15% overhead) and solicit feedback from the business (whenever possible) as to how many users can acceptably be affected by a server outage. Table 7.5 gives an example based on my sample environment of 400 concurrent users. The table contains calculations ranging from 5% to 60%. I've omitted 0 simply because it's impossible to have an outage without affecting at least some users. I have also not gone higher than 55% (220) due to a limitation in the page pool size, which in turn restricts the size of the Registry (I will talk more about this shortly.). In practice, the upper limit on concurrent connections per Terminal Server is usually around 200.

Table 7.5   *Percentages of Total Concurrent Users*

5%	10%	15%	25%	50%	55%
20	40	60	100	200	220

Author's Note

On a Terminal Server, each concurrent user's profile must be loaded into the registry; therefore, a maximum registry size introduces a limitation on the number of concurrent users on a Terminal Server. This limitation is due to the fact that Windows has a maximum of 2GB RAM allocated for kernel memory, regardless of how much physical memory is on the server. A portion of this RAM is reserved for memory allocated to kernel-mode components (page pool) and kernel-thread stack space (page table entries, also known as PTEs).

If a system runs out of PTEs, it can't allocate stack space and will crash with a Blue Screen of Death. If the server runs out of page pool space, you'll typically receive Registry Full error messages and new user connections will not be accepted, even if processor and memory utilization itself is low. On a Windows 2000 server, you can reduce the space allocated for PTEs, which by default is higher than for the page pool. By lowering the memory allocated for PTEs, you can increase the page pool size, allowing more space for the registry and hence more concurrent connections. The Microsoft Knowledge Base article Q247904 provides a detailed explanation of how to do this (although I warn you that it's not for the faint of heart). In Windows 2000, the maximum available PTE space is allocated by default. Even if you run out of PTEs, you can't increase this space. On Windows NT 4.0, the maximum PTE space is not allocated by default, but a smaller value is calculated based on the memory on the server. You can increase the number of PTEs on a TSE 4.0 server, and hence the space allocated. I talk more about this topic in Chapter 12, "Terminal Server Configuration and Tuning." ◆

Referring to the table, select two numbers representing your acceptable and maximum risk-tolerance factors. For example, say that out of the 400 concurrent users, your business would be most comfortable with having only 60 users affected by a server outage, but would be able to tolerate an impact of up to 100 users before it would have a significant impact on the business. Taking these values and adding the 10–15% overhead, you'll have the target range for determining the number of users per server. This is not necessarily the maximum capacity that the servers will support, but is the range that you'll initially size for.

In my example, adding the 15% overhead I would get a user count between 70 and 115. This range will be used in the next section along with the other information gathered during the requirements phase to develop an initial plan for the hardware requirements of the Terminal Server environment.

Sizing the Users per Server

In this step you will bring together the data that you've collected to determine an estimate for the planned users-per-server ratio. At this point, you're not yet estimating the specifics of the server such as processor and memory requirements. That information will be determined in the next section.

Of course, the estimated number of users per server is by no means final. It's likely that you'll need to make adjustments once you've calculated your processor and memory requirements, and have had the opportunity to perform some actual load testing on the server configuration. Remember, at this point you're only planning an initial estimate, so leave room to make any necessary adjustments before deciding on the final system requirements.

Normally I perform two calculations at this step—one based on the lower users-per-server risk estimate, and the other based on the higher estimate. By providing both extremes, the business has the opportunity to make a decision based on users-per-server risk, rather than the estimated hardware costs. It also allows you to perform testing based on two different hardware configurations to determine what's optimal for the environment. If the gap is very narrow between these two numbers, you may want to use the higher value. For example, I could simply take 100 as the targeted number of users per server and go from there. I usually record the following information (where UL is the lower users-per-server number and UH is the higher). Notice that these numbers include my 15% buffer.

UL = 70

UH = 115

Author's Note

While it's possible to calculate the number of servers needed based on your users-per-server estimate, until you have had the opportunity to perform load testing on your hardware configuration, any estimates you create are likely to change.

See the later section "Determining the Number of Required Servers" for more information. ◆

Hardware Sizing

Now that you have an estimate of the number of concurrent users per server, the next step is to determine the hardware requirements that will support this environment. It's important to remember that this information should be used as a guideline in developing your hardware configuration, but shouldn't be treated as the final word on the subject. The only way to ensure that the calculated estimates will meet your requirements is to perform some load testing once you have Terminal Server installed on the proposed hardware.

I highly recommend that you consult the Microsoft Windows Hardware Compatibility List (HCL) prior to selecting any type of hardware to ensure that it's supported. You don't want to have to worry about your server hardware causing unexpected stability or performance issues. The most current HCL is available on the Microsoft Web site at www.microsoft.com/hcl. ◆

Processors

Probably the single most important factor when looking at your Terminal Server's processor configuration is deciding on the number of processors that each server will have. While Microsoft describes a single-processor server as the minimum configuration for a Terminal Server, I recommend that you *never* plan to implement a single processor server in a production environment, except possibly in the smallest of environments.

Using the data from Table 7.6, which summarizes the average number of users supported per processor, you can estimate the average processor requirements for each of your servers based on your user types.

Table 7.6   Average Supported Users per Processor

Processor Type	Light Users	Medium Users	Heavy Users
Pentium Pro 200	35	25	13
Pentium II 300	45	30	18
Pentium III 500	60	40	23

Of course, the benchmark for processor performance is always being raised as Intel continues to deliver faster and more powerful processors. Coupled with this fact are additional processor options such as increased cache size, bus speed, and other performance-enhancing features. The users-per-processor estimates in Table 7.6 should be treated as nothing more than a starting point for estimating the size of your servers. During the load testing phase, you'll be able to establish a more realistic users-per-processor ratio specific to your environment. Usually I won't take the clock speed of the processor into consideration unless it's a change of at least 25%. So I would typically treat a PIII 600 as a 500 when calculating users, but for a PIII 750, I would increase the users-per-processor by approximately 30–45%, and a PIII 1 GHz would effectively double the users-per-processor. ◆

Now let's look at a couple of examples of how you could use the data from Table 7.6 to estimate the processor requirements for your server.

Returning again to sizing an environment for 460 concurrent users, I have the lower and upper estimates for the number of users per server at 70 and 115, respectively. Using the data from Table 7.6 and the assumption that all users are classified as heavy users, I could calculate the number of processors per server as follows:

Proc# = 70/23 = 3 (for 70 users per server)

Proc# = 115/23 = 5 (for 115 users per server)

Of course, I wouldn't have a server with three or five processors, so I need to round the number of processors in each case either up or down. I *always* suggest that you round down to the nearest power of two (unless it's a single processor; then round up to two). So instead of three processors I would use two, and instead of five processors I would use four.

In doing so, you should also adjust the expected number of users per server accordingly, based on the values in Table 7.6. This would mean that I would now be sizing the servers as shown in Table 7.7.

Table 7.7   *Adjusted Users-per-Server Estimate Based on the Number of Processors*

Pentium III Processors	Original Estimate	New Estimate
2	70	2 × 23 = 46
4	115	4 × 23 = 96

Don't be alarmed by the fact that the users-per-server estimate has now dropped off to accommodate the processor estimates, particularly for the dual-processor configuration, which has gone from 70 users per server down to 46. Remember, these numbers are going to be used only to size the server that you'll use to perform load testing. It's not necessarily the final configuration that you're going to implement. Only after completing the testing can you determine the final users-per-server total, and from there decide on the actual number of servers that will make up the environment.

For completeness I'll also demonstrate these calculations based on a percentage breakdown of users based on their type, instead of simply assuming that they're all heavy users. Earlier in this chapter I said that my sample environment had a percentage breakdown of users as follows:

- 4% light users
- 42% medium users
- 54% heavy users

My calculation for the number of Pentium III processors required for 70 users per server with the given percentage distribution would then be as follows:

Proc#   = $((70 \times 4\%)/60) + ((70 \times 42\%)/40) + ((70 \times 54\%)/23)$

         = $(0.05) + (0.74) + (1.64)$

         = 2.43

Rounding this number down, I estimate that it would require dual Pentium III processors to support 70 users with the user percentage distribution given above. As I mentioned earlier, it's usually simpler to base your sizing estimates on treating all users as heavy users, instead of trying to divide them into individual categories.

RAM

No matter how many processors you have or how fast they are, without adequate memory your server will take a significant performance hit. The most common cause of a Terminal Server failure is inadequate memory to support the number of concurrent users on the system.

There are three areas to consider when calculating the amount of physical RAM required on the server:

- **Operating system requirements.** The operating system requires a certain amount of memory in order to function. I recommend the following based on the Terminal Server version:

TS 2000	150MB
TSE 4.0	80MB

- **Per-user requirements.** A certain amount of RAM will be required to support each user's session on a Terminal Server. In general, there are two ways to approach estimating the RAM requirements for each server. The first method is to look at the individual requirements based on the type of users running in the environment. Usually you can allocate memory as follows:

Light user	10MB
Medium user	15MB
Heavy user	20MB

  These requirements may seem high in comparison to some recommendations from other sources, but I've always found that providing a slightly higher estimate on memory requirements will help to ensure that the server functions as robustly as possible. Using these numbers, you can then calculate the user RAM requirements for your implementation.

As with the processor calculations, you can either calculate memory requirements based on the percentage breakdown of the different user types that will be accessing the server, or simply base the calculations on the assumption that all users are heavy users. In this situation, you simply multiply the number of users per server by 20MB to get the system's memory requirements. This could result in an overestimate of the memory requirements for the server, but typically this results in a slightly higher users-per-server ratio than you had originally anticipated.

- **Additional application memory requirements.** I've found that if users will be running three or fewer *32-bit* applications, memory sizing based on the per user requirements listed above is sufficient without augmenting the memory totals. If heavy users will run more than three 32-bit applications, or any users will run any 16-bit or DOS applications, you'll need to perform some additional calculations to take the memory requirements of those applications into consideration. The memory calculations for the different application types are summarized as follows:

DOS apps	2MB RAM per DOS application
16-bit apps	4MB RAM per WOW (Windows on Win32) session plus 2MB for each additional 16-bit app run within that WOW session.
32-bit apps	2MB–4MB RAM per application is usually a fair estimate as an average between all of the 32-bit apps being used, although a more accurate measurement can be taken by simply looking at the memory usage for the application through Task Manager while running on a regular Windows 2000 Professional desktop computer.

Using my adjusted users-per-server estimate from the processors section, I would calculate my environment's memory requirements as follows:

1. First I get the amount of RAM required for my operating system. I'll be implementing Windows 2000 Terminal Services, so I need 150MB per server.

2. Next I calculate the per-user memory requirements. For completeness I'll calculate using both methods described above. First I will assume that all users are heavy users, so on a server with 46 user sessions I would calculate this total RAM requirement:

   $46 \times 20MB = 920MB$

   And for my 96 user sessions I would have this amount:

   $96 \times 20MB = 1920MB$

Now, if I break down the user totals into the percentage of user types (4% light, 42% medium, 54% heavy) my calculations for the 46 users per server would be as follows:

$(46 \times 4\% \times 10MB) + (46 \times 42\% \times 15MB) + (46 \times 54\% \times 20MB)$

$= 18.4MB + 289.8MB + 496.8MB$

$= 805MB$

3. Now I calculate the additional RAM required to support the applications in the environment. If I assume that all users are heavy users, then I will calculate the requirements for all of them to run six 32-bit applications and one 16-bit application as described back in Table 7.2. I'll use 2MB as the estimate for memory requirements in this situation for 32-bit applications.

The application memory requirements for 46 users per server would be as follows:

$(46 \times 6 \times 2MB) + (46 \times 1 \times 4MB)$

$= 552MB + 184MB$

$= 736MB$

And for 96 users per server:

$(96 \times 6 \times 2MB) + (96 \times 1 \times 4MB)$

$= 1152MB + 384MB$

$= 1536MB$

4. Now, all that's left is to total the memory requirements for each Terminal Server. For my 46 users-per-server example, I get the following total:

$150MB + 920MB + 736MB = 1806MB$

From this I can estimate that I would need around 2GB of memory per server in order to support 46 concurrent heavy users accessing the required applications.

For my 96 users-per-server example I would have this total:

$150MB + 1920MB + 1536MB = 3606MB$

Therefore, I can estimate that I need approximately 4GB of memory per server in order to support 96 concurrent heavy users accessing the required applications.

Disk Subsystem

Your decision on the disk subsystem to use for your servers is based on a standard recommendation instead of a calculated per-user value. In a properly sized environment you should never encounter any bottlenecks as a result of high disk utilization. It's much more likely that you'll become memory or CPU-bound first.

The following issues should be considered when deciding on your disk configuration:

- Always use SCSI disk drives in conjunction with SCSI or RAID controllers.

- Divide your disk requirements into three areas—operating system, pagefile, and application files. When possible, configure your environment to service the operating system and pagefile with one controller and the application files with the other. If you want to provide disk redundancy in your environment, place the OS and pagefile onto a set of mirrored (RAID 1) drives and not within a RAID 5 configuration. The application files can be run from a RAID 5 configuration, although RAID 1 is usually sufficient, particularly if a hot spare configuration is supported.

Author's Note

My personal preference is not to introduce RAID 5 unless the environment is configured in such a way that a server cannot be offline for an extended period of time (server uptime must be maximized). Because there's no permanent user data being stored on the Terminal Server, a high level of redundancy isn't necessarily required on the server. If a server happens to lose both disks in a mirrored configuration, the server could be recoverable fairly quickly based on a standard server cloning and build process (see Chapter 18, "Server Operations and Support," for a discussion of server imaging). In most situations, having a small stock of spare drives on hand or configured as hot spares will provide the necessary redundancy at the disk level for your servers. ◆

Network Interface Cards

Chapter 5, "Network Planning," talks about the requirements for planning and testing a network configuration that supports your Terminal Server implementation, and the overall importance of network performance and availability in your Terminal Server environment. If network connectivity is unavailable, all the processing power in the world won't help your users. When deciding on the network interface card to use in your server, take the following issues into consideration:

- Select a card from a well known and supported manufacturer. The *de facto* standard in many Terminal Server implementations is the Intel PRO/100+ card or an equivalent card from the server hardware vendor (such as the NC3122 dual-port Fast Ethernet card from Compaq).

- Chose an adapter that has current drivers for your OS and supports advanced features such as adapter fault tolerance (AFT) or hot-swapping to increase server uptime and network availability.

Author's Note

Because of the relatively low cost of network adapters, I usually recommend that dual NIC cards be implemented with some form of teaming or fault tolerance to improve availability. When looking to implement card teaming, always look to use well known and supported hardware, such as Intel or Compaq. Poor hardware or driver support can cause stability issues with NIC teaming◆

Servers Versus Workstations

Today, with the availability of high performance and multiple processors in workstation computers, the performance gap between them and the server is practically nonexistent. The only difference between many high-end workstations and low-end servers is usually hardware redundancy such as RAID controllers, and hot-swappable components such as hard drivers or power supplies.

In many Terminal Server configurations, the workstation computer may fit the role of a small to medium server, with a lower cost per user than true server hardware. The main limitations that exist in many workstations are their limited support for multiple processors (usually two) and RAM (usually 1–2GB).

The workstation hardware is a viable option because, in most Terminal Server implementations, the servers will contain no dynamic user data. Couple this with a plan for redundancy at the server level and there's no longer the requirement for system redundancy such as RAID arrays or swappable power supplies. Of course, some features such as dual NIC cards are still available, although the fault tolerance in the environment is handled by the presence of multiple redundant Terminal Servers. If you lose a Terminal Server, no problem—there are still x number of other Terminal Servers in the environment that users can log onto.

Author's Note

In situations where the server uptime must be maximized, server-class hardware may be the only option to minimize the downtime due to hardware failure. This simply means the introduction of the hardware redundancy features, not necessarily an increase in the number of processors, RAM, or other components. ◆

Load Testing

After gathering and analyzing your requirements and developing a sizing estimate for your server hardware, the next step is to perform some baseline testing on this configuration with your applications to determine what adjustments need to be made in order to best satisfy the requirements of your implementation. For example, you may determine that one of the applications you plan to deploy is very processor-intensive, forcing you to decrease the anticipated user load per server or increase the processing power of each server. This is the type of thing that you want to know before you buy all the hardware for your implementation.

Author's Note

Depending on whether you're introducing new applications or migrating them from the local desktop, you may already have a good idea as to the behavior of the applications and their typical memory and CPU resource requirements. You should still test these in a Terminal Server environment before committing to one hardware configuration or another.

Many big-name hardware vendors will be happy to provide you with an evaluation machine configured to your specifications for a limited demo or trial period, particularly if you make it clear that you are also going to be trying a competitor's configuration. ♦

Plan to test your proposed hardware configuration as early in the project as possible and have this configuration finalized prior to the beginning of the proper server build and user testing. If you leave this testing until after you've started the user testing and piloting, you run the risk of having to modify your hardware requirements very late in the implementation.

Typically, two types of server-load testing are performed. The first involves testing with a small set of test users. The second involves performing some automated testing to develop results based on high user-connectivity scenarios.

User and Application Testing

The first phase occurs after you have installed the base operating system (Terminal Server and MetaFrame) and a core set of applications that represent the majority of the usage in your environment. Don't spend too much time tweaking and tuning the system, since you're looking only for a reasonable expectation of how the hardware and software will perform. Get a few users (possibly only the members of your project, at this point) to log onto the system in a controlled fashion while monitoring some standard performance counters (see Table 7.8 for a list of some standard counters to monitor). During this monitoring, look for changes in such things as memory or processor utilization.

Plan to monitor the system with one user, then two, then four, and try to estimate how you think the system should react to the increase in users. What you're looking for is some indication that the user sessions and their application usage will scale in a reasonably linear fashion. For example, moving from two users to four users should double (or less than double) the resources currently in use in the environment. This will help to validate that you've sized your servers correctly. A drastic change in resource consumption with a small change in user load could indicate a poorly behaved application or some other issue that may force you to adjust your server requirements.

Author's Note

You may have noticed that I've omitted any network counters from Table 7.8. While issues with your network may severely hamper your users' computing experience on the Terminal Server, there's very little in the way of server configuration that you can do to correct this problem. As I mentioned earlier, I recommend going with a network card teaming strategy to introduce redundancy in the network cards and also provide a small performance improvement. If there are issues with your network, they need to be addressed separately. See Chapter 5 for a discussion of this topic.

I have yet to see a server sized in such a way that it encounters a network utilization bottleneck prior to developing a bottleneck in another area such as memory. ♦

Table 7.8   Sample Performance Monitor Counters to Capture During Load Testing

Object	Counter	Comments
System	% Total Processor Time	Monitors the total percentage of processor usage for all processors combined. A sustained usage of 85% or higher indicates that the server is either underpowered or possibly low on memory (if the % pagefile usage is also high).
	Processor Queue Length	Measures the number of threads currently waiting in the processor queue for execution time. All processors on a server share a single processor queue. A sustained queue length of 15 or greater usually indicates that the server is operating at its user capacity.

continues ▶

Table 7.8   *continued*

Object	Counter	Comments
Memory	Available Bytes	Represents the total amount of virtual memory that's currently available for use. A continuous decline in available bytes may indicate an application that's leaking memory and will eventually lead to exhausted memory resources. The virtual memory manager attempts to maintain a minimum amount of available physical memory for use (around 4MB), so as the consumption of available bytes increases, the VM tries to swap more information to the pagefile. A sustained availability of less than 5MB (5,242,880 bytes) indicates that all physical memory is in use, and pagefile usage will be increasing.
	% Committed Bytes in use	Represents the ratio of committed memory to the total available memory of the system (physical & pagefile). When this percentage is over 90%, the system is getting dangerously close to exhausting all available memory.
	Pages Input/sec	Monitors the number of pages read from the pagefile that weren't already in memory when referenced. When this counter rises above 65 pages per second, the system is performing too much paging and a continued increase will almost certainly result in a system crash. A steady increase in this counter is an indication that you have insufficient memory in the server to handle the current user load. It may also indicate an application is running that's leaking memory.
Paging File	% Usage	Measures the percentage of the pagefile that's currently in use with information that has been paged from physical memory. A steady increase in the percentage used indicates that the server has insufficient physical memory available to service the current user load. A usage above 85% usually indicates that the server will run out of virtual memory. You must increase the virtual memory, the physical memory, or both.

Object	Counter	Comments
Physical Disk	Current Disk Queue Length	This counter includes both waiting requests and requests currently being serviced by the disk at the time of the data capture. To calculate the number of requests currently outstanding, sub-tract the current queue length from the number of spindles on the disk. Multi-spindle drives service multiple requests simultaneously. A queue length consis-tently over 2 usually indicates a disk subsystem bottleneck.
	% Disk Time	Indicates the percentage of time that the disk is busy servicing read and write requests. An average percentage that's consistently in the 70–80% range is a good indication of a disk perfor-mance problem.
		Don't take % Disk Time as the only factor, however, since it's possible that a long queue may developing while the percentage disk time remains below the maximum.

Figure 7.2 shows an example of Performance Monitor running with the listed counters on a test Terminal Server.

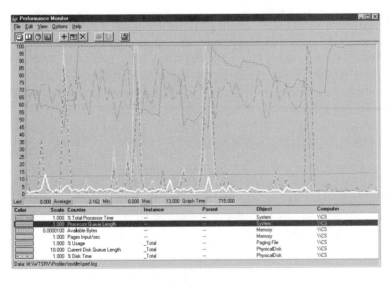

Figure 7.2   *Performance Monitor with the listed counters.*

Automated Server Load Testing

After performing initial testing with a small set of users, you may also want to develop some rough estimates on how you should expect the server to behave in a situation with an increased user load. One way to do this is to perform some automated server-load testing, using a load-testing tool.

Two tools are available to help you in doing this. The first is the *Capacity Planning Tool* provided as part of the Windows 2000 Server Resource Kit, or as a link from within the Microsoft document "Windows 2000 Terminal Services Capacity and Scaling," which is available at the following address:

    www.microsoft.com/windows2000/library/technologies/terminal/tscaling.asp

This document includes some detailed information on capacity and scaling tests performed using this tool.

Citrix also provides a tool called the *Citrix Server Sizing Kit*, free from the Citrix Developer's Network (CDN). The CDN can be accessed from a link on the main Citrix Web site (www.citrix.com). Citrix includes documentation on how to configure and use this tool, along with some sample scripts for use with the Microsoft Office products.

Automated testing is usually done simply to validate that the server sizing is in the ballpark with regard to the system requirements and to get an idea as to how it will behave under heavy user loads. (Of course, automated testing can never fully replicate the behavior of real users.)

Author's Note

Unless you're concerned about the results that you've seen during the user testing with your configuration, I usually recommend that you not perform automated testing. If you're going to perform automated testing, I recommend keeping it as simple as possible and not worrying too much about developing a completely customized configuration.

Automated testing can require a large amount of setup and configuration time in order to generate truly accurate results.

It is recommended that you avoid using third-party load or application testing tools, such as Rational Software Team Test or Mercury Interactive's WinRunner. These types of tools are developed for use in automating and managing the testing life cycle for application development and typically run very poorly (if at all) in a Terminal Server environment. ◆

Determining the Number of Required Servers

Once all of the sizing and load testing is finally complete, you should be able to comfortably predict the number of users that a server in your environment will be able to support. Now you're ready to look at the number of servers that will be required in your environment.

In order to perform the calculation, you'll need the total number of con-current user sessions *including* the 10–15% overhead, in addition to your estimated number of users per server.

If S is the number of servers, Cu is the number of concurrent users, and U is the number of users per server, then the calculation is simply this:

$S = Cu/U$

Looking one last time at my estimated number of users per server, let's assume that after performing my load testing I determined that I could sup-port 55 and 105 users, respectively, on each of my server configurations, well over the proposed 46 and 96 users with which I went into the testing phase. Based on these values, the number of servers that I would need to support 55 users per server with a total of 460 concurrent users would be as follows:

$S = 460/55$

$= 8.4$, which I will round down to 8

So it would seem that I need 8 servers in my environment to support 460 concurrent users, with 55 users per server. But I'm not quite finished yet. These calculations represent the number of servers required when each is operating at 100%, and don't take into consideration the requirements for system availability in my environment. If for some reason there's a server failure, the environment won't have sufficient capacity to allow those users who were kicked off the failed server to log back onto the environment. In order to ensure environment availability, I should augment the calculated number of servers by approximately 25%.

So, increasing my server count of 8 by 25%, I would end up increasing the number of servers to 10, resulting in a reduced average number of users per server from 55 to around 46, but having sufficient capacity to be able to lose 2 servers and still support the entire concurrent user load.

Author's Note

Don't be fooled by the assumption that fewer servers will directly result in reduced administration requirements. In a properly configured environment, the additional overhead required to support 10 servers versus 5 servers is very small. The increased availability of the 10–server configuration usually results in greater administrative flexibility, allowing you more time to troubleshoot or perform maintenance on a server without affecting the user community. ◆

One final thing to note is how many servers are available for maintenance during peak and off-peak hours (refer to the "System Availability" section). In my example, even during peak hours, 1–2 servers could be offline with-out affecting the environment. During the off-peak hours, when my concur-rent user load drops to only 175 users, I can take more than half of the servers offline.

8

Server Management Planning

In this chapter:

- **The Model for Terminal Server Management**
  Regardless of whether the environment contains two or two hundred Terminal Servers, a sound management plan is required in order to maximize the scalability, stability, and availability of the environment.

- **The Theory of Terminal Server Management**
  One of the goals of developing the management process for your Terminal Server environment should be to make it scalable so that as the environment grows, the processes continue to function with minimal change.

- **Security Management**
  A proper security implementation is a critical component of any Terminal Server installation.

- **Application Management**
  When preparing your server management plan, one of the areas to investigate in detail is application management.

The Model for Terminal Server Management

This chapter discusses how to plan the technical management of a Terminal Server environment. Regardless of whether the environment contains two or two hundred Terminal Servers, a sound management plan is required to maximize the scalability, stability, and availability of the environment. Proper hardware planning alone will *not* accomplish this objective.

When considering other computing systems after which you could model your environment, you won't turn to the traditional Windows server infrastructure, but instead to other centralized operating environments, such as mainframes or UNIX. The following list describes some of the common systems-management practices found in these environments:

- A security implementation and administrative authority that's limited to only a handful of trained staff, who have a clear understanding of the environment and the importance of ensuring that it's functioning for the end user.

- Rigorous change-control processes to ensure that only tested and scheduled changes are implemented into production.

- Thorough operations documentation and monitoring mechanisms to ensure the availability of the environment.

Unfortunately, finding a complete implementation of any one of these practices—let alone all three—within a typical Windows-based networking system is uncommon. The problem has little to do with the operating system, but instead has more to do with the history of the desktop PC and the relative youth of Windows in comparison to mainframes and UNIX. Most Windows implementations contain the following variations of the management practices listed above:

- Windows servers usually have a clear division between user and administrator. Users have access to only selected resources; administrators have full access to the system. Unfortunately, these implementations rarely further subdivide users into more granular groupings. If you're not a user, you're an administrator—leading to a large number of administrators.

- As a consequence of the large number of administrators, there is rarely any true accountability for the production environment. As a result, change-management processes are very lax and rarely enforced. When a change is needed, it's usually implemented with only minimum testing and with little or no notification. Change management is often viewed as a corporate bureaucracy that's more about wasting time than accomplishing work. This mentality arises from the fact that most changes in a Windows environment are relatively easy to implement, low risk, and easily recoverable if there are issues. Also, many companies have an unusually high tolerance for failures and downtime in their Windows server environments. If a file or mail server is down for a half hour, there is rarely any true issue. This situation is beginning to change in Windows environments where service-level agreements and mission-critical systems are more common, and greater than 99% uptime is a requirement.

- Very rarely is the idea of the traditional operator extended to the management of the PC server. Although a PC server may reside within a data center, the server is usually managed only by the PC administrators, and the extent of the operator support for such servers is simply to reboot the machine if issues arise.

Author's Note

This is not to say that all Windows environments are poorly managed. I have had the opportunity to witness some corporate environments that were extremely well managed, with clear systems-management practices in place. Unfortunately, this is more the exception than the rule. ✦

While developing your Terminal Server management plan, keep in mind that you are *not* implementing a traditional Windows server environment. To be successful, you'll most likely be implementing server-management practices that currently don't exist within your organization.

Warning

One common problem for an organization with implementation-management rules for their Windows 2000 or NT infrastructure is assuming that Terminal Server should fall under these same rules and requirements. Things such as administrative privileges and management software are deemed necessary, yet are either not suited or not required in a Terminal Server environment. If your organization provides implementation rules for Windows, you must make it clear that Terminal Server is a completely independent product with its own variation of management requirements specifically suited to meet its needs. ✦

Although Terminal Server and MetaFrame theoretically have almost unlimited scaling potential, the true limiting factors for how large an environment can scale are how well it can be managed and whether the management practices can scale as effectively as the hardware or software scales.

The Theory of Terminal Server Management

One of the goals of developing the management process for your Terminal Server environment should be to make it scalable so that as your environment grows, your processes continue to function with no (or minimal) change. Reinventing the systems-management wheel every time you want to expand your Terminal Server infrastructure would be both time-consuming and a poor use of resources.

Author's Note

Deferring the establishment of systems-management standards until after the implementation is complete is a common "time-saving" tactic, but invariably results in increased administration, and as a consequence reduces the time available after the deployment to develop the required standards. Having an idea from the beginning as to how you will manage the environment will help immensely in planning the overall implementation. ◆

Build-on-Demand Management

The most common Terminal Server management approach that people undertake when first implementing their environment is known as *build-on-demand management (BOD)*. In this approach, each Terminal Server is treated as an individual management entity that's supported independently of all others. If a new server is required in this environment, it's built from scratch (hopefully using a set of documented guidelines to ensure that it's configured properly). If an application is required in Terminal Server, it's manually installed on each of the servers that will run it.

Build-on-demand management develops as a result of the natural progression of learning when a Terminal Server environment is first created. It's difficult to develop effective management practices until you're familiar with the steps involved in constructing a functional environment. As you progress through the iterations of building the Terminal Server as desired, you develop a documented approach that can be followed to reproduce the environment you've created. After you move on to adding and testing the desired applications, the document continues to grow to include this new knowledge until eventually you have a complete history of how you progressed from start to finish.

When the Terminal Server environment is small (from two to eight servers), the BOD strategy is a viable option for maintaining the environment. As you move beyond six servers, you'll find that more and more work is required to ensure consistency within the environment. With BOD, every time you manually build a server or install an application you run the risk of introducing subtle configuration differences that can result in application anomalies or even errors. Always having to question the consistency of the production environment adds an additional layer of complexity when attempting to troubleshoot a production problem. BOD introduces a constraint on the scalability of your environment.

A common suggestion that I often hear to overcome the difficulties of managing an increasing number of servers is simply to upgrade the existing hardware to support an increased user load per server. As discussed in

Chapter 7, "Server Hardware Planning," the acceptable ratio of users to servers really depends largely on the risk tolerance of the business. If a server goes down, what's an acceptable minimum number of users that can be affected? Increasing the number of users on a single Terminal Server machine can impact the resilience of the environment. To ensure an optimal configuration, you need to develop a server management strategy to meet the needs of the business and the environment, not build an environment to accommodate the management strategy.

Virtual Server Management

For the large-scale Terminal Server implementations common in many enterprise environments, I use a management strategy known as *virtual server management (VSMgr)*. I use the term *virtual server (VS)* to describe two or more Terminal Servers that are grouped together and managed conceptually as a single server entity. The idea behind VSMgr is to develop a management infrastructure that maintains consistency regardless of the number of physical servers involved, thereby reducing the complexity of managing a large Terminal Server environment.

The idea is that whenever a change is made to the virtual server, it's automatically reflected in all of the servers that make up the virtual server. Whether a VS represents two or two hundred Terminal Servers, the method by which the environment is maintained is identical. Figure 8.1 shows the conceptual layout of a virtual server environment consisting of many physical servers grouped into three virtual servers.

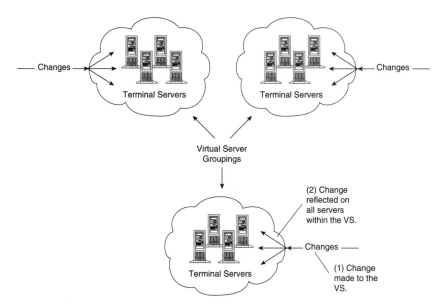

Figure 8.1 *The virtual server environment.*

When constructing a virtual server, the goal is to maximize the number of physical servers contained in the virtual server. Try to group servers together that share a common application base. This helps to minimize the number of virtual servers that exist and, as a result, reduces the management requirements for the environment. Ideally, all servers within a virtual server will be running the same software and most often will have the same hardware configuration (although this isn't strictly required in most circumstances). This setup will simplify the creation of the virtual server and avoid the requirement of introducing exceptions within the virtual server for particular application changes or hardware considerations.

Of course, the ideal scenario would be to have all your Terminal Servers within a single virtual server. Then you would be managing the entire environment as a single entity. In most large-scale implementations, however, you'll probably have multiple virtual servers, particularly if applications are grouped on different servers and published using MetaFrame, or multiple Terminal Server farms exist to support different user groups or departments within your company.

Author's Note

Very often people equate the idea of a virtual server to Citrix's server farm strategy (see Chapter 3, "Citrix MetaFrame" for more information on Citrix server farms). While they share a common goal of simplifying the management of the environment, there are conceptual differences between the two strategies. The Citrix server farm provides a way to group applications together and manage the delivery of those applications to the client. The virtual server provides a way to group servers into more manageable units. It wouldn't be uncommon for a single Citrix server farm to contain multiple virtual servers, each containing one or more servers publishing a common group of applications into the associated server farm.

Theoretically, there's no limit on the number of Terminal Servers that you can put into a single virtual server, but practical limits may be imposed, depending on the software that you use to manage this environment. ◆

Virtual Server Management Components

In the practical implementation of the virtual server management model, a single contact point for the VS is usually created, known as the *virtual server master* (*VSM*). Don't confuse this with the ICA master browser discussed in Chapter 3. Although a VSM can also be an ICA master browser, there is no requirement or dependency involved in this. Figure 8.2 shows the same virtual server groups from Figure 8.1, except that the virtual server master has now been explicitly listed. The VSM can be thought of as the *management* interface to the servers within the virtual server.

Author's Note

If you read the first edition of this book, you may notice that I've dropped the virtual server domain (VSD) terminology from my discussion of the virtual server model. A number of readers suggested that the additional terminology was confusing because a virtual server and a virtual server domain were essentially the same thing. I hope this change helps to make things a little clearer. ◆

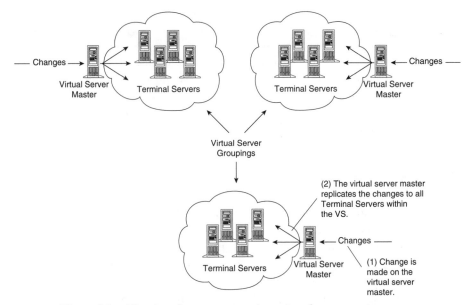

Figure 8.2   *The virtual server master in a virtual server environment.*

Any changes that you want to make to all servers in the virtual server are made only on the VSM. These changes are then propagated from the VSM to all the other servers in the virtual server. The VSM has the following configuration characteristics:

- It has the same software configuration as all other servers in the virtual server.

- It's not normally accessible by users and doesn't participate in any load balancing or application publishing.

- It usually is configured to allow only administrators to log onto it, not regular users.

- It has any necessary software components installed that are required to manage the virtual server. This software and the job that it performs are discussed shortly.

- The physical servers in the virtual server should have no dependencies on a specific VSM. Although the designated VSM is the management node, none of the servers in the virtual server actually "know" this. By "knowing," I mean that they have no dependency on the VSM being a particular name or IP address. Thus, the interchanging of VSMs or the possible unavailability of the VSM has no impact on the functioning (and ideally the management) of the virtual server.

Author's Note

You should try to build redundancy into your environment. This is an important factor in eliminating the single point of failure that the virtual server concept can impose. The ideal (and achievable) solution is to have an environment in which any server in the virtual server can become the VSM very quickly. This would allow you to introduce a new VSM into the environment seamlessly if the current VSM failed. ◆

Although no one tool integrates all the features required to support the practical application of the virtual server model, the requirements for implementing virtual servers can be broken down into components for which suitable tools can be acquired. Table 8.1 summarizes the main component requirements for implementing the VS management model and includes some examples of software available to perform the listed function. In Chapter 9, "Software Planning," I talk more about file and registry replication, application deployment, and server cloning. I also provide an example of server health monitoring in Chapter 18, "Server Operations and Support."

Table 8.1   Component Requirements for the Virtual Server Management Model

Component	Functional Requirement	Examples
Environment Hiding	Hide the details of the underlying configuration from the end user. Remove any dependencies on particular servers within a VS.	Citrix Load Balancing, Published Applications, and Program Neighborhood. Microsoft Network Load Balancing.
File Replication	The distribution of application or other files to the VS, including file permission updates.	Custom-written batch scripts. Tricerat's Reflect (www.tricerat.com), Legato's Octopus (www.legato.com), Opalis' RendezVous (www.opalis.com).

Component	Functional Requirement	Examples
Registry Replication	The distribution of registry changes to servers in the VS.	Custom-written scripts. Tricerat's Reflect (www.tricerat.com).
Application Deployment	The automatic deployment of application installations to all servers within the VS.	Custom-written scripts. Windows 2000 Software Installation (SI) Citrix Installation Management Services (IMS), Wise Solutions' Install Master (www.wisesolutions.com), Veritas' WinINSTALL (www.veritas.com).
Server "Cloning"	Allows the creation of production server images that can be used to build test and pilot servers or to expand a virtual server. Also can be used as part of a disaster-recovery scenario. Helps to ensure consistency in the VS.	Windows Unattended Installation, Norton's Ghost (www.symantec.com), PowerQuest's Drive Image Pro (www.powerquest.com), StorageSoft's ImageCast (www.imagecast.com).
Health Monitoring	Allows for real-time monitoring of the health of the servers within your VS.	Performance Monitor, NetIQ's AppManager (www.netiq.com), RippleTech's LogCaster (www.rippletech.com), Mission Critical Software's OnePoint Operations Manager (www.missioncritical.com).

Security Management

A proper security implementation is a critical component (if not *the* critical component) of any Terminal Server installation. Although security is a concern even for a traditional Windows server, the differences in user interaction between the two mean that Terminal Server requires greater diligence in implementing stringent security measures. Typical Windows security usually works as follows:

- Windows desktop computers are usually implemented with very limited security features, although it's not uncommon for the end user to have administrative privileges on his or her desktop.

- Windows servers are usually implemented using the "chocolate egg" approach, with a hard outer shell that, once penetrated, reveals a very soft interior. Many Windows servers rely on share-level and file-level security to protect them against unauthorized access. A typical file and print server or Web server is accessed in a very well-defined way, servicing specific external user requests through file shares or HTTP ports. Security is concentrated at these interaction points and is usually adequate for the situation.

The Terminal Server, on the other hand, allows users to interact with the server in very unpredictable ways. Unlike other Windows servers, you must provide a security mechanism that protects the Terminal Server both externally and internally. After the user has established a connection, he or she has an interactive presence on the server with direct access to the resources shared between all users, such as disk and memory. The actions of one user can have an impact on all other users on the system unless the proper steps are taken to protect against this possibility. This requirement covers *all* users, including system and network administrators.

To ensure a secure Terminal Server environment, you must provide a complete security solution—not only at the connection point, but also for the entire server, from the file system and the registry through to system rights such as shutting down a server or killing a running process. Any system change can have an impact on all users, so you need to ensure that only those people who are authorized can make these changes.

Terminal Server security management can be divided into five components:

- Limiting administrative privileges
- Connection security
- File security
- Registry security
- Auditing
- Domain-level and local security policies

Limiting Administrative Privileges

People often make the comparison between the UNIX *root* account and the Windows *administrator* account. Both have global access over the entire environment and, as a result, should be limited to the fewest people possible. While this is usually very rigorously enforced in most UNIX environments, within Windows it's not uncommon for 2–5% of all the users in an environment to have administrative access, either directly through the administrator account or as a member of the Domain Admin group. The most common defense for this setup is that it's required for the person to do his or her job, even though this person isn't performing a truly administrative job function.

Regardless of how many administrators exist in your environment today, you *must not* allow these users to have administrative authority on your Terminal Servers unless they're qualified to do so. The more Terminal Server administrators you have, the greater the risk of an undesirable change affecting your production environment. You need to develop your own security model specifically for your Terminal Server environment.

Table 8.2 shows a typical user-group hierarchy for a Terminal Server implementation, along with a brief description of each group and the users who are typically granted such access. By no means is your hierarchy limited to the groups listed. This is presented only as a guide for your system planning. The only requirement is an Administrators group with very limited membership and a User group that has only the minimum access required in order to function properly within the environment.

Table 8.2   Terminal Server User Access Hierarchy

Local Terminal Server User Group	Description
System	Permissions granted to the underlying operating system.
Administrators	These users are responsible for performing software deployments and server configuration changes in the production environment. Typically there will be from 2–5 users maximum with this security level. Any existing Windows administrators *should not* be granted access to this group by default.
Server Operators	Users at this level will have the authority to monitor the various system functions and perform such tasks as shutting down a server or terminating a process. They *will not* have the ability to make any system changes or perform application installation.
User Support	These users have the ability to perform basic support functions such as shadowing another user's session or logging an active user off. They don't have the ability to restart a server or perform any other server maintenance.
Users	These users have only the ability to execute the available applications on a Terminal Server. They don't have write permissions anywhere on the Terminal Server except for specific areas such as their personal temp directory. Domain groups such as Domain Admins and Administrators belong to this group by default. If a member of any of these groups requires greater access, it has to be granted explicitly.

Figure 8.3 shows an example of the local security groups configured on a Windows 2000 Terminal Server.

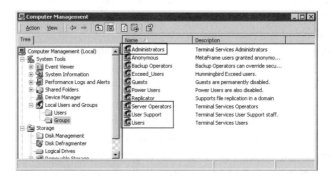

Figure 8.3   *Local Windows 2000 Terminal Server security group example.*

One of my clients had included Domain Admins in its group of administrative users for its Terminal Servers because this was the standard for any Windows server in the environment. Unknown to the true Terminal Server administrators, a few of these people were in the habit of issuing a shutdown instead of a logoff when exiting client sessions, since this is what they usually did on their local desktops. They didn't know that this was actually performing a shutdown on the server itself, causing all other connected users to lose their sessions. It was only after an administrator heard about users periodically losing their connections that the problem was discovered and eventually corrected. ✦

Connection Security

Connection security is applied when the user is first authenticated on the server to which he or she wants to connect. After the user has provided the necessary user ID and password, the Terminal Server will query its connection security with the user's credentials to determine whether the user is authorized to establish a Terminal Server connection, and if so, what connection privileges have been granted for this user. Connection privileges are maintained separately from other system privileges and control not only whether a user can establish a connection but also how the user can interact with other user sessions, such as with the Remote Control feature. Figure 8.4 shows the available Terminal Server connection privileges. Connection security must be defined for each connection type. For example, an RDP-TCP connection type and an ICA-TCP connection type would both have to be configured separately.

Tip

You can't create multiple instances of the same connection type on a single network interface card (NIC). For example, if you had two NICs in your server, you could define one instance of RDP-TCP on each of them, but you could not create two instances of RDP-TCP on the same NIC. ◆

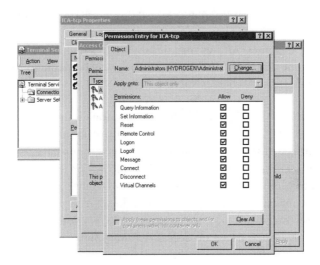

Figure 8.4   *Terminal Server connection privileges.*

The following list provides a brief description of each of the connection permissions that you can set. The permissions apply only to the specified connection type. For example, having access to remote control for RDP-TCP connections doesn't automatically grant remote control access for ICA-TCP connections.

- **Query Information.** Allows connections to be queried for information.
- **Set Information.** Controls access to setting connection properties.
- **Reset.** Allows resetting of connections. When reset, a connection is immediately terminated without warning and without performing a clean logoff.
- **Remote Control.** Allows the user to establish a remote control session with another connection of the same type.
- **Logon.** Provides access to log onto a Terminal Server session.
- **Logoff.** Grants permission to log off other user sessions. As with a Reset, the user is given no warning that his or her session is being logged off. Logoff provides a more graceful termination than a reset.
- **Message.** Allows the user to send messages to other connections.

- **Connect.** Allows a user to connect to another user's session. The user must provide the target user's password (unless that user is also logged onto the target session) to establish the connection. This permission is not required for a user to be able to log onto a terminal session or to reconnect to one of his or her disconnected sessions.

- **Disconnect.** Controls access to disconnecting another user's session. A disconnected session remains active on the server even though the user is no longer connected.

- **Virtual Channel.** Allows for additional virtual channels to be accessible within the connection. Virtual channels are available to developers through Terminal Server-specific APIs.

When planning your Terminal Server connection security, try to keep it as simple as possible. Once set, connection security should rarely if ever need to be modified. Based on the four default user groups (five if you include the System account) listed in Table 8.2, Table 8.3 provides a common security configuration that I've used in multiple Terminal Server implementations. The connection security is based on local groups defined on the Terminal Server. In this way, the necessary global groups can be assigned into the local groups based on access requirements.

Table 8.3   Terminal Server Connection Permissions

Local Terminal Server User Group	Permissions
System	Full control.
Administrators	Full control.
Server Operators	User access + Remote Control + Reset + Logoff privileges.
User Support	User access + Remote Control + Reset + Logoff privileges.
Users	User access.

Tip

Remember that the listed permissions only pertain to connection security and are completely independent of any of the permissions that you may define for other resources on the server, such as file or registry security. ◆

With the listed connection permissions in place, administrators have complete control to monitor and maintain the Terminal Server connections as required. Both the Server Operators and User Support groups have the ability to remotely control, reset, or log off another user's session. These features are available to allow the operator/support person to provide user support if required. The regular user has only the standard user access permissions. In addition to granting the access to log onto the Terminal Server, this also gives them the Query Information, Logon, Message, and Connect options.

Notice that in Table 8.3 both operators and support staff are granted the basic user access plus additional security permissions in order to access the restricted features. Under TS 2000, these specific permission attributes are accessed by selecting the Advanced button from the Permissions tab in the Connection Properties dialog box. On TSE 4.0, the same permission attributes can be found by double-clicking the appropriate user group from within the security dialog box for the connection permissions (under the Security menu option). For a complete discussion of how to configure connection security, see Chapter 12, "Terminal Server Configuration and Tuning."

File Security

To develop a secure Terminal Server environment, you must understand how Terminal Server file security is configured and managed. If you're not already familiar with Windows NTFS file security (including the new Windows 2000 additions), I suggest that you review Appendix C, "File and Folder Security Primer," before continuing.

> ### Tip
>
> *When implementing Terminal Server, you must format all server drives as NTFS. Because users run interactive sessions on the Terminal Server, any drive that's formatted as FAT would be completely accessible by all users.* ◆

Most of the default file-system permissions set during a Terminal Server 4.0 installation provide the regular users with too much access, allowing them to manipulate or add files to the system and potentially causing system issues. Users require very little write access to a Terminal Server and read/execute access to only certain areas. The default file system permissions under Windows 2000 are much more restrictive and require very little change from the default to accommodate the Terminal Services permission requirements.

Looking back at Table 8.2, notice that only the administrators have the ability to make any modifications to the configuration of the Terminal Server; all other user groups have only read access. Unfortunately, configuring file security is not as simple as assigning full control to administrators and read access to everyone else (although it's fairly close).

When implementing file security, I follow these four rules:

- Divide the server into two logical drives—the system drive and the application drive. This allows a more clear division between where applications reside and are accessed and the operating system itself. It also means that the system can be re-created if necessary without losing the application files.

- Restrict access to read-only and then grant or revoke permissions as required. The optimal scenario would be to completely eliminate user access and then grant it only as required, but the large number of system files that must be accessible to the end user makes this extremely time-consuming. My solution is to establish read-only permissions and then modify or revoke the permissions where necessary. Revoked permissions usually involve accessing the Terminal Server and MetaFrame administrative utilities.

- Script all security changes so that they're reproducible. I manage all file security settings that I create through batch scripts as much as possible, using the CACLS command-line file security utility provided with Terminal Server. A script ensures that the exact changes can be reapplied if necessary, and it also provides a documented list of what changes have been implemented. The XCACLS tool that comes with the Resource Kit provides additional functionality and granularity that can sometimes be useful.

- Implement all file security prior to installing any applications onto the Terminal Server. While some people may argue that this makes it more difficult to determine whether an application issue is security-related, I have always found that with the use of security auditing these types of issues can be resolved quickly. It also eliminates the problem of an application working properly during testing, only to find that implementing security causes the application to break. All testing should be performed with the security settings already in place.

Author's Note

A Zero Administration Kit is available for Terminal Server 4.0 (ZAK4WTS) on the Microsoft Web site. This kit is intended to supplement the ZAK for NT Workstation documentation. ZAK4WTS provides two components designed specifically for Terminal Server 4.0:

- *Automatic lockdown of the file system permissions on the system drive.*
- *A set of system policies designed to restrict a user's desktop on TSE 4.0.*

Be aware that when you execute ZAK4WTS2.exe, which comes as part of the supplement, it immediately begins performing the file-permission lockdown on the machine, regardless of whether it's a Terminal Server or a workstation. Unfortunately, you must run this file to retrieve the policy files. Don't run this script on a production server, as it will prevent users from running applications that they had been able to run before. Always run this on a test machine. This script also deletes all entries from %systemroot%\Profiles\All Users\Start Menu\Programs\Startup before the file-permission script executes.

When you run ZAK4WTS2.exe, it creates a POL and SCRIPTS folder under WTSRV\ZAK. The policies and lockdown scripts are copied here. Then the ACLS.CMD file runs; this uses CACLS to update the permissions and perform other updates. After the permissions have been applied, the HIDE.CMD script runs. This sets the Hide attribute on almost every file on the system drive.

I discuss the policies in Chapter 16, "Group and System Policy Configuration." The ACLS.CMD file performs the following system and permission changes:

- *Assigns the Everyone group Read-only access to the entire drive.*
- *Removes access to NT accessories (Notepad, etc.).*
- *Everyone is given Change permission to the Temp directory on %systemroot%. A file called secure.dir is placed in this directory; users are not given access to it. With this file in place, users can't delete the directory.*
- *Everyone is given Change permission on the Profiles folder.*
- *Access to .INF, .EXE. and .HLP files under System are denied for non-administrators.*

Personally, I feel that these permissions still provide too much access to certain areas, while limiting access too much in others. The best use for ZAK, aside from the POL files, is to use the file permissions as a tool to better understand what you can do in your environment, instead of blindly implementing to secure your environment. ZAK is not a replacement for a proper understanding of what's required to establish a secure Terminal Server environment. ◆

To maintain consistency between the different areas of security, the same local security groups used for connection security will also be used for file security. This does introduce some redundancy, since Server Operators, User Support, and Users all have identical file permissions. But it also puts a more flexible security model in place—for example, to grant Server Operators additional privileges without modifying either of the other two groups' rights. Table 8.4 gives an example of the modified security permissions for an NT 4.0 Terminal Server system drive.

Table 8.4   Modified Terminal Server 4.0 Permissions Example

System Directory	Permissions	Comments
Root (\)	*Full Control* Administrators, System	Replaces permissions on all subdirectories.
	Read Server Operators, User Support, Users	
\Recycler	*Full Control* Administrators, System	A unique Recycle container is generated for each user who needs one. It's based on the user's SID and is accessible only by the user or an administrator.
	Change Server Operators, User Support, Users	
\WTSRV\Config	*Full Control* Administrators, System	Required only by administrators.

The associated CACLS script to implement the permissions listed in Table 8.4 is shown below. In this example, drive X: is the system drive for the Terminal Server.

Tip

Appendix D, "Suggested System and Application Volume Security Permissions," provides a suggested base configuration for security on the two volumes, along with a CACLS script. ◆

```
@ ECHO OFF
ECHO Setting security permissions on system volume.  Please wait...
ECHO Y¦CACLS X:\* /T /c /g Administrators:F SYSTEM:F
➥Users:R "Server Operators":R "User Support":R
CACLS X:\Recycler /e /c /g Users:C "Server Operators":C "User Support":C
CACLS X:\WTSRV\Config /e /c /T /r Users "Server Operators" "User Support"
```

Windows 2000 introduces some new naming conventions for the file-system permission attributes, as well as some additional attributes (see Appendix C). Table 8.5 lists each Windows 2000 attribute next to the NT 4.0 attribute that would grant the equivalent permission, with a brief description of each.

Table 8.5   *Auditable File System Events*

Windows 2000 Attribute Name	NT 4.0 Attribute Name	Description
Traverse Folder/ Execute File	Execute	Allows you to execute files and traverse into a folder.
List Folder/Read Data	Read	Allows you to read either a folder or file object.
Read Attributes	Read	Allows viewing the basic file properties: Read-Only, Archive, System, and Hidden.
Read Extended Attributes	Read	Allows viewing the extended attributes of a file. Extended attributes are custom file properties based on the file type. Microsoft Word and Excel store extended attributes with their files.
Create Files/Write Data	Write	Allows new files to be created and overwrite existing data in a file. Doesn't allow adding data to an existing file.
Create Folders/ Append Data	Write	Allows creating subfolders and adding data to the end of an existing file. Doesn't allow changing data within a file.
Write Attributes	Write	Allows modifying the basic attributes.
Write Extended Attributes	Write	Allows modifying the extended attributes.
Delete Subfolders and Files	No equivalent	Provides permission to delete the contents of a folder. This overrides any conflicting permissions in that folder. For example, if you have this attribute on a folder and a file within that folder doesn't provide you with explicit delete access, you can still delete it.
Delete	Delete	This attribute provides permission to delete an object. If you have Delete permission on a folder but not on its contents, you can't delete the folder until it has been emptied.

continues ▶

Table 8.5   continued

Windows 2000 Attribute Name	NT 4.0 Attribute Name	Description
Read Permissions	Read	Allows access to read the NTFS permissions for a file or folder.
Change Permissions	Change Permissions	Allows access to modify the NTFS permissions for a file or folder.
Take Ownership	Take Ownership	Allows you to take ownership of a folder or file.

Registry Security

Containing all of the critical configuration information for a Terminal Server, the registry is a vital component of your server, and as such needs to be protected as much as possible. Just as with the file system, the fact that users are running interactively on the server means that extra steps must be taken to protect the registry from unplanned modifications.

Tip

If you're not already familiar with basic Windows Registry security, review Appendix E, "Registry Security Primer," before continuing. ♦

While the registry has security settings similar to those of the file system, the assignment of security in the registry is much more difficult. The problem is that in certain situations, applications may have a legitimate reason for writing into certain areas of the registry. Because of this, registry security must be handled on almost a key-by-key basis. The complexity of this can make it a daunting task. Fortunately, some characteristics of the registry can help to make this task a little easier.

Warning

Although I've had success with security modifications to the registry, this doesn't guarantee that these changes will work under all circumstances. It's possible that certain applications or operating system components may not function properly when forced to run in a more secure environment.

Review any changes carefully before making them and ensure that you have a backup of the registry that can be restored if necessary. Always perform these changes on a test server in case the modification causes issues with the operating system. ♦

Concentrate your security management only on the HKEY_LOCAL_MACHINE\ SOFTWARE key in the registry. The other root keys under LOCAL_MACHINE (HARDWARE, SAM, and SYSTEM) are configured during Terminal Server installation to limit non-administrator accounts to read-only access.

The contents and security of the keys under HKEY_USERS are handled by local and roaming profiles (regular and mandatory). Most Terminal Server implementations utilize roaming profiles to ensure that users have a consistent desktop and application configuration regardless of which Terminal Server they connect to. The majority of the information configured in the profile is set during the installation of the applications that will be used by the end user.

> **Tip**
>
> *In Chapter 17, "User Profile and Account Planning," I talk in detail about different user profile configurations and how they can be implemented and managed.* ◆

I will now briefly discuss the security around the HKEY_LOCAL_MACHINE\SOFTWARE key. Given the nature of Terminal Server as an execution environment from which users run applications, and the fact that users are not granted the permission to add any new software, certain permissions can be set in the registry that you wouldn't normally set on an NT/Windows 2000 desktop. A couple of examples of subkeys under the SOFTWARE key are Classes and Microsoft, discussed in the following sections.

Classes Key

The Classes key (HKEY_CLASSES_ROOT) contains information on file associations and all registered objects and controls. While the default permissions for this key list both the Users and Everyone groups as having only Read access, the special groups INTERACTIVE (on NT 4.0) and TERMINAL SERVER USER (on Windows 2000) are set with the equivalent of change permissions. Both of these are special group SIDs and are automatically assigned to any user who has an interactive logon on a Terminal Server. In most Terminal Server environments, you don't want users to be able to modify file associations or registered OLE or ActiveX controls. To prevent unauthorized changes, you may want to update the permissions for these special groups to be read-only. Figure 8.5 shows the default permissions for the INTERACTIVE group on the root of the Classes key on an NT 4.0 Terminal Server. The Classes key is one of the few areas of the registry where you can define permissions at the root and propagate them down through all subkeys.

Warning

Restricting access to the Classes *key to read-only will have an impact on some applications, in particular Internet Explorer, which makes class and object modifications to this key during execution. See Chapter 19, "Application Integration," for a discussion of this topic.* ◆

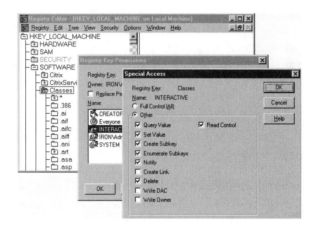

Figure 8.5   *The INTERACTIVE group's permissions for the* Classes *key.*

Microsoft Key

The Microsoft key contains the majority of the configuration information for all the Microsoft products that you might install on Terminal Server, as well as many of the core components of the operating system itself. By default, the majority of the subkeys are accessible with write permission by the Everyone group, except for Windows NT\CurrentVersion, which allows the Everyone group read-only access throughout all of its subkeys.

Author's Note

You've probably noticed that most of these keys include permissions for the Power Users group. The default permissions for the Power Users group on a Terminal Server are identical to those for a regular NT/2000 workstation. This includes allowing a power user to shut down a Terminal Server. Normally I remove the reference to Power Users from the registry security, but you may decide to leave these permissions in place. If you do this, I suggest that you keep careful track of whether any members have been assigned to the local Power Users group. ◆

Of course, the Classes and Microsoft keys are only a small portion of the total number of keys available. There are usually around 10–15 subkeys immediately under the SOFTWARE key after a Terminal Server installation. Most of these are fairly straightforward to configure and can usually be set with read-only access for users.

> **Warning**
>
> *Although you may be tempted to define the permissions at the parent key and propagate them down throughout all subkeys, you should review carefully before proceeding with the change, as it may cause issues with one or more of the applications on the server. See Appendix F, "Terminal Server Registry Security Permissions," for an example of how security permissions can be configured on a Terminal Server. Luckily, very little needs to be done on a Windows 2000 Terminal Server when Windows 2000 user security has been implemented. I talk more about this option in the "Windows 2000 Terminal Services" section of Chapter 10, "Terminal Server Installation."* ◆

Scripting Registry Security Changes

Just as with file system permissions, the permissions for the registry are manageable using a command-line tool. This tool is called REGINI and is available as part of the Windows NT Server/2000 Resource Kits. It's not available as part of the standard Terminal Server operating system. Unfortunately, REGINI is not as robust in its functionality as CACLS is for the file system. These are the two main differences:

- You can't modify existing security permissions on a registry key. Your only option is to replace them. This means that if you want to change the security for a key, you must know all the permissions that you want to set, not just the one you're changing.

- You can't automatically propagate your permission changes down through all the subkeys under a key. You must explicitly list each key you want to update, along with the complete set of permissions.

While it's certainly more effort to prepare a security script for the registry using REGINI, the end result is still a documented and reproducible history of the registry permission changes you've made. The following is an example of a text file that could be passed to REGINI to update the security on a subkey under HKEY_LOCAL_MACHINE\SOFTWARE\Microsoft:

```
HKEY_LOCAL_MACHINE\Software\Microsoft\TestApp [1 5 8 17]
    TestParms [1 5 8 17 22]
```

The permissions to assign are specified by the integers separated by spaces within the square brackets. Each integer corresponds to a particular user group and security setting. Unfortunately, you can't define your own groups within REGINI and must rely on the ones that it "understands" for setting security privileges. Usually, this isn't too much of a problem, since you'll most likely be setting user privileges to read-only and administrators to full control. Table 8.6 lists the user group/permission settings for each of the numbers listed in the example above.

Table 8.6   Example of REGINI Permission Settings

Integer Value	Group	Permission
1	Administrators	Full Control
5	CREATOR OWNER	Full Control
8	Everyone	Read
17	SYSTEM	Full Control
22	INTERACTIVE	Read

Tip

The most current list of groups/permissions supported is available by simply running REGINI from a command line with no input file. ◆

Comparing the sample file with the entries in Table 8.6, it's easy to deduce that the permissions for the subkey TestApp would be set as follows:

Administrators	Full Control
CREATOR OWNER	Full Control
Everyone	Read
SYSTEM	Full Control

The subkey TestParms under TestApp would be assigned these permissions:

Administrators	Full Control
CREATOR OWNER	Full Control
Everyone	Read
SYSTEM	Full Control
INTERACTIVE	Read

Tip

The task of determining and setting the registry permissions can be an extensive one. In Appendix F, I outline in detail my suggestions for registry security modifications and accompany these with REGINI batch scripts to apply the changes. ◆

Restricting Registry Tool Access

The question has been raised before as to why access to the registry editing tools (REGEDIT, REGEDT32) cannot simply be restricted instead of spending all this time modifying registry permissions. My preference has always been to do both. By making it as difficult as possible for a non-administrator to make changes to the registry, you help to improve its stability. In order to lock down access to the registry, following are a couple of suggestions:

- Allow only administrators to have read and execute access on the REGEDIT and REGEDT32 executables. This will prevent users from running the applications on the Terminal Server. It won't prevent them from executing these files from another location, however, such as a share point on the network.

- To eliminate users' ability to use these tools, you can add a registry policy to their profiles. Add this key:

  ```
  HKEY_CURRENT_USER\Software\Microsoft
  ↪Windows\CurrentVersion\Policies\System
  ```

  Under this key, add the DWORD entry DisableRegistryTools with a value of 1. This change is most often made for mandatory roaming profiles, although it can be set up to automatically be added to roaming profiles for non-administrators using system or group policies (see Chapter 16). With this policy in place, the user will receive the error message shown in Figure 8.6 when attempting to run either of these registry tools. Note that this doesn't prevent the user from running other tools that may manipulate the registry, such as command-line tools or Policy Editor (POLEDIT). It does prevent the user from simply renaming one of the registry tools and then attempting to launch it.

Figure 8.6   *Eliminating non-administrator access to the Windows registry tools.*

While these suggestions make editing the registry much more difficult, they don't absolutely prevent the user from using some form of tool to access the registry. The only way to ensure a completely secure environment is to implement the proper registry security and auditing, which I will discuss next.

Auditing

In addition to planning for the necessary security settings, I also recommend ensuring that these areas are audited to detect anomalies in application or user behavior. You need to ensure that you have implemented sufficient auditing to allow monitoring for unauthorized change attempts, while at the same time being selective enough in the events being monitored so that the log file doesn't become overwhelming to view and impossible to manage. I recommend that auditing be enabled for Everyone, so that events are captured regardless of who is on (or attempting to get on) the system.

Before auditing can be enabled for any of the Terminal Server security areas discussed, you must first enable object auditing. On NT 4 Terminal Server, this is done through User Manager, under the Policies, Auditing menu selection. On Windows 2000 Terminal Server, you use the Local Security Policy (or Domain Security Policy in an Active Directory environment) utility under the Audit Policy folder. Figure 8.7 shows the Local Audit Policy for a Windows 2000 Terminal Server.

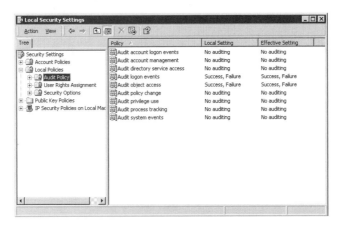

Figure 8.7   *Windows 2000 Terminal Server local audit policy.*

Connection Auditing

One of the features available only on Windows 2000 Terminal Server is *connection auditing*. Connection auditing monitors actions that one user session performs against another, or performs directly on the connection configuration, such as modifying connection properties. Figure 8.8 shows the auditing dialog box for an ICA-TCP connection entry. The selected entries also represent my recommendations for the events to audit. The connection auditing simply tracks the success or failure of performing a particular connection action.

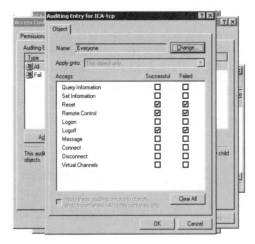

Figure 8.8 *Windows 2000 Terminal Server connection auditing.*

File Auditing

I recommend that file auditing be enabled on both your system and application volumes. Table 8.7 lists one suggestion for auditing properties for the
application volume on the server.

Table 8.7 *Suggested Application Volume File-Auditing Properties*

Permission	Audit Setting
Traverse Folder/Execute File	<None>
List Folder/Read Data	<None>
Create Files/Write Data	Failure
Create Folders/Append Data	Failure
Delete Subfolders and Files	Success Failure
Delete	Success Failure
Change Permissions	Success Failure
Take Ownership	Success Failure

This auditing configuration is based on the fact that the application volume
is essentially read-only except when applications are being updated or
installed. Auditing in this situation has been configured to capture attempts
to update or modify the information on this volume. Certain applications
may also be restricted based on security groups, so auditing is in place to
see whether users are attempting to run applications that they haven't been
granted access to run. The listed auditing properties are suitable for this
situation. You need to set up your final auditing based on the security
requirements of your administrators.

Registry Auditing

Windows 2000 has added only one new auditable event over NT 4.0, the *Write Owner* property. This property manages who has the ability to take ownership of a registry key, much like file ownership. Registry auditing is enabled through REGEDT32; Figure 8.9 shows the auditing entry dialog box along with my recommended settings for auditing of the registry. The same auditing settings can be applied to either a Windows 2000 or an NT 4.0 Terminal Server.

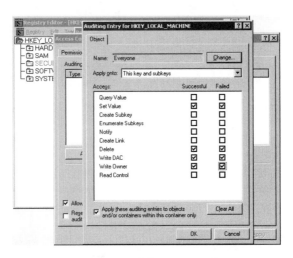

Figure 8.9   *Recommended registry-auditing entries.*

You should enable auditing on both the HKEY_LOCAL_MACHINE and HKEY_USERS hives. Remember that all of the other hives are merely pointers to subkeys within either of these two hives.

The reason behind establishing this auditing is based on the fact that the Users group will have read access to the majority of the registry. For this reason, the events corresponding to the read access set (Query Value, Enumerate Subkeys, Notify, Read Control) were omitted. All other events are configured to capture changes made to the registry. Because the environment should remain fairly static unless application changes are being made, you want to be aware of all changes that may be occurring.

The implementation details for auditing connections, the file system and the registry are discussed in Chapter 12.

Event Monitoring

Auditing is of little value if you're not diligent in monitoring the security events as they arise and taking the appropriate action. Suspicious behavior discovered two weeks after it has occurred doesn't put you in a position to react in a timely manner to the problem. Depending on the size of your Terminal Server environment, it may be nearly impossible to manually review the event log on each machine looking for issues. Fortunately, event log monitoring tools exist that provide immediate notification (for example, email, page, or system message) when a particular event is detected in the event log. Following are some of the products that provide real-time event monitoring:

- NetIQ's *AppManager* (www.netiq.com)
- Aelita's *EventAdmin* (www.aelita.com)
- RippleTech's *LogCaster* (www.rippletech.com)
- Mission Critical Software's *OnePoint Operations Manager* (www.missioncritical.com)

AppManager, LogCaster, and OnePoint are commonly known as *systems and application management solutions*. These products provide varying degrees of centralized management of an entire Windows server environment, allowing for the monitoring of a wide variety of environmental conditions such as server loads, hung services, event logs, or memory utilization. Configurable thresholds can be defined that will cause the products to issue alerts and/or execute proactive tasks to try and correct the problem. All of the listed products provide free trial downloads from their Web sites. Chapter 18 talks in more detail about systems and application-management products.

Domain-Level and Local Security Policies

A final area of server security involves defining security policies for your Terminal Server. These policies include such things as restrictions on who can shut down a server or manage auditing and security logs.

> **Tip**
>
> *Account policies are discussed in the "User Profile, Policy, and Account Planning" section of Chapter 6, "Client Planning."* ◆

Security policies are divided into three groups: Audit Policies, which we have already discussed; User Rights Assignments; and Security Options. Figure 8.10 shows the local policies on a Windows 2000 Terminal Server.

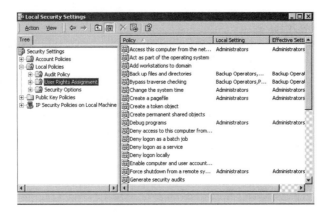

Figure 8.10   *Local security policies on a Windows 2000 Terminal Server.*

On an NT 4.0 Terminal Server, the Audit and User Rights policies are available under User Manager for Domains. When editing local server policies, make sure that you have pointed User Manager at the local computer and not the NT domain. In order to access some of the options that are readily visible under the Security Options folder on a Windows 2000 Terminal Server, you have to use Policy Editor (POLEDIT) on an NT 4.0 Terminal Server. The remaining options are available only by directly manipulating the registry. System and Group policies are discussed in Chapter 16; user rights are covered in the "Terminal Server Security Configuration" section of Chapter 12.

Application Management

When preparing your server management plan, one area that will need to be investigated in detail is application management. The following sections briefly discuss some of the areas that relate directly to server management and defer the remainder of the conversation until Chapter 9.

These are the major application-management considerations that will have a direct impact on your server planning:

- Server reboot scheduling
- Test and pilot server management

Server Reboot Scheduling

Issues with an application's stability or resource requirements on the desktop are very quickly amplified when run on Terminal Server. Problems such as memory leaks can have a significant impact on the availability of a Terminal Server as they slowly (or quickly, as the case may be) consume the available resources, eventually resulting in "low on virtual memory" errors and system crashes. The only reliable way to ensure that issues like this will not impact your server environment is to establish a server reboot schedule. The frequency of the reboots depends largely on how many applications are being served and the overall stability of the environment during your testing and pilot phase. Using some of the load-testing criteria from Chapter 7, "Server Hardware Planning," you can monitor your servers to determine the extent of resource issues (most often memory) during piloting and plan any necessary reboot scheduling that may be required.

Whenever discussions of the reboot requirements arise, the first reaction is almost invariably one of disbelief. Comparisons between the average uptime of a SQL server or IIS server are common, but not valid. It's like comparing apples and oranges, because the operating environments are not the same. Possibly a better comparison would be to look at the average uptime of a Windows *desktop* running the applications that are targeted for Terminal Server.

Author's Note

I haven't yet encountered an enterprise Terminal Server deployment where a scheduled reboot wasn't implemented in some fashion, whether daily, weekly, monthly, or even longer. Applications are not the only culprits of memory leaks. The operating system itself can be guilty of this behavior. ◆

To ensure the continued reliability of your Terminal Server environment, the requirements for a reboot schedule should be implemented as part of your server-management plan, particularly if memory allocation issues exist with your applications.

Author's Note

Scheduled reboots can be developed in such a way as to minimize the impact a user may experience when system restarts are scheduled to occur. This can be an important requirement in situations where a Terminal Server environment is expected to be operational 24 hours a day, 7 days a week.

I have worked on projects where "intelligent" reboot scheduling was implemented so that it would automatically detect if users were still on the system, warn them about the planned shutdown, disable future logons, and then wait until the users logout or their sessions time out before initiating the shutdown. ◆

Test and Pilot Server Management

A necessary requirement of your environment will be one or more test and pilot Terminal Servers. The number and types of servers required will depend on the size of your production environment and the number of in-house or custom applications that you're serving. Custom-developed applications tend to have a much more frequent release schedule than prepackaged products such as Web browsers or word processors. This is usually because of application fixes, but can also be because of code changes to accommodate new business requirements. Twice-monthly or monthly releases are very common in many organizations.

Following are some rules that I use to determine the number of test and pilot servers:

- One test server for every 4–8 applications that are being tested *concurrently* for deployment. The number of servers that you can test concurrently depends on the changes that are being tested. Fewer servers can simplify managing the test environment but can introduce the possibility of conflicts between programs during this phase. Very often test Terminal Servers are built using lower-capacity hardware than what is run in production. Redundancy features are usually not a requirement and can drastically reduce the cost of the hardware. To reduce costs, perform a separate server sizing for your test environment, rather than simply purchasing additional production hardware.

- One pilot server for every three test servers, or as user capacity allows. In most situations you'll need only one or two pilot servers, depending on how many users you can handle per server and how many concurrent pilot users will be on the system. The exact number will depend on your production configuration, since these machines should mirror production. Because of this, pilot servers usually run on the same hardware as the production servers, although this isn't a requirement.

A distinction is usually made between these two types of servers in both their configuration and management when compared to production.

Test Servers

The test server is usually made available to application developers so that they can system test their application changes during development. Test servers are usually configured identically to production servers, with the following exceptions:

- Database server settings point to development or test servers and not production.

- One or more members of the development team will have write permission to their application area on the server so that they can promote changes as required for testing. Write access is usually limited to the given area and at no time should administrative access be handed over to any member of the development team.

There will usually be more test servers than pilot servers.

Author's Note

A development region is a good area to begin training junior Terminal Server administrators. They can familiarize themselves with the configuration and management aspects of the environment without affecting production. Depending on the amount of application development work within the organization, this can be a full-time job! ◆

Pilot Servers

When the development team has completed system testing, they'll announce that they're ready to enter user testing or piloting. At this stage, you need to be able to provide a server that completely mirrors the production environment but doesn't service production users. This is your *pilot server*. Pilot servers have the following characteristics:

- They're configured the same as any one of your standard production servers (with the possible exception of the piloted application, which may be configured to access a pilot or test data region; this may be necessary if the application is scheduled for release in conjunction with a back-end database change).

- The development team will *not* have any kind of write access that they don't normally have in a true production server. Their application should be released into the pilot region by an administrator, following the standard application-release process. Very often the development team will release their complete application deployment into a form of "staging area," where the administrator will issue the deployment. This not only allows piloting of the application, but also the release process prior to the production deployment.

It's not uncommon in a load-balanced environment to temporarily use an actual production server for piloting. During this time the server is removed from production load balancing and only the piloting users are granted access to it. In this situation, adequate precautions must be taken to ensure that the server is configured properly prior to being promoted back into production.

Tip

The testing and piloting processes are discussed in more detail in Chapter 9. ◆

9

Software Planning

In this chapter:

- **Software Planning Overview**
  As the final part of the planning process for your Terminal Server implementation, list and categorize all the software that you plan to deploy on the Terminal Servers.

- **Administration and System Support Software**
  These tools are an important part of software planning but their need in the environment is often overlooked until near the end of the project, or when an issue arises that requires the tools.

- **Application Software**
  Although the exact number and type of applications that you will deploy is dependent on the requirements of your project, a standard methodology can be applied to capture the required information, making the scheduling and implementation of the applications more manageable.

- **Change Management**
  As part of the development of your software management procedures, document the process that application developers and others will need to follow to have a program implemented within the Terminal Server environment.

Software Planning Overview

As the final part of the planning process for your Terminal Server implementation, you need to list and categorize all the software that you plan to deploy on the Terminal Servers. This includes not only the applications that you want to deliver to users, but any server support software that you'll use to manage the environment.

After developing the two application lists, you need to prioritize the order in which the applications will be installed. I usually arrange applications for installation as follows:

1. **Common application components.** These usually consist of low-level middleware components such as ODBC drivers or SQL drivers (Sybase, Oracle, etc.) that are required by both the applications and the administrative utilities. The Microsoft Data Access Components (MDAC) is a good example of an application installed during this step.

Author's Note

It's worth noting that MDAC 2.5 ships as part of Windows 2000. ◆

2. **Administrative support software.** Next I install the necessary support software that will be used by the administrators. This usually includes such tools as the Server Resource Kit and a resource management tool such as NetIQ.

3. **Common user application software.** Next comes the common user application software that will be installed on all Terminal Servers, or software that's a required component of one or more other applications. In most cases this includes office productivity tools, Web browsers, and so on. I always include the installation of Internet Explorer during this phase, since its existence is a requirement for other Microsoft applications such as Office 2000.

4. **User applications.** The final installation step handles the remaining applications that will be used by the user. Microsoft Office, Lotus Notes, and custom client/server applications are examples.

Chapter 19, "Application Integration," discusses the steps involved in the installation and configuration of applications on Terminal Server.

Administration and System Support Software

Administrative and system support tools are an important part of software planning but their need in the environment is very often overlooked until near the end of the project, or when an issue arises that requires these tools. I always recommend that administrative support tools be identified early on so any additional hardware or software requirements can be addressed and resolved prior to the project entering any form of piloting or testing phase. Some components, such as service packs or hotfixes, need to be addressed even before you begin the operating system installation, so that you have a clear and documented idea of how the server should be built.

Tip

During the investigation of your planned support software, maintain a list of all of the common components or additional resources that they may require. For example, Citrix's Resource Management Services requires the installation of MDAC, while Microsoft's Network Load Balancing recommends having dual network cards in the server. ◆

Service Packs and Hotfixes

Both Microsoft and Citrix periodically release service packs, hotfixes, and patches for their products, and I strongly suggest that you keep up to date on these as they become available. Table 9.1 lists the locations where important update information on these fixes can be found:

Table 9.1   Component Update Locations

Component	Location(s)
Windows 2000	www.microsoft.com/windows2000/downloads
Windows NT 4.0 Terminal Server	www.microsoft.com/ntserver/terminalserver
MetaFrame 1.8	www.citrix.com/support/ftp_meta18new.htm

Author's Note

Updates are also available for Terminal Server from the windowsupdate.microsoft.com *site. This site is automatically accessed if an administrator clicks the Windows Update option on the Start menu. The available updates are displayed based on the version of the operating system that you're running. This update feature works for both Windows 2000 and NT 4.0 Terminal Server.* ◆

I recommend that you collect the most recent information to build your list of fixes and service packs to install. My approach is usually to install the latest available service packs but hold off on hotfixes unless your configuration is exhibiting a behavioral problem that one of these fixes will correct.

Warning

Many hotfixes are not extensively regression tested, only unit tested. When installing a hotfix onto your server, you always run the risk of introducing a new problem into your environment while you're fixing another. I recommend that you always scan one of the Thin Client newsgroups for feedback on an existing hotfix prior to installing it on your servers. ◆

Load Balancing

As I mentioned earlier in this book when talking about scalability (both in Chapter 2, "Microsoft Windows Terminal Server," and Chapter 3, "Citrix MetaFrame"), various options exist for delivering load balancing to your Terminal Server environment. The decision on what tool to utilize depends mainly on the flexibility and functionality that you need. In an RDP-only environment you may want to use Microsoft's Network Load Balancing extension for Windows 2000 Advanced (or higher) server, or Windows Load Balancing Services on an NT 4.0 Terminal Server. NCD's ThinPATH Load Balancing can also be used in an RDP or ICA environment.

In an enterprise ICA environment, you'll most likely use Citrix's Load Balancing option pack on each of your servers. Both Citrix's and NCD's load balancing solutions are completely software-based and require no additional hardware. If you're going to use Microsoft's NLB, implementing dual network interface cards (in a type of multi-homed configuration) is recommended.

Author's Note

As you may recall from Chapter 7, "Server Hardware Planning," I typically recommend implementing dual network cards in a "teamed" or load-balanced configuration on a Terminal Server, mainly to provide redundancy. ◆

I always treat load balancing as a core operating system component and try to install it very early in the building of the Terminal Server (before installing other applications).

Cloning and Server Replication

In Chapter 8, "Server Management Planning," I talked about the theory of Terminal Server management and explained that one of the keys to successful management of a large scale implementation was being able to build a server quickly from a standard "image." This functionality is important for two reasons. One, it provides a means of establishing an effective disaster-recovery plan that would allow you to quickly re-create your exact environment, given the proper hardware and supporting infrastructure. Second, it allows you to expand the environment easily, or roll back to a previous configuration in a consistent fashion.

A number of different means exist for cloning a server. Utilities such as Symantec's Norton Ghost allow you to capture an entire snapshot of a drive and save it to a file that can then be imaged onto another machine. Other methods of cloning involve the use of backup software in conjunction with a second operating system installation that's used to restore the backup server image onto the new hardware. The exact process depends on the software used.

I've found cloning to be an invaluable process for managing a Terminal Server environment. Using cloning, a Terminal Server can typically be built from an image in 30–60 minutes. The result is a completely functional server containing all of the applications installed prior to the creation of the image.

Author's Note

There are a number of issues to consider when using the cloning technique to build multiple Windows 2000/NT servers. Foremost is the question of SID uniqueness on the cloned server. When Windows is installed, a unique security identifier (SID) is generated for that machine. This SID plus an incremented value known as the relative ID (RID) are used to create local security group and user SIDs. If an image of this server is cloned onto another computer, that second computer will have the same computer and account SIDs that existed on the first computer, introducing a potential security problem in a workgroup environment. The local SID also plays a much greater role in a Windows 2000 environment than it did in NT 4.0.

Fortunately, Microsoft now supports a technique for cloning complete installations of Windows 2000 from one server to another. Using a utility available in the Windows 2000 Server Resource Kit called SysPrep, you can prepare a Windows 2000 Terminal Server for replication and have a unique SID automatically generated on the target server when it reboots. SysPrep doesn't perform the actual imaging, but prepares a server to be imaged. Once SysPrep is run, any imaging tool can then be used to create and distribute the server clone. The SysPrep tool that ships with the Windows 2000 Server Resource Kit cannot be used to clone TSE 4.0 servers. For a TSE 4.0 server, you must rely on SID generation tools, such as symantec's GhostWalker or NewSID from www.sysinternals.com to assist in the cloning process. in Chapter 18, "Server Operations and Support," server cloning is discussed in more detail for both TS 2000 and TSE 4.0. ◆

Application Deployment

Depending on the size of the Terminal Server environment you plan to deploy, you may want to consider the use of application deployment tools to assist in the timely and *consistent* delivery of applications to all your Terminal Servers. The key consideration here is consistency. In a small environment (2–5 servers), you have a fairly good chance of being able to perform manual installations of an application on each of the servers and maintain a consistent configuration. But if you have a medium-to-large Terminal Server environment (10 or more servers), the odds of making a mistake on at least one of these machines during the application installation goes up dramatically.

In this situation, it's necessary to implement an application-deployment process that involves the use of some form of automated tool. Following are some examples of tools that can be used:

- **SysDiff.** Provided as part of the Resource kit, the SysDiff tool is used to generate what's called a "difference" file, which contains information on an application installation that can then be applied against another machine to reproduce the exact installation. There are several steps to using SysDiff: Generate a base snapshot of the server before the app is installed, install the desired application, generate the difference file based on the snapshot and the current state, and then use the difference file to install the application on another machine. You can also use SysDiff to generate only a list of differences in registry and INI files.

- **Citrix Installation Management Services(IMS).** IMS allows you to install an application on a single MetaFrame server and have that application automatically installed on any of the other MetaFrame servers in the server farm. Conceptually, it works similarly to SysDiff in that it generates what's called a *package*, containing the information on how an application was installed on the server. The difference between the SysDiff and IMS is that IMS then pushes that application installation to any MetaFrame server running the installation service that's part of IMS. This service is responsible for reading the package and performing the installation. Package distribution in IMS is managed through the MetaFrame Published Application Manager.

Author's Note

The Windows Installer feature of Windows 2000 is not available to users running on a Terminal Server, so you need to make sure that all the necessary application components are installed—not just the installation points. You can still create MSI or custom transformation files (when supported) so that you've preconfigured an installation that can simply be run without any intervention by an administrator.

Chapter 19 provides more details on application installation. ◆

Registry and File Replication

After implementation, there will very likely be situations when you'll want to change the registry or file system on each of your Terminal Servers. The need for consistency is as important here as in a full application installation, particularly when your environment consists of a large number of Terminal Servers. Many tools and scripting languages are available to automate the replication of file or registry changes to all of your servers.

For example, the ROBOCOPY utility from the Windows 2000 Server Resource Kit provides an automated way to maintain an identical set of files between two servers. Another option is to use XCOPY, which is included with all versions of Windows, and can be used to script the replication of files from a source to a target server.

Using the REGDMP and REGINI utilities from the Resource Kit, you can extract the desired registry changes from one server's registry and then import those changes into another. Scripting languages such as KiXtart, which provide robust registry editing support, can also be used to create customized scripts to replicate the necessary changes to the remote servers.

Author's Note

A number of commercial products provide file and/or registry replication features. One example is Tricerat Software (www.tricerat.com). ◆

Server Monitoring and Health Checking

Being proactive about the health of your Terminal Servers before they cause a system failure is an important part of Terminal Server administration. Unfortunately, I've seen many implementations of Terminal Server in which inadequate consideration has been given to the tools and processes that would aid in managing the environment. Reacting to problems *after* they've brought down a server is far too common.

Numerous tools exist that have been specifically designed to run on a Terminal Server. The following describes some key considerations for choosing a monitoring tool:

- **Terminal Server and MetaFrame "aware."** These tools tend to be better tuned to operate in a thin client environment without introducing too much additional overhead. They also usually have default configurations that are better suited for monitoring a Terminal Server in comparison to a regular Windows server.

- **A robust notification system.** A monitoring tool is of little use if there's no way to configure it to send a notification to one or more administrators if a system problem is detected. At a minimum, it should support SNMP (Simple Network Management Protocol) and SMTP (Simple Mail Transfer Protocol).

- **Proactive error-correcting logic.** Some of the more robust monitoring tools can react to problems by attempting to correct them. An excellent example is a situation in which a service fails and the monitoring software automatically tries to restart the service.

- **Report generation.** Reports should be easily producible based on the performance data that has been collected. This information is helpful not only for troubleshooting, but for trend analysis and future capacity planning.

Two common tools that I've used are Citrix's Resource Management Services (RMS) and NetIQ's AppManager. AppManager is a robust systems-management and application-management product that provides support for both Terminal Server (4.0 and 2000) and MetaFrame. It provides all the functionality summarized above in addition to a number of other features such as event log monitoring, automatic resetting of Terminal Server sessions, and the ability to push tasks out to each server where it's run. Using such a feature, you could have maintenance or application scripts scheduled to run at a given time locally on a server. For more information on AppManager, see `www.netiq.com`.

RMS is geared specifically for working in a MetaFrame environment, where it provides detailed information on the health of a MetaFrame server as well as information such as which applications have been run, how often, by whom, and what resources they consumed (% CPU, RAM, and so on). RMS also provides the ability to generate billing information based on resource usage on the server. Figure 9.1 shows an example of the RMS data analysis tool with a CPU percentage graph taken from the sampled data.

Author's Note

RMS can also be an invaluable tool during the server-sizing and capacity-planning phase, to help ensure that you've sized your servers appropriately. For more information, see Chapter 7. ◆

A common requirement of most resource-monitoring tools is the need for a database management system (DBMS) to store the collected data. The size and type of DBMS supported depends on the product being used. For example, RMS works with most ODBC-compliant database systems, including Microsoft Jet database files. Of course, in a production implementation you'll want to ensure that a supported professional DBMS such as Microsoft SQL Server or Oracle is available to store the data that has been gathered from the Terminal Servers.

Make sure that such requirements are flagged early and tasked in your project plan. It's likely that you'll need to engage the assistance of a database administrator so that the necessary tables can be created and made available for populating by the monitoring product.

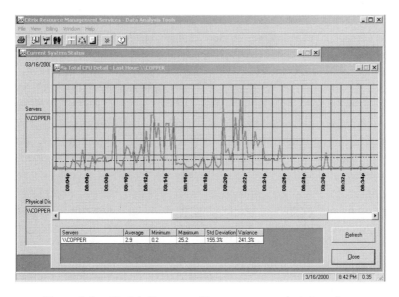

Figure 9.1   *Citrix's Resource Management analysis interface.*

Antivirus Software

With the proliferation of computer viruses, particularly macro-based viruses, the desire for an antivirus solution as part of a Terminal Server implementation is growing stronger. While a properly locked down Terminal Server prevents a regular user (non-administrator) who accidentally becomes infected from introducing a problem onto a Terminal Server, there's still the problem of the user's personal files or user profile becoming infected. Even if virus scanning is actively taking place on the file and mail servers, there's always the potential for a user to, through FTP or some other means, encounter an infected file.

Luckily, as the popularity of Terminal Server grows, so does the support from antivirus software manufacturers for the Terminal Server environment. Performance can be a major factor in an antivirus solution. A poorly configured antivirus program can very easily consume huge amounts of system resources, particularly when live scanning is enabled. The following list shows some of the antivirus software products that have been used on Terminal Server:

- **Trend Micro's ServerProtect.** Versions 4.7 and 4.8 have been labeled by Trend Micro as being compatible with Terminal Server. Version 5 is currently being tested. Their Web site is www.antivirus.com.

- **McAfee NetShield.** Although no official information on compatibility has been provided by McAffee, version 4.03 of NetShield runs on Terminal Server. Their Website is www.mcaffee.com.

When looking at testing an antivirus product, always try to work with the latest version of the product. Older versions are more likely to introduce issues and possibly system crashes into the environment.

When configuring a virus-scanning tool, configure only inbound scanning if possible, and make sure that you're targeting macro-enabled documents such as .DOC or .XLS. Once configured, all the virus-scanning configuration options should be locked down so that the end user can't modify the configuration and possibly affect virus scanning on the entire server.

After the antivirus software has been installed, spend some time collecting performance data to get an idea as to the overhead that the program introduces. Practically all antivirus developers provide some form of limited trial download, so you should be able to evaluate a few products to get a fairly good idea of which product will work best in your environment.

Windows Server Resource Kit

I've found the Windows 2000 Server Resource Kit to be one of the most valuable tools to assist in the administration of a Terminal Server environment. Tools such as SysPrep (mentioned earlier for use with server cloning) or RegDmp and RegIni (registry changes and replication) are just two examples of what's available.

A number of tools are designed specifically for Terminal Server. This list describes a few of them:

- **TSReg.** This tool, shown in Figure 9.2, allows the very granular tuning of sections of the RDP client's registry, which pertain to the bitmap and glyph caching. Using this tool, you can modify settings such as the cache size.

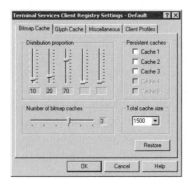

Figure 9.2 *Terminal Server client registry tuner.*

- **DRMapSrv.** This command-line tool can be used to automate the process of creating shares on the client's drive using the NET SHARE command and then accessing them from within a Terminal Server session using NET USE. It automates the manual process that's usually required if you want to provide client drive mapping with the RDP client.

- **Winsta.** This simple GUI tool provides a list of users who are logged onto the Terminal Server where the tool is run. It provides a simple way of quickly seeing who may be on the server. It's similar to the QWINSTA command-line tool that's part of the Terminal Server command set, but it doesn't allow you to query information on a remote server. This tool only runs on TS 2000.

- **Terminal Server Capacity Planning Tools.** This set of utilities is used to simulate the load on a Terminal Server. Additional documentation relating to this utility can also be found at the following address:

  `www.microsoft.com/windows2000/library/technologies/terminal/tscaling.asp`

Scripting Tools

Scripting can play an important role in the development and management of your Terminal Servers, particularly when deploying a large number of applications across multiple servers. Scripting is particularly important for the creation of domain or machine logon scripts, as certain per-user options can be set to assist in the smooth operation of an application. A number of scripting languages are available, and the decision is really a matter of personal preference and familiarity on the administrator's part, since you need to be able to manage and update these scripts as necessary. These are some of the supported features that you should look for in a scripting language:

- **Registry manipulation.** This is a very useful feature when creating customized application-compatibility scripts.

- **File read and write.** The ability to read and write to a text file can be very useful for such tasks as information logging or application-file configuration.

- **Structured programming.** Basic programming features such as IF...ENDIF and LOOP structures are important for developing robust and useful scripts.

In addition to third-party scripting languages such as KiXtart or Perl, Microsoft now provides more robust scripting support through its Windows Script Host (WSH). WSH is language independent and includes support for both VBScript and Jscript. Using VBScript with WSH, you can produce robust scripting solutions, including the development of your own custom COM objects. For a thorough treatment on WSH, I highly recommend the book *Windows 2000—Windows Script Host*, written by Tim Hill and published by MTP.

Application Software

While the exact number and type of applications that you'll be deploying is dependent on the requirements of your project, a standard methodology can be applied to capture the required information, making the scheduling and actual implementation of the applications more manageable.

When planning to install an application, gather the following information:

- Are any customization tools available for the application to automate the installation and/or lock down the user's access to certain components that may not be suitable for Terminal Server? Two such utilities that I commonly use are the Internet Explorer Administration Kit (IEAK) and the Office 2000 Resource Kit. Both of these allow the customization of their respective products prior to installation. Certain features such as the animated Office Assistant or the Internet Connection Wizard can be turned off. The IEAK also provides custom policy templates that can be used on a TSE 4.0 implementation. Chapter 16, "Group and System Policy Configuration," provides more details about policies in TS 2000 and TSE 4.0.

- How is user-specific information for the application maintained? In the registry, through INI files, or through other customized or proprietary files? Is per-user information saved, or does the application assume that only one user can run the program at a time? This is common with custom-built applications, but many commercial programs also exhibit this behavior.

- What additional drivers does this program need? Components such as ODBC drivers, the Borland database engine, or Oracle SQLNet drivers are a few examples. Collect this information so that you can develop a list of common components that you will install on the server prior to installing the application.

- Are any other applications dependent upon this program? Are certain configuration features assumed to be available? The most common scenario involving this issue has to do with Web browsers or office productivity tools such as Microsoft Excel. This is usually a consideration when custom-built applications are being implemented that interact with programs like Excel for displaying data results or creating graphs. These dependencies need to be flagged so these applications can be installed first on the Terminal Server. If multiple apps depend on a common component, this information will help ensure that the requirements of one don't conflict with the requirements of another.

After collecting the necessary information, arrange and prioritize the installation of each component, ensuring that all dependencies have been accounted for. From the results, you can schedule dates and times for the installation of each component. This method can be extremely valuable, particularly if additional human resources must be scheduled to assist in the application installation. Table 9.2 shows a sample prioritization from one of my recent projects. The numbers in the "Dependencies" column refer to any other applications in the list that an application depends on. For example, the custom C++ client/server application is dependent on application 1, which is MDAC 2.1.

Table 9.2   Sample Application-Installation Priority List

#	Application	Dependencies
1	MDAC 2.1	None
2	Citrix Resource Management Services	1
3	SQL Server 7.0 Client	None
4	Internet Explorer 5.0	None
5	Office 2000 (Word and Excel only)	4
6	Custom C++ client/server application.	1
7	Custom PowerBuilder client/server application.	3

Application Installation Standards

Although the actual process for application installation is covered in Chapter 19, one area that should be flagged during the planning stage is a standard for the location of installed application files.

Many of the commercial Windows applications default to installing in the %systemdrive%\Program Files directory. In a Terminal Server environment, you don't want to place these files onto the system drive. Instead you want all your applications to be installed on the dedicated application volume. I also suggest that you create a standard location where you will maintain custom or in-house developed applications, separate from any commercial products you install. I usually suggest this structure:

- Y:\Program Files for commercial applications such as Microsoft Office.

- Y:\Custom Program Files for custom-developed applications specific to your company. I like to use this name because the eight-character short name is likely to be custom~1, something that's easy to remember.

This information should be clearly communicated to all administrators involved in the project to eliminate the accidental deployment of an application on the system drive.

Pay particular attention to updates to the system path. Many in-house developed applications assume that their specific application directory will be listed in the system path. In a Terminal Server environment, you should avoid this whenever possible. By keeping the system path size to a minimum, you reduce the chances of a misplaced DLL or other application file affecting the functionality of another program. It will also reduce the overhead of directory searches, which are performed on all entries in the PATH when the system is searching for a file.

Author's Note

Although it's important to minimize the size of the PATH command in your Terminal Server environment, don't get into the habit of placing all your DLLs and other common files into a single location such as System32. With that technique, you still have the problem of applications that need different versions of the same files. Maintaining everything in a single directory doesn't allow for this flexibility; neither can you place these alternate files in another directory and add that to the path. Where would you put it?

Consider this example: You have two directories, dbdlls and dbdlls_old. The first contains new database drivers and the second contains an older version of these files. The files in the two directories are named identically. You want to make them both available, so you put them into the PATH command as shown:

```
PATH=x:\winnt;x:\winnt\system32;y:\dbdlls;y:\dbdlls_old
```

Because Windows traverses the path from left to right, as soon as it finds the DLL or executable that it's looking for in dbdlls, it stops and uses that file. It won't skip over a directory, nor will it allow you to select the second file as opposed to the first. Reversing the order doesn't help the situation. So what do you do?

One option is to place a copy of the old DLLs in the working directory for the application, since it always looks there first before searching the path for the file. Multiple applications with the same requirement may introduce significant administrative overhead as well as wasting disk space.

An alternative that I commonly employ is a special feature of directory paths known as relative paths. You may have used this feature when working from a Windows command prompt. The key to relative paths is two special directory entries (. and ..). The single dot points back to itself; the double dots point to the parent directory (or the current directory, if you're at the root directory).

Using these relative paths, I'll add the following standard entries to the system PATH:

```
..\BIN;..\..\BIN
```

These relative entries mean that the contents of the BIN directory, located under the parent of the current directory, as well as the contents of the BIN directory under its parent, are both accessible.

By using relative paths in conjunction with a standard for directory naming and application deployment, I can keep the number of entries in the system PATH command to a minimum. In order to do this, custom-built applications must go into a standard directory structure. The following hierarchy demonstrates how this might be done on the application volume:

```
BIN
Program Files
     Microsoft Office
     Internet Explorer
Custom Program Files
     BIN
     Custom App_01
     Custom App_02
Old Program Files
     BIN                    <- the old DB dlls could be placed here
          Custom_App 03
          Custom_App_04
```

At the root of the structure, the BIN directory contains DLLs or administrative tools that are common to all applications located in the directories below the root. Here I commonly place tools that I use frequently from the command prompt. I try to avoid adding files to System32 whenever possible. The other BIN directories would then contain files that were common to all programs underneath.

Because of the relative paths added to the system path, if the required file isn't found within the application's working directory, the next location to look is a child BIN directory, then the BIN directory of the parent, and finally the BIN directory of its parent if necessary.

Returning to my earlier example with the dbdlls and dbdlls_old directories, using the relative path directory shown above, I could place all of the new DLLs into the Y:\Custom Program Files\Bin directory, while placing the old DLLs into the Y:\Old Program Files\Bin directory. All apps that require those DLLs could then be placed in the Old Program Files folder. If the application was later updated to work with the new DLLs, its folder could simply be moved back up to the Y:\Custom Program Files folder. The only change would be an update to the shortcut for the application. In its new location it would automatically pick up the new DLLs from the Y:\Custom Program Files\Bin location.

I've found this configuration most useful in organizations that insist on standardizing a certain build or version number of database DLLs, particularly when they decide that they're ready to move to a newer version of the files. Using this approach, applications can be migrated to the newer DLL set once tested, without causing problems for any other applications that haven't yet been certified.

This approach is certainly not ideal in all situations, particularly if you have only a few custom-built apps in your environment, but may be something to consider if you're deploying a large number of in-house applications within your Terminal Server environment.

At the very least, you should ensure that you keep the system PATH command entries as short as possible. ◆

Change Management

As part of your software planning, you should develop change and release management procedures. A critical part of maintaining a stable Terminal Server environment is having the proper software testing and validation procedures in place that must be completed prior to the software's deployment. System downtime as a result of a poor software deployment is completely avoidable in a Terminal Server environment.

Author's Note

I once encountered an incident that serves to reiterate this fact. A custom-developed application was presented to me for deployment into a production environment. I informed the project team that the application would have to go onto a test server before it would even be scheduled for deployment into production. Even though the developers were adamant about the fact that the program was very small and had caused no problems on the desktop, I wouldn't allow a production deployment without it going onto a test server first. I informed them that desktop validation is not a substitute for Terminal Server validation.

After installing the application on a test server, the program was working perfectly. Only a short time later, however, I discovered that a number of other applications had stopped functioning properly, including one of the mission-critical applications for the organization. The reason was that the install program for the new application had placed a database driver file in the SYSTEM32 directory that was being picked up by this application (and others) instead of the file out of the standard database driver directory on the Terminal Server. This was a simple mistake made by the programming team while creating the install program and hadn't been picked up during testing on the desktop (since they didn't run the other applications). To correct the problem, I just moved this file into the application's working directory where it would be available only to this application.

Luckily, this problem was detected on a test server, and I was able to correct the problem before the actual production deployment, which went without incident. This certainly wouldn't have been the case if I hadn't insisted on the testing in the first place. Before you put any software into your production environment, be sure to test it first. ◆

Planning for Testing and Pilot Users

An area where you should start planning early is in the selection of your test and pilot users. Choosing the right users for this task is an important ingredient in implementing an application successfully. These users are not the same ones that you might employ to do some load testing prior to deployment. These are the veteran users who will become involved in the very early days of your implementation. They'll be key in validating the acceptable level of performance and functionality for an application and will help pave the way for the success of the software implementation. You won't want to choose these people lightly. A suitable pilot user should have the following qualifications:

- **Advanced user of the application.** An advanced user will be able to recognize immediately any variances from the normal operating behavior of an application. When looking for the advanced user, talk with both the desktop support staff who serve these users as well as the manager and other staff in that department.

- **Comfortable with change.** You may find that many advanced users are also very resistant to change. These people don't make good pilot users. In many cases, they know how to do their jobs very well, but are unable to adapt well to new situations. They've learned their jobs through repetition more than through knowledge.

Warning

No matter how tempting it may be, don't make false promises to solicit the cooperation of an advanced user who is uncomfortable with change. He or she will expect you to live up to those promises. More specifically, don't promise better performance unless you can deliver it. I say this because it's done so often it's almost cliché. Always be honest about why you're doing something. ◆

- **Positive attitude toward the success of the project.** The user needs to have a clear idea as to why the project is being undertaken and must believe in the benefits it will bring, regardless of the problems that may arise in getting there. Because this user will most likely be well known and respected among his or her peers, you can't have this person complaining loudly to anyone who will listen about any problems he or she might have encountered during the testing. This is a sure-fire way of planting the seeds of resistance to your Terminal Server implementation. At the same time, positive feedback may increase the desire to move to the new environment. This is something that needs to be watched very carefully.

- **Excellent listener and communicator.** Not only must pilot users be able to relay accurately any problems they may be having, but they must be able to follow instructions given to them.

Don't hesitate to drop or replace a pilot user who hasn't measured up to your expectations. This is not to say that he or she should be removed just for being critical of the system. On the contrary, objective criticism can be very beneficial in delivering a robust environment. Users who provide little or no feedback or who abuse the testing privileges should be prime candidates for immediate replacement.

See Chapter 6, "Client Planning," for more information on client deployment and support planning.

Software Testing

Software testing and deployment in your Terminal Server environment will go through two distinct phases. The first is during the Terminal Server implementation, and the second is once you've gone into a production mode:

- **Terminal Server Implementation Phase.** During this phase, you'll be migrating one or more applications from the user's desktop into the Terminal Server environment as well as introducing new applications. The key difference between this phase and the next is that the Terminal Server environment, being new, is more open to change. Until Terminal Server is rolled into production, its configuration is very malleable. This provides you with the flexibility to ensure not only that the environment is robust and stable, but that whatever is required to get the applications working is done properly. The biggest benefit is that you have some room for error. You can make some mistakes and not bring the world crashing down with you. Use this opportunity to its fullest potential. Take the time to understand what's happening and experiment with more than one solution to a problem. When your Terminal Server environment goes live, you'll no longer have this luxury.

- **Production Maintenance Phase.** At this point you're running a production Terminal Server environment with many users running key applications. The number one priority now is to maintain stability. Any changes you introduce must not have a negative effect on the existing users. You need to have a process in place for testing new software before it gets near the production environment. Production won't be the place for doing testing or last-minute changes. A set of one or more non-production Terminal Servers should be available for testing all changes.

The approach you take to implement software differs only slightly between these two phases. Figure 9.3 outlines the process of adding and testing software in the Terminal Server environment. The steps shaded in gray are the same whether you're implementing a new Terminal Server environment or managing an existing one.

For specifics on software installation, see Chapter 19.

Author's Note

An important part of every step is the proper documentation of what was done to configure an application to run on Terminal Server. Even if the installation was very straightforward and without any issues, you should mention this somewhere so that, if the software ever needs to be installed again, someone can look up this information and quickly re-create the installation. ◆

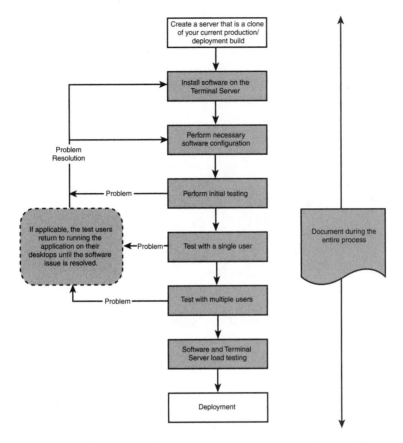

Figure 9.3   *Software installation and testing procedure on Terminal Server.*

Creating the Terminal Server Production Mirror

During the implementation phase, the production mirror will not necessarily be a clone of a production server, but should be a clone of the most recent build you're currently working with. See the earlier section "Cloning and Server Replication" for more information.

By using a cloned image of your latest "production" server, you ensure that if the application installs and functions properly, it will work in the production environment. Testing a new application on a generic installation of Terminal Server is not sufficient to guarantee its stability in your production configuration.

Tip

It's certainly reasonable to use this test server to test more than one software package concurrently, although I suggest that you handle this with care. It's best if you can keep to only two or three packages being tested on a single server at a time—fewer, if possible. The problem with having many applications being tested at once is that if a problem occurs, such as intermittent performance degradations or crashes, it becomes more difficult to narrow down the actual culprit. ◆

Application Installation and Configuration

Many applications, particularly custom applications or older 16-bit or 32-bit applications, need to be configured differently or augmented with scripting to get them to function properly or to resolve performance issues when run on Terminal Server. The installation and configuration of applications in your environment will usually take up the majority of the project time. See Chapter 19 for a complete discussion of installing and configuring applications.

It's worth reiterating the importance of documentation, particularly during the installation of your applications, since it's unlikely that any subtle changes made to an application will be remembered by you, or easily re-created by someone else.

Initial Application Testing

After you have the software installed on your test server, you should do some initial testing. You'll be able to examine general-purpose applications, such as Microsoft Word, better than custom applications developed for a specific department. In many cases, you may not be able to test much more than the logon screen for the application.

Tip

Although you may not be able to run the application, when possible you should attempt to verify connectivity to back end database systems such as SQL Server prior to having the test user become involved. ◆

Single-User Testing

Before you can run, you need to learn to walk. This is why initially you should introduce only a single user to the software on Terminal Server. Make sure that the process of switching back and forth between Terminal Server and the desktop is clear to the user. This will minimize its impact if the application in Terminal Server is not working properly. I highly recommend that you demonstrate the back-out procedures to anyone who may have concerns with downtime, such as a tester's manager. This rollback plan is another benefit to software deployment during the Terminal Server implementation.

Warning

If an application is being migrated from a user's desktop, don't remove the user's desktop version of the application until the Terminal Server version is in production. During testing, the desktop software will be the user's immediate back-out if there are problems on Terminal Server. ◆

A frequent question is, "How long should I test with one user?" My response is typically, "Until you're comfortable that multiple users could work in the same environment with the same or fewer issues than the single user." If a single user is having frequent problems, there's no reason to believe that adding more users will make the problem disappear. More likely, multiple users will start to exhibit the same problem.

Testing with a single user will very often eliminate the majority of the issues that would also be encountered by multiple users.

Multiuser Testing

When the application is working properly for the single test user, the next step is to increase this to two or three users. The reason is to ensure that the software continues to function when multiple instances are being run on the same computer (the Terminal Server). A classic problem area is in applications that create temp files or user files in a location that's not unique for multiple users on a Terminal Server. In many instances this is the application directory itself, but you'll normally discover this when testing with a single user since he or she should not have write access to the application directory. Don't let yourself fall into the trap of trying to add too many users too quickly. Always start slowly when performing initial testing. The more users you have testing, the more work required to ensure that they're working properly and to provide any required user support.

Another potential problem area is the registry, where the software may place user-specific application information in HKEY_LOCAL_MACHINE instead of HKEY_CURRENT_USER. All users can then access the same information, causing problems in the application. Again, if access to the registry is being controlled, this problem will be uncovered during the single user testing.

Author's Note

Until Terminal Server becomes more widely used, many software manufacturers will be able to provide only minimal (if any) support for their product when run on a Terminal Server. You'll have much more success if you can describe the problem specifically for the manufacturer. For example, if a software package insists on writing a temporary file into a specific location and this is causing conflicts on Terminal Server, ask the vendor if there's a way to modify the location of this file. This will be more easily answered than simply asking why the program won't run on Terminal Server.

In a number of situations, I haven't even revealed to the support people that I'm attempting to use their product on Terminal Server. When I do, the response is usually "Sorry, we don't support our product on that platform," even though the issue usually has to do with a user having more restrictive access and not with the operating system itself. ◆

Because of the increased possibility of problems when you first begin testing with multiple users, don't add too many users during the initial testing. "Too many" usually means more than five. With five or fewer users, the support responsibilities are still manageable by a single support person. More than five and your testing group may become much more difficult to support.

Warning

Never put an application into production on a Terminal Server if you have done testing only with a single user. ◆

Software Load Testing and Terminal Server

After the application has gone through multiuser testing successfully, the only outstanding task is to examine the load that the software will introduce to the Terminal Server. This can actually be started during single-user testing because severe performance problems may be noticed immediately. Using a tool such as Citrix RMS can be very helpful in estimating the resource requirements on a per-user basis. At the very least, basic load monitoring should be performed during the multiuser test phase.

Deployment

The final step is the actual deployment. By the time you're ready to deploy, there should be no doubt as to whether the application will work. The deployment should be no more than a formality.

Release Management

As part of the development of your change-management procedures, document the process that application developers and others need to follow if they want to have a program implemented within the Terminal Server environment. Regardless of which release procedures exist today, you need to establish a guideline that everyone will have to follow. Otherwise you run the risk of allowing releases to be scheduled before they've been tested properly in a test Terminal Server environment. Figure 9.4 describes the release-management process that I commonly implement.

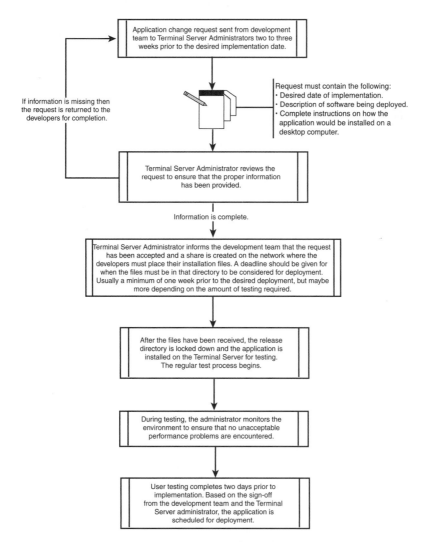

Figure 9.4 *Example of a possible Terminal Server release-management process.*

One of the key requirements is insisting that the development team clearly document exactly how the application should be installed. You shouldn't necessarily expect that the documentation will clearly explain how to deploy the application onto Terminal Server, but instead how the development team would normally install it on a desktop. You can then review this procedure and make any necessary adjustments to accommodate your Terminal Server requirements.

You should never allow a development team to install an application onto your environment without your direct involvement, and ideally with you at the controls. Unsupervised access to install any application is an almost certain invitation for trouble.

Part III

Implementing Terminal Server and MetaFrame

10

Terminal Server Installation

In this chapter:

- **Before You Begin**
  To help ensure a smooth Terminal Server installation, you should have a list of all the necessary information and configuration options that you plan to select during the installation.

- **Windows NT Server 4.0, Terminal Server Edition Installation**
  This section provides both a veteran NT administrator's summary and a step-by-step walkthrough of a TSE 4.0 installation.

- **Windows 2000 Terminal Services Installation**
  This section provides both a veteran Windows 2000 administrator's summary and a step-by-step walkthrough of a TS 2000 installation.

Before You Begin

This chapter discusses the actual installation of both versions of Terminal Server. For readers who are already familiar with the installation of Windows NT or 2000 Server, I have included a summary section for each operating system that outlines the key areas that may differ between a Terminal Server and a standard Windows server installation. The post-installation configuration and tuning for Terminal Server is discussed in Chapter 12, "Terminal Server Configuration and Tuning."

> **Tip**
>
> *For a complete discussion of planning the server hardware you will use to run Terminal Server, see Chapter 7, "Server Hardware Planning."* ◆

During the installation of Terminal Server, avoid adding components that are not directly required to achieve the objective of a bootable operating system. The rule I always use is this:

If it's not required to boot the operating system, leave it until later.

The following are some examples of components that are not required in order to create a bootable installation of Terminal Server:

- **Custom video drivers.** The standard VGA drivers for Terminal Server are often sufficient.

- **Internet Explorer.** You *should not* install IE 4.0 as part of the NT 4.0 Terminal Server installation. For Windows 2000, IE 5 is considered a core OS component and will always be installed.

  See Chapter 19, "Application Integration" for a complete discussion of installing and configuring IE in a Terminal Server environment.

- **Additional network services or protocols.** Services such as Simple Network Transfer Protocol (SNMP) are not normally required during the installation.

- **Accessories.** Many of the accessories, such as screen savers, should never be installed.

Installation Checklist

Before beginning the installation, you should have the following information on hand, most of which you would normally have before beginning a standard Windows server install:

- **Types of adapters (SCSI, RAID, network) and other devices present on your server, and any vendor drivers they may require during the installation.** I recommend using the drivers that ship with Terminal Server whenever possible during the installation, and then upgrading these drivers to the most current version after the installation is complete. This information is more critical to Terminal Server 4.0, since Windows 2000 will provide plug and play support for most current hardware.

- **Type of Client Access Licenses (CALs) you will use, and how many licenses.** For Windows 2000, you should also know where your Terminal Services license server will reside. See the Windows 2000 installation section for more details on this issue.

- **Drive configuration details.** You should know how the physical disks will be configured for running Terminal Server and what partition layout you plan to use. If necessary, review Chapter 7 for more information on this topic. The system should not have any disk compression software installed.

- **Networking specifications.** You should have all the necessary networking information in hand, such as IP addresses, subnet masks, and WINS/DNS addresses.

Upgrading an Existing Operating System

If you're currently running WinFrame or Terminal Server 4.0, you may be considering upgrading to a newer version of Terminal Server in order to preserve any system, application, or security settings that you already have in place. Table 10.1 summarizes the available upgrade options.

Author's Note

While the upgrade path from WinFrame 1.x to Terminal Server 4.0 is officially supported, I recommend performing a clean install instead of an upgrade whenever possible. The time saved with an upgrade rarely justifies the questions of stability that will almost always arise. Whenever a problem is encountered, there will always be the question of whether it's because of the upgrade. If you ever require support from either Microsoft or Citrix, one of the first tasks they'll require is for you to perform a clean install in an attempt to duplicate the problem.

The major changes in the underlying operating system (OS) from 3.51 to 4.0 may also raise issues with applications that were installed on the server prior to the upgrade.

Although Microsoft officially supports an upgrade from Terminal Server 4.0 to Windows 2000, the same can almost be said for this configuration. Unless absolutely necessary, I recommend performing a clean installation of Windows 2000 in order to implement Terminal Services, instead of simply upgrading an existing TSE 4.0 server. ♦

Table 10.1   Upgrade Options for Terminal Server

Existing OS	Target OS Support	Comments
WinFrame 1.x	Terminal Server 4.0	After upgrading, only the RDP protocol will be supported unless you also install MetaFrame. An upgrade directly from WinFrame to Windows 2000 is *not* supported. If you want to upgrade, you must first upgrade to TSE 4.0 and then upgrade again to Windows 2000.
OEM WinFrame	Not supported.	Upgrades from OEM versions of WinFrame such as NCD's WinCenter are not supported.

continues ▶

Table 10.1   continued

Existing OS	Target OS Support	Comments
Terminal Server 4.0	Windows 2000 Terminal Server	Fully supported.
NT Server 3.51/4.0	Not supported.	Upgrades from a standard NT Server to Terminal Server *are not* supported because any applications on the server will not be properly configured to run in a multiuser environment after the upgrade. Because Terminal Servers won't be performing a typical server role, a clean install in this situation is always recommended.

Windows NT Server 4.0, Terminal Server Edition Installation

The installation of Terminal Server is very similar to a typical NT Server 4.0 installation. For readers who are well versed in the installation of NT Server 4.0, I've listed the differences in the following section, "Veteran NT Administrator's Summary." I've also included a step-by-step walkthrough of the installation for readers who want more information on the installation options.

There are three main methods of initiating the Terminal Server installation:

- Use the three Terminal Server 3[1/2]-inch installation disks. If you don't have the floppy disks, you can build them by running WINNT32 /OX from the i386 directory on the CD.

- Perform the install over an existing NT installation by using the WINNT32 command.

- Start from DOS using the WINNT command.

Tip

You can also install TSE 4.0 by booting directly from the CD-ROM, if your hardware supports that option. Successfully booting from the CD is dependent on your hardware configuration, particularly when a RAID controller is not directly supported by the operating system. ◆

My preference is to use the installation disks (or the CD-ROM when possible) provided with Terminal Server, because you can partition and format the target hard drives as necessary. With the other two installation methods, you can't reformat the drive containing the installation files. You would use the other methods only if you don't have a CD-ROM drive (or the CD-ROM media) on the server and need to perform the install across the network. In this case, you could boot the server in DOS, format the system partition, and then install TSE 4.0 across the network, converting the drive to NTFS from FAT in the process. The following sections assume the standard install, booting from floppy disks.

Veteran NT Administrator's Summary

For readers who are experienced administrators and are familiar with the standard process of installing NT Server 4.0, I have included this summary to outline the key areas of the installation that you'll need to review. If you're new (or fairly new) to the installation of NT Server, I recommend reviewing the following outline step by step at least once to familiarize yourself with the options presented and why certain options have been chosen.

Boot Partition Size

When prompted to allocate space for the boot partition, I recommend that you install Terminal Server on a separate partition (or physical disk) from where you will install your applications. I've found that this helps in managing the deployment and maintenance of the applications as well as in managing file security.

Although you will typically implement the production pagefile on a separate partition or physical disk from the OS (see Chapter 7 for a discussion on pagefile location), whenever possible I recommend ensuring that space exists on the system partition equal to the physical memory on the server. This allows room for the creation of a crash-dump file if necessary. Although this option is rarely used in a Terminal Server environment, in the situation where a persistent problem is occurring it may assist in the troubleshooting of the problem by the appropriate vendor's technical support.

When calculating the space required, I use 200MB as an estimate for the required space for the OS alone. Next, I add the physical memory on the server. Finally, I multiply this number by 1.5 to determine the total space required. Of course, this calculation isn't perfect. For example, if I have a server with 4GB of physical memory, my calculations would suggest that I need a boot drive of approximately this size:

$$(0.2GB + 4GB) \times 1.5 = 6.3GB$$

But under NT 4.0, the maximum size of the boot partition is limited to 4GB at installation. In this situation, I would simply allocate the maximum of 4GB for the boot partition and sacrifice the ability to store crash-dump logs (not that big of an issue by any means). In Chapter 12, I talk more about pagefile optimization.

Tip

Under NT 4.0, the boot partition is limited to a maximum of 4GB because during the installation it must first format the partition as FAT16—even if it will be converted to NTFS. The limitations of FAT16 are the cause for this 4GB limit. Under Windows 2000, this problem doesn't exist, since the installation program can immediately format the partition as NTFS. ◆

Boot Partition File System

When selecting the file system to use on any Terminal Server drive, you should *always* select NTFS. You may be used to formatting your NT Server boot partition as FAT for both performance and recovery reasons, since it can easily be protected through share-level permissions and local logon policies. With Terminal Server, share permissions are inadequate for protecting the file system from regular users. Remember that all TSE 4.0 clients are logging on *locally*. This means that they have direct access to all disks on your server. The only way to protect these disks is by using NTFS so that you can apply file-level security, something you can't do with FAT.

You should *never* format any of your Terminal Server drives as FAT. There's no way to restrict access or audit usage, leaving the drive completely open to any user who may log onto your Terminal Server. I recommend not doing this even in a test or development environment, because you can't properly simulate the different access rights that users have. You have no way of knowing whether more restrictive permissions will cause application issues or change any of your testing or development results.

Server Client Access Licensing Modes

On the licensing mode screen, you're prompted to select the mode for the server client access license, not the Terminal Server client access license, and even though you have the option of selecting Per Server or Per Seat, *only* the Per Seat option is a valid licensing scenario with Terminal Server. For more information on Terminal Server licensing, see the "Terminal Server Licensing Requirements" section of Chapter 2, "Microsoft Windows Terminal Server."

Terminal Server Client Access License Count

When prompted, you should enter the total number of Terminal Server client (desktop) access licenses you have purchased. This represents the *total* number of users who are legally allowed to connect to this Terminal Server, not just the concurrent total. As discussed in Chapter 2, these licenses are recorded but not tracked with TSE 4.0. You can modify this number at any time after the installation by using the Terminal Server License Manager.

Server Type

When selecting the server type for your Terminal Server, you should always select Stand-Alone Server. As mentioned in Chapter 2, Terminal Server should not be configured as anything other than an application (stand-alone) server except in the smallest of environments. Assigning additional computing responsibilities to a Terminal Server will degrade its application-servicing abilities.

Internet Explorer 4.0 Installation

I highly recommend that you *do not* install IE4 as part of the OS installation, but wait until the server has been built and then add the desired Web browser during the application installation or server configuration phase.

Author's Note

I have experienced problems with installing IE during the OS setup on some machines that have greater than 1GB of RAM. In these situations, everything appeared to install properly, but IE simply generated an exception error (Dr Watson) when you tried to run it after the installation. The issue appears to be caused by Terminal Server running with an incorrect pagefile (temppf.sys). The solution in this case was to recreate a properly sized pagefile on the system partition, reboot, and then reinstall IE4. Because of this issue, and the fact that people will typically be installing IE5 now instead of IE4, I have found that a more reliable base server can be built if IE4 is simply not installed during the OS setup. ◆

IIS 3.0 Installation

The version of Internet Information Server (IIS) that ships with TSE 4.0 is still 3.0, the same that ships with NT Server 4.0. I wouldn't recommend running IIS on your Terminal Server for the same reasons that I have discussed before with other server-based applications. IIS utilizes resources that may be better served by your Terminal Server clients. There's rarely a reason for using a server as both a Terminal Server and a Web server.

Display Resolution

When prompted to configure the video display for your server, I *highly* recommend that you simply use the default of VGA, and adjust it as desired when the installation is complete and your server has rebooted.

The resolution on the console of your Terminal Server will have *no* impact on the maximum resolution of the user's client session. You can have your Terminal Server running at 640 × 480 with 16 colors, and a client can still connect to the server with a desktop session of 1024 × 768 with 256 colors.

Finishing the Installation

Once the Terminal Server installation is complete, you're ready to perform the rest of the configuration on the server. If you're planning to implement Citrix MetaFrame in your environment, I recommend proceeding to Chapter 11, "MetaFrame Installation," and then continuing with Chapter 12, "Terminal Server Configuration and Tuning" to complete the build of your server.

Part 1: Beginning the Setup

The following procedure assumes that you're booting from the installation disks. To install Terminal Server, perform the following steps:

1. Place the Terminal Server Setup Boot Disk into drive A: and start the server. When prompted, insert Setup Disk #2 and press Enter. After the core drivers required for the Terminal Server installation to boot are loaded, the screen font changes and the Windows NT name, version, and build number appear. The second line identifies this as Terminal Server, followed by the build number.

2. The Windows Terminal Server Setup window appears; press Enter to continue the installation.

3. Specify whether you want TSE 4.0 to autodetect your mass storage devices, or you want to select them manually (either from the provided list or from a disk provided by the hardware vendor). Unless the hardware vendor tells you otherwise, I recommend selecting the Auto Detect option. Even if you have newer drivers for an existing device, unless the existing driver that ships with TSE 4.0 is known to cause problems, you should wait until TSE 4.0 is installed and functioning before you update the drivers. You should also use the vendor's disk if TSE 4.0 doesn't ship with the necessary drivers.

Author's Note

I've had problems adding drivers from a floppy disk during an installation when booting directly from the CD-ROM. The installation simply refused to acknowledge that the driver disk was in the drive. When I performed the installation using the boot floppies instead of the CD-ROM, I was able to add the additional drivers without any problems. ◆

4. After selecting the Auto Detect option, when prompted, insert Terminal Server Setup Disk #3 into drive A: and press Enter.

5. After finding all detectable mass storage devices, if any other storage devices must be added, press S to specify them manually. If your server contains a RAID controller, you'll probably be required to add the necessary drivers manually from the vendor's driver disk.

6. When all the mass storage devices you need are listed, press Enter to continue. After Setup has completed loading some additional drivers, you'll be prompted to insert the Terminal Server CD-ROM.

7. Next, review the End-User License Agreement onscreen. Press the F8 key to continue with the installation if you accept the terms of the agreement.

8. TSE 4.0 searches for any previous installations of Windows NT or WinFrame. If you attempt to upgrade Terminal Server over an existing regular Windows NT server, a dialog box appears, explicitly stating that upgrades of this nature are not supported and suggesting that you perform a clean install instead. TSE 4.0 setup ignores an NT Workstation installation if it exists on your server. I suggest that you choose to install a fresh copy of Terminal Server.

9. The installation program next asks you to identify computer type, video display, mouse, keyboard, and keyboard layout. Most likely the proper settings will already be displayed for your server. You *should not* change these settings unless you're absolutely sure that what's shown needs to be corrected. The one setting you shouldn't change is the video display, which defaults to VGA. Remember that during the installation, you're attempting to build a bootable Terminal Server; settings such as the video display can be modified after the server is up and functional. When you're satisfied with the choices listed, press Enter to continue.

10. The next screen prompts you to select and configure the system boot partition. You don't need to worry about setting up any non-system partitions (application drives) right now; you can do this by running Disk Administrator after you've completed the Terminal Server installation.

I highly recommend that you install Terminal Server on a separate partition (or physical disk) from where you'll maintain your installed applications. I've found that this helps not only in managing the deployment and maintenance of applications, but in configuring security on the Terminal Server.

When deciding how much space to allocate for the boot partition, make sure that you set aside sufficient space not only for the operating system, but also for application files that must be installed on the system partition, and, more importantly, space for a pagefile. See the earlier section "Boot Partition Size" for a discussion on how to calculate the space needed.

11. After you have created a system partition of the desired size, highlight it and press Enter. If this is a newly created partition, you need to format it before it can be used. You have two possible file systems: FAT and NTFS. For any Terminal Server drive, you should *always* select NTFS.

> **Warning**
>
> *Many NT administrators may suggest formatting the system partition of an NT server as FAT for performance and recovery reasons, because share permissions provide sufficient security across a network to protect these drives from unauthorized access. With Terminal Server, share permissions are inadequate for protecting the file system from regular users, as discussed in the earlier section "Boot Partition File System." You should never format any of your Terminal Server drives as FAT. ◆*

12. Specify where you want to install Terminal Server. I recommend that you use the default setting, which is \WTSRV. Press Enter to continue.

13. The installation process prompts you to determine whether it should perform an exhaustive secondary examination of all existing partitions. Selecting Enter performs this test in addition to the standard corruption test. If you press Esc, only the standard check is performed.

14. When the disk tests are complete, files are copied to the server. When all files have been copied, you're prompted to remove the floppy disk and the CD from their drives. Press Enter to restart the server and continue with the installation.

Part 2: The GUI Setup

After the server has restarted and the additional files have been copied, you'll begin the GUI portion of the installation. This portion starts by presenting the three parts that need to be completed for the installation:

- Gathering information about your computer
- Installing Windows NT Networking
- Finishing Setup

To proceed, perform the following steps:

1. Click the Next button to begin gathering information about your computer. Provide your name and the name of the company when prompted. Click Next.

2. The next dialog box prompts you to select the appropriate CAL mode. This is *not* the licensing for Terminal Server client sessions. You'll provide your Terminal Server licensing information in the next part of the installation. A Microsoft CAL is required for each computer that you want to access any of the additional services that a Terminal Server can provide, such as RAS or File and Print. While the dialog box provides two options, Per Server and Per Seat, only Per Seat is a valid license option with Terminal Server. For more information on Terminal Server licensing see the "Terminal Server Licensing Requirements" section of Chapter 2. Select the Per Seat radio button, and click Next to continue.

Tip

The two license options differ as follows:

- *Per Server. For this CAL mode, you purchase client licenses and apply them to the Terminal Server. The maximum number of concurrent connections equals the number of licenses purchased. Any client can connect to the server, but the total number can't exceed the CAL count.*

- *Per Seat. With this mode, you purchase a CAL for each computer that will access an NT server product (TSE 4.0 or regular NT Server). You only have to buy this license once, and it permits the client to connect to any number of available servers.* ◆

---

3. Next you're prompted to enter the number of TSE 4.0 client (desktop) access licenses you have purchased. This represents the *total* number of users who are legally allowed to connect to this Terminal Server, not just the concurrent total. As discussed in Chapter 2, these licenses are recorded but not tracked with TSE 4.0. You can modify this number at any time after the installation by using the Terminal Server License Manager.

4. After entering the license information, you're asked to select a computer name for the server. The name can be from 1–15 characters in length and must be unique in your environment.

5. The next dialog box prompts you to select a type for your server. The three options are

   • Primary Domain Controller

   • Backup Domain Controller

   • Stand-Alone Server

   As discussed in Chapter 2, Terminal Server should not be configured as anything other than an application (stand-alone) server. You should select Stand-Alone Server, and then click Next.

6. Setup prompts you to enter a password for the local administrator's account. Select something that's not easily guessed and, ideally, contains a combination of letters and numbers. If necessary, write down the password and store it in a safe place. Click Next.

7. The next step gives you the option to create an Emergency Repair Disk (ERD). Although I recommend that you always have a current ERD, I usually wait until I've finished the installation and have all the drives formatted and configured as I want before creating the ERD.

8. The next dialog box allows you to choose which optional components you want to install. Take a few minutes to review the options to make sure you're installing only the components that are really necessary. Following are some components that you *should not* install on your Terminal Server:

   • **Screen savers.** Screen savers can introduce a significant load on a Terminal Server, affecting all users. If a screen saver must be used, use only the blank screen saver.

   • **Communications.** The communications components should be omitted, as they're of little use in a multiuser environment.

   • **Games.** Although games can certainly be good for passing idle time, they introduce additional load on a Terminal Server.

   • **Multimedia.** Unless you're planning to provide sound to the local desktops through the MetaFrame client, I suggest that you omit the multimedia features.

- **Windows Messaging.** If you want to use the Windows Messaging provided with the Terminal Server installation, I suggest that you wait until the installation is complete and then select Add/Remove Programs from the Control Panel to add this feature.

9. You now have the option of installing Internet Explorer 4.0, which is included with Terminal Server. I highly recommend that you *do not* install IE4 at this point, but instead wait until the OS installation is complete and then add the desired browser during the application installation phase.

Part 3: Configuring Network Components

The next phase of the installation handles the configuration of the networking components of TSE 4.0. Click Next to continue.

1. Your first choice deals with how your server will connect to the network. The three choices are hard-wired, remote, or both. We'll configure this server to participate on a network with a hard-wired connection. You would only select the Remote option if this server were required to dial in to become a member of a network. Almost all Terminal Server installations will participate on a network via the hard-wired scenario. Select Hard-Wired and click Next.

2. You now have the option of installing Microsoft IIS. I don't recommend running IIS on your Terminal Server; see the earlier section "IIS 3.0 Installation" for my rationale.

3. Choose the network adapters that are present on your server. Terminal Server provides an autodetect feature that will attempt to find all installed network cards. If you want to use this feature, click the Start Search button. If you want to select from a list or you have an updated driver disk for your card, click the Select from List button. After selecting the drivers for all the network cards on your server, click Next.

> **Warning**
>
> *Autodetection may cause your server installation to freeze, forcing you to restart the installation. The network card is one piece of hardware that you should ensure is on the Terminal Server hardware compatibility list (HCL). Name-brand cards by manufacturers such as Compaq, 3Com, or Intel will very rarely cause problems, and all provide frequently updated drivers on their Web sites. You can check the latest Windows HCL at* http://www.microsoft.com/hcl.

continues ▶

▶ *continued*

Be aware that while the autodetect feature will usually find a card by one of these manufacturers, the available driver on TSE 4.0 may not be appropriate for the exact card configuration, and may prevent the card from functioning properly. I recommend that you retrieve the latest drivers for the card either from a CD-ROM or via the Internet and use these when installing the network adapter support. ◆

4. Select the network protocols to be installed on the Terminal Server. The TCP/IP protocol is required, as it is the only protocol that TSE 4.0 can use to communicate with RDP clients. If your server will be communicating with MetaFrame ICA clients or other network devices that require a protocol other than TCP/IP, you should plan to install these additional protocols after the OS installation is complete. At this time you should install only the protocols necessary to get the server booted and functioning.

5. Select the Network Services that you want installed. Any services that are required for your Terminal Server to function will appear grayed out and cannot be removed. Unless required for your particular environment, I recommend leaving the service list as is and returning to the Network option of Control Panel to add any additional services *after* the server installation is complete.

   After you click Next, the selected networking components will be installed.

6. During the component install, files will be copied and you'll be prompted to answer any necessary configuration questions. TCP/IP is mandatory, so you'll always need to specify the information for that. When the situation permits, I usually use DHCP to automatically assign an IP address during the build and test process of a server, particularly in an environment where Microsoft WINS/DNS are available to provide dynamic updating of these resources. When the server goes into piloting or production, a static address can be assigned if desired.

   DHCP addressing can also be useful if servers will be built using an imaging tool such as Norton Ghost. This way, when a new server is created it won't conflict with another server.

7. After configuring all the necessary network components, you'll be prompted to verify your network bindings. After this is done, click Next to continue. If you've configured your network properly, the Network Services will start.

8. At this point, you must decide whether this computer will participate in a domain or workgroup. Usually I leave it in the workgroup until the installation is complete and then add it into the desired domain. Of course, until it has been added to the domain, you'll be able to access it only through a local user account.

Author's Note

I recommend taking an image of the server immediately after installation (once you're confident that it's booting properly), so that you'll have a base config that you can easily revert to if necessary. In order to image the server, Microsoft requires that you first remove it from the domain. See the "Server Cloning," section " in Chapter 18. ◆

Part 4: Finishing the Setup

After selecting either a domain or workgroup, you've completed the network portion of the NT installation. The only part that remains is step 4, aptly named "Finishing the Setup":

1. The next dialog box prompts you to choose the appropriate time zone. Select the applicable zone and click OK.

2. Next, you're prompted to verify the video adapter and adjust the resolution if you want. If the installation program was able to autodetect your adapter, it will display the appropriate chipset in the dialog box; otherwise, it will select standard VGA. I recommend leaving the default for now and adjusting as desired when the installation is complete and your server has rebooted. (For details, see the earlier section "Display Resolution.") Even if you have drivers for your video adapter, wait until the server is functioning properly before you add them.

3. If you opted to create an ERD during installation, you'll be prompted to insert a blank formatted 3[1/2]-inch disk into your drive. Do so and the necessary repair files will be placed on the disk.

4. The final step prompts you to restart the computer. After you restart, your base installation of TSE 4.0 is complete.

Before you begin installing applications or allowing users access to the server, some additional configuration and tuning steps are required. Chapter 12 reviews all these changes. If you're planning to implement Citrix MetaFrame, see both Chapters 11 and 12.

Windows 2000 Terminal Services Installation

Because Terminal Services are integrated into Windows 2000, the setup screens are nearly identical to those in a typical Windows 2000 server installation. The following "Veteran Windows 2000 Administrator's Summary" section is provided for readers who want to see only those installation options that differ from a standard Windows 2000 server install. I've also included a step-by-step walkthrough of the installation for those who want more information on the installation options.

Just as with Windows NT, there are three main methods of initiating the installation:

- Initiate the installation from boot floppies. Windows 2000 requires four installation disks, NT requires three. Installation disks are built by running MAKEBOOT.EXE (for 16-bit operating systems) or MAKEBT32.EXE (for 32-bit operating systems) from the BOOTDISK directory on the installation CD. You'll need four blank, formatted floppy disks.

- Perform the install over an existing NT installation using the WINNT32 command.

- Start from DOS using the WINNT command.

Tip

You can also install TS 2000 by booting directly from the CD-ROM, if your hardware supports that option. ✦

My preference is to use the installation disks (or the CD-ROM itself) provided with Terminal Server, because you can partition and format the target hard drives as necessary. With the other two installation methods, you can't reformat the drive containing the installation files.

Author's Note

To install Terminal Services, you don't immediately need a Terminal Services License server, as discussed in Chapter 2. You have 90 days after the installation of Terminal Services to have the appropriate license server in place. Chapter 12 talks about configuring a Terminal Services License server. ✦

Veteran Windows 2000 Administrator's Summary

For readers who are experienced administrators and are familiar with the standard process of installing Windows 2000 Server, I have included this summary to outline the key areas in the installation that you'll need to take into consideration when planning to implement Terminal Services that may differ from your typical Win2000 server install.

If you're new (or fairly new) to the installation of Windows 2000 Server, I recommend reviewing the following outline step by step at least once to familiarize yourself with the options presented and why certain options have been chosen.

Boot Partition Size

When prompted to allocate space for the boot partition, I recommend that you install Windows 2000 on a separate partition (or physical disk) from where you will install your applications. I've found that this helps in managing the deployment and maintenance of the applications as well as in managing file security.

As I recommended in Chapter 7, you should store your production server's pagefile on a separate partition or physical disk. When calculating the space required for the boot partition, whenever possible you should also allocate space equal to the amount of physical RAM on the server to accommodate a dump file if ever required. While this option is rarely exercised in a Terminal Server environment, in a situation where a persistent, reproducible problem is occurring it may assist the appropriate vendor's technical support in troubleshooting the problem.

When calculating the space required, I use 850MB as an estimate for the required space for the OS alone. Next, I add the physical memory size on the server. Finally, I multiple this number by 1.5 to determine the total space required. So for example, on a system with 2GB of memory, the boot partition would be as follows:

$$(.85GB + 2GB) \times 1.5 = 4.28GB$$

Boot Partition File System

When selecting the file system to use on any Terminal Server drive, you should *always* select NTFS. You may be accustomed to formatting your boot partition as FAT for both performance and recovery reasons, since it can easily be protected through share-level permissions and local logon policies. When running Terminal Services, share permissions are inadequate for protecting the file system from regular users. Remember that all Terminal

Services clients are logging on *locally*. This means that they have direct access to all disks on your server. The only way to protect these disks is by using NTFS so that you can apply file-level security, something you can't do with FAT.

I recommend not doing this even in a test or development environment, because you can't properly simulate the different access rights that users have. You have no way of knowing whether more restrictive permissions will cause application issues or change any of your testing or development results.

Server Client Access Licensing Modes

On the licensing mode screen, you're prompted to select the mode for the Windows 2000 Server client access license, *not* the Terminal Services client access license. For Windows 2000, Terminal Services licenses are handled by a special license server. The license server doesn't need to be available prior to the installation of Terminal Services, but must be available within 90 days of the install. Chapter 12 describes how to configure a Terminal Services License server.

Even though this screen provides the option of selecting Per Server or Per Seat, *only* the Per Seat option is a valid licensing scenario when implementing Terminal Services in Application Server mode, which is the mode that you will select later in the installation to signal that this server will be allow multiuser access. For more information on Terminal Server licensing, see the "Terminal Server Licensing Requirements" section of Chapter 2.

Windows 2000 Components

In the Windows 2000 Components dialog box, select the specific components that you want to install on the server. I recommend that you only select those options that are required in order to create a bootable base server. Many options can be added after you have the server up and running. Table 10.2 summarizes my recommendations for which components should be selected and deselected.

Tip

Don't install any components that you won't need on your Terminal Server. This will help to maximize the available system resources. ◆

Table 10.2   Suggested Windows 2000 Components to Install

Component	Comments
Accessories and Utilities	Deselect Communications, Games, and Multimedia. If you need any of these components, they can be added individually after the installation is complete.
	Under Accessories, deselect the Desktop Wallpaper option. A wallpaper background adds unnecessary bandwidth and processing requirements, as the data needs to be transmitted to the client. All other options under can remain selected.
Certificate Services	Deselect.
Cluster Service	Deselect.
Indexing Service	Deselect.
Internet Information Services	Deselect.
Management and Monitoring Tools	Deselect the Connection Management components. Select Network Monitoring. If you don't need SNMP, deselect this option as well.
Message Queuing Services	Deselect.
Networking Services	Deselect. None of the networking services should be run on a Terminal Server.
Other Network File and Print Services	Deselect.
Remote Installation Services	Deselect.
Remote Storage	Deselect.
Script Debugger.	This installs the debugger support for the Windows Script Host (WSH). If you plan to use WSH in your environment, you can select this option.
Terminal Services	Select. This is the service that provides multi-session connectivity.
Terminal Services Licensing	Deselect. (Chapter 12 discusses the creation of a Terminal Services licensing server. You shouldn't install the licensing service on a Terminal Server.)
Windows Media Services	Deselect.

Terminal Services Setup

In the Terminal Services setup dialog box are two options, Remote Administration Mode and Application Server Mode. As discussed in Chapter 2, under Windows 2000 you can configure a server to provide remote administration services. This allows an administrator to connect to a regular Windows 2000 server using an RDP client and then perform remote management tasks as if logged onto the console. This doesn't modify the performance configuration for the server to support application serving. Only two concurrent remote sessions can be connected to the server at a time. To provide the multi-session features, you must select Application Server mode.

Author's Note

Providing remote administration services on a server doesn't require any special Terminal Services licensing. The licensing for the two concurrent connections is included as part of the OS. ◆

Application Compatibility Permissions

The Application Compatibility Permissions dialog box for Terminal Services setup provides two options:

- **Configure permissions compatible with Windows 2000 users.** This option provides for a more secure Terminal Server environment, enforcing more restrictive security on the registry and file system. Depending on the applications that you plan to implement, it may require greater effort to function properly in the environment.

- **Configure permissions compatible with Terminal Server 4.0 users.** This setting configures the server with the same permission configuration found on an NT 4.0 Terminal Server. While this reduces the effort required to get many applications working on TS 2000, *it grants full control to portions of the registry and file system* for regular users and, as a result, introduces potential security concerns.

I highly recommend selecting the Windows 2000 user permissions. This option provides a more secure Terminal Server environment and reduces the time that you must spend enforcing the necessary security yourself. Chapter 19 assumes that you have implemented the Windows 2000 user permissions.

Finishing the Installation

After the Windows 2000 Terminal Services installation is complete, you're ready to perform the rest of the configuration on the server. If you're planning to implement Citrix MetaFrame in your environment, I recommend proceeding to Chapters 11 and 12.

Part 1: Beginning the Setup

The following steps assume that you're booting from the installation disks. To install Windows 2000 Terminal Services, perform the following steps:

1. Place the Windows 2000 Server or Advanced Server Setup Boot Disk into drive A: and start the server. Immediately after the screen turns blue, you'll have the option of pressing F6 if you have any special SCSI or RAID controller drivers that may need to be installed. Don't do this unless your hardware manufacturer has informed you that this is required in order to install Windows 2000. When prompted, insert Setup Disk #2, then #3, and finally #4 when prompted in order to load the core drivers required for Windows 2000 to load.

2. The Windows 2000 Server Welcome to Setup window appears; press Enter to continue the installation.

3. When prompted, insert the Windows 2000 Server CD and press Enter to continue.

4. Next comes the End-User License Agreement. After reviewing it, press the F8 key to continue with the installation if you accept the terms of the agreement.

5. The next screen prompts you to select and configure the system boot partition. You don't need to worry about setting up any non-system partitions (application drives) right now; you can do this by running Computer Management after you've completed the Windows 2000 Terminal Services installation.

   I highly recommend that you install Windows 2000 on a separate partition (or physical disk) from where you'll maintain your installed applications. I've found that this helps in not only managing the deployment and maintenance of applications, but in configuring security on the server.

   When deciding how much space to allocate for the boot partition, make sure that you set aside sufficient space not only for the operating system, but also for application files that must be installed on the system partition.

As discussed in Chapter 7, you should store the pagefile on a separate partition or physical disk instead of on the system partition. Even so, consider allocating sufficient space on the boot partition to accommodate a crash-dump file if one is ever required. This option would normally be enabled only if you were troubleshooting a recurring problem with the assistance of the appropriate vendor's technical support department.

When estimating the space required for the boot partition I normally use this formula:

(850MB + *<physical memory on server>*) * 1.5 = partition size

850MB is a typical estimate for the Windows 2000 operating system.

6. After you have created a system partition of the desired size, highlight it and press Enter. If this is a newly created partition, you need to format it before it can be used. You have two possible file systems: FAT and NTFS. For any Terminal Server drive, you should *always* select NTFS. Notice that for Windows 2000 the default file system is NTFS, while under NT 4.0 it was FAT.

> **Warning**
>
> *Many Windows administrators commonly suggest formatting the system partition as FAT for performance and recovery reasons, because share permissions provide sufficient security across a network to protect these drives from unauthorized access. When implementing Terminal Services, share permissions are inadequate for protecting the file system from regular users, since the users are logged on locally. You should never format any of your Terminal Server drives as FAT.* ◆

Immediately after completing the format, the setup program will copy the necessary files to the drive in order to continue the setup, and then will reboot.

Part 2: The GUI Setup

After the server has restarted, the GUI portion of the installation will begin:

1. After restarting, Setup begins the plug and play detect phase and installs the necessary drivers for your hardware. To ensure that all the components on your server are successfully detected and the proper drivers installed, you should verify that they appear on the Windows 2000 hardware compatibility list. You can check the latest Windows HCL at http://www.microsoft.com/hcl.

After the necessary drivers have been loaded, the Regional Settings dialog box opens. Here you can specify the appropriate settings for your region, such as number, currency, time, and date formats. Press Next to continue.

2. Provide the name and organization information. This is used simply to show who has licensed the software. Press Next to continue.

3. Provide the product key for Windows 2000 Server. This key is usually located on the back of the CD jewel case.

4. The next dialog box prompts you to select the appropriate CAL mode. This is *not* the licensing for Terminal Services client sessions, but the Microsoft CAL. Terminal Services licensing is provided by a license server that doesn't need to be available prior to the installation of Terminal Services, but must be available within 90 days of the install. See Chapter 12 for details on how to configure a Terminal Services License server.

    A Microsoft CAL is required for each computer that you want to access any of the additional services that a Terminal Server can provide, such as RAS or File and Print. While the dialog box provides two options, Per Server and Per Seat, only Per Seat is a valid license option with Terminal Services. For more information on Terminal Server licensing, see the "Terminal Server Licensing Requirements" section of Chapter 2. Select the Per Seat radio button, and then click Next to continue.

5. Next you're prompted to provide both the name of the server and the local administrator's password. Select something that's not easily guessed and, ideally, contains a combination of letters and numbers. If necessary, write down the password and store it in a safe place. Click Next.

6. The Windows 2000 Components dialog box appears next. Here you can select which additional components should be installed along with the base operating system. (Refer to the earlier section "Windows 2000 Components" for a complete list of which options should and should not be included.) After selecting the desired components click Next to continue.

7. Next you're asked to confirm the date, time, and time zone. Enter the appropriate values and then click Next to continue.

8. The next dialog box is for the Terminal Services setup. To provide multi-session support, select Application Server Mode and click Next. For more information on the remote administration mode, see Chapter 2.

9. The Application Compatibility Permissions dialog box for Terminal Services provides two options: configured as permissions compatible with Windows 2000 users, or permissions compatible with Terminal Server 4.0 users.

I recommend selecting the Windows 2000 user permissions. This option provides a more secure Terminal Server environment. The discussion of application integration in Chapter 19 assumes that you have implemented the Windows 2000 user permissions.

> *Tip*
>
> *You can change these permission settings after Terminal Services have been installed by running the Terminal Services Configuration application (under Administrative Tools on the Start menu) and selecting Permission Compatibility under the Server Settings folder.* ♦

10. The network services start, and you're prompted to choose either Typical or Custom network settings. The Typical option assumes that you want to use DHCP for TPC/IP addressing, client for Microsoft networking and file and print sharing. The Custom option gives you complete control over configuring the server's networking. If you want to provide a static IP address you must click the Custom radio button; otherwise, simply choose Typical for now and then click Next.

11. If you selected Custom in the preceding step, the next screen allows you to view and modify the properties for the default network components that will be installed. Highlight Internet Protocol (TCP/IP) and click the Properties button. Enter the necessary TCP/IP address information and then click OK when finished. Leave all other properties the same and click Next to continue.

12. At this point, you must decide whether this computer will participate in a domain or workgroup. Usually I leave it in the workgroup until the installation is complete and then add it into the desired domain.

After you select the domain or workgroup, Setup installs the necessary components and performs the final setup configuration.

Author's Note

I usually recommend taking an image of the server immediately after installation (once you're confident that it's booting properly), so that you'll have a base configuration that you can easily revert to if necessary. In order to image the server, Microsoft requires that you first remove it from the domain. ◆

Before you begin installing applications or allowing users access to your server, some additional configuration and tuning steps are required. Chapter 12 reviews these changes. If you're planning to implement Citrix MetaFrame, see both Chapters 11 and 12.

11

MetaFrame Installation

In this chapter:

- **Before You Begin**
  A few points that you should review prior to your MetaFrame installation.
- **Installing MetaFrame**
  A step-by-step explanation of the MetaFrame installation.
- **Unattended Setup Mode**
  The installation of MetaFrame can be fully automated using an unattended setup file.
- **Uninstalling MetaFrame**
  MetaFrame can be easily uninstalled through the Add/Remove Programs icon in the Control Panel.

Before You Begin

Citrix's setup process for MetaFrame is both quick and straightforward, requiring only one true configuration option during installation that can't be done after the product has been installed. This chapter covers only the installation of MetaFrame. Chapter 12, "Terminal Server Configuration and Tuning," discusses the post-installation configuration specific to MetaFrame that should be performed.

> **Tip**
>
> *The steps for installing MetaFrame 1.8 are identical for both Terminal Server 4.0 and Windows 2000 Terminal Services.* ◆

There are only a few points that you should review prior to performing the MetaFrame installation on your Terminal Server:

- Perform the MetaFrame installation prior to adding any applications or making any other operating system changes. Ideally, MetaFrame should be added immediately after installing Terminal Server and prior to performing any Terminal Server configuration or tuning. One of the options presented during the MetaFrame installation is the ability to reassign the system and application drives from C: and D:—for example, to X: and Y:. Applications installed prior to this change most likely won't function after the drive letters have changed. (I talk more about this later in this chapter.) If MetaFrame requires any particular Windows service pack (which it currently doesn't), you'll need to add the service pack first. Otherwise, you can add any necessary service packs and hotfixes after you complete the MetaFrame installation.

- Although not a requirement, I recommend that you install all the network protocols on the Terminal Server that you plan to use to provide ICA connectivity. For example, if you'll have clients connecting using IPX, you should ensure that the protocol is available on the Terminal Server prior to installing MetaFrame. The MetaFrame setup program automatically detects the existence of these protocols and enables you to create Terminal Server connections during the install. Don't install any protocols if they're not required, because they'll introduce additional load on the Terminal Server. When possible, I recommend using only TCP/IP.

- If Remote Access Services (RAS) is installed on the server, you should remove any modems from the RAS modem pool that you want available for ICA dial-in connections. Modems can be assigned to either RAS or ICA dial-in, but not both. If you're going to use a multiport serial adapter, you should install the necessary drivers prior to installing MetaFrame. If possible, try to split RAS off from the Terminal Server and run it separately. This provides a better use of resources on the Terminal Server.

Installing MetaFrame

To install MetaFrame, perform the following steps:

1. Log on at the server console. Make sure that no users are logged on to your server, and issue the following command from a command prompt:

   ```
   change logon /disable
   ```

This will disable Terminal Server logons for all client sessions (except the local console), ensuring that users won't be able to log on while you're performing the MetaFrame installation. This isn't a mandatory step in the installation, but it's worth doing unless you're 100% sure that no one will be logging on. For a complete description of the change logon command, see Appendix A, "Terminal Server/MetaFrame Command Reference." Once the server reboots at the end of the MetaFrame installation, logons will automatically be re-enabled.

2. Insert the MetaFrame CD into the drive on your server. The Citrix MetaFrame CD-ROM dialog box should appear. Select the MetaFrame Setup icon to begin the installation. The MetaFrame license agreement dialog box will appear. You need to accept the terms of this agreement before you can install MetaFrame. After you click the I Agree option, the MetaFrame Welcome dialog box opens, as shown in Figure 11.1, displaying a brief description of MetaFrame and reminding you to close all other running programs. Click Next to continue. If the CD doesn't autorun, or if you're performing the installation across the net-work, you can begin the installation by running SETUP.EXE, located in the i386 directory on the CD.

Figure 11.1   *The MetaFrame Welcome dialog box.*

3. Click Next in the Setting Up MetaFrame dialog box to begin copying the files and making the necessary system changes.

4. When the file copy has completed, the MetaFrame 1.8 Licensing dialog box opens. The Licensing dialog box provides the opportunity to add any Citrix licenses that you have to your MetaFrame installation. This

includes the MetaFrame base license, any user license packs, or other licenses, such as load balancing or SecureICA. All of these licenses will be in the following form:

CTX-0000-0000-0000-000000

Although you can add licenses here, you don't activate them until after you've completed the installation. I suggest that you wait until after you've completed the installation and then add any licenses that you have, using the Citrix Licensing application. From there you'll be able to both add and activate all of your licenses. Until you've added at least the base license, MetaFrame allows only a single user logon. For a full description of the Citrix Licensing program, see Chapter 3, "Citrix MetaFrame." In Chapter 12, I discuss adding and activating Citrix licenses.

5. Click Next to bring up the Network ICA Connections dialog box (see Figure 11.2). This dialog box allows you to select the network proto-cols on which the setup program will create ICA connections. Because TCP/IP is required for Terminal Server, this protocol is always selected by MetaFrame. It's selected and grayed out in the dialog box. If you have IPX, SPX, or NetBIOS protocols installed, the appropriate check box will be enabled and selected by default; otherwise it will be grayed out. Deselect any protocols that you're not going to use, and then select Next to continue. If you decide later that you want to allow ICA connections for additional protocols, you can do so from within the Terminal Services Manager. As mentioned earlier, you shouldn't be run-ning any protocols on the Terminal Server that aren't required, and if possible you should try to run only TCP/IP.

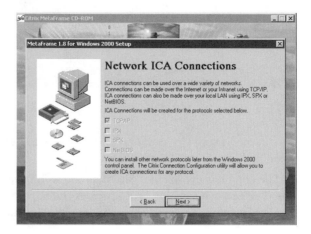

Figure 11.2 *Network ICA connections.*

6. The TAPI Modem Setup dialog box appears next (see Figure 11.3). In this dialog box, you can add and configure one or more modems on your server to be used for asynchronous ICA connections. This is functionally equivalent to double-clicking on the Phone and Modem Options icon in the Control Panel. I discuss remote access connectivity in Chapter 14, "ICA Client Installation and Configuration." If you want to add any modems, click the Add Modems button. Otherwise, click Next. As I suggested at the beginning of this chapter, you should try to run Remote Access Services on a separate server if possible, to maximize resources on the Terminal Server.

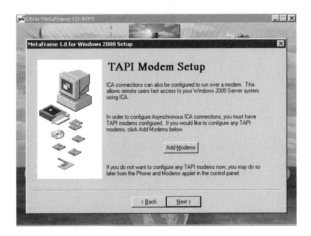

Figure 11.3 *The TAPI Modem Setup dialog box.*

7. If you added any modems in the previous dialog box or you already have one or more TAPI devices installed prior to your MetaFrame install, the next dialog box is Asynchronous ICA Connections. Select any devices that you want to configure for ICA connections, and then select Next.

8. If this is the first time installing MetaFrame on your Terminal Server or your system drive is currently C:\, the next dialog box describes MetaFrame's drive-mapping capabilities, as shown in Figure 11.4.

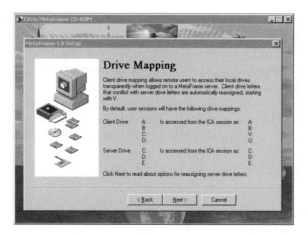

Figure 11.4 *Drive-mapping description.*

MetaFrame drive mapping allows you to configure how drives will appear to users while they're logged onto the server. The following table is an example of how drives are commonly configured and how they would appear during a user's session on the server:

How Drives Are Configured on Their Respective Computers	How Drives Appear Within the MetaFrame Client Session
A:(local floppy drive)	A:
C:(local hard drive)	V:
D:(local hard drive)	U:
E:(local hard drive)	E:
C:(local MetaFrame drive)	C:
D:(local MetaFrame drive)	D:

What this means is that from within a user's MetaFrame session, the C: drive would correspond to the C: drive on the server itself. The user's local C: drive would be available through the drive letter V:.

If a client drive letter doesn't conflict with a drive letter on the MetaFrame server, it will keep the same drive letter, as the E: drive demonstrates in the preceding table. Client drive letters that conflict with server drives are mapped to drive letters starting with V: and working *backward*. The one mapping exception is server floppy drives, which are never available to client sessions.

In the preceding table, the client floppy drive would map to the same drive letter in the MetaFrame session, whereas the client hard drives (C: and D:) would map to V: and U:, respectively. This is because the server drives are also labeled as C: and D:. By reassigning the server drive letters you can avoid this conflict.

The following table demonstrates what happens when the server drives are remapped to higher drive letters. In this example, the primary drive mapping starts at X: on the MetaFrame server.

How Drives Are Configured on Their Respective Computers	How Drives Appear Within the MetaFrame Client Session
A:(local diskette drive)	A:
C:(local hard drive)	C:
D:(local hard drive)	D:
E:(local hard drive)	E:
X:(local MetaFrame drive)	X:
Y:(local MetaFrame drive)	Y:

Tip

Whenever installing MetaFrame, I will always reassign server drive letters, most often starting at X:. This not only helps to avoid conflicts with client drive mappings, but helps to avoid issues with other standard network mappings that may be in use within a company. The exact decision on what werver drive letters to use will depend on the standard letters currently in use in your organization. For example, many companies that use Netware have drive letters, such as Z: already assigned to mandatory network shares, so these would be a poor choice for Terminal Server drives (unless you were not planning to support Netware connectivity from within Terminal Server.)

If drive remapping is not implemented, users will probably try to save information to drive C: (since that's what they've been conditioned to do), but because it's a Terminal Server system drive, it will be locked down in such a way that the user won't have write access, resulting in an "access denied" error. It can also be very difficult to train users to understand that drive C: is actually V: in Terminal Server. ◆

9. After reviewing the explanation of client drive mapping and clicking Next, you will be presented with the Server Drive Reassignment dialog box, as shown in Figure 11.5. At this point, you decide whether you're going to assign the server alternative drive letters. If you are, click on the Remap the Server Drives check box and then select the starting drive letter from the drop-down list. Click Next when you're finished.

> ### Warning
>
> *The server drive-mapping function will most likely fail if you've performed any kind of fault-tolerant configuration in Disk Administrator prior to installing MetaFrame. I recommend that you not use software fault tolerance, but if you must, you should perform the configuration after installing MetaFrame.*
>
> *Be aware that this is a one-way operation. After drive letters have been remapped, you can't map them back without reformatting and reinstalling the OS or manually correcting the registry. The "Administrator's Guide for Citrix MetaFrame Application Server for Windows 2000 Servers" lists the registry keys that are updated, but I don't recommend this, as you'll have no guarantee of stability.*
>
> *And finally, you should not perform the MetaFrame drive remapping if you already have installed any applications on the Terminal Server. The change in drive letters will render these programs inoperable. This applies only to non–operating-system programs such as Office 2000. Operating system applications will be properly updated by MetaFrame to reference the new drive letters.* ◆

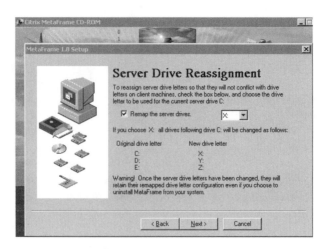

Figure 11.5 *Server drive reassignment.*

10. When the final System Reboot dialog box appears, remove the CD from the drive and then click Finish. The install creates the anonymous user accounts, remaps the drive letters (if you have selected this option), and finally reboots the server to complete the installation of MetaFrame.

Figure 11.6 shows a typical TS 2000 administrator's desktop after installing MetaFrame. The ICA toolbar will automatically be started (for administrators only) and the Program Neighborhood and ICA Activation Wizard icons will have been added to the desktop.

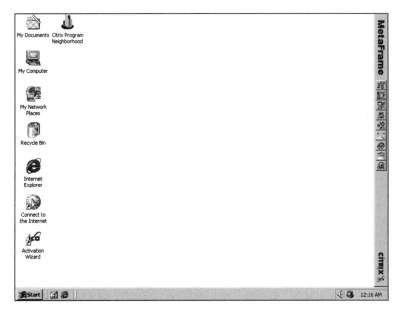

Figure 11.6 *MetaFrame additions to the TS 2000 desktop.*

Now that you have Terminal Server and MetaFrame installed, the next step is to move on to Chapter 12, where I describe the configuration and tuning changes that should be made for both Terminal Server and MetaFrame.

Unattended Setup Mode

Citrix provides the capability to install or upgrade MetaFrame without any input from you. This is known as the *unattended setup mode*. Not only is it helpful in speeding up the installation process, but it can help to ensure that your MetaFrame installations are consistent.

To perform an unattended setup, you need to issue the setup command from a command prompt or from the Run command on the Start menu. The syntax for running in unattended setup mode is as follows:

```
Z:\i386\setup /u[:answerfile]
```

where z: is the location of your MetaFrame install files and *answerfile* is the name of the optional answer file that you have created. A typical answer file would look like this:

```
[MetaFrame License Agreement]
AcceptLicense=Yes
[License Serial Numbers]
CTX-XXXX-XXXX-XXXX-XXXXXX=
[ICA Network Protocols]
TCP=Yes
IPX=No
SPX=No
NETBIOS=No
[Drive Reassignment]
ReassignDriveLetters=Yes
NewDriveLetter=X
[Options]
RebootOnFinish=Yes
```

As you can see, the answer file is a plain text file that uses an INI file format structure. Each of the keys has the following function:

- **MetaFrame License Agreement.** If you accept the terms of the end-user license agreement, set the value AcceptLicense to Yes. If not, you'll be prompted with the acceptance question during the installation. The default value is No.

- **License Serial Numbers.** This key contains a list of serial number values, which are followed by the equal (=) sign. The serial numbers are assigned in the order in which they're listed, so you must ensure that you have the base license listed first. As mentioned earlier, the licenses are only added to the server during this phase; they're not activated. That must be done separately, as described in Chapter 12.

- **ICA Network Protocols.** This key allows you to specify which ICA connections are created for which protocols. The four options are TCP, IPX, SPX, and NetBIOS. You specify which ones to install by including the value followed by either Yes or No. If you specify Yes for a network protocol that's not installed on the Terminal Server, the installation simply ignores it. The default value is Yes for all protocols.

- **Drive Reassignment.** This key allows you to specify whether drives will be reassigned or not (Yes or No), and if so, what the starting drive letter will be. When specifying the starting drive letter, *do not* include the colon (:). For example, you would specify the starting drive X: as follows:

```
[Drive Reassignment]
ReassignDriveLetters=Yes
NewDriveLetter=X
```

The default value is `ReassignDriveLetter=No`.

- **Options.** The `Options` key handles additional actions that are performed during an unattended install. Currently the only supported action is to automatically restart the server after MetaFrame has been installed. The default value is `Yes`.

As with normal INI files, the answer file is completely non–case sensitive. If you don't include an answer file when using the `/u` parameter, the MetaFrame installation will use the default answers just described.

> **Tip**
>
> *A sample unattended setup file can be found in the i386 directory on the MetaFrame CD. The file is called UNATTEND.TXT.* ◆

Uninstalling MetaFrame

It's worth noting that you can uninstall MetaFrame at any time. This will remove *all* ICA functionality from the system, including any installed licenses or published-application information. If you decide to reinstall MetaFrame over an existing installation, all published-application information will be retained, but any existing licenses (excluding Resource Management Services or Installation Management Services) will be lost.

To remove MetaFrame, follow these steps:

1. Log on at the console, ensuring that there are no users logged onto the server. If necessary, issue the `change logon /disable` command to prevent users from logging on while you uninstall the software.

2. Run Add/Remove Programs from the Control Panel.

3. Select MetaFrame from the list and click the Add/Remove button.

4. The Uninstall Wizard opens (see Figure 11.7). Follow the instructions presented in each of the dialog boxes to complete the uninstall.

If for some reason MetaFrame doesn't appear in the Add/Remove Programs list, you can also uninstall by issuing the `RMVICA` command from a command prompt.

Figure 11.7 *Uninstalling MetaFrame.*

Author's Note

Uninstalling MetaFrame will not revert any converted drives back to their original drive letters. If you have reassigned the server drives starting at X:, they'll remain that way even after MetaFrame has been removed. ◆

Terminal Server Configuration and Tuning

In this chapter:

- **Before you begin**
  A few points that you should review prior to beginning to configure your Terminal Server.

- **Service Packs and Hotfixes**
  An inevitable part of your Terminal Server and MetaFrame administration will be the testing and implementing of service packs and hotfixes.

- **Terminal Server Licensing Configuration**
  Both Windows 2000 and MetaFrame require some license management prior to their production implementation.

- **Terminal Server Stability and Availability**
  Changes can be made to a Terminal Server that can help to provide improved stability and availability.

- **Terminal Server Performance Tuning**
  After the operating system installation, a number of changes can be made to Terminal Server to help boost its overall performance.

- **Terminal Server Security Configuration**
  Now that you have completed the basic performance tuning and server configuration, the next step is to apply the basic Terminal Server security to your system.

- **Connection Configuration**
  With the necessary security groups in place, you can now configure the desired RDP or ICA connections on your server.

- **Additional MetaFrame Configuration Options**
  If You're running MetaFrame on Terminal Server, you may want to adjust a few final server settings, depending on your configuration.

- **Printer Drivers**

  When configuring Terminal Server, one of the areas frequently over-looked is the installation of the printer drivers. This is necessary on a Terminal Server because regular users don't have sufficient privileges to install their own drivers.

Before You Begin

> **Tip**
>
> *If you're going to be implementing MetaFrame and haven't already done so, I highly recommend that you install MetaFrame before doing any configuration or performance security tuning. See Chapter 11, "MetaFrame Installation," for more information on how this is done.* ◆

In this chapter, I review many of the Terminal Server and MetaFrame changes that need to be implemented *prior* to installing any applications or allowing any end-user access to the system. It has always been my prefer-ence to implement these changes first, perform the necessary testing to ensure stability, and then move on to add the required applications. I have found that issues are much easier to troubleshoot when following this approach. I would discourage the testing of applications on a completely unsecured system with the intent of adding security later. In almost every situation, this will cause the application to fail, resulting in a hurried mission to "unsecure" whatever components are required in order to get the program to function again.

Whenever possible, you should perform the core server configuration first, and then work to configure your applications to fit this environment—not the other way around. This helps to ensure a clear understanding not only of the server, but of the applications in your environment.

Chapter 19, "Application Integration," talks specifically about the instal-lation and tuning of applications within Terminal Server.

Preventing Client Connections

Until you're ready to allow user connections to your Terminal Server, you need to restrict client connections. There are easy ways to do this:

- If you'll be performing all of your configuration directly from the server's console, you can disable RDP/ICA connections using the Terminal Server Connection Configuration utility on TSE 4.0, or Terminal Services Configuration on TS 2000. In either case, simply right-click the protocol and select Disable. Anyone who attempts to connect to the server will receive an error message. When RDP connec-tions are disabled, the message is similar to Figure 12.1. ICA's message simply states that the server is not accepting connections.

Tip

Disabling logons will not disconnect or log out any users who are currently on the system. ◆

Figure 12.1   *User message when RDP connections are disabled.*

- If you want to perform at least some of your server configuration through a client connection, the first option is not feasible. The alternative is to simply restrict access to only the local Administrators group and SYSTEM. For TSE 4.0, highlight the connection, right-click, and select Permissions. Now remove Users, Guests, and the Everyone group, leaving only Administrators and SYSTEM. Under TS 2000, right-click the connection and select Properties; then select the Permissions tab. Highlight Users and Guests and click Remove, leaving only Administrators and SYSTEM, as shown in Figure 12.2. *Be sure to configure security for all the available display protocols.* I'll look specifically at configuring Terminal Server security, including ICA and RDP connections, later in this chapter.

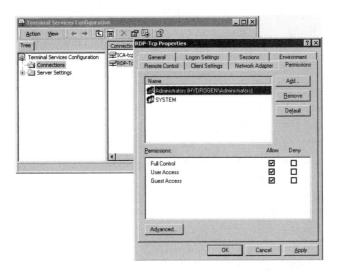

Figure 12.2   *Restricting connection access to administrators only.*

Domain Membership

Although not a requirement, it's usually easier to perform the necessary server configuration if the Terminal Server is a member of the appropriate Windows domain. This can make it easier to access certain network resources for any additional tools or files that may be required, such as service packs or hotfixes. It will also allow you to configure the necessary domain security access to the Terminal Server.

Performing Systematic Changes

One of the most important things that you should remember when configuring your server is to perform systematic changes. Always know what changes are being made and why. You should always document the changes made to ensure that not only you, but anyone else who becomes involved, knows what has been done. This point cannot be stressed too much. For more information on change management, please see Chapter 9, "Software Planning."

I recommend that you review this entire chapter before you begin to make any changes. This will give you an idea as to what changes can be done and allow you to decide what changes you will make and when. You shouldn't simply proceed from the beginning of the chapter to the end, applying every change listed. Many changes need only be made in certain situations, and some only if certain issues arise when you begin to test your implementation.

Service Packs and Hotfixes

An inevitable part of your Terminal Server and MetaFrame administration will be the testing and implementing of service packs (SPs) and hotfixes (HFs) from both Microsoft and Citrix. I encourage you to regularly check the Web sites of both companies for the latest information on new SPs and HFs. This is particularly important with Citrix, which issues regular updates that, in many cases, can resolve very specific problems that arise from particular Citrix implementations. Both Citrix and Microsoft occasionally introduce new features with a hotfix or service pack, so you need to be aware of hotfixes as well.

Information on Citrix hotfixes is available under both Knowledge Base and FTP links. Follow the Support link from the Citrix home page at http://www.citrix.com.

For information on service packs for Terminal Server, see the Terminal Server home page at http://www.microsoft.com/ntserver/terminalserver.

When installing hotfixes and service packs on a new Terminal Server, I typically apply all Windows updates first, and then apply the necessary MetaFrame updates.

On an existing Terminal Server, pay particular attention when applying a new Microsoft update, as it may have an impact on any existing MetaFrame hotfixes on the system. Always apply a new service pack or hotfix to a test server prior to performing any updates on a production system.

Warning

Don't apply a service pack or hotfix simply because it's available. Always take the time to review problems it corrects or features it introduces, and decide whether it is a necessary requirement for your environment. Not all fixes—particularly those from Citrix—are required for your server to function properly. ◆

Author's Note

Always standardize your service packs and hotfixes across all your Terminal Servers. Inconsistencies can lead to strange problems in communication between servers, particularly with Citrix hotfixes that modify the behavior of the ICA browser service. ◆

Terminal Server 4.0

At the time of this writing, the current service pack (SP) for TSE 4.0 is SP5. I recommend installing this service pack because it fixes a number of stability issues and makes a change to how client connections are initiated, helping to prevent situations in which users cannot connect to a server under heavy user logon scenarios.

Windows 2000

There are currently no service packs available for TS 2000, but at least one update is available on the Microsoft site.

MetaFrame

At the time of this writing, there are no hotfixes available for MetaFrame 1.8 for TS 2000, but Service Pack 1 exists for MetaFrame 1.8 for TSE 4.0.

Citrix hotfixes are managed using the HOTFIX command. Each hotfix includes a README file containing complete instructions on how to apply the hotfix.

Determining Hotfix and Service Pack Versions

You can determine your current service pack and hotfix levels as follows:

- **Terminal Server:** Select Run from the Start menu and enter WINVER.EXE. This will open the About Windows dialog box, which lists the current Windows Service Pack level (if any). The most reliable way to determine which Microsoft hotfixes have been installed on a Terminal Server is to inspect the following registry key:

  ```
  HKLM\Software\Microsoft\Windows NT\CurrentVersion\HotFix
  ```

  For each hotfix, you'll see the registry key corresponding to the Knowledge Base article number; for example, Q253934. To determine whether the hotfix is installed, click it and inspect the value called Installed. If the value is 0x1, the hotfix has been applied to the server. If you have MetaFrame installed, you can see the Microsoft hotfixes from within Citrix Server Administration by clicking the server and then selecting the Information tab as shown in Figure 12.3. The Microsoft hotfixes appear as the Knowledge Base Q hotfix names.

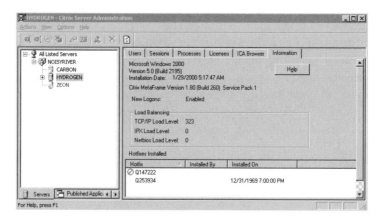

Figure 12.3   *Viewing hotfix information within Citrix Server Administration.*

- **MetaFrame:** As I have already discussed, if you have MetaFrame installed, you can view both service packs and hotfixes through the Citrix Server Administration. If you have any MetaFrame hotfixes or service packs on your system, you can also use the command-line tool HOTFIX. Typing HOTFIX from a command prompt displays information similar to that shown in Figure 12.4.

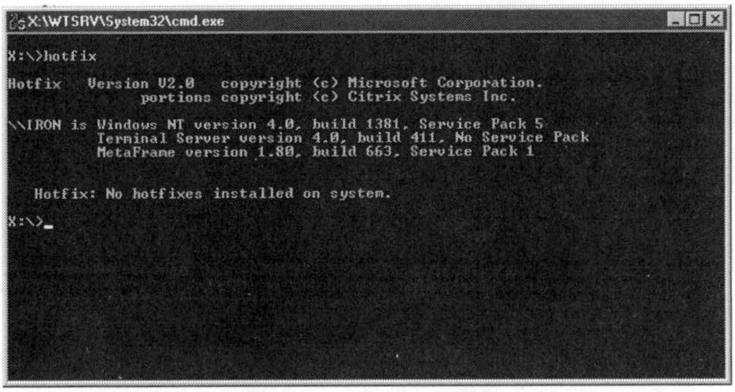

Figure 12.4   *The Citrix HOTFIX command.*

Terminal Server Licensing Configuration

Both Windows 2000 and MetaFrame require some license management prior to production implementation. Fortunately, both also allow a grace period in which the Terminal Server can be tested and configured before the license must be activated. I highly recommend that you take advantage of this grace period to build and test your Terminal Server prior to activating any licenses (or bringing license servers online), since it's very likely that you'll need to rebuild your server prior to implementation.

MetaFrame requires an actual activation process that's discussed in Chapter 3, "Citrix MetaFrame" while Windows 2000 Terminal Services requires the implementation of a Terminal Services Licensing server, which provides licenses to Terminal Server clients on demand. Terminal Server 4.0 has no license-enforcement mechanism—only a license-reporting service. Chapter 2, "Microsoft Windows Terminal Server" also discusses the licensing requirements for Terminal Server.

Windows 2000 Terminal Services Licensing

The type of licensing server that must be implemented with Windows 2000 depends on the Windows domain implementation. In a Windows NT domain, with only member Windows 2000 servers, the *Terminal Services Licensing (TSL)* service can reside on any Windows 2000 server. I advise that you not run this service on a Terminal Server because of the additional server load it introduces. If you're implementing TS 2000 in a Windows 2000 domain, you must run TSL on a Windows 2000 domain controller.

You install TSL as follows:

1. Open Add/Remove Programs from within the Control Panel.

2. Click the Add/Remove Windows Components button.

3. Scroll down to the bottom of the list box and select Terminal Services Licensing (see Figure 12.5). Click Next to continue.

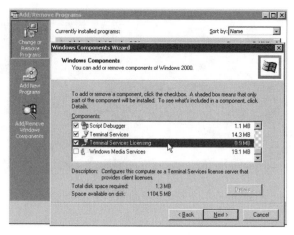

Figure 12.5 *Installing the Terminal Services Licensing component.*

4. If you have Terminal Services installed on the server in either *application server* mode or *remote administration* mode, the Terminal Services setup dialog box appears. Make sure that the correct mode is selected and click Next to continue.

5. The Terminal Services Licensing Setup dialog box appears next (see Figure 12.6). Here you have the option of configuring your license server to service either the entire enterprise or a single domain or workgroup. In an NT 4.0 domain, you must select the domain/workgroup option. If a license server is configured to service a domain, it can only service Terminal Servers within the same domain. Under most circumstances, you'll select the domain/workgroup option unless you have a large number of Windows 2000 domains. (See Chapter 8, "Server Management Planning," for more information on planning your licensing server configuration.)

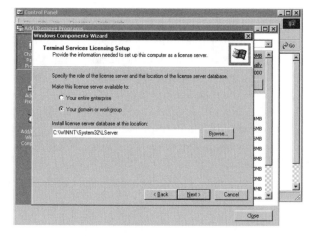

Figure 12.6 *Installing the Terminal Services Licensing component.*

6. After you have decided on the scope of the license server, specify where you will maintain the license database. The necessary licensing service files are copied to the server, and the installation will complete. The licensing service becomes available immediately; you do *not* need to reboot the server.

Activation

After installing TSL, you need to activate it through Microsoft before it can service licenses. The licensing server is activated using the Terminal Services Licensing application, located under Administrative Tools on the Start menu.

Once started, the tool queries for all available license servers and lists those that it has found. The status of each server is listed (activated or not). If you click a server, the right pane displays which licenses exist, which are available, and how many are in use.

To activate a server, simply right-click the server name and select Activate Server. The Licensing Wizard will guide you through the activation process. You can activate the server through a number of methods: using a direct Internet connection, through the Microsoft activate site on the Web at https://activate.microsoft.com, by fax, or by telephone. The Internet and Web activation methods require the least amount of time and provide immediate access to the activation code.

After you provide Microsoft with the necessary information, including the product ID for your Windows 2000 server, you'll receive a license server ID. Figure 12.7 shows the screen where you enter this ID after you have completed the activation process on the Microsoft Web site.

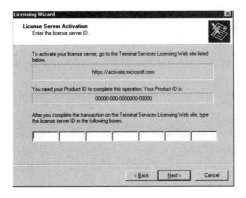

Figure 12.7   *Activating the Terminal Services Licensing server.*

After activating the Terminal Services License server, you're ready to install the client license pack. License packs contain the actual licenses that are issued to Terminal Services clients that connect to Terminal Servers.

Terminal Server Client License Packs

You install client licenses on a license server by right-clicking the server name and selecting Install Licenses. License installation is very similar to the server activation. With each client license pack comes a license code that's sent to Microsoft, and in return you receive an activation code that you enter on the license server to add those licenses. For more information on Terminal Server licensing, see Chapter 2.

> **Author's Note**
>
> *License activation codes are only valid on the license server that was used to register them with Microsoft. If you have multiple license servers, you need to activate your licenses using the appropriate server activation code for the corresponding server.* ◆

MetaFrame License Installation and Activation

Just as with Terminal Server licensing, Citrix provides a grace period before licenses must be activated with Citrix. Even with the grace period, however, most Citrix products require that the licenses be *installed* before the Citrix feature is accessible. A good example of this principle is Citrix Load Balancing (CLB), which has no installable component, but simply requires the installation of the CLB license for it to become available. Usually within 30 days of installing the license you must activate it, or it will cease to function. All Citrix user licenses must also be installed before they are usable.

All Citrix licensing is managed through the Citrix Licensing application located under MetaFrame Tools on the Start menu. This program lists all the installed licenses, the license numbers, activation status, and the user license count (when appropriate). Figure 12.8 shows Citrix Licensing with a number of installed licenses. Notice that none of them are yet activated.

> **Author's Note**
>
> *Until you've installed the base licenses for MetaFrame, whenever an administrator logs onto the server he or she will receive a message stating that the server is operating in single-user mode because no licenses have been installed. After licenses are installed, the administrator will receive a message stating how much time remains until the licenses expire unless activated.* ◆

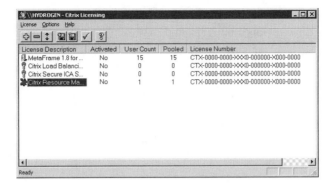

Figure 12.8   *Installed Citrix licenses.*

Installing Citrix Licenses

Installing a Citrix license is a straightforward process:

1. From within Citrix Licensing, select Add from the License menu.

2. Enter the serial number for the license you're adding. The serial number is either located on the CD-ROM jewel case or on a license card, and usually has the format XXX-HHH-HHHH-HHHH-HHHHHH, where X is a letter and H is a hexadecimal number.

After adding the serial number, you'll receive a message similar to the one shown in Figure 12.9.

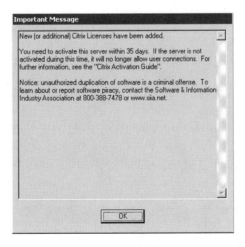

Figure 12.9   *License installation message.*

The license is added to Citrix Licensing. Appended to the end of your serial number is an eight-digit hexadecimal number (known as the *machine* or *server code*) that forms the complete license number submitted to Citrix during the activation phase. This suffix is generated uniquely every time a license is installed, even if the same license is reinstalled on the same server.

Warning

If you remove a license and later reinstall it, you have to submit the newly generated machine code to Citrix to receive a new server activation code. A previous activation code won't work if the license was reinstalled.. ◆

Unlike MetaFrame and WinFrame (1.7 and 1.8), which use paper-based licenses, WinFrame 1.6 maintained all of its licensing information on 3$1/2$-inch floppy disks. The Citrix Licensing tool allows the conversion of disk-based licenses to paper-based licenses. This action is irreversible, and the licenses can't be placed back onto the floppy disk.

To add a disk-based license, insert the floppy disk, select the Add from Disk option from the License menu, and enter the drive letter. If a Citrix license exists on the floppy disk, the license will be converted to a paper license and added to the list in the Citrix Licensing program with its own eight-digit prefix appended to the end. Once added, it's activated in the same way as a regular Citrix license.

Author's Note

I highly recommend that you not activate any licenses until you have your base Terminal Server configuration complete. You should use at least some of the grace period to ensure that you have everything configured the way you want. During the grace period, the Citrix software will function exactly as it would if it were activated. ◆

Activating Citrix Licenses

Citrix licenses are activated through Citrix's online Product Activation System, accessible on the Internet through a Web browser or through the Activation Wizard. The secure Web site is accessed through `http://www.citrix.com/activate`.

Author's Note

The TSE 4.0 Activation Wizard also has the option to connect to a Citrix license activation server via dial-up or through an ICA connection over the Internet. These methods are no longer supported; although they will connect you to a server, you'll receive a message that the activation system has been disabled and be directed instead to activate using the Web site. ◆

The online system maintains a history of all your previously activated licenses and includes an option to reactivate these licenses if necessary. Only the serial numbers of the licenses are maintained, not the corresponding machine code.

Terminal Server Stability and Availability

One of the first things you'll want to do after applying the necessary service packs and hotfixes is review and perform a few changes to your Terminal Server to help improve stability and availability. A number of these changes have to do with disabling a certain default behavior of Windows that's detrimental to the overall performance of a Terminal Server.

Configure the Pagefile

If you haven't already done so, you should now configure the pagefile as desired for your Terminal Server. As discussed in Chapter 10, "Terminal Server Installation," you will normally want to configure your pagefile to exist on a separate volume (or drive) from your system and application volumes. This will help to prevent pagefile fragmentation and improve performance.

After installing Terminal Server, the approximate default pagefile size, depending on the version, is as follows:

Operating System	Initial Size (MB)	Maximum Size (MB)
Windows 2000 TS	$1^1/2 \times$ RAM	$3 \times$ RAM
Windows 4.0 TSE	$2^1/2 \times$ RAM	$3^1/2 \times$ RAM

The pagefile configuration screen is identical for both versions of Terminal Server, although they are accessed in a slightly different way:

- On a TS 2000 server, open the System applet in the Control Panel, select the Advanced tab, and then click the Performance Options button. Now click the Change button for Virtual Memory.

- On a TSE 4.0 server, open the System applet in the Control Panel, click the Performance tab, and then click the Change button for Virtual Memory.

A dialog box opens in which you can modify the pagefile information for the server (see Figure 12.10). Select the volume where you will place the pagefile and enter the initial and maximum sizes. (These should be the same.) Now select the system volume and set the pagefile to zero. A message warns you that debug information can't be created if a STOP error occurs. Click OK and the operation will complete. Click OK when you're finished.

You must reboot the server for the changes to take effect.

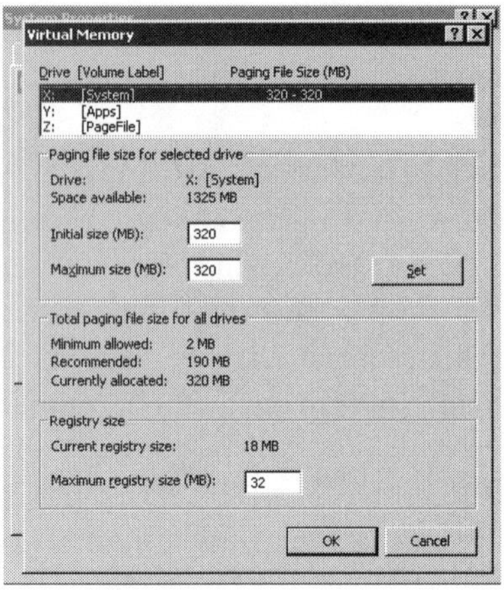

Figure 12.10   *Windows 2000 Virtual Memory dialog box.*

Increase the Registry Size

A critical change that you *will* need to make is to increase your server's *registry size limit* (*RSL*). The number of concurrent users that you expect to have on the server will dictate how large you must set the registry size. Typically each user hive loaded in the registry takes 400–600KB, but can be as high as 2–3MB if per-user file associations have been enabled on a TSE 4.0 Server. See the PERUSER command in Appndix A, "Terminal Server/MetaFrame Command Reference" for complete information on this option. Based on this average, you can determine the registry size using the following calculation:

600KB × (number of users) = maximum registry size

For example, if you expect to have 120 concurrent users on the server, you calculate the registry size as follows:

600KB × 120 = 72000KB = 72MB (approx.)

Table 12.1 lists the maximum paged pool size based on the Terminal Server version and the corresponding maximum possible registry size. As the table shows, 153.6MB is the upper limit on the registry size on a TSE 4.0 server. Based on the assumption of 400–600KB per user, this would limit a TSE 4.0 server to a maximum number of concurrent users somewhere between 200 and 300, taking into consideration that other system information must also be maintained in the registry in addition to user profiles. The Microsoft document "Windows 2000 Terminal Services Capacity and Scaling" provides an example where a limit of 210 users was encountered due to the page pool size limitation. See the following address:

```
www.microsoft.com/windows2000/library/technologies/terminal/tscaling.asp
```

Table 12.1   Maximum Registry Size by Terminal Server Version

Terminal Server Version	Maximum Paged Pool Size	Maximum Registry Size Limit
NT 4.0	192MB	153.6MB
Windows 2000	370–400MB	296–320MB

If you attempt to set the RSL to greater than 80% of the current paged pool size on the server, you'll receive a message similar to the one shown in Figure 12.11. Clicking OK causes Windows to do two things:

- Increase the maximum size of your pagefile as required.
- Increase the paged pool size (up to the maximum listed in Table 12.1) so that it is 20% greater than the RSL value you have specified. This paged pool size is then hard-coded into the registry. Once this value is hard-coded, Windows no longer dynamically adjusts the paged pool size based on the physical memory in the system.

If you attempt to set the RSL greater than the maximum value listed in Table 12.1, Windows simply uses the listed maximum.

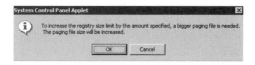

Figure 12.11   *Message displayed when attempting to set the RSL greater than 80%.*

The registry size is configured on both TSE 4.0 and TS 2000 in the same location as their respective pagefiles are set (refer to Figure 12.10).

> ### Tip
>
> *One of the problems that you can encounter on a Terminal Server is registry file fragmentation as a result of users continuously logging on and off. This can result in degraded system performance and an artificially inflated registry size.*
>
> *To ensure optimal performance, institute an automated process that defragments the registry. While Windows provides no built-in mechanism for "compacting" the registry, a couple of solutions are available.*
>
> *The first is to use the REGBACK and REGREST utilities from the Windows Resource Kit as follows:*
>
> ```
> regback x:\%systemroot%\RegBack
> regrest x:\%systemroot%\RegBack x:\%systemroot%\RegBack\old
> ```
>
> *The RegBack and RegBack\old directories must exist prior to running these programs. After running these, reboot the server. As part of the backup process, REGBACK optimizes the size of the backed-up registry keys, in effect "compacting" them. REGREST simply copies the compacted files over top of the original fragmented files during bootup.*
>
> *The second option is to use the PageDefrag utility from the SysInternals Web site (www.SysInternals.com). This tool allows you to view the current state of fragmentation in both the registry and pagefile and provides the option of automatically scheduling a defragmentation of both during bootup. Currently PageDefrag is only documented as being supported on NT 4.0. This is an excellent tool, even if it's used for nothing other than to determine the current state of fragmentation on the pagefile and registry.* ◆

Disable Dr Watson

Very few people have not encountered the good doctor at least once during their use of Windows. Dr Watson is the default application debugger in Windows that's launched to handle all unhandled application errors. Most often, these are memory exception errors that occur when an application attempts to access a memory location that hasn't been allocated for it by the operating system.

When the exception is raised, Windows automatically starts Dr Watson to gather information about the application error. This usually involves writing a crash dump file and a log file containing information such as the application's stack and symbol table contents. The current options for Dr Watson on your Terminal Server can be viewed anytime by running DRWTSN32.EXE from a command prompt. The default configuration for Dr Watson is the same in TSE 4.0 and TS 2000, with the exception that TS 2000 doesn't turn on the visual notification option. The options managed by this application are stored in this registry key:

```
\\HKEY_LOCAL_MACHINE\Software\Microsoft\Dr Watson
```

Note that this key doesn't exist until the first time you actually run DRWTSN32.EXE.

Unless you're debugging a recurring application problem, I suggest completely disabling the use of Dr Watson. Windows looks in the following registry location to determine what debugger it should run:

```
HKEY_LOCAL_MACHINE\Software\Microsoft\Windows NT\CurrentVersion\AeDebug
```

The particular value in question is Debugger. Windows looks here for a valid debugger to run. After a clean Windows installation, the value usually contains the following text:

```
drwtsn32 -p %ld -e %ld -g
```

To disable Dr Watson, simply delete this registry key. You can also delete the Dr Watson key mentioned earlier, which is located under this key:

```
\\HKEY_LOCAL_MACHINE\Software\Microsoft\DrWatson
```

Tip

If you ever want to restore the Dr Watson registry values, simply run DRWTSN32 –I from a command prompt.

By default, when the registry values are created, Dr Watson will default to writing crash dump and log file information to the %WINDIR% location. If you're debugging a user's problem, you'll want to ensure that these entries are pointed to a location where the user will have write access. You can either set this manually by running DRWTSN32 or you can run the Dr Watson application-compatibility script. This will redirect these dump files to the user's root directory. For more information on the root directory and application compatibility scripts, please see Chapter 19 ◆

Suppress Hard Error Messages

Until the release of Service Pack 5 for TSE 4.0, attempting to reset a disconnected session (ICA or RDP) containing a hard error message dialog box awaiting a user response would result in the reset failing and the connection going into a "down" state (visible from within Terminal Server Administration) or hanging until the server was rebooted. While "down," the session and its connection are completely inaccessible.

This was a problem, particularly in environments where the connections were configured to automatically reset disconnected sessions after a set period of idle time. If a session contained one of these hard errors, it would not reset cleanly and would end up in the "down" state. The result was a situation in which a server would quickly develop a large number of downed connections.

Author's Note

I encountered this exact problem at one client sight. Users were periodically receiving two different types of error messages as a result of two applications (one 16-bit, the other 32-bit). One was a Dr Watson error (with a memory dump), and the other was an invalid path specification. Many users reacted to these messages, particularly the Dr Watson, since it appeared to be frozen while it wrote the log, by disconnecting their sessions and then immediately logging back in. The server had been configured to immediately reset disconnected sessions, resulting in the session going "down." User education in combination with removing Dr Watson and implementing this fix helped to eliminate the problem. ◆

As I mentioned earlier, this problem is corrected in Service Pack 5 for TSE 4.0, and doesn't occur in TS 2000. In the past, I usually modified this option once the server was ready to enter the final testing and piloting stage. All hard errors would be written to the system log, so if you had implemented a management system you could monitor these logs for particular errors.

I wouldn't recommend doing this prior to installing applications, as it may prevent immediate visual notification of application problems from occurring, and make problem resolution more difficult.

To modify Terminal Server's displaying of hard errors, you need to modify the ErrorMode value in this registry key:

```
HKEY_LOCAL_MACHINE\SYSTEM\CurrentControlSet\Control\Windows
```

The three possible values for ErrorMode are 0, 1, and 2. 0 is the default and displays all error messages. 1 suppresses only system errors, but displays all application-generated errors. 2 suppresses all hard errors, writing them only to the system event log.

Tip

For specific information on the problem that was fixed in TSE 4.0 with SP5, see the Microsoft Knowledge Base article Q229012, "Disconnected Winstation Sessions that Generate a 'Hard Error' Dialog Box Cannot be Reset." ◆

Configure the Server Recovery Options

One important part of availability is configuring the server to automatically recover in the event that the system halts with a *STOP* error, also known as the infamous *Blue Screen of Death (BSOD)*. If the server isn't configured to recover, it may remain inaccessible for an extended period of time, particularly in a large server farm where additional server monitoring hasn't been implemented.

You should verify that the server is configured to automatically recover from a STOP error. This is done from within the System applet of Control Panel. On TSE 4.0 it's on the Startup/Shutdown tab, and on TS 2000 it's on the Startup and Recovery option of the Advanced tab. Figure 12.12 shows the default recovery options that I recommend.

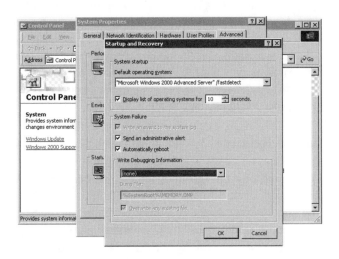

Figure 12.12   *Server recovery options.*

An event should always be written to the system log. If you're using a separate monitoring tool for the server, you can also disable the Send an Administrative Alert option. I recommend that the debug file not be written under normal circumstances. If you encounter a problem with recurring BSODs, you can enable this option to capture the necessary information. Figure 12.13 shows a sample event for a system STOP.

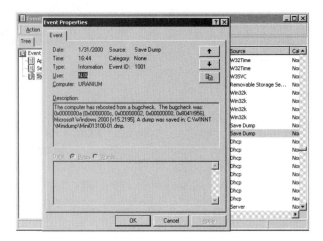

Figure 12.13   *A STOP error logged in the system log.*

Tip

Although you can change the location of the dump file, Terminal Server will always write the debug information to the %systemroot% partition first, and then move it to the location that you have specified. This is because Terminal Server writes the dump to a pagefile on the system partition first. If you want to enable the full memory dump, you must have sufficient space on your system partition to accommodate the creation of a pagefile equal to the amount of physical memory on your server plus one to two megabytes. ◆

Set Up Scheduled Reboots

As discussed in Chapter 8, it's very likely that you'll need to configure the automatic rebooting of your Terminal Servers. Problems such as memory leaks can have a significant impact on the availability of a Terminal Server as they slowly (or quickly, as the case may be) consume the available resources, eventually resulting in "low on virtual memory" errors and system crashes. The only reliable way to ensure that issues like this won't affect your server environment is to establish a server reboot schedule. The frequency and sophistication of this schedule depends on the applications in your environment and the system behavior that you observe during testing and piloting.

Author's Note

I have frequently worked on projects where a nightly reboot was necessary to ensure that application issues didn't slowly grow to the point of affecting the system performance. In all of these situations, a large number of applications were being deployed, and many of them were custom-built apps that performed poor memory management. I recommend that some form of reboot schedule be implemented for any Terminal Server project. The stability of the environment will dictate whether it will be nightly, weekly, or even monthly. ◆

Conveniently, Terminal Server comes with a command-line tool called TSSHUTDN on TS 2000 and SHUTDOWN on TSE 4.0. This command can be used in conjunction with the Scheduler Service and the AT command to schedule an automatic shutdown and restart of your Terminal Servers. The full syntax of the TSSHUTDN/SHUTDOWN commands is described in Appendix A, and is the same for both Terminal Server and MetaFrame. The simplest implementation is as follows:

```
TSSHUTDN /reboot
```

This command shuts down and restarts the Terminal Server 60 seconds after being executed. Immediately after starting, it issues a message to all users on the Terminal Server, stating that the system will restart in 60 seconds. It sends another message at the 30–second mark and then restarts the server. For example, to schedule a Terminal Server to automatically reboot at 11 p.m. every night with a two minute wait period, you could issue the following AT command:

```
at 23:00 /every:M,T,W,Th,F,S,Su "tsshutdn 120 /reboot"
```

Normally, I recommend that the reboot scheduling not be implemented until you're ready to perform some preliminary testing with applications on your Terminal Server. Then, with the assistance of some server-monitoring tool, you can determine the requirements for reboot scheduling. If the applications are well-behaved, it's possible that you may only need to perform reboots once every couple of weeks.

The simplest way to determine the state of the system is to see what the pagefile usage and process counts are after users have logged off the system. If you see a steady increase in pagefile usage that doesn't drop off when users have logged out, or you see hung processes or sessions, you need to look for reboots to clear these up.

Disable MetaFrame Client Auto-Updating

One useful feature of MetaFrame is the ability to automatically update an ICA client to the latest version from a client database. Unfortunately, until you've had a chance to properly configure the client for your environment, it can introduce potential problems, particularly if people connect to the server and select the option to update their ICA client when they lack the necessary local security privileges to complete the action successfully. Until you're ready to implement this feature, I recommend that you turn off the auto-update functionality. Chapter 14, "ICA Client Installation and Configuration," explains how to configure this client auto-update functionality.

The auto-update feature is managed through the ICA Client Update Configuration utility located under MetaFrame Tools on the Start menu. To disable auto-updating, select the Properties option from the Database menu and deselect the Enabled check box (see Figure 12.14). This will turn off updating from the listed client database.

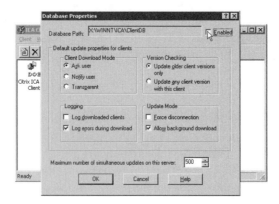

Figure 12.14   *Disabling ICA client auto-updating.*

Turn Off Network Interface Card Auto-Detect

Another recommended change is to verify that the network interface card (NIC) on the server has been configured specifically for the appropriate speed and duplex as opposed to having it set to auto-detect these features. Most network administrators agree that this is preferred, particularly in a switched environment.

The exact interface for making this change depends on the NIC manufacturer, but in general the change is made as follows:

- On a TS 2000 server, select Network and Dial-Up Connections from the Control Panel; then double-click your Local Area Connection. Next, click the Properties button. The top portion of the dialog box shows the NIC information along with a Configure button. Clicking this button brings up the properties for the NIC. Figure 12.15 shows an example of the properties for an Intel Pro/100B card. The property changes you make here take effect immediately and don't require a reboot.

- On a TSE 4.0 server, open the Network applet in the Control Panel and then select the Adapters tab. Highlight the NIC and click the Properties button. You should then be able to configure network speed and duplex mode. You'll need to reboot the server before this change will take effect.

Warning

Make sure that you configure the NIC to match the specifications of the network. Improperly configuring the NIC can result in severe network performance degradation. ◆

Figure 12.15   *Configuration settings for the Intel Pro/100B network interface card.*

Add the User and Server Name in the My Computer Icon

One change that I have found to be helpful–for the support staff more than the users—is to provide the user ID and server name in the text portion of the My Computer icon. The support staff commonly asks, "What's your user ID and what Terminal Server are you currently on?" By providing this information for the user, you give him or her an easy and consistent way to provide a response. The REGINI script shown in Listing 12.1 updates the appropriate registry key to include the user ID and server name in parentheses after the My Computer text on a TSE 4.0 server.

Warning

Be sure to back up at least the CLSID registry key prior to doing this, to ensure that you can recover the original information if necessary—particularly for the TS 2000 script, since it replaces localized information. ◆

Listing 12.1   *A REGINI file to update the registry key.*

```
HKEY_LOCAL_MACHINE\Software\Classes
   CLSID
      {20D04FE0-3AEA-1069-A2D8-08002B30309D}
         = DELETE
         = REG_EXPAND_SZ "My Computer (%USERNAME% : %COMPUTERNAME%)"
```

This script can also be downloaded from the Web site for this book (www.newriders.com/1578702399). The file is called MyComputerUpdate_ TSE40.ini. To execute this script, simply issue the following command from a command prompt:

```
Regini MyComputerUpdate_TSE40.ini
```

Listing 12.2 shows the TS 2000 script.

Listing 12.2   *REGINI script for TS 2000.*

```
HKEY_LOCAL_MACHINE\Software\Classes
   CLSID
      {20D04FE0-3AEA-1069-A2D8-08002B30309D}
         LocalizedString = DELETE
         LocalizedString= REG_EXPAND_SZ "My Computer (%USERNAME% : %COMPUTERNAME%)"
```

This script is called MyComputerUpdate_TS 2000.ini.

Of course, these scripts are just examples; you can change how the information appears. Both scripts can be found in the MyCmpUpd.zip file on the books Web site.

Terminal Server Performance Tuning

Once the basic stability and availability options have been set, you can make a number of changes to Terminal Server to help boost its overall performance. When necessary, the following sections point out configuration changes that are specific to one version of Terminal Server or the other. Otherwise, the system changes are valid for both.

Disable Active Desktop

When Internet Explorer is installed on a TSE 4.0 server, the Active Desktop feature is not supported and should *never* be enabled. In Chapter 19, I discuss installing Internet Explorer 5 on TSE 4.0.

On TS 2000, IE5 is automatically installed and the Active Desktop feature is enabled. I recommend disabling the Active Desktop, as it can consume unnecessary resources and doesn't add any real value to the use of applications on the server.

To disable the Active Desktop, launch Terminal Services Configuration from the Administrative Tools option on the Start menu. Then click the Server Settings folder, double-click the Active Desktop option, and disable it as shown in Figure 12.16.

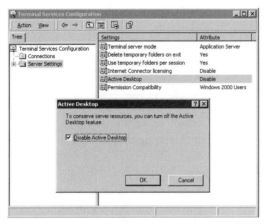

Figure 12.16   *Disabling the Active Desktop option on TS 2000.*

After this option is disabled, any new logons to the server will not have any of the Active Desktop options available to them. This doesn't affect users who are currently logged on when you make the change. They'll still have Active Desktop functionality until they log off and back onto the server.

Disable NT Executive Paging

On Terminal Servers with large amounts of physical memory, you can provide a response boost to the server by forcing drivers (user-mode and kernel-mode) and system code to remain in memory, even if they were written to be "pageable." Even on large memory systems, these pageable components will be swapped out to disk unless this option is set.

> **Warning**
>
> *This option consumes additional physical memory, so you should ensure that your server is not operating at full physical memory utilization under regular user load before configuring this setting. Doing so will result in less physical memory being available for the user sessions and increased pagefile usage.* ◆

The following registry key handles this option:

```
HKEY_LOCAL_MACHINE\SYSTEM\CurrentControlSet\Control\Session Manager\
➥Memory Management
```

The value to modify is `DisablePagingExecutive`. Setting this value to 1 turns off the paging of these drivers and system code to disk.

Disable Last Access Time Update on Directory Listings

By default, Windows updates the last access time on each directory when listed. You can provide a slight disk-read performance increase by disabling this option, since users on a Terminal Server will mostly be performing file reads on the server. You can turn off this default behavior. For this registry key:

```
HKLM\System\CurrentControlSet\Control\FileSystem
```

add this value:

```
NTFSDisableLastAccessUpdate REG_DWORD
```

(which doesn't exist by default) and set it to `0x1`.

A reboot is required in order for this change to take effect.

Adjust L2 Cache Settings

There has been much debate about whether manually setting the L2 cache size makes any difference at all with the performance of a Windows server in general, and the reasons why Windows wouldn't be able to automatically detect the L2 cache itself. People have claimed to receive performance increases of 8% or more when implementing this change, but I have personally never seen any change in performance when implementing this feature. I have included this information for completeness, since it is very likely that you will hear this recommendation at one point or another.

I suggest making this change only on a TS 4.0 server, not a TS 2000 server, which should be able to determine the system's L2 cache size itself.

You can use a registry entry to specify how much L2 cache exists on your system *per processor*. The REG_DWORD registry value is `SecondLevelDataCache` and is located under this registry key:

```
HKEY_LOCAL_MACHINE\SYSTEM\CurrentControlSet\Control\Session Manager\
↪Memory Management
```

The default value is `0x0` (hexadecimal), which is supposed to configure Windows to autodetect the L2 cache. If you have 512KB of L2 cache per processor, for example, you enter 512 in hexadecimal (`0x200`) for this registry value. You have to reboot for this change to take effect.

Disable Roaming User Profile Caching

The normal behavior of a Windows server is to cache a roaming profile on the server to speed up accessibility to it the next time the user logs onto that server. Because of the potential for a large number of users to connect to a Terminal Server over time, it's suggested that you disable the caching of the roaming profiles by setting the registry value `DeleteRoamingCache` to `0x1`.

If the value doesn't exist you can add it, with the data type of REG_DWORD. This value is located under this registry key:

```
HKEY_LOCAL_MACHINE\SOFTWARE\Microsoft\Windows NT\CurrentVersion\Winlogon
```

Modify Server Optimization Setting

After installation, both TSE 4.0 and TS 2000 need to have their server optimization settings tuned for operation as a Terminal Server.

TSE 4.0's default configuration is optimized to operate as an NT Workstation, which minimizes the memory used in network connectivity and attempts to maximize paging to conserve as much free physical RAM as possible. The idea is that a workstation will typically have a small amount of RAM, and this will help to maximize the RAM available for running applications.

Unfortunately, this can have a significant impact on a Terminal Server's performance, particularly as the user load increases. You end up with the server prematurely swapping data from memory to disk, even though physical memory is still available. This problem is easily detected by running Performance Monitor and examining the percentage of the pagefile in use compared with the free physical memory.

I highly recommend changing this memory-tuning model to better suit the Terminal Server. Under TSE 4.0, open Control Panel and go to the Server property in the Network applet. Then select Maximize Throughput for Network Applications (see Figure 12.17).

Unless you have LAN Manager 2.x clients on your network, you should also disable Make Browser Broadcasts to LAN Manager 2.x Clients.

This tuning change should also be performed under TS 2000. A Windows 2000 server (with or without Terminal Services) defaults to the Maximizing Data Throughput for File Sharing configuration. This option is ideal for file and print servers, but not for a Terminal Server.

Under Windows 2000, this change is made in the File and Printer Sharing for Microsoft Networks properties page, as shown in Figure 12.18.

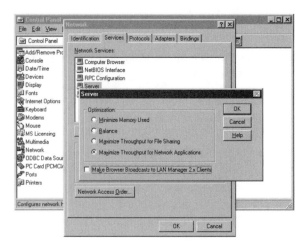

Figure 12.17   *TSE 4.0 server service properties.*

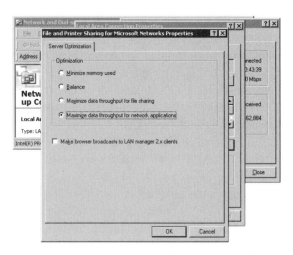

Figure 12.18   *TS 2000 file and printer sharing for Microsoft networking properties.*

Author's Note

Windows 2000 Professional is configured to use the Maximize Data Throughput for Network Applications option. ◆

Modify Foreground Thread Timeslices

Back in Chapter 2, I discussed the differences in thread priorities for Terminal Server in comparison to a typical Windows server, and mentioned that many more foreground threads exist on the server because of the multiple concurrent user sessions.

On TSE 4.0, the foreground task timeslice needs to be adjusted to better suit a Terminal Server environment, in which multiple users will be running multiple foreground and background applications. By default, TSE 4.0 is configured to boost the timeslice of foreground applications to be longer than background processes. This should be adjusted to ensure that foreground processes receive no boost. This is done on the Performance tab of the System applet in the Control Panel. The Boost slider should be set to None instead of Maximum. When Terminal Services is installed on a Windows 2000 Server, this is automatically adjusted to assign no boost to foreground applications. This option is under the Advanced tab of the System applet in the Control Panel (see Figure 12.19). The Optimize Performance for Background Services radio button should be selected.

Figure 12.19   *Application performance optimization.*

In both situations, the configuration has the same effect, which is to configure the server to use standard timeslices for foreground applications, resulting in more responsive application access for all users. When the opposite configuration is chosen (Maximum on TSE 4.0 and Applications on TS 2000), the servers operate with much longer foreground timeslices. This results in a poor configuration for a Terminal Server, since many foreground threads will be queued while awaiting their processor timeslice. Long timeslices result in "sluggish" application response on a terminal server. For more information on the behavior of these settings with regards to NT 4.0 and Windows 2000, I recommend that you review the article "Win2k Quantums" on the System Internals Web site (http://www.sysinternals.com/nt5.htm)

Increase Idle Connections

Chapter 2 also discusses the Terminal Server architecture and how by default it's configured with two idle connection sessions that are immediately available for servicing user connections. Figure 12.20 shows the two idle sessions in the Terminal Services Manager.

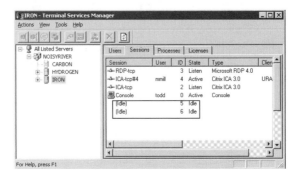

Figure 12.20   *Idle connection sessions on a Terminal Server.*

When a request for a connection is received on the appropriate protocol listening port (ICA or RDP), if an idle session is available it's used immediately to initiate the user's connection. This provides the user with rapid response to a Terminal Server session.

As soon as a user has connected to the available session, the server creates a new session that remains idle until the next connection request is received. The Terminal Server always attempts to have the configured number of idle sessions available for use.

You can increase the number of available idle sessions to assist in supporting users during peak logon times—at the cost of some additional memory overhead in maintaining these additional connections during normal operation. The idle session count is managed through this registry key:

```
HKEY_LOCAL_MACHINE\SYSTEM\Current ControlSet\Control\Terminal Server
```

The value to modify is `IdleWinstationPoolCount`, and the default `REG_DWORD` value is `0x2`. This value can be increased or decreased as desired to configure the number of idle sessions. Setting this value to `0x0` simply means that no sessions are preloaded for use by connecting clients. Unfortunately, this change is not dynamic, so a system reboot is required for the changes to take effect.

Unless users complain about a significant delay in the time required for the session logon screen to appear, I would leave the idle count at the default of 2.

Author's Note

Modifying the idle connection count was most useful during the pre–Service Pack 5 days of TSE 4.0. This technique resolved a problem in which users would receive a message stating that the server was not available if both idle sessions were in the process of establishing a user session, but hadn't yet reached the point where the system would initiate the creation of a new idle session.

If you have a TSE 4.0 server with SP4 or earlier, you can easily reproduce this problem by simply opening two Telnet sessions to the Terminal Server on port 1494 (ICA) or 3389 (RDP). For RDP, the Telnet session will simply remain blank; the ICA session will periodically display ICA on the screen. In both cases, the Telnet connections eventually time out. While these Telnet sessions are active, both connections are in the ConQ state in Terminal Server Administration. This stands for connection query and is the state in which the session is trying to initiate the connection with the client. Of course, neither Telnet session is responding, so the pending connection never actually continues. If you try to establish a third Telnet session while the first two are active, it will fail. If you try to connect to the server with either the RDP or ICA client, you receive a message that the server is not available. Until the Telnet sessions time out or are terminated, the Terminal Server is completely inaccessible. Of course, active sessions on the server are not affected—just new connections.

This problem no longer exists with either TS 2000 or TSE 4.0 with SP5, so new idle sessions will be created, even if a connection is "hung" in the ConQ state. ◆

Enable MetaFrame SuperCache

Beginning in the MetaFrame 1.8 hotfix ME180010 for TSE 4.0, and in the release version of MetaFrame 1.8 for TS 2000, Citrix includes an advanced caching technique known as *SuperCache* that can produce large performance improvements over slow connections or for applications that perform a redisplay of large areas of the screen in response to a localized screen update. The default MetaFrame cache displays bitmaps from top to bottom; SuperCache displays them from left to right.

SuperCache is enabled by default in MF/TS 2000, but you must manually enable SuperCache when running MetaFrame on a TSE 4.0 server. SuperCache is enabled by issuing the following command from a command prompt:

```
Keysync ICAThinwireFlags /Enable:2
```

To disable SuperCache, simply repeat the same command with `/Disable:2` instead of `/Enable:2`.

If you don't have the necessary hotfix installed that includes this feature for MF/TSE 4.0, you receive an error message when executing the command. If the update was successful, a message indicates that the registry key was updated and the binary and ASCII registry keys are now in synch.

You can determine whether a server currently has SuperCache enabled by issuing this command:

```
Keysync /Q
```

If the text `Key ICAThinwireFlags value is 3 (0x3)` is present, SuperCache is enabled. If the value is 1 instead of 3, SuperCache is not currently active.

Terminal Server Security Configuration

Now that you have completed the basic performance tuning and server configuration, the next step is to apply the basic Terminal Server security to your system.

Local Security Groups and Users

The first step is to create the necessary local security groups and adjust the local user accounts and group memberships as required. On either a TSE 4.0 or a TS 2000 server, I typically perform the following local security group and account configuration:

- Rename the local administrator and guest accounts. You should select an alternate name for your administrator that you can remember but that wouldn't be immediately obvious to a would-be hacker. This simple change makes it much more difficult for someone to guess the administrator's password, since they won't even know what the local administrator's account name is. The same goes for the guest account. Even though it's disabled, I like to rename it to something more obscure.

- Remove the Domain Admin group from the local Administrators group and add the appropriate domain Terminal Server administrator's group. Chapter 8 discusses the importance of limiting administrative access to your Terminal Servers to as few people as possible in order to ensure system stability, including regular domain administrators.

- Remove Domain Guests from the local Guests group.

- Remove the Domain Users group from the local Users group and add in the appropriate domain Terminal Server user's group. This change is really only necessary if you limit access to Terminal Servers to a specific group of users instead of all users in your organization.

- Create any additional support groups. This typically includes two groups, one for server operators and the other for user support staff. These groups normally grant additional file system or connection security privileges in order to allow them to perform their job function. For example, members of the user support staff group have connection privileges to shadow other users—something that a regular user doesn't have. Local group names would be something like Server Operators and User Support. I use these groups when discussing the different security configuration options later in this section.

Local groups and user accounts are managed on TS 2000 by right-clicking the My Computer icon and selecting Manage from the menu list to display the Computer Management application, as shown in Figure 12.21.

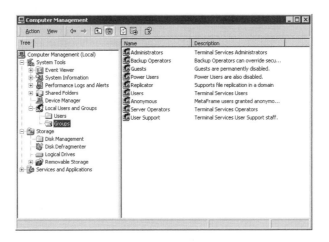

Figure 12.21   *Additional local security groups visible in Computer Management.*

On a TSE 4.0 server, you use User Manager for Domains to modify the local groups and user accounts.

Author's Note

After opening User Manager, make sure that you're pointing at the local users and groups. If you're logged on as the local administrator, this will automatically be set, but if you're logged on as a domain user, you'll need to select the desired Terminal Server name using the Select Domain option on the User menu. For example, if the server is called IRON, specify \\IRON as the domain name. ◆

File Security

Chapter 8 discusses the default file-security configuration on a TSE 4.0 server and how the permissions reflect the default configuration for Windows NT Workstation 4.0. Unfortunately, this configuration provides the Everyone group with much more access to the file system than you'll want on your Terminal Server. A necessary step in configuring your Terminal Server is to adjust these system drive permissions.

A Windows 2000 Terminal Server provides a much more secure file system if the Windows 2000 permissions were chosen when installing Terminal Services instead of TSE 4.0–compatible permissions (see Chapter 10). Even so, some minor file system security updates must be performed on the server to ensure that it's secure.

For both versions of Terminal Server, you need to ensure that the application and pagefile volumes have been secured. Basically the permissions are set as Read-Only for users and Full Control for both the administrators and SYSTEM. Limit users' write access as much as possible. The less access a user has, the less likely he or she is to negatively impact the environment.

For full details on the suggested security permissions that should be set on the file system, as well as sample CACLS command-line scripts, see Appendix D, "Terminal Server System and Application Volume Security Permissions."

Registry Security

While the registry's security requirements are similar to those of the file system, the process of assigning security in the registry can be much more difficult. The problem is that in certain situations an application can have a legitimate reason for writing to the registry. Fortunately, more and more applications are adhering to the standard of writing machine-specific information to HKEY_LOCAL_MACHINE while maintaining user-specific information in the user's personal profile (HKEY_CURRENT_USER).

As I discuss in Chapter 8, the majority of the registry security changes are concentrated in the HKEY_LOCAL_MACHINE\Software key. The other root keys (HARDWARE, SAM, SYSTEM) are configured during the Terminal Server installation to grant only Read access to non-administrator accounts.

Just as with the file system, Windows 2000 Terminal Server by default provides a much more secure registry than an NT 4.0 Terminal Server.

For full details on the suggested security permissions that should be set in the registry system, see Appendix F, "Terminal Server Registry Security Permissions."

Security Auditing

An important part of any secure environment is not only having the means to log system activity, but effectively monitoring these logs and flagging suspicious activity when it occurs. Unfortunately, most organizations are quick to implement the logging portion, but rarely establish any effective method of monitoring. As a result, the systems log huge amounts of security information that's rarely—if ever—examined. The log files themselves are usually so small that information is quickly overwritten, eliminating any possibility of examining the security information even if a problem is detected.

This section takes a look at the areas of security auditing that are available in Windows, providing some suggestions on events that you may want to audit. Even if you're not planning to implement any real form of auditing in your environment, understanding how auditing works is an important tool when performing application integration (see Chapter 19 for more information), as it can help you to determine files or directories that may require modified security permissions in order to allow the application to work properly.

If you're going to implement security auditing, you need to consider carefully which events you want to audit. Although it's easy to configure your environment to audit all events, the resulting logs will be difficult to review and manage, defeating the purpose of auditing. Finding the proper level of auditing for your environment requires a bit of work, but it's an exercise that I highly recommend. My simple rule is this: If you're not planning on proactively monitoring an event, don't waste your time auditing it. Other people may disagree with this philosophy, but in most situations, by the time you discover there's a security problem, the pertinent log information is very likely gone.

System Auditing

The first step is to enable auditing on the system itself. On TSE 4.0, auditing is enabled through User Manager for Domains. The Audit Policy dialog box shown in Figure 12.22 is accessed by selecting Audit from the Policies menu.

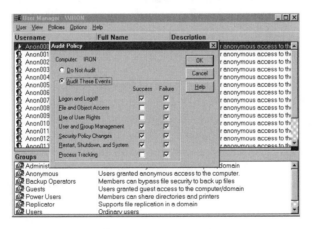

Figure 12.22   *The TSE 4.0 Audit Policy dialog box.*

On TS 2000, auditing is accessed through the Local Security Settings application found under Administrative Tools on the Start menu. The audit policy information is found under the Local Policies folder, as shown in Figure 12.23.

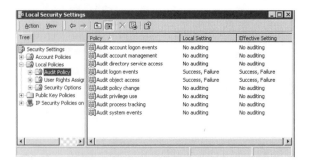

Figure 12.23   *The TS 2000 Audit Policy information.*

The following list describes the auditable events in the Audit Policy dialog box. The TS 2000 names are shown with the TSE 4.0 names in parentheses.

- Account Logon Events (no TSE 4.0 equivalent)—This audit policy should not be confused with the Logon Events policy. This policy logs an event whenever an account on *this* server is used to authenticate on this or any other server. It's typically enabled on a domain controller. You don't need to audit this policy on a Terminal Server.

- Account Management (User and Group Management)—The result of the creation, deletion, or modification of a *local* user account or group will be logged when this audit event is selected. I recommend tracking both successes and failures.

- Directory Service Access (no TSE 4.0 equivalent)—Access to an Active Directory object that has its own system access control list (SACL) is audited using this policy. This audit policy is valid only on a domain controller, so doesn't need to be set on a Terminal Server.

- Logon Events (Logon and Logoff)—Whenever a user attempts to log on or log off the Terminal Server, an event is written to the log. This differs from the Account Logon Events audit policy, which generates a log entry on the server where the *user account resides*. Logon Events auditing generates a log entry on the server where the logon was *attempted*. I recommend that you audit both success and failure. Successful logons let you audit the logon activities for users, and failures may indicate an attempt by someone to access a restricted resource. Figure 12.24 shows an audit entry created when an invalid logon attempt was performed on a Terminal Server. MetaFrame includes a command-line tool called AUDITLOG, which generates output from the security event log based on the logon/logoff information in the security log. See Appendix A for more information.

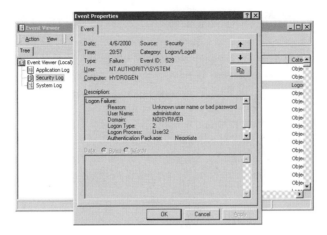

Figure 12.24   *Invalid logon attempt in the security audit log.*

- Object Access (File and Object Access)—Access to standard objects such as files, folders, printers, or the registry are audited using this policy. The object must have its own SACL defined before it will be audited. I recommend auditing failures, which will indicate users with insufficient privileges attempting to access a resource. Mapping successes offers little value except in isolated situations, because users can successfully access a large number of objects during a single session.

- Policy Change (Security Policy Changes)—This setting covers any changes made to the security policies, which are composed of the user rights policies and the audit policies on a Terminal Server. Because of the sensitive nature of this security information and the fact that it should rarely change, both success and failure should always be audited.

- Privilege Use (Use of User Rights)—This audits the use of a user right on the Terminal Server, such as taking ownership of an object or changing the system time. Failure should be tracked for this policy.

- Process Tracking (Process Tracking)—This policy tracks actions such as process (including program) starting and stopping. Indirect object access tracked includes such things as a process or thread from an application that manipulates an object in some way. Failures should normally be audited for this policy.

- System Events (Restart, Shutdown, and System)—When a user attempts to restart or shut down a system, this policy is triggered. Any event that affects the system security or the security log is also tracked with this event. I recommend auditing both success and failure.

Author's Note

Do not be too surprised if you see a large number of restart and shutdown attempts made on your Terminal Servers shortly after you first implement. If users had previous experience with Windows, they may be accustomed to "shutting down" when they're finished working on their computers for the day. This will be very common among users who use the Alt+F4 key combination to terminate Windows. Even on Terminal Server, using Alt+F4 presents the user with the Windows Security dialog box, where he or she has the option to shut down (unless you have disabled this through system policies, which I discuss next). Although regular users have insufficient privileges to complete this operation, the shutdown or restart attempt will still be logged. ◆

Auditing will introduce an additional performance overhead, so unless you are willing to actively monitor your audit logs and feel that their use is necessary, you can provide a performance boost by not implementing auditing. Of course, the performance gains will have to be worth not having the audit information available. While I have suggested some events to audit, the ones that you implement depend on the information that you're interested in tracking and that you feel is necessary. You should monitor your security logs carefully to see if there is extraneous information that can be eliminated.

Tip

*The AUDITPOL tool from the Windows Server Resource Kit can be used to update system auditing policies on any computer from a command prompt. For more information on the AUDITPOL command, see the appropriate Resource Kit documentation (NT 4.0 or Windows 2000) or type **AUDITPOL /?** from a command prompt.* ◆

File System Auditing

After you have enabled object access auditing, you can set up the desired file system auditing. If object access is not being audited (see the preceding section regarding system auditing), any file auditing you configure is simply ignored.

File auditing is enabled on the appropriate operating system as follows:

- TSE 4.0: Right-click a file object (drive, folder, or file), select Properties, click, the Security tab, and then click the Auditing button.

- TS 2000: Right click a file object (drive, folder, or file), select Properties, click the Security tab, click the Advanced button, and then click the Auditing tab.

As Figure 12.25 shows, the auditing options available correspond to the file system security attributes. For more information on the specific attributes, see Appendix C, "File and Folder Security Primer."

Figure 12.25   *File auditing options on TS 2000.*

Tables 12.2 and 12.3 list my suggested auditing settings for the system and application volumes on a TS 2000 server. Tables 12.4 and 12.5 list the corresponding auditing settings for a TSE 4.0 server. If a specific permission is not listed, I haven't set any auditing on it.

On the system volume, you may want to create separate audit settings for the profile directory, since users will be writing, editing, and deleting information from that location. On TSE 4.0, the profile directory is %systemroot%\Profiles; on TS 2000, the profile directory is %systemdrive%\Documents and Settings.

On TSE 4.0, you may also want to change the auditing settings on the TEMP directory, which is located in %systemdrive%\Temp, for the same reason; users will be writing and deleting from there.

Table 12.2   *TS 2000 System Volume Auditing*

TS 2000 Permission	Audit Setting
Create Files/Write Data	Failure
Create Folders/Append Data	Failure
Delete Subfolders and Files	Success Failure
Delete	Success Failure
Change Permissions	Success Failure
Take Ownership	Success Failure

Table 12.3   TS 2000 Application Volume Auditing

TS 2000 Permission	Audit Setting
Create Files/Write Data	Failure
Create Folders/Append Data	Failure
Delete Subfolders and Files	Success Failure
Delete	Success Failure
Change Permissions	Success Failure
Take Ownership	Success Failure

Table 12.4   TSE 4.0 System Volume Auditing

TSE 4.0 Permission	Audit Setting
Write	Failure (see Author's Note)
Delete	Success Failure
Change Permissions	Success Failure
Take Ownership	Success Failure

Table 12.5   TSE 4.0 Application Volume Auditing

TSE 4.0 Permission	Audit Setting
Write	Failure (see Author's Note)
Delete	Success Failure
Change Permissions	Success Failure
Take Ownership	Success Failure

Author's Note

When failure auditing is enabled for the Write permission on TSE 4.0, a large number of Event 560 entries will appear in the security log. Many of these entries are created during the user's logon. This is an issue with NT 4.0 that's documented in Knowledge Base article Q172509. Normally I won't set any auditing on the Write event unless troubleshooting an application error, simply to keep the security event log at a manageable size.

This is not an issue in Windows 2000. ◆

Registry Auditing

Unlike file auditing, which introduces a number of new auditable events with Windows 2000, registry auditing has only one new event over NT 4.0. The Write Owner property monitors if someone tries to take ownership of a registry object, much like ownership on a file object.

Typically auditing is only enabled on the HKEY_LOCAL_MACHINE hive and all subkeys. The auditable events are set similar to those shown in Figure 12.26.

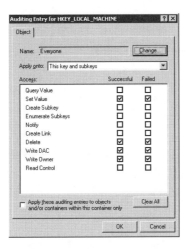

Figure 12.26   *Registry auditing suggestions.*

For both NT 4.0 and Windows 2000, registry auditing is enabled through REGEDT32. Depending on the operating system, the Auditing dialog box is accessed as follows:

- For TSE 4.0, open REGEDT32, select the key that you want to audit, and then click Auditing on the Security menu.

- For TS 2000, open REGEDT32, select Permissions, click the Advanced button, and then select the Auditing tab.

Click the Add button to add the users or groups, and then select the events to audit. On a Windows 2000 server, you may need to select the Reset Auditing Entries... check box to configure all child objects and enable propagation of inheritable audit entries.

You may receive a message indicating that all subkeys could not be updated. This is okay, as it will fail to update subkeys for which you don't have access, such as the HKLM\SECURITY key or the HKLM\SAM\SAM key. Auditing on the relevant keys will be updated properly.

You shouldn't monitor the success of either the Query event or the Enumerate Subkeys event, as both generate a large number of event entries very quickly, and should only be enabled when attempting to troubleshoot or resolve a specific issue.

> **Tip**
>
> *Using system policies on TSE 4.0 or Group Policy on TS 2000, you can restrict access to the registry editing tools.*
>
> *For Group Policy, this is located under User Configuration\Administrative Templates\System; for system policies, it's located in User\System\Restrictions.*
>
> *For more information on managing system policies or group policies, see Chapter 16, "Group and System Policy Configuration." ♦*

User Rights

User rights are a special set of privileges that define which basic operating system functions a user or group of users can perform. Review the user rights configuration on your server to ensure that the appropriate groups have been defined. Table 12.6 lists the available user rights, along with the suggested users and groups that should have access. If the policy is preceded by an asterisk (*), it's new to Windows 2000; otherwise the policies exist both in Windows 2000 and NT 4.0.

On TSE 4.0, user rights are accessed from within User Manager for Domains and located under the Policies menu. On TS 2000, the Local Security Settings application should be used. User rights are located under the Local Policies folder.

> **Tip**
>
> *For a detailed explanation of each of the user rights, see the electronic Group Policy Reference included in the Windows 2000 Server Resource Kit documentation. ♦*

Table 12.6   Suggested User Rights Configuration

Policy	Users/Groups
Access this computer from the network	Administrators
	This right is not required for a user to log onto a Terminal Server. It's only required if the Terminal Server is sharing a folder or printer, which it normally shouldn't.
Act as part of the operating system	None
Add workstations to domain	None
Back up files and directories	Backup Operators, Administrators
Bypass traverse checking	Everyone, Users, Power Users, Backup Operators, Administrators

Policy	Users/Groups
Change the system time	Administrators
Create a pagefile	Administrators
Create a token object	None
Create permanent shared objects	None
Debug programs	Administrators
*Deny access to this computer from the network	None
*Deny logon as a batch job	None
*Deny logon as a service	None
*Deny logon locally	None
*Enable computer and user accounts to be trusted for delegation	None
Force shutdown from a remote system	Administrators
Generate security audits	None
Increase quotas	Administrators
Increase scheduling priority	Administrators
Load and unload device drivers	Administrators
Lock pages in memory	None
Log on as a batch job	None
Log on as a service	None
Log on locally	Administrators, Users, TsInternetUser
	This right is required in order to log onto a Terminal Server.
Manage auditing and security log	Administrators
Modify firmware environment values	Administrators
Profile single process	Administrators
Profile system performance	Administrators
*Remove computer from docking station	Administrators
Replace a process level token	None
Restore files and directories	Backup Operators, Administrators
Shut down the system	Backup Operators, Administrators
*Synchronize directory service data	None
Take ownership of files or other objects	Administrators

Group and System Policies

Group policies (TS 2000) and system policies (TSE 4.0) provide you with the ability to apply restrictions and standards to a Terminal Server and/or a group of users. Using policies, you have granular control over large portions of the behavior of your system, both from a security and a stability standpoint.

Chapter 16 talks in detail about group and system policies.

Connection Configuration

With the necessary security groups in place, you can now configure the desired RDP or ICA connections on your server. The configuration steps differ slightly, depending on the Terminal Server version you're implementing. Windows 2000 has the more sophisticated Terminal Services Configuration tool; Windows NT 4.0 has the original Terminal Server Connection Configuration Tool.

TS 2000 Connection Creation

If you have MetaFrame installed, you have two different tools at your disposal for creating and managing connections. Both tools provide the same functionality, although the information is displayed differently. Figure 12.27 shows the Terminal Services Configuration tool and the Citrix Connection Configuration tool.

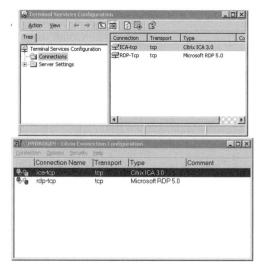

Figure 12.27 *Terminal Server and Citrix connection creation tools.*

The tool that you decide to use really comes down to personal preference. If you're already familiar with the Citrix tool from earlier versions of MetaFrame or WinFrame, you'll probably find it much easier to use than the Microsoft tool, since the information has been organized differently. If you're new to thin-client operating systems, you should probably use Terminal Services Configuration tool, since the interface is standardized with other Windows property controls.

> **Tip**
>
> *The Terminal Services Configuration tool also provides a wizard to guide you through the creation of a new connection; the Citrix Connection Configuration tool simply provides the properties dialog box where you can modify the settings as required.* ◆

The following procedure demonstrates the creation of an ICA connection using the Terminal Services Configuration application (the steps to create an RDP connection are practically identical):

1. Open the Terminal Services Configuration tool, which is found under the Administrative Tools option on the Start menu.

2. Right-click the Connections folder and select Create New Connection from the pop-up menu. The connection creation wizard opens. Click Next to begin.

3. First you'll select the appropriate connection type, either RDP 5.0 or ICA 3.0. Select the desired protocol (ICA in this example) and click Next.

4. The next dialog box asks you to select the encryption level corresponding to the protocol type. Unless you have SecureICA installed, you'll only have None and Basic as your encryption options. Figure 12.28 shows the high encryption options available when SecureICA has been installed on the MetaFrame server. On this screen you'll also see the Use Standard Windows Authentication check box. When this option is selected, the standard Windows GINA is used for authentication, even if an alternate method has been installed on the server. Normally you'll leave this option deselected.

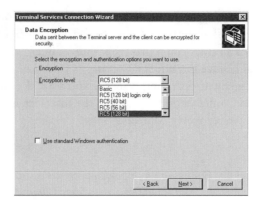

Figure 12.28 *ICA encryption options available when SecureICA has been installed.*

5. After choosing the encryption level, configure the remote control (also known as shadowing) options. The default is to use the options as set within the individual user's account. I recommend that you standardize on the shadowing method at the connection level, overriding the per-user settings. To do this, click the option Use Remote Control with the Following Settings, as shown in Figure 12.29. If you select Require User's Permission, the user will receive a request asking if you can "shadow" him or her, with a yes/no answer. The user must say yes before you can start remotely controlling his or her session.

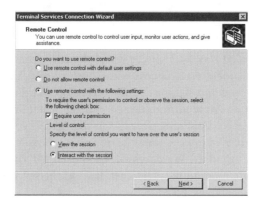

Figure 12.29 *Remote control options.*

6. On the next screen, select the transport type, along with a name. The name can be anything, but usually something short. For example, you could use ICA-tcp.

7. Specify the network adapter on which you want to configure the connections. You must also choose whether to allow unlimited connections or assign a specific number. I highly recommend that you assign a fixed number rather than setting this as unlimited. The maximum connection count should be set to the maximum number of users that you have sized your servers to handle. Figure 12.30 shows an example.

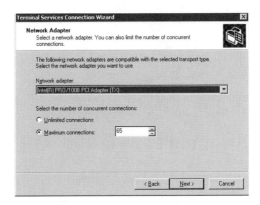

Figure 12.30   *Setting the network adapter and connection count settings.*

After the new connection has been created, you should change a couple of additional settings:

1. If you will be publishing applications using Program Neighborhood (ICA only), right-click the new connection and select Properties. Click the Logon Settings tab and ensure that the Always Prompt for Password check box is not selected. When selected, it will force clients to always be prompted for their password, even if they have hard-coded it on their client. This option will override the authentication feature of the ICA Program Neighborhood, forcing a user to log onto each server before they can run a program.

2. Select the Sessions tab. Here is where you specify the default timeout options for the connections. Figure 12.31 shows my suggested timeout options; you may need to adjust these, depending on your company's policies regarding idle sessions.

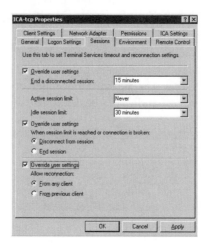

Figure 12.31 *Session timeout settings.*

The settings in Figure 12.31 do the following:

- A disconnected session will be terminated (reset) automatically after 15 minutes.

- An active session will never timeout.

- An idle session will timeout after 30 minutes and automatically be disconnected. At this point the disconnect timer would kick in, so it would remain disconnected for 15 minutes before finally being terminated.

- The last option at the bottom of the dialog box allows the client to reconnect a disconnected session from any client workstation, instead of only from the session where he or she was last logged on.

3. Select the Environment tab and click the Disable Wallpaper option. This will conserve resources by preventing desktop wallpaper from being displayed.

4. Click the Client Settings tab (see Figure 12.32). Here you can configure which client devices are automatically mapped. You should disable all devices that you won't need, such as sound or COM port mappings. These settings apply to all users who use these connections, so make sure that the changes are appropriate for everyone.

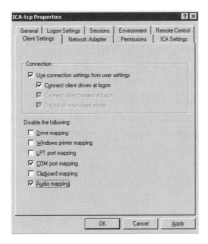

Figure 12.32 *Client settings.*

5. Click the Permissions tab. Here you specify which user groups will have access to connect through this connection type, and what privileges they'll have to interact with other user sessions of the same connection type. First remove the Guests and Everyone groups, so that only Administrators, SYSTEM, and Users exist. Now add any other local security groups that you have. In Figure 12.33, I have added Server Operators and User Support groups. Click each new entry and make sure that it has both the User and Guest permission sets selected.

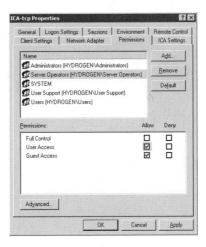

Figure 12.33 *Selecting the permission sets for the Server Operators group.*

6. Click the Advanced button and double-click the Server Operators entry to display the individual permission attributes. In addition to the currently selected attributes, click Allow for Reset, Remote Control, Logoff, and Disconnect as shown in Figure 12.34. This combination allows a server operator to perform additional functions on other connections of the same type, such as resetting a hung session or assisting a user through remote control. I haven't selected the Set Information option in this example, since I don't want the operators to be able to change the configuration of the connection. You may want to assign the User Support group the same permissions as a server operator or be more restrictive and allow them only a subset of these privileges, such as Remote Control and Logoff.

7. Click OK to save the changes. Once the permissions have been set, the connection is ready for use.

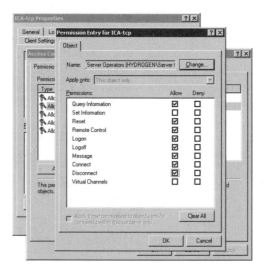

Figure 12.34 *Special permissions for the Server Operators group.*

TSE 4.0 Connection Creation

The options available for a created connection on a TSE 4.0 server are similar to those on a TS 2000 server, but the interface tools are different. The Microsoft Terminal Server Connection Configuration and Citrix Connection Configuration tools are practically identical. The following steps demonstrate how a connection would be created using the Terminal Server Connection Configuration (TSCC) utility:

1. Launch TSCC from the Administrative Tools option on the Start menu. Initiate a new connection by selecting New from the Connection menu.

2. In the new connection interface shown in Figure 12.35, configure the required options: name, transport type, protocol type, LAN adapter, and connection count. The presentation protocol types are ICA 3.0 and RDP 4.0. When you select the protocol type, a name is suggested automatically, such as ica-tcp.

When you're done with these settings, click the Advanced button.

Tip

You should always define an upper limit on the connection count. I recommend setting it equal to the maximum user load sized for your server. ◆

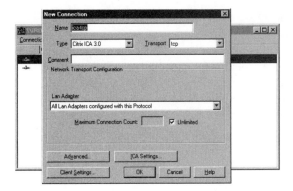

Figure 12.35   *The New Connection dialog box.*

3. Here you'll set the majority of the session information. Figure 12.36 shows my suggested default settings. Timeouts are configured so that after 30 minutes an idle session will be disconnected, and a disconnected session is automatically reset after 15 minutes of idle time. A reset ends the session. Shadowing has been enabled and users will be prompted to accept the shadow request before they can be shadowed. The user will be prompted for a password, even if he or she has set up the client to remember the password. Wallpaper has also been disabled to save resources. After all of the desired settings are in place, click OK to close the dialog box and save the changes.

4. Click the Client Settings button. From here you can enable or disable any of the client mappings, including overriding specific mapping options such as audio and LPT port mapping. I recommend disabling all unnecessary mappings such as audio or COM to conserve bandwidth and other resources. Click OK when the changes have been made.

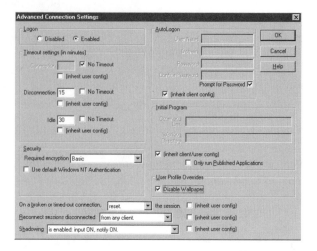

Figure 12.36   *Advanced setting options.*

5. The ICA Settings button contains only information on how to configure the audio quality. Click this button and specify the appropriate settings if you're providing audio support; otherwise, you don't need to worry about this option.

6. After all of the desired changes have been made, click OK to create the connection.

After creating the connection, you need to configure the security permissions for the connection:

1. Highlight the appropriate protocol and select Permissions from the Security menu to open the dialog box shown in Figure 12.37.

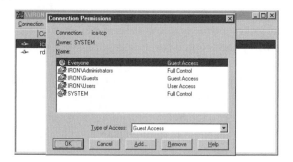

Figure 12.37   *Connection security settings.*

2. Remove the Guest and Everyone groups. Then add any other desired local groups and select the User Access type from the drop-down list.

3. Double-click a local group, set the individual permission attributes for that group, and click OK. Do this for each local group that you added in step 2.

For example, for the Server Operators group I would enable the Reset, Shadow, Logoff, and Disconnect options. This allows the Server Operators group to perform additional operations on other connections of the same type. For example, the server operator can reset or shadow another user's session. For the User Support group, I allow only the Remote Control option, so that these users could shadow other users, but would have no other special privileges.

Once the permissions have been set, the connection is ready for use.

Additional Connection Security Features

A couple of additional features are available to help improve the security of a Terminal Server connection. The first is disabling the default behavior of the RDP client to display the name of the person who last logged on. Under this key:

```
HKLM\Software\Microsoft\Windows NT\CurrentVersion\WinLogon
```

change the value DontDisplayLastName from 0x0 to 0x1.

As mentioned earlier, the ICA client will never display the ID of the user who last logged on.

The other security feature is only available on Windows 2000, and involves enabling security auditing on the Terminal Services connections. To find connection auditing, open the Permissions dialog box for a connection, click the Advanced button, and then select the Auditing tab. Auditing for connections is configured exactly as it is for other object auditing, such as the file system or the registry. Figure 12.38 shows my suggested connection auditing settings. These settings allow you to monitor who is resetting, logging off, or attempting to shadow other users.

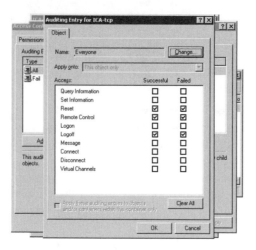

Figure 12.38   *Suggested connection auditing settings.*

Additional MetaFrame Configuration Options

If you're running MetaFrame on your Terminal Server, you may want to adjust a few final server settings, depending on your configuration:

- ICA browser service tuning
- ICA gateway creation
- Load balancing tuning
- Server farm membership
- Drive-mapping adjustments for NetWare

ICA Browser Configuration and Tuning

If you're going to load-balance your MetaFrame servers or you have multiple servers in your environment, you'll need to modify the default ICA browser configuration on your servers to optimize their performance. If you're implementing one or more dedicated ICA master browser servers, you'll also need to configure the browser service to identify these master browsers. For a complete discussion on the ICA browser service and master browsers, see Chapter 3.

To access the ICA browser service settings, click the Start button and select MetaFrame Tools, Citrix Server Administration. After the servers in your environment appear, highlight the server in the left pane and then click the ICA Browser tab on the right as shown in Figure 12.39.

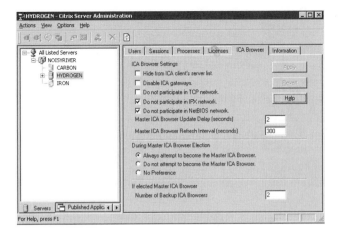

Figure 12.39   *ICA browser settings.*

For a complete description of each of the available options, simply click the Help button in this dialog box. A summary of the browser settings will appear. ◆

I typically apply the following changes to the ICA browser configuration:

• Hide from ICA Client's Server List—If users will access the Terminal Server environment only through published applications (the preferred method), you can hide the server from the client's list. While it doesn't prevent users from typing the name of the server on the client, it does prevent the simple point-and-click approach.

If you configure a MetaFrame server to be hidden from the server list, it also won't appear within the Load Balancing Administration application, although it will appear in the Citrix Server Administration application. If you're going to hide the servers, you may want to wait until after you have tuned the load-balancing configuration (discussed shortly). ◆

• **Master ICA Browser Update Delay.** This is the delay interval between when a client connects or disconnects from *this* server and when *this* server sends the update information to the current master browser. This is important to ensure that the master browser maintains accurate load-balancing statistics. I typically leave this set at 2 seconds.

- **Master ICA Browser Refresh Interval.** This interval determines how often the server sends update information to the master browser. The default is once every 30 minutes (1800 seconds). In a load-balanced environment I usually lower this to 5 minutes (300 seconds). Note that this refresh has nothing to do with the update delay setting. The server sends information to the master browser every time someone connects, disconnects, or after the refresh interval has expired. If you're using the default load-balancing configuration (discussed next), this configuration is adequate, since the load-balancing calculations are based solely on connection count, which is updated automatically. Only if you're applying addition factors into the calculations, such as CPU or memory utilization, will you want to ensure that the refresh interval is set low enough to maintain reliable statistics when users are not connecting or disconnecting.

- **During Master ICA Browser Election.** Chapter 3 discusses the idea of creating dedicated ICA master browser servers in large server farm environments, or environments with a large number of concurrent users. In these implementations, select the appropriate ICA browser election behavior for the server. If this server is going to be a dedicated master browser, select Always Attempt to Become the Master ICA Browser; for a regular MetaFrame server that's publishing applications, select Do Not Attempt to Become the Master ICA Browser.

  Even if you have two or more servers that will make up a master browser pool, you can still configure them all to attempt to become the master browser. A regular election will take place between those servers and one will be elected. See Chapter 3 for details on ICA master browser elections.

- **Number of Backup ICA Browsers.** The final option is to configure how many backup master browsers will be selected if this server becomes a master browser. The default is two, which is usually adequate for most environments. I recommend not adjusting this value. Setting it too high forces the master browser to maintain backup information on multiple servers, increasing resource requirements on both the master and the selected backup servers. You can't control which other MetaFrame servers will be selected to maintain backup browser information.

After setting the desired options, click Apply to have them take effect. Clicking Revert restores the options that were selected when you first opened the ICA browser property page.

ICA Gateways

ICA gateways are also configured through the Citrix Server Administration utility. Instead of clicking an individual server, click the All Listed Servers icon in the left pane. You can then click the ICA Gateways tab in the right pane to bring up the property page, as shown in Figure 12.40. (For more information on ICA gateways, refer to Chapter 3.)

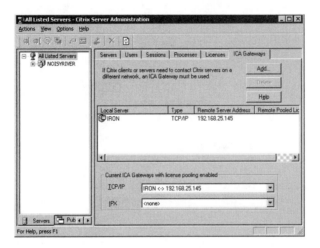

Figure 12.40 *ICA gateways property page.*

Before creating an ICA gateway, make sure that you have the following information:

- The Citrix server on the local network that will act as the local gateway link. This can be any Citrix server and doesn't have to be the elected master browser.

- The hostname or IP address of the Citrix server on the remote network that will act as the remote link. This can be any Citrix server and doesn't have to be the elected master browser server.

- Whether license pooling is required between the two networks. An ICA gateway that also pools licenses is commonly called a *license gateway*. Only one license gateway can exist on a subnet, which prevents license pooling between more than two subnets.

Once you have this information, you can click the Add button to begin. In the resulting dialog box, you can select the local Citrix server from the list box as well as provide the IP address (or hostname) of the remote Citrix server. If you'll be implementing license pooling, select the License Pooling check box (see Figure 12.41). Click OK to create the gateway.

> *Tip*
>
> *If you're planning to implement license pooling across the gateway, you must also configure the reverse ICA gateway setup from the remote network back to this local network. This establishes the two-way communications required in order to allow pooling to function properly.* ◆

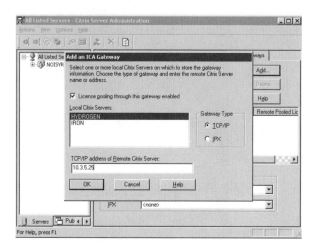

Figure 12.41   *Adding an ICA gateway.*

Citrix Load Balancing

If you're utilizing load balancing in your environment, you'll need to do some basic tuning. This configuration is done using the Load Balancing Administration (LBA) tool, which can be found under MetaFrame Tools on the Start menu. Once launched, it lists all the available servers that have Citrix Load Balancing installed.

> *Tip*
>
> *If a server doesn't appear on the list but does have load balancing installed, check whether its ICA browser settings are set to hide it from the server lists. If the browser settings are hiding the server, you need to deselect that option in order to view the settings (see the earlier section "ICA Browser Configuration and Tuning"), or run the Load Balancing Administration tool directly on that server.* ◆

After LBA starts, selecting an individual server displays the server-specific settings in the right pane, as shown in Figure 12.42.

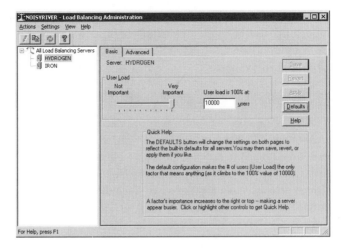

Figure 12.42   *Load Balancing Administration.*

The Basic tab displays the default configuration for a load-balanced server. In most cases, this is where 90% of the tuning occurs for a load-balanced server. As Figure 12.42 shows, the only option on this tab is the configuration of the user load setting.

By default, the number of users is the only factor considered in load balancing; the upper limit is set to 10,000 users. The actual maximum user load on a server is the smaller of these two:

• The total number of user licenses available (local plus any pooled licenses).

• The maximum number of users the server can support. This is either the sum of all the defined connections on the server or the upper limit defined in LBA (if the connection count is set to unlimited).

Author's Note

As I mentioned earlier in this chapter when talking about creating connections, you should always set an upper limit on your connection count. ◆

Normally I set the maximum user load in the LBA to be the maximum number of users sized for the server instead of leaving the 10000 default.

Tip

If you have a mixed environment with servers of different capacities, set the user limits appropriately to ensure an even distribution of users across the servers based on their capacity limits. ◆

While the basic load-balancing configuration should be more than sufficient in most situations, you have the option of very finely tuning the calculations used in determining a server's load. The Advanced tab contains the settings that you would need to adjust.

Author's Note

Normally advanced tuning is required only in situations where you have applications that are unpredictable in their use of processor and memory utilization. I highly recommend that you not make any adjustments on the Advanced tab unless you have the time to thoroughly test the impact of such changes. Simply modifying the default settings could easily skew the load calculations and degrade the efficiency of Citrix's load distribution. ◆

Figure 12.43 shows the Advanced tab.

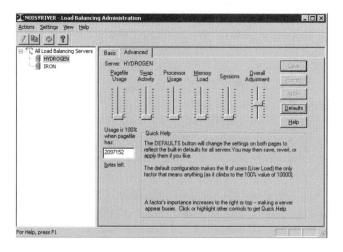

Figure 12.43   *Advanced Load Balancing Administration settings.*

Each of the listed factors is assigned a relative importance that determines how much influence that factor will have when accepting user connections. Increasing a setting increases its influence on the overall load calculation. Raising the importance of one factor won't influence how important any of the other factors are in the calculation. If all of the settings are at Very Important, for example, they're all given the same weight.

The following list describes each of the adjustable factors:

- **Pagefile Usage.** By default, load is assumed to be 100% when the pagefile has only 2MB remaining. The Pagefile Usage slider represents the importance of the ratio of the current pagefile size to the allowed minimum space left in the pagefile. If you are running a mixed environment of MetaFrame 1.8 and 1.0 servers, there is a known issue with the default pagefile usage setting and trying to load balance applications accross the two server types. Search the Citrix Knowledgebase for the article "MetaFrame Stops Load Balancing" for details.

- **Swap Activity.** Importance of the number of times the pagefile is accessed per second.

- **Processor Usage.** Importance of the percentage of time the processor is busy. Increase this setting if any applications run on a MetaFrame server are very processor-intensive. This is usually the first factor that's changed when setting advanced options.

- **Memory Load.** Importance of the ratio of total physical memory to available memory.

- **Sessions.** Importance of the ratio of total Terminal Server sessions to free sessions. The number of available sessions for a server is set using the Connection Configuration Manager. When licenses are not pooled, the maximum allowable number of sessions is dictated by the number of licenses on the server. MetaFrame never attempts to add a user to a server that has no free sessions.

- **Overall Adjustment.** This slider raises or lowers the overall calculated load on the server. When in the middle at 50%, there are no adjustments. Lowering the slider makes the server appear less busy, while raising it makes it appear busier.

> *Tip*
>
> *When adjusting the load calculations on a server, many times it's easiest to simply use the Overall Adjustment factor and raise or lower accordingly.* ◆

Server Farm Membership

Typically people will add a server to a server farm when they begin to publish applications, but this can be done sooner if you prefer. Normally I add a server to the desired server farm after the build is completed and I want to perform some initial client/server testing to ensure that Program Neighborhood and the server farm are configured properly.

Server farm membership is managed through the Published Application Manager (AppMgr) application, found under MetaFrame Tools on the Start menu. The first time you launch AppMgr, you should be prompted to create or join a server farm as shown in Figure 12.44. If not, simply select Join or Create Server Farm from the Configure menu.

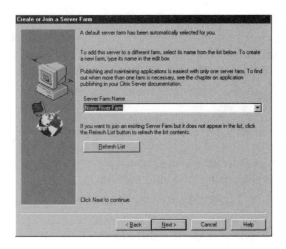

Figure 12.44   *This wizard guides you through the process of creating or joining a Citrix server farm.*

After you click Next, if a server farm already exists, it will appear in the drop-down list. Otherwise, you need to type a name for the new server farm you're creating. After clicking Next (and selecting Yes if it's a new farm), you're finished. The server is now a member of the selected server farm. The farm name appears in square brackets ([ ]) next to the name of the server in the title bar for AppMgr.

Removing a Server from a Server Farm
After adding a server to a server farm, you might expect to be able to remove a server from a server farm, or even delete an entire server farm. Neither of these tasks is easily accomplished.

No option is available for deleting a server farm. The reason isn't immediately obvious but makes sense once it's explained. A server farm is actually "deleted" when no servers belong to it. This is because there is no central location where a farm "exists." The farm only exists because at least one server advertises the fact that it belongs to that server farm. If that one server is shut down, the farm simply "disappears" until the next time that server is brought up. So if you actually want to delete a farm, you must assign all the servers that belong to it to another server farm. Once this is done, the original farm is "deleted."

Of course, the next obvious question is how to remove a server from a server farm. At this time, this feature is not actually supported by Citrix *at all*. There is no option to "leave a farm." However, I have successfully removed a server from a farm by performing the following steps.

> **Warning**
>
> *This workaround is not officially supported, so use it at your own risk.* ◆

1. In AppMgr, remove all the applications that this server is publishing in the farm. You don't want these apps publishing after you have switched back to the domain scope.

2. If this server belongs to a server farm that has other servers in it, move this server into a "temporary" farm. This is a new farm to which only this server will belong. To change the farm membership, select Server Farm from the Configure menu in AppMgr, and then click the Change Server Farm button. When prompted, enter the name of a new farm.

3. Now that the server belongs to the new farm, you can switch its scope to a domain instead of a server farm. Choose View, Select Scope, click the Use Only NT Domains button, and then select the appropriate domain. Now exit the AppMgr so that the application changes are written to the registry. By changing it to the domain scope, you prevent an error message from appearing the next time you run AppMgr.

4. The server farm membership is dictated by the single registry value called `Neighborhood`, located under this key:

   `HKLM\System\CurrentControlSet\Services\ICABrowser\Parameters`

   You'll see your temporary server farm name there. Change it to an empty string.

5. The last step is to stop and start the ICA browser service. You can do this from a command prompt by running these commands:

   NET STOP ICABrowser

   NET START ICABrowser

   The server now belongs to no server farm and the temporary farm has been deleted.

NetWare Drive-Mapping Conflicts

When you offer connectivity to NetWare volumes on your Terminal Server, some extra settings are available that enable you to control where the NetWare SYS:LOGIN directory is mapped during a user logon and also where automatic client drive mapping should begin for drives that couldn't be matched up with their local assignment.

By default, MetaFrame begins at C: and works up to find the first available drive to which to map the SYS:LOGIN directory. At the same time it searches down, starting at V:, to find the first available drive to map any client drives that couldn't be mapped to their matching drive letters in Terminal Server.

This logic for drive assignment can cause great confusion for users, particularly when you have reassigned the server drive letters to begin at something other than C: (such as X:). In this case, you would expect that all client drives would match up with their corresponding drive letter in Terminal Server. When you're also running NetWare login scripts that map NetWare drives, however, this isn't always the case.

The problem is that MetaFrame client drive mapping and the NetWare login script run in parallel. Therefore it's possible that a user could have the following scenario during one logon:

```
SYS:LOGIN mapped to the server drive C:
Client C: mapped to server drive V:
```

During a different logon, the same user might have the following:

```
Client C: mapped to the server drive C:
SYS:LOGIN mapped to the server drive D:
```

This inconsistency would be extremely confusing for users (and many administrators).

To remedy this problem, you need to make a change to the registry. Open REGEDT32 and traverse to this key:

```
HKEY_LOCAL_MACHINE\SYSTEM\CurrentControlSet\Control\Terminal Server
```

Now add the following new value to this key:

```
InitialNetWareDrive:REG_SZ
```

Assign the drive letter that will be used for the SYS:LOGIN directory mapping. Don't include the colon (:). The letter F is usually a safe choice as few (if any) users will have a local disk F:. If you *have not* reassigned the server drive letters, I suggest that you set this drive letter higher up the alphabet, such as L: or M:.

Next, traverse to this key:

```
HKEY_LOCAL_MACHINE\SYSTEM\CurrentControlSet\Control\Citrix
```

Add the following new value:

```
InitialClientDrive:REG_SZ
```

This specifies where MetaFrame will begin assigning client drives that couldn't be matched up with their local drive letters. Normally this would start at V:, and has the potential to conflict with the NetWare drive letter (since it's mapping upwards). You should set this drive to be one less than the one that you assigned for NetWare earlier. If the NetWare value is M:, for example, set the client value to be L:. This will ensure that the settings don't conflict with each other during a user's logon.

Printer Drivers

When configuring a Terminal Server, one of the areas frequently overlooked is the installation of the printer drivers that will be required by the users. This is necessary because, on a Terminal Server, regular users don't have sufficient privileges to install their own drivers. For a user to be able to print, the required driver must already be installed on the server.

While this is often looked upon as an inconvenience (which in many cases it is), it is necessary to help ensure a stable Terminal Server environment. Printer drivers should be considered an operating system component, and like any other feature should be tested prior to production implementation. There are situations where a printer driver that works properly on a desktop computer will behave poorly on Terminal Server and in some instances can cause blue screen STOP errors.

Tip

Before adding any printer driver to your system that's not supplied with either the operating system CD or as part of a service pack, you should check with the vendor to ensure that the driver is compatible with Terminal Server. A number of printer drivers have been known to cause problems, in particular the Hewlett-Packard LaserJet 5P/MP, 6P/MP, and 2000C, which can all generate blue screen STOP errors, and the HP4000 driver, which has been known to hang the spooler. See Microsoft Knowledge Base article Q191666 for more information on stop errors with HP drivers. Hewlett-Packard also provides a fix for the 2000C problems on their Web site, along with a complete list of which drivers are supported on Terminal Server. ◆

To ensure that you have all of the necessary drivers available, you need to consider both printer access scenarios that are available to the users:

- **Network connected printers.** These printers are accessible on the network that a user connects to from within the Terminal Server session, either through a logon script or manually mapped using the Add Printer option.

- **ICA or RDP client-printer mappings.** In this situation, a printer that's configured on the user's local desktop is automatically mapped so that it's accessible from within the Terminal Server session. RDP allows you to map only a locally attached printer; ICA also allows you to map any locally attached network printers.

Network Printer Drivers

The process of connecting to and using a networked printer is fairly straightforward. Here's one method:

1. Click Start, Settings, Printers.

2. Double-click the Add Printer icon.

3. Follow the steps in the wizard, being sure to select Network Printer when requested.

When connecting to a network printer, if the required driver is not already installed, it's automatically downloaded from the print server and installed. As you may have guessed, however, this won't work properly for anyone who's not an administrator.

The brute-force method of installing all of the necessary printer drivers on your Terminal Server could go as follows:

1. Log onto the Terminal Server as an administrator.

2. Click Start, Run and type the following:

   \\<print server>

   where *<print server>* is the appropriate hostname for the server containing the printer queues. After running this command, a window opens, listing all the shared printers available on that print server.

3. Double-click each of the listed printers to establish a connection. The printer driver automatically downloads if necessary.

4. After all of the desired printer drivers have been installed, go back to the Printers folder and delete all the connections you just created. Deleting your connection won't remove the driver once it has been installed.

Author's Note

If you're running TSE 4.0 with Service Pack 5, printer drivers from a print server may not download and install as expected. This is because SP5 enables a security feature that allows a driver to be installed only from a trusted source. See my tip at the end of the "Printer Drivers" section for complete information, including how to allow users to install their own printer drivers if you decide to do so. ◆

Of course, this wouldn't be called brute-force if it wasn't excruciatingly tedious when you have a large number of print servers and/or queues. This is an excellent example of a situation where a script file would be helpful. Following is a sample KiXtart script that automatically connects to the listed print server and enumerates all available printers, then connects to them one by one and automatically installs the driver if necessary. The script also disconnects automatically from each of the printers that it connects to.

Additional functionality could be added, including enumerating and processing all available print servers, but this example demonstrates the basic functionality. A downloadable copy of this script is available on the Web site for this book (www.newriders.com/1578702399) in the file PrnConn.zip.

Tip

You will also need to download the KiXtart interpreter in order to run this script. One location is http://netnet.net/~swilson/kix. *I have tested this script with version 3.62. The zip file also includes PrnConn.cmd. You can simply edit this file and provide the name of the desired print server.* ◆

```
;
; PrnConn
;
; Enumerates all printer shares off of the listed server and then
; performs a connect/disconnect so that the associated printer driver
; is loaded. Ideal for preloading the required printer drivers on a
; Terminal Server so that users can use them.
;
; This script has been tested on both Windows 2000 Terminal Services
; and Windows NT 4.0, Terminal Server Edition (SP5).
;
; Created By: Todd W. Mathers
; Last Updated: April 2000
; KiXtart Version: 3.62

BREAK ON

; Variable Def
;$PrintServer = "\\<server name>"   ; this variable is passed as a parameter
$ShareList   = "sharelist.txt"   ; output from net view call
$Line        = ""              ; a line from the $ShareList file
$ShareName   = ""              ; printer sharename
$PrinterName = ""              ; actual printer's name

; if the server value was not passed as a parameter then
; generate an error and exit
if $PrintServer = ""
    ? "PrnConn - Enumerates and connects to all printers on the given server
➥name."
    ?
    ? 'Usage: kix32 prnconn.kix $$PrintServer="\\<server name>"'
    ?
    ? "  where <server name> is the name of server with printer shares "
    ? "                      you want to connect to. Quotes (') "
    ? "                      are required."
else
```

```
; populate $ShareList with output from "net view"
shell "cmd /c net view " + $PrintServer + " > " + $ShareList

; now we need to parse the $ShareList file and pick out all
; printer share names. We will connect/disconnect as we
; find each one

if Open(6, $ShareList) = 0
   ; skip the first 7 lines since they are just
   ; header information from the net view output
   $i = 1
   while $i =< 8
      $Line = ReadLine(6)
      $i = $i + 1
   loop
   $Line = ReadLine(6)
   while @ERROR = 0
      $Line = ReadLine(6)
      ; now check the text from column 13
      ; if it contains only the word Print, then we have
      ; a printer share. If not, then we will store the line
      ; in $ShareName as a possible sharename

      if RTrim(LTrim(SubStr($Line, 13, 12))) = "Print"
         ; this is a printer share
         ; now check the share name for this row
         ; if it is blank then we use the sharename from the previous
         ; iteration, since net view will wrap the type and other
         ; info to a new line if the share name is > 12 chars
         $TempName = RTrim(LTrim(SubStr($Line, 1, 12)))
         if $TempName <> ""
            ; a sharename exists so get it
            $ShareName = $TempName
         else
            ; the sharename on this row was empty
            ; so we use the $ShareName from the previous iteration
         endif
         ; next we must get the actual printer name from the
         ; comment field, this is used to perform the disconnect
         $PrinterName = RTrim(SubStr($Line, 36, Len($Line)))

         ; now connect/disconnect from the share

         ? $ShareName
         $x = AddPrinterConnection($PrintServer + "\" + $ShareName)
         if $x = 0
            "    Connected."
            $x = DelPrinterConnection($PrintServer + "\" + $ShareName)
            if $x = 0
               "    Disconnected."
            else
               "    Disconnect failed."
            endif
```

```
            else
              "   Connection failed."
            endif
          else
            ; the type name "Print" was not found in the proper
            ; location, so we will store this row in $ShareName with
            ; the assumption that it contains the sharename for a printer
            ; type that has wrapped to the next line. we will know as soon
            ; as we process the next row whether this is true or not
            $ShareName = RTrim($Line)
          endif
        loop
        $x = Close (3)
      else
        ? "The output file from the 'net use' command called " + $ShareList + "
  ↩could not be found."
      endif
    endif
```

Client Printer Mapping

In order to provide the necessary drivers for client printer mapping, you need to understand the process by which client printers are detected and connected through the appropriate client (RDP or ICA). The mapping steps differ slightly between the two clients. The RDP 5 client works as follows when logging onto a TS 2000 server:

1. A user with a locally attached printer logs onto a Terminal Server with an RDP client.

2a. If the user is running a 2000/NT client, the associated printer driver on the client is automatically uploaded and installed if it doesn't already exist on the Terminal Server. Of course this will fail if the user doesn't have administrative privileges to install the printer driver.

2b. If the user is running Windows 95/98, printer drivers cannot be uploaded since they're not compatible with Windows 2000. Instead, the operating system looks in the [Previous Names] section of %systemroot%\Inf\Ntprint.inf to find a cross-reference between the Windows 95/98 driver name and the associated Windows 2000 printer driver. An example would look like this:

```
"HP LaserJet 4/4M PS"          =    "HP LaserJet 4/4M PostScript"
"HP LaserJet 4L/4ML PostScript" =   "HP LaserJet 4ML PostScript"
"HP LaserJet 4P/4MP PS"         =   "HP LaserJet 4P/4MP PostScript"
"HP LaserJet 4Si/4Si MX PS"     =   "HP LaserJet 4Si/4SiMX PS"
"HP LaserJet 5L"                =   "HP LaserJet 5L PCL"
"HP LaserJet 6L"                =   "HP LaserJet 6L PCL"
"HP LaserJet 6P/6MP PostScript" =   "HP LaserJet 6P/6MP - PostScript"
```

The driver name on the left side is for Windows 95/98; the right side is the Windows 2000 driver name. If the Windows 95/98 driver name is not found or the Windows 2000 driver is not installed, the client printer won't be mapped.

The ICA client works slightly differently for client printer mapping:

1. A user with a locally attached or network printer connection logs onto a Terminal Server with an ICA client.

2. The server is examined to see whether the associated printer driver is installed. If it is, the client printer connection is created.

3a. If the driver is not installed and the client printer is a mapped network printer, the driver is taken from the printer server and installed onto the Terminal Server. If you're running TSE 4.0 with SP5, this option won't work by default. See my note at the end of this section for information on how to "re-enable" this feature.

3b. If the driver is not installed and it's a locally connected printer, the %systemroot%\Inf\NTPrint.inf file is checked to see whether the driver is part of the base OS. If it is and the installation media is available, the driver is silently installed and the printer is mapped. Admin access is required for the driver to be installed.

4. If the driver is not part of the base OS or the installation media is not available, Citrix resorts to inspecting the files WTSPRNT.INF and WTSUPRN.INF in the %systemroot%\system32 directory for the information shown in Table 12.7 (in the order listed). As soon as a match is found, that information is used to create the printer mapping. These two files contain a cross-reference list, similar to the [Previous Names] section in the NTPrint.inf file. WTSPRNT.INF is installed by MetaFrame and should not be edited. WTSUPRN.INF is created by the administrator and won't be overwritten by a MetaFrame upgrade.

Table 12.7   ICA Client Printer Cross-Reference Inspection Order

Inspection Order	Search For	In File
1.	*<client name>#<printer name>*	WTSUPRN.INF
2.	*<printer name>*	WTSUPRN.INF
3.	*<client name>#<printer name>*	WTSPRNT.INF
4.	*<printer name>*	WTSPRNT.INF
5.	*<client name>#<client printer driver name>*	WTSUPRN.INF
6.	*<client printer driver name>*	WTSUPRN.INF
7.	*<client name>#<client printer driver name>*	WTSPRNT.INF
8.	*<client printer driver name>*	WTSPRNT.INF

This thorough inspection list means that you have some extra flexibility in configuring which driver should be used with which figure. Following is an excerpt from the WTSPRNT.INF file:

```
;
;       WTSPRNT.INF — DO  NOT  CHANGE
;
; This file is supplied by Citrix as a reference and best guess for
; client printer selections.  The file wtsuprn.inf is the user file
; for client printer mapping and takes precedence over this file.
; An example file, wtsuprn.txt is supplied as a template.
;
; This file may be overwritten during software upgrades!
;
[Identification]
        OptionType = PRINTER
[ClientPrinters]
"HP LaserJet 4/4M"                          = "HP LaserJet 4"
"HP LaserJet 4P/4MP"                        = "HP LaserJet 4P"
"HP LaserJet 4 Plus/4M Plus"                = "HP LaserJet 4 Plus"
"HP LaserJet 4Si/4Si MX"                    = "HP LaserJet 4Si"
"HP LaserJet 4V/4MV"                        = "HP LaserJet 4V"
"HP LaserJet 5/5M - Enhanced"              = "HP LaserJet 5"
"HP LaserJet 5/5M - Standard"              = "HP LaserJet 5"
"HP LaserJet 5L (PCL)"                      = "HP LaserJet 5L"
"HP LaserJet 5P/5MP (HP)"                   = "HP LaserJet 5P"
"HP LaserJet 1100"                      = "HP LaserJet 1100 (MS)"
"HP DeskJet 895C Series Printer"            = "HP DeskJet 895Cxi"
"Fax"                                       = ""
```

> **Tip**
>
> *You'll also need to update the cross reference in the WTSUPRN.INF file if the user is running Windows 95/98. This is because many of the 95/98 driver names don't correspond to their NT/2000 equivalent. This means that MetaFrame won't be able to find the corresponding driver even if it's installed on the server. In this case, you need the cross reference so that MetaFrame knows what to look for.* ◆

When attempting to provide the necessary driver information for a client printer mapping, you have two options:

- Install the necessary printer driver.
- Update the cross-reference in the appropriate file (NTPrint.inf or WTSUPRN.INF) so that the user will use a driver that already exists on the system to print to the printer.

In many situations, I prefer the second option. I don't need to install a new driver to support a possible one-off printer, and I can use an existing driver that I already know is stable rather than introducing a new driver that may cause issues.

When feasible, I recommend handling client printer drivers as exceptions requiring a request from the user (including the printer and printer driver name) before the necessary file or driver addition occurs.

Tip

If you would rather allow users to install their own printer drivers (which I don't recommend for stability reasons), you can enable this option by changing the value for AddPrinterDrivers *to* 0x0. *This value is located under the following registry key:*

```
HKLM\CurrentControlSet\Control\Print\Providers\LanMan Print Services\Servers
```

On TSE 4.0 with Service Pack 5, the option to only allow drivers to be installed from a trusted resource is enabled by default. I recommend using this option if you're going to allow users to install their own drivers, since it will ensure that you can maintain some control over exactly which drivers go onto the Terminal Server. The two values that manage this are LoadTrustedDrivers *and* TrustedDriverPath. *Both are located under the same key as* AddPrinterDrivers.

When LoadTrustedDrivers *has the value* 0x1, *only printer drivers located in one of the* TrustedDriverPath *locations can be installed. By default this is set to* %systemroot%\system32\Spool\drivers\w32x86. *You can add multiple trusted driver paths simply by separating them with a semicolon (;).* ♦

RDP Client Installation and Configuration

In this chapter:

- **RDP Client Installation**
  Although the installation of the Microsoft Terminal Server client is straightforward, a number of configuration options are available when creating connections.

- **RDP Client Applications**
  Two RDP clients are provided with Terminal Server: the Terminal Services Client and the Client Connection Manager.

- **RDP Client Configuration**
  The RDP client is best suited for a desktop-replacement implementation scenario, although it can be configured for application replacement with some limitations.

- **RDP Client Deployment Options**
  The RDP client can be configured for both manual and automated deployment, although a manual implementation is most common during the early stages of a Terminal Server project.

RDP Client Installation

Chapter 6, "Client Planning," discusses in detail both the ICA and RDP clients, the various implementation categories that exist (desktop and application replacement, desktop integration), and the planning and support issues you must consider when planning a Terminal Server implementation. This chapter looks at the steps for installating the RDP client, and provides more detailed examples of how you would configure the client in each of the implementation categories.

Author's Note

The installation of both ICA and RDP clients is very straightforward, but don't let this ease of installation lead you to believe that a formal implementation plan for your clients is not a necessity. "Easily installed" doesn't mean simplistic or trivial. ◆

The exact location of the RDP client installation files depends on which version of Terminal Server (TSE 4.0 or TS 2000) you're deploying:

- If you are deploying TSE 4.0, the client installation files are on the CD in the D:\Clients\TSClient directory (where D: is the CD-ROM drive). This directory doesn't exist on the Windows 2000 Server CD.

- In either version, you can create client installation floppy disks by using the Terminal Services Client Creator (discussed shortly).

- After the installation of either version of Terminal Server, the RDP client files (and the ICA client files if MetaFrame has been installed) are in the %systemroot%\System32\Clients folder. These folders are used by the Client Creator program to build the disks. A Net directory also exists and can be used for performing network installations or pushing out the client using Active Directory (Windows 2000 only).

Tip

If you're considering setting up a distribution share point on the network from which the appropriate support staff will have access to the client files, I recommend that you do this on a proper file server and not on a Terminal Server. The easiest way to do this is to copy the contents of the Net directory. This also allows you to perform certain client customizations that will then be included automatically in any installation that originates from that location. I'll discuss client customization shortly.

If you're implementing TSE 4.0, I don't recommend sharing out the OS CD itself. The Clients directory contains a number of clients and tools for Windows NT, including DOS and OS/2 LAN Manager clients; server tools such as Server and User Manager that run on Windows 95 or 98; and even the Remote Boot service for Windows NT Server. ◆

Creating Client Installation Disks

Client installation floppy disks for Terminal Server are easily created using the Terminal Services Client Creator program located under Administrative Tools. When you start the program, the Create Installation Disk(s) dialog box opens (see Figure 13.1). Here you simply select the type of client floppy disks you want to create and then click OK to begin the process of copying the necessary files to floppy disk. Two blank, formatted 3½-inch floppy disks are required for the 32-bit client, and four if you want to create the 16-bit client install disks.

> **Tip**
>
> *Make sure that the client disks are blank or that you select the Format option; otherwise, the Client Creator generates an error saying that it couldn't copy the listed file. It won't say that there was insufficient disk space.* ♦

Figure 13.1   *The Create Installation Disk(s) dialog box.*

Creating a Client Distribution Share Point

As mentioned earlier, if you're going to provide a distribution share point on the network where the installation files will be available, I highly recommend that this be done on a dedicated file server and not a Terminal Server.

This is essential if you're planning to distribute the client using Active Directory, since you'll want to specify a persistent share point during the creation of the package using Veritas' WinINSTALL LE. I discuss the distribution of the client using Active Directory in the later section "Client Distribution with Active Directory."

Disk-Based or Share Point Client Installation

Follow these steps to install the Microsoft RDP Terminal Services client from floppy disk or from a share point on the network:

1. Run SETUP.EXE from the installation location and enter the required name and organization information. Click OK. After ensuring that the information is correct, click OK again.

2. After reviewing the End User License Agreement (EULA) click I Agree if you accept the agreement.

3. Verify the location where you'll install the client. This location should have been defined as part of the client planning, so make sure that you're using that standard location. This can be very important with regard to support and for simplifying future upgrade plans. Click the large button with the icon to begin the installation.

4. Indicate whether you want to apply the initial settings to all users or just to you. If you're installing on an end-user machine, I suggest selecting all users, to simplify management and allow the creation of a standard TS client for all users on that machine. If you're placing this client on a power user's or administrator's desktop, select individual settings so that each person who logs onto the client can maintain his or her personal information.

Setup copies the necessary files to the client computer. Once the copying is done, the client installation is complete. There's no need to reboot the computer before starting to use the RDP client.

Client Distribution with Active Directory

If you want to deploy the RDP (or ICA) client to users running Windows 2000 Professional in a Windows 2000 domain, you can utilize the Windows Installer component and group policy to automate the deployment to the end user. In general, the creation and deployment of a client package would work as follows:

1. The Windows Installer package is created on a clean workstation using the Veritas WinINSTALL LE application that ships with Windows 2000. Microsoft provides a very helpful Knowledge Base article (#Q236573) that describes step by step how to use WinINSTALL to do this.

2. After you've created the .MSI package, the next step is to create a group policy for an organizational unit in the Active Directory that will contain the users who should receive the client package (see Figure 13.2).

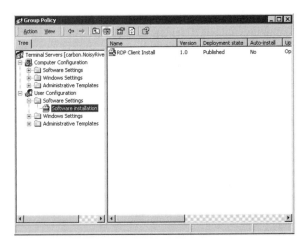

Figure 13.2 *Assigning an installation package within a group policy.*

3. Depending on how you've configured the package, you can have it auto-install, or you can simply make it available in the Add/Remove Programs utility under the Control Panel.

A discussion on the use of group policies to deploy software is beyond the scope of this book, but detailed information is available in the Windows 2000 Help. Simply look for Windows Installer in the Help index.

> ### Tip
>
> *New Riders Publishing offers a complete book on Windows 2000 deployment, "Windows 2000 Deployment & Desktop Management," ISBN 0-7357-0975-0.* ◆

RDP Client Applications

Chapter 2, "Microsoft Windows Terminal Server," briefly mentions the two RDP clients that are provided with Terminal Server: the Terminal Services Client and the Client Connection Manager. The following sections describe these clients in more detail.

Terminal Services Client

The *Terminal Services Client* (TSC) really serves two functions:

- It can be used as a simple tool for establishing a connection to a Terminal Server. When you start TSC, a dialog box appears, similar to the one shown in Figure 13.3. The lower half of the dialog box lists all the Terminal Servers found in the current domain. To establish a connection, select one of the servers, choose the resolution size, and click the Connect button. The Server drop-down list shows a history of the servers that you've previously connected to. If the server you want isn't in the list, you can type the name in the text box.

  Having the appropriate name service (DNS or WINS) configured in your environment ensures that all the valid Terminal Servers are displayed. Very little configuration is involved in the TSC, and on its own it's not a very useful application to deploy to end users unless you're implementing as described in the next bullet point. Requiring the user to select a server (and desired resolution) every time he or she connects is not only unnecessary, but it may cause problems if users shouldn't be connecting to some servers in the environment, such as test or development servers. A better solution is to provide users with shortcuts that they simply double-click to establish Terminal Server connections. These shortcuts are created using the Client Connection Manager (CCM), discussed in the next section.

Figure 13.3   *The Terminal Services Client application.*

- More importantly, TSC works in combination with the Client Connection Manager (CCM) application (described in the next section) to allow the creation of shortcuts to sessions configured in CCM. The following command line would launch TSC and automatically have it run the client connection labeled ORCA in the CCM:

```
"C:\Program Files\Terminal Server Client\MSTSC.EXE" "ORCA"
```

MSTSC.EXE is the executable that starts the Terminal Services Client.

The next section discusses the creation of these connections and their shortcuts.

Client Connection Manager

The *Client Connection Manager* (CCM) is the true RDP client program, with the following capabilities (see Figure 13.4):

- Create and save connection configurations for specific Terminal Servers.

- Create shortcuts to these connections on the desktop.

- Specify connection properties such as window size, whether to open in a window or full screen, and connection speed.

- Configure a connection to launch a specific program automatically. When connecting in this way, the user is immediately presented with the application after he or she logs on, and doesn't have direct access to a Windows desktop. This isn't the same as accessing a published application with the ICA protocol. With the RDP client, you must hardcode the path and application name on the client. With ICA published applications, this information is managed on the server, not on the client. For more information on published applications, see Chapter 3, "Citrix MetaFrame."

- Store user ID, password, and domain information that are automatically provided when the user connects. This allows the session to be logged onto a Terminal Server automatically.

Figure 13.4 *The RDP Client Connection Manager (CCM).*

Author's Note

Allowing users to automatically log onto a server with cached ID and password information is a definite security concern and something that I do not recommend. A Terminal Server can easily be configured to require that users always provide a password, regardless of the information that they have stored on their clients. I describe how this is done in Chapter 12, "Terminal Server Configuration and Tuning." ◆

RDP Client Configuration

The following sections describe how to configure the RDP client to support the three implementation scenarios (desktop replacement, application replacement, and desktop integration) discussed in Chapter 6. Currently, I feel that the RDP client is best suited for use in a desktop-replacement scenario, although application replacement can be implemented with some limitations. Non–Windows client support for RDP is available only through the use of Windows emulators or third-party RDP clients, such as SCO's Tarantella or HOB's Java client.

Desktop-Replacement Connections

The simplest configuration for an RDP connection is a desktop-replacement scenario. These are the steps for setting up a standard server connection:

1. Launch CCM and click New Connection on the File menu. This will launch the Client Connection Manager Wizard. Click Next to begin.

2. Figure 13.5 shows the initial screen in the wizard. Enter a description for the connection (you can include spaces). You also enter the name or IP address of the Terminal Server or network load-balanced environment. If you don't know the name of the server, click the Browse button to list all available Windows domains. Then you can drill into the desired domain to see the available Terminal Servers. (You must have access to a domain to see its Terminal Servers.) After entering the desired information, click Next to continue.

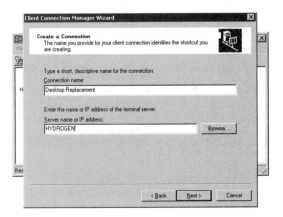

Figure 13.5   *Entering the connection description and server name.*

3. In the next screen, you can enter automatic logon information. If you do, you're required to provide all the information; for example, you cannot provide only the domain name. As I mentioned earlier, because of the obvious security reasons, I don't recommend using this feature. If a Terminal Server has been configured to always prompt for a password, any settings entered here will be ignored.

Warning

If you have disabled Remember Last Logon on a Terminal Server, the automatic logon feature won't work with the RDP client even if the server connections have been configured to allow this. This is because the TSC passes the auto-logon information to the server in the same way that it passes the information for displaying who last logged onto the server from the client. Because this is disabled on the server, the information isn't processed properly. For more information on how to enable or disable the Remember Last Logon feature, refer to Chapter 12. ◆

4. In the next dialog box, you select the screen options for the session (see Figure 13.6). Only screen sizes that are equal to or smaller than the client's actual screen resolution will be available for selection.

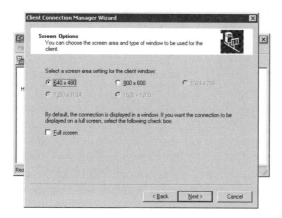

Figure 13.6   *Setting the screen options.*

When configuring the client for desktop replacement, click the screen size that matches the local client's, and then click the Full Screen check box. Selecting Full Screen completely hides the local desktop behind the Terminal Server session. Table 13.1 lists the shortcut keys that are most useful in a full-screen Terminal Server session.

Table 13.1   *Common RDP Session Shortcut Keys*

Desired Function	Local Desktop Shortcut Key	Terminal Server Session Shortcut Key
Move forward between active programs	Alt+Tab	Alt+Page Up
Move backward between active programs	Alt+Shift+Tab	Alt+Page Down
Cycle through programs in their start order	Alt+Esc	Alt+Insert
Display the Start menu	Ctrl+Esc	Alt+Home
Display the Windows security dialog (Windows Professional/ Workstation only)	Ctrl+Alt+Delete	Ctrl+Alt+End
Display the active window's Control menu	Alt+Spacebar	Alt+Delete
Toggle the client between a window and full-screen session	Not applicable	Ctrl+Alt+Break

> **Tip**
>
> *For your RDP session to use the full screen, you must select the proper desktop screen resolution. For example, if you have a client with a resolution of 1024 × 768 and you select Full Screen but have selected 800 × 600 as the screen area, the usable desktop space within the session will be only 800 × 600, and the remaining area will simply appear black.* ◆

5. On the next screen, you can configure the compression and bitmap caching settings for the RDP client (see Figure 13.7). If you'll be connecting over a slow dial-up or WAN link, I recommend selecting both options. If you're on a fast LAN connection, select only the Compression option. Compression will introduce only a small additional load on both the client *and* the server. In Chapter 5, "Network Planning," I demonstrate how the different client options can affect the average bandwidth utilization for both RDP and ICA. After selecting the desired options, click Next.

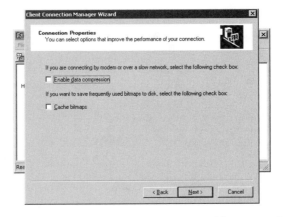

Figure 13.7   *Setting up data compression and bitmap caching.*

6. Next you can specify an application to start automatically after the user has logged onto Terminal Server. For a desktop-replacement scenario, leave this screen blank. For more details on this dialog, see the later section "Application-Replacement Connections."

7. The next screen allows you to select the icon and folder to be used when CCM automatically creates the shortcut to this new connection. The default folder is the Terminal Services Client folder in the common Start menu. Enter the desired options and click Next.

8. The final screen presents a brief summary of the connection you've just created. Click Finish to complete the setup.

The icon for the newly created connection now appears in the CCM and in the folder that you selected in step 7. You can modify the properties for this connection at any time by right-clicking the icon and selecting Properties. To test the new connection, double-click it. The logon for the full-screen Terminal Server session should now appear.

Creating the Desktop Shortcut

To create a desktop shortcut to the new connection, right-click the connection and select Create Shortcut on Desktop. As mentioned earlier, the application that's actually responsible for launching a session from a shortcut is the Terminal Services Client (MSTSC.EXE). Executing this program with the associated connection description launches that session. For example, to launch my connection to the server with the description "Helium Server," the shortcut would look like this:

```
"C:\Program Files\Terminal Services Client\MSTSC.EXE" "Helium Server"
```

Notice that the quotes are required for both the path to the executable and the connection description.

Author's Note

Typically, when employing a desktop replacement scenario, you'll configure the local desktop to launch the RDP client automatically and initiate the Terminal Server connection when the user logs on or starts the local computer. This configuration usually works best when all the computers in a certain area are being employed merely as a form of Windows Terminal. Call center or shop-floor implementations are both common examples, since all the users of the computer are running completely from within a Terminal Server desktop and don't need access to the local desktop.

The exact method of launching the RDP session depends on the client operating system, but a simple example is to add the session shortcut to the startup menu. Another option might be to add a value called "RDPClient" with the data string containing your shortcut information. For example, add this value:

```
"C:\Program Files\Terminal Services Client\MSTSC.EXE" "Helium Server"
```

to this registry key:

```
HKLM\Software\Microsoft\Windows\CurrentVersion\Run ◆
```

Application-Replacement Connections

With the RDP client, the only option currently available to support an application-replacement implementation is to configure an RDP connection to include the application name and path (described in the earlier section

"Desktop Replacement Connections"—see step 6 of the RDP client installation instructions). Figure 13.8 shows a sample configuration of an RDP connection that automatically launches Microsoft Word. Notice that the environment variables %HOMEDRIVE% and %HOMEPATH% have been defined as part of the application setup on the *local client*. These variables are not defined on the client, but are defined on the server. This is possible because the client passes the information to the server to execute the desired program. The server takes the variables and expands them before processing. I talk more about %HOMEDRIVE% and %HOMEPATH% in Chapter 19, "Application Integration."

Author's Note

When setting up the Terminal Server Client to launch a specific application, no validation is performed with respect to the application directory, working directory, or filename. Test a connection immediately after setting it up to ensure that it's working properly. Otherwise, when run, the Terminal Server session will simply flash on the screen and then disappear. ♦

Figure 13.8 *Configuring application replacement with the RDP client.*

If a user launches a shortcut for that connection, Microsoft Word appears (see Figure 13.9). Notice the two title bars—one for Word, and the other for the Terminal Server client. I've seen this cause confusion for users on more than one occasion. The only way to overcome this problem is through education, and training the users to understand why there are two title bars.

Figure 13.9   *Microsoft Word launched directly from an RDP client.*

For more information on planning the client portion of an application-replacement scenario, see the section "Deployment Scenarios with RDP and ICA" in Chapter 6. This section discusses some of the issues that exist with the RDP client when using it in an application-replacement scenario.

Author's Note

Don't rely on configuring a user's client to launch only a specific application as a means of preventing the user from accessing other applications on the Terminal Server. If you want to grant access only to certain applications while denying access to others, implement the necessary file system security as discussed in Chapter 12. If you plan to implement an application-replacement scenario, I recommend that you look at deploying Citrix MetaFrame and leveraging its published application feature. ◆

Desktop-Integration Connections

The only options currently available for providing RDP support on a non–Windows operating system is through Windows emulation software such as WINE (WINdows Emulator) on UNIX, the RDP Java client from HOB (http://www.hob.de/www_us), or SCO's Tarantella (http://www.tarantella.com).

RDP Client Deployment Options

Chapter 6 talks about the different client deployment options. In general, they're broken down into manual and automated:

- **Manual.** This involves someone physically visiting the client's desktop to install and configure the client software as required. In almost every situation, some standard configuration is developed, documented, and then automated to a degree so that the support person must perform only minimal work to get the client working properly. A standard configuration can be deployed with the RDP client; unfortunately, it's not very automated. Within CCM, the Export and Export All options on the File menu enable you to export the connections from one installation of CCM and import them into another installation. The options are imported into the new client by selecting Import from the File menu.

  An easier way to automate the configuration of the RDP client is to export the contents of this registry key:

  ```
  HKEY_CURRENT_USER\Software\Microsoft\Terminal Server Client
  ```

  Note that the key is Terminal *Server* Client. This key contains all the connection settings for the RDP client. If you export this key as a .REG file using REGEDIT, you can then very quickly import the contents onto the client on which you're performing the installation. The import can be done either by double-clicking it in Explorer or running the command REGEDIT *<filename>*.REG from a command prompt or within a batch file.

- **Automated.** This installation involves the use of a deployment tool such as Systems Management Server (SMS) packages, or as I discussed earlier in this chapter, Windows 2000 group policies and Active Directory.

  When planning to automate your client deployment, it's critical that you take the time to ensure that the client is functioning properly—not only from a location local to the servers, but from a remote network location if necessary (depending on the user's location). While this certainly sounds logical, for some reason I repeatedly encounter implementations that have spent only a minimal amount of time testing the user's client configuration. In a manual implementation this is bad enough, but when the client deployment is automated, you may have hundreds of users with the RDP or ICA client before you determine that there's an issue.

Author's Note

Citrix provides the ability to easily customize and create an unattended installation of the ICA client. MetaFrame also has the ability to automatically update a user's ICA client when the user logs onto the server. For more information on these features, see Chapter 14, "ICA Client Installation and Configuration." ◆

ICA Client Installation and Configuration

In this chapter:

- **ICA Client Installation**
  Citrix provides a straightforward process for installing its ICA client on any of the supported platforms.

- **ICA Client Applications**
  Citrix provides two different ICA client applications: Program Neighborhood for its Win32 client and the Remote Application Manager for other platforms (with the exception of the Java and Web clients).

- **ICA Client Configuration**
  For each of the implementation scenarios (desktop replacement, application replacement, and desktop integration), the client can be configured using both Program Neighborhood and the Remote Application Manager.

- **Deploying the ICA Client**
  Citrix provides two features to help in the customization and deployment of the ICA client: the client installation customization (sometimes known as ReadyConnect) and the Automatic Client Update utility.

ICA Client Installation

Chapter 6, "Client Planning," talks in detail about both the ICA and RDP clients, the various implementation categories that exist (desktop replacement, application replacement, and desktop integration), and the planning and support considerations for which you must account when planning your Terminal Server implementation. This chapter looks at the steps for installing the ICA client and configuring the client to provide support for each of the implementation categories.

Author's Note

As mentioned in Chapter 13, "RDP Client Installation and Configuration," don't let the ease of installation for the ICA and RDP clients lead you to believe that a formal implementation plan is not required for your client deployment.

One problem I often encounter with poorly planned client installations is an inconsistency in the configuration of the keyboard mappings for the ICA client (these are not configurable in the RDP client). Very often the ICA client hotkeys must be modified to avoid a conflict with another application. A 3270 host emulator is a good example of this problem, since it required certain PF and PA key combinations that very often match the default keys for the ICA client. Unless this modification has been considered during the client planning and configuration phases, it can be difficult to correct after the implementation is underway. ◆

All the Citrix ICA clients available at the time of the MetaFrame 1.8 release are accessible from at least one of the following locations:

- On the MetaFrame CD in the directory D:\i386\FILES\system32\clients\ICA (where D: is the CD-ROM drive). Each of the clients has its own subdirectory: ICA16, ICA32, ICADOS, ICADOS32, ICAJava, ICAMAC, ICAUNIX (which contains a subdirectory for each of the supported UNIX versions), and ICAWeb.

- The installation files for the various PC clients (DOS, Windows 16-bit and 32-bit) can be accessed from floppy disks generated using the ICA Client Creator application.

- The client files should be in the directory %SystemRoot%\System32\Clients\ICA on a Terminal Server that has MetaFrame installed.

Author's Note

I recommend that you periodically check the Citrix Web site (www.citrix.com) for the latest information on what clients and versions are available. Client updates are infrequent, but they do occur. At the time of this writing, the current ICA client version shipping with MetaFrame 1.8 for Windows 2000 was 4.21.779. ◆

In addition to the standard installation options that are available—similar to those provided with the Client Connection Manager (CCM) for RDP—MetaFrame provides additional functionality, such as the capacity to completely customize the default settings for a client installation or automate client updates during a user's session connection. I talk more about configuring these features later in this chapter.

Creating ICA Client Installation Disks

The client floppy disk creation for ICA clients is nearly identical to the one for RDP clients. ICA client disks are created by running the ICA Client Creator program located under the MetaFrame Tools folder on the Start menu.

After you start the program, the dialog box Create Installation Disk(s) appears, as shown in Figure 14.1. Although this dialog box has the same name as in the Terminal Services Client Creator, it contains a list of ICA clients that you can create. Simply select the type of client disks you want to create and then click OK to begin.

Figure 14.1   *The ICA Create Installation Disk(s) dialog box.*

Installing the MetaFrame Client

Following are the steps for installing the Windows 32-bit Citrix MetaFrame client. Although the installation instructions vary slightly for other ICA clients, depending on the client operating system, the general requirements are the same and the actual client configuration is very similar. The only exceptions are the Web and Java clients, discussed further in Chapter 15, "Web Computing with MetaFrame."

1. Run Setup.exe from the installation location. The first screen reminds you to shut down any other running applications prior to proceeding with the client installation. Click Next when ready.

2. The next screen displays the Citrix client software license agreement.

Review the details and then click Yes to continue if you accept the terms of the agreement.

3. If you have an older version of the ICA client installed, you have the option to either upgrade or install in a new location. If you have an existing client, I recommend performing an upgrade and replacing the client. All ICA clients are fully compatible with all Citrix WinFrame and MetaFrame servers, although certain client features such as sound are available only on servers that support that feature. Make your selection and then click Next to continue.

4. If you're performing the installation in a separate directory or installing for the first time, you're prompted to select the location to install the files. Just as with the RDP client, you probably have already developed a standard installation location for the client to help ensure consistency within the environment. Provide the desired destination directory and then click Next.

5. The next dialog box prompts you to enter or validate the unique client name for this installation. The client name is used by MetaFrame to manage local drives, printers, and other resources; if two clients have the same client name, conflicts may arise between local resources on the machines. After entering the client name, click Next to continue.

Tip

On the PC platform, you can modify the client name at any time by using the Citrix client software or by updating the WFCNAME.INI file located in the root directory of drive C:. You must close and reopen the client software to pick up any changes to the WFCNAME.INI file. If possible, lock down access to that file to prevent tampering by users. ◆

---

6. Setup then copies the necessary files to the client computer. When this process is finished, the client installation is complete. Unlike previous versions of the ICA client, all versions of the client that include the Program Neighborhood (since the release of MetaFrame 1.8 and later) require a reboot of the computer before they can be used.

ICA Client Applications

Chapter 3, "Citrix MetaFrame," talks about the two different ICA clients that are available, depending on the platform on which you're running the ICA client. The Windows 32-bit client has the *Program Neighborhood* (PN) client; other platforms have the *Remote Application Manager*. Special versions of Program Neighborhood are available for both the Java and Web clients, but I'll defer my discussion on these until Chapter 15, where I look at them in more detail.

Author's Note

If you're running an older version of the Citrix ICA client on the Win32 platform, you'll have the Remote Application Manager instead of Program Neighborhood. The PN client only became available with the release of MetaFrame 1.8. ◆

Common ICA Client Properties

Before discussing the details about the Remote Application Manager and Program Neighborhood, the following sections point out the properties and settings that are common to both clients. Many of these features are available in all versions of the ICA client.

General Settings

The general settings of an ICA client allow the changing of general information pertaining to the behavior of the client, such as the following options:

- Setting or modifying the client name.

- Assigning a serial number. A serial number is only required if you're running the ICA client supplied with the *ICA PC Client Pack*, in which case you must include the serial number in order to log onto the MetaFrame server.

- Setting the default keyboard layout to values such as Dutch, British, or Canadian French.

- Alternate keyboard type such as the original PC/XT keyboard or a language-specific keyboard such as Japanese.

- Dial-in settings, which allows you to specify whether the Connect To screen or terminal window appears during the dial-in.

- The option to allow automatic client updates, which controls whether the client will respond to a client-update request issued from a MetaFrame server. For a client to be properly updated, this option must be enabled. Unfortunately, this setting can't currently be overridden by anything on the server side. This means that if a user has sufficient privileges on the desktop, he or she could disable this option and prevent client updates from occurring.

Bitmap Caching

Most ICA clients provide the ability to modify the bitmap cache settings, including the size and location of the actual cache as well as the minimum size bitmap that will be cached (the default is 8KB). The cache size is typically a percentage of the total disk volume size where the cache is located. On a large volume, even 1% can be quite significant. If you encounter a large amount of disk thrashing during logon, it can mean that the cache has grown too large. The easiest solution is to clear the cache by clicking the "Clear cache now" button.

Hotkeys

Because the standard key combinations such as Alt+Esc and Alt+Tab are in use on a local desktop, the MetaFrame client allows you to specify alternate key combinations to perform the same function from within a Terminal Server session (see Figure 14.2). A standard set of hotkey combinations should be developed that will not conflict with any of the applications that the user may be running within Terminal Server. For example, many terminal emulation programs such as 3270 host emulators use keys such as Shift or Ctrl+F1 to represent traditional 3270 PA or PF key mappings. These key combinations (Shift+F1, Ctrl+F1) would be overridden by the corresponding Citrix client hotkeys unless the client keys were mapped differently.

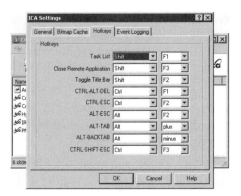

Figure 14.2   *Client Hotkeys tab.*

Figure 14.3 shows the key combinations that seem to introduce the least number of conflicts with other applications. I disable a number of hotkeys and utilize the Alt+ combination with all others; I've found that most users use key combinations such as Alt+Esc so rarely that few people even notice when it's not available. Of course, you need to provide a standard keyboard set that's suitable for your environment, and this should be finalized during the client planning phase prior to deploying any clients to the end user.

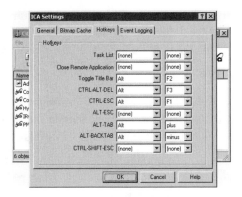

Figure 14.3 *The author's suggested ICA hotkey combinations.*

Server Location

One of the most important ICA client features is the server location list, as shown in Figure 14.4. Chapter 3 discusses the details of the ICA browser service and the role it plays in providing server and application information to an ICA client. An ICA client attempts to generate a server and published application list by locating a master browser to query for information. A master browser is also contacted when a client is connecting to a load-balanced application so that it can be directed to the server with the least load.

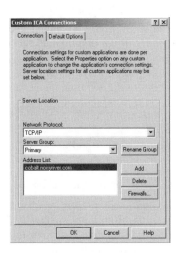

Figure 14.4 *Server location settings.*

The client attempts to locate a master browser by issuing UDP broadcasts unless one or more MetaFrame server addresses are supplied in the server location list. When the list is populated, the client contacts the servers on that list in order to obtain the necessary information, rather than issuing the broadcast. This can be an important feature, since the network support staff will typically request that broadcasts be minimized as much as possible. The Server Location settings must be populated when the ICA clients and the MetaFrame servers exist on different networks unless an ICA gateway exists between the client network and the MetaFrame server network, since the UDP broadcasts typically won't cross a router.

Author's Note

Server location entries are not required if you're connecting directly to a server with its name or network address. In this situation, the client doesn't query for a master browser but simply attempts to connect to the named server. ◆

Up to three groups of five servers can be defined for each of the available protocols that your clients will use to create MetaFrame server connections. By default, the groups are labeled Primary, Backup1, and Backup2, but you can rename them by highlighting the existing name and clicking the Rename Group button.

The client queries all servers in the Primary group for the necessary browser information; if no response is received within the given time interval, the client repeats the request with the Backup1 group and finally the Backup2 group, if necessary. If no response is received from any of the servers in any of the groups, the client fails with an error message similar to the one shown in Figure 14.5.

Figure 14.5   *Error received by the client when no servers are available.*

The backup groups are most often used when a separate MetaFrame environment exists on a different network that would support users if the primary environment is unavailable. This could be a fail-over site for disaster recovery or a corporate or branch office that would normally not support these users but could do so if necessary.

An ICA client attempts to contact a master ICA browser when performing any of the following actions:

- Connecting to a published application
- Gathering information about a server farm
- Returning a list of MetaFrame servers or published applications

When populating the server location list, I recommend that you specify *at least* two MetaFrame servers (more if you have them) for each of the appropriate protocols. This strategy provides redundancy in case one of the servers in the list is unavailable. The ICA client sends a directed message to each of the servers simultaneously, and the first response received is used in locating the master browser. Multiple servers ensure that the client receives a response.

If you're implementing multiple MetaFrame sites and it's appropriate to your configuration, you should consider designating one or more of these remote sites as backup server locations.

Tip

If you're using the TCP/IP protocol and broadcasts are not a major concern in your environment, consider using broadcast addresses instead of specific server addresses. This setup directs the client to issue a UDP datagram to all servers on that subnet, ensuring that if there are any active MetaFrame servers, the client will receive a response. For example, if you have MetaFrame servers on the 192.168.10.0 network, the broadcast address would be 192.168.10.255. This allows you to further generalize clients and not tie them to the existence of particular servers. It also allows for the designation of particular networks as possible future fail-over or disaster-recovery sites and their inclusion in the client configuration without requiring specific server IP addresses. I would recommend consulting with your network support staff prior to implementing this change, to ensure that it won't introduce any network utilization problems. ◆

Author's Note

A common misconception is that the server list must contain the name of the master browser in order to work properly. This is not true. The list only needs to contain the names of MetaFrame servers on the same network as the master browser that the client needs to contact. The servers in the list must be ICA aware. You can't list Terminal Servers if they're not running MetaFrame, but you can include any WinFrame servers that exist in your environment. ◆

Event Logging

If you're encountering problems with a user accessing a MetaFrame server, you can configure Event Logging to record information about the user's session so that you can review and debug it (see Figure 14.6). When gathering data, select the option Append to Existing Event Log; otherwise the log will be overwritten every time the user logs onto MetaFrame. Normally you'll only want to log connections, disconnections, and errors. The other options, Data Transmitted, Data Received, and Keyboard and Mouse Data, will fill the logs very quickly. Never enable these other options by default, as it will have a large negative impact on the client's performance.

Figure 14.6   *Event logging options.*

Remote Application Manager

The Remote Application Manager is used to create various ICA client connections and is almost functionally identical to the CCM for the RDP client. Figure 14.7 shows the main Remote Application Manager dialog box that appears when you start the application on Linux.

Author's Note

The executable name for the Remote Application Manager varies, depending on the client OS. For example, the Win16 client is called wfcmgr16.exe, while on UNIX it's wfcmgr. The WF in wfcmgr is a holdover from the days of WinFrame, and the name has remained to maintain consistency with previous versions of the Remote Application Manager. ◆

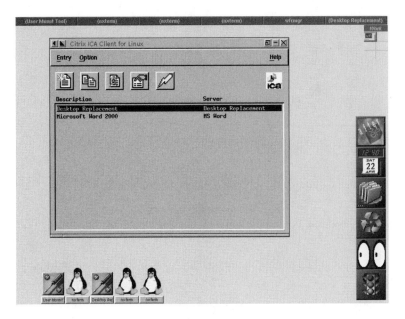

Figure 14.7   *The Citrix Remote Application Manager for Linux.*

Just as with the CCM, you can configure the Remote Application Manager client to launch a complete desktop or a specific application. With the ICA client, you have two different ways of accessing the application: You can specify the server name and the path to the application as you would with CCM, or you can select the desired application from the list of published applications available in your MetaFrame environment.

Warning

Just as with applications accessed through CCM, if the program being used allows the launching of another program, users may have access to applications that you didn't intend to them to use. ◆

In addition to the properties specific to each MetaFrame connection (discussed shortly), you can set some global options in the Remote Application Manager to affect all configured session connections. Selecting Settings from the Options menu opens the Settings dialog box, as shown in Figure 14.8.

Figure 14.8 *The Win16 Remote Application Manager settings.*

Six settings tabs enable you to configure various aspects of the Remote Application Manager. Most of these options are discussed in the earlier section "Common ICA Client Properties." Where additional functionality is available I'll mention it in the following discussion; otherwise, the behavior is exactly as described in the earlier section.

- **Preferences.** This corresponds to the "General Settings" information discussed in the "Common ICA Client Properties" section.

- **Disk Cache.** When clearing the cache using the Clear Cache Now button, you won't be prompted for verification before the cache is actually cleared.

- **Hotkeys.** Behavior is as described earlier.

- **Server Location.** One thing to note is that *all* MetaFrame connections that you create in the Remote Application Manager will use this server location list to access the desired published application. This introduces a limitation on accessing published applications on multiple subnets unless you implement ICA gateways. For more information on ICA gateways, refer to Chapter 3.

- **Event Logging.** Behavior is as described earlier.

- **Profile.** This tab allows you to modify the configuration of the Remote Application Manager itself by setting such things as the default location and size of the dialog box and the default font to use.

Program Neighborhood

With the introduction of MetaFrame 1.8 and the Citrix concept of a server farm came the new ICA client, Program Neighborhood (PN). PN combines the features originally provided with the Remote Application Manager (discussed in the preceding section) with the single sign-on and application-management features found in the Citrix server farm. Figure 14.9 shows the main PN application window.

Author's Note

With MetaFrame 1.8, single sign-on support is limited to a single server farm. This means that a user logs on to the server farm once and is automatically authenticated for all servers within that farm. If a user wants to access multiple server farms, he or she needs to log onto each one individually. MetaFrame 2.0 is expected to provide true single sign-on when used in conjunction with Windows 2000 Active Directory. ◆

Figure 14.9 *Program Neighborhood.*

This combination of features seems to introduce a large amount of confusion when configuring the client to provide the desired access to published applications and, more importantly, the application sets available through one or more Citrix server farms.

When describing Program Neighborhood, I've always found it easiest to break it down into three pieces:

- **Custom ICA Connections.** This is the component of PN that's nearly identical to the functionality provided by the original Remote Application Manager. Here you define connections to a specific server or published application. Some settings exist that apply only to these custom connections.

- **Application Sets.** These are the custom groupings of applications made available through the Citrix server farm. A user is granted access to one or more applications based on his or her group membership and which applications have been published within a server farm. The user can have multiple application sets from multiple server farms, all accessible from within the Application Sets grouping. Individual application sets can have their own personal settings.

- **Common Settings.** Certain settings are common to both custom connections and application sets. Very often people get confused as to
  which settings apply to what type of connection, which usually leads to
  a misconfigured client.

Common Settings

I'll begin by looking at the common settings that apply to both custom ICA
connections and application sets. The common settings can be accessed at
any time by selecting ICA Settings from the Tools menu. This brings up a
dialog box with a subset of the settings discussed in the earlier section
"Common ICA Client Properties." The four listed tabs are as follows:

- **General.** Behavior is as described earlier.
- **Bitmap Cache.** When manually clearing the cache, you'll be warned to
  ensure that all active ICA connections are closed prior to clearing the
  cache. By default, the bitmap cache is stored in the user's profile in the
  folder Application Data\ICAClient\Cache.
- **Hotkeys.** Behavior is as described earlier.
- **Event Logging.** Behavior is as described earlier.

Custom ICA Connections

Double-clicking the Custom ICA Connections icon within the PN window
opens a custom connection folder similar to the one shown in Figure 14.10.
From here you create connections to servers and published applications that
are specific to the client only. These connections have no relationship to
application sets (described shortly), and don't utilize the single sign-on
authentication feature of PN.

Figure 14.10 *Custom ICA connections.*

In addition to the common settings, custom settings also exist that are specific to custom ICA connections. These settings are accessed by clicking the Settings button on the toolbar or by right-clicking anywhere in the connection view window and selecting Custom Connections Settings.

Figure 14.11 shows the settings that are common to *all* custom connections.

Figure 14.11   *Custom ICA connections global settings.*

The settings window contains two tabs:

- **Connection.** This tab corresponds to the server location information mentioned in the earlier section "Common ICA Client Properties."

  Just as with the connections in the Remote Application Manager, *all* MetaFrame connections that you create under Custom ICA Connections will use this server location list to access the desired master browser information. This introduces a limitation on accessing published applications on multiple subnets unless you implement ICA gateways or utilize Citrix server farms and application sets (described shortly). For more information on ICA gateways, see Chapter 3.

This tab also contains the Firewalls button that you use to configure default settings for connecting to a MetaFrame server located behind a firewall. I discuss this further in Chapter 15.

- **Default Options.** These are default settings for sound, screen size, and color depth that are applied to all new connections. These settings can be changed for a specific connection by modifying its properties. For each connection that has been created, you can modify its individual properties by right-clicking the connection and selecting Properties. For more about the creation and management of connections, see the later section "ICA Client Configuration."

Application Sets

A new feature introduced with the Program Neighborhood client is the concept of an *application set*. Application sets are groups of published applications within a server farm to which a user has been granted access by an administrator. Chapter 19, "Application Integration," describes the creation and management of applications within one or more Citrix server farms.

Following are some characteristics of application sets:

- All applications within an application set reside within the same server farm. You can't combine applications from different farms into a single set.

- A single user can simultaneously access multiple application sets from different server farms.

- Each application set maintains its own settings, which include its own server location list. This allows a user to access multiple application sets located on different networks.

- Single sign-on applies only to an application set. To access multiple application sets, a user must log onto each set individually. A single sign-on doesn't apply to multiple application sets.

After an application set has been created, it appears in the main PN window, as shown in Figure 14.12. You can review or modify the client properties for an application set simply by right-clicking the application set icon and selecting Application Set Settings. These settings are initially configured during the creation of a new application set.

Figure 14.12 *An application set in Program Neighborhood.*

Refer to Chapter 3 for a complete discussion on Citrix server farms and application availability.

ICA Client Configuration

As mentioned in Chapter 6, in almost all production environments where you're using MetaFrame, you should have clients configured to access a published application or published desktop, and never a MetaFrame server or application directly. This abstraction allows for the addition or subtraction of servers on the back end without any changes being required on the client. If a user is receiving his or her applications through an application set, the only configuration required on the client is the application set definition itself. Once that's complete, applications are simply managed through security groups. If a user belongs to a group with access to an application, Program Neighborhood automatically makes the icon available to the user in his or her application set.

For each of the implementation scenarios (desktop replacement, application replacement, or desktop integration), the following sections look at how the client would be configured using both Program Neighborhood and the Remote Application Manager (for non–Win32 clients).

Desktop-Replacement Connections

A complete desktop is accessible from a MetaFrame client in one of two ways. It can be referenced directly by server name (see my earlier comments on why you shouldn't do this), or it can be accessed by a published application name (the preferred method), exactly as an individual program would be.

Desktop Replacement with Remote Application Manager

To create a MetaFrame session with the Remote Application Manager, do the following:

1. Launch Remote Application Manager. If you're accessing this program for the first time, it will ask if you want to create a new entry. If an entry already exists or you selected No, click New on the Entry menu.

2. The first dialog box asks what type of connection you want to create (see Figure 14.13). You can choose one of the following:

   - **Network.** The server will be accessed through a LAN or Dial-Up Networking connection.

   - **Dial-In.** The server will be accessed directly through a modem. This is different from Dial-Up Networking (DUN), which establishes the local computer as a node on the network. An ICA dial-in connection connects directly with the Terminal Server.

   - **Serial.** The server will be accessed through a direct serial cable connection.

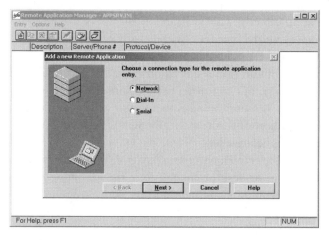

Figure 14.13   *Choosing the connection type in the Remote Application Manager.*

For this example, I'll select Network, which is the most common form of connecting.

After selecting the connection type, click Next.

3. The next dialog box prompts for a description for the connection. Select the protocol that you'll use. If you'll access the server directly by name, select the Server option; otherwise, select the Published Application option to access a published desktop (see Figure 14.14). Select the server or published application from the appropriate drop-down list and then click Next.

Troubleshooting Tip

If the server or application you want isn't listed in the drop-down list, it most likely means that the server is located across a router or is unavailable. If you know the name, type it. If you can then connect successfully, the server is not visible to the current ICA master browser. If it's located on the other side of a router, you'll need to populate the client's server location list as described earlier or use an ICA gateway to make it visible in the list. See Chapter 3 for a discussion on ICA browsing and ICA gateways.

In a TCP/IP network, if the server can't be connected by name, try using the IP address of the server. If this works, there's an issue with your WINS/DNS resolution, which isn't properly resolving your MetaFrame server's name. ◆

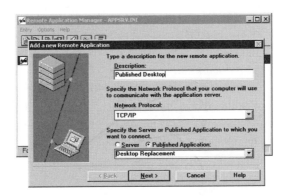

Figure 14.14 *Entering the connection description, protocol, and server or published application name.*

Warning

The Remote Application Manager lists all protocols that the ICA client supports, even if the client computer or the server doesn't support them. When selecting a protocol, choose one that's actually in use. If you receive the message Cannot connect to Citrix server: Protocol Driver Error *when testing the new connection, you probably selected a protocol that's not supported by either the client or the server.* ◆

4. The next dialog box specifies whether the user will communicate with the application server through a SOCKS proxy server. If so, enable the Connect via SOCKS Proxy option and then enter the necessary server address and port number. I talk more about Terminal Server and proxy/firewalls in Chapter 15. Click Next.

5. The next dialog box lets you select the type of network connection you have: a fast network connection or a low-bandwidth connection. If you're on a LAN or a fast WAN, select the fast network option. On a DUN connection or a slow WAN connection, use the low-bandwidth option. Click Next after choosing the connection type.

6. Regardless of the connection type, the next dialog box prompts you to enter a user ID, password, and domain if you want to automatically log onto the MetaFrame session. Enter only a domain name if you want a consistent domain name to appear every time the client connects. Normally the MetaFrame server lists the domain of the last person who logged onto that server. If the server has autologon disabled for security reasons, these settings are ignored.

Warning

For security reasons, I don't recommend using this automatic login feature. Anyone who uses this workstation could then connect to the MetaFrame server as the user whose information has been provided in these fields.

This feature can be disabled on the Terminal Server when configuring the ICA connections. See Chapter 12, "Terminal Server Configuration and Tuning," for details on how to disable this option. ◆

Warning

If the Remember Last Logon feature is disabled on the Terminal Server, the Citrix client still allows you to autologon or pass the domain information through. Citrix clients never display the name of the user who last logged onto the server from a particular client. ◆

7. In the next dialog box, you specify the screen resolution for the client as well as whether audio support is enabled or disabled (see Figure 14.15). To modify the screen resolution to some setting other than the default, click the Change button, disable the Use Default option, and then select the desired resolution. If you're accessing a published application, you can select the Seamless Windows option. For a desktop-replacement scenario, I recommend selecting the Full Screen option.

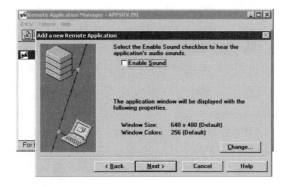

Figure 14.15   *Specifying the sound and resolution options.*

Tip

When you select Full Screen with the Citrix client, you actually get a MetaFrame session that appears full screen. It automatically adjusts to the resolution of your desktop. For example, if you're running at 800 × 600, you get a full-screen Terminal Server session running at 800 × 600. ◆

---

8. Next, specify the path to the executable and its working directory. In a desktop replacement scenario, leave this information blank. If you have selected a published desktop, this screen won't appear.

9. In the next dialog box, specify the icon and the program group where the connection shortcut will be created. Clicking Next takes you to the final dialog box, which summarizes the connection you've created. Click Finish to complete the connection setup.

10. After completing the setup, the connection appears in the Remote Application Manager's main dialog box. To modify the properties for a connection, highlight it and select Properties from the Entry menu.

You can create icons or batch files to access a Remote Application Manager entry directly, instead of having the user start the Remote Application Manager and click the desired server. A helper application for ICA can directly launch the connection entry. On the Win16 platform, this file is called WFCRUN16.EXE.

The usage is very straightforward. Simply precede the application with the description for the connection that you created. For example, if you had a server connection with the description MFSrv01, to launch it directly using the 16-bit executable you would enter this command for the command-line property:

```
WFCRUN16.Exe "MFSrv01"
```

Quotes are mandatory if the description contains spaces.

Desktop Replacement with Program Neighborhood

Program Neighborhood offers two ways to implement desktop replacement: by using the Custom ICA Connection option or through a server farm and application set. The following sections describe the configuration steps for both methods.

Custom ICA Connection

A custom ICA connection would be created as follows:

1. From the root of the Program Neighborhood, double-click the Custom ICA Connection icon; then double-click the Add ICA Connection icon.

2. The first screen prompts you to select the type of connection you want to create: Local Area Network (LAN), Wide Area Network (WAN), Dial-Up Networking (DUN), or ICA Dial-In. The DUN option simply initiates a Microsoft DUN PPP or RAS connection prior to attempting to connect to the desired Citrix server. ICA dial-in establishes a direct dial-in to a MetaFrame server. When the WAN option is selected, additional compression features are enabled to maximize the available bandwidth; these features are not normally enabled for a regular LAN connection.

   For this example, I'll select the LAN option.

   After selecting the connection type, click Next.

3. Next, you can provide a description, select the network protocol to use, and select the server or published application name (see Figure 14.16). As mentioned earlier, whenever possible you should use published applications, even for accessing a complete Terminal Server desktop. Select the appropriate option, specify the desired server or published desktop, and click Next.

Troubleshooting Tip

If the server or application you want isn't listed in the drop-down list, it most likely means that the server is located across a router or is unavailable. If you know the name, type it. If you can then connect successfully, the server is not visible to the current ICA master browser. If it's located on the other side of a router, you'll need to populate the client's server location list as described earlier or use an ICA gateway to make it visible in the list. See Chapter 3 for a discussion on ICA browsing and ICA gateways.

In a TCP/IP network, if the server can't be connected by name, try using the IP address of the server. If this works, there's an issue with your WINS/DNS resolution, which isn't properly resolving your MetaFrame server's name. ◆

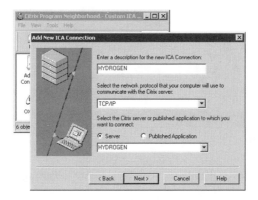

Figure 14.16   *Selecting new ICA connection properties.*

4. Next you specify whether the user will communicate with the application server through a SOCKS proxy server (see Figure 14.17). If so, enable the Connect via SOCKS Proxy option and then enter the necessary server address and port number. For more about Terminal Server and proxy/firewalls, see Chapter 15. Click Next.

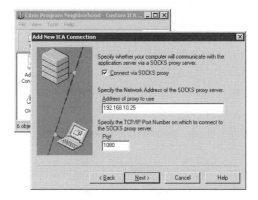

Figure 14.17   *SOCKS proxy option for a custom ICA connection.*

5. Specify whether the application will run in a seamless window or in a remote desktop window. When accessing a complete desktop, select the remote desktop window option. For more information on seamless windows, see Chapter 3.

6. Next you can enter a user ID, password, and domain if you want to automatically log onto the MetaFrame session. Enter only a domain name if you want a consistent domain name to appear every time the client connects. Normally the MetaFrame server lists the domain of the last person who logged onto that server. If the server has autologon disabled, these settings are ignored.

Warning

For security reasons, I don't recommend using the Automatic Login feature. It can very easily allow anyone with access to the client's workstation to log onto a MetaFrame server with their ID. ◆

Author's Note

If the Remember Last Logon feature is disabled on the Terminal Server, the Citrix client will still allow you to autologon or pass the domain information through. Citrix clients never display the name of the user who last logged onto the server from a particular client. ◆

7. Next you're asked to specify the color depth and resolution for the connection. If necessary, deselect the Use Default check box and select the desired values. For a full desktop connection, always select Full Screen. You'll need to scroll to the bottom of the Window Size drop-down list to find the full screen option.

8. The final screen simply informs you that the connection was successfully created; clicking the Finish button completes the connection creation and adds the connection icon to the Custom ICA Connections window.

9. To create a shortcut for this connection, right-click the icon and select Create Desktop Shortcut.

Application Sets
The creation of a desktop connection within an application set requires the following steps:

- Creation of the published desktop within the server farm, and the assignment of a domain group to manage its access.

- The configuration of the client to access the defined application set.

- Assignment of the user to the appropriate domain group.

The first time you run Program Neighborhood, you're prompted to select a default application set. If this wasn't done initially, you need to add the necessary application set for the client manually. Follow these steps to add an application set:

1. Open Program Neighborhood, and if necessary click the Up toolbar option until you see the Find New Application Set icon. Double-click this icon to begin the process of adding a new application set.

2. The first screen prompts you to select a method of connecting to the application set. The only options you have are LAN, WAN, and Dial-Up Networking. You don't have the direct Citrix dial-in option, because an application set assumes that you'll access one or more published applications on multiple servers. Citrix dial-in would connect you directly to only one server.

3. After selecting the network configuration to use, you're prompted to enter a name for the application set and to select an existing set from the drop-down list (see Figure 14.18). Notice that you're provided with the option of defining the server location for this application set. This server location applies *only* to this application set, which means that you can have multiple application sets, all corresponding to MetaFrame servers located on separate networks. See the earlier section "Common ICA Client Properties" for more information on the server location.

Figure 14.18   *Finding a new application set.*

4. In the next dialog box, you can specify display options that override the defaults set for the application set. You can enable sound if required, as well as specify the color depth and the desktop size.

Tip

I recommend using the server-set defaults. This strategy helps to simplify the environment and prevent "one-offs" in which one user's application set is configured one way, and another user has something different. ◆

5. The final screen confirms the creation of the application set. After you click Finish, the corresponding icon is added to Program Neighborhood.

After an application set has been added, you can set it as the default by right-clicking the icon and selecting Set as Default. The icon for the default application set displays a check mark. Whenever Program Neighborhood starts, it automatically attempts to connect to the default application set. Once connected, it displays the Program Neighborhood logon dialog box and requests the user ID, password, and domain. After you have logged on, the applications available with this default application set are displayed when Program Neighborhood starts up. Figure 14.19 shows the Desktop Replacement published-application icon within Program Neighborhood.

> **Tip**
>
> *The Remember Password option in the Program Neighborhood logon can be disabled so that users are required to enter a password. See the later section "ICA Client Settings—The APPSRV.INI and PN.INI Files" for information on how to do this.* ◆

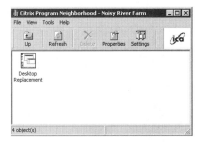

Figure 14.19   *Application-set icons are available when logged onto Program Neighborhood.*

Double-clicking the Application Set Manager icon returns you to the Program Neighborhood window, where you can add new application sets or create custom ICA connections. To return to the default application window, click the Up button on the toolbar until you reach this uppermost window.

> **Author's Note**
>
> *If no default application set is selected, the user isn't prompted with the Program Neighborhood logon dialog box until he or she double-clicks a specific application within an application set.* ◆

After the application set has been defined on the client and the desktop session has been published, it's simply a matter of assigning the user to the corresponding group; the desktop icon will automatically become available when the user logs onto that application set (refer to Figure 14.19).

Application-Replacement Connections

One of Citrix's strong suits is its capacity to provide robust application-integration features, which are ideal in an application-replacement scenario.

Published Applications and Seamless Windows

While the RDP client currently only supports configuring a specific application connection directly on the client, the ICA client supports a Citrix feature known as *published applications*, a superior method of delivering individual applications (as well as complete desktops) to the end user. Published applications provide centralized access control and management as well as transparent load balancing. To configure a published application on a client, you just select its name from a published application list. You don't need to know the executable path or working directory, or even on which server(s) the application is available.

As recommended in Chapter 6, whenever performing an application-integration project with MetaFrame, you should implement published applications and not provide the executable name and working directory within the client software. All Citrix clients support accessing published applications.

Three presentation methods are available for a published application:

- The published application is presented within a client window boundary, as shown in Figure 14.20. This is exactly the same as you would get with the RDP client.

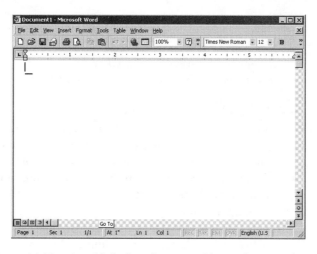

Figure 14.20 *A published application within a client window.*

- The published application displays without its own title bar but remains within a client window boundary. This is identical to the previous configuration except that the application's title bar is hidden. This helps to create the illusion that the application is actually running locally to the client (see Figure 14.21). The one complaint that I often hear from users working in this scenario is that they can't resize the application window. This is because it's actually the ICA session client window, which can't be resized. This can be particularly troublesome for applications such as Internet Explorer or Microsoft Word, which many users want to size to suit their personal preference.

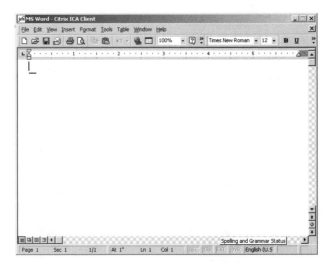

Figure 14.21   *A published application within a client window, but without its personal title bar.*

- The published application is presented within a seamless window. The seamless window overcomes the problems that exist with the previous two methods by eliminating the client window boundaries and allowing the application to visually function as if it were running locally. In fact, combining this with integration features such as printer and drive mappings results in an application that is nearly indistinguishable from a locally running application.

For more information on published applications and seamless windows, see Chapter 3. Chapter 19 discusses the steps in configuring and publishing applications in a MetaFrame environment.

Application Replacement with Remote Application Manager

With the Remote Application Manager, a client is configured to access a published application in the same way as described for a desktop-replacement scenario. (See the earlier section "Desktop Replacement with Remote Application Manager.") In the third step of the procedure, select the Published Application option and then select the desired application from the drop-down list (see Figure 14.22).

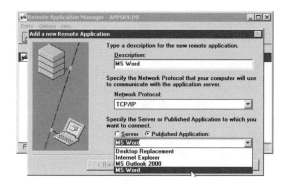

Figure 14.22   *Selecting a published application.*

Application Replacement with Program Neighborhood

The steps for configuring an individual application within Program Neighborhood are identical to those for configuring the complete desktop. (See the earlier section "Desktop Replacement with Program Neighborhood.") In the third step of the custom ICA connection configuration procedure, select the desired published application from the drop-down list.

When using application sets, after the application has been published within the server farm, you simply add the user to the application's access group and the icon will automatically appear within the Program Neighborhood window (see Figure 14.23).

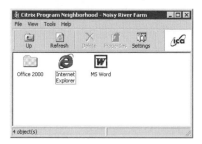

Figure 14.23   *Applications automatically appear in the Program Neighborhood window.*

Desktop Integration Connections

The wide support for heterogeneous computing environments provided by Citrix makes it currently the only real solution for cross-platform access to a Terminal Server environment. The consistency in the user interface between different clients also means that it's very straightforward to configure a non–Windows client to access either a complete Windows desktop or an individual application, both using the published application feature of MetaFrame.

Figure 14.24 demonstrates how a published desktop or individual application can be accessed from non–Windows clients. A similar interface is available for other clients such as those for DOS or Macintosh. Unfortunately, Program Neighborhood is only supported with the Windows 32-bit, Java, and Web clients, and the seamless windows feature is supported only on the Win32 client. I discuss the Java and Web clients in Chapter 15.

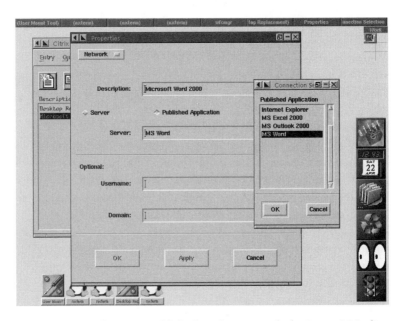

Figure 14.24   *Selecting a published application with the Linux ICA client.*

Deploying the ICA Client

Citrix provides two features to help in the customization and deployment of the ICA client:

- **Installation customization.** The ICA client installation is fully configurable, enabling you to test and then configure the client installation files so that they automatically deliver certain features on setup, such as server location lists, custom ICA connection entries, or standard application sets.

- **Automatic Client Update.** Updates or changes to the ICA client can be delivered to a client automatically using Citrix's Automatic Client Update feature. Client information is maintained in a database that's consulted when a client connects, to determine whether a client update is required. You can use this mechanism to deliver configuration changes as well, including application-set changes or server location list updates.

ICA Client Settings—The APPSRV.INI and PN.INI Files

Before I get into the discussion of how to customize the ICA client installation, it's important to understand how the ICA client maintains both the global and connection-specific settings for a client.

All configuration information for an ICA client is centered around four .INI files:

- **MODULE.INI.** This file maintains default settings for the client transport, protocol, Winstation, and virtual drivers. It also contains default settings for user interface features such as scan codes for the hotkey shift states. Rarely does the information in this file need modifications.

- **PN.INI.** This file contains the settings information for Program Neighborhood application sets that have been configured on the client. For example, if a client has an application set defined for a Citrix server farm called Noisy River Farm, the PN.INI entry might look something like this:

```
[Program Neighborhood]
Noisy River Farm=
[Noisy River Farm]
DesiredHRES=4294967295
DesiredVRES=4294967295
PNName=Noisy River Farm
ConnectType=1
MaximumCompression=Off
UseAlternateAddress=0
NoAutoDetectProtocol=Off
PNProtocolMask=1
Compress=On
PersistentCacheEnabled=Off
```

```
MouseTimer=0
KeyboardTimer=0
AudioBandwidthLimit=1
NoDeskInt=Off
PNCacheRefresh=Off
DefaultVideoType=1
UseDefaultSound=On
DefaultSoundType=1
ClientAudio=Off
UseDefaultEncryption=On
EncryptionLevelSession=1
UseDefaultWinColor=On
DesiredColor=0
UseDefaultWinSize=Off
DesiredWinType=8
TWIMode=On
SavePNPassword=Off
TcpBrowserAddress=192.168.1.255
```

- **APPSRV.INI.** This file maintains the bulk of the client configuration information, including hotkey settings, server location settings for custom connections, custom connection entries, as well as certain Program Neighborhood settings, such as the default application set. A custom connection entry in this file would look something like this:

```
[ApplicationServers]
HYDROGEN=
[HYDROGEN]
TransportDriver=TCP/IP
DesiredHRES=4294967295
DesiredVRES=4294967295
ScreenPercent=0
Description=HYDROGEN
Address=HYDROGEN
IconPath=C:\program files\Citrix\ICA Client\pn.exe
IconIndex=1
ConnectType=1
MaximumCompression=Off
Compress=On
PersistentCacheEnabled=Off
MouseTimer=0
KeyboardTimer=0
AudioBandwidthLimit=1
UseDefaultSound=Off
DefaultSoundType=1
UseDefaultEncryption=On
EncryptionLevel=1
UseDefaultWinColor=Off
UseDefaultWinSize=Off
DesiredWinType=7
TWIMode=Off
SavePNPassword=On
DesiredColor=2
ClientAudio=Off
```

- **WFCLIENT.INI.** This file contains the information used during the initialization of the ICA client. Normally this information won't need changing.

For the Win32 ICA client, both the PN.INI and APPSRV.INI files are located in each user's personal area. On Windows 2000 Professional, for example, this information would be located by default in the directory C:\Documents and Settings\%username%\Application Data\ICAClient. If a user doesn't have these files in his or her personal area, the ICA client automatically copies them from the application's installation directory.

Author's Note

As I mentioned earlier, there is also the WFCNAME.INI file located in the root of the C: drive. This contains only the client name, similar to the following:

```
[WFClient]
ClientName=URANIUM
```

This file is generated during the client installation. ♦

Customizing the ICA Client Installation

The idea behind customizing the installation is to enter the desired settings into the files described in the preceding section, and then have these changes automatically picked up when the client is first run. This feature was once known as *ReadyConnect*, but now is commonly referred to simply as *ICA client customization*.

With a custom installation, you can preconfigure information on such features as Program Neighborhood application sets, custom connections, hotkey configurations, server locations, or other preferences. In this way, you can create custom ICA client installation files that contain exactly the information that you want distributed to your MetaFrame clients.

Follow these steps to create a custom client installation set:

1. If you'll be running installations from a server or you're creating this installation set for use with the Automatic Client Update (ACU) utility, create a directory that will contain the completed custom installation set. Into this directory, copy the standard client installation files for the client you're targeting, using the MetaFrame CD or the latest client downloaded from the Internet.

   If you're going to run the client installation from disks, you can use the ICA Client Creator to create a standard set of installation files that you'll modify to build the custom connection set.

2. Using either the files from your newly created directory or the disks created using the ICA Client Creator, install the client on a test client.

3. Run the appropriate client (Remote Application Manager or Program Neighborhood) and make any desired configuration changes for the client. This includes defining all the desired application sets and optionally selecting a default, adding any required custom connections, and modifying the hotkey configuration.

All the changes that you make will be stored in the files discussed earlier (WFCLIENT.INI, MODULE.INI, PN.INI, and APPSRV.INI). The location of these updated files depends on which client and operating system version were used. For example, if Program Neighborhood was used, the updated files will be located in the *personal area* of whoever performed the custom configuration.

Tip

Options are available to hide the administrative icons within Program Neighborhood (Application Set Manager, Custom Connections, and New Application Sets). These icons can be turned off by adding the following entries to the [WFClient] *portion of the APPSRV.INI file:*

```
[WFClient]
ApplicationSetManagerIconOff=ON
CustomConnectionsIconOff=ON
FindNewApplicationSetIconOff=ON
```

Setting the value to ON *hides the icon; setting it to* OFF *makes it visible again. Other icons exist for controlling the interface, such as this one:*

```
DragOutOff=ON
```

This prevents users from dragging icons onto their desktop.

```
NoSavePwordOption=On
```

This turns off the save password option on the Program Neighborhood logon window. Additional restrictions can be placed on the Program Neighborhood menus by using a "greyed" version of PN. This is the PN executable modified to disable all menu options. You can find this version on the Thin Net Web site at http://thethin.net/downloads.cfm. *Information on how these changes were made is available at* http://thethin.net/visual.cfm. *You should be aware that this modified executable is not supported by Citrix.* ◆

4. Replace the files on the floppy disks (the first disk) or in the target directory with the four updated files from step 3. You'll need to copy these files to the target and rename them as follows:

WFCLIENT.INI becomes WFCLIENT.SRC

MODULE.INI becomes MODULE.SRC

APPSRV.INI becomes APPSRV.SRC

PN.INI becomes PN.SRC

Now, when you perform an installation using the custom disks or directory, the target client automatically loads the preconfigured client files. I recommend that you review the contents of these files prior to using the custom installation set to ensure that you don't have any user-specific information such as a user ID and/or domain. This information is maintained in each user's individual APPSRV.INI file, so you don't want to propagate an APPSRV.SRC file containing a specific user's information. In particular, look to edit the cache and log file paths.

In addition to performing individual installations, these customized files can also be used with the ACU utility, described in the next section.

> **Tip**
>
> *When you're ready to use your customized files with ACU, simply start ACU, select New from the Client menu, navigate to the directory containing the customized files, and select the UPDATE.INI file. You can then configure this ACU as described in the next section.* ✦

Automatic Client Update

Chapter 3 describes the Automatic Client Update (ACU) utility, which allows an administrator to configure a MetaFrame server to issue client updates to a user automatically when the user logs onto the server. ACU provides a simple solution to the problem of keeping the MetaFrame client up to date on a user's desktop.

> **Author's Note**
>
> *For an ICA client to support ACU, it must be version 581 or higher. Prior versions are not recognized by this utility.* ✦

Starting the ACU Utility

To run this utility, select MetaFrame Tools (Common), ICA Client Update Configuration on the Start menu. As with other standard object containers, you can change the view from the View menu. Of note is the Details view, which displays information on all installed clients, including those that are enabled or disabled (see Figure 14.25).

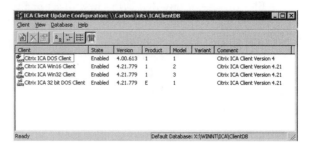

Figure 14.25   *The ICA Automatic Client Update main window in the Details view.*

The ACU main window displays all ICA client files that have been installed and are available for automatic update on the client. This client information is stored in a configuration database, as discussed in the next section.

The ACU Database

By default, the ICA client files and their configuration information are stored in a central database on the MetaFrame server. During the MetaFrame setup, this database is created and the 32-bit Windows, 16-bit Windows, and DOS ICA clients (16-bit and 32-bit) are added.

By default, this database is located in the directory %systemroot%\ICA\ ClientDB on the MetaFrame server. In a multiple-server environment, this configuration isn't very practical, since you would be required to configure the client database on each of your Terminal Servers. Luckily, Citrix allows you to modify the location of this database so that multiple MetaFrame servers can access a single client update database. The only requirement is that this client database be configured on a network share.

To configure a central client database, perform the following steps:

1. Create the required share on a file server.

2. Copy the contents of %systemroot\ICA\ClientDB from a MetaFrame server to the central file server share created in step 1.

3. Open the Client Update Configuration utility, select Open from the Database menu, and enter the complete *UNC path* to your new share, including the DBCONFIG.INI file. Don't use a mapped drive letter, as it won't necessarily be available to anyone but you. The title bar for the utility should now show the UNC path to the client database.

4. Select Set Default from the Database menu. A dialog box similar to the one shown in Figure 14.26 should appear. Here you can set this database as the default not only for the current MetaFrame server, but for all other MetaFrame servers under your administration. To do so, enable the check box Set as Default Database on Local Machine, and then select all of the other desired servers from those listed.

Figure 14.27 shows the properties for a client database. To access this dialog box, simply select Properties from the Database menu.

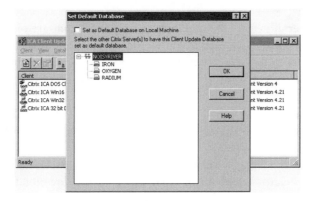

Figure 14.26 *Setting the default ACU client database.*

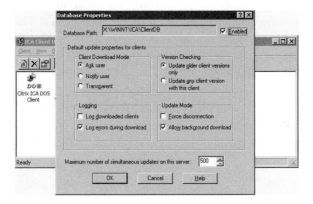

Figure 14.27 *Properties for a client database.*

From here you can configure these options:

- **Whether client updates are enabled or disabled for this database.** When the database is disabled, no client updates happen from this database. Disabling updates from here is easier than disabling each client individually. Even if an individual client shows its state as being enabled, updates won't occur if the database itself is disabled.

- **Whether the user is notified of the client update.** If you want to ensure that a user receives an update, select Notify or Transparent. Note that this change affects *all* users who connect to the server—even administrators.

- **Whether all clients are updated, or only those that are older than the current version.** Normally you would only update older clients, but you can elect to deploy a change to everyone. When All Clients is selected, a user may find that his or her client is updated multiple times, depending on how often the user logs on and off, and how long you keep this option enabled. I recommend not selecting the All Clients option unless absolutely necessary, and then keeping it active for as short a time as possible.

- **Update logging.** The ACU utility can be configured to log successful client updates or only errors that occur during download. This information is written to the Event Log of the server that performs the actual update.

- **Whether a client can continue to work with an outdated client until the next time the client connects to a MetaFrame server.** The other option is for the server to force immediate *disconnect* (not logoff) so that when reconnected the client automatically picks up the client changes.

- **Setting the number of maximum concurrent updates.** You should change this setting to closely match the estimated number of concurrent users that you expect on each MetaFrame server. Performing client updates requires server resources, so you want to set this value relatively low, instead of setting it to equal the upper limits of your server.

Warning

The Delete command for the database must be used with great care, especially in an environment where multiple MetaFrame servers are sharing the same client update database. An accidental deletion could leave all servers without client update capabilities.

I strongly suggest that you restrict permissions on the client database directory to Read-Only for Everyone, except a single NT group that has the minimal number of users in it. Write access to this directory should be strictly controlled. I recommend that even traditional administration groups such as Domain Admins not have write control to this database. There's little reason for a domain administrator to be writing anything into the ICA client database. ✦

Adding a New Client to ACU

During the installation of MetaFrame, the clients for 32-bit and 16-bit Windows and DOS are created automatically. You can add new clients by selecting New from the Client menu, which starts the New Client Wizard. This opens the Description dialog box, which requires you to provide a client installation file (usually called UPDATE.INI). This can be a file that's part of a custom ICA client that you've created (discussed earlier in this chapter), a file from an OEM vendor, or a file directly from Citrix.

If this new client is a customized client, the UPDATE.INI file will be located in the Disk1 directory. Enter the path or click Browse to navigate to the file. The file must be a valid client UPDATE.INI file. Following is a sample UPDATE.INI file taken from the 32-bit ICA client:

```
;*********************************************************************
;** Update.ini: Citrix ICA Client for Windows (Win32)
;**
;** This file is used to describe the ICA Client Update capabilities
;** for the Citrix ICA Client for Windows (Win32)
;**
;*********************************************************************

[ICAClient]
ProductID=1
Model=3
Version=4.21.779
Enabled=yes
ClientDescription=Citrix ICA Win32 Client
UpdateDescription=Citrix ICA Client Version 4.21
IconPath=clientn.ico

[Intel]
UpdateHelper=cudhlpn.dll

[Update.ini]
DoNotUpdate=yes

[appsrv.ini]
DoNotUpdate=yes

[wfcmoven.exe]
UpdateImmediate=yes
```

```
[wfica32.exe]
FileExistenceRequired=yes

[migraten.exe]
ExecuteFile=yes
```

Author's Note

If you're creating a customized client that will be used to update an existing client with new APPSRV.INI information, you must edit the UPDATE.INI file and modify the DoNotUpdate=Yes *setting for the* [appsrv.ini] *value to* DoNotUpdate=No. *Otherwise, an existing APPSRV.INI file won't be overwritten.* ◆

After you select the proper file, the client information is filled in automatically. You can provide your own description for the client in the Comment text box.

The next dialog box asks you to set the Update Options. These options are identical to the database defaults discussed earlier, with the exception of the option Display This Message on the User Terminal. This option allows you to add comments regarding this client update, possibly explaining why it's being done. Despite the name, this message is displayed to the user only if he or she clicks the More Info button presented before the update begins.

Next you set the Event Logging options. Again, these options are identical to those described earlier for the database properties.

Tip

The source name recorded in the Event Log for all messages written by the ACU is CLTMGR. ◆

The final dialog box is for enabling the client. Click the Enable check box to activate the newly created Automatic Client Update package, which automatically disables all other client packages with the same product ID and model number.

As a user logs onto a MetaFrame server, he or she may be required to update the client, as shown in Figure 14.28. In this example, the user has the option of postponing the update and waiting for the download, or having the download run in the background.

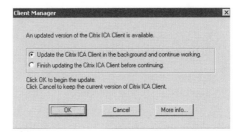

Figure 14.28   *An ICA client being prompted to update its client software.*

Modifying an Existing ACU Client

You can modify the properties of an existing ACU file by simply right-clicking the icon for the client and selecting Properties. This brings up the Properties dialog box, in which you can edit any of the options set during the creation of the client.

The only information available here that isn't displayed when a new client is created is the Client Files tab. This tab displays all the files that make up the client. Although these files are viewable, the list can't be modified in any way.

Author's Note

The ICA client is also well suited to automated deployment using alternative methods such as Microsoft's Systems Management Service (SMS) or Active Directory (if you're targeting Windows 2000 Professional desktops in a Windows 2000 domain). ◆

Web Computing with MetaFrame

In this chapter:

- **Component Overview**
  Citrix MetaFrame provides the ability to access one or more
  MetaFrame published applications through a Web browser interface.

- **Application Launching and Embedding**
  Citrix provides two ways of accessing a Web-enabled application—
  either by launching the application in a separate window or by embedding it within the confines of the Web page. Collectively, this is known
  as Application Launching and Embedding (ALE).

- **Citrix NFuse: Program Neighborhood for the Web**
  NFuse is the collective name for a number of components that work
  together to deliver Program Neighborhood application set support to
  users through a Web browser interface.

- **Citrix ICA Web Client Configuration**
  Two different categories of ICA Web clients exist: the Web browser
  "helper" applications and the ALE clients. Helper applications
  handle launching an application, and ALE clients provide application
  embedding support.

- **MetaFrame Server Configuration for Web Computing**
  The changes required to your MetaFrame server configuration depend
  on where your users are located and whether you will implement NFuse.

- **Web Server Configuration**
  You need to configure the appropriate MIME type information for the
  ICA protocol, as well as set up the ICA Java client and install and con-
  figure the NFuse Java objects, depending on your implementation plans.

- **MetaFrame and Firewall Considerations**
  A question that's becoming more and more common is how to configure a MetaFrame server and client to function properly through a firewall using network address translation. This section discusses the
  requirements and provides a sample configuration using CheckPoint
  FireWall-1.

Component Overview

Web-enabling an application is simply the process of providing access to it
through a Web browser. Normally, a Web-enabled application is developed
explicitly for the purpose of running from within a Web browser. Citrix
MetaFrame provides an alternative by bringing a robust set of tools to
Terminal Server, which allow for the accessing of one or more MetaFrame
published applications through a Web browser interface without any coding
changes required to the application.

A Web-enabled MetaFrame environment is made up of four components:

- **The MetaFrame server.** One or more MetaFrame servers in the
  environment publish the applications that are accessed through
  the browser.

- **The Web server.** The Web server hosts the pages containing the links
  that launch the published applications. These links actually point to
  ICA files also stored on the Web server. The files are downloaded
  to the browser and then used by the ICA client to connect to the
  application.

- **The Web browser.** The Web browser is responsible for displaying the
  appropriate pages published by the server. The browser itself relies on
  the appropriate ICA helper application to process the ICA file associated with the application link.

- **The ICA client.** Citrix provides a special set of ICA Web clients. These
  ALE (Application Launching and Embedding) clients can be used to
  connect to a Web-enabled MetaFrame environment via a Web browser.
  Four types of ALE clients exist: an ActiveX control for 32-bit Internet
  Explorer, a Netscape plug-in (16- and 32-bit), and a Java applet. Most
  of the existing ICA clients also ship with a "helper" application that
  can be used to access Web-enabled applications. Regardless of the
  client, the basic function remains the same: processing the contents
  of the ICA file and establishing the connection to the appropriate
  published application.

Figure 15.1 illustrates how the components work to establish a published application connection through a Web browser from any supported ICA client operating system.

1. The user requests the Web page from the server.

2. The page is displayed within the user's Web browser.

3. After an application link is clicked, the associated ICA file is downloaded to the client and processed by the ICA client.

4. Based on the information in the ICA file, the ICA client connects to the appropriate published application within the MetaFrame environment.

5. A regular MetaFrame published-application session is opened between the client and the server.

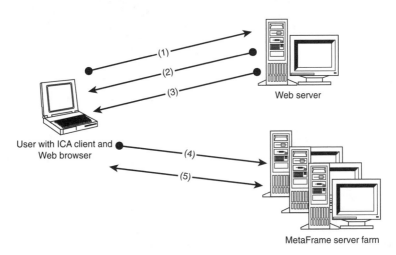

Figure 15.1 *MetaFrame Web computing components and the steps to launching an application.*

Later sections of this chapter look at each of these components in more detail and discuss the configuration changes required in order to implement a successful Web-based application environment.

Application Launching and Embedding

Citrix provides two ways of accessing a Web-enabled application: either by launching the application in a separate window or by embedding it within the confines of the Web page. Collectively, this is known as Application Launching and Embedding (ALE), as mentioned earlier. The type of ICA client being used determines whether launching or embedding is supported.

Application Launching

When an application is launched from a Web page, it appears as a separate window on the client's desktop and functions just as a regular published application. Figure 15.2 demonstrates Microsoft Word being launched from a link on a Web page.

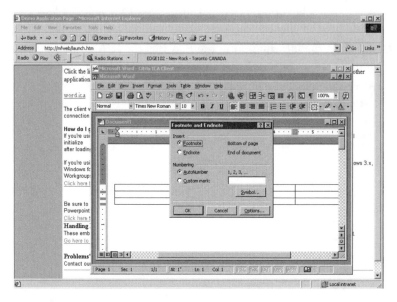

Figure 15.2   *Microsoft Word being launched from a Web page.*

Application launching utilizes the helper application that's available with the latest version of most ICA clients and doesn't rely on the special ICA Web clients (also known as *ALE clients*). The features available to the launched application depend on what's supported by the ICA client in use. For example, if you're using the Linux ICA client, a launched application will support the features available to that client.

When application launching is employed on the Win32 platform, you can also utilize the seamless windows feature. This allows the program to appear as if it were running locally. For more information on the seamless windows feature, refer to the "ICA Client Features" section of Chapter 3, "Citrix MetaFrame."

Application Embedding

When an application is embedded, it's placed within the confines of the Web page itself. This is used most often when the published application is directly related to the content of a Web page. Figure 15.3 demonstrates Microsoft Word embedded in a Web page.

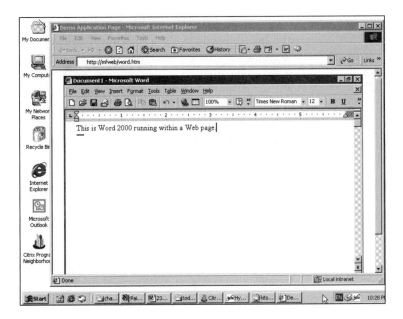

Figure 15.3   *Microsoft Word embedded in a Web page.*

To embed an application, the user must be using one of the Citrix ALE clients. Currently, three such clients exist:

- An ActiveX control for Internet Explorer 3.0x or higher running on 32-bit Windows
- A Netscape plug-in for Netscape Navigator 2.2 or higher and Communicator 4.x or higher, running on either 16- or 32-bit Windows
- A Java applet that will run within any browser that supports the Java Development Kit (JDK) 1.1

The features available to an embedded client are restricted to those that are supported by the ALE client in use. For a complete list of supported features by ICA client, see Chapter 6, "Client Planning."

Citrix NFuse: Program Neighborhood for the Web

NFuse is the collective name for a number of components that work together to deliver Program Neighborhood application-set support to users through a Web browser interface. Until the introduction of NFuse, Web-enabled applications were accessed through statically created links on a Web page. NFuse now allows an administrator to manage a user's access to applications just as if the user were running Program Neighborhood directly from the desktop, using the Win32 or Java ICA clients.

When NFuse has been implemented on a Web server, a user is first presented with a logon page, which requires him or her to provide authentication credentials for a Windows domain. These credentials are then used by NFuse to determine which application set access the user has and dynamically generate the HTML page containing links to the applications within this application set.

Warning

The logon information communicated between the Web browser and the Web server (running NFuse) is standard HTTP. Unless the HTTP has been encrypted with SSL (Secure Sockets Layer), the information will be transmitted in clear text. In an Internet implementation, this is a definite security concern. An excellent document on this topic is available at the Citrix Web site: "Security Guidelines for NFuse 1.0." Before implementing NFuse, I highly recommend that you review this document to ensure that you have a clear understanding of the possible security concerns in NFuse. This document can be found at the following address:
`ftp.citrix.com/doclib/NfuseSecurity.pdf` ◆

Figure 15.4 shows the updated components and steps involved in connecting to a Web-enabled application with NFuse. This is an update of Figure 15.1.

1. The user requests the initial Web page from the server.

2. The logon page is displayed within the user's Web browser (see Figure 15.5).

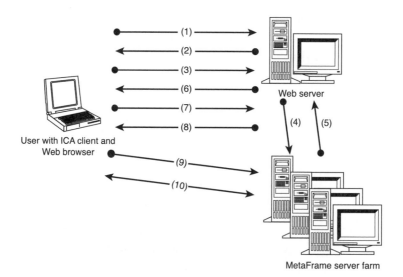

Figure 15.4 *MetaFrame Web computing components and the steps to launch an application when using NFuse.*

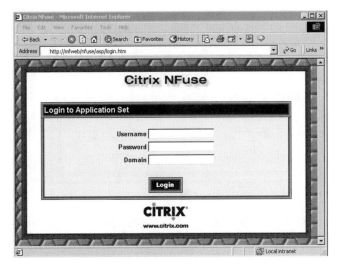

Figure 15.5 *An NFuse logon Web page.*

3. After the necessary information is entered (user ID, password, and possibly the domain), the user's Web browser sends the credentials back to the Web server.

4. The NFuse Java objects running on the Web server pass the information to a corresponding NFuse service running on a MetaFrame server.

5. The NFuse service takes the information and communicates with the Program Neighborhood service on that MetaFrame server to get the necessary application-set information. This information is then passed by the NFuse service back to the NFuse Java objects, which generate the corresponding HTML page containing links to the applications in the set. The links on the page point to ICA template files that, when clicked, will provide the information to establish the connection to the appropriate application.

6. The generated HTML page is returned to the client's Web browser to be displayed locally. Figure 15.6 shows an example.

7. After the desired application is clicked, the request for the corresponding ICA is sent back to the Web server.

8. NFuse replaces the substitution tags in the ICA file with the necessary information specific to the user, and the file is then passed back to the client.

9. Based on the information in the ICA file, the ICA client connects to the appropriate published application within the MetaFrame environment.

10. A regular MetaFrame published-application session is opened between the client and the server.

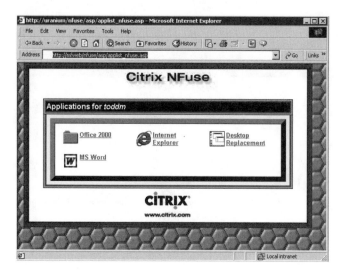

Figure 15.6   *An NFuse-generated application set in a Web page.*

Author's Note

The MetaFrame server that communicates with the NFuse objects on the Web server in steps 4 and 5 doesn't have to be the same server with which the user establishes the connection in step 9. The NFuse service simply acts as a liaison between the Citrix Program Neighborhood service running on the MetaFrame server and the NFuse objects on the Web server. ◆

NFuse provides an application programming interface (API) to the Java objects, allowing experienced Web developers to have more control over the construction and behavior of the NFuse Web site. Using the API, you can manipulate the contents of both the HTML pages and the ICA files that your users may access. Currently, the NFuse API is accessible via the following APIs:

- Microsoft's Active Server Pages (ASP)
- Sun's JavaServer pages
- Citrix's proprietary HTML substitution tags
- Custom-developed Java server applets (servlets)

Author's Note

Citrix's substitution tags are available for Webmasters who are unfamiliar with Web server scripting. The use of these tags also requires a Citrix-provided Java servlet or ASP support files in order to perform the desired NFuse actions. ◆

To implement NFuse, you must perform some configuration steps on each of the components shown in Figure 15.4 (the client browser, the Web server, and the MetaFrame server). The following sections look at each of these areas in turn and discuss the configuration requirements for both a standard Web-enabled application environment and an NFuse environment.

Citrix ICA Web Client Configuration

There are two different categories of ICA Web clients. *Helper applications* are provided with the following ICA clients:

- Win32 and Win16
- Macintosh
- UNIX and Linux
- Java application

A helper application's job is simple: Take an ICA file as input, parse the information, and establish a connection with the appropriate MetaFrame server. The Win32 and Win16 applications are called WFICA32.EXE and WFICA16.EXE, respectively. The UNIX/Linux application is simply called wfica, and the Macintosh and Java ICA clients are themselves the helper program.

Author's Note

These helper applications are also known as Citrix ICA client engines. If you look at the association for an ICA file after installing the latest ICA client on a Windows system, you'll see this as the description for the WFICA32 or WFICA16 client. ◆

The following is an example of an ICA file that could be processed by one of these clients. This ICA file launches Internet Explorer, which has been configured as a published application. To process the file, you could simply execute the helper application followed by the ICA filename.

```
[WFClient]
Version=2
; The TcpBrowserAddress corresponds to an entry in the server location list.
; This is so the helper application knows where to look to find the master
; ICA browser, so that it can then connect to the published application,
; which in this case is Internet Explorer.
TcpBrowserAddress=192.168.1.5

[ApplicationServers]
Internet Explorer=

[Internet Explorer]
```

```
Address=Internet Explorer
; The # sign before the program name signals that this is a
; published application.
InitialProgram=#Internet Explorer
DesiredHRES=640
DesiredVRES=480
DesiredColor=2
TransportDriver=TCP/IP
WinStationDriver=ICA 3.0
```

The second Citrix Web client type is the Citrix ALE client, which I discussed earlier. The ALE client's sole purpose is to process ICA files directly within a Web browser; these clients can't be run outside a Web browser. Following are the ALE clients that are currently available:

- ActiveX control for Internet Explorer (IE)
- 32-bit and 16-bit plug-in for Netscape or older versions of IE
- Java applet

When a user clicks a link on a Web page pointing to an ICA file, a Citrix ALE client parses the file and establishes the connection with the published application. The following JavaScript example for the ActiveX control creates a Web page that automatically initiates a connection using the ICA file just shown. If necessary, the ActiveX control is downloaded from Citrix prior to starting the session. In the later section "Web Server Configuration," I talk in more detail about generating the HTML pages to support your Web-enabled applications.

```
<script language="JavaScript">
<!—
var icaFile = "remoteIE.ica";
var width = 640;
var height = 480;
var start = "Auto";
var border = "On";
var hspace = 2;
var vspace = 2;
var cabLoc = "http://www.citrix.com/bin/cab/wfica.cab#Version=4,2,274,317";
// The following is the ActiveX tag:
var activeXHTML = '<CENTER><OBJECT
➥classid="clsid:238f6f83-b8b4-11cf-8771-00a024541ee3"
➥data="' + icaFile + '" CODEBASE="' + cabLoc + '" width=' + width
➥+ ' height=' + height + ' hspace=' + hspace + ' vspace=' + vspace
➥+ '> <param name="Start" value="' + start + '">
➥<param name="Border" value="' + border + '"></OBJECT></CENTER>';
{document.write(plugInHTML);}
//—>
</script>
```

Normally the ALE client is preferred when establishing connections to Web-enabled applications, but you might want to use a helper application in the following situations:

- You're using NFuse and you want to have seamless application connections on a Win32 client. In this case, you'll want to install the Win32 ICA client on the user's desktop.

- You want to have a launched application instead of an embedded application. The Java applet supports only embedded applications. If you want to have a launched Java application, you need to use the Java application helper instead of the ALE Java applet.

- You're running on a non–Windows system and don't want to use the Java applet. In this case, you can use the appropriate client helper program instead.

- You're running a Web browser other than Internet Explorer or Netscape Navigator/Communicator. Other browsers are supported in certain situations but must rely on the helper applications to launch a published application. I discuss the supported Web browsers shortly.

ICA Client Version Requirements

The required version of either the helper or ALE client depends on whether you will be implementing Citrix NFuse. NFuse requires the latest version of these clients in order to function, but the more traditional implementation of Web-enabled applications, using the JavaScript example just shown, function with older versions of the clients. Table 15.1 lists the minimum ICA client versions required in order to use the NFuse product, which I discuss shortly.

Author's Note

Remember that all ICA clients can be downloaded for free from the Citrix Web site (www.citrix.com). I recommend that you deploy the latest ICA client even if you're not planning to deploy NFuse immediately, because that option will then be open to you without requiring any future client-update planning. ◆

Table 15.1   Minimum Required ICA/ALE Client Versions for Use with NFuse

ICA/ALE Client	Version Number
Win32	4.21.779
Win16	4.20.779
Macintosh	4.10.23
Linux	3.0

continues ▶

Table 15.1   continued

ICA/ALE Client	Version Number
UNIX	3.0.85
Java application	4.11
ActiveX control (ALE)	4.20.779
Plug-in 16/32-bit (ALE)	4.20.779
Java applet (ALE)	4.11

Installing an ALE Client

Helper applications are installed during the regular ICA client installation, discussed in Chapter 14, "ICA Client Installation and Configuration." The installation of the ALE client is straightforward, requiring minimal or no input from the end user. The ActiveX control and the Netscape plug-in can be installed in one of two ways:

- **From the Citrix ICA Web Client installation source.** The ActiveX control is installed by running WFICA32.EXE /SETUP from the ActiveX directory in the installation location. The plug-in is installed by running either WFPLUG16.EXE or WFPLUG32.EXE from the NSPlugin directory. In both cases, you need to stop the browser before performing the installation and restart the browser afterwards to begin using the new client. The client must be installed in this manner in order to launch an application.

- **Automatically over an intranet or the Internet.** You can configure your Web page to download the necessary client files automatically to the user if he or she doesn't already have them when connecting to your site. If the user is using IE, the ActiveX control can be downloaded and started automatically. The Netscape plug-in will be downloaded but will require the user to initiate the installation process manually. After this is done, the user will be able to begin using the Web client. The auto-loaded client will only function with embedded applications. It cannot be used for application launching. In order to support launching, the ActiveX or Plug-in client must be manually installed as described in the previous bullet.

The ActiveX HTML source looks similar to the following, which retrieves the ActiveX control from the Citrix site if required:

```
<CENTER><OBJECT classid="clsid:238f6f83-b8b4-11cf-8771-00a024541ee3"
➥data="remoteIE.ica" CODEBASE="http://www.citrix.com/bin/cab/wfica.cab#
➥Version=4,2,274,317" width=640 height=480 hspace=2 vspace=2>
➥<param name="Start" value="Auto"><param name="Border"
➥value="On"></OBJECT></CENTER>
```

The plug-in source looks like this:

```
<CENTER><EMBED SRC="remoteIE.ica" pluginspage="http://www.citrix.com/demoroom/
⇒plugin.htm" width=640 height=480 start=Auto border=On hspace=2
⇒vspace=2></CENTER>
```

The Java applet requires no explicit installation on the client. Instead, it's installed and configured on the Web server, where it's accessed when the user clicks a link configured to run with the Java applet. To use the Java applet, the browser must support the JDK 1.1 or higher. A 1.0 version of the Java client is available from the Citrix Web site if you need to support older browsers (such as Netscape Navigator 3.x) that don't have a 1.1-compliant JDK.

Author's Note

If you want to run the Java client in application mode, you need to install the ICA Java client on the user's local computer. I discuss these installation steps in the next section. ◆

ICA Java Client

The Citrix ICA Java client allows you to access a published application from a *Java Virtual Machine (JVM)*. This can be a JVM running on any operating system, a Web browser that supports Java applets, or a Java-based device. A number of browsers are supported not only on Windows platforms, but also on UNIX, Macintosh, and OS/2.

Depending on how you use the Java client, it runs in one of two modes: application or applet mode. Both operation modes use the same set of class files.

- **Application mode.** In this mode, the Java client resides on the user's computer, along with a valid JVM. A published application is usually accessed by executing the Java client from the command line, with the help of the JVM. The application on the MetaFrame server then starts as its own window on the client desktop. I discuss application mode in more detail in the "Java Helper Application" section later in this chapter. To run in application mode, the JVM must support the JDK 1.1 or higher.

- **Applet mode.** As discussed earlier, in this mode the Java client resides on a Web server. Users access MetaFrame sessions by using a Web browser that has Java support. To run in applet mode, the browser must support JDK 1.1 or higher.

Troubleshooting Tip

Neither Internet Explorer 3.x or earlier nor Netscape Navigator 3.x or earlier have a 1.1-compliant JDK. To access a MetaFrame Java applet using one of these browsers, you need the JDK 1.0-compliant version of the Citrix ICA Java client. This is available from Citrix's Web site. ◆

The ICA Java client doesn't provide full support for all the ICA client features found with the Windows clients. The supported features are as follows:

- Client audio, printer, and COM port mapping
- Clipboard sharing (text only, no graphics)
- Multiple server location entries (also known as the business recovery option)
- Data compression and SpeedScreen2
- Auto-reconnect to an existing session and shadowing
- Encryption (only basic encryption)
- Program Neighborhood

The Java client has the following limitations:

- No support for seamless windows
- No persistent bitmap caching
- Supports only 256 colors (not 16)
- Supports only the TCP/IP protocol
- No support for client drive mappings

Installing the Java Client

To access a published application or Program Neighborhood through a Java applet, the necessary Java classes need to be installed on the Web server. If you'll be running the Java client directly on a user's desktop, you need to install the classes locally. For either situation, the installation is the same and is performed as follows.

Author's Note

Because the exact JVM implementations differ between operating systems, the installation steps are not identical for all of them. I've included notes for both Windows and Linux in this example. For specific installation information on other platforms, review the documentation that accompanies the ICA Java client installation files. ◆

1. Create the directory in which you will install the client. In this example, I'll use the directories d:\JICA11 for Windows and usr/lib/jica11 for Linux. If you're installing the client on a Web server, make sure that this directory is accessible by your users. A common location is in a jica11 directory off the root Web directory.

2. Copy Setup.class into this directory. This file can be found on the MetaFrame CD in the ICACLNT\ICAJAVA directory. It can also be downloaded from the Citrix Web site.

3. Run Setup.class and install the Java classes into this directory. You run Setup.class by launching it with the appropriate JVM for your operating system. The general syntax is as follows:

   ```
   <full path>\<jvm> setup
   ```

   where `<full path>` is the full path to the `<jvm>`. On the Win32 platform, Microsoft's JVM is JVIEW.EXE and is located in the %systemroot% directory. On Linux, the Sun JVM (downloadable from www.sun.com) is java.

4. Running Setup.class starts the InstallShield Installation Wizard (see Figure 15.7), which guides you through installing the classes. You'll be prompted to provide the destination for the class files. Specify the directory that you created in step 1. All required files are then installed into the destination location.

5. As part of the installation, two batch scripts are created in the destination directory that can be used to start the Java Program Neighborhood or launch individual ICA files (Java helper application). I'll talk about both of these shortly.

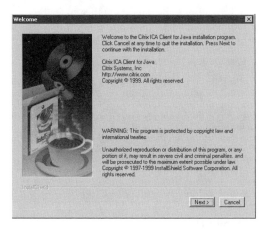

Figure 15.7   *The Citrix ICA Java client installation wizard.*

If you're installing the client on a Web server, you need to create a Web page that will launch either an individual published application or Program Neighborhood with the Java applet when visited by users. I talk about this in the later section "Web Server Configuration."

Java Program Neighborhood

During the installation, the setup program detects the OS that the client is running as well as the JVM being used and generates the appropriate script file to launch the Java version of Program Neighborhood. The created script is called pnsession.<ext>, where <ext> is the appropriate batch extension for the client OS. For example, on Windows the script would have the extension .BAT. On Linux, no extension would be assigned, and the script would simply be called pnsession. When using Microsoft's JVM, the Program Neighborhood script would look similar to the following:

```
@echo off
REM This file was generated by InstallShield
REM Created on Fri Feb 18 13:01:17 EST 2000 by toddm
"jview" /cp:p "D:\JICA11\.;D:\JICA11\JICAEngJ.jar" com.citrix.pn %1 %2 %3 %4 %5
➥%6 %7 %8 %9
```

Online help is available from within Program Neighborhood, but to make it work properly you must modify the generated script by adding the /d: or -d option, depending on your JVM. For the Microsoft script just shown, I would add the following immediately after the "jview" text:

```
/d:install.root=D:\JICA11\
```

On Linux, using Sun's java JVM, I would add the following:

```
-dinstall.root=/usr/lib/jica11/
```

Without this entry, you'll get the message shown in Figure 15.8 when you attempt to open the PN help.

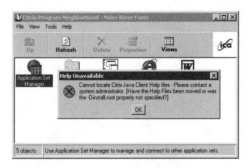

Figure 15.8   *Java PN help error message.*

To run the script, simply open a command prompt and run PNSESSION.BAT. The main Program Neighborhood window (see Figure 15.9) should open, appearing almost identical to the one available with the native Win32 client.

Figure 15.9   *Java Program Neighborhood.*

Many of the features and functions found in the Win32 PN are also available in the Java PN. For more information on Program Neighborhood, see Chapters 3 and 14.

The following restrictions apply to the Java PN in comparison with the Win32 version:

- Only the TCP/IP protocol is supported.

- Seamless window sessions are not supported.

- Dial-up ICA connections are not supported.

- A default server farm must always be selected.

- Bitmap caching is not configurable, although the Java client does utilize SpeedScreen.

Java Helper Application
The other script file created during the Java client setup is the ICA helper script called jicasession.<ext>, where <ext> is the appropriate batch extension for the client OS. For example, on Windows the script would have the extension .BAT. On Linux, no extension would be assigned, and the script would simply be called jicasession. When using Microsoft's JVM, the helper script would look similar to the following:

```
@echo off
REM This file was generated by InstallShield
REM Created on Fri Feb 18 13:01:16 EST 2000 by toddm
"jview" /cp:p "D:\JICA11\.;D:\JICA11\JICAJ.jar" com.citrix.JICA %1 %2 %3 %4 %5
➡ %6 %7 %8 %9
```

Notice that this script uses the JICAJ.JAR file instead of the one containing Program Neighborhood. To test the script after installation, simply open a command prompt and change into the directory containing your Java client files. Then execute this command:

```
jicasession -address:<MF Server>
```

where *<MF Server>* is the name of a MetaFrame server.

For example, to connect to a MetaFrame server called ORCA, I would enter this command:

```
jicasession -address:ORCA -width:800 -height:600
```

This will open a connection to the ORCA server with a window size of 800×600. A number of parameters exist for the Java client, in both application and applet modes. Table 15.2 lists some of the commonly used parameters. Each parameter is preceded by a hyphen (-) and uses a semicolon (:) as the separator between the parameter and the actual data value. For a complete list of options, consult the "ICA Java Client Parameters" section of the HTML help file installed with the ICA Java client. It can be found in the help subdirectory where you installed the Java client.

Table 15.2   Common Java Helper Application Options

Parameter	Description
Address	Specifies the name of a server or published application. If this is a published application, you must also specify the InitialProgram parameter.
InitialProgram	The name of the program to run after connecting to the server. If this is a published application, you must include the # symbol at the beginning of the name. For example, if the application is called IE, you enter #IE.
WorkDirectory	The working directory for the initial program. If InitialProgram is a published application, this is not required.
IniDir	Specifies a directory location where INI file information can be stored for the Java client. Using this parameter allows the storing of client printer information so that it can be reloaded automatically in later sessions.
TCPBrowserAddressX	Used when a client is on a different subnet than the Citrix servers containing the published application. You provide the IP address or fully qualified domain name of a Citrix server on the target subnet. X is either blank or a number from 2 to 15, signifying the server location for business recovery. Blank through 5 are the primary group, 6 through 10 are the secondary group, and 11 through 15 are the tertiary group.
Username	Specifies a username to use during logon.
Domain	Specifies the domain to use during logon.
Password	The password for the user.

Of course, if you provide the password from the command line, it will appear in plaintext. I recommend that you never provide a password from a command line or a script file. ✦

You can also pass a predefined ICA file to `jicasession` by simply passing it as a parameter without any switches. For example, to connect to a MetaFrame server using an ICA file called remoteIE.ica, you would enter the following:

```
jicasession remoteIE.ica
```

Entering `jicasession` without any parameters launches the GUI command prompt. This is a graphical window where you can enter any of the parameters you normally would enter from a command prompt. This is mainly used to allow Macintosh users to enter the various parameters because they don't have a command prompt from which to run the Java client in application mode. ✦

Java Security Issues

Because of network security restrictions that exist in Java, Web browsers normally are unable to access other computers on the network when running a Java applet. Only resources on the same machine as the Java classes are accessible. Under these conditions, an attempt by the ICA Java applet to connect to a MetaFrame server across the network will fail because of the security violation. Figure 15.10 shows the message that appears in this situation.

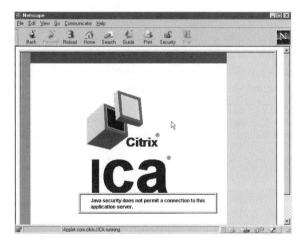

Figure 15.10   *Java security denying access to a MetaFrame server on the network.*

Fortunately, you can deal with this security restriction in three ways:

- **Locate your Web server and your MetaFrame server on the same physical machine.** This way, when the Java applet is started, it accesses the Web pages and MetaFrame server locally. This is allowed by Java security. Of course, this doesn't allow you to access a published application load-balanced across multiple servers. While this technique will resolve the security issue, I don't recommend it, since it not only introduces additional load on the MetaFrame server (since you're now also running the Web service), but also limits your ability to expand Web-enabled applications beyond the one server.

- **Maintain your Web server separate from your MetaFrame server, but locate the ICA Java classes on the MetaFrame server.** The links on the Web page will reference the Java classes, which reside on the MetaFrame server. Java security will allow the applet to connect to the MetaFrame server. While this separates the Web service from the MetaFrame server, just as in the preceding option it limits connections to that specific server and doesn't take into consideration accessing a published application.

- **Use "signed" Java class archives.** These specially "signed" files verify that they came from Citrix and have not been altered in any way by someone else. Browsers that understand signed Java archives allow connections to a Citrix server that's not the same machine as the Web server that contains the ICA Java classes. To access published applications, you must use the appropriate signed Java class archive. I discuss these archives next.

Signed Java Class Archives

The Setup.class installation file includes six different signed Java class archives. Which archive is used depends on the type of browser or JVM used by the client and whether Program Neighborhood functionality is desired. If the browser or JVM doesn't support any of these archive types, they can still access the extracted class files, although they will be restricted by the Java security issues described in the preceding section. The class files can be extracted using a tool such as WinZip that understands Java archives. The six archives available are as follows:

- **JICAEngM.cab.** Signed cabinet (CAB) file containing Program Neighborhood. It can be used by any browser or JVM that supports running Java programs from CAB files. CAB files allow Internet Explorer to work around Java network security, which prevents Java applications running on one machine from accessing resources on another. The security safety level for active content must be set to Medium in IE in order to use the signed CAB file.

- **JICAEngJ.jar.** Signed Java Archive (JAR) file containing Program Neighborhood, which can be used by any browser or JVM that supports running Java programs from JAR files. For example, this JAR allows the HotJava browser to work around Java network security. This JAR is the default used by the setup program when creating the helper and Program Neighborhood scripts (discussed shortly).
- **JICAEngN.jar.** JAR file containing Program Neighborhood, specifically for the Netscape browsers.
- **JICAM.cab.** Internet Explorer CAB file without Program Neighborhood support.
- **JICAJ.jar.** JAR file without Program Neighborhood support.
- **JICAN.jar.** Netscape JAR file without Program Neighborhood support.

I discuss using the appropriate Java class archive in an HTML file in the "Web Server Configuration" section of this chapter.

Supported Web Browsers

The list of supported Web browsers for accessing Web-enabled applications depends on whether you'll use NFuse to provide your users with access to published applications or if you'll provide application links on a Web page.

NFuse Browser Support

Table 15.3 lists the supported Web browser and ICA/ALE client combinations when using NFuse. As you can see, currently only Internet Explorer and Netscape Navigator/Communicator are supported with NFuse.

Table 15.3   Supported Web Browsers for Use with NFuse

ICA/ALE Client	Supported Web Browsers
Win32	Internet Explorer 4.0+
Java application	Netscape Navigator 4.01+
Java applet (ALE) ActiveX Control (ALE) Plug-in 16-bit or 32-bit (ALE)	
Win16	Internet Explorer 4.01+
	Netscape Navigator 4.08+
Macintosh	Netscape Navigator 4.01+
	Netscape Communicator 4.61+
UNIX/Linux	Netscape Navigator 4.01+
	Netscape Communicator 4.61+

Web-Enabled Published-Application Browser Support

When accessing a published application directly from a link on a Web page, almost any Web browser is supported. Table 15.4 lists the supported ALE/Web browser combinations in this situation and indicates whether launching or embedding is supported.

Table 15.4   ALE Clients and Supported Web Browsers in Non–NFuse Configurations

ALE Client	Launching/Embedding	Supported Web Browsers
ActiveX control	Both	Internet Explorer 3.x or higher on a Windows 32-bit OS.
Plug-in	Both	Netscape Navigator 2.02 or higher on 16-bit or 32-bit Windows.
Java applet	Embedding only	If using signed archives, it depends on whether the browser supports a signed archive. Netscape, Internet Explorer, and Sun HotJava all support signed archives. If you're using unsigned archives, any browser that supports JDK 1.1 should be usable.

Tip

In order to use the ActiveX or Netscape plug-in to launch an application, the Web client must first be installed on the user's desktop using WFICA32.EXE 1 setup, WFPLUG16.EXE, or WFPLUG32.EXE. The client cannot be automatically loaded as it can with an embedded application. See the section "Installing an ALE Client" earlier in this chapter for more information. ♦

Even if a browser doesn't support an ALE client, it can still provide application *launching* if the browser supports configurable MIME types. Application embedding is supported only with the Citrix ALE clients. The MIME type is configured with the following information:

Mime type:	Application/x-ica
File extension:	.ica
View/helper program:	Specify an appropriate helper application, depending on the ICA client. For example, the helper application for the Win32 client is WFICA32.EXE, and the Java client's helper is `jicasession`.

Author's Note

The latest versions of all ICA clients supported by NFuse (refer to Table 15.1, earlier in this chapter)—except for the Java and Macintosh clients—automatically configure their helper applications to work with Internet Explorer or Netscape during installation. If you want to use the Java or Macintosh clients, or if you want to configure a different browser to use a helper application, you must configure the proper MIME type for your browser manually. ◆

Configuring the Web Browser

Unless your Web browser requires a manually configured MIME type to support application launching, you're not required to perform any specific Web browser configuration prior to accessing a Web-enabled published application. You can also manually install the ActiveX control or the Netscape plug-in using the Web installation files, as discussed in the earlier section "Installing an ALE Client."

Exactly how you configure a MIME type depends on which browser you're using. For example, with Netscape you define the helper application by selecting the View, Preferences menu option. Figure 15.11 shows the configuration of the MIME type for Netscape so that the application script JICASESSION.BAT will be used to launch published applications from a Web page using the ICA Java application.

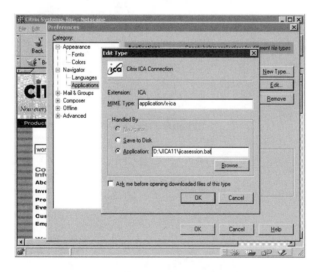

Figure 15.11   *The ICA Java client defined as a helper application for Netscape Communicator.*

To perform a similar configuration with Internet Explorer on a 32-bit
Windows OS, you must edit the file type properties for the OS. This is done
by opening a folder and selecting Tools, Folder Options from the menu.
Then select the File Types tab and click New Type to open a screen similar
to the one shown in Figure 15.12. For IE on Macintosh, the MIME settings
are found under the Edit, Preferences menu option. You'll need to configure
a new File Helper under the Receiving Files section in the left panel.

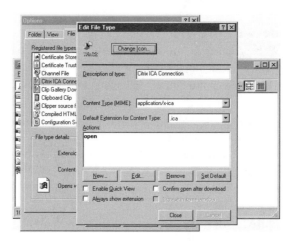

Figure 15.12   *Configuring the ICA helper application
for Internet Explorer on an NT 4.0 workstation.*

If you'll be using the Java client as an applet with Internet Explorer, set the
security safety level in order to properly use signed CAB files, as shown in
Figure 15.13.

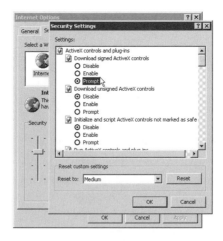

Figure 15.13   *Setting the security safety level in IE5 to support signed CAB files.*

MetaFrame Server Configuration for Web Computing

The changes required to your MetaFrame server configuration depend on where your users are located and whether you'll be implementing NFuse. If users will be within the corporate intranet and will access applications directly from links on a Web page (no NFuse), you probably won't be required to make any changes. Here are a couple of general configuration points to check:

- Ensure that TCP/IP ICA connections exist. Web clients can access a MetaFrame server only over TCP/IP connections.

- Make sure that you have properly published the application that you'll be making available to the Web clients. Chapter 19, "Application Integration," explains how to create a published application.

If you plan to provide access to users over the Internet, you need to review both your server and network configuration to ensure that you have adequate security measures in place. Some areas to review include the following:

- Make sure that you have implemented the suggested system security, as discussed in Chapter 12, "Terminal Server Configuration and Tuning."

- Try to position your MetaFrame servers behind a firewall, and preferably within a subnet that has access to only specific resources located on other internal networks (or no access, if possible). Provide access to only specific MetaFrame ports (1494 for application connections) through the firewall. In this situation, you'll most likely use network address translation (NAT). As a result, you'll be required to perform some additional configuration on your MetaFrame servers to ensure that users can access the servers properly. Consider implementing a virtual private network (VPN) solution between the clients and the network where the MetaFrame servers reside. See the later section "MetaFrame and Firewall Considerations" for more information on the MetaFrame requirements for firewall access.

- Establish rigorous monitoring practices for the security logs on these MetaFrame servers. This can provide valuable early-warning information in case of any potential security issues.

- Restrict connections on the MetaFrame servers to run only published applications, and *do not* publish any complete desktop scenarios. In this situation, a full desktop should be accessible only from the console.

- Involve the people from within your business who are responsible for corporate security, specifically Internet security.

NFuse MetaFrame Server Configuration

Only one main change is involved in configuring your MetaFrame servers to support NFuse—installing the NFuse MetaFrame service on one or more MetaFrame servers within your environment. This service provides the communication link between the NFuse Java objects on the Web server and the Program Neighborhood and browser services, which manage the user authentication and application-set information, as shown in Figure 15.14.

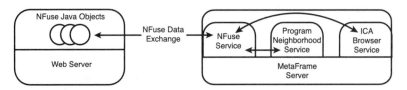

Figure 15.14   *The NFuse MetaFrame service's role in the communication process.*

Installing the NFuse MetaFrame Service

The installation file for the NFuse MF service is contained in the file NFuseForMF.exe, which can be downloaded from the Citrix Web site (www.citrix.com).

> **Author's Note**
>
> *Although NFuse requires that this service be installed on only one MetaFrame server, consider using multiple servers for redundancy and fail-over. If you're implementing dedicated ICA master browser servers, I recommend adding the NFuse service to each of these servers. I discuss NFuse redundancy in the next section.* ◆

The NFuse service is installed as follows:

1. Log on to the MF server where you will install this service. Change to installation mode by typing **change user /install** at a command prompt. Alternatively, you can launch NFuseForMF.exe from the Add/Remove Programs applet in the Control Panel.

2. Accept the terms of the license agreement. The component selection screen appears next, in which you can choose to install the NFuse service and the Web Site Wizard. You don't need to install the wizard on a MetaFrame server. This application will run in any Win32 environment. You normally won't run this from an MF server; more likely, you'll run it on a Web development machine. Deselect Web Site Wizard, and then click Next.

3. The next screen prompts you to select a listening port for the NFuse service, as shown in Figure 15.15. The default port is 80, which is the well-known port for HTTP. This was selected as the default because

most firewalls already have this port open for HTTP services. I recommend using this port unless you also have your MetaFrame server operating as a Web server, in which case you're required to select an alternate port.

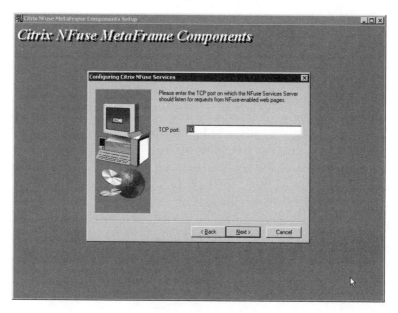

Figure 15.15   *NFuse service listening port selection.*

Tip

You can use the NETSTAT -A *command from a command prompt to get a list of currently active TCP/IP ports on your MetaFrame server. If you're selecting an alternate port for the NFuse service, make sure that it's not already in use or a "well-known" port such as Telnet (23) or FTP (21), unless you're certain that those services won't be required on your MetaFrame server.*

You can find a list of well-known ports in the services file located in the directory %systemroot%\system32\drivers\etc.

After installation, you can change the port number used by this service by stopping the service, typing NFUSE.EXE /Rxx *(where xx is the new port number), and restarting the service. You can also update the information directly in the registry. The NFuse service properties are maintained in this registry key:*

```
HKEY_LOCAL_MACHINE\SYSTEM\CurrentControlSet\Services\CtxHttp
```

The NFUSE.EXE /U *command can also be used to completely remove this registry key.* ◆

4. After you select the port, a summary screen indicates the actions that will be taken. Click Next to complete the NFuse service installation. The service starts operating immediately. You're not required to restart the MF server. You can verify that the service is running by typing NET START from a command prompt. You should see Citrix NFuse Service in the list.

Redundancy and Fail-Over Considerations

One of the shortcomings with the first release of NFuse is the lack of redundancy available as an integrated part of the NFuse Java component on the Web server. Currently, you must hard-code (either for all Web pages or for each individual page) the address of a MetaFrame server running the NFuse service. Although this may be acceptable for managing load distribution between a few servers, it doesn't provide any protection against the failure of one of these servers, resulting in a loss of service for the associated Web page(s). Figure 15.16 shows the error that a user would receive if the specified MetaFrame server (or the NFuse service) were unavailable.

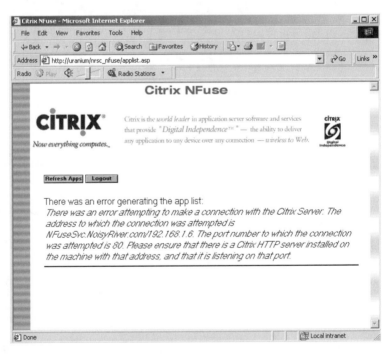

Figure 15.16 *Error received when the NFuse service is unavailable.*

Fortunately, there are some options for providing some simple redundancy to help improve the availability of the NFuse service. Here are two of the options:

- **Employ Microsoft network load balancing.** Although this would provide load balancing and fail-over management for the NFuse service, the additional complexity involved may not warrant its use.

- **DNS round-robin.** A means of providing simple redundancy and very basic load distribution, implementing DNS round-robin allows you to specify multiple servers under a single DNS name. Although it doesn't dynamically remove a failed server from the list (users would still periodically attempt to hit that downed server), it allows the user to eventually establish his or her NFuse session. Figure 15.17 demonstrates how this could be configured using Windows 2000 DNS. Notice that in this example I've created a virtual hostname (nfusesvc. noisyriver.com) that I'll use when configuring my Web server. The hostname can be associated with one or more MetaFrame servers running the NFuse service.

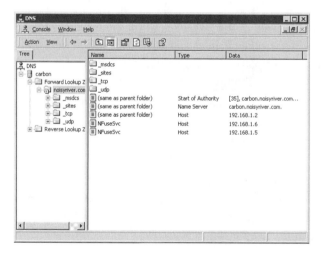

Figure 15.17 *Configuring DNS round-robin for multiple NFuse-enabled MetaFrame servers.*

If you'll be using DNS round-robin and your Web server is a Windows 2000 server, you will need to make two changes to ensure that round-robin will work properly. The first is a change on the Web server itself, and the other is with the DNS server.

On the Web server, you need to modify the time-to-live (TTL) for the server's local DNS cache. Otherwise, repeated hits to a DNS name will result in attempts to contact the same host. All Windows 2000 products employ a local DNS cache that was not present in previous versions of Windows. The registry key is

```
HKEY_LOCAL_MACHINE\SYSTEM\CurrentControlSet\Services\Dnscache\Parameters
```

The value to modify is `MaxCacheEntryTtlLimit`. Setting this value to 1 causes cached entries to time out after one second, forcing a query of the DNS server for repeated lookups of the same hostname. You must stop and restart the DNS Client service for this change to take effect. You should also flush the existing contents of the cache using the command

```
ipconfig /flushdns
```

You can view the current contents of the cache by typing this:

```
ipconfig /displaydns
```

If you're using a Windows DNS server, you need to ensure that `LocalNetPriority` is not enabled. This feature forces the DNS server to return the best-fit host address to a client. If the client is located on the same network as at least one of the addresses in the round-robin list, that address is always returned to the client. You can disable this feature by adding the `REG_DWORD` value `LocalNetPriority` to this registry key:

```
HKEY_LOCAL_MACHINE\SYSTEM\CurrentControlSet\Services\DNS\Parameters
```

Set the value to 0, which will disable this feature. You'll have to stop and restart the DNS Server service for this change to take effect. On a Windows 2000 DNS server, this option is enabled by default.

Web Server Configuration

Three configuration tasks may be required in order to set up your Web server to support Web-enabled MetaFrame applications:

- MIME type configuration is required whether or not you'll be implementing NFuse.
- Installation of the ICA Java client is required in order to support the Java applet on the client browser.
- Installation and configuration of the NFuse Java objects is required only if you're implementing NFuse.

MIME Type Configuration

When a Web server passes a file to a client's Web browser, it tells the browser what type of file it is, so that the browser can select the appropriate application to process the file. The Web server can recognize a file type by mapping the file's extension to a list of Multipurpose Internet Mail Extension (MIME) types. For a Web client to be able to process an ICA file, you need to register the proper MIME type information on the Web server. Here's the MIME type information:

MIME type: application/x-ica

File extension: .ica

Microsoft Internet Information Server (IIS) 4.0/5.0

You configure the MIME type information on an IIS server by opening the Microsoft Management Console (MMC), right-clicking the Internet Information Services entry, and selecting Properties from the menu. Then click the Edit button for the Computer MIME map and click the New Type button to open the dialog box shown in Figure 15.18.

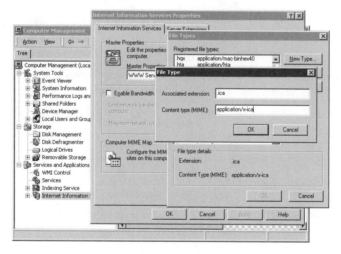

Figure 15.18   *MIME type configuration in IIS 5 on Windows 2000.*

Apache

For Apache, you use the AddType directive in the httpd.conf configuration file to add the ICA MIME type. The syntax is as follows:

```
AddType application/x-ica ica
```

You need to stop and restart Apache for the changes to take effect.

ICA Java Client Configuration

If you plan to provide access to published applications using the ICA Java client running as a Java applet, you must install the client on the Web server. The installation instructions are identical to those given in the earlier section "Installing the Java Client," with one exception. Make sure that you install the class files in a directory that's accessible by all clients from a Web browser. If you're running IIS, you could place the Java files in a directory called JICA11 off the Inetpub\wwwroot directory.

After the ICA Java class files have been installed, you only need to configure the Web page to access the appropriate signed Java archive. I talk about Web page creation shortly.

NFuse Web Server Configuration

Different NFuse Web server installation files are available, depending on the operating system and Web server software you're running. On Windows, NFuse supports Microsoft IIS 4.0 and higher; on UNIX, NFuse supports Netscape Enterprise Server and Apache Web server. Both sets of installation files can be downloaded from the Citrix Web site (www.citrix.com). For 2000/NT, the installation file is called NFuseWebExt.exe; for UNIX it's NFuseForUNIX.tar.gz.

> **Warning**
>
> *As I mentioned earlier in the chapter, unless SSL is being used to encrypt the HTTP data between a Web browser and an NFuse-enabled Web server, the user credentials (user ID, password, and domain) will be transmitted in clear text. The NFuse logon page should never be hosted on an unsecured Web server.* ◆

Microsoft Internet Information Server

> **Warning**
>
> *The installation of the NFuse Web component requires that the IIS service be stopped on the server. Make sure that your Web server is not currently servicing user requests before you perform this installation.* ◆

Do the following to install the NFuse Web extensions on IIS:

1. Log on to your IIS server and launch NFuseWebExt.exe.

2. If the ISS services are currently running, the setup program warns you that they must be stopped for installation to continue. If you say Yes, all necessary services will be stopped before the installation continues.

3. After selecting the destination location for the installation files, choose typical or custom installation. I recommend that you install the sample files along with the NFuse components.

4. In the dialog box shown in Figure 15.19, provide the name and port for the MetaFrame server that's currently running the NFuse service. Enter the appropriate hostname and click Next.

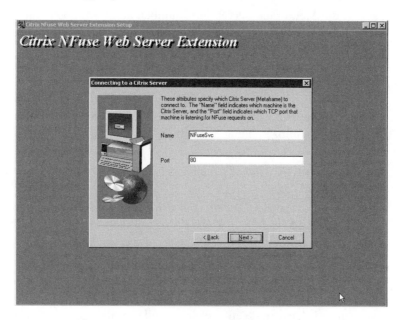

Figure 15.19   *Selecting the MetaFrame host and port where the NFuse service is running.*

5. Indicate where the root URL is located on the physical file system. Be sure to enter the complete path.

6. The next screen summarizes the selections you made. When you're satisfied, click Next to complete the installation. After installation is complete, the IIS service is automatically restarted. You don't have to restart the Windows server.

The values entered during the installation, plus some other system-wide settings for NFuse, are located in the file NFuse.properties, which can be found in the %systemroot%\java\trustlib directory on an NT server. The following is a sample of the contents of this file:

```
CitrixPN_ContentType=text/html
SessionFieldLocations=Script,Template,Url,Post,Cookie,Properties
Timeout=60
Version=Preview
SessionField.NFuse_CitrixServer=NFuseSvc
SessionField.NFuse_CitrixServerPort=80
SessionField.NFuse_IconCache=/NFuseIcons/
SessionField.NFuse_TemplatesDir=C:\\Inetpub\\wwwroot\\NFuse
URLMapping./=C:\\Inetpub\\wwwroot
```

Notice that the MetaFrame server, port number, and URL home information are stored here. Changes to this file don't take effect until you stop and restart the Web server.

Apache Server on Red Hat Linux
The installation of the NFuse component for Linux is fairly straightforward. After downloading and extracting NFuseForUNIX.tar.gz, start the text-based setup program by running setupNFuse.

1. After selecting to install the NFuse components and accepting the license agreement, select the Web server software that you're running and press Enter.

2. You must provide the full path to the document root for the Web server. The Apache default is /usr/local/apache/htdocs. Provide the correct path and then press Enter to continue.

3. Provide the location for the NFuse Java objects. The default is /usr/local/jserv/NFuse. Press Enter after entering the desired path.

4. You're asked whether you want to install the sample NFuse Web site. I recommend that you do so because it will provide you with some sample pages on which you can base your site. The default target location is the NFuse directory under your Web root.

5. Provide the virtual directory for servlets on your server.

6. Specify the directory in which NFuse icons will be stored to assist in generating the user-specific Web pages. The default is Nfuseicons off the Web root. I recommend providing an alternate name for this directory, because it's set up as writeable by everyone.

7. Provide the hostname for the MetaFrame server on which the NFuse service is running.

8. The final prompt asks you to provide the port number for the NFuse service. After the necessary files are copied, you're returned to the main setup screen, where you can exit the installation.

9. The final step you need to perform is to update the CLASSPATH line in the appropriate .profile file to include the full path to nfuse.jar, ctxxml4j.jar, and NFuse.properties.

10. Restart Apache for the changes to take effect.

The values entered during the installation, plus some other system-wide settings for NFuse, are located in the file NFuse.properties, which can be found in the directory that you specified for the NFuse Java objects during the installation. By default, this is /usr/local/jserv/NFuse. The following is a sample of the contents of this file:

```
Version=Preview
SessionFieldLocations=Script,Template,Url,Post,Cookie,Properties
SessionField.NFuse_ContentType=text/html
URLMapping./=/usr/local/apache/htdocs
SessionField.NFuse_IconCache=/NFuseIcons/
SessionField.NFuse_TemplatesDir=/usr/local/apache/htdocs/NFuseTemplates
SessionField.NFuse_CitrixServer=NFuseSvc
SessionField.NFuse_CitrixServerPort=80
DTDDirectory=/usr/local/jserv/NFuse/
Timeout=60
```

Notice that the MetaFrame server, port number, and URL home information are stored here. Changes to this file won't take effect until you stop and restart the Web server.

Developing the HTML Page

Now that you have the ICA client, MetaFrame, and Web servers configured, the final step is the creation of the Web page and ICA files that users will use to connect to the available published applications.

Two different tools are available for creating the HTML and ICA files. Which one you use depends on whether you're implementing NFuse. The two tools are as follows:

- **Citrix ALE Wizard.** This tool is provided as part of the Published Application Manager on each MetaFrame server. It's used if you're not implementing NFuse.

- **Citrix Web Site Wizard.** This tool is provided as part of the NFuse MetaFrame installation component. It allows you to create a simple NFuse interface that you can then customize or use as is.

Citrix ALE Wizard

To make your published application available to Web clients, you must create a Web page with the proper information in it. Citrix provides the ALE Wizard to assist you in creating both a properly configured HTML file and an accompanying ICA file if required. You don't have to use this wizard to create your Web page, but the generated file does demonstrate what HTML tags you need to use and provides a nice template that you can then customize as required.

The ALE Wizard is accessed from within the Published Application Manager, located under Start, Programs, MetaFrame Tools (Common). To create a Web page using the ALE Wizard, follow these steps:

1. To start the ALE Wizard, right-click the icon for the application that you want to place in the Web page. Select the Write HTML File option, as shown in Figure 15.20. (You can also find this option under the Application menu.)

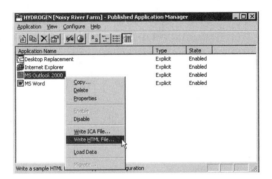

Figure 15.20   *Selecting the Write HTML File option.*

2. The first dialog box prompts you to decide how much assistance you need. If this is your first time using this tool, I suggest that you select A Lot! Please Explain Everything. This option provides detailed information on every dialog box. In contrast, the other option, Not Much. I've Done This Before, displays the minimum dialog boxes required to generate the HTML and ICA file. For this example, select the A Lot! option, and then click Next.

3. Decide whether to use an existing ICA file or create a new one. In this example, I'll select Create a New ICA File.

4. The dialog box shown in Figure 15.21 appears. Here you specify the size and color depth at which to display the application when it's accessed through the Web page. I chose 640×480 and 256 colors.

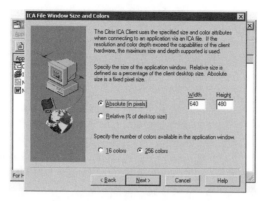

Figure 15.21 *The ICA File Window Size and Colors dialog box.*

5. The next screen lets you select the required encryption for the MetaFrame session. Even though you can select any encryption level, the actual level used depends on what encryption is available on the MetaFrame server that's publishing the application. If you need strong encryption, make sure that the MetaFrame server has been configured with the SecureICA option pack. Select the desired level and then click Next.

6. You're prompted to provide a name for the ICA file. When choosing a name, it's suggested that you select one that's eight characters or less to ensure that all browsers will be able to access it properly. Be sure to include the .ICA extension.

7. The next dialog box prompts you to specify whether the application is embedded or launched. If you select Launched, skip ahead to step 10; otherwise, continue with step 8.

8. If you selected Embedded, you have the choice of creating a page based on the Netscape plug-in/ActiveX control or the Java ALE client (see Figure 15.22). Choose the desired client type and click Next. For this example, I'll choose the Java client.

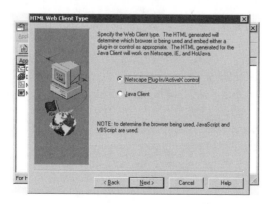

Figure 15.22 *Selecting the desired ALE client type for an embedded application.*

Tip

In order for the Java ALE client to work, the ICA Java client must be installed on the Web server. Refer back to the "Web Server Configuration" section of this chapter for more information. ◆

9. Specify the size of the window on the Web page. This is the space allocated on the page for the application, not the dimensions of the application itself. The application will be contained within this window. I recommend that you specify this size to equal the window size that you selected in step 4. Enter the width and height and click Next.

10. The next dialog box asks whether you want to create a verbose page. The verbose page includes comments and additional content that help explain how the page is configured. The non-verbose page contains only the HTML source required to display the application window or link.

11. The final dialog box prompts you to provide a name for your Web page (see Figure 15.23). Again, it is suggested that you use a filename consisting of eight characters or fewer to ensure compatibility with all browsers. Remember to include the .HTM or .HTML extension. I recommend that you give this page the same filename that you assigned to the ICA file in step 6.

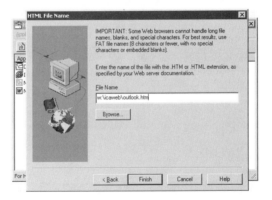

Figure 15.23   *Specifying the HTML filename.*

After you click Finish, a screen explains that the generated Web page is only a template and requires editing before it can be used in a production environment. In particular, you need to update the CODEBASE property in the HTML file to point to the location where you installed the Java classes. Here is the resulting HTML file that I created for embedding Outlook Express within a Web page using the Java client:

```
<!DOCTYPE HTML PUBLIC "-//IETF//DTD HTML//EN">
<html>
<head>
<meta http-equiv="Content-Type" content="text/html; charset=iso-8859-1">
```

```
<meta name="METAMARKER" content="null">
<title>Demo Application Page</title>


<script language="VBScript">
<!—
option explicit
dim majorver
dim ua
dim ie3
dim ie4
dim aol
dim minorver4
dim update
dim winplat
dim nav
dim intButton
set nav = navigator
ua = "Mozilla/2.0 (compatible; MSIE 3.02; Windows NT)"
minorver4 = ""

if len(ua) >=1 then 'nav object is supported
    winplat = mid(ua,instr(ua,"Windows") + 8, 2)
    majorver = mid(ua,instr(ua,"MSIE") + 5, 1)
    ie3 = majorver = 3 and (winplat = "NT" or winplat = "95" or winplat = "32")
    ie4 = majorver = 4 and (winplat = "NT" or winplat = "95" or winplat = "32")
    update = instr(ua,"Update a")
    aol = instr(ua,"AOL")

    if ie4 then minorver4 = mid(ua,instr(ua,"MSIE") + 7, 3)
end if
—>
</script>

</head>

<body>
<script language="Javascript">
<!—
  var browserType=navigator.userAgent;
  if (browserType.indexOf("Mozilla")!=-1 &&browserType.indexOf("/4.")!=-1)
    {
        document.write("<applet codebase=. code='com.citrix.JICA.class'
        ↪ archive='JICAEngN.jar'  width=640 height=480><!—");
    }
  else
    {
        document.write("<applet codebase=. code='com.citrix.JICA.class'
        ↪ archive='JICAEng.zip' width=640 height=480><!—");
    }
// —>
</script>
        <applet codebase=. code='com.citrix.JICA.class' archive='JICAEngJ.jar'
```

```
    ↪ width=640 height=480>
<script language="Javascript">
<!—
  var browserType=navigator.userAgent;
  if (browserType.indexOf("Mozilla")!=-1 ¦¦ browserType.indexOf("MSIE")!= -1)
    { document.write("—>"); }
—>
</script>

        <param name=cabbase value='JICAEngM.cab'>

        <!param name=Address       value="n.n.n.n">
        <param name=Address        value="Outlook Express">

        <param name=TCPBrowserAddress     value="192.168.1.5">

        <param name=Start      value="auto">

        <!param name="Username"   value="whatever">
        <!param name="Domain"     value="whatever">
        <!param name="Password"   value="whatever">

        <param name="InitialProgram" value="#Outlook Express">
        <!param name="WorkDirectory"  value="dir">

        <!param name=EndSessionTimeout value=n>
        <param name=Border value=on>
        <!param name=BorderWidth value=6>
        <!param name=ICAPortNumber value="whatever">
        <!param name=LargeCacheSize value="6543210">
</applet>
</body>
</html>
```

Tip

An exclamation point (!) before the <param name> tag simply comments out that information. ◆

Notice that the file contains JavaScript to use the appropriate signed Java archive based on the user's Web browser.

To test the resulting files, you should do the following:

- Update the HTML file to point to the location where you installed the ICA Java client files. For example, if they're located in the directory JICA11 off the root directory for the Web server, the CODEBASE entries would be updated to read as follows:

  ```
  codebase=/JICA11/
  ```

And the CABBASE value for the Java CAB file would be updated to read this way:

```
"/jica11/JICAEngM.cab"
```

- Copy the files (HTML and ICA) to the desired location under the root of the Web server. You should place both of these files in the same directory.
- Launch your Web browser and point it to the desired file.

To test the generated files, make sure that they're located in the same directory and then access the HTML page through a Web browser. Figure 15.24 shows the Web page that I generated with Outlook Express embedded within the Web page.

Figure 15.24 *Outlook Express running as an embedded application within a Web page.*

The following is the accompanying ICA file that was also generated by the ALE wizard for my embedded Outlook Express example. Notice that the browser address entry is automatically populated with the IP address. You can modify this to use the server name instead.

```
[WFClient]
Version=2
TcpBrowserAddress=192.168.1.5

[ApplicationServers]
Outlook Express=

[Outlook Express]
```

```
Address=Outlook Express
InitialProgram=#Outlook Express
DesiredHRES=640
DesiredVRES=480
DesiredColor=2
TransportDriver=TCP/IP
WinStationDriver=ICA 3.0
```

Citrix Web Site Wizard

NFuse's answer to the ALE wizard is the *Web Site Wizard* (*WSW*). The Web Site Wizard is a separate component that, although a part of the MetaFrame installation component, can be run on any 32-bit operating system. The installation of the wizard is straightforward. Launch the NFuse MetaFrame component (NFuseForMF.exe). When you reach the screen where you select the components to install, select only the Web Site Wizard (see Figure 15.25). If you run the setup on a non–MF server, only this option will be selected by default. You will be able to start using WSW immediately, because a reboot is not required.

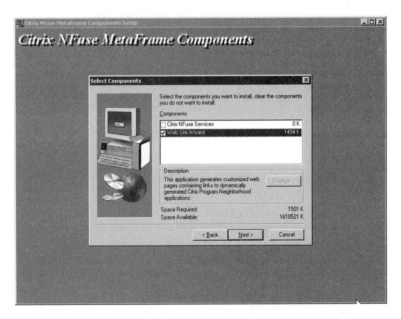

Figure 15.25 *Selecting the Web Site Wizard to install.*

The wizard is automatically added to the Web Site Wizard folder under Programs on the Start menu. When launched, it guides you through eight steps to creating a simple interface to your NFuse environment:

1. The first screen simply introduces you to the wizard.

2. The second screen enables you to override the default MetaFrame server and port that you provided during the NFuse Java object installation on the Web server. I don't recommend doing this unless you're directing this page at a specific server, such as a test or development MetaFrame machine. Managing load using a strategy such as DNS round-robin helps to remove this dependency from the Web pages.

3. Next you can select a scheme for your Web site. The choices are fairly standard but provide a starting point for developing your own custom sites.

4. In the fourth dialog box, specify how the Web site will be generated (see Figure 15.26). You can choose between Citrix-enhanced HTML tags and scripting-based using Active Server Pages or JavaServer pages. When possible, I recommend using the scripting-based implementation appropriate for your Web server.

Figure 15.26   *Selecting the layout model for your Web site.*

5. The fifth dialog box allows you to specify whether the application will be launched or embedded within the Web page (see Figure 15.27). The decision depends on how you're planning to implement your NFuse environment. Typically, when you're using NFuse, applications are launched so that they run independently of the browser and allow users to continue surfing to other locations without losing their application sessions. If users are running the Win32 ICA client, a launched

application can also be configured to run seamlessly. When selecting the embedded mode, you can specify which ALE client is supported, or you can configure it so that the user can decide which client to use.

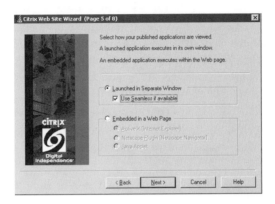

Figure 15.27   *Specify how the applications are viewed.*

6. The next dialog box contains the options that control how application links will appear on the Web page. Here are the available options:

   • **Show Icon.** Displays the application's icon on the page. This option provides a nice visual cue to the user.

   • **Show Name.** Displays the application's name as well.

   • **Show Details.** Displays the associated description for the published application. Normally you won't need to provide this information to the user.

   • **Show Folders.** When publishing applications to a server farm, you have the option of creating them in subfolders in the application set. This way, you can group common applications within a folder. When Show Folders is selected, users have links on their pages that take them to the corresponding folder containing the application links. If this option is deselected, all applications appear on a single page.

   • **Allow user to view application settings.** Checking this option creates a View Settings button on the generated Web site that, when clicked, displays the settings for each application. Users won't need this information under most circumstances, but it may be helpful during testing to possibly assist in debugging.

7. In the next-to-last dialog box, you choose how users will authenticate in your environment (see Figure 15.28). By default, the Allow Explicit Logins option is selected because this is the most common configuration in which to use NFuse. You can force users to authenticate against a specific domain; however, the information is simply generated within the resulting Web page, so it's not really hidden from users who might want to find out what domain they're authenticating against. By requiring a user to provide the domain information, you're demanding one more piece of information that an unauthorized user needs in order to gain access to your environment.

You can allow guest logons by providing a user ID, password, and domain in the appropriate fields. This information will be written into the appropriate file and used to automatically log on with those credentials. For example, when using Microsoft Active Server Pages, the guest credentials are stored in the file GUESTAPPS.ASP, which contains the plaintext information on this guest account, including the password. *Never* configure the guest account to automatically connect with a user ID that may have anything other than guest privileges.

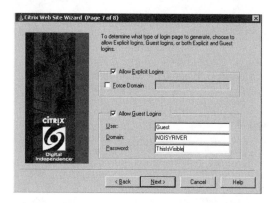

Figure 15.28   *Selecting the form of user authentication to employ.*

8. In the final dialog box, verify the options you've selected and provide a destination location for the files that will be generated automatically to support an NFuse Web environment.

Figures 15.29 and 15.30 demonstrate an example of the automatically generated NFuse logon screen and an application-set page that was automatically generated based on the user's credentials.

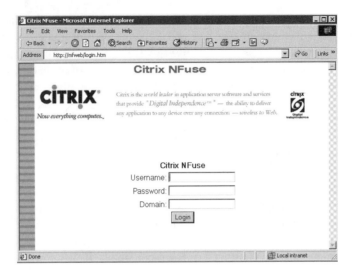

Figure 15.29   *The NFuse logon prompt.*

Figure 15.30   *The user's automatically generated
application-set page, including folders.*

As mentioned earlier, NFuse uses a template ICA file, which it populates
with the necessary information before passing it to the client to be used to
establish the connection. The following is a sample template created by the
Web Site Wizard. Each of the substitution tags in the file is contained in
square brackets ([]) and begins with the word NFuse.

```
<[NFuse_setSessionField NFuse_ContentType=application/x-ica]>

<[NFuse_setSessionField NFuse_WindowType=seamless]>
```

```
[WFClient]
Version=2
ClientName=[NFuse_ClientName]

[ApplicationServers]
[NFuse_AppName]=

[[NFuse_AppName]]
Address=[NFuse_IPV4Address]
InitialProgram=#[NFuse_AppName]
DesiredColor=[NFuse_WindowColors]
TransportDriver=TCP/IP
WinStationDriver=ICA 3.0
Username=[NFuse_User]
Domain=[NFuse_Domain]
Password=[NFuse_PasswordScrambled]
[NFuse_IcaWindow]

[NFuse_IcaEncryption]

[EncRC5-0]
DriverNameWin32=pdc0n.dll

[EncRC5-40]
DriverNameWin32=pdc40n.dll

[EncRC5-54]
DriverNameWin32=pdc54n.dll

[EncRC5-128]
DriverNameWin32=pdc128n.dll
```

Within this template file, you perform any of the customizations that you want for all connections to your MetaFrame server. A number of parameters can be added to this file, allowing you to set options such as persistent cache size, use of sound, and tuning of the mouse and keyboard response.

Of particular interest in this example is this entry:

```
Address=[NFuse_IPV4Address]
```

It specifies the server that the user will connect to in order to run the published application. One of the features of NFuse is the server-side communication with the master ICA browser in order to find published application information. This entry tells NFuse that it should determine what server the user should connect to instead of the user doing it.

Alternatively, you can modify the template file so that the user's ICA client is responsible for locating the master browser and selecting the server on which to run the published application. This is done simply by changing the entry to read as follows:

```
Address=[NFuse_AppName]
```

This forces the client to broadcast for the published application. You can enter one or more server location values by including the `TCPBrowserAddress` entries. The following shows an example of adding two server addresses:

```
TCPBrowserAddress=192.168.10.25
TCPBrowserAddress2=192.168.10.26
```

For more information on ICA browsing and server location entries, see Chapter 3.

> **Tip**
>
> *For a complete list of available template options, review the NFuse online PDF*
> *document available on the Citrix Web site at this address:*
>
> `http://download.citrix.com/pub/server/nfuse/NFuseAdmin.pdf` ◆

MetaFrame and Firewall Considerations

Figure 15.31 demonstrates a simple configuration involving an external firewall connected to the Internet, and one or more internal MetaFrame servers that people on the Internet want to access. To add to this, network address translation (NAT) is involved, meaning that addresses on the internal network are not visible to users on the external side. The only way for someone on the Internet to access an internal resource is through a public IP address (shown as the second external address in the diagram) that the firewall product translates and routes to the corresponding server on the internal side.

> **Author's Note**
>
> *To demonstrate how a MetaFrame environment and a firewall would be config-*
> *ured for client access via the Internet, I have purposely kept the configuration in*
> *this section fairly simple. Most corporate environments would employ a much*
> *more advanced firewall configuration, but the basic requirements for TCP and*
> *UDP port access would still apply.* ◆

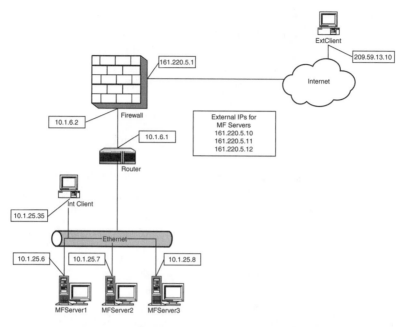

Figure 15.31 *Simple firewall design involving MetaFrame.*

In this example, I have three MetaFrame servers on the internal network that I want to be accessible externally. Table 15.5 lists the internal and external addresses for the objects in this example.

Table 15.5 *Internal and External IP Addresses for the Firewall Example*

Host	Internal IP Address	External IP Address
MFServer1	10.1.25.6	161.220.5.10
MFServer2	10.1.25.7	161.220.5.11
MFServer3	10.1.25.8	161.220.5.12
FireWall	10.1.6.2	161.220.5.1
ExtClient	N/A	209.59.13.10
IntClient	10.1.25.35	N/A

Published Application Accessibility Requirements

Although the diagram in Figure 15.31 (see the preceding section) is straightforward, the process involved in configuring this environment to work properly is not quite as trivial when a MetaFrame server is involved. The problem is not in the connectivity between a client and a specific server, since the process of configuring this with NAT is identical to that for setting up an FTP or Web server. The problem arises when you want to allow access to published applications or desktops in a load-balanced configuration. The difficulty lies in how the ICA client and the ICA master browser perform this communication.

I'll start by demonstrating how the internal client would communicate with a master browser. Let's assume that the MFServer3 is the master browser and that the IntClient has MFServer1 in its server location list.

1. IntClient contacts MFServer1, requesting the location of the master browser.

2. MFServer1 returns the IP address for MFServer3 (10.1.25.8).

3. IntClient contacts 10.1.25.8 and requests the desired published application.

4. 10.1.25.8 returns the IP address for MFServer2 (10.1.25.7), which is where the application is located.

5. IntClient connects to 10.1.25.7 and runs the published application.

Now let's repeat this process with the ExtClient, with the assumption that NAT is in place on the firewall. We'll assume that ExtClient also has MFServer1's external IP address (161.220.5.10) in its server location list.

1. ExtClient attempts to contact MFServer1, requesting the location of the master browser. The firewall translates the external address to the internal one and routes the request to MFServer1.

2. MFServer1 returns the IP address for MFServer3 (10.1.25.8) to ExtClient. The firewall handles routing the request back to the client, but the payload still contains the internal address to MFServer3.

3. ExtClient attempts to contact 10.1.25.8, at which point the connection fails.

Obviously, the problem arises when MFServer1 returns the internal IP address to MFServer3. The firewall won't perform NAT on this address since it's not in the source or destination portion of the packet, but instead is in the payload.

What we really want is for MFServer1 to return the *external* address for MFServer3 to ExtClient so that the client can properly contact that server. Fortunately, Citrix provides a means of doing this.

Author's Note

This problem doesn't occur if an external client attempts to connect directly to a MetaFrame server instead of requesting a server from the master browser. For example, if ExtClient had a connection set explicitly for the server MFServer3, it would establish that connection without issue. The IP address translation issue that I'm discussing here deals only with communication between the master ICA browser and the ICA client when attempting to access published applications across a firewall. ♦

The resolution to this problem is actually broken down into two parts: a server component and a client component. You configure the MetaFrame server to maintain information on its equivalent external IP address, and configure the client to request the MetaFrame server's alternate address from the master browser.

MetaFrame Server Configuration

For each MetaFrame server that will be available externally, you need to define its alternate address. This information is maintained on the server and is passed to the ICA master browser so that it can be passed to a client if requested.

The alternate address is configured using the command-line tool ALTADDR. For example, to set the alternate (external) IP address for MFServer1, you would enter the following command while logged onto MFServer1:

```
altaddr /set 161.220.5.10
```

You can set the alternate address on a different server by including the /server: option. While logged onto MFServer1, you could set the alternate address on MFServer2 as follows:

```
altaddr /server:MFServer2 /set 161.220.5.11
```

After the alternate address has been set, the information is made available to the master browser, which can then pass it on to the client if requested. The master browser returns this information only when requested, so that clients on the internal network can still access the same MetaFrame servers. Otherwise, you would only be able to use the servers in one situation or the other, but not both.

For a complete list of the ALTADDR parameters, see Appendix A, "Terminal Server/MetaFrame Command Reference."

ICA Client Configuration

To use the alternate address for a MetaFrame server, the client must explicitly request it. The exact location where this is done varies slightly from client to client, but in general it's configured on the same screen as where you specify the server location list information. For Program Neighborhood clients (Win32 and Java), you can specify this in two locations: one for the custom connections and the other for each created Program Neighborhood application set. Unless you're accessing published applications through a firewall where NAT is involved, you don't need to configure the alternate address request. Figure 15.32 shows where you set this option for an application set on the Win32 client.

Figure 15.32   *Setting the alternate address request for an application set.*

NFuse Configuration

If you're implementing NFuse in a firewall implementation, you also need to modify the template ICA file to support alternate addresses. The changes you make will depend on whether the NFuse Java objects are responsible for contacting the master browser, or the client will do this by itself.

If the Java objects are communicating with the master browser, replace this entry:

```
[[NFuse_AppName]]
Address=[NFuse_IPV4Address]
```

with this:

```
[[NFuse_AppName]]
Address=[NFuse_IPV4AddressAlternate]
```

If the ICA client will be responsible for communicating with the master browser, add the UseAlternateAddress option to the [[NFuse_AppName]] section, along with one or more TCPBrowserAddress entries. For example:

```
[[NFuse_AppName]]
Address=[NFuse_AppName]
TCPBrowserAddress=161.220.5.10
TCPBrowserAddress2=161.220.5.11
TCPBrowserAddress2=161.220.5.12
UseAlternateAddress=1
```

Sample Configuration with CheckPoint FireWall-1

To complete this chapter, I would like to provide a brief demonstration of how the basic configuration shown in Figure 15.33 could be implemented using the popular firewall software CheckPoint FireWall-1.

Author's Note

Of course, an alternate implementation is to employ a VPN solution at the firewall and require all clients that want to access the MetaFrame server to first connect with the appropriate VPN client. ◆

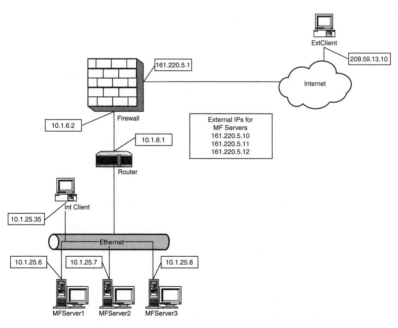

Figure 15.33   *Simple firewall implementation with MetaFrame and CheckPoint Firewall-1.*

> **Warning**
>
> *Please be aware that this is only a demonstration of the steps required to perform the configuration. It's not a recommendation as to how best to configure your production firewall. I highly recommend that someone skilled in the administration of firewall software and Internet security configure your environment for production use (with any necessary corporate approval, of course). ◆*

To review, the goal is to allow clients over the Internet to connect to any one of the three MetaFrame servers, which are physically located behind the firewall. There are three public or external IP addresses that I'll map using network address translation through to the internal servers. There are four basic steps:

1. Include static ARP entries on the firewall to manage the three external IP addresses. This will allow the external firewall interface to receive data for all three external IPs.

> **Tip**
>
> *Address Resolution Protocol (ARP) maps an IP address to a physical machine address that's recognized on the local network. Hosts on a network maintain a list of dynamic and sometimes static ARP entries that tell it where an IP is located on their network. ◆*

2. Set up static routes on the firewall so that it directs requests for the three external IP addresses into the internal network instead of back out onto the Internet, which it will do based on its dynamic routing table.

3. Configure the necessary objects in FireWall-1, and apply the security and NAT policies.

4. Configure the MetaFrame servers with their alternate addresses so that they can properly service external clients.

I'll review each of these steps with the assumption that FireWall-1 is installed and running on an NT 4.0 or Windows 2000 server.

Update the ARP Cache on the Firewall

The first step is to configure the existing external interface on the firewall to act as a proxy for the three external IP addresses. To do this, you need the MAC (Media Access Control) address of the external network card. This can be done by typing `ipconfig /all` from a command prompt on the firewall. I'll assume that the MAC for my interface is `00-c0-7a-2a-11-6d`.

Windows does not support proxy ARPing using the ARP –s command, as you could do on a UNIX server. Instead, you need to create a file in the folder *<FW-1 Install Path>*\State, called LOCAL.ARP. This file should contain across reference between the external IP addresses and MAC addresses of the external NIC. In my example, this file contains the following entries:

```
161.220.5.10      00-c0-7a-2a-11-6d
161.220.5.11      00-c0-7a-2a-11-6d
161.220.5.12      00-c0-7a-2a-11-6d
```

The next time the security policy is installed on Firewall-1, these ARP proxy settings will take effect.

Author's Note

When a gateway receives a packet, it checks its local ARP cache to find the MAC address that matches the packet's destination IP address. If no local entry is found, an ARP broadcast tries to find the machine with that IP, which will respond to the request. This information is then stored in the gateway's local cache for future reference. The reference is kept for only a fixed length of time. After the time expires, the reference is flushed from the cache. ✦

Add Static Routes

Next you set up the required static routes, which will direct packets destined for the external IP address to their internal equivalents. The route add command will be used, along with the -p option, which marks the entries as persistent so that they'll remain even after a server reboot. The static routes would be added as follows:

```
route add 161.220.5.10 10.1.6.1 -p
route add 161.220.5.11 10.1.6.1 -p
route add 161.220.5.12 10.1.6.1 -p
```

Notice that I've directed all of these to the appropriate internal router interface instead of the destination MetaFrame servers. Attempting to route directly to the MetaFrame servers would result in a "destination unreachable" message.

It may seem strange that routes are being added for the external IP addresses into the internal network, but this is required because NAT on Firewall-1 doesn't occur until the packet is *leaving* the gateway. This means that until the point where it leaves the firewall, it still has the external IP. Firewall-1 processes a packet in the following order:

1. The packet passes through the security policy.

2. The packet is routed based on routing information at the operating system level.

3. NAT is applied as the packet leaves the gateway.

4. The packet once again passes through the security policies as it leaves the gateway (after NAT has taken place).

Configure the Required Firewall-1 Policies

Next, you need to create the necessary objects and define the appropriate security policies and NAT rules. The objects to create are listed in Table 15.6.

Table 15.6   *Firewall-1 Objects to Be Created*

Object Name	Type	Description
MFServer1-Ext	Workstation	Represents the external
MFServer2-Ext	Workstation	interface for each
MFServer3-Ext	Workstation	MetaFrame server.
MFServer1-Int	Workstation	Represents the internal
MFServer2-Int	Workstation	interface for each
MFServer3-Int	Workstation	MetaFrame server.
ICATCP	Service	Represents the ICA service itself.
ICAUDP	Service	Represents the UDP requests for master browser information. If you will implement NFuse, you don't need to define this service.

Each of these objects is created by selecting the Manage, Network Objects menu option. Click New and then Workstation to open the properties dialog box, as shown in Figure 15.34. It contains the information for MFServer1-Ext. You need to repeat this for each of the external and internal objects. Be sure to select the Internal location option when updating the internal IP addresses.

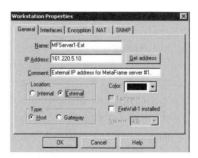

Figure 15.34   *The Workstation Properties dialog box for Firewall-1 workstation objects.*

To create the ICA services, simply select the Manage, Services menu item. A list of all the existing services appears. Click the New button and select the network protocol to assign to your service. Begin by selecting TCP to display the dialog box shown in Figure 15.35, which contains the information for the ICA connection service. Notice that I'm using port 1494, the default listening port for ICA.

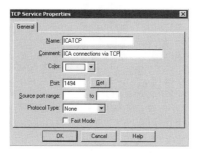

Figure 15.35 *Configuring the ICA TCP service.*

To give users access to published applications, you also need to define the ICAUDP service, as shown in Figure 15.36. If you'll be using NFuse, the service definition is not required because the remote users won't be required to contact the master ICA browser; the NFuse Java objects on your Web server are configured by default to perform this service.

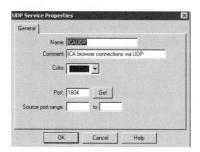

Figure 15.36 *Configuring the ICA UDP service.*

Now that all of the required objects have been defined, the necessary security and NAT policies can be created. The security policies would look like this:

Source	Destination	Service	Action	Tracking
Any	MFServer1-Ext	ICATCP ICAUDP	Accept	Long
Any	MFServer2-Ext	ICATCP ICAUDP	Accept	Long
Any	MFServer3-Ext	ICATCP ICAUDP	Accept	Long
Any	MFServer1-Int	ICATCP ICAUDP	Accept	Long
Any	MFServer2-Int	ICATCP ICAUDP	Accept	Long
Any	MFServer3-Int	ICATCP ICAUDP	Accept	Long
Any	Any	Any	Drop	Long

The first three policies allow anyone on the Internet to connect to one of the external MetaFrame IP addresses using either the ICATCP or the ICAUDP service. The next three policies are actually tested after the packet leaves the firewall. These allow a packet with a source IP located on the Internet to access an internal MetaFrame server's IP address. The last policy is simply a catchall that drops all traffic not destined for the MetaFrame servers. You need to fit these policies into your firewall configuration where appropriate. A security policy is inserted by clicking the row number for an existing policy, right-clicking the policy, and then selecting Insert Rule Above or Add Rule Below. You can then modify the policy by right-clicking the appropriate cell and setting the contents as desired.

Here are the corresponding NAT rules:

Source	Destination	Service
	Original Packets	
Any	MFServer1-Ext	Any
Any	MFServer2-Ext	Any
Any	MFServer3-Ext	Any
Internal Network	Any	Any
	Translated Packets	
Original	Mfserver1-Int(S)	Original
Original	MFServer2-Int(S)	Original
Original	MFServer3-Int(S)	Original
Firewall(H)	Original	Original

Any connection directed to a MetaFrame server's external IP address is automatically translated to the internal address as it leaves the firewall's internal interface. Any replies made by the MetaFrame server are automatically translated. You don't need to define an explicit rule for this unless you want connections initiating from a MetaFrame server to appear as if they were coming from the external address. The last rule hides all internal addresses behind the firewall's external interface IP address. The (S) and (H) refer to Static and Hide, respectively, and describe what form of NAT is taking place.

NAT rules are added using the same technique that was employed for creating security policies.

Author's Note

Remember that NAT is not applied until after the packet has passed the security policy inspection. Once translated, the packet will be inspected again on its way out of the interface. This is why the security policies explicitly state both the internal and external rules. ◆

Alternate Addressing on the MetaFrame Servers

The final piece required in order to allow external clients to communicate with the internal MetaFrame servers (via published applications) is to set up the appropriate alternate addressing. Remember that this is required whether you're allowing users to access the ICA browser or you're doing it through NFuse. These alternate addresses are returned by the master ICA browser to tell the client what MetaFrame server to connect to in order to run its desired published application. For more information on why this is required, see the earlier section "Published Application Accessibility Requirements."

The following commands set the alternate address on the three MetaFrame servers. You can run these on any one of the servers. Also note that you need to use the "real" server name with this command and not the object names you defined within Firewall-1.

```
altaddr /server:MFServer1 /set 161.220.5.10
altaddr /server:MFServer2 /set 161.220.5.11
altaddr /server:MFServer3 /set 161.220.5.11
```

Your MetaFrame/firewall configuration is now complete. If you're having issues with connecting to any of the MetaFrame servers, I suggest that you review the Firewall-1 audit logs. These logs provide valuable information on what might be happening to connection attempts that are failing.

Here are three things to remember when troubleshooting a problem:

- Before attempting to access a published application, you should try to hit a MetaFrame server directly. This will validate that the necessary NAT and security rules are functioning for the ICATCP component.

- Security policies are always checked first and in order from first to last. The first rule that matches a packet is used and the rest are ignored. The same applies for NAT.

- Address translation doesn't occur until the packet is leaving the firewall, so all security rules and routing information must be based on the address the packet contains when it *enters* the firewall.

Author's Note

An excellent (and one of the only) reference for FireWall-1 administration is CheckPoint FireWall-1 Administration Guide *by Marcus Goncalves and Steven Brown (McGraw-Hill, 1999, ISBN 0-0713-4229-X).* ◆

Group and System Policy Configuration

In this chapter:

- **Introduction to Policies**
  An important part of any Terminal Server implementation is having a clear understanding of the role that policies play in the configuration of your environment.

- **Environment Preparation**
  Performing some simple preparation work prior to beginning your policy development can save time and help you to better plan your environment.

- **Creating and Managing NT 4.0 System Policies**
  Policies are managed on NT 4.0 Terminal Servers (and Windows 2000 Terminal Servers in an NT 4.0 domain) using the System Policy Editor utility.

- **Creating and Managing Windows 2000 Group Policies**
  As part of Windows 2000's Active Directory, Microsoft has provided a robust and centralized policies implementation known as Group Policy.

Introduction to Policies

An important part of any Terminal Server implementation is having a clear understanding of the role that policies play in the configuration of your TSE 4.0 or TS 2000 environment.

While a profile (discussed in Chapter 17, "User Profile and Account Configuration") is used to store the desktop and application settings for a user, it doesn't provide a mechanism for controlling which features are actually available to the user. This is where *policies* come in. Policies are used to control the features and restrictions for one or more users. For example, a policy may be implemented that removes the Shutdown option from the Start menu and replaces it with a "Log off" option for all non-administrative users. A policy may also be used to redirect a user's My Documents folder to an alternate location on the network instead of storing it locally on the server.

Policies are not simply about imposing restrictions, but more importantly provide a means to easily configure a Windows environment to function exactly as required. Profiles and policies work together to provide the environment in which your Terminal Server users will work.

> **Warning**
>
> *If you intend to implement policies, review the entire contents of this chapter before beginning your implementation. Unless implemented properly, a policy that you create may affect a user's settings not only when the user is logged onto a Terminal Server, but also when he or she is logged onto any other Windows workstation or server.* ✦

Policy development can be broken down into two main categories:

- *Local server policies* govern how the server behaves for all users who log onto it, including administrators.

- *User-specific policies* are applied based on the group membership for the user. These policies usually affect only the regular Terminal Server users and include restrictions such as no access to run registry editing tools, or the removal of Start menu options such as Shutdown or the Run command.

Environment Preparation

Before getting into the details of how to create and manage policies, I suggest you do some preparation work. If you prefer, you can skip this section and return after you have reviewed the specifics on policies and are ready to perform the actual implementation.

Domain Security Groups

If you haven't already done so, you should create the base Terminal Server domain security groups. In Chapter 8, "Server Management Planning," I discuss the creation of the local security groups and the role that they play in managing the file, registry, and connection security. Domain groups are commonly placed into these local groups when assigning access to your Terminal Servers. Domain groups are also a key part in the implementation of policies, as you will soon see.

The following table describes the domain security groups that I use in the examples in this chapter:

Domain Security Group	Description
TSE_Sec_Admins	Terminal Server administrators. These users have full control over the configuration of a Terminal Server.
TSE_Sec_Operators	Terminal Server operators. These users have the privileges needed to support a Terminal Server, such as shutdown/restart or killing a running task. They don't have the ability to install or modify software or the operating system.
TSE_Sec_Users	Terminal Server users. These users have only the minimum access needed to work within the Terminal Server environment.

Network Policy Share

If you're deploying Terminal Servers in an NT 4.0 domain, you'll want to create a share to contain the system policies for your Terminal Server implementation. I recommend using a name such as TSEPolicies to ensure that people know that the information it contains is specific to Terminal Server. The share and directory permissions should both have the following settings:

SYSTEM	Full Control
TSE_Sec_Admins	Full Control
TSE_Sec_Operators	Read
TSE_Sec_Users	Read

Users need only Read access to be able to process the policy information that you create.

Author's Note

An alternative to managing system policies from a single network share is to place them locally on each Terminal Server. While this increases the management required to ensure that the policies are up to date, it also provides a performance increase during logon. This performance boost can be significant if the policy information being loaded by each user is quite large.

To use local system policy files, you simply need to point to a local server drive instead of a network UNC path when defining the file location. For more on this topic, see the later discussion of configuring the actual policies. ✦

Terminal Server Organizational Units

In a pure Windows 2000 environment where you'll be using group policies, you should create an organizational unit structure similar to the one shown in Figure 16.1. This configuration allows the assignment of group policies that are specific to Terminal Servers, without affecting other Windows 2000 servers. It also provides a means of grouping the servers and Terminal Server domain groups into one area to ease the administrative work.

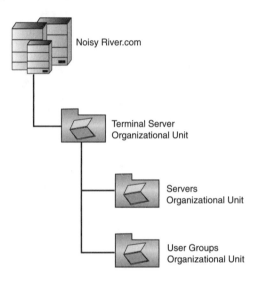

Figure 16.1   *Terminal Server organizational unit example.*

Creating and Managing NT 4.0 System Policies

Policies are managed on NT 4.0 Terminal Servers (and Windows 2000 Terminal Servers in an NT 4.0 domain) using the System Policy Editor (PolEdit) utility. Figure 16.2 shows the main interface window for PolEdit.

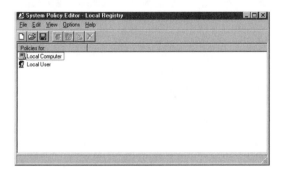

Figure 16.2   *Terminal Server 4.0 System Policy Editor.*

Author's Note

In many cases, the enforcement of a policy is based on a change that's made within the system's registry. The policy management tools provide a graphical interface to managing registry changes, instead of you having to script or manually make these changes yourself. ✦

When creating policies in an NT 4.0 environment, I usually break it down into four steps:

1. Create the policies associated with the Terminal Server computer itself. This configures how the Terminal Server will behave from a system standpoint, including where it looks to retrieve the policy information for users logging onto the Terminal Server.

2. Define the default policies associated with all users who log onto the Terminal Server. Although these settings apply to all users, they're not directly related to the default user profile (discussed in the next chapter). Usually only one or two options are created for this default policy since they will apply to all users, including administrators.

3. Create policies for specific user groups. These policies are based on a user's group membership and usually make up the bulk of the restrictions that are implemented in the Terminal Server environment.

4. Define the implementation priority for the policies you have created. Terminal Server applies all appropriate policies from lowest priority to highest, so you need to ensure that you have defined the priorities properly to avoid accidentally assigning policies to the wrong users.

Author's Note

I was once involved in a project in which most of the policies were implemented against the default user policy, and then certain restrictions were "turned off" for Terminal Server administrators. This ensured that any domain user logging onto the server (regardless of account domain) would receive these policy settings. ✦

Creating the Local Terminal Server Policy

Creating the local Terminal Server policy is critical to the proper operation of system policies in an NT 4.0 domain, since it's here that you define where the Terminal Server will look to retrieve the policy information for user-specific policies. By default, the Terminal Server will look to the NETLOGON share on a domain controller to retrieve policy information when a user logs on. Unless you're going to have the same policies for both regular NT and Terminal Server (you probably won't), you need to tell the Terminal Server to look in an alternate location.

Warning

Don't create Terminal Server specific policies in the NETLOGON location. If you do, these policies will be picked up by your Terminal Server users even when they are not logging onto Terminal Server. This can have a negative impact on their local desktop settings, and possibly render that environment unusable.

I recommend that you always redirect your Terminal Server policies to an alternate location. ◆

The steps for creating the local Terminal Server policies are as follows:

1. Log onto the Terminal Server with an administrative account and run the command to start the System Policy Editor (POLEDIT).

2. From the File menu, select Open Registry to display the local computer and local user icons. Don't make any changes to the local user policy, as these will only apply to the HKEY_CURRENT_USER registry key and won't be applied to any other users who log onto the server.

3. Double-click the local computer icon to open its properties, as shown in Figure 16.3. Setting these policies updates the appropriate registry entries for HKEY_LOCAL_MACHINE.

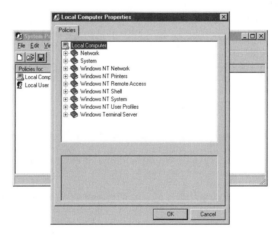

Figure 16.3 *Local computer properties in the System Policy Editor.*

4. The first option to set is where the Terminal Server will retrieve user-specific policy information. To do this, select Network\System Policies Update\Remote Update. Select the Manual update mode and enter the UNC path to the policies share that you created (see the earlier section "Environment Preparation" for more information on this topic). Be sure to include the name of the policy file that will be loaded. This file doesn't have to exist at this point. I recommend using the name TSConfig.pol instead of NTConfig.pol, which is the default name for regular NT policy files. Figure 16.4 shows these settings.

Tip

Instead of a UNC path, you could use a local server path. Don't forget to include the policy filename. ◆

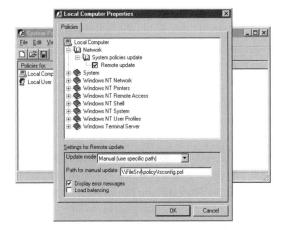

Figure 16.4   *Configuring the Remote Update policy.*

5. To save the changes, click OK to close the properties dialog box, and then choose File, Save.

6. After you have updated the Terminal Server policy location, make any other configuration changes appropriate for your environment. Table 16.1 lists some of the suggested policies that you should implement on the Terminal Server.

   Remember that any policies that you define for the local computer will apply to all users who log on, regardless of whether the user is an administrator.

Table 16.1   *Suggested Policies for the Local Terminal Server*

Path	Comments
Windows NT System\Logon	**Logon Banner** displays a message prior to the user receiving the logon prompt for the server. Usually this is a legal notice regarding the privacy of the system. This message will not be displayed if you access the server through Program Neighborhood.
	Do Not Display Last Logged On User Name prevents a user's logon name from appearing automatically.

continues ▶

Table 16.1   continued

Path	Comments
Windows NT System\File System	Enabling the **Do Not Update Last Access Time** entry greatly improves file system performance, since it no longer has to update the access time on a read operation.
Windows NT User Profiles	Enabling the **Delete Cached Copies of Roaming Profiles** option helps to reduce the amount of disk space consumed by profiles left on the server. Every time a user logs off, his or her cached local profile will be removed.

Author's Note

If you are implementing Windows 2000 Terminal Services in an NT 4.0 domain, a local group policy can still be created on the Terminal Server using the GPEDIT.MSC snap-in for the Microsoft Management Console (MMC). As the name implies, any settings in this group policy will apply only the local Terminal Server on which it was created. The local group policy is applied when the server first boots up, and again at each scheduled refresh interval.

Any system policies created using POLEDIT will be applied as expected when the user logs onto the Terminal Server. Whenever the local group policy is refreshed, the systems are automatically reapplied. I will talk more about Windows 2000 group policy later in this chapter. For a complete description of system and group policy interaction in a mixed Windows environment, see the complete group policy documentation in the Windows 2000 Resource Kit. ◆

Creating the Default User Policies

The next step is to create the default policies that will apply to all users who log onto your Terminal Server. These settings are applied regardless of which access privileges the user has, so make sure that the changes you make should apply to all users.

To apply these default policies you need to create a new policy with the following procedure:

1. Log onto the Terminal Server with an administrative account and start the System Policy Editor.

2. Choose File, New Policy. Two icons are created: Default Computer and Default User. Any properties set within either of these policies will apply to all users who log onto the Terminal Server and will override any settings that have been made in the local registry. Normally I don't make any changes for the Default computer, since the necessary changes are usually applied directly to the registry.

3. To update the default user properties, double-click Default User to open a property dialog box similar to the one discussed earlier for the local computer. One difference that you'll notice with all property values in the policy is that by default they appear with a gray box instead of an empty (white) box (see Figure 16.5).

For these values, three different settings are available: enabled, disabled, and not defined. When the value is not defined it appears in gray, and the default setting of a lower priority policy remains in affect. The enabled/disabled option will override any values that may have been defined in lower priority policies. (I'll discuss policy priorities shortly.)

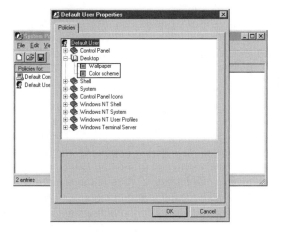

Figure 16.5 *Policy values.*

4. As I've already mentioned, there are very few options that you will want to implement that will affect all users. In Windows NT System, for example, I normally disable the Parse Autoexec.bat option and the Show Welcome Tips at Logon option (really more of a personal preference than a technical requirement). By disabling the parsing of the autoexec.bat, you prevent any environment variables defined in this file from being loaded into the system. This can help to simplify troubleshooting of application issues.

5. After making the desired changes to the default policy, select File, Save, and use the filename that you defined earlier as the policy name (see the earlier section "Creating the Local Terminal Server Policy"—I recommended using the name TSConfig.pol). Make sure you save it into the share location that you created for your policies so that the Terminal Server will be able to pick it up.

Creating Group-Specific User Policies

After you have defined the default policies for all users, the next step is to create the policies that will be applied to users based on their group membership. This is where you'll do the bulk of your customization based on the different types of users.

Normally I create the following group-specific policies:

- **TSE_Sec_Users.** These policies apply to all users who log onto Terminal Server.

- **TSE_Sec_Admins.** This policy applies to all Terminal Server administrators and exists to ensure that no other policy prevents an admin from accessing his or her required functions.

- **Special user group policies.** These policies are created only when you have special subgroups of users who require certain policies. An example might be a department that requires a very restrictive Terminal Server desktop that doesn't include any desktop icons.

Here's an example of how you might create the TSE_Sec_Users group policy:

1. If you have already created the TSConfig.pol file, make sure it's open by selecting Open Policy from the File menu.

2. Select Add Group from the Edit menu and either type or select the desired group by clicking the Browse button. For this example, I'll select the TSE_Sec_Users group, which corresponds to all regular Terminal Server users. After you have chosen the group, an icon for that group is added to the policy window, as shown in Figure 16.6. In this example, I have changed the view type to Detail so that the complete icon name is displayed.

Figure 16.6   *The new policy for the selected domain group.*

3. To modify the policies for the new group, double-click the icon and update the properties as discussed in the previous sections. Table 16.2 lists some of the common properties that I set for regular Terminal Server users.

Table 16.2   Suggested Policies for Regular Terminal Server Users

Path	Comments
Control Panel\Display	Enable this option to restrict a user's access to the Display properties dialog box. Normally I select all tabs, preventing users from having any access to the display properties. Users shouldn't be able to set background properties or specify a screen saver. You may want to allow them to access the Appearance tab to change colors if you feel that's appropriate.
Desktop\Wallpaper	I enable this option and specify (None) as the wallpaper name. This prevents users from specifying a wallpaper that will increase the amount of graphical data transmitted between the client and server.
Shell\Restrictions	The options I select here depend on how restrictive I want to make the user's environment.
System\Restrictions	I always enable the **Disable Registry Editing Tools** option. While it doesn't prevent users from running scripts or other tools to access the registry, it eliminates easy access to the REGEDT32 and REGEDIT applications.
Windows NT Shell\Restrictions	Depending on the implementation, I usually enable the option **Remove Common Program Groups from Start Menu**. This provides users with a list of only the applications that are specifically set for them to access. Another option that I normally select is **Remove Disconnect Item from Start Menu**. While this doesn't eliminate the situation in which users disconnect instead of logging off, it does help to cut this down. It also simplifies the Start menu. I always select the option **Prevent Users from Changing File Type Associations**. When all users share common file associations, you don't want one user changing the associations for an application such as Word, which would be updated for all users.
Windows NT User Profiles	Here you can set some of the management options for user profiles.
	The **Limit Profile Size** option is used to set a quota limit on the size of a user's profile. Once set, the user can't log off if his or her profile exceeds the defined limit. Consider carefully whether you want to implement this feature and what limit you want to set. If you enable this option, you can set a custom message that appears when the quota limit is reached. When the quota limit is reached, an error icon appears

continues ▶

Table 16.2   continued

Path	Comments
	in the system tray. If clicked by the user, it displays a list of files sorted from largest to smallest. (Files less than 2KB in size are not displayed.) If the **Include Registry in File List** option is selected, the ntuser.dat file is also displayed. Normally the user is only notified that he or she has exceeded the quota limit when attempting to log off. If you set the **Notify User** option, however, the user is notified immediately if the quote limit is exceeded. The notice can be repeated every x minutes if you desire.
	The average size of a user profile is typically under 5MB, but can be even less if you also utilize the **Exclude Directories in Roaming Profile** option. This allows you to specify subdirectories under the user's profile that are not copied back to the remote profile location when the user logs off. If cached roaming profiles are configured to be deleted, these excluded directories will be removed immediately.
	In Windows 2000, by default the History, Local Settings, Temp, and Temporary Internet Files folders are excluded from a user's roaming profile. No directories are excluded by default for Windows NT. Enabling the **Exclude Directories in Roaming Profile** option automatically places Temporary Internet Files and Temp in the list.

4. After you've made all the desired policy changes, click OK and then select File, Save to save your changes. Make sure you specify the appropriate location to save the file. For example, I would use the location \\FileSrv\Policy\TSConfig.pol, which is where I configured my Terminal Server to pick up the policies during user logons (see the earlier section "Environment Preparation"). After the file has been saved successfully, the location appears in the title bar for the System Policy Editor. As mentioned earlier, you could also use a file location on the Terminal Server, such as X:\WTSRV\UsrPol\TSConfig.pol, where UsrPol is a directory under the %systemroot% where the policies could be stored.

Now that the file has been saved, the next time a user in the TSE_Sec_Users group logs onto the configured Terminal Server, he or she will pick up the policies that have been defined.

You should now go back and define a system policy for the TSE_Sec_Admins group. This policy will differ from the TSE_Sec_Users policy in that all options, except for those that you want to apply to administrators—such as excluding directories from roaming profiles—should be disabled explicitly (that is, set to be blank and not gray). This means going through all options and making the appropriate selection. I explain the reason for this in the next section; for now, it's sufficient to say that without this policy, if an administrator accidentally belongs to both the TSE_Sec_Admins and TSE_Sec_Users group, he or she would pick up the policy definition for the Users group and would have the same restrictions imposed as a regular user.

Defining Policy Priorities

As mentioned earlier, policies are assigned a priority and are applied from lowest to highest. Figure 16.7 shows the standard priorities for processing policies.

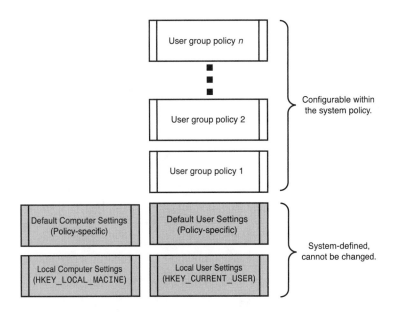

Figure 16.7 *Policy priorities.*

As the figure implies, the priority for the user group policies is configurable. This can be done within the System Policy Editor by selecting Group Priority from the Options menu. This will open the priority dialog box, as shown in Figure 16.8. From here you order your policies as desired. For a user who belongs to multiple groups, policies are applied from lowest (the bottom) to highest (the top); the higher policies override settings applied lower in the list.

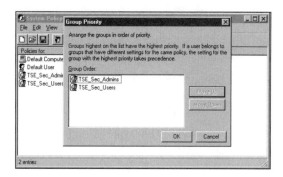

Figure 16.8   *Setting policy priorities in the System Policy Editor.*

I recommend that you always place the TSE_Sec_Admins group at the top and TSE_Sec_Users group at the bottom. If you need to create any other special profile groups, they should be ordered between these two. This way, users always have the minimum policies set for TSE_Sec_Users applied before any other special policies. In this configuration, an administrator can belong to multiple groups, but the policies defined in the TSE_Sec_Admins group will always be applied last, ensuring that the necessary options have not been restricted. This is why I suggested that you explicitly exclude all undesired restrictions in that admin policy.

Using System Policy Editor Templates

The policy configuration options listed in the System Policy Editor—for example, the Windows NT User Profile settings—are not hard-coded within the System Policy Editor, but instead are read from policy editor *template* files that are loaded when the System Policy Editor starts up. Additional template files can be added or removed by selecting Policy Template from the Options menu. Figure 16.9 shows this dialog box with the two default templates (COMMON.ADM and WINNT.ADM) loaded.

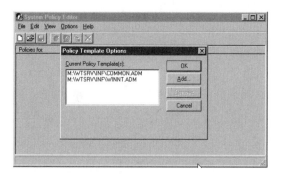

Figure 16.9   *Policy Editor template files.*

All template files are plain text and therefore can be edited using a text editor such as Notepad. A number of custom template files have been created specifically for use within a Terminal Server environment and are available from The ThinNet Web site at http://thethin.net/tsdownload.cfm.

Consider including the CPANEL and WTS template files in your system policy. To do this, download the appropriate files (CPANEL.ZIP and WTSADMIN.ZIP) and extract the contents into a directory where the System Policy Editor always has access to them. I recommend adding these to the %systemroot%\INF directory, which is where the COMMON and WINNT templates exist. Then, from within the System Policy Editor, add the two template files as shown in Figure 16.10.

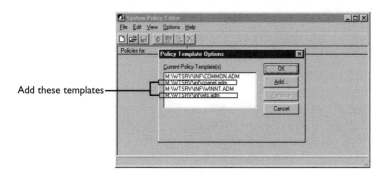

Figure 16.10 *Adding custom Terminal Server policy templates.*

After adding the new templates, if you open your TSConfig.pol file and double-click any defined policy, you'll see the additional policy options (Control Panel Icons and Windows Terminal Server) that are now available to be set.

Tip

Many of the Microsoft Office applications, including Internet Explorer, provide administrative templates that can be loaded and used to enable restrictions and specific configuration options that pertain to the application. Some template files are also provided with the Zero Administration Kit (ZAK) for TSE 4.0 and can be used to lock down additional operating system features. ✦

Creating and Managing Windows 2000 Group Policies

As part of Windows 2000's Active Directory, Microsoft has provided an advanced policies implementation known as *group policy*. Although it's conceptually similar to the policy feature available in NT, group policy provides a much more robust and centralized way of managing Windows policies. Figure 16.11 shows an example of the user configuration options available within a group policy.

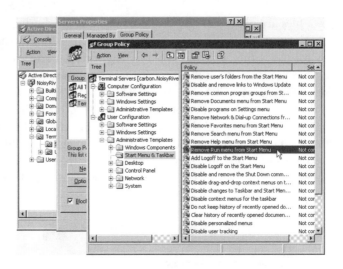

Figure 16.11   *Windows 2000 group policy.*

Each group policy is made up of two components, the Computer Configuration and the User Configuration, and can be applied to objects contained in a site, a domain, or an organizational unit. Policies implemented higher in the Active Directory apply to all objects that are lower, unless special override features have been put in place. In Figure 16.12, for example, if a policy is applied for the domain NoisyRiver.com, it affects all objects underneath it, including those within the Terminal Server organizational unit (OU). On the other hand, if a policy is applied for the Servers OU within Terminal Server, it applies only to objects contained within it, and no other objects within the directory.

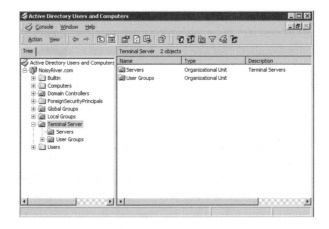

Figure 16.12   *Active Directory example.*

Author's Note

Windows 2000 group policy can only be applied to objects within an Active Directory or locally on a Windows 2000 computer (where it is called a local group policy). Group policies can't be applied to NT 4.0 computers. ✦

When configuring group policies for a TS 2000 environment, I usually follow these five steps:

1. Create the necessary organizational unit to which the Terminal Server policies will be applied. This step is required unless you'll be applying your policies to all servers/users in your domain, which you might do if you have a domain specifically designated for Terminal Servers.

Author's Note

Please be aware that I'm using this OU configuration simply to demonstrate the steps involved in configuring group policy. It's not a recommendation on the best practices for an AD configuration, which could easily be a book in itself—and is, actually: Windows 2000 Active Directory, *also published in 2000 by New Riders Publishing, ISBN 0-7357-0870-3.* ✦

2. Create the policies associated with the Terminal Server computers. These policies dictate the configuration for the server itself.

3. Define the default policies that will apply to all users who log onto the Terminal Server, including administrators.

4. Create the user-specific policies that are applied to users based on their group membership.

5. Ensure that the proper policy priorities have been set so that they're applied in the desired order.

Creating the Terminal Server Organizational Unit

Earlier in this chapter, I discussed the OU that would be used when setting group policies (see the section "Terminal Server Organizational Units"). To create the Terminal Server OU, from within the Active Directory Users and Computers, simply right-click the domain and then select New, Organizational Unit. Similarly, you create the Servers and User Groups OUs by right-clicking the new Terminal Server OU and selecting New, Organizational Unit.

Figure 16.13 shows the OU configuration that I'm going to use to demonstrate group policies. As the figure shows, the policies will be applied only to the Servers OU. They're applied to this OU and not the User Groups OU or Terminal Server OU for the following three reasons:

- The policies applied to the Servers OU will be configured in such a way as to affect users only when they log onto a Terminal Server within this OU.

- If the policies had been applied to the User Groups OU, they would affect all users, regardless of whether they logged onto Terminal Server or a regular Windows 2000 machine.

- Similarly, if the policies were applied to the Terminal Server OU, they would cascade down and affect all groups in the User Groups OU as well as the servers in the Servers OU.

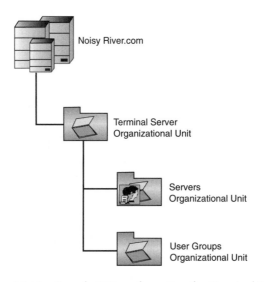

Figure 16.13　*Sample OU configuration for Terminal Server.*

Creating the Terminal Server Computer Policy

Create the base Terminal Server computer policy as follows:

1. Launch the Active Directory Users and Computers and drill down into the Terminal Server OU. Right-click the Servers OU and select Properties to open the Servers Properties dialog box.

2. Click the Group Policy tab (see Figure 16.14). Here you'll manage the group policies for all Terminal Servers in your environment.

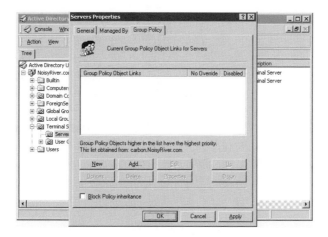

Figure 16.14   *Group policy for the Servers organizational unit.*

You now have three options:

- Create a new *group policy object* (*GPO*).
- Add an existing GPO that may be linked to another site, domain, or OU.
- Enable the Block Policy inheritance option. This will prevent policies defined in parent objects from affecting objects in this OU, unless an override option has been enabled that forces these changes to occur. I normally enable this option, as it prevents policies that may not have been configured explicitly for Terminal Server from being applied accidentally.

3. Click the New button to create a new policy. Its name is automatically added to the GPO link list. Right-click the object, select Rename, and change the name to Terminal Server.

4. With the Terminal Server policy highlighted, click the Properties button. The general properties for this policy are set in the resulting dialog box. There are three tabs of information for a policy:

- The General tab provides a summary of the policy's creation and modification history and allows you to disable the Computer or User settings. Because this is going to be the Terminal Server policy, click the Disable User Configuration Settings option (see Figure 16.15). This will help to speed up the application of the policy on a server by skipping all of the user settings.

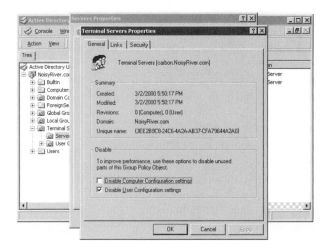

Figure 16.15   *General properties for a group policy.*

- The Links tab shows which other sites, domains, or OUs are using this policy. Because the policy in this example is new, only the current OU has this policy assigned.

- On the Security tab, you define who can access, manage, and apply these policies. This includes the Terminal Server computers themselves; unless they're authorized to apply a policy, the policy won't be applied to the server.

Figure 16.16 shows the adjusted list of user permissions that I've set for this example. My list includes only TSE_Sec_Admins who are authorized to manage the policy; Authenticated Users, which ensures that all servers in the OU are able to apply the given policies; and the SYSTEM account.

Warning

Before changing your security, make sure that you're a member of the TSE_Sec_Admins group, or you'll end up locking yourself out of the policy as soon as you close the dialog box. ◆

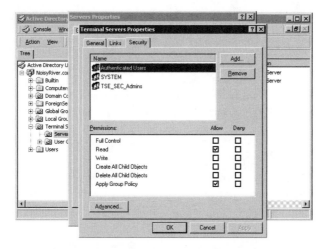

Figure 16.16   *Policy management security properties.*

Table 16.3 shows the permissions that should be assigned to each of these groups.

Table 16.3   *Terminal Servers Policy Security Permissions*

Permission	Authenticated Users	SYSTEM	TSE_Sec_Admins
Full Control			
Read	Allow	Allow	Allow
Write		Allow	Allow
Create Child Objects		Allow	Allow
Delete Child Objects		Allow	Allow
Apply Group Policy	Allow		

Author's Note

Notice that the administrators group has not been assigned the Apply Group Policy permission. When this permission set to Allow for a user, any user group policies that have been defined will be applied to the user. Note that the Apply Group Policy permission need only be enabled in one of the groups that a user belongs to for the policy to be applied. For the Terminal Servers poilcy earlier, this doesn't really matter, since only computer configuration settings are being applied. If this policy also included user configuration options, however, and I wanted to ensure that a member of the TSE_Sec_Admins group would not have the user policy applied, I would explicitly set the Apply Group Policy privilege to Deny. This is necessary because an Administrator is also a member of the Authenticated

continues ▶

▶ *continued*

Users group, which does have this permission set, and so would have the policy applied. Remember that Deny overrides any other permission setting from a different group.

This is also the reason why no one has been assigned the Full Control permission—the Apply permission is included as part of Full Control. ◆

5. Now you can set the actual policy options. After closing the Properties dialog box, you return to the Group Policy tab in the Server Properties dialog box. Now highlight the Terminal Servers policy that you just created and click the Edit button. The Group Policy window opens (see Figure 16.17).

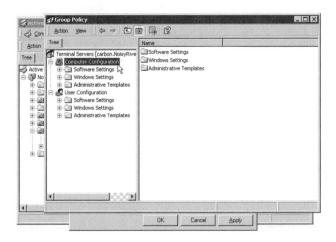

Figure 16.17   *Group Policy configuration window.*

The first change that must be made is so that any user configuration settings that are defined in other group policies are applied to any user who logs onto one of the Terminal Servers in the organizational unit. Normally only the computer configuration settings are applied to the computers within an OU, and any user configuration settings are simply ignored. Policy information for users normally comes from the OUs containing those users. For a Terminal Server environment, this default behavior should be modified so that user configuration settings within the Terminal Servers OU *are* applied to users when they log on. This way, you can define special policies that apply only when the user is on a Terminal Server—not when the user logs onto a regular (non-Terminal Server) computer.

To modify the default behavior, the Loopback Processing Mode option must be enabled. This is found in Computer Configuration\Administrative Templates\System\Group Policy. Two operating modes are available:

- The Merge option finds any policies that have been defined for the user in other OUs and combines those policies with the policies in this OU.

- The Replace option replaces the policies defined for the user with the computer's policies. Normally I use the Replace option to ensure that only the appropriate policies are applied to the user while he or she is logged onto the Terminal Server (see Figure 16.18).

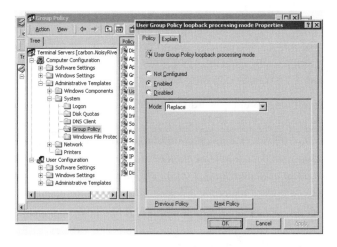

Figure 16.18   *Enabling the loopback processing mode for the server's policy.*

6. After enabling the loopback mode, the only other option that I usually set for the base Terminal Server policy is Delete Cached Copies of Roaming Profiles, which is located in Administrative Templates\System\Logon. Enabling this option ensures that all locally cached roaming profiles are cleared when the user logs off. This helps to conserve disk space on the Terminal Server, particularly if you have a large user base that may log onto your servers.

After updating the desired settings, simply close the Group Policy dialog box. The changes are automatically saved as you edit them. The group policy is applied automatically to any computers that exist within the Servers OU the next time they reboot, or at regularly scheduled intervals. By default, this update is done every 90 minutes plus a random interval from 0 to 30 minutes. You can modify the refresh rate for the policy by updating the Group Policy Refresh Interval for Computers option located under Computer Configuration\Administrative Templates\System\Group Policy. You can also refresh a policy immediately by issuing one of the following commands from a command prompt (you must be logged onto the server on which you want the policies updated).

- To refresh the Computer Configuration settings on the current computer, run this command:

```
secedit /refreshpolicy MACHINE_POLICY
```

- To refresh the User Configuration settings for the user account currently logged on, run this command:

```
secedit /refreshpolicy USER_POLICY
```

If the update fails, an entry is added to the server's Application event log.

Author's Note

The Windows 2000 Server Resource Kit includes a detailed description of all definable group policy options. You can also find an explanation for many of the policy options located under the Administrative Templates folder by clicking the Explain tab located within the properties for the setting. ◆

Defining the Default User Policy

After creating the base server group policy, the next step is to create the default user policy that will be applied to all users who log onto a Terminal Server (including administrators). The steps to configure this are almost identical to those for setting up the server policy:

1. Return to the Group Policy tab under the Servers OU properties and click New to create a new policy. Label this one All TSE Users.

2. Open the properties dialog box for this policy and disable the Computer Configuration settings (this policy will contain only user settings).

3. Click the Security tab and adjust the security groups so that you have the appropriate Terminal Server security groups. As mentioned before, my security configuration is made up of Authenticated Users, TSE_Sec_Admins, and SYSTEM. The permissions in this situation are slightly different, however, as shown in Table 16.4. This time the

administrators are explicitly set to apply the group policy. This is because this group policy will affect all Terminal Server users. If this was a policy specific to a particular user group, I would set the Apply permission for the administrators to Deny.

Table 16.4   Policy Security Permissions for All Terminal Server Users

Permission	Authenticated Users	SYSTEM	TSE_Sec_Admins
Full Control			Allow
Read	Allow	Allow	Allow
Write		Allow	Allow
Create Child Objects		Allow	Allow
Delete Child Objects		Allow	Allow
Apply Group Policy	Allow		Allow

4. After setting the appropriate permissions, click OK. Then select Edit to open the Group Policy Settings dialog box. Table 16.5 lists some of the common policies that I implement, which affect all users. All of these options are set under the User Configuration\Administrative Templates folder.

Table 16.5   Common Policy Settings for All Terminal Server Users

Path	Comments
Windows Components\Windows Explorer	Enable the setting **Do Not Track Shell Shortcuts During Roaming.** Normally Windows stores both a relative and an absolute path (UNC) to a shortcut. If the file isn't found with the relative path, the absolute is used. Enabling this option ensures that users are not trying to access a shortcut across the network to a remote computer if it's not found locally.
	Enable the option **Disable UI to Change Menu Animation Settings.** Menu animation introduces additional traffic between the client and the server. Enabling this option ensures that users can't turn on animation.

continues ▶

Table 16.5   continued

Path	Comments
Start Menu & Taskbar	Enable the options **Add Logoff to the Start Menu** and **Disable and Remove the Shut Down Command.** I like to set these options for all users so that even an administrator can't easily shut down a server. This helps to reduce the chance of an accidental reboot. An administrator can still shutdown a server by using the TSSHUTDN command.
	Enable the option **Do Not Use the Search-Based Method When Resolving Shell Shortcuts.** Normally Windows attempts to do a comprehensive search of the target drive in order to find a shortcut if it cannot be resolved directly or by searching for the file ID (only on NTFS). Disabling this option prevents this exhaustive search behavior and instead Windows simply says that the file could not be found.
Control Panel\Display	I always enable the **No Screen Saver** option. Screen savers should not be run on a Terminal Server as they introduce unnecessary overhead.
System\Group Policy	The default refresh interval for applying user policy updates is every 90 minutes plus a random 0–30 minute increment. Policies are always applied when a user first logs on. When a policy is applied, the user's session will flicker momentarily and any open menus will close. While this isn't really a problem, I personally think the interval is too short in a production environment, so I enable the option **Group Policy Refresh Interval for Users** and set the refresh time to 1440 (24 hours).

Creating Group-Specific Terminal Server User Policies

Within these group-specific policies you'll place the majority of the restrictions on the regular Terminal Server user. Normally I create a third policy called Regular Terminal Server Users or some other descriptive name that helps to identify it as a user-only policy. The steps to creating the policy are the same as for creating the policy for all users, except that you should configure the permissions as shown in Table 16.6. Notice that in this case the administrators have the Deny permission explicitly set on the Apply Group Policy setting. This ensures that these policies never apply to anyone in the TSE_Sec_Admins group.

Table 16.6   Policy Security Permissions for Regular Terminal Server Users

Permission	Authenticated Users	SYSTEM	TSE_Sec_Admins
Full Control			
Read	Allow	Allow	Allow
Write		Allow	Allow
Create Child Objects		Allow	Allow
Delete Child Objects		Allow	Allow
Apply Group Policy	Allow		Deny

Table 16.7 summarizes the policy options that I normally enable for regular Terminal Server users. All of these options are located under the User Configuration folder.

Table 16.7   Policy Settings for Regular Terminal Server Users

Path	Comments
Windows Settings\Folder Redirection	An important part of configuring a user's Terminal Server environment is the redirection of certain folders to a centralized network location—in particular, the My Documents folder, which by default is contained as part of the user's profile. I discuss profiles in Chapter 17, but it's important to note here that the My Documents folder tends to become quite large over time. By redirecting this folder to a network location, only the network path is stored in the profile, reducing its size and decreasing the user's logon and logoff times. I normally redirect both Application Data and My

continues ▶

Table 16.7   continued

Path	Comments
	Documents. To do this, right-click the option and then select Basic from the drop-down list. Provide the network path to the folder. Normally I direct this to the same location as the user's home share location. For example, if your users' home shares are on \\FileSrv\Home, then for My Documents you would enter `\\FileSrv\Home\%username%\My Documents`. You *do not* need to enclose this in quotes.
	While you can include the %username% variable in the path, this option doesn't currently support using other environment variables such as %homeshare%, even though such support would make this option more versatile.
	If you want to redirect folders to multiple locations, you can specify where to redirect the folders based on the user's group by choosing the Advanced setting instead of the Basic setting.
Administrative Templates\Windows Components\Windows Explorer	Two options are enabled here for regular users. **Removes the Folder Options Menu Item from the Tools Menu** prevents users from accessing the Windows Explorer properties. **Hide Hardware Tab** removes the hardware option from the properties panel for all local devices as well as from the Control Panel.
Administrative Templates\Start Menu & Taskbar	Three options are set here: **Disable and Remove Links to Window Update** **Remove Network & Dial-up Connections from Start Menu** **Disable Changes to Taskbar and Start Menu Settings**
Administrative Templates\Desktop	Only one option is set here: **Prohibit User from Changing My Documents Path**. This change is usually done in combination with setting the folder redirection listed earlier.

Path	Comments
Administrative Templates\Control Panel	The **Disable Control Panel** option is enabled.
Administrative Templates\System	Enable the **Disable Registry Editing Tools** option.

As mentioned before, this isn't a comprehensive list of what options to enable in a Terminal Server configuration, but a suggestion as to what options you're likely to employ. While the list is extensive, it's certainly worth the time to review all the options in group policy and employ the ones that will help to ensure that you deploy a manageable and secure Terminal Server environment.

Setting Group Policy Priorities

After all of the desired policies have been created, the final step is to establish an order of priority in which the policies are applied. Policies are applied starting at the lowest and working up to the top. If a policy setting has been defined in multiple group policy objects, the one with higher priority determines exactly how the setting is configured. Figure 16.19 demonstrates how I normally order my three GPOs.

The Terminal Servers GPO applies only to the servers themselves, and therefore can have the lowest priority. Next comes the GPO for regular users, where the majority of the restrictions are applied. Any member of the administrators group will not have any of these settings applied. The group policy with the highest priority is the one that affects all Terminal Server users, including administrators.

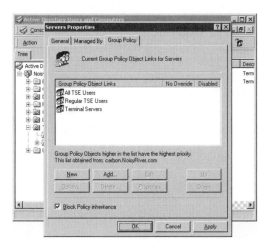

Figure 16.19   *Group policy object priorities.*

Group Policy Templates

Just as with the System Policy Editor (discussed earlier in this chapter), you can import administrative template files into Windows 2000 group policies to allow for the addition of new policy options. The template files even have the same extension (.ADM) as the System Policy Editor files, but don't contain the same information, and are actually a newer version. GPO template files can't be loaded in the System Policy Editor, but PolEdit template files can be loaded into group policies with one major restriction: Any settings that are applied by a policy that's set using an old format template will not be removable from the target user or computer. When a new template is used in a group policy and a policy is removed, the Active Directory will actually remove all references to that policy from the user and/or computer that was assigned the GPO. Any old .ADM templates loaded into a group policy will appear with a red icon instead of a blue one.

A template is loaded by opening a group policy for Terminal Server, right-clicking Administrative Templates, and then selecting the template to load. The Office 2000 Resource kit ships with .ADM files designed for use in Windows 2000 Active Directory. An updated PolEdit is also included that reads and processes these new template files. Figure 16.20 shows an example of the custom templates for Office 2000 loaded into a group policy.

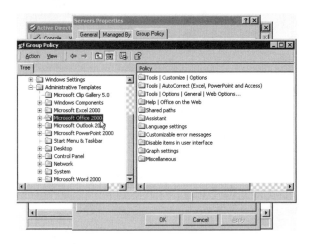

Figure 16.20   *Office 2000 administrative templates in a group policy.*

17

User Profile and Account Configuration

In this chapter:

- **Introduction to Profiles**
  User profiles manage the appearance of the desktop to the user.
  Windows provides three profile options that control the extent of the
  profile's accessibility and the user's control over the profile contents.

- **Environment Preparation**
  Prior to beginning your profile implementation, some environment
  preparation work should be done.

- **Creating and Managing User Profiles**
  When developing user profiles for an implementation, I usually follow
  a standard process that involves three stages in profile creation: creating the default profile, custom roaming profiles, and finally any
  required mandatory profiles. Once created, a process must also be
  developed so that changes can be deployed easily to the necessary
  target profiles.

Introduction to Profiles

Every user of a Windows NT/2000 computer has a *user profile*. A user profile contains a combination of the user's desktop settings (such as icons,
screen colors, or window positions) and user-specific information (such as
network or printer connections). A profile also contains a copy of the contents of the HKEY_CURRENT_USER registry information, which is automatically
loaded when the user logs on. This registry key contains application information specific to that user.

In both Windows NT and 2000, three types of profiles are available:

- Local profiles
- Roaming profiles
- Mandatory roaming profiles

While all profile types manage the same information, the main difference between the three types is the extent of the profile's accessibility and the amount of control the user has over saving changes back to the profile so that the changes can be accessed later.

Author's Note

Mandatory roaming profiles are provided with Windows 2000 only for backward compatibility with an NT 4.0–based domain. In Windows 2000, this is replaced with a combination of the roaming profile and group policies. I discuss these features in more detail later in this chapter. ◆

Local Profiles

The first time you log onto a Windows NT/2000 computer, a *personal profile* is created for you by saving a copy of the computer's local default profile to the hard drive of the local computer. Any changes that you make to your desktop or your environment are saved to this profile when you log off. The next time you log onto that computer, this profile is automatically loaded and appears exactly as you left it. Of course, because the profile is stored on the local computer, logging onto a different computer doesn't give you the same profile. Either a profile that previously existed for you on that other machine is used, or a new one is created from the default profile on that computer. If you travel around and log onto a number of computers, you'll have a distinct local profile on each of them.

The *local profile* behaves the same way on a Terminal Server. The first time a user logs onto a Terminal Server, he or she is presented with a default profile, which the user can freely customize. The next time the user logs onto that same server, that profile is picked up automatically, along with any of the changes instituted by the user in the previous session. As you may have guessed, if the user logs onto a *different* Terminal Server, he or she won't pick up the local profile that was saved on the other Terminal Server. This will most certainly cause problems if your Terminal Server environment is composed of multiple Terminal Servers.

Local profiles are the default profile type used unless a roaming profile (regular or mandatory) has been defined for a user. The exact location where local profiles are stored depends on the operating system, as summarized in Table 17.1.

Table 17.1   *Local Profile Location Based on Operating System*

Operating System	Profile Location
Windows NT 4.0	%systemroot%\Profiles
Windows 2000 (upgrade from NT 4.0)	%systemroot%\Profiles
Windows 2000 (clean install)	%SystemDrive%\Documents and Settings

Figure 17.1 shows an example of the Documents and Settings directory on a Terminal Server. Notice that it contains folders for a number of users, including the local administrators, the default user, and even a folder for All Users, which contains common profile information for all users who log onto the server. The Profiles folder on a TSE 4.0 server contains the equivalent information of the Documents and Setting folder except that the Default User folder isn't hidden, as it is on TS 2000 (its visible in the figure because I have configured Explorer to show hidden files).

> **Tip**
>
> *Only administrators and the corresponding user have access to a profile; regular users can't access other users' profile folders.* ✦

Figure 17.1   *The Documents and Settings folder on a TS 2000 server.*

Microsoft recommends that you not manage a local profile by directly manipulating the profile folder, but instead access it from the User Profiles tab in the System applet in the Control Panel. In addition to viewing a list of the existing profiles, you use this dialog box to perform profile manipulation (discussed later in this chapter). Figure 17.2 shows how the profiles from Figure 17.1 would appear in the User Profiles tab.

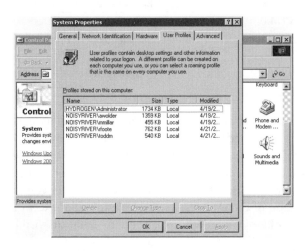

Figure 17.2   *The User Profiles tab from the System applet.*

Roaming Profiles

The biggest problem with local profiles is that they're tied to a specific Terminal Server and don't "travel" with the user from server to server. For a profile to "travel" with the user independent of the Terminal Server, a *roaming profile* is required. The roaming profile is a user profile stored in a network location instead of on the local computer, so regardless of the server that a user logs onto, his or her profile comes from a single location. Any changes the user makes while logged on are saved to the profile stored on the network so that it's accessible from whatever server the user logs onto next.

Roaming profiles are processed in Windows as follows:

1. A user with a roaming profile logs onto a Terminal Server.

2. The Terminal Server checks whether the user has a local (cached) copy of his or her profile stored on the server. If so, the local copy is compared with the server copy to see which is newer (the comparison is based on the last updated timestamp). If the server copy is newer, the

server profile is copied down to the local machine. If the profiles are the same, the local copy is used. On NT 4.0, if the local copy is newer, the user receives a message stating that the cached profile is newer than the server-based profile and asking the user which profile to use. On Windows 2000, the user isn't prompted to select a profile, but instead is automatically assigned the newer local profile. This is done because of differences in the merge algorithm in Windows 2000, which help in synchronizing changes back to the server. I'll discuss this synchronization shortly.

3. If the user has no cached profile on the local server, the network-based profile is copied to the local server. It remains on the local server until the next time it's updated, deleted manually by an administrator, or deleted automatically (see Chapter 12, "Terminal Server Configuration and Tuning," for information on setting this option).

4. After the appropriate profile has been placed on the local server, the registry information stored in the file NTUSER.DAT is loaded into the registry hive HKEY_USERS. Figure 17.3 shows this hive with three users who are currently logged onto the Terminal Server. The default user's profile is also loaded, from the NTUSER.DAT file in the Default Profile directory.

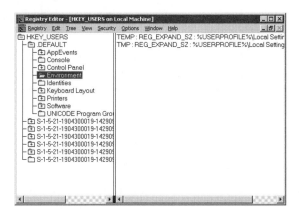

Figure 17.3   HKEY_USERS *registry entry with current logon sessions.*

5. Any desktop changes that occur to the profile are stored locally while the user is logged on. When the user logs off the Terminal Server, his or her information is unloaded from the registry and written back to the NTUSER.DAT file on the local computer. On NT 4.0, the entire profile is then written back to the network, replacing any previous profile stored there.

On Windows 2000, the individual files within the profile are compared with those in the profile on the server (see Figure 17.4).

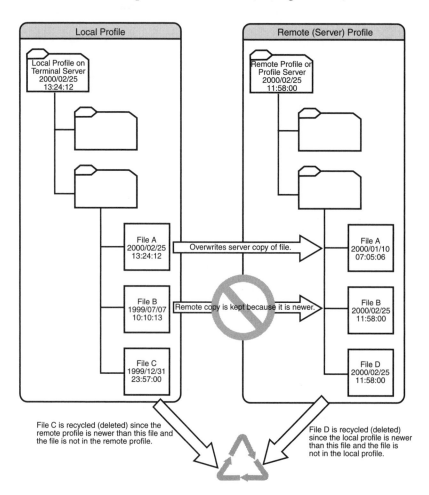

Figure 17.4 *Windows 2000 local and remote profile comparison mechanism.*

The files are handled as follows:

- If a file exists in both the local and the remote profile, the file with the newer timestamp is kept. In Figure 17.4, FileA in the local profile will overwrite FileA on the server, while FileB on the server is kept because it's newer than the one in the local profile.

- If a file exists in the local profile but not on the server, the timestamp of the *remote profile* is compared with the timestamp of the file. If the profile is newer, it means that the file was deleted in another instance of the profile on a different computer, so the file is deleted from this profile as well. If the file is newer, it's copied to the remote profile. FileC in this example will be deleted from the local profile, because the server profile's timestamp is newer than the timestamp on the local file.

- If the file exists in the remote profile but not in the local profile, the timestamp of the file is compared with the timestamp of the *local profile*. If the local profile is newer, the file must have been deleted from the local profile, so it's also deleted from the remote profile. If the file is newer, it must have been added in another instance of the profile on a different computer, so the file is kept in the remote profile. FileD in this example will be deleted from the server profile, since its timestamp is older than the timestamp on the local profile, so Windows assumes that it was deleted from the local profile.

If you watch the HKEY_USERS registry hive when a user logs off, you'll see the user's associated registry key disappear.

Roaming Profile and Home Directory Preferences

Chapter 2, "Microsoft Windows Terminal Server," talks about the customized User Manager for Domains available in a Windows NT domain environment, which contains additional configuration information specific to Terminal Server (as shown in Figure 17.5).

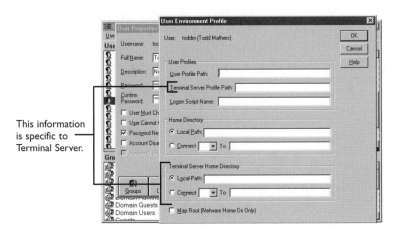

Figure 17.5   *Terminal Server User Manager for Domains.*

In a Windows 2000 domain, the Active Directory Users and Computers component for managing user account properties contains configuration options specific to Terminal Server clients, as shown in Figure 17.6.

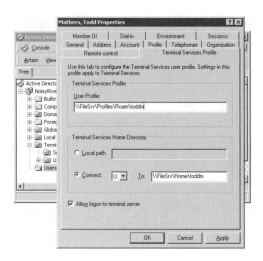

Figure 17.6 *TS 2000 user properties.*

In both situations, you can define a user profile and home directory that's specific to Terminal Server and separate from the standard Windows profile and home directory paths.

Figure 17.7 shows the process flow that Terminal Server follows when determining a profile and home directory to use. The process is repeated independently for both the profile and the home directory, so it's possible that a Terminal Server home directory would be defined but not the Terminal Server profile. If the home directory is set to an empty local path, by default it will point to the same location as the user's profile. If a user logs onto a regular Windows workstation computer (NT 4.0 or Windows 2000), the Terminal Server profile and home directory are *never* used. They only apply when logging onto a Terminal Server.

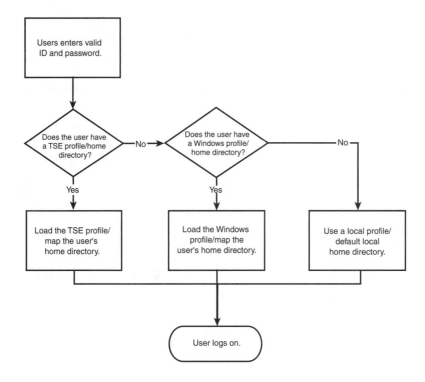

Figure 17.7   *The user profile/home directory decision tree for Terminal Server.*

Mandatory Roaming Profiles

Although a roaming profile provides the user with a consistent desktop regardless of which Terminal Server he or she uses, it can still introduce a number of administrative challenges:

- Giving users the ability to modify and control their own desktops and application settings can cause the type of support calls that you intended to reduce (or eliminate) with the introduction of Terminal Server.

- An additional user support requirement is immediately created, since you must now work to ensure that the user's roaming profile is available when necessary. A loss in application or other desktop settings will most likely result in a support call from the user.

- Roaming profiles introduce additional complexity in how updates to application or other registry settings are effectively propagated to all users.

Microsoft provides a solution to these issues through the *mandatory roaming profile*. A mandatory roaming profile behaves exactly like a standard roaming profile with one exception: Changes made by the user during a session *are not* saved to the profile stored on the server when the user logs out. The next time the user logs on, he or she will once again receive the original profile from the server. Removing the user's ability to save profile changes gives you the capacity to assign the same profile to multiple users, and as a result provides a single location where profile changes will automatically be updated for all associated users. This approach is most common in a situation where a number of task-based workers perform the same job function and you want to ensure that they all have a consistent user interface. This helps to simplify not only support, but issues such as training. It can also help to reduce the amount of time users spend customizing their environments with such features as custom icons or wallpaper.

Author's Note

Microsoft recommends that the mandatory profile be used only in an NT 4.0 or mixed-mode Windows 2000 domain. In a pure Windows 2000 domain, a regular roaming profile should be used in conjunction with the appropriate group policies. One of the main reasons that Microsoft recommends not using a mandatory profile is because of differences that may exist in a user's desktop hardware from one computer to another. Their recommendation is based on the assumption that the mandatory profile is being used to enforce a standard on the user's local Windows computer, not on a Terminal Server. Hardware differences aren't a concern in a Terminal Server environment if consistent hardware has been implemented.

In a Terminal Server environment, I've found that when you want to provide a static profile in which a user can't make any changes, the mandatory profile is still much easier to implement than a regular roaming profile with group policies. I discuss this in more detail in the sections on creating and managing mandatory profiles, later in this chapter. ◆

Mandatory roaming profiles are processed in almost exactly the same way as regular roaming profiles:

1. A user with a mandatory profile logs onto a Terminal Server.

2. The Terminal Server checks whether the user has a cached copy of the profile on the server. If so, the cached copy is compared with the server-based profile to see if they're the same. If they are, the local copy is used. If they aren't, or no local copy of the profile exists, the server-based profile is copied to the Terminal Server and used. The cached

profile remains until the next time the profile on the remote server is updated, or until it's deleted from the Terminal Server either automatically or manually by an administrator.

3. The registry information that's stored with the profile in the NTUSER.MAN file is loaded into the registry hive HKEY_USERS.

4. Any desktop changes that are made during the user's session are saved to the registry, but *are not* written back to disk when the user logs out. When the user logs off, the registry information is simply unloaded. The profile *is not* written back to the remote profile share location.

Environment Preparation

Before getting into the details of how to create and manage profiles, I suggest you do some preparation work ahead of time. If you prefer, you can skip this section and return after you have reviewed the specifics on profiles and are ready to perform the actual implementation.

Author's Note

If the wording and the steps in this environment preparation section seem familiar, it's probably because you have already read the equivalent section in Chapter 16, "Group and System Policy Configuration." The process of preparing for profile setup is essentially the same as that required for policy setup. If you have policies in place as described in Chapter 16, you will need only to ensure that you have the profile and home directory shares as discussed shortly. I recommend that you keep the policy, profile, and home directories separate from each other. This will help to simplify the security requirements for both the shares and the directories. ◆

Profile/Policy Implementation Options

The first step is to decide which implementation method to use. Your choice really depends on two factors:

- The Terminal Server operating system you're running
- The type of Windows domain you're running

Table 17.2 summarizes the choices you have for profile and policies based on these factors.

Table 17.2   Profile and Policy Options

	Terminal Server Version	
Domain	TS 2000	TSE 4.0
Windows NT 4.0/3.51	Roaming/mandatory profiles NT 4.0 policies	Roaming/mandatory profiles NT 4.0 policies
Windows 2000 (native mode)	Roaming/mandatory profiles Group policies	Roaming/mandatory profiles NT 4.0 policies
Windows 2000 (mixed mode)	Roaming/mandatory profiles NT 4.0 policies	Roaming/mandatory profiles NT 4.0 policies

Remember that in a Windows 2000 mixed mode environment, you have a Windows 2000 domain controller in addition to one or more NT 4.0 backup domain controllers in your environment.

Author's Note

Unless absolutely necessary, I recommend that you avoid implementing a Terminal Server environment that allows production users to use local profiles. If users can maintain information locally on a Terminal Server, they're faced with potentially different configurations, depending on which server they connect to. This problem only gets worse as you add more servers to your environment; the user's changes to the desktop will seem to "disappear" if he or she logs onto a different server and will magically reappear on returning to the first server. ♦

Domain Security Groups

If you haven't already done so, you should create the local Terminal Server security groups as discussed in Chapter 8, "Server Management Planning." Within these local groups you should place the corresponding domain global groups that will actually contain the user accounts. The following table summarizes the global security groups that I'll use in the discussions. These are the same groups that I talk about in Chapter 16, "Group and System Policy Configuration." In an NT 4.0 domain, I suggest using TSE or some other common prefix to ensure that these groups are listed together within User Manager for Domains.

Domain Security Group	Description
TSE_Sec_Admins	Terminal Server administrators. These users have full control over the configuration of a Terminal Server.
TSE_Sec_Operators	Terminal Server operators. These users have the privileges needed to support a Terminal Server, such as shutdown/restart or killing a running task. They don't have the ability to install or modify software or the operating system.
TSE_Sec_Users	Terminal Server users. These users have only the minimum access needed to work within the Terminal Server environment.

Profile Directory Share

The next step should be to establish a location on the network where you will manage your profile information. For both TSE 4.0 and TS 2000, you'll want to establish a share location where you will store these profiles. Figure 17.8 shows a sample profile hierarchy for maintaining both roaming and mandatory roaming profiles. All mandatory profiles are normally maintained in a single directory since they're shared by multiple users, while each user must have his or her own personal profile directory for a regular roaming profile. You're not required to create each user's roaming profile directory; these are created automatically the first time a user attempts to access his or her roaming profile.

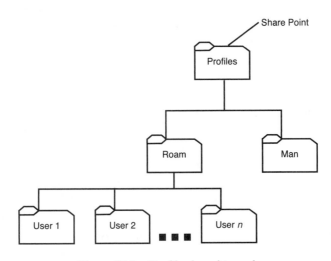

Figure 17.8   *Profile share hierarchy.*

After the directories and shares have been created, assign the appropriate permissions to them. The permissions should be set as shown in the following table. (Note that the share and directory names match those shown in Figure 17.8. This was done to keep the example simple. You are certainly free to use alternate names on your system.)

Share/Directory Name	Permissions
Profiles (Share)	System: Full Control
	TSE_Sec_Admins: Full Control
	TSE_Sec_Operators: Full Control
	TSE_Sec_Users: Full Control
Profiles (directory)	System: Full Control
	TSE_Sec_Admins: Full Control
	TSE_Sec_Operators: Change
	TSE_Sec_Users: Read & Execute
Man (directory)	System: Full Control
	TSE_Sec_Admins: Full Control
	TSE_Sec_Operators: Change
	TSE_Sec_Users: Read & Execute
Roam (directory)	System: Full Control
	TSE_Sec_Admins: Full Control
	TSE_Sec_Operators: Change
	TSE_Sec_Users: Read & Execute, Write

When the personal profile directory is created for a user, the operating system assigns full control to the individual user and SYSTEM. So, even though all users have Read access at the root of the Roam directory, they won't be able to view the contents of another user's profile.

Home Directory Share

In addition to creating a location for the user profiles, you should create a share to contain the home directory for each user. A unique home directory is required for each user in order to provide a location for user-specific application and system information within Terminal Server. If a home directory location isn't specified for a user's account, the default setting is to use the profile directory. This *is not* a desired result, particularly for roaming profiles, because the contents of the home directory could grow quite large and would increase the time required to both download and the upload the profile changes. As a result, this could also introduce disk space problems on your Terminal Servers.

The share permissions should be set as follows:

SYSTEM	Full Control
TSE_Sec_Admins	Full Control
TSE_Sec_Operators	Full Control
TSE_Sec_Users	Full Control

The directory permissions should be set like this:

SYSTEM	Full Control
TSE_Sec_Admins	Full Control
TSE_Sec_Operators	Change
TSE_Sec_Users	Read

Just as with user profiles, you don't need to create the individual user directories; they're created automatically when the user's account is configured to point to the appropriate directory. After the system creates the user's home directory, the user is assigned full control.

Creating and Managing User Profiles

When developing the user profiles for an implementation, I usually perform the following three steps:

1. Configure default settings within the local default profile on the Terminal Server. This is important for two reasons:

   - First, this is the profile that every user will load the first time he or she logs onto a Terminal Server, unless the user has been set up with a mandatory profile, or a roaming profile has been pre-loaded to his or her remote profile location.

   - It's also the profile that a user will receive if, for whatever reason, his or her roaming profile is unavailable (the profile server is down, for example). In certain situations, a user may also receive this default profile if the mandatory profile is unavailable.

2. Create any custom roaming profiles that will be deployed to a user's personal roaming profile area prior to the user's first logon. This is a way to bypass the user picking up the default profile and immediately using a customized profile that you have created.

3. Create any required mandatory roaming profiles. This is really just a modification to a custom roaming profile.

Author's Note

An integral part of configuring roaming and mandatory profiles is the implementation of a number of associated policies, as discussed in Chapter 16. I recommend that you don't undertake the final creation of profiles until you have reviewed both chapters and have a complete understanding of the steps involved. ◆

Creating Template User Accounts

A common practice when creating and managing profiles is to use what I call *template user accounts*. These are special user accounts created solely for the purpose of configuring a user profile. In most cases, these accounts will have administrative privileges on the Terminal Server so that all the necessary configuration options can be performed. Domain privileges may be required, depending on what's being configured. For security reasons, I recommend disabling any template accounts when they're not required. This ensures that the account cannot be used until it has been enabled by a valid administrator (an auditable event).

Typically I assign names to these templates account so that their function is immediately obvious. For example, a template account that's used to manage a mandatory profile for the Accounting department may be named something like TSE_Template_Accounting.

Configuring the Local Default Profile

The first step is to configure the local default profile so that it contains the necessary information that you want as standard for *all* users the first time they connect to the Terminal Server. Unfortunately, there's no way to specify a different default profile based on a user's group membership, so you have to ensure that only common settings are placed within the default profile.

Author's Note

If you need certain options to be set for a user based on his or her group membership, you can script this as part of the user's logon script. Ensuring that certain folders exist or that shortcuts appear on the desktop can all be done from within the logon script. ◆

To configure the default local profile, follow these steps:

1. Create a template account with a name such as TSE_Template_Default. This account must have administrative privileges on the Terminal Server. Assign a standard Terminal Server home directory for the account (for example, \\FileSrv\Home\%username%), but leave the Terminal Server Profile field blank.

2. If this account already exists, make sure that there's no local profile for this account on the Terminal Server by running the System applet under Control Panel and reviewing the User Profiles tab.

3. Log onto the Terminal Server with the template account. This will assign a copy of the current default profile to the user.

4. Now configure the session as you want it to appear for any user the first time he or she logs on. Following are some settings you may want to configure:

    •   Background color or default font.

    •   Regional settings such as date, time, and currency formats.

    •   Per-user Start menu settings. This could include applications listed under Accessories, such as System Tools.

5. After configuring the profile, log off as the template account and then log back on using an administrator's account (you can use the local Admin account if you want).

6. Open the System applet from Control Panel and select the User Profiles tab. You should see the local profile for the template account (see Figure 17.9). Click on the profile and select the Copy To button. The Copy To dialog box opens.

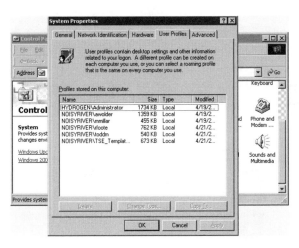

Figure 17.9   *Template account profile in the User Profiles tab.*

7. Click the Change button under Permitted to Use and select the Everyone group. You must do this to ensure that the users will have rights to access the registry component of the profile.

8. Under the Copy Profile To section, enter the location where the current default profile is located on the Terminal Server. On a Windows 2000 server, this would be %systemdrive%\Documents and Settings\Default User; on NT 4.0, it would be %systemroot%\Profiles\Default User.

9. After the contents have been copied, delete the existing profile for the template account and then log back on with that account. You should now automatically receive the settings that are stored in the default user profile.

10. When you're confident that the settings have been saved properly, disable the template account until you're ready to use it again.

Now that the default profile has been configured, any user who logs onto this server for the first time will automatically receive these settings as part of his or her newly created roaming profile.

Tip

You can also directly manipulate the registry settings for the default profile (or any user profile) without having to load, edit, and save the entire profile. As mentioned earlier, the contents of the HKEY_CURRENT_USER registry hive are stored in the NTUser.dat file located in the user's profile directory. You can load the contents of this file into the registry, modify any desired settings, and then save the changes back to the file. The steps to do this are as follows:

1. *Open REGEDT32, select the HKEY_USERS hive, and click the HKEY_USERS text.*

2. *From the Registry menu, select Load Hive. When the dialog box appears, traverse to the default user's profile directory and select the NTUSER.DAT file, as shown in Figure 17.10.*

Figure 17.10 *Loading the contents of NTUSER.DAT in the registry.*

3. *When prompted, enter a name for the new key. Be sure to select a name that's not already in use. (One suggestion is DEFAULTUSR.)*

4. *After the contents of NTUSER.DAT are loaded into the registry, you can then modify any of the desired registry values.*

5. *When you're finished, save the changes back to the NTUSER.DAT file: Select the name that you assigned the key (for example, DEFAULTUSR); then choose the Unload Hive option from the Registry menu. This will automatically unload the updated information back into the NTUSER.DAT file.* ◆

Assigning Roaming Profiles

The assignment of a roaming profile to a user is straightforward. All that's required is to configure the user's account to access a roaming Terminal Server profile. Figure 17.11 shows an example, with the user's profile location set as follows:

\\FileSrv\Profiles\Roam\%username%

Windows automatically resolves the %username% value to the corresponding user's ID. Why use the %username% variable instead of explicitly entering the user's ID? With the variable, if you decide to create a new account by copying this one, the roaming profile (and home directory) locations automatically change to reflect the new user's ID. Otherwise, the new user's profile would be directed to the original user's profile.

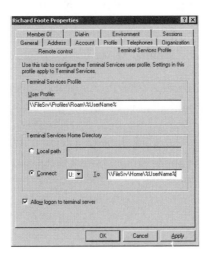

Figure 17.11   *A roaming profile assignment in a user's account.*

After the roaming profile location has been set, the first time the user logs onto a Terminal Server, Windows checks the network location for the profile. If it doesn't exist, the default user profile on the Terminal Server is used to create the new profile. From that point on, the user retrieves his or her profile from the appropriate network location.

Managing Group-Specific Default Roaming Profiles

In many situations, you would rather assign a previously configured profile to a user or group of users, rather than having the users load the default profile from a Terminal Server. As I mentioned earlier, there's no way to designate a default user profile based on a user's group membership. Because of this deficiency, a process has to be developed wherein a user's profile is copied to the appropriate network location prior to the user logging onto a Terminal Server for the first time.

There are two steps in managing these customized default profiles:

- Creation of the profile
- Distribution to the appropriate network location

The following sections describe these steps.

Configuring the Custom Roaming Profile

The steps in creating a custom roaming profile are nearly identical to those for modifying the default user's profile:

1. Create a template account for managing this profile. For example, if you're creating a profile for users in the Sales department, you could create a template account called TSE_Template_Sales. This account must have administrative privileges on the Terminal Server. You should assign a standard Terminal Server home directory (for example, \\FileSrv\Home\
   %username%), but leave the Profile entry empty for now.

2. Log onto the Terminal Server with the template account and perform any desired profile configuration. After you're finished, log off the template account and log back on with a regular administrator account.

3. Open the System applet from Control Panel and select the User Profiles tab. Click the profile and select the Copy To button. The Copy To dialog box opens, as shown in Figure 17.12.

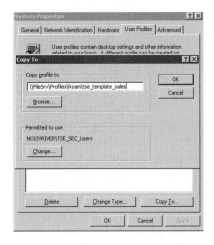

Figure 17.12 *A template account profile on the User Profiles tab.*

4. Click the Change button under Permitted to Use and select the Terminal Server users group (in my case it would be TSE_SEC_Users). You must do this to ensure that the users will have rights to access the registry component of the profile.

5. Now provide a destination for the profile copy. I recommend that you copy this to the network location where other roaming profiles are stored. For example, I would specify this location as the destination:

\\FileSrv\Profiles\Roaming\tse_template_sales

6. You should make one other permission change to this profile so that Terminal Server operators will be able to deploy copies to users if necessary. Go to the profile directory on the server and add an operators group (for example, TSE_Sec_Operators) with Read & Execute permission, as shown in Figure 17.13.

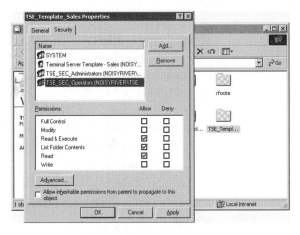

Figure 17.13 *Updated permissions on the template profile directory.*

7. The last step is to update the template account so that it now uses the profile that you copied to the server. This allows you to make future changes to this profile simply by logging on as the template user, making the changes, and then logging off.

Deploying the Group-Specific Roaming Profile

Now that you have created the customized profile, the next step is to deploy the profile to the appropriate users prior to them logging onto Terminal Server. There are two steps in this process:

1. Copy the template profile to the user's profile directory.

2. Update the security permissions on the folder so that the corresponding user has Full Control access.

For a few users, this can be done manually without too much effort. If you have to do this for 50 users, however, it would obviously be very time-consuming. It's much easier to script this change to create these profiles automatically.

The following is a sample batch script that takes the user ID as a parameter and performs the necessary folder copying and permission updates to create that user's profile. This script assumes that the profiles are stored under the \\FileSrv\Profiles\Roam share.

```
@echo off

REM Copy template profile to user profile
xcopy \\FileSrv\Profiles\Roam\TSE_Template_Sales
➥\\FileSrv\Profiles\Roam\%1 /E /I /H /K /X

REM Now update security
Xcacls \\carbon\Profiles\Roam\%1 /E /G %1:F /Y
Xcacls \\carbon\Profiles\Roam\%1\* /T /E /G %1:F /Y
```

Managing Changes in a Roaming Profile

One of the more difficult tasks in managing roaming profiles is when a change needs to be replicated to each individual profile. For example, suppose you have 500 users, each with his or her own profile, and they've been working in your Terminal Server environment for the past two months. You now want to install a new application onto the Terminal Servers and deploy it to all users. You have two requirements for this deployment:

- The necessary application registry entries need to be replicated to each user's profile so that the user can launch the application.

- You want to add a shortcut for this application onto each user's desktop.

While the first requirement seems by far the most difficult, in fact Terminal Server provides an implementation feature that makes this step quite easy. I'll defer a complete discussion of application deployment until Chapter 19, "Application Integration," but meanwhile I'll mention here that Terminal Server provides a special mode of operation known as *install mode*. When in this mode, the Terminal Server records every HKEY_CURRENT_USER (HKCU) registry key change that's made using the *standard API calls* (direct updates to the registry through other means are not captured), and store this information so that it can be applied to each user who logs onto the Terminal Server when it's put back into *execute mode*. There are a few caveats, but in general that's how this feature operates. When a user logs onto the server, Terminal Server compares the last synchronize time of the user's HKCU registry with the last update time of the information stored on the server. If the server version is newer, the changes are automatically applied to the user's HKCU.

Unfortunately, the management of the user's personal profile isn't quite as easy. Unless you have the luxury of being able to delete a user's roaming profile and assign the user a new default profile, you need to develop a way of making updates as required without affecting the user's current environment. When changes need to be made to the roaming profile for multiple users, a few options are available, depending on what needs updating:

- **Group policies.** You can use the appropriate group policy to update a number of features in the user's profile, particularly when the change pertains to features such as regional settings, display backgrounds, and so on. Group policies generally aren't helpful when you want to manage shortcuts on the user's desktop.

- **Logon/startup scripts.** Logon or startup scripts can be very helpful when updating the Start menu or the user's desktop. The addition of an application shortcut to a user's desktop can be achieved easily through such a script. Typically, what I do is create a directory on the application volume of a server where I keep shortcuts that need to be deployed. Then I make a short addition to the startup script so that the shortcut is copied to the appropriate area, depending on the user's group membership. Here's an example script that would copy the Microsoft Project shortcut, depending on the user's group membership. I normally place a call to any additional customization scripts at the end of the USRLOGON.CMD script, which runs for every user who logs onto Terminal Server and is responsible for launching the necessary application-compatibility scripts. This script is located in the %systemroot%\System32 directory. Before you make changes to this file, however, review the section in Chapter 19 pertaining to application-compatibility scripts.

For this script to work, users need Read access to the Y:\shortcuts directory. Because the script is actually running as the user when he or she logs on, the user will have access to update the files in his or her Desktop directory. I also make use of the %userprofile% environment variable, which automatically points to the user's proper profile directory. Be sure to include the quotes around the copy parameters to ensure that any spaces are handled properly.

```
REM Sample script to update a user's desktop
REM with a shortcut when he or she logs on.
REM ifmember is a Windows 2000 Server ResKit tool

ifmember TSE_Sales_User
if not errorlevel 1 exit

REM User is a member of the Sales group if
REM we reach here, so update profile.
If exist "%USERPROFILE%\Desktop\MSProject.lnk" goto END
Copy "y:\shortcuts\MSProject.lnk" "%USERPROFILE%\Desktop\MSProject.lnk"
:END
```

Creating and Assigning Mandatory Roaming Profiles

The creation and assignment of the mandatory roaming profile is nearly identical to that of the standard roaming profile. These are the differences:

- The profile is assigned a standard name such as SALES or MARKET-ING instead of an individual user's name.

- The profile has an extension assigned to it, either .MAN or .PDM. .MAN is the standard extension to use when creating new mandatory profiles, while .PDM is used when migrating profiles from NT 3.51 to Windows NT 4.0/2000 or maintaining profiles for both operating systems simultaneously.

- Multiple users are assigned the same mandatory profile since it can't be updated by a user. This means that you don't have to worry about one user making a change to the profile that is then picked up by the other users who have also been assigned that profile. It also means that any environment changes that the users make will be lost when they log off, and the original profile defaults reloaded the next time they log on.

Figure 17.14 shows a user account configured with a mandatory roaming profile called SALES.MAN in a Windows 2000 domain.

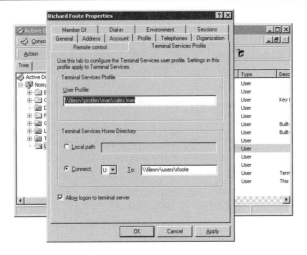

Figure 17.14   *Mandatory profile assigned in a user's account.*

Author's Note

Previous versions of Windows NT as well as WinFrame use the .MAN extension to distinguish mandatory profiles from regular roaming profiles. Terminal Server supports both the .MAN extension and the .PDM extension. Microsoft supports both naming standards to allow for backward compatibility with previous versions of Windows NT. This support can be very useful if you're going to migrate your existing WinFrame environment to Terminal Server/MetaFrame or you'll be maintaining a mixed environment of both server types.

Consider the scenario in which you're going to be slowly introducing Terminal Server into your environment, which currently contains only WinFrame servers. You want to perform piloting with a few users, but you also want to provide them with the ability to go back to WinFrame immediately if there are any issues. They currently have mandatory profiles on WinFrame, and you want them to use mandatory profiles on Terminal Server as well. The issue is that you won't always be available immediately to reset users' profiles if they have a problem. So how do you allow them to pilot while ensuring that they can switch back to WinFrame when necessary?

Luckily, Terminal Server provides the ability to manage both NT 3.51 and NT 4.0/2000 profiles based on the same name. It works as follows:

1. *You've assigned WinFrame users the profile \\PILOT\Profiles\man\Sales.man in the WinFrame profile path.*

2. *If the WinFrame user logs onto the Terminal Server, Terminal Server looks in the \\PILOT\Profiles\man location for the Terminal Server profile called Sales.man. When it finds the WinFrame profile (because it's a file and not a directory), Terminal Server automatically switches to look for the profile (directory) called Sales.pdm.*

continues ▶

▶ *continued*

3. *To allow pilot users to switch automatically between Terminal Server and WinFrame, you only need to create the Terminal Server profile called Sales.pdm, which is located in the same directory as the WinFrame Sales.man. Sales.man is a file, whereas Sales.pdm is a directory.*

Unless you're migrating from NT 3.51 or maintaining a mixed environment, you should use the .MAN extension. One advantage to using .MAN is that if the user's mandatory profile is unavailable (for example, it doesn't exist or the server isn't available), users won't be able to log on. Instead, the user receives a message stating that his or her mandatory profile is unavailable. If the .PDM extension is used and the profile isn't available, the user can still log on and will receive a copy of the local default profile. Considering that mandatory profiles are typically implemented to ensure a consistent interface for all users assigned that profile, the default behavior when using .PDM is usually unacceptable. ✦

Creating a Mandatory Roaming Profile

To create a mandatory profile, follow steps 1 through 7 outlined earlier for creating a custom roaming profile (see the earlier section "Configuring the Custom Roaming Profile"). You should still save the new profile into the Roam directory. After creating the roaming profile, perform the following additional steps to configure it as a mandatory profile:

1. Copy the profile from the roaming location to the mandatory profile location that you've created. For example, I have a mandatory profile location of \\FileSrv\Profiles\Man. Make sure that you do this *after* you've copied the local profile from the Terminal Server to the network and updated the access permissions to include TSE_Sec_Users. Otherwise, users won't be able to load the registry portion of the mandatory profile. (See steps 3 through 5 in the procedure for creating the roaming profile.)

2. Go into the mandatory profile folder where you copied the roaming profile (the folder is called Man in my example). Now go into the Man folder and add the .PDM (or .MAN) extension to the roaming profile folder. Figure 17.15 shows an example of this.

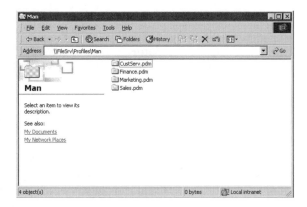

Figure 17.15   *Assigning the PDM extension to a profile folder.*

3. Now go into the new .PDM template folder and rename the NTUSER.DAT file to NTUSER.MAN. Unlike the folder, which can have either the .PDM extension or the .MAN extension, the NTUSER file *must* have the .MAN extension for Windows to recognize it properly.

4. Validate that the proper permissions have been set on the mandatory profile directory. SYSTEM and TSE_Sec_Admins should have Full Control, while TSE_Sec_Users requires only Read & Execute access.

5. Assign this profile to the users who will be using it from within their user account, just as you would with a regular roaming profile. Because this is a mandatory profile, multiple users can be assigned to it. Don't forget to include the .PDM extension when specifying the profile name.

Now anytime a user who has been assigned a mandatory profile logs on, he or she will always receive the same consistent user interface.

Managing Changes in a Mandatory Roaming Profile

In some ways, the management of the mandatory profile is simplified by the fact that a single copy of the profile can serve any number of users. This makes changes such as the addition of a shortcut to the desktop or the Start menu very easy. Changes to the mandatory profile can be done simply by logging on as the associated template account, for example TSE_Template_ Sales, and making the desired changes to the profile, which are then copied back to the template account's roaming profile on the network. This profile can then be copied to the mandatory profile location, and the folder and NTUSER.DAT file renamed accordingly. The next time a user who has been assigned the mandatory profile logs on, he or she will pick up the changes that you have introduced. This is much simpler than trying to implement similar profile changes with a regular roaming profile.

The major drawback to the mandatory profile is actually due to its major benefit, which is protection from any changes by the user. This is a problem when new applications are introduced into the environment or applications want to store user-specific information in the user's personal registry settings. For these applications to operate properly with a mandatory profile, much more work must be done during the application-integration phase to ensure that the necessary registry entries are part of the mandatory profile. In many cases, this requires extensions to application-compatibility scripts that write user-specific information into the registry every time a user logs onto the Terminal Server. The registry capture features of the CHANGE USER /INSTALL feature help to some degree, but customized configuration is almost always required.

18

Server Operations and Support

In this chapter:

- **Terminal Server Operations**
  After your Terminal Server implementation is complete, the main job becomes one of operations—ensuring that the environment is available and that users are able to work without difficulty.

- **Server and User Session Management**
  Probably the most common task required of a Terminal Server operator or support person is the support of active user sessions.

- **Server Health Monitoring**
  Being able to receive timely information on the status of the servers (both Terminal Servers and other dependent servers) in your environment is critical to maximizing its uptime and availability to users.

- **Server Maintenance**
  As a part of the overall operations support of a Terminal Server environment, some additional server maintenance functions can also be performed.

Terminal Server Operations

After your Terminal Server implementation is complete, the main job becomes one of operations—ensuring that the environment is available and that users are able to work without difficulty. Although most Terminal Server environments will continue to be managed by the same people who were involved in the implementation, a distinction should be made between the role of the operator and that of the administrator. The administrators group is usually responsible for coordinating changes and updates to the environment; the operations group is responsible for monitoring the day-to-day stability of the environment. When talking about operations, I usually include any help desk support staff that may exist in the organization.

These people are usually the first line of contact when a user has an issue, and their level of expertise with the environment dictates how many support calls filter through to the operators or administrators of the environment.

The requirements for Terminal Server operations and support can be divided into three main tasks:

- **Server and user session management.** This involves managing the availability of servers and supporting active user sessions on a Terminal Server. Either the GUI-based tools or command-line utilities are commonly used to perform this job function. Some common tasks include adding or removing a server from a farm, shadowing a user for support, or resetting a user's hung session. User account management such as password resets or group membership changes would also fall into this category.

- **Server health monitoring.** Using either third-party tools or utilities from the Resource Kit, the operator takes on the role of proactively monitoring the status of all Terminal Servers so that potential problems can be flagged early and resolved before they cause system degradation or unscheduled downtime. This task is extremely important for any organization that must guarantee a minimum level of service to their customers.

- **Server maintenance.** Some general server maintenance functions that can be performed on a Terminal Server include the installation of support and Resource Kit files, the use of disk defragmenting software, and server cloning.

The remainder of this chapter looks at each of these categories in more detail and provides some examples of how to use the tools to perform the necessary tasks.

Server and User Session Management

Probably the most common task required of a Terminal Server operator or support person is the support of active user sessions. Much of this support can be performed using either the available command-line tools or the appropriate GUI tool. The GUI support tool used will depend on whether you are running MetaFrame. If you are running only Terminal Services with RDP, you can use *Terminal Services Manager* (or Terminal Server Administration on TSE 4.0). If you are also running MetaFrame on your Terminal Server, you should use the Citrix tool, *Citrix Server Administration*. Table 18.1 lists some of the most common tasks that are performed and what tool is required in order to do it.

Author's Note

Usually I recommend that access to these tools be restricted through file security to only members of the local administrators and operators group. Even though connection security will prevent a regular user from performing an unauthorized action such as shadowing, I suggest restricting access anyways. Every running instance of these programs does produce overhead as it queries the master browser and other servers in the environment for information. ♦

Table 18.1 Common Operator/Support Tasks and the Tool Required

Task	Terminal Services Manager	Citrix Server Admin	Command-Line Tool
Generate a list of all available servers.	Yes	Yes	Qserver
Generate a list of all users on a server.	Yes	Yes	Quser /Server:<server ➥name>
Generate a list of all users in the environment.	Yes	Yes	Not without scripting.
Shadow/Remote Control a user's session.	Yes	Yes	Shadow <session ID or ➥name>[/SERVER:<server ➥name>] The remote server option is only supported with ICA, not RDP.
Log a user off.	Yes	Yes	Logoff [<session ID or ➥name>][/SERVER:<server ➥name>] If you don't specify a session ID or name, you're logged off.
List Citrix server farms.	No	Yes	Qserver /serverfarm
View ICA gateway info.	No	Yes	Qserver /gateway

Terminal Services Manager

The *Terminal Services Manager* (*TSM*) application is located under Administrative Tools on the Start menu. It can also be launched from a command prompt using TSADMIN.EXE. The executable name is the same for both TS 2000 and TSE 4.0. Figure 18.1 shows a typical Terminal Services Manager session. The management window is divided into two panes. The left pane contains a list of domains, Terminal Servers in each domain, and the user sessions on each server. The right pane contains different tabs, depending on which object is currently selected in the left pane.

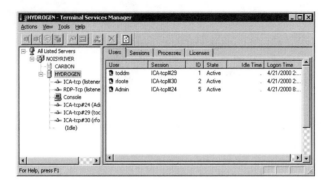

Figure 18.1   *Terminal Services Manager.*

Table 18.2 summarizes the tabs that are available based on the object selected in the left pane. Depending on your access level, only a subset of these tabs may be visible.

Table 18.2   TSM Tabs

Object Selected	Tabs Available
All Listed Servers	Servers
	Users
	Sessions
	Processes
	Licenses
Specific domain (for example, NOISYRIVER)	Servers
	Users
	Sessions
	Processes
	Licenses
Specific server (for example, HYDROGEN)	Users
	Sessions
	Processes
	Licenses
Specific connection (for example, ICA-tcp#3)	Processes
	Information
	Modules (ICA only)
	Cache (ICA only)

The following sections discuss the information on each of the tabs.

Servers

The Servers tab lists the recognized Terminal Servers (in the selected domain or in all domains), along with the corresponding IP and/or IPX address and the number of active connections for each server. If you right-click a listed server name, a pop-up menu displays a Connect and Disconnect option. These settings have only to do with whether TSM tracks the information on that server. When you select Disconnect, the server immediately disappears from the list in the right pane. The server is still listed in the left pane but is grayed out. A server is also grayed out if you don't have access to query the information on that server or the server is unavailable.

Users

Under the Users tab is a list of all users, and if you're at the domain level or higher, you'll also see the associated server that the user is logged onto. Other user-specific information is also displayed, such as the user's session name, session ID, and current connection state. Figure 18.2 shows some of the common connection states; in this example, the user called "bobuser" is currently disconnected, "rfoote" and "toddm" are active, and the admin user is remotely controlling one of the other sessions.

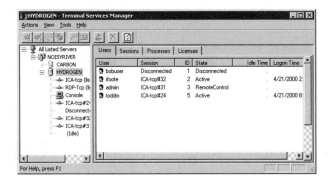

Figure 18.2   *The Users tab.*

Right-clicking a user entry lists the actions that you can perform directly on that user account, such as connecting, disconnecting, or resetting the session; sending the user a message; remotely controlling the session; or logging off the user. Certain options may be grayed out if the user is currently disconnected or controlling someone else. If a user tries to perform an unauthorized action such as logging someone else off, an access-denied message appears.

Sessions

The Sessions tab displays information very similar to that shown under the Users tab. Three additional pieces of information are available:

- Non-user sessions are listed, including the idle and protocol listening sessions.
- The exact type of client session (ICA or RDP) is shown.
- The user's local client name is listed with the session information.

Aside from this, the other information on the Sessions tab is the same as for the Users tab, including the options available on the pop-up menu that appears when you right-click.

Processes

From this tab you can view all the active processes on all your Terminal Servers. For each process you can view the owner (user), session ID and name, process ID (PID), and the process name. With sufficient privileges, you can end any task by right-clicking and selecting End Process. Regular users receive an access-denied error if they attempt to end any process other than their own.

By default, all processes are listed, including the ones owned by SYS-TEM. You can remove all SYSTEM processes from the display by deselecting the Show System Processes option on the View menu. You may have noticed additional processes running in the Console session—ones that don't correspond to any applications being run by a user on the console. These processes correspond to any services that may be running on a Terminal Server, such as TERMSRV.EXE (Terminal Services) or SPOOLSV.EXE (the print spooler service).

Author's Note

While being able to view all running processes on any of your Terminal Servers can be very helpful, in a large environment with many users, it can take quite a while for TSM to display all the processes. I recommend that you avoid listing all processes for all domains—or even a single domain—unless absolutely necessary. Instead, you should select a specific server and inspect its processes. ♦

Licenses

The Licenses tab provides information on any Citrix licenses installed on the servers, as shown in Figure 18.3. This is an information-only display; you can't modify any of the Citrix licenses from here. To update Citrix licenses, you need to run the *Citrix Licensing* tool. To view Terminal Server licensing, you need to run either *Terminal Services Licensing* (for TS 2000) or *Terminal Server License Manager* (for TSE 4.0).

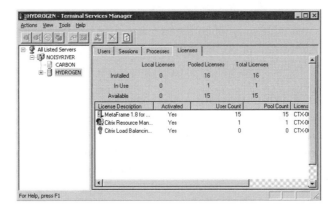

Figure 18.3 *The Licenses tab.*

Information

Figure 18.4 shows the Information tab. This is available only when looking at an individual user's session on a Terminal Server. The tab presents a summary of the user's client information. None of the data presented here can be modified.

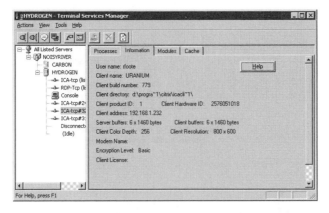

Figure 18.4 *The user session's Information tab.*

Modules

This tab presents a list of the modules that make up the ICA client that the user is running. If the user is accessing the Terminal Server using an RDP client, the Modules tab is not available.

Cache

This tab is available only when the user has connected using an ICA client. It provides information on the session's client and bitmap cache. No information can be changed on this tab.

Citrix Server Administration

Citrix Server Administration (CSA) can be launched from the MetaFrame Tools menu or by running the executable MFADMIN.EXE from a command prompt. At first glance, CSA looks very similar to the Terminal Services Manager, but with additional functionality specific to a Citrix ICA environment. Figure 18.5 shows the All Listed Servers view.

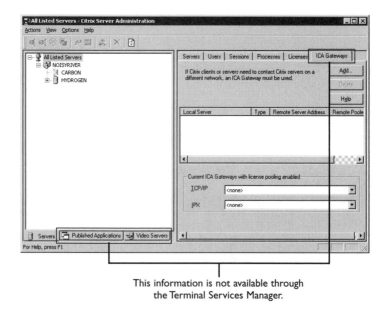

This information is not available through
the Terminal Services Manager.

Figure 18.5   *The All Listed Servers view in Citrix Server Administration.*

In addition to the user information supplied by TSM, within CSA you can view published applications and their associated server farms. You can also view any servers that are running VideoFrame. These are commonly referred to as *video servers*. From the All Listed Servers view, you can manage any ICA gateways that may exist in your environment. Table 18.3 summarizes the tabs that are available based on the object selected in the left pane. Tabs that differ from those available with Terminal Services Manager are shown in bold. Depending on your access level, only a subset of these tabs may be visible.

Table 18.3   *CSA Tabs*

Object Selected	Tabs Available
All Listed Servers	Servers
	Users
	Sessions
	Processes
	Licenses
	ICA Gateways
Specific domain (for example, NOISYRIVER)	Servers
	Users
	Sessions
	Processes
	Licenses
Specific server (for example, HYDROGEN)	Users
	Sessions
	Processes
	Licenses
	ICA Browser Information
Specific connection (for example, ICA-tcp#3)	Processes
	Information
	Modules (ICA only)
	Cache (ICA only)

ICA Gateways

This tab is where you manage ICA gateways in your environment. An ICA gateway is created between Citrix servers located on different physical networks so that they can share browser information. Without a gateway, the Citrix servers in one environment can't "see" the Citrix servers in the other. For a complete discussion on the ICA master browser and ICA gateways, see Chapter 3, "Citrix MetaFrame." Chapter 12, "Terminal Server Configuration and Tuning," provides an example of configuring an ICA gateway.

ICA Browser

From the ICA Browser tab, you can control the behavior of the browser service running on the selected server. Figure 18.6 shows the options that are available. Normally you'll only need to configure these options when you first set up your MetaFrame server. For a complete discussion on the ICA master browser, see Chapter 3. In Chapter 12, I provide suggestions on how you should configure the ICA browser on each of your MetaFrame servers.

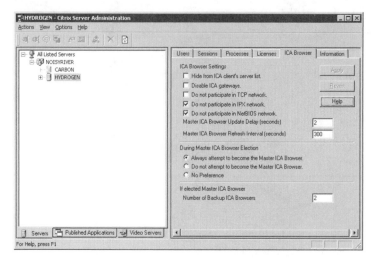

Figure 18.6   *The ICA Browser property settings.*

Information (for the Server Object)

CSA displays an Information tab when a server object is selected. As Figure 18.7 shows, this tab displays information on the version level of Terminal Server and MetaFrame, as well as any hotfixes that may have been installed. If the server is also running Citrix Load Balancing Services, the current load levels are also displayed. For information on installing hotfixes on a Terminal Server, see Chapter 12.

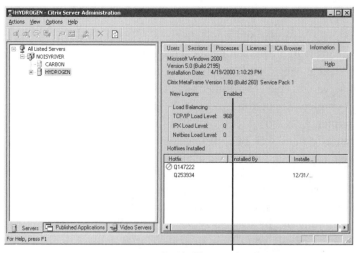

See the Tip regarding this option.

Figure 18.7   *Server Information tab.*

Tip

The Information tab also lists the current status for new logons (Enabled or Disabled). This status can be toggled on or off by right-clicking the server name and selecting the appropriate option from the menu, as shown in Figure 18.8. If logons have been turned off and a user attempts to connect to this server, the user will receive the message Remote logins are currently disabled.

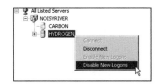

Figure 18.8   *Setting the status for new logons.*

This option is intended to prevent users from logging onto a server while doing what's commonly called "drain-stopping," which is where you prevent new users from logging onto a server but allow the current users to remain active. This way, once all of the active users have logged off, the server will be empty and can then be taken offline safely without affecting any users.

There is one "gotcha" involved with this technique. If you disable logons on a Terminal Server that's publishing applications, there will be a delay between when you perform the disable and when the master browser receives this change. Until the master browser is aware that logons have been disabled for the Terminal Server , it will continue to assume that the server is participating in application publishing and as a result continue to direct users to that server. If this happens, the user will receive an error message stating Logins have been disabled. *When the master browser finally receives the change in logon availability, it automatically removes that Terminal Server from its application-publishing list.*

You'll be able to tell that the master browser has received this information because the Load Balancing load level for a Terminal Server with disabled logons displays as 10002. *You can view a server's load level by running* QSERVER /APP *or* QSERVER /SERVERFARM *from a command prompt.*

The refresh interval for the Terminal Server to send information to the master browser is set on the ICA Browser tab. The default value for the ICA Browser Refresh Interval setting is 60 minutes (3600 seconds). In Chapter 12 I talk about modifying this setting to decrease the refresh interval, but unless you set it very low (which I don't recommend), there's still a timeframe in which the user may hit this server.

continues ▶

▶ *continued*

To avoid this problem altogether, you can force the server to send its updated information to the master browser immediately by using the following command:

```
Qserver [<servername>] /update
```

The server name is optional; if you omit it, however, all MetaFrame servers will pass updated info to the master browser. If you specify the name, only that specific server will be updated. You can validate that the update was sent by running this command:

```
Qserver <servername> /stats
```

If you run the command both before and after the update, you'll notice that the SendBrowserUpdate option is incremented by one. When using /stats *you must include the* servername, *even if it's the local server.* ♦

Published Applications

Figure 18.9 shows the Published Applications window in which you can view the existing server farms in your environment and see what applications are published within each farm. For each published application, this window shows on what servers the app is published, which users are currently connected, and the settings and authorized groups for that application (on the Information tab). Very little information can actually be changed on this screen aside from enabling and disabling new logons to a server.

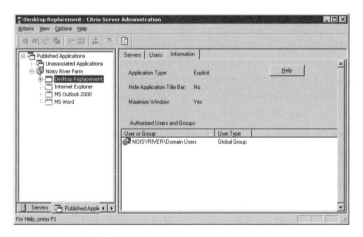

Figure 18.9   *Published application settings.*

Video Servers

The Video Servers pane displays all available VideoFrame servers, along with the name and number of video streams currently active and the clients processing each active stream.

Command-Line Tools

The graphical tools are not the only way to perform server and user session management. All of that functionality (and more) can be found through the available command-line tools. It's not uncommon for many veteran Terminal Server administrators to work almost exclusively from a command shell instead of using the GUI tools. Personally, I find the command line much faster to use when looking for specific information, particularly in a large Terminal Server environment. The ability to use these commands within batch scripts also allows for the automation of certain features, as I'll demonstrate shortly. For some changes, such as configuring the ICA browser or gateway settings, I use the GUI tool (instead of the registry), but as I mentioned, these settings are usually done during the configuration and tuning portion of the server build and don't normally change very frequently.

Earlier in the chapter, Table 18.1 listed some of the common operator/support staff tasks performed in Terminal Server, along with the corresponding command-line tool that performs the same function. These tools are as follows:

- QSERVER (query server) is probably one of the command-line tools used most often. This tool allows you to query and set much of the information that pertains to the Terminal Server. The following are typical QSERVER commands:

    To display information for only the servers that support TCP/IP:

    `QSERVER /TCP`

    To view all of the published applications:

    `QSERVER /APP`

    To view a list of all the server farms and the MetaFrame servers participating in each one:

    `QSERVER /SERVERFARM`

    There are also functions available with QSERVER that have no GUI equivalent. As I already mentioned, you can force an immediate update of the master browser data:

    `QSERVER [<servername>] /UPDATE`

You can also force an ICA browser election:

```
QSERVER /ELECTION
```

- QUSER (query user) is another important command. This allows you to retrieve a list of the sessions currently logged onto either the local or a remote Terminal Server. To list the active sessions on the local computer, simply run this command:

```
QUSER
```

You can query a remote server by adding the /SERVER:<servername> parameter. The colon (:) is required.

- QWINSTA (query winstation) is used to query for session-related information. Figure 18.10 shows a sample output from running the QWINSTA command.

Figure 18.10   QWINSTA *output.*

- QPROCESS (query process) by default lists only the processes that correspond to the person running the utility. You can very easily list the processes for a particular username, however, by running this:

```
QPROCESS <userid>
```

This version lists all (non-system) processes on a server:

```
QPROCESS *
```

- SHADOW allows you to initiate a shadow session on the local or a remote Terminal Server. The syntax is simple:

```
SHADOW <session name or ID> [/SERVER:<server name>]
```

Run QUSER to get the user's session ID, and then you can use the SHADOW command to begin shadowing.

> *Tip*
>
> *To be able to shadow another user, your screen resolution and color depth must be at least equal to or greater than that of the person you intend to shadow. For example, if the user has a screen resolution of 800 × 600 and color depth of 256, your corresponding settings cannot be less. Both of the options must be equal to or greater, so 1024 × 768 at 256 colors would work, but 1024 × 768 at 16 colors would not.* ♦

- CHANGE LOGON is the last command I'll mention here. With CHANGE LOGON you can enable and disable new logons to a Terminal Server. There are three available parameters:

/QUERY	Shows the current status of logons.
/ENABLE	Enables new logons.
/DISABLE	Disables new logons.

  Just as with the GUI tool, after the change is made it's not updated on the master ICA browser until the next browser update interval is reached. Your change can be updated immediately by running QSERVER <servername> /UPDATE.

Normally I combine these functions into a simple batch script that I can run when I want to move servers in and out of the environment. My disable script would look like this:

```
@ECHO OFF
CHANGE LOGON /DISABLE
QSERVER %COMPUTERNAME% /UPDATE
```

Unfortunately, the CHANGE LOGON command only functions on the computer you're currently logged onto. You can't turn logons on and off from a remote system as you can with the GUI tool.

For an explanation of all of the available command-line options, see Appendix A, "Terminal Server/MetaFrame Command Reference."

Server Health Monitoring

Being able to receive timely information on the status of the servers (both Terminal Servers and other dependent servers) in your environment is critical to maximizing uptime and availability to your users. Regardless of the number of Terminal Servers in your environment, some form of monitoring should exist; otherwise, you're forced to react to problems only *after* they have affected users.

With some form of systems and application management, you can receive alerts about issues as they arise but before they have reached a critical state. The following sections look briefly at three methods of monitoring the health of your environment and how you could configure these systems to notify you when certain issues arise. The thresholds for establishing alert notification are based on the values discussed in Chapter 7, "Server Hardware Planning," when talking about the sizing of a computer. Typically I use these values as a starting point for an environment and then tune accordingly to meet the specific needs of the environment.

Two of the methods that I discuss involve the use of commercial products from Citrix and NetIQ; the third works exclusively with the performance and alerting tools in Windows 2000. My goal in providing this information is not to give a complete lesson on how to use these products, but more of an overview of how they can be used in a Terminal Server environment and the basics of what types of features you should expect from these types of products.

An unfortunate situation that I've seen a number of times is that, while it's not hard to see the benefits that can be gained by using these types of tools, many companies don't see a justifiable value either in dollars or man-hours in implementing such a solution. Hopefully you will be able to use the information in the following discussion to aid in justifying the use of these types of tools in a Terminal Server implementation.

Citrix Resource Management Services

Citrix *Resource Management Services (RMS)* is actually a result of a licensing agreement between Citrix and a company called Lakeside Software (www.lakesidesoftware.com). RMS was developed from Lakeside's original product, called SysTrack.

Figure 18.11 shows a typical RMS configuration. Each Terminal Server runs the RMS data collection service (RESMGMT.EXE), which is responsible for collecting the relevant system data and sending it to (almost) any ODBC-compliant database management system. The diagram shows a Microsoft SQL Server, but an alternate DBMS could be used.

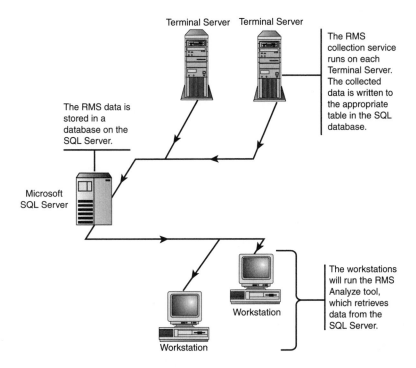

Terminal Server   Terminal Server

The RMS collection service runs on each Terminal Server. The collected data is written to the appropriate table in the SQL database.

The RMS data is stored in a database on the SQL Server.

Microsoft SQL Server

The workstations will run the RMS Analyze tool, which retrieves data from the SQL Server.

Workstation

Workstation

Figure 18.11   *A typical Resource Management Services configuration.*

You can then use the RMS Analyze tool to view the data stored in the DBMS. Typically this is done from your desktop and not on the Terminal Server itself. From within the Analyze tool, you configure the desired thresholds for alarms—the appropriate actions to take as well as running reports against the stored data. Multiple copies of this tool can be run simultaneously against the database; for example, to allow the real-time monitoring of the system from both an operator's location and a help desk site.

Tip

When thresholds are set within the Analyze tool, the information is stored on a per-user basis in the HKEY_CURRENT_USER *registry key. They don't apply globally to any other instances of the tool that may be running. So unless you're using roaming profiles for your local desktop logons, your RMS settings may differ from machine to machine. The solution is to export your threshold settings and then instruct the users of Analyze to import these settings instead of creating their own.*

Typically, a company using RMS will have a dedicated monitoring workstation where the Analyze tool is run and where thresholds and alert notifications are maintained.

continues ▶

▶ *continued*

> *The RMS settings are stored under the following registry key:*
>
> `HKCU\Software\VB and VBA Program Settings\CitrixRMS\Analyze`
>
> *You'll notice that some things, such as the ODBC connection string, are stored in plaintext, meaning that any passwords used in connecting to the database will be visible. One way to minimize this problem is to create a "generic" account with read-only access to the RMS database. Only the data collection service actually requires write access to the tables in the database.* ◆

Configuring Alert Thresholds

The first step is configuring the thresholds that correspond to the requirements of your environment. These thresholds are used to control the status lights for each monitored server. Thresholds control when a light turns red, yellow, or green. RMS comes with a default set of thresholds, but you'll most likely need to tune them to meet your specific system requirements.

Thresholds are set by selecting Options from the View menu and then choosing the Alarms tab. As Figure 18.12 shows, a list of all servers currently running RMS appears, along with the alarm profile assigned to each. All new servers initially use the default profile.

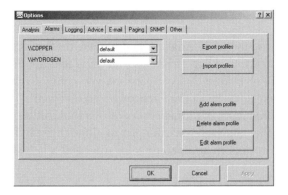

Figure 18.12   *The Alarms tab in the Options dialog box.*

To modify the default settings, you need to create a new profile:

1. Select the Add Alarm Profile button.

2. When prompted, assign a name to the new profile. Normally, you'll have a single profile for all production servers unless you have a mixed hardware environment, in which case you may need to adjust the thresholds. For my example, I'll create a profile called Prod_Servers.

3. Next you select a profile from which to inherit the initial settings. Choose default and then click OK to create the new profile.

4. Click the Edit Alarm Profile button. A dialog box containing the new profile opens, as shown in Figure 18.13. Select the new profile from the drop-down list at the top of the dialog box to display the settings for that profile.

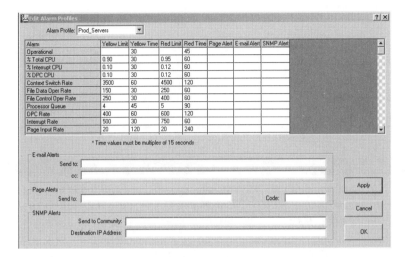

Figure 18.13   *Editing the alarm profile.*

Now you're ready to edit the thresholds. All threshold limits are either a percentage or a value; all threshold times are in 15-second increments. This increment is necessary because the Analyze tool retrieves samples from the database every 15 seconds.

Table 18.4 lists some suggested threshold changes based on the discussion in Chapter 7. After monitoring these values for a while, you'll be able to decide whether these thresholds should be adjusted up or down based on your specific environment requirements. I suggest that you perform some load testing while monitoring these alerts to ensure that you're receiving the proper notifications with sufficient time to react to them. If a particular alarm is not listed in the table, its setting can be left as the default. There is no explicit way in RMS to disable an alert, but you can effectively disable one by setting the threshold and timer values very high.

Table 18.4   Suggested RMS Threshold Adjustments

Alarm	Yellow Limit	Yellow Time	Red Limit	Red Time
% Total CPU	0.85	30	0.95	60
Processor Queue	10	30	12	60
Available Bytes	5242880	45	4194304	60
Page Input Rate	50	120	60	240
Page Output Rate	50	120	60	240
Pagefile Usage	0.75	15	0.85	30
Commit Ratio	0.80	30	0.90	30
% Disk Time	0.70	60	0.85	60
Disk Queue Length	2	30	2	90

Author's Note

As I've said previously, these are simply suggested thresholds and may not necessarily be appropriate for your environment. In particular, the Available Bytes threshold really depends on the physical memory in your server and how much notice you want before the available physical memory begins to run low. A common suggestion is to set the yellow threshold at around 10% and the red threshold around 5%. ◆

The Yellow Time and Red Time values are a common area of confusion when first working with RMS. Basically, the time monitoring in RMS works as follows.

Whenever a set of data is retrieved from the database, RMS checks to see whether any of the defined thresholds have been exceeded. If so, the appropriate counter is set (yellow, or both yellow and red).

When the next set of data is retrieved, the values are compared again with the thresholds. If the value has fallen below the threshold, the corresponding counter is "turned off." If it's still above the threshold, the counter continues, or if the Yellow Time or Red Time has been reached, the appropriate alert is raised. If both a Yellow and Red alert time have been met, Red takes precedence. Consider the following example with the Commit Ratio having thresholds as shown in Table 18.4. Table 18.5 lists six samples and the expected alert behavior for each.

Table 18.5   *Suggested RMS Threshold Adjustments*

Interval	Sample	Alert Color	Notes
1	79.8%	Green	First sample is below the yellow threshold.
2	81.1%	Green	This is above the yellow threshold, so the yellow timer is set. The alert remains green.
3	82.5%	Yellow	At the end of the next 15-second interval, it's still above the yellow threshold, so now the alert turns yellow. The yellow timer is set again.
4	90.6%	Yellow	The sample is above both the yellow and red thresholds, so both the yellow and red timers are set. The alert remains yellow.
5	83.7%	Yellow	This sample is above the yellow threshold, but below the red. The red timer is turned off.
6	77.5%	Green	The final sample falls below the yellow threshold, so the alert is once again set to green.

After entering the desired thresholds, you can configure the form of alert you'll use by clicking the appropriate cell in the list of alert settings. When an alert is selected, a check mark appears in the cell, as shown in Figure 18.14.

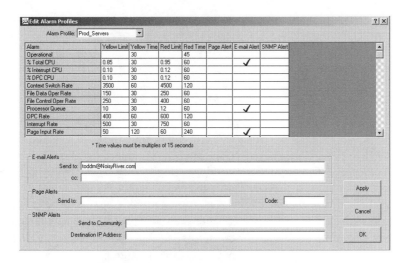

Figure 18.14   *Setting the alert options.*

Tip

Notification is only sent out when a red alert is raised. Yellow alerts only update the color on the Analyze display. ◆

After you have finished configuring the alarm profile options, click OK to return to the Alarms tab on the Options dialog box. You can then assign your new alarm profile to each of the desired servers.

The configuration details for each of the three supported alert options (SMTP mail, SNMP, and pager) can be found on the appropriate tab in the Options dialog box, as shown in Figure 18.15.

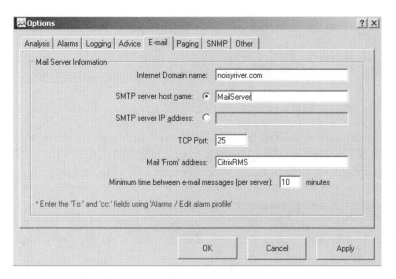

Figure 18.15   *Configuring the SMTP mail option.*

NetIQ AppManager

The *AppManager (AM)* tool from NetIQ consists of a number of product options that together form a suite of tools available for use. Some of the various product plug-ins available include Terminal Server and MetaFrame, Windows 2000/NT, Microsoft Exchange, and Compaq Insight Manager.

Not only does AM monitor the status of your environment and alert you to problems, it can also take a proactive role in attempting to correct these problems, such as automatically attempting to restart a downed service (such as the ICA Browser service) or launching a batch script based on an alert condition. A number of systems administration tasks can also be managed directly from within AppManager, such as rebooting a server, adding a local group, checking a service pack level, or stopping and restarting a service. AM also maintains a complete inventory of your system configurations.

Author's Note

AppManager was the first application to be certified for Windows 2000 Advanced Server. Details on AppManager can be found at www.netiq.com. ◆

Figure 18.16 shows a typical AppManager configuration. The repository for AM must be a Microsoft SQL Server database, and it contains all of the information used to configure and control AppManager. This includes information such as the collected monitoring data, alert configuration information (known as *knowledge scripts*), and any raised events. The following list describes the individual components:

- The *management server*, which typically resides on the repository server (but can be run separately), is responsible for controlling the agents that run on each of the monitored servers. Statistics gathered on the agents are transmitted back to the management server, which in turn sends the information to the repository. Based on information in the repository, it will also perform actions such as adding a new monitoring job to an agent. The management server raises any alarm conditions that occur on an agent. Unlike RMS, which relies on the Analyze tool to be running in order to raise events, AppManager continuously monitors the system even when no client application is running. This also means that threshold information is maintained in a single location and therefore is the same regardless of where you run an operator console.

- The *AppManager agent* is a service that runs on each Terminal Server. The agents communicate solely with the management server and don't talk directly to the repository.

- The AppManager environment is controlled through the use of the *operator console* application. This application communicates directly with the repository, updating information on which knowledge scripts to run on which agents, what data to collect, and other configuration options. This information is then picked up by the management server and processed accordingly.

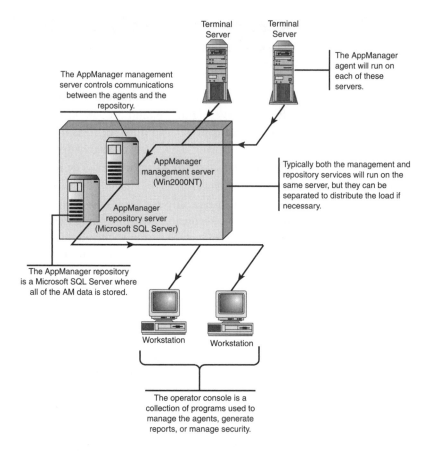

Figure 18.16   *Typical NetIQ environment configuration.*

The AppManager Operator Console

From the operator console, you perform all threshold configuration for your managed Terminal Servers. Unlike RMS, which has a predefined set of monitored objects that you can't change, AppManager provides a wide assortment of monitoring options. To monitor a particular component of your Terminal Server, you must create a corresponding job on the server. Until you do so, no monitoring is taking place. A *job* is an instance of a knowledge script that's run by the AppManager agent. Figure 18.17 shows the operator console with a property sheet open for a knowledge script.

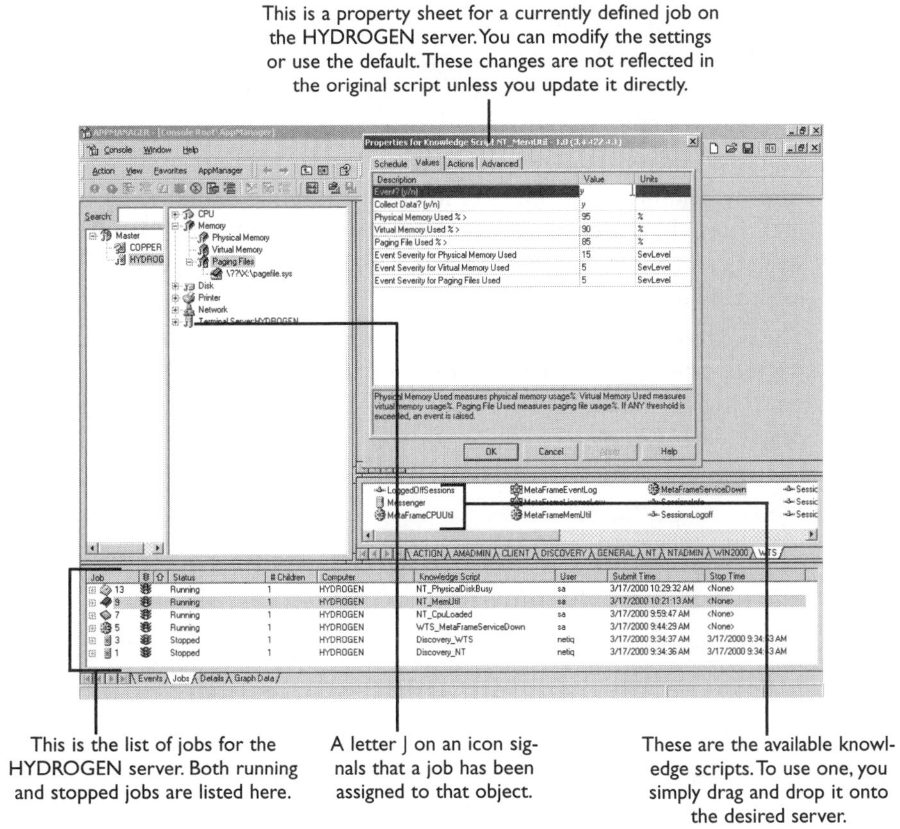

This is a property sheet for a currently defined job on
the HYDROGEN server. You can modify the settings
or use the default. These changes are not reflected in
the original script unless you update it directly.

This is the list of jobs for the
HYDROGEN server. Both running
and stopped jobs are listed here.

A letter J on an icon signals that a job has been
assigned to that object.

These are the available knowledge scripts. To use one, you
simply drag and drop it onto
the desired server.

Figure 18.17   *The NetIQ operator console.*

Author's Note

*When an agent is first installed on a Terminal Server, two default jobs are
configured to run once. These "discovery" jobs are responsible for collecting the
configuration and resource information on the server. These jobs must run in
order to determine things such as number and type of processors, physical RAM,
or network card type.* ◆

Creating Jobs

The creation of a job is straightforward. You simply select the desired
knowledge script (KS) from the appropriate pane and drag it over the server
object or individual component object of the server. Dragging an object to
the Master icon applies the job to all servers. The following steps demonstrate how to set up a job to monitor the CPU % on my HYDROGEN
Terminal Server.

1. I first click the NT KS tab, select the CpuLoaded script, and drag it over to the server or its CPU object. If the object is a valid destination for the KS, it will turn into a green circle. After I drop the script, the properties open automatically. This is where the job can be customized for this server.

2. The first tab allows me to set the schedule for how often the job will run. By default it will run continuously, collecting data every 5 minutes. I usually lower this interval to between 1 and 3 minutes. This way it can collect multiple samples within a 10-minute period. For this example I'll set it to 3.

3. The next tab is the Values tab, where you configure the threshold for the job, plus options such as whether data should be collected for reporting purposes. Figure 18.18 shows the adjusted CPU settings as described in Chapter 7.

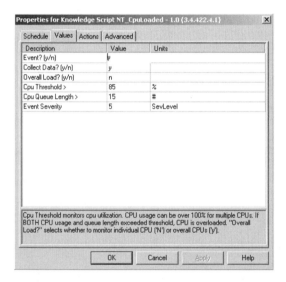

Figure 18.18   *CpuLoaded job threshold parameters.*

4. On the Actions tab, configure the appropriate response to a threshold being exceeded. By default, this is set to AKP_NULL, which means that nothing is done. By clicking the drop-down list, you can select from a number of available actions, including running a batch command, sending SMTP mail, sending an SNMP trap—even rebooting the system. After the desired action is selected, click the Properties button to configure it. Figure 18.19 shows the properties for the SMTPMail action.

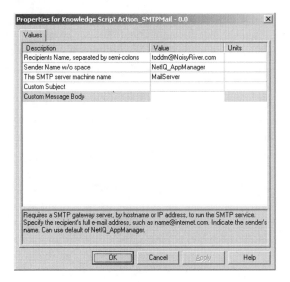

Figure 18.19 *SMTPMail action properties.*

5. The final tab is the Advanced tab. From here you control the characteristics of how events are handled. By default, the option Collapse Duplicate Events into a Single Event is selected. What this means is that multiple occurrences of an event within the time interval will be collapsed into the original event and shown as a count increment. This allows multiple occurrences to be captured, but an event is not raised for every instance. Figure 18.20 shows my typical configuration for this job.

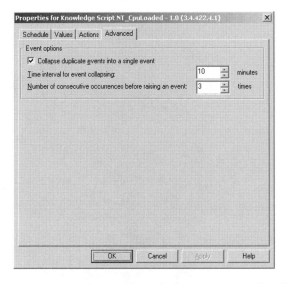

Figure 18.20 *Configuring how duplicate events are handled.*

With my sampling interval set to 3 minutes, the event handling, based on the options selected in Figure 18.20, would work as follows. Assuming that my CPU% is above the threshold, the first two occurrences of the event will be ignored (6 minutes will have passed). On the third occurrence (at 9 minutes), the event will be raised and an SMTP mail message will be sent. As you can see from Figure 18.20, three occurrences of the event must be raised before the SMTP mail alert will be sent.

After the event has been raised, AppManager starts the 10-minute event-collapsing timer. Any *valid* event (every third event) raised during that time is collapsed and no new email will be sent. The events at the 12- and 15-minute mark are ignored (these are the first and second event instances), and the next *valid* event at the 18-minute mark (the third) also falls within the 10-minute collapse interval. At this point, the original event counter is incremented by one and the timer is once again reset to 10 minutes. No new email is sent. The only way that a new email will go out is if the next *valid* event does not occur within the 10-minute interval.

Table 18.6 shows some suggested job settings for AppManager in addition to the CPU utilization that I described earlier.

Table 18.6   Suggested AppManager Job Settings

Knowledge Script	Interval	Values	Event Collapsing
NT_MemUtil	Every 2 min.	Collect Data	Collapse
		Physical Mem Used: 95	Interval:
		Virtual Mem Used: 85	10 min.
		Paging File Used: 85	Occurrence
		Physical Mem Sev.: 15	Count: 2
		Virtual Mem Sev.: 5	
		Paging File Sev.: 5	
NT_Physical DiskBusy	Every 5 min.	Collect Data	Collapse
		Disk Op. Time: 85	Interval: 10 min.
		Queue Length: 2	Occurrence
		Event Severity: 5	Count: 1

There are two things to note with regard to the knowledge script NT_MemUtil. First, you'll need to adjust the actual physical memory percentage to correspond to your desired threshold for notification. For example, if you wanted the percentage setting to alert you when 15MB of physical RAM was remaining, the calculation would be as follows:

100 – (15MB / physical RAM)

Second, be aware that the event descriptions may not be 100% accurate, although this may have been corrected by the time you read this. In the release that I tested, the Virtual Memory Used actually represented the percentage of the pagefile in use while the Paging File Used corresponded to the percentage of total memory in use (commit ratio). I also adjust the severity so that high physical memory generates a yellow alert, while high virtual or paging memory raises a red alert.

In addition to using the predefined knowledge scripts, you can monitor the individual Performance Monitor counters to achieve a more granular breakdown of the system performance. This is done using the General_Counter knowledge script.

Author's Note

One of the most powerful features of AppManager is the ability to run batch commands when certain events are raised. This can allow you to execute proactive measures to prevent a server from going down or affecting the users currently on that server.

For example, in addition to sending a page to an operator when the paging file goes above 85% usage, you may also run a batch script that would disable logons on that server, preventing any other users from logging onto this degraded system. You could even send a message to the users on that server telling them of the temporary degradation in performance and that the system is being corrected. ♦

Graphing Data

When you define a job to collect data, you can then display that data in a graph or report. To display a graph, you simply click the Graph Data tab along the bottom of the AppManager console, highlight the desired data, right-click, and select Create Graph. Figure 18.21 shows an example of a graph containing CPU and memory utilization data. The gaps in the graph are due to differences in how often the data was being sampled.

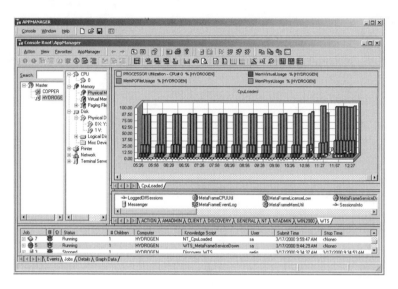

Figure 18.21   *CPU and memory utilization graph examples using AppManager.*

Performance Monitor

While RMS and AppManager (and other, comparable third-party tools) would certainly help to make an operator or administrator's life easier, not everyone will be fortunate enough to be able to implement such a solution. Fortunately other tools at your disposal can execute sufficient monitoring so that you can take a more proactive role in your Terminal Server support.

The most obvious tool is Performance Monitor (called PerfMon for short, and simply called Performance on Windows 2000), which is available as part of Windows. This tool can be found under Administrative Tools on the Start menu. Figure 18.22 shows Performance Monitor with the counters suggested in Chapter 7. Table 18.7 summarizes these monitored objects. I've also included the thresholds to watch for, and I will discuss the creation of alert logs shortly.

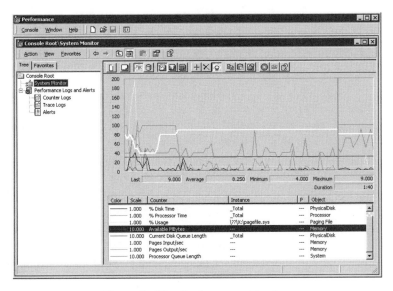

Figure 18.22   *Performance Monitor.*

Table 18.7   Suggested Performance Monitor Counters

Object	Counter	Threshold
Processor	% Processor Time (total)	>85%
System	Processor Queue Length	>15
Memory	Available Megabytes	<4MB
	Pages Input/sec	>65
	Pages Output/sec	>65
Paging File	% Usage (total)	>85%
Physical Disk	% Disk Time (total)	>80%
	Current Disk Queue Length	>2

Author's Note

As I've mentioned before, the actual threshold that you will set for the available memory will depend on when you wish to be alerted. For example, on a system with 1GB of physical memory, you may wish to set a threshold that is triggered when it falls below 5% (50MB). ♦

Normally, when you want to view the status of the system, you run PerfMon and add the appropriate counters to the system monitor. Then you watch the different objects to determine whether there was an issue. Of course, it's not very likely that you'll be sitting in front of PerfMon all day, so you need a mechanism for monitoring the system and automatically alerting you when an issue arises. Fortunately, Microsoft provides an alerting and logging system to do just that. The steps to setting this up are summarized as follows:

1. Create the appropriate counter log containing the counters that you want to monitor if an alert is raised. You'll probably create a counter log with the counters listed earlier in Table 18.7, but you can also create specific logs based on which alert is raised. For example, if a processor alert occurs, you may have a custom log that tracks the % Processor Time for all Terminal Services sessions currently active on the server.

2. Create the alert log, which will contain the counters from step 1 with the appropriate thresholds. When this alert is running and one of the counters goes above or below the defined threshold, an alert message is usually sent, and the counter log is started to keep a history of what was going on.

Creating the Counter Log

To create a counter log, follow these steps:

1. After opening the Performance tool, expand the Performance Logs and Alerts tree, right-click Counter Logs, and select New Log Settings.

2. When prompted, enter a name for this log. I'll use TSE Performance Log.

3. On the properties page, add the desired counters. For this example, I'll simply enter all the counters listed earlier in Table 18.7.

4. Review the Log File tab to see whether any settings need to be changed (see Figure 18.23):

   - By default, performance logs are written to %systemdrive%\PerfLogs. You can change this location if you want.

   - A default filename is created for the output log, but you can define a special suffix to be appended to each file. This allows unique log files to be created based on when the counter log is started. I recommend that you select the option mmddhhmm as the file extension so that a timestamp is associated with each log.

   - You can also specify the type of file that's created; by default, the files are binary, but you can select a text-based, comma-delimited, or tab-delimited file. In this way, you can import data directly into a graphing tool such as Excel.

   - Finally, you can specify the logfile size. By default, the file will grow until it runs out of disk space.

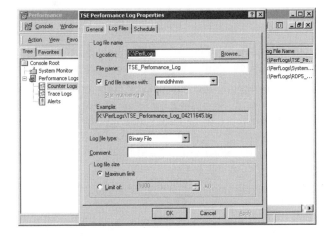

Figure 18.23   *Log File tab for the Counter Log settings.*

5. The final tab is the Schedule tab. From here you can configure the time intervals when the log will run. For this example, I don't want the log to start automatically, so the Start Log setting should be set to manual. Normally I also set a stop time of 2–4 hours, so the logfile won't continue indefinitely. Figure 18.24 shows these options.

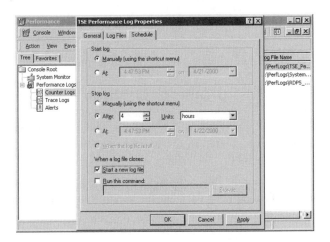

Figure 18.24   *Schedule tab for the counter log settings.*

6. After you click OK, the new counter log appears in the list.

Creating the Alert Process

Now that the counter log exists, the next step is to create the alert process:

1. Right-click the Alerts object and select New Alert Settings. When prompted, provide a name; I'll use Server Alerts.

2. The Alerts property dialog box opens. From here you select the counters to monitor and the sample interval. For each counter that you add, set the threshold value to be either above or below the specified value. I'll create an entry for each of the counters listed earlier in Table 18.7. Figure 18.25 shows these entered values.

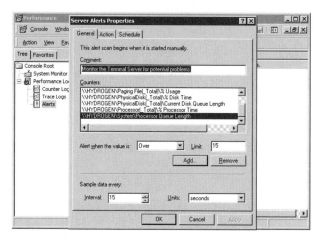

Figure 18.25   *Counters to monitor in the Alerts object.*

3. After the counters have been defined, the next step is to configure the actions that will be taken. I'll configure two actions: send a network message to my management workstation, and start the Terminal Server Performance Log created in the preceding section. Figure 18.26 shows these settings.

4. On the schedule tab, I recommend setting both the start and the stop to manual. Typically, you'll start the alert monitor and leave it running under normal conditions.

To start the alert monitor, simply right-click the new entry and select Start. The icon should change from red to green. If a threshold is exceeded, the management server receives a message similar to the one shown in Figure 18.27 and the counter log is activated. You can confirm this by opening Performance and clicking the Counter Log object. The icon for the Terminal Server Performance Log should be green.

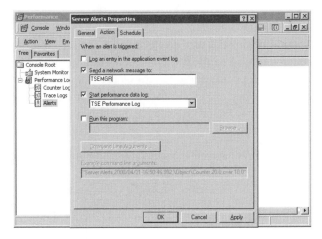

Figure 18.26   *Action settings in the Alerts object.*

Figure 18.27   *Sample message sent by the Alert monitor.*

You can view the contents of this log by clicking System Monitor, then clicking the View Log File Data icon, and selecting the log you want to open. Click the plus (+) icon next to the counters you want to display. Figure 18.28 shows the System Monitor with a sample counter log loaded.

Click this button to load a counter log.────┐   ┌── Then click this button to load the desired counters.

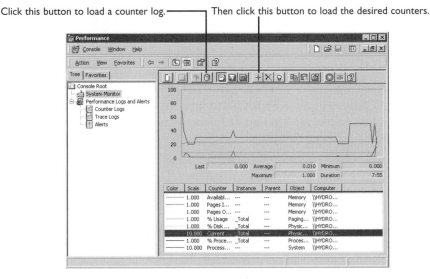

Figure 18.28   *System monitor data from a counter log.*

Server Maintenance

The final section of this chapter discusses a few of the common Terminal Server maintenance and support functions that are performed as part of server operations. Typically these functions are not critical to the operation of the environment, but are useful for troubleshooting, recovery, or to help maximize the performance of the system. I will look briefly at these topics:

- Disk defragmenting
- Windows 2000/NT Server Resource Kit and support tools
- Server cloning

Disk Defragmentation

Over time, as files (and folders) are created and deleted on a disk volume, the files tend to become *fragmented*. When a file is fragmented, it doesn't occupy a single contiguous space on the disk, but instead is broken into multiple pieces (clusters) that are spread out across the disk. The result is the need for multiple disk reads in order to retrieve all the information for a file. Fragmentation is also a problem with write operations. As files are deleted, small "holes" of free space develop on the disk. When a new file is written, the file system attempts to fill these holes with the contents of the file. If the file is too large to occupy the first hole, a portion of the file's contents are written to the first hole, and the remainder is written to the next available hole(s).

As a volume becomes more and more fragmented, the performance of the server can be adversely affected, particularly when a large number of read and write operations are occurring. Typically, file servers are the most susceptible to high amounts of fragmentation as users read, write, and delete files. On a Terminal Server, the amount of fragmentation is much lower, since users have very limited access to perform write and delete operations on the server. On a Terminal Server that has been configured as suggested in Chapter 7 with separate disks (or partitions) for the operating system, applications, and pagefile, the amount of fragmentation is usually broken down as follows:

- **System volume.** This is where the most fragmentation usually occurs, since each user's profile and temporary folders are stored here. Typically I suggest performing a defragment on the system volume once every month or so, although the frequency for your environment will depend on your fragmentation reports. Ideally you should schedule the defrag to occur when the server is out of production or during off-peak times, so as not to affect users.

- **Pagefile volume.** Very little file fragmentation occurs on this partition, since the only file here is the pagefile. The pagefile itself can become internally fragmented (because of how Windows manages it), but commercial utilities can defragment the pagefile. A freeware tool called PageDeFrag is also available from www.sysinternals.com.

- **Application volume.** Very little fragmentation should occur on the application volume, since users should have no (or only minimal) write or delete access. I suggest defragmenting the application volume after you have completed the installation and configuration of all the applications on your Terminal Server. A scheduled defrag is not normally required.

Defragmentation Software

Software solutions are available to remedy the situation of fragmented volumes. Windows 2000 ships with a tool called Disk Defragmenter, which is a limited version of the full commercial product called Diskeeper from Executive Software. To start Disk Defragmenter, right-click the disk you want to analyze or defragment, select Properties, click the Tools tab, and then click the Defragment Now button. A dialog box appears, similar to the one shown in Figure 18.29.

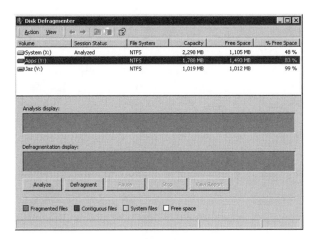

Figure 18.29   *Disk Defragmenter in Windows 2000.*

Before defragmenting a disk, you should first analyze the drive to determine whether the defrag is required. Simply select the drive you want to analyze at the top, then click the Analyze button. A pop-up box indicates whether the volume should be defragged; if you want to continue with the defrag, click the Defragment button to begin the defragging process.

While the Disk Defragmenter tool that's included in Windows 2000 is useful, a number of key features are missing that limit its usefulness in a large implementation:

- It can defragment/analyze only one volume at a time.
- Defrags can't be scheduled.
- The defrag settings can't be configured from a command prompt.

Probably the biggest limitation is the fact that it can't be scheduled for launched from a command prompt. This means that in order to defragment a volume, you need to log onto the Terminal Server, launch the tool, and then perform the defrag one at a time on each of the volumes.

In order to be able to use these more robust features (or to defragment a Terminal Server 4.0 system, which doesn't ship with a defrag tool) you need to look at third-party defragmentation tools. Currently the only defragmentation tool that provides support for Terminal Server (NT and 2000) is Diskeeper 5.0. Diskeeper 5.0 is the first (and currently the only) defragmentation tool certified for use on Windows 2000. Diskeeper provides a number of enhancements over the basic version that ships with Windows 2000. Figure 18.30 shows the Diskeeper interface. Diskeeper 5.0 includes the "Set It and Forget It" schedule feature, which allows you to configure Diskeeper for scheduled defrag operations. Diskeeper also has a boot-time defragmentation option, which defrags the pagefile if necessary, as well as the ability to defrag multiple volumes simultaneously. An NT 4.0 version of Diskeeper is also available that will work on TSE 4.0, although it has been reported that the Diskeeper management application is only accessible from the server console. An evaluation copy of Diskeeper can be downloaded from www.diskeeper.com.

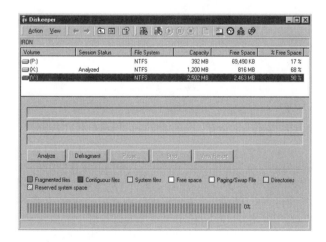

Figure 18.30   *Diskeeper 5.0 interface.*

Windows Server Resource Kit and Support Tools

As I've mentioned several times, probably the most useful set of tools that any Terminal Server administrator could have is the Windows 2000/NT Server Resource Kit. While the documentation alone can save you hours of time, the robust set of tools can assist you in almost every area of server administration. One of the tools that I'll discuss in more detail later in this chapter is the SYSPREP tool that's used to prepare a Windows 2000 system for cloning. SYSPREP is included as part of the Windows 2000 Server Resource Kit.

The installation of the NT 4 Server Resource Kit is fairly straightforward. If you're going to be installing the Windows 2000 Server Resource Kit, however, note the following:

- If you're installing across the network, make sure that you launch SETUP.EXE through a UNC path (such as \\steel\cdrom\setup.exe) and not from a mapped drive letter. Using a mapped drive causes the installation to fail with an internal error just before it begins to copy the files. Using a UNC path solves this problem. This is a known bug in Windows 2000 and is being investigated by Microsoft.

- The Windows 2000 Server Resource Kit can only be installed on a Windows 2000 computer. It won't install on an NT 4.0 system.

In addition to the Windows 2000 Server Resource Kit, a number of support tools are also included on the Windows 2000 Server CD. These tools are completely independent of the Resource Kit tools, and are intended to provide you with features geared specifically for troubleshooting and managing problems in a Windows 2000 environment.

The installation files are in the Support\Tools folder on the Windows 2000 Server CD. Just as with the Resource Kit, if you're installing these on a Windows 2000 server across the network, you must run SETUP from a UNC path and not from a mapped network drive. You can find the latest information on the Resource Kits at this address:

```
www.microsoft.com/windows2000/library/resources/reskit/default.asp
```

Server Cloning

Chapter 9, "Software Planning," talks about the advantages of using server cloning in a Terminal Server implementation to quickly build up an environment from a single base image. Using cloning, you can ensure that all your Terminal Servers have an identical configuration. The advantages of cloning quickly become apparent in a large server deployment scenario, since a single server can be used during the installation and testing of the operating system and software. When the time comes to test the configuration on multiple servers, you simply place the cloned server's image onto the other hardware, and voilà, you have a multiple-server environment. While alternatives exist, such as scripted installations, I always select cloning if given the choice. Cloning can be ideal in a disaster-recovery situation to get an environment back online as quickly as possible.

Figure 18.31 demonstrates how server imaging can be integrated into the build process for the Terminal Server environment. Of course, the environment could be created without the imaging step, but if a problem is encountered, it's very likely that you'd need to start over from the beginning to rebuild the server. If you've been maintaining server images, you can easily roll back to the point where you had a stable server configuration. For example, say you discover a problem during the application-installation phase that has left your Terminal Server unstable. You would be able to quickly rebuild your server from the last image and reevaluate the application-installation process without having to completely rebuild the server from scratch. This process can be a valuable time-saver, even in a small Terminal Server implementation.

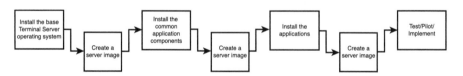

Figure 18.31   *Server cloning in a Terminal Server implementation.*

The exact method of cloning depends on the version of Terminal Server that you're implementing. In a TS 2000 implementation, you can use the Microsoft SYSPREP utility that ships with the Windows 2000 Server Resource Kit to help prepare the server for cloning. Microsoft fully supports cloning of Windows 2000 Terminal Servers when this utility is used.

Unfortunately, while a version of SYSPREP exists for NT 4.0, it's supported only for NT Workstation and regular NT servers running as member servers. Support *is not* included for TSE 4.0. While Microsoft doesn't officially support cloning a TSE 4.0 server, tools do exist that allow you to reliably clone one of these servers and create new servers from this image. When a server ID (SID) generation tool is used, a fully functional TSE 4.0 server can be constructed. I'll discuss the TSE 4.0 cloning techniques shortly, but first I'll look at the Windows 2000 Terminal Services cloning process.

Author's Note

I've worked on a number of TSE 4.0 projects where cloning has been used (either with cloning tools such as Norton Ghost or backup software such as ArcServe) and have never encountered a system problem that was related to the use of cloning. ◆

Tip

The first time you boot a cloned server that has had the drive letters reassigned using MetaFrame, you may find that the drives have been reset back to their defaults of C:, D:, and so on. This behavior is normal and is easily corrected by running Disk Administrator on TSE 4.0, or through Disk Management under Computer Management on TS 2000, and resetting the drives back to their correct drive letters. All application and system references to the reassigned drive letters will still be correct. Only the assigned drive letters need correction. ◆

Cloning a TS 2000 Server

The first step in cloning a TS 2000 server is to run SYSPREP to prepare the server for cloning. Follow these steps:

1. Create a directory called SYSPREP off the root of %systemdrive% and copy the files SYSPREP.EXE and SETUPCL.EXE into it. Both files are located in the directory where the Windows 2000 Server Resource Kit was installed.

2. Remove the server from the domain. (This way, when the cloned server is booted up, it won't attempt to join the domain with a computer name that's already in use.)

3. Run SYSPREP on the server. The confirmation dialog box shown in Figure 18.32 asks you to verify that you want to run SYSPREP.

Figure 18.32 *SYSPREP confirmation dialog box.*

4. After you click OK, SYSPREP prepares the system for cloning and, when completed, automatically shuts down the server. At this point, you're ready to capture the clone image either by using a cloning software package or by rebooting the server into a second OS and performing a traditional backup.

After you have captured the image, the next time you reboot the server from which you took the image or boot up any server that you clone from the image, SYSPREP automatically initiates a mini-installation of Windows 2000. This mini-install prompts you for a subset of the information that you would provide when installing a fresh copy of Windows 2000. This information includes the desired regional settings, the product license key, the computer name, the administrative password, the date and time, the desired network components to install, and whether you want to join a domain. After all the required information has been provided, the server automatically reboots and the cloned server's setup is complete. The SysPrep directory off the %systemdrive% is deleted automatically.

> **Warning**
>
> *If you have modified the security of the registry from its default settings, you need to reapply this security on the cloned server. The current version of SYSPREP (1.1) won't modify the registry security, which means that after a new server ID (SID) has been generated for the computer, the SIDs for the users and groups in the registry no longer correspond to a valid local group. Instead, you get Account Unknown entries when you view the registry security. This is a known bug in SYSPREP. For complete details, refer to Microsoft Knowledge Base article Q251042.* ◆

You can speed up the configuration of a cloned server by using the Windows 2000 Server Resource Kit tool SETUPMGR.EXE to create an answer file that's used by SYSPREP the first time a cloned server starts up.

When you launch SETUPMGR, it guides you through a wizard that generates an answer file called SYSPREP.INF. You then place this file into the %systemdrive%\SysPrep folder along with the other two executables. When the cloned server is booted for the first time, SYSPREP runs and uses the answer file to configure the server. You can configure all the desired options within SETUPMGR, including the following:

- The default server name to use.
- The administrative password to use. Note that if you provide a password, it will be stored in plaintext in the generated SYSPREP.INF file.
- Default console display resolution and color depth.
- Whether the server will automatically join a domain or workgroup. If you're going to be completely automating the creation of the cloned image, you should configure the answer file so that the server remains in a workgroup. This way, you'll have the opportunity to rename it and add it to the domain immediately after the first boot.
- The server's timezone.

A sample answer file looks something like this:

```
;SetupMgrTag
[Unattended]
    OemSkipEula=Yes
    TargetPath=\WINNT

[GuiUnattended]
    AdminPassword=this_is_plain_text
    OEMSkipRegional=1
    TimeZone=35
    OemSkipWelcome=1

[UserData]
    FullName=TWM
    OrgName="Noisy River Software Corp."
    ComputerName=NOISYRIVERSRV

[Display]
    BitsPerPel=8
    Xresolution=800
    YResolution=600
    Vrefresh=60

[LicenseFilePrintData]
    AutoMode=PerSeat

[RegionalSettings]
    LanguageGroup=1

[SetupMgr]
    DistFolder=X:\sysprep\i386
    DistShare=win2000dist

[Identification]
    JoinWorkgroup=METAFRAME

[Networking]
    InstallDefaultComponents=No

[NetClients]
    MS_MSClient=params.MS_MSClient
```

Cloning a TSE 4.0 Server

The procedure for cloning an NT 4.0 Terminal Server is slightly more
involved than the one for TS 2000. These are the steps that I suggest
following for cloning a TSE 4.0 server:

1. Remove the Terminal Server from the domain and assign it to a workgroup. I also suggest that you rename the server so that a newly cloned
   server from this image won't be in conflict with an existing machine.
   This can also provide a visual reminder to you that it's a newly created
   server in the environment.

2. Capture the server image using the desired cloning or backup software. For example, if you're using Norton Ghost, boot the server using a network-enabled DOS disk and then run Ghost to write an image of the server's disk to a file located on a network share.

3. After you've captured the server image, use it to create one or more cloned servers. If a cloned server will be assigned a static IP address (instead of DHCP), disconnect it from the network until you've had the chance to update the IP address so that a duplicate-address conflict doesn't occur.

4. After the cloned server has booted, the first thing you should do is generate a new unique SID. Many cloning packages provide their own SID-generating software. A freeware 32-bit SID changer is also available from www.sysinternals.com. The utility is called NewSID, and it generates a new SID and automatically renames a server.

5. When a unique SID and name have been assigned to the server, add it to the desired Windows domain. At this point, the cloned Terminal Server is now ready for use.

19

Application Integration

In this chapter:

- **The Challenge of Application Integration**
  The greatest challenges that you are likely to face during your Terminal Server project will not involve the configuration and implementation of your servers, but instead will be the installation, testing, and deployment of the applications you want to run on those servers.

- **Terminal Server Application Support Features**
  In order to ensure that the majority of applications will function properly, Terminal Server incorporates a number of application support features that you must understand in order to be an effective application integrator.

- **Application Integration Tools and Techniques**
  As an application integrator, you will need to employ a common set of tools and techniques to assist in configuring applications to run properly within Terminal Server.

- **The Application Integration Process**
  Before looking at a few examples of installing and configuring different applications on Terminal Server, I would first like to outline the general process that you should follow when performing application integration, particularly during a new Terminal Server implementation.

- **Application Installation Examples**
  To finish this chapter, I walk through the installation of a few applications on Terminal Server.

The Challenge of Application Integration

It probably comes as no surprise that the greatest challenges you're likely to face during your Terminal Server project will involve not the configuration and implementation of the servers, but instead the installation, testing, and deployment of the applications you want to run on those servers. The purpose of implementing Terminal Server is to centralize the management and servicing of these applications, so it's vitally important that they be configured to work with as little loss of functionality as possible (or no loss).

In the role of an *application integrator* (*AI*), you're likely to face a combination of both technical and managerial challenges, such as these issues:

- **Release management.** One area where many AIs seem to have difficulty is in the establishment and enforcement of release management procedures. One reason is simply that the PC computing environment has traditionally had poor release management control. For your Terminal Server environment to remain stable, you must adopt the release procedures that are common in more traditional multiuser environments, such as mainframe and UNIX. As I have stated many times throughout this book, it's a *requirement* that you put the proper release-management procedures in place, regardless of whether you're deploying 2 or 20 applications. If there's no control over the releasing of software into the Terminal Server environment, it's only a matter of time before a release causes your environment to fail. Please see Chapter 9, "Software Planning," for more information on release management.

- **Application stability.** Although application stability is not strictly an issue for the AI (it's more of a concern for Terminal Server operators), the AI must keep this requirement in mind when installing and configuring the application. On the desktop, an application failure affects only one person and usually results in no more than a few harsh words directed by the user to the computer. On a Terminal Server, however, an application failure could immediately affect 20, 50, 100, or more users. In this situation, the harsh words will very likely be directed at the Terminal Server operators and administrators.

  As an AI, you must ensure that the installed application is configured to be as stable as possible. It must also interoperate with any other programs that users may be running on Terminal Server. Of course, you have little control over an application that's inherently buggy, but if this is the case, it's likely that these problems existed on the desktop.

  One thing that you'll learn very quickly is that whenever an issue comes up with any application running in the Terminal Server environment, the problem will immediately be attributed to Terminal Server, and not to the application.

- **Multiple simultaneous users.** The most obvious challenge you'll face is configuring applications to function properly when run simultaneously in multiple user sessions on the same computer. Although we're slowly starting to see the development of applications designed specifically to run in a Terminal Server environment (particularly with the new requirements for Windows 2000 application certification), most applications on the market today were not developed with that purpose in mind. I've found that most apps still function properly, but in some situations additional work and "fiddling" are required to overcome specific problems. Typically, if an application has been designed using proper Windows development techniques, such as storing program-specific information in HKEY_LOCAL_MACHINE while maintaining user-specific information in HKEY_CURRENT_USER, it should run on Terminal Server with few problems.

  A number of products available on the market support Terminal Server; WRQ's Reflection and Microsoft Office 2000 are just two examples.

- **Enhanced security.** Very often the enhanced security requirements of Terminal Server pose more of a problem to the AI than the multiuser requirements. Security issues can introduce unexpected problems, particularly when the AI has been testing with an administrative account instead of a regular user account. Whenever you encounter a situation where the program runs for an administrator but not for a user, it's almost always a security-related problem.

Author's Note

I can't count the number of times I've reviewed a Terminal Server implementation where the administrators have said, "We originally had the system locked down, but we couldn't get the applications to run, so we gave everyone full control and now it works fine." Although this certainly fixes the immediate problem of getting the programs to function properly, it is not a solution. In fact, this is likely to cause more problems down the road. Every time you give a user elevated security access to the Terminal Server, you're introducing the potential for a problem. It is only a matter of time before the user either installs something or modifies something that causes an application failure. ◆

My goal in this chapter is to provide the information you need to become a successful application integrator in a Terminal Server environment. I discuss the application support features available in Terminal Server, the tools and techniques that will assist you, and the process that I typically follow when installing an application. Finally, I provide a step-by-step walk-through of how to install and configure some of the most common applications in a fictitious implementation scenario. Although no amount of documentation can prepare you for every situation, I hope that, with the information in this chapter, you will be able to resolve most of the application problems you encounter.

Here are the three rules I follow when performing application integration:

- **Have patience.** Although many applications can be installed on the first try, most can't. You might need to try a few configurations to find the one that's right for your environment. Don't always settle for the first solution that comes along.

- **Automate as much as possible.** If you have the option of preconfiguring something or automating a process that would normally require user interaction, do so. The more the Terminal Server user must do before he can run an application, the more likely that he won't do it properly. If a user must run a setup program before he can use the program for the first time, put it in a batch script and ensure that it runs before the application does.

- **Test, test, test.** Always test the applications with a restricted user account. Testing an application with an administrative account is only useful to ensure that it runs at all. Ninety-nine percent of the users in your environment are not administrators, so don't waste a lot of time testing with an admin account.

Terminal Server Application Support Features

To ensure that the majority of applications will function properly, Terminal Server incorporates a number of application support features that you must understand in order to be an effective application integrator. Before installing any applications, you should have a clear understanding of why these features are required and how you can use them to your advantage.

The User Home Drive and Root Drive

Chapter 2, "Microsoft Windows Terminal Server," talks about the management tools included with Terminal Server, including the special options available for configuring a user's account for operation on a Terminal Server. Both Active Directory Users and Computers on TS 2000 and User Manager for Domains on TSE 4.0 provide these features. Figure 19.1 shows the Terminal Services Profile tab for a user's account properties. This is where the user's Terminal Server home directory and profile are defined.

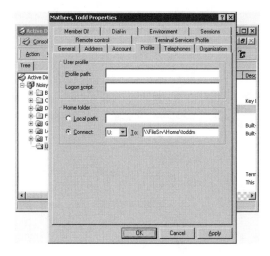

Figure 19.1   *Defining the Terminal Services home directory.*

The home directory is of particular importance in a Terminal Server environment because it's where the user-specific application and environment data is stored. Terminal Server uses the home directory to store a personal copy of WIN.INI and SYSTEM.INI for each user who may be running a 16-bit application. (I talk more about the information maintained in the home directory shortly.)

The Terminal Server home directory and profile paths are referenced only when a user is logged onto a Terminal Server. When the user is logged onto a non–Terminal Server environment (such as a Windows 2000 Professional desktop), this information is ignored. Figure 19.2 shows the simple process flow used by Terminal Server to determine where the user's home directory is located.

If a Terminal Server home directory has been defined, it's used. If not, and a regular Windows home directory has been defined, that's used instead. If neither has been defined, Terminal Server defaults to using the user's local profile path. On Windows 2000, this would be %systemdrive%\Documents and Settings\%username%. On NT 4.0, it would be %systemroot%\Profiles\%username% by default.

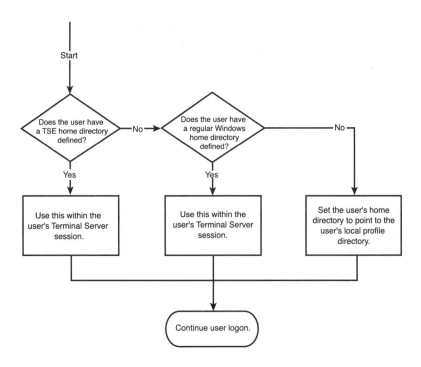

Figure 19.2   *Determining the user's Terminal Server home path.*

You can view the current location of a user's home directory simply by
opening a command prompt from within that session and running SET to
view the current environment variables. In both TSE 4.0 and TS 2000,
you see the entries HOMEDRIVE and HOMEPATH. TS 2000 also uses the variable
HOMESHARE, which points to the exact location where the user's home directory is located. Assuming that the share point is \\FileSrv\Users, a sample
output on Windows 2000 would look something like this:

```
HOMEDRIVE=U:
HOMEPATH=\
HOMESHARE=\\FileSrv\users\toddm
```

On NT 4.0 Terminal Server, it would be slightly different:

```
HOMEDRIVE=U:
HOMEPATH=\toddm
```

The difference is that the HOMEPATH on Windows 2000 is simply the root (\),
while on NT 4.0 it's the path from the share point into the specific directory
(\toddm). This is because Windows 2000 supports a feature commonly
called *map root,* which allows you to map a drive letter to a specific directory located *below* a defined share point. You can't do this on NT 4.0. You
can map a directory only to an explicitly defined share point.

Author's Note

Though I use the drive letter U: in my discussion of the home directory, you can use any drive letter you wish when defining the home drive of a user's account. ◆

So, on Windows 2000, if I went to U:\, I would still be within my personal home drive (\\FileSrv\Users\toddm), but if I went to U:\ on NT 4.0, I would actually be one directory above my home directory, in the root of the share (\\FileSrv\Users). Although the default security would prevent me from accessing any other user's home directory, I would still be able to generate a list of all of the other users.

So now that we have the desired home directory information configured for the user's Terminal Server session, we should be ready to go, right? Not quite. The multiuser features of Terminal Server work to complicate this process further. Consider the following example:

- I'm installing an application on TSE 4.0. During the installation, the setup program asks me to provide a working directory where user information will be stored. What directory should I specify? Of course, I want to use the user's home directory. But how do I tell the installation program where this is, since I need the directory to change depending on the individual user? Ideally, I'd like to provide U:\%username%, but most applications don't do variable expansion. Since TSE 4.0 doesn't support the map root feature, I don't have an easy solution to this problem.

- Now assume that I'm trying to install the same application on TS 2000. Initially it would appear that the installation will be much easier, because when the application prompts me to provide the directory where the user data is stored, I can simply tell it to use U:\, which will map to the root of the user's personal home directory. Of course, this solution will work only if all Terminal Server users have U: defined as the working drive. In a large organization in which users are spread out over a number of departments or possibly different geographical areas, it's very likely that users have a different home drive letter. How would we accommodate this?

Microsoft's solution to both of these problems (actually, it was originally developed to solve the TSE 4.0 issue) was to create a new drive definition specific to Terminal Server called the *root drive* (this is *not* the same as %systemroot%). The purpose of the root drive is to provide a consistent drive letter that points directly to the user's home directory (just as U: would in Windows 2000), regardless of what the user's drive letter is within his or her user account. Not only would this solve the fairly trivial problems just stated, but it would allow for the distribution of certain application components into a user's home drive while addressing the home drive with a consistent drive letter.

For example, with Word 97, you need to alter the location where NORMAL.DOT and other template files are stored so that they're on the user's home drive and not on the system or application drive. This is so that each user can modify his or her own templates without conflicting with other users' templates. You must configure Word so that it will look to the user's home drive for the template files.

Typically, the Terminal Server root drive is designated as W:, but it can be set to be any drive letter you want. It must be a drive letter that's not required by any of the applications you'll be running on Terminal Server because it will be deleted and reassigned to point at the user's home directory.

The root drive normally is not defined until the first time you run an application compatibility script (as discussed in the next section). You can create the root drive immediately by running this batch script:

```
%SystemRoot%\Application Compatibility Scripts\chkroot.cmd
```

Notepad opens, as shown in Figure 19.3. To set the root drive letter, simply enter the letter and a colon immediately after the equal sign (=). For example, if you want to use W:, enter this:

```
Set RootDrive=W:
```

For the remainder of this chapter, I assume that the root drive is W:.

Figure 19.3 *Setting the root drive letter.*

The next time you log on after setting the root drive (or the first time you run an application compatibility script), the SUBST command will be used to map to your home directory. For example, if my home directory is currently U:\users\toddm, the SUBST command would be as follows:

```
Subst W: U:\users\toddm
```

The actual drive letter substitution is done in the USRLOGON.CMD compatibility script. This script is automatically run for each user every time the user logs onto Terminal Server. It appears momentarily as a minimized DOS window before the logon completes.

In a Windows 2000 environment, if you know for certain that all users will be configured with the same drive letter for the Terminal Server home drive, you can disable the root drive substitution to a second drive letter and simply use the one defined in the user accounts. For example, if you know that all users' home directories are U:\, you can disable the substitution of W: = U: that would normally occur. I discuss how to do this in the next section. ♦

Application Compatibility Scripts

To help resolve many of the common problems that applications have when trying to run on Terminal Server, Microsoft has developed an intricate group of batch scripts called *application compatibility scripts (ACS)*. These scripts are used to perform any necessary file and registry modifications in order to allow an application to function properly on Terminal Server.

The majority of the files that collectively make up the ACS are located in the directory %systemroot%\Application Compatibility Scripts. The main batch script, which is called by every user who logs onto Terminal Server (whether remotely or from the console), is located in the System32 directory and is called USRLOGON.CMD.

The ACS has three main functions:

- **Configure the environment.** This includes defining the ROOTDRIVE (as described in the preceding section), as well as setting a number of other environment variables that may be used in the compatibility scripts, such as the user's start menu location (USER_START_MENU).

- **Run scripts immediately after an application has been installed.** These scripts run once in order to perform some post-installation changes that must be made to an application. While all installation scripts do not require it, I recommend that you always have the server in install mode (discussed in the next section) prior to running an installation ACS. These scripts are located in the Install subdirectory under the ACS directory.

- **Run scripts during a user's logon.** These scripts need to be run every time a user logs on in order to ensure that the necessary file and registry changes have been made to support any applications the user might run. Logon ACSs are located in the Logon subdirectory, also under the ACS directory.

Typically, application compatibility scripts are invoked the first time you install an application onto the Terminal Server. Not all applications require compatibility scripts (IE5 and Office 2000 don't), and Microsoft provides only a limited set of scripts for those that do. In some situations, you may need to define your own compatibility scripts; I discuss this in more detail shortly. Before you can develop your own scripts, you need a clear understanding of how the ACS environment operates, and you must know the exact functions of the files that comprise the ACS. Table 19.1 lists and describes the main scripts that make up the ACS environment.

Table 19.1   The Main Application Compatibility Scripts

Script Name	Location Under %systemroot%	Description
Usrlogon.cmd	System32	Called during every user's logon and by the ChkRoot script. It's responsible for calling all the other required scripts. It also performs the SUBST command to map the root drive.
Usrlogn1.cmd	System32	Called by UsrLogon.cmd. Initially, this file doesn't exist. When it does exist (either by running a compatibility script or manually created), it will contain calls to only those compatibility scripts that *do not* require the root drive to be defined.
Usrlogn2.cmd	System32	Called by UsrLogon.cmd. Initially, this file doesn't exist. When it does exist, it contains calls to any compatibility scripts that *do* require the root drive to be defined.
SetPaths.cmd	Application Compatibility Scripts	Called by UsrLogon.cmd. This script defines a number of environment variables that are used during the running of the application compatibility scripts, such as the common and per-user startup folder locations.
RootDrv.cmd	Application Compatibility Scripts	Called by UsrLogon.cmd. This script simply calls RootDrv2.cmd if it exists.
RootDrv2.cmd	Application Compatibility Scripts	Called by RootDrv.cmd. This script sets the environment variable %rootdrive% to the desired drive letter so that UsrLogon.cmd can perform the proper substitution. RootDrv2.cmd is created by the ChkRoot.cmd script.

Script Name	Location Under %systemroot%	Description
ChkRoot.cmd	Application Compatibility Scripts	Called by the various application compatibility scripts to verify that the root drive has been set. If it hasn't been set, this creates the RootDrv2.cmd file and prompts the user to specify the drive letter to use as the root drive.
End.cmd	Application Compatibility Scripts	Called by UsrLogon.cmd. This script performs no function. It simply sets @ECHO OFF.

Terminal Server also comes with a set of three "helper" executables that are used by the compatibility scripts to retrieve and update registry and file information. These helper application names all begin with the AC (application compatibility) prefix. The helper applications are as follows:

- **ACINIUPD.EXE.** This tool is used to update INI files. Its usage is as follows:

```
aciniupd.exe [/e] [/k] [/u] [/v] <ini filename> <section name> <key name>
➥<new value>
```

/e tells ACINIUPD to update the value for the given section and key name. An existing value is replaced by the new value given.

/k tells the tool to update the given key name in the section with the name specified in <new value>. This replaces the key name, not the key's value.

/u signals the tool to update the INI file in the user's Windows directory instead of in %systemroot%.

/v means to run in verbose mode. The default is to run silently.

- **ACREGL.EXE.** This utility searches the registry for the provided key and value and outputs them to a file as a SET statement with the provided environment variable name. This is primarily used to retrieve specific information from the registry and make it available as an environment variable that can then be used by the compatibility scripts. Its usage is as follows:

```
acregl.exe <output filename> <set variable name> <registry key> <registry value>
➥<options>
```

The registry key must start with either HKCU (HKEY_CURRENT_USER) or HKLM (HKEY_LOCAL_MACHINE) and must be enclosed in a string, such as "HKLM\Software\Microsoft".

The <options> value can be an empty string (""), STRIPCHAR*c*n, or STRIPPATH. STRIPCHAR*c*n, starting from the right side of the string, strips *n* instances of the character *c*. Anything to the right of *c* is dropped. STRIPPATH removes the full path from a filename, so X:\WinNT\ System32\UsrLogon.cmd would become simply UsrLogon.cmd.

- **ACSR.EXE.** This tool performs search-and-replace on the given input file, sending the results to the provided output file. The syntax is simple:

  ```
  acsr.exe <search string> <replace string> <input file> <output file>
  ```

  Every occurrence of `<search string>` is replaced with the `<replace string>` value and saved to the `<output file>` location.

Author's Note

I've included the information regarding these helper programs more as a guide to reviewing the existing compatibility scripts than as a primer for using them to create your own scripts.

Personally, I prefer to use a scripting language such as KiXtart when writing custom compatibility scripts. This allows much more flexibility and control over exactly what's happening when compared to using these fairly limited tools. ♦

As mentioned earlier, the ACS is usually invoked the first time an application is installed on a Terminal Server. This includes the creation of the RootDrv2.cmd script, which defines the root drive environment variable, which in turn allows UsrLogon.cmd to perform the substitution on it.

I recommend that you configure the root drive *prior* to performing the installation of your first application on the Terminal Server. This provides three advantages:

- You can perform any desired script creation or server configuration that depends on the root drive prior to installing the applications.
- You can reference the root drive during the installation of the first application. When the first application is installed, unless an ACS has already been executed then the root drive won't be defined until after the app is installed and its ACS has been run.
- The root drive is available to those applications that don't have an ACS. Normally, unless at least one ACS is run, the root drive won't be defined. A good example is Office 2000, which doesn't require an ACS. Unless you manually run the script (or install another application that has an ACS) to create the root drive, it won't be available to Office 2000 after it has been installed.

You can trigger the creation of the root drive simply by calling the ChkRoot.cmd script located in the Application Compatibility Script directory. This launches Notepad and prompts you to provide the root drive letter, including the colon (:). After you enter this information, the RootDrv2.cmd file is created. The next time you log onto Terminal Server, the root drive will be available. You can easily check this either through My Computer or by opening a command prompt and typing **subst**. You should see this entry:

```
<root drive> = <home drive><home path>
```

Even with a list of all the components that make up the ACS, it's not necessarily clear how these pieces fit together. The flow chart in Figure 19.4 summarizes how the different application compatibility scripts interact from the main program, UsrLogon.cmd.

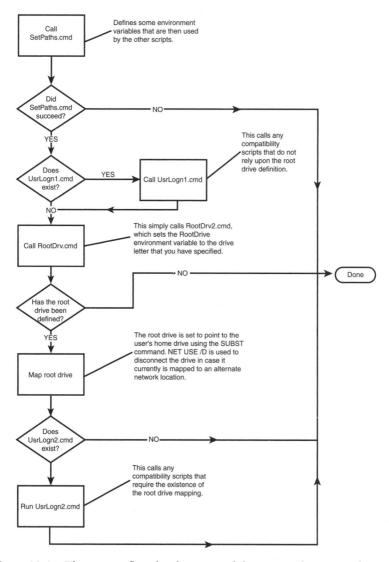

Figure 19.4 *The process flow for the compatibility scripts during user logon.*

Sample Application Compatibility Scripts

Now that you have a clear idea of how the compatibility scripts fit together, I'll end this section by dissecting an ACS to see exactly what information it contains.

The first example uses the Microsoft SNA client, a common component installed on a Terminal Server when delivering host emulation. I'll bypass the exact details involved in the client installation, because I want to wait until I've covered the remainder of the material in this section before getting into the details of an application installation. For now I'll simply say this:

- The server is put into installation mode.

- The SNA client software is installed.

- The appropriate SNA client install script is run. Install scripts are always run after the application has been installed. If necessary, this script configures the system so that the appropriate logon script is run for each user.

- After the install script has been run, the server can be placed back into execute mode and rebooted if necessary.

The corresponding SNA installation script looks like this:

```
@ECHO OFF
REM *** SNA40CLI.CMD - Batch file to register SNA Client 4.0 ***

Rem ####################################################################

If Not "A%SNAROOT%A" == "AA" Goto Cont1
Echo.
Echo    Unable to complete Multi-user Application Tuning because the
Echo    SNAROOT environment variable isn't set.  This could occur if
Echo    the command shell being used to run this script was opened
Echo    before the SNA Client 4.0 was installed.
Echo.
Pause
Goto Cont2

Rem ####################################################################

:Cont1
Register %SNAROOT%\SNADMOD.DLL /SYSTEM >Nul: 2>&1
Register %SNAROOT%\SNAMANAG.DLL /SYSTEM >Nul: 2>&1
Register %SNAROOT%\WAPPC32.DLL /SYSTEM >Nul: 2>&1
Register %SNAROOT%\DBGTRACE.DLL /SYSTEM >Nul: 2>&1
Register %SNAROOT%\MNGBASE.DLL /SYSTEM >Nul: 2>&1
Register %SNAROOT%\SNATRC.DLL /SYSTEM >Nul: 2>&1
Register %SNAROOT%\SNALM.DLL /SYSTEM >Nul: 2>&1
Register %SNAROOT%\SNANW.DLL /SYSTEM >Nul: 2>&1
```

```
Register %SNAROOT%\SNAIP.DLL /SYSTEM >Nul: 2>&1
Register %SNAROOT%\SNABASE.EXE /SYSTEM >Nul: 2>&1

Echo SNA Server 4.0 Multi-user Application Tuning Complete
Pause

:Cont2
```

Notice that this script doesn't make use of the %rootdrive% environment variable discussed earlier. This one simply registers a set of DLL and executable files as system global so that multiple instances of the SNA client will share these components. There's no component that runs every time the user logs on.

The next script is the installation script associated with ODBC. This ACS does make use of the %rootdrive% environment variable, updating it so that the ODBC log files point to a user's home directory. The script looks like this:

```
@echo off
Rem
Rem  This script updates the location of ODBC log files.
Rem

Rem #################################################################

Rem
Rem Verify that %RootDrive% has been configured and set it for this script.
Rem

Call "%SystemRoot%\Application Compatibility Scripts\ChkRoot.Cmd"
If "%_CHKROOT%" == "FAIL" Goto Done

Rem #################################################################

Rem If not currently in Install Mode, change to Install Mode.
Set __OrigMode=Install
ChgUsr /query > Nul:
if Not ErrorLevel 101 Goto Begin
Set __OrigMode=Exec
Change User /Install > Nul:
:Begin

..\acsr "#ROOTDRIVE#" "%RootDrive%" Template\ODBC.Key ODBC.Key
regini ODBC.Key > Nul:

Rem If original mode was Execute, change back to Execute Mode.
If "%__OrigMode%" == "Exec" Change User /Execute > Nul:
Set __OrigMode=


Echo.
Echo   When configuring SQL data sources, click the Options button on
Echo   the User DSN tab and then the Profiling button. Change the Query
```

```
Echo    Log and Statistics Log files to be saved on the user's root
Echo    drive (%RootDrive%).
Echo.
Echo    Additionally, an administrator may configure a data source for
Echo    all users. First, open a command window and enter the command
Echo    "Change User /Install". Next, configure the data source.
Echo    Finally, enter the command "Change User /Execute" in the
Echo    command window to return to Execute Mode.
Echo.

Echo ODBC Multi-user Application Tuning Complete
Pause

:Done
```

Notice that two things differ between this script and the one for the SNA client. First, this script checks to see that %rootdrive% has been defined. This is done by calling the ChkRoot.cmd script. If the script fails, this script simply exits without any warning. If the root drive has been defined, the script ensures that the server is in install mode (if it isn't already). The current server mode is "remembered" so that it can be set back after this script completes. The installation and execution modes are discussed in the next section. Now the script performs the actual changes.

First, the script uses the ACSR tool to replace the #ROOTDRIVE# reference in the ODBC.key file located in the Template directory and writes the resulting file into the directory where the ACS is located. The resulting ODBC.key file is shown next. This is simply a text file that's passed as input into the REGINI utility so that the necessary registry keys can be updated.

```
HKEY_CURRENT_USER\Software\ODBC\ODBC.INI\ODBC
    TraceFile = DELETE

HKEY_LOCAL_MACHINE\Software\ODBC\ODBC.INI\ODBC
    TraceFile = DELETE

HKEY_CURRENT_USER\Software\ODBC\ODBC.INI\ODBC
    TraceFile = W:\SQL.LOG

HKEY_LOCAL_MACHINE\Software\ODBC\ODBC.INI\ODBC
    TraceFile = W:\SQL.LOG
```

The first two statements delete the listed value, and the last two re-create it. After the registry has been updated, the server is set back into the proper execution state, and the script finishes.

I recommend that you take the time to review a few of the existing compatibility scripts to get an idea as to how different applications might need to be modified to operate in a Terminal Server environment. Although some of the scripts can be quite extensive, their general function remains the same.

Author's Note

You may have noticed that there is an uninstall directory alongside the install and logon directories. The scripts in this folder are run simply to remove the reference to the corresponding application compatibility script from either the usrlogn1.cmd or usrlogn2.cmd script. This doesn't actually uninstall the software from the server. You still need to use Add/Remove Programs for that. ◆

Installation and Execution Modes

Another application integration feature available with Terminal Server is the existence of two special modes of operation: execution mode and installation mode. By default, the Terminal Server operates in execution mode for all users, including administrators. As you may have guessed, the server is put into installation mode when an application is being installed on the server.

There are two ways in which to control the mode of operation. The first is to use the CHANGE USER command from a system prompt as follows:

CHANGE USER /INSTALL puts the session into install mode.

CHANGE USER /EXECUTE puts the session into execute mode.

The other option is to use the Add/Remove Programs applet in Control Panel. When adding or removing a program, the server automatically performs the switch between execute and install modes.

In Windows 2000 Terminal Services, the operating system itself doesn't allow you to install many applications unless the server has been placed into install mode. Figure 19.5 shows the message that you receive when you try to do this. This doesn't work for all applications, but many of the most popular commercial applications are caught by the operating system. This feature is not available in TSE 4.0.

Figure 19.5 *The TS 2000 warning message you see when attempting an installation while in execute mode.*

Installation Mode Behavior

When the server is placed into installation mode, it performs the following tasks during an application installation:

- All registry entries created under HKEY_CURRENT_USER *using the standard Windows APIs* are copied into this registry key:

  ```
  HKLM\Software\Microsoft\Windows NT\CurrentVersion\Terminal Server\
  ⇒Install\Software
  ```

- Any changes to INI files are written to the appropriate INI file in the %systemroot% directory.

- The times that the registry and files were last updated while in install mode are stored under this key:

  ```
  HKLM\Software\Microsoft\Windows NT\CurrentVersion\Terminal Server\Install\
  ⇒IniFile Times
  ```

Author's Note

The key point to remember is that the Terminal Server captures changes that are made to the registry or INI files only if they have been made using the standard Windows API functions. Registry changes made using REGEDT32 while Terminal Server is in install mode will not be captured and recorded under the Terminal Server *registry key.* ✦

Execute Mode Behavior

When the Terminal Server is running in execution mode, the following may occur:

- If an application attempts to read an entry from HKEY_CURRENT_USER that doesn't exist, Terminal Server checks to see if a copy of the key exists under this registry entry:

  ```
  HKLM\Software\Microsoft\Windows NT\CurrentVersion\Terminal Server\Install\
  ⇒Software
  ```

  If it does exist, this key and all subkeys are copied to the corresponding area location under HKEY_CURRENT_USER.

- If an application tries to read from an INI file in the %systemroot% directory, Terminal Server transparently redirects that request to look in the user's personal Windows directory located under his or her home drive (for example, W:\Windows). If the INI file doesn't exist in the user's directory but does exist in %systemroot%, Terminal Server copies it into the user's Windows directory.

- Whenever a user logs onto the server, Terminal Server compares the last update time of the registry keys in `Terminal Server\Install` and the INI files with the user's last synchronization time. The user's registry synch time is stored in the value `LastUserIniSyncTime` in this registry key:

  `HKCU\Software\Microsoft\CurrentVersion\Terminal Server`

The synch times for the INI files are stored in the file INIFILE.UPD, located in the user's personal Windows directory on his or her home drive.

If any entries are out of date, they're updated for the user. By default, any out-of-date registry keys are deleted before the new registry keys are loaded into the current user's registry. The changes in the INI files are either merged with the existing ones or completely replaced. The default is to replace them. I talk about modifying the default behavior for both registry and INI files in the section "Program Compatibility Flags." The previous version of the INI file is renamed with the .CTX extension.

Tip

You can force an update of all existing INI files by deleting the INIFILE.UPD file from the user's Windows directory. ✦

Exploiting the Installation Mode Behavior

Once you understand the behavior of a Terminal Server when operating in install mode, you can exploit this behavior to help preconfigure many applications with common settings that you want to have automatically picked up by the user the first time he or she runs the application. Install mode is not simply for performing the initial installation of the application. It can be used at any time to change the configuration of most 32-bit or 16-bit applications. For example, you could run a Microsoft Office application such as Word while in install mode to set any defaults that you want the users to have, such as turning off animation or modifying the default directory locations. This is an effective alternative to using the Office profile (.OPS) files.

The one caveat that is worth repeating is that changes are captured while in install mode only if the application is using standard Windows API calls to perform the registry/INI file updates. If an application directly manipulates an INI file through file system read and write operations, Terminal Server is not aware that the changes have occurred and will not update the last-modified date in the registry. This prevents the changes from being incorporated into an existing INI file in the user's home directory. Note that if the user doesn't already have the INI file, it would still be copied to his or her home directory, even if the last-update time had not been updated.

Program Compatibility Flags

Terminal Server provides the ability to modify the behavior of specific applications as well as the registry and INI file mappings that I discussed in the preceding section. This is done through the use of *program compatibility flags (PCFs)*. PCFs are a special set of registry values that tell Terminal Server what to do with a specific program, registry key, or INI file. These three registry keys are located under this key:

```
HKLM\Software\Microsoft\Windows NT\CurrentVersion\Terminal Server\
➥Compatibility
```

These are the specific keys:

- **Applications.** This key contains a list of subkeys corresponding to executable names, each containing specific values that dictate how the application should be handled when run. For example, the subkey EXCEL would contain options specific to EXCEL.EXE.

- **IniFiles.** This key contains a list of values, each corresponding to an INI filename in the %systemroot% folder. Each has an associated flag that determines how file replication should be handled. There are two entries by default—one for SYSTEM.INI and another for WIN.INI. The .INI extension is not included in the value name.

- **Registry entries.** This key contains a list of values corresponding to registry keys located under HKLM\SOFTWARE. The value of each entry determines how registry replication is handled while the Terminal Server is in execute mode. Three entries usually exist: Classes, Microsoft\Windows NT, and Microsoft\Windows\CurrentVersion\Explorer\Shell Folders.

Depending on the key, certain compatibility flags are available to use in modifying the entries' behavior. All PCFs are REG_DWORD hexadecimal entries. If multiple entries are set for a particular value, you need to sum the individual hex values to determine the actual hex number to enter. If you're uncomfortable with performing hexadecimal arithmetic, use the Calculator application to perform hex calculations in scientific mode.

IniFiles and *Registry* Entries Registry Keys

Table 19.2 lists the valid flags for the IniFiles and Registry Entries keys.

Table 19.2   INI and Registry Compatibility Flags

Flag	Valid for...	Description
0x00000004	INI files	Flags a 16-bit Windows application.
0x00000008	Registry keys	Flags a 32-bit Windows application.

Flag	Valid for...	Description
0x00000040	INI files and registry keys	Synchronizes values to system version. For INI files, this means that new entries from the system version of the INI file are merged with the user's version. Normally, the user's version is deleted and replaced with the system version.
		For registry entries, this flag means that new keys and values from the system registry are added, but existing keys and values are not deleted. The default is to delete any keys and values that are out of date with the system version.
0x00000080	INI files only	Don't substitute the user's Windows directory for the system directory. This means that the user's personal Windows directory is not substituted, and the %systemroot% directory is used instead.
0x00000100	Registry keys only	Disables registry mapping for the given key. This automatically includes all subkeys.

Multiple flags can be entered for a single value by summing them (in hex) to get the final flag value. The IniFiles folder on the Terminal Server contains the following two entries:

```
SYSTEM:REG_DWORD:0x44
WIN:REG_DWORD:0x44
```

As noted in Table 19.2, INI synchronization is on for the 16-bit files SYSTEM.INI and WIN.INI. Any changes made while you are in install mode will be merged with any existing information in the user's SYSTEM.INI or WIN.INI. All other INI files will be replaced.

Under the Registry Keys key is the following entry:

```
Microsoft\Windows NT:REG_DWORD:0x108
```

Referring again to Table 19.2, notice that registry mapping has been disabled for the 32-bit Windows NT key.

Author's Note

Typically, you won't need to modify any of these entries. However, if there's a particular registry key or INI file that you don't want users to have in their personal area (registry or Windows directory), you can exclude it from synchronization and then set it to read-only so that users can't modify the system version. ◆

Applications Registry Key

For a specific application, up to four registry values can be created that control its behavior while running on Terminal Server. Figure 19.6 shows the registry entries for the Microsoft Access application (MSACCESS.EXE). Notice that the .EXE extension is not included in the key name.

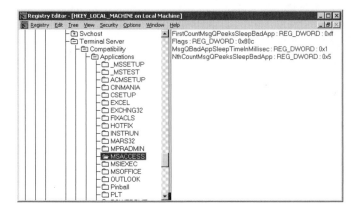

Figure 19.6   *Program compatibility flags for Microsoft Access.*

As the figure shows, there are four registry values for MSACCESS:

- FirstCountMsgQPeeksSleepBadApp
- MsgQBadAppSleepTimeInMillisec
- NthCountMsgQPeeksSleepBadApp
- Flags

The first three entries are used to tune an application to function optimally on Terminal Server. You shouldn't modify or set any of these values for an application unless you're experiencing a real performance issue. I'll talk more about these settings shortly.

The fourth entry is the Flags value. It contains a hex value that provides Terminal Server with information about the application and indicates whether any special actions are required, such as disabling registry mapping. Table 19.3 lists the entries for the Flags value. As with the INI and registry settings, multiple values are set simply by summing the hex values to come up with the new hex value. For example, if you want to flag that the entry is for both the 16-bit and 32-bit applications, you sum 0x04 and 0x08, resulting in 0x0c in hex.

Table 19.3   Valid Flag Settings for an Application

Flag	Description
0x00000001	DOS application.
0x00000002	OS/2 application.
0x00000004	Windows 16-bit application.
0x00000008	Windows 32-bit application.
0x00000010	Substitutes the username for the computer name. If the application requests the computer name using the GetComputerName API, Terminal Server returns the username instead. This setting is typically used with applications that equate the NetBIOS name for the machine with an individual user.
0x00000020	Returns the Terminal Server build number instead of the Windows build number. For Windows 2000, the build numbers are the same. On TSE 4.0, the Terminal Server component has a different build number than the OS.
0x00000040	This indicates that INI file or registry data should be synchronized with any new data, instead of the existing data being *replaced by* the new information.
0x00000080	For this application, don't substitute the user's personal Windows directory for the system directory. This means that the user's personal Windows directory is not substituted, and the %systemroot% directory is used instead when this application makes reference to an INI file.
0x00000100	Disables registry mapping for this application.
0x00000200	Enables per-object mapping for user and system global objects associated with this application.
0x00000400	Returns the %systemroot% directory to the application instead of the user's personal Windows directory. This overrides the server's default behavior when running in execute mode. This applies only to the specific application.
0x00000800	Limits the physical memory reported to the application. This flag is typically used when an application has problems running on a system with a large amount of physical memory. When specified, the default memory reported is 32MB. You can modify this value by including the PhysicalMemoryLimit value in the program compatibility key. This value should also be of type REG_DWORD.
0x00001000	Logs the creation of named objects by the specified application. This flag is used to assist in debugging an application that's not running properly on Terminal Server. Normally, when an application runs, objects are created within the user's name space by appending the session ID to the object name. This can cause certain applications that expect to find a fixed object name to fail. Using the

continues ▶

Table 19.3   continued

Flag	Description
	REGISTER command, you can tell the Windows Object Manager not to append the session ID to an object created by a specified DLL or EXE. Using this flag, you can generate a list of the objects created by an application, along with the associated DLL. From this, you can get a list of the DLLs that must be registered.
	For logging to take place, you must create a system environment variable called CITRIX_COMPAT_LOGPATH and assign it a valid directory where the log will be created. The logfile *<app name>*.log will be created in the specified location.
	This flag should be set only while debugging because it will degrade the application's performance.
	For more information on the REGISTER command, see Appendix A, "Terminal Server/MetaFrame Command Reference."
0x20000000	Indicates that the application should not be put to sleep when it polls the keyboard unsuccessfully. This option normally should not be set because it can cause significant performance degradation.

Notice in Figure 19.6 that the value for the `Flags` entry is `0x80c`. Consulting Table 19.3, this equates to the following:

- For both 16-bit and 32-bit applications (`0x008 + 0x004 = 0x00c`)
- Limits the physical memory reported (`0x800`)

This is easily validated by adding the results to get `0x80c`.

Now that you're familiar with the various flags available for an application, the next thing to look at is the settings used for tuning a "badly behaved" application.

A "bad" application can exhibit unusually high or low processor utilization. If an application is run on a Terminal Server and a corresponding key does not exist for it under the Compatibility\Applications registry, it will automatically be throttled by Terminal Server if it queries the message queue too often within a default time period. The result is an application that runs very slowly even though the system resource utilization (such as CPU and disk) is low. Software installation programs will commonly fall into this category. A common solution is to add a registry key corresponding to the application's executable name with values that correspond to the MSACCESS key. The descriptions for these registry values are as follows:

- FirstCountMsgQPeeksSleepBadApp. This represents the number of times the application can query the message queue before Terminal Server initially flags it as "bad." Lowering this value causes the application to be flagged more quickly, decreasing its processor utilization.

- MsgQBadAppSleepTimeInMillisec. Once Terminal Server has decided that an application is "bad," this is the number of milliseconds that the application must "sleep" before it can query the message queue again. Increasing this value forces the application to sleep longer.

- NthCountMsgQPeeksSleepBadApp. Once Terminal Server has flagged an application as "bad," this is the number of times the application can query the message queue before it is once again put to sleep. Typically, this value is less than the FirstCountMsgQPeeksSleepBadApp value.

Looking again at Figure 19.6 for the MSACCESS entry, the values for the three settings are as follows:

```
FirstCountMsgQPeeksSleepBadApp = 0xff (255 decimal)

MsgQBadAppSleepTimeInMillisec = 0x1 (1 decimal)

NthCountMsgQPeeksSleepBadApp = 0x5 (5 decimal)
```

So after 255 consecutive queries of the message queue, Access will be put to sleep for 1 millisecond, and thereafter for every 5 queries.

> **Tip**
>
> *These tuning values apply only to 16-bit or 32-bit Windows applications. If they're set for a DOS application, they're simply ignored. To tune a DOS application, you need to use the DOSKBD utility. This allows you to configure keyboard polling detection for the DOS application. For more information on DOSKBD, see Appendix A.* ◆

As mentioned earlier, you shouldn't create or modify any of these program compatibility flags unless you have an application that's behaving "badly." If the application is running unusually slowly, even though system utilization is low, then add an entry and assign values equal to those for the MSACCESS key. If an application exhibits unusually high processor utilization, I recommend performing the following steps to tune the application:

1. Launch PerfMon and monitor CPU utilization.

2. Start the offending application and record the baseline performance while running the application. Ideally, you should run it for 5–10 minutes.

3. Exit the application and create the corresponding entry or entries in the registry under the `Applications` key. You can either type the entries or save the `Setup` key and then add it back in with the name of your application. The default values for `Setup` are as follows:

    `FirstCountMsgQPeeksSleepBadApp = 0xf` (15 decimal)

    `MsgQBadAppSleepTimeInMillisec = 0x1` (1 decimal)

    `NthCountMsgQPeeksSleepBadApp = 0x5` (5 decimal)

    `Flags = 0xc` (16-bit and 32-bit)

4. Rerun the application and compare the new PerfMon results with the baseline.

5. Exit the application and change the application settings to something like this:

    `FirstCountMsgQPeeksSleepBadApp = 0xf` (15 decimal)

    `MsgQBadAppSleepTimeInMillisec = 0x64` (100 decimal)

    `NthCountMsgQPeeksSleepBadApp = 0x5` (5 decimal)

6. Run the application again and compare the reduction in processor utilization to the responsiveness of the application. You may want to compare this to adjustments in the `FirstCount` value to see if one provides a larger improvement over the other. Unfortunately, this is not an exact science, so it might take some time to develop the ideal tuning values for a particular application. You'll likely have to settle for some excess utilization to ensure that the program is responsive enough that users will be able to use it.

Luckily, additional tuning isn't usually required with most applications that run on Terminal Server.

Author's Note

Be careful with applications that are CPU-intensive. Many of these applications, even with the use of program compatibility flags, are simply poor candidates for a Terminal Server environment. Compatibility flags won't always rein in a poorly behaved application. ◆

Temporary Directories

The last application support feature that I'll look at is Terminal Server's handling of each individual user's temporary directory location. Normally, every user who logs onto a Windows 2000 or NT computer has a temporary directory defined with the environment variables TEMP and TMP, where temporary data can be stored that can be deleted when the user logs off.

The only difference on a Terminal Server is that multiple temporary directories exist at the same time and must be managed individually. The default configuration varies between TSE 4.0 and TS 2000. I'll begin by looking at TSE 4.0 because the same functionality is available in TS 2000.

TSE 4.0 Temporary Directories

The default temporary directory location for all users on TSE 4.0 is the %systemdrive%\Temp directory. If you open the system properties from Control Panel and then select the Environment tab, the TEMP and TMP values appear similar to those shown in Figure 19.7.

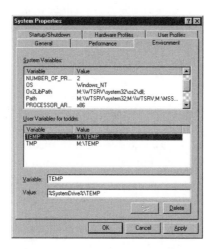

Figure 19.7   *Default temporary directory location settings on TSE 4.0.*

To give multiple simultaneous users access to the temporary directory, Terminal Server provides a feature known as *per-session temporary folders.* Every time a user logs on, Terminal Server creates a directory corresponding to the user's session number underneath the TEMP directory. The user's TMP and TEMP variables are then updated automatically to point to this location. If you open a command prompt and type **SET,** you see the modified values for these environment variables. For example, you might see this:

```
TEMP=M:\TEMP\1
TMP=M:\TEMP\1
```

The directory 1 corresponds to the current session number. If these were my temp directories and I did a QUSER from a command prompt, I would see something like this:

```
USERNAME            SESSIONNAME       ID  STATE   IDLE TIME  LOGON TIME
administrator       console            0  active        .    3/27/00 13:36
>toddm              ica-tcp#1          1  active        .    3/27/00 13:45
```

The permissions on the directory are set to allow access only by the specific user and SYSTEM. When the user logs off, Terminal Server automatically deletes the associated temporary directory.

Whenever you reference a user's temporary directory, be sure to use the TEMP or TMP environment variables. Never hardcode the complete path (M:\TEMP\1) because it's very likely that the next time the user logs on, he or she will have a different temp directory, such as M:\TEMP\7.

Author's Note

If a user session is disconnected or reset without being properly logged off, Terminal Server won't clean out the temporary directory. The next time a user logs on with the matching session ID, he or she will be pointed to this orphaned temporary directory. The file permissions will not have been reset, though, so the user won't have access to this temporary folder. Any attempt by an application to write to that location will fail with an access-denied message. ◆

The temporary directory-mapping feature can be disabled using the FLATTEMP command. However, I do *not* recommend doing this unless you have an alternative user-specific location where a user's temporary files can be stored. This should be somewhere local to the server and should not be located on a network drive. For more information on FLATTEMP, see Appendix A.

TS 2000 Temporary Directories

The default temporary directory location for all users on TS 2000 is the %userprofile%\Temp directory. From Control Panel, open the system properties. Select Advanced and then click the Environment Variables button to display the TEMP and TMP values set in the user variables (see Figure 19.8).

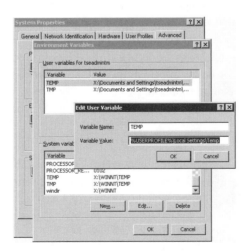

Figure 19.8 *Default temporary directory location settings on TS 2000.*

The one difference between TS 2000 and TSE 4.0 that you'll notice immediately is that no explicit user TEMP and TMP variables were listed for TSE 4.0.

Even though TS 2000 defaults to a different location for the temporary folders, the support for temporary folder remapping still exists and is enabled by default. As with TSE 4.0, every time a user logs on, Terminal Server creates a subdirectory under the listed temp folder path corresponding to the user's session ID number. If you open a command prompt and type SET, you see the full TEMP and TMP paths. If I were logged onto session 3, for example, these would be my environment variables:

```
TEMP=X:\DOCUME~1\TODDM\LOCALS~1\Temp\3

TMP=X:\DOCUME~1\TODDM\LOCALS~1\Temp\3
```

The short name (eight-character maximum) is used to ensure that DOS and Win16 applications can use the same environment variables.

Because the folder is created under the user's profile, access is available only to Administrators, SYSTEM, and the user. Upon logoff, the folder is automatically deleted (unless this option was changed in Terminal Services Configuration).

Since each user's temp directory is already located with his or her profile, it's possible to turn off the per-session mapping feature either using the FLATTEMP command or through Terminal Services Configuration. Take note that if this is turned off, the contents of the user's temporary directory are *not* deleted when he or she logs out, even if the corresponding option is enabled in Terminal Services Configuration.

As with TSE 4.0, when referencing the temporary directory for an application, use the TEMP or TMP environment variables whenever possible.

Application Integration Tools and Techniques

As an application integrator, you should have and understand the following common set of tools and techniques to assist in configuring applications to run properly within Terminal Server:

- Windows 2000/NT Server Resource Kit
- Scripting
- Registry and file security auditing
- Software packaging and deployment

The difficulties you encounter when attempting to install and run the application decide the extent to which you need to utilize these tools and techniques. The following sections provide more details.

Windows 2000/NT Server Resource Kit

I personally have found the resource kit to be an invaluable tool not only for application integration, but also for Terminal Server deployment and administration. Following are some of the available tools that you'll probably find useful:

- **SysDiff.** Allows you to create a snapshot file containing all the changes that were made as a result of a software installation. This can be valuable in software packaging and deployment.

- **SysPrep.** Designed to be used prior to creating a disk image of a Windows 2000 computer (including TS 2000) Terminal Server. This disk image can then be used to restore the server or quickly build additional servers that are exact replicas of the first. This tool is included with the Windows 2000 Server Resource Kit. Chapter 18, "Server Operations and Support," provides an example of using SysPrep to clone a TS 2000 server.

- **AppSec.** Allows you to restrict a user's access to a limited set of applications.

- **IfMember.** A simple tool that tests whether the currently logged-on user is a member of the specified group. This tool is commonly used in custom batch scripts run from UsrLogn1.cmd or UsrLogn2.cmd to control whether a certain script is run based on group membership.

- **Xcacls.** A more granular version of CACLS that allows you to set a number of individual permission attributes.

The most commonly used tools from an application standpoint are typically the IfMember function, Xcacls, and SysDiff.

Registry and File Monitoring

At some point during the installation of your applications, you may find it necessary to capture the changes that an application or its installation is making to either the registry or the file system.

One of the best tools I've found for capturing registry changes is REGMON. Developed by Mark Russinovich and Bryce Cogswell, this application allows you to monitor and record all access to the Windows registry. Figure 19.9 shows an example of NTREGMON. This information was gathered after clicking the My Documents icon and moving other icons around on the desktop.

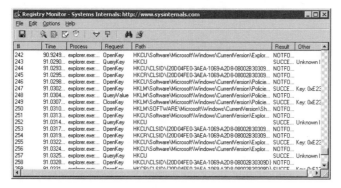

Figure 19.9   *A sample registry-information capture from REGMON.*

Author's Note

To find more information on REGMON, visit the System Internals Web site at `http://www.sysinternals.com.` ◆

As you might expect, the amount of information captured by REGMON can grow quite large very quickly. Fortunately, REGMON includes a number of filtering options that allow you to monitor only changes made to the registry for a specific application.

Author's Note

When monitoring the registry changes made during an application installation, you should wait until the first prompt appears in the install program before starting REGMON. You can then use a tool such as TList from the resource kit or HandleEx (also from SysInternals) to get the actual name of the executing process. Typically, when running an InstallShield installation, the executing name will not be SETUP.EXE. ◆

A utility almost identical to REGMON is also available from SysInternals for monitoring file system activity. This utility is called FILEMON. Figure 19.10 shows a sample capture from FILEMON.

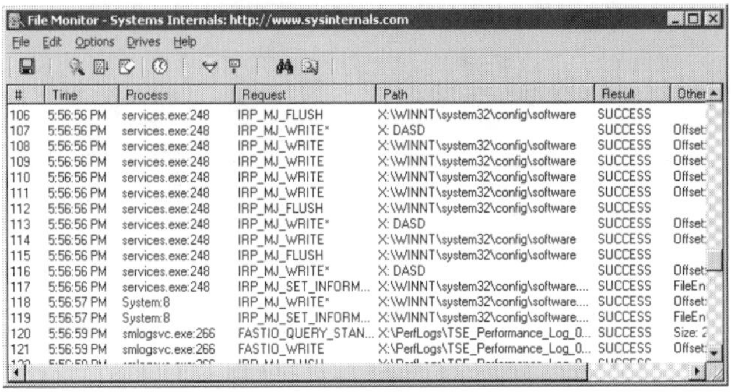

Figure 19.10   *A sample file-system information capture from FILEMON.*

Scripting

When developing scripts (application compatibility or otherwise) to assist in the implementation of an application, I prefer to use a more powerful and robust scripting language than the traditional Windows shell batch language.

A number of popular scripting languages are available, including VBScript and JavaScript, which are available as part of the Windows Script Host (WSH). WSH is included with Windows 2000 and can be downloaded for NT 4.0. Whatever scripting language you choose, it should support the following features:

- **Windows group membership testing.** This feature allows you to generate scripts that perform certain actions based on whether the user is a member of a specific group.

- **Registry and file manipulation.** You'll likely need to create scripts to perform certain functions on a registry value or a file.

- **Programming constructs such as IF...ENDIF and WHILE...LOOP.** These constructs provide flexibility in the scripts created and make it much easier to develop and maintain than the IF...ENDIF and GOTO constructs in the standard Windows shell batch language.

- **Relatively easy to understand and use.** Although all languages require at least basic programming experience to be used effectively, the scripting language should be as easy as possible to use. Two particular features lend themselves to ease of use:

  - **Interpreted instead of compiled.** Many people have difficulty understanding and maintaining scripts that require compiling in some way. Although they're slower to execute, interpreters are generally easy to use. Plain-text files fed into the interpreter usually mean that the source is readily available for updating or reviewing.

- **Loosely typed instead of strongly typed language.** Although they can cause problems when attempting to debug a script, loosely typed scripting languages are generally easier for the novice script writer to work with. Of course, the resulting code may not be the most elegant code written, but it usually works.

Author's Note

As I've mentioned a few times throughout this book, a scripting language that I use extensively is KiXtart, developed by Ruud Van Velsen of Microsoft Benelux. KiXtart is available in both the Windows 2000 and NT Server Resource Kits. The most current release of KiXtart is available on a number of Web sites, including `http://netnet.net/~swilson/kix/.` ◆

Registry and File Security Auditing

When configuring an application to run on Terminal Server, one of the most common problems you'll encounter will be due to the increased security of the Terminal Server in comparison to a regular Windows desktop. The fastest way to resolve these types of issues is to use Windows' file and security auditing to log a user's attempt to access the restricted resource (usually by writing to it). If an application works properly for an administrator but not for a regular user, you most likely have a permissions issue.

Typically, you would troubleshoot using security auditing as follows:

1. If you're unsure where the security problem lies (file or registry), begin with the file system. Most security-related issues are a result of the tighter file system security on Terminal Server (if you have opted to use the system security).

2. Enable auditing for a specific test user account. This helps reduce the amount of information going into the event log, making it easier to flag the security problem.

3. After auditing has been enabled, log on as the test user and perform a test security violation to ensure that auditing is working properly. For the file system, try writing a file to %systemroot%. For the registry, try updating a property on a service. In both cases, the user should receive an access-denied message, and a security entry should be added to the server's event log.

4. Run the application until you encounter the problem you're trying to resolve. Don't continue using or even exit the application. Immediately inspect the security log to see if any entries have been generated. If there are no entries, the security problem doesn't lie with the file system. Perform a similar security check on the registry.

When configuring auditing on the file system, begin by auditing the %systemroot% folder, all subfolders, and the application folder itself. If there is a security violation on the file system, this process will almost surely find it. You may also want to include any common Program Files folders from the system drive.

For registry auditing, look at the SOFTWARE key under HKEY_LOCAL_MACHINE. You'll receive an error if you attempt to cascade the security down from SOFTWARE, but the auditing will still be set.

After you have resolved your security issue, be sure to reset the auditing to the standards that have been designated for your Terminal Server environment.

> **Author's Note**
>
> For information on configuring file and registry security auditing, see Chapter 12, "Terminal Server Configuration and Tuning." ◆

Software Packaging and Deployment

As part of the process of installing and testing the application on Terminal Server, you should also be developing the process by which these applications will be installed across the other Terminal Servers in your environment. If your environment is small (fewer than five servers), you'll probably use some form of imaging to perform the initial rollout and then simply perform manual installations of programs as the need arises. For larger environments, or situations in which you want to ensure the highest level of consistency among your servers, you'll need to perform some form of application packaging so that it can be "pushed" out to the other Terminal Servers in your environment.

A number of installation-packaging options are available to assist in automating this process. Here are three examples:

- **SysDiff.** This is available as part of the Windows 2000/NT Server Resource Kit, allowing you to create installation packages for applications.

- **Citrix Installation Management Services (IMS).** IMS is an add-on tool from Citrix that enables you to package and deploy applications through the published application interface.

- **WinINSTALL LE.** Included as part of Windows 2000, this tool is typically used to create Microsoft Installer Packages (MSI files), which can then be used to perform standard installations or pushed out through Active Directory.

Although each product has its own specific options and features, each performs the same basic five steps in order to create and apply the application installation package:

1. Take a "snapshot" of the system prior to installing the application.

2. Install the desired application on the server.

3. Create the installation package based on the changes on the current system, in comparison to the system snapshot in step 1.

4. Modify the package as required.

5. Apply the package to another system to duplicate the installation of the application on the first system.

These forms of application packaging are well suited for a Terminal Server environment because of the consistency in hardware and software—particularly if you built your server environment using system cloning.

After the package has been created, it's simply a matter of deploying the package onto the desired Terminal Servers. The simplest method is to log onto each server and execute the package. Because it's fully automated, you can ensure consistency from one server to another. The only drawback is that you must actually log onto each server, which may take some time—particularly in a large or distributed Terminal Server environment.

The Application Integration Process

Before looking at a few examples of installing and configuring different applications on Terminal Server, I want to outline the general process that should be followed when performing application integration, particularly during a new Terminal Server implementation. Although there are no hard and fast rules, a general set of guidelines to follow will help minimize both the problems encountered and the time required to resolve them. I typically break the process of application integration into three fairly intuitive parts:

- Preparation
- Installation
- Deployment

The following sections describe each stage.

Preparation

All too often, insufficient time is taken during a Terminal Server deployment to properly plan for the software implementation. Usually this results from the desire to simply get started installing the applications on the Terminal Server. As with any project, taking the time to plan for the software installation can save you much more time down the road. During the preparation phase, I strive to achieve the following objectives:

1. Generate a complete list of all applications that will be installed on the Terminal Servers. This list should include everything from standard applications to helper applications such as Adobe Acrobat. From this will come the list of dependencies that exist between these applications. If a custom-built program launches Excel to display graph information, for example, a dependency exists between that custom app and Excel. All 16-bit and DOS applications, in addition to any 32-bit applications that are known to be processor or memory-intensive, need to be clearly flagged so that special attention can be paid to them during installation. If possible, 32-bit alternatives to any 16-bit or DOS applications should be investigated.

2. Determine the list of core components that are required on the system. This should be a subset of the application list in step 1, and will be based on the dependencies. For each of the applications, you should also list any additional software components that might be required in order to complete the installation. For example, Internet Explorer is typically modified using the IE Admin Kit prior to installing it on Terminal Server. A typical core component list might look similar to Table 19.4.

Table 19.4   *Sample Core Component List with Additional Tool/Component Requirements*

Component	Additional Components/Tools Required
Internet Explorer 5.0	IE Administrators Kit
Microsoft Data Access Components (MDAC)	None
Oracle SQLNet client	None
Microsoft SQL Server client	None
ODBC data source connections	Depends on MDAC being installed

These components are then prioritized. This makes up the list of initial applications that will be installed on the Terminal Server.

3. Establish the secondary list based on the remaining applications that must be installed on the system. Usually there are few or no dependencies between the applications on this list, so the installation order is really based on the availability of any application support staff who might be required to assist in the installation. In addition, you should list any tools or utilities that might be required in order to install a particular application. For example, to install Office 2000 on Terminal Server, you must have the Office 2000 Resource Kit. Table 19.5 shows a sample secondary application list with dependencies.

Table 19.5   *Sample Secondary Application List with Additional Tool/Component Requirements*

Component	Additional Components/Tools Required
Office 2000	Office 2000 Resource Kit. An ODBC data source must exist for an Access connection. IE 5.0 must be installed on the Terminal Server.
Hummingbird Exceed 6.2	None
Custom Visual Basic client/server application	Oracle SQLNet client
Custom PowerBuilder client/server application	Microsoft SQL Server client

4. Make sure that a simple testing process is in place to validate the applications after they've been installed on Terminal Server. Always take the time to test each application individually instead of waiting until they've all been installed. Although you probably won't be able to do extensive user testing at this stage, you should still plan to do some basic testing. For example, with IE5 you might have a list of Web sites to hit to test different types of content. You might have proxy settings that need to be validated or custom intranets that need to be accessible. For each application, you should do the following:

- Test with an administrative account.
- Test with a regular user's account.
- Test with multiple simultaneous user accounts.
- Correct any related issues.

At this point, you're looking for security-related issues that you can address before moving forward. See the earlier section "Registry and File Security Auditing" for suggestions on how to track down security-related application issues.

Installation

During the installation phase. Take the time to document the steps you're taking during the installation. Not only does this provide a repeatable method of installation, but it also helps you think through what you're doing, reinforcing that the installation steps are appropriate. During the installation of each application, I typically follow these four steps, described in the following sections:

1. Customize the application installation, if necessary.
2. Install the application.
3. Test.
4. Create an image or backup of the server when the applications are working properly.

Step 1: Customizing the Application Installation

When possible, I perform any required customization for the application. This includes developing an installation package or customized settings specific to Terminal Server. The IE admin kit is an example of such a tool. When given the option, disable or remove application features that are not required or that might cause performance issues on Terminal Server. Settings such as animation, sound, splash screens, and other optional graphics should all be disabled.

Step 2: Installing the Application

Now I finally perform the actual application installation. Remember the following when installing an application:

- Always make sure that you're in installation mode, either by running setup from Add/Remove Programs or by running CHANGE USER /INSTALL from a command prompt.
- Install applications from the server console. Although this isn't strictly necessary for all applications, it's a good practice to follow, particularly when you're installing MSI packages. A bug currently exists in Windows 2000 that prevents you from running an MSI install package

from a mapped network drive. Launching the installation from the UNC network path works fine, but using a mapped drive letter results in the Internal Error 2755 message similar to the one shown in Figure 19.11. In this example, the F: drive is mapped to a network share.

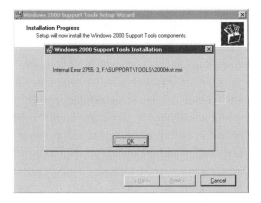

Figure 19.11   *You receive an error message when attempting to run an MSI install package from a mapped network drive.*

- When installing an application on a MetaFrame server, don't configure the application to have any dependencies on any locally mapped client drive (such as C:). Utilize the user's root drive or another network resource instead.

- If the installation doesn't require a reboot, make sure that you return the server to execute mode, either by closing the Add/Remove Programs applet or by executing CHANGE USER /EXECUTE from a command prompt.

Step 3: Testing the Application

When testing the application, I suggest that you run it first from the console to ensure that it will work properly for an administrator, and then log off and log back on from a client session to complete the testing. You should work through the test process you developed earlier, testing first with an administrative account, again with a regular user account, and finally with multiple regular user accounts.

As I mentioned earlier, you should test each application immediately after installation. This way, you can catch most of the problems as you move forward instead of having to deal with multiple problems after all the applications have been installed. Realistically, you won't catch all the issues that might arise (true user testing is required for this), but you should be able to weed out many of the errors that are common to applications run for the first time on Terminal Server. See the later section "Common Application-Integration Issues" for details.

Step 4: Creating a Server Image

A worthwhile strategy to follow when installing applications on a Terminal Server is to create a snapshot of the system after the desired applications have been installed and are working properly. This serves two purposes. First, it allows you to create checkpoints that you can roll back to if you encounter problems further down the deployment path, without having to start from the beginning. Second, it provides a single reliable source that can be used to quickly create multiple servers with a consistent configuration. See the " Server Cloning" section in Chapter 18 for more information.

Common Application-Integration Issues

The following sections discuss some of the most common problems you might encounter while trying to get applications to run in the multiuser environment.

The Application Runs for an Administrator But Not for a Regular User
Typically, this is caused by a security issue with either the file system or the registry. Here are three things you should try:

- Some applications attempt to write certain information into the registry the first time they run, based on whether a certain registry key exists. You can try putting the server into install mode, running the application as an administrator, and then exiting and returning the server to execute mode. Try rerunning the application as a regular user.

- Failing that, use security auditing on the file system and registry to pinpoint the offending file, folder, or key. After it is found, you may need to alter the permissions in order for the application to run properly. If you do so, make sure that you assign only the minimal permissions required. Users shouldn't need full control of any object in order to use it. Resist the temptation to simply grant full control to everything for users. Although this might allow the application to run, it creates an unsecured and eventually unstable server.

Author's Note

I once installed a 16-bit application that insisted on writing a temporary file to the same directory as the application. After attempting to work through the issue with the vendor, I discovered that there was no way to change this behavior through any form of configuration file. This "functionality" was hard-coded into the application. The vendor had the 32-bit version of its application scheduled for release in a couple of months, and no updates to the 16-bit application were being made.

As a workaround to the problem, I created a batch script that was launched instead of directly launching the executable. This batch file placed a copy of the executable (about 1.2MB) into the user's %TEMP% directory and then launched it from there. This allowed the required temp file to be created with the executable and at the same time allowed multiple instances of the application to run. The executable and the temp file were automatically deleted along with the temporary directory when the user logged off.

Although this wasn't necessarily the ideal solution, it did allow the client to use the 16-bit application until the 32-bit version became available. ◆

- If this is a 16-bit application, it is possible that it wrote information directly to WIN.INI or SYSTEM.INI instead of using the proper Windows APIs. Check the date/time stamp on these files. If this is the case, you can force a refresh of these files by putting the server into install mode and then running SYSEDIT. Make a trivial change to both WIN.INI and SYSTEM.INI and save. Exit and change back to execute mode. The next time the user logs on, he or she should receive the refreshed INI files.

Only a Single Application Instance Will Run
Usually this is caused by one of two issues:

- The file or registry is not tightly secured, and the application is writing temporary information to a central location that prevents another instance of the program from starting.

- When first started, the application might be launching a common process that attaches to a specific port or named pipe, which then services all other instances of the application. Usually this occurs when you're running a client/server application that has a component that runs as a service. Additional instances of the application detect this common process by searching the object name space. If it's not found, it's assumed to not be running, and a new common process is started. When this process attempts to run, it finds that the port is already in use, so it fails. This problem arises because Terminal Server appends the session ID as a suffix to a created object's name. So the first user starts the common process, but it's assigned an object name that doesn't correspond to what other instances of the program are looking for.

This problem can be resolved by registering the executable or DLL responsible for creating that object as system global. When this is done, objects are created without the session prefix. Now applications launched in different user sessions will be able to "see" this common process.

To determine which executables or DLLs to register, you should enable object logging for the application using the program compatibility flags discussed earlier in this chapter. Launch a second instance of the program to see what objects are created before the application fails. The associated DLL and any dependent files may need to be registered.

Author's Note

The Microsoft SNA client (3.0 and 4.0) exhibits this problem. A good way to become familiar with object logging and registering objects globally is to install the SNA client without running the compatibility script (which registers the necessary files globally). Then execute the client to observe the errors, and look at the object to see what's being created. You can then compare this with the associated compatibility script to see what files are being registered and what files are registering objects in the log. ◆

The Application Works for a While and Then Crashes or Works Erratically
This might be the result of a sharing violation if you don't have your file system or registry locked down tightly. The application might be using a single location for storing temporary data that's eventually being stomped on by other users. Use REGMON and FILEMON to monitor the registry and the file that's active for the specific application. Be sure to filter only on that application. Look for entries being written to HKLM or the system or application partitions.

User Data Is Maintained in the Application's .INI File
Many 16-bit applications maintain data in an INI file located in the application's binary directory, and some try to maintain user information there as well. Typically this is information such as a working directory or a list of last-used files. Try the following:

- Relocate the INI file to %systemroot%, allowing the execution-mode feature of INI file replication to provide each user with his own copy of the file in his Windows directory.

- Enter generic user information and be sure to use the root drive for any user's working location.

The Application Expects a Hard-Coded Installation Path

This is usually a bigger problem with custom-built applications that assume they'll be installed in a fixed location, such as C:\ProgramA. It can also be a problem with certain commercially available applications. Many apps now default to installing in the Program Files folder on the system partition. Even though you have the option of selecting an alternative location, certain files might still be written to this default location. If the hard-coding requirement exists only for the installation program, you can try using the SUBST command to map C: to your actual application drive. Assuming that your application drive is Y:, you could do the following:

```
REM Make sure that C: is not mapped to anything else.
net use /d c:
subst c: /d
REM Now point it at the application drive.
subst c: y:\
```

This option may work if hard-coding exists in the application itself, although this usually gives rise to a conflict with ICA client-mapped drives. Typically, you'll need to solicit the assistance of the application developers to resolve this problem.

Author's Note

Don't be surprised if a software vendor simply tells you that they don't support their product on Terminal Server, particularly if it requires a change in their application to function properly.

You're much more likely to have success if you tell them which component of their application is causing a problem instead of simply saying, "I'm trying to get it to run on Terminal Server."

I once had an application that was hard-coded to install and run from the C: drive. When I contacted the vendor, I told them that our configuration didn't allow for any applications to be installed on the C: drive, that they had to be installed on an application drive. When they asked what operating system I was using, I said Windows NT 4.0 (this was a TSE 4.0 implementation). This was not really a lie, because the application would not have allowed me to install it on an alternative partition on a regular NT workstation either.

The vendor provided a fix a week later that allowed the application to be installed and run from an alternative location. The application then installed and worked perfectly on the Terminal Server. Would the vendor have been so cooperative if I had said I was trying to run the app on Terminal Server? ◆

Deployment

The final step required when installing an application is actually making it available to the end user—first for user testing and piloting, and then eventually for production deployment. As you know, there are two ways of doing this:

- As part of a full desktop (desktop replacement)
- As an individual application (application replacement)

Author's Note

Chapter 6, "Client Planning," provides a complete discussion of the deployment scenarios available through Terminal Server. ◆

Desktop Replacement

At this point, the only thing that remains to be done is to ensure that the application's shortcut is available to the user the next time he or she logs on. If the application will be accessible by all users, you can simply add it to the desired folder under All Users.

If you want this shortcut made available to only a certain set of users, you have a couple of options:

- You can add the shortcut to the All Users folder but restrict access to users who are members of a certain group. Unfortunately, all users will be able to list the contents of the All Users folder, so they'll see the shortcut but won't have permissions to execute it.

- You could programmatically add the icon to the user's profile through a simple application compatibility script. In pseudo-code, the script could execute the following:

```
if user is member of group X
    copy the shortcut to their personal start menu
else
    delete the shortcut from their personal start menu if it exists
endif
```

This would allow you to control access to the shortcut simply by adding them to or removing them from a security group.

Application Replacement

With the RDP client, the only option you have for application replacement is to configure an RDP client shortcut using the Client Connection Manager. Figure 19.12 shows an example of how you would configure the connection properties to access Microsoft Word 2000 on a Terminal Server using the RDP client.

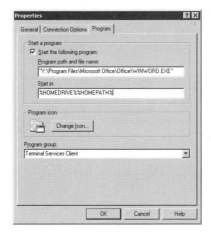

Figure 19.12   *Properties for the Word 2000 RDP application shortcut.*

For more information on the RDP Client Connection Manager, see Chapter 6, "Client Planning," and Chapter 2, "Microsoft Windows Terminal Server."

MetaFrame Published Applications

The steps involved in publishing an application are straightforward. Published applications are created and modified using the Published Application Manager, located under MetaFrame Tools on the Start menu. After it's started, it lists all published applications currently available in the server farm (or domain, if you're not a part of a server farm), as shown in Figure 19.13. If you have multiple Citrix servers in your environment, you can also view published applications on a server-by-server basis. This is done by choosing View, Select Citrix Server from the menu. If you have the Load Balancing option pack installed on two or more Citrix servers, you can configure a published application to be load-balanced across these servers.

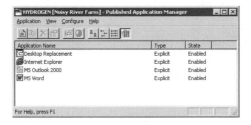

Figure 19.13   *Citrix Published Application Manager.*

I'll demonstrate the creation of a published application in a server farm using Microsoft Outlook as an example. My farm name is Noisy River Farm, and my application drive is Y:\. The published application is created as follows:

1. Select the Application, New menu item to start the Published Application Wizard. The first dialog box prompts you for a descriptive name for the application. This is the name that will appear in the published application list. I'll enter MS Outlook 2000. You can also enter a description if you want.

2. The next dialog box asks you to define the application type. The two options are Explicit and Anonymous. Choose Explicit if you want to force the user to enter a valid Windows user ID and password before being able to run the application. Anonymous requires no ID or password and automatically logs the user on using one of the available anonymous accounts. When publishing an application to a server farm, always select Explicit. Program Neighborhood takes care of the necessary authentication.

3. In the third dialog box, which is shown in Figure 19.14, you enter the command line and working directory for the application. You can use the Browse button to search for the executable if you don't know the specific command line. My Outlook executable is located in Y:\Program Files\Microsoft Office\Office\OUTLOOK.EXE.

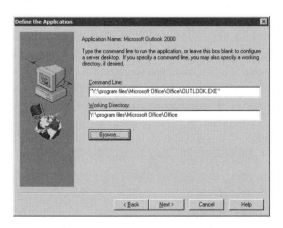

Figure 19.14 *Defining the command line and working directory for the published application.*

4. Next you specify the window properties for the application. You have the option of showing or hiding the window's title bar, as well as forcing the application to maximize at startup. Typically, I select both options. When the application is being run in a seamless window on the client, these settings are ignored. Click Next to continue.

5. In the next dialog box, shown in Figure 19.15, you set the Program Neighborhood options. These settings are applied when a client running Program Neighborhood connects to this application. Normally I disable both video and sound. The Minimum Requirement option allows you to specify what a client *must* have to see this application in the PN. For example, if you want to ensure that only clients with high encryption can run this application, you could select RC5(128) as the encryption type and click the associated Minimum Requirement check box. The Window Size option is ignored if the user is running the application in seamless mode.

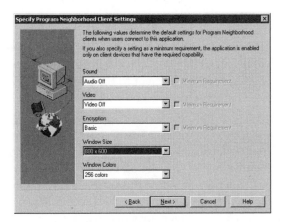

Figure 19.15   *Program Neighborhood client settings for the application.*

6. In the next dialog box, specify where the application icon will appear for a Program Neighborhood client. You can specify that the icon will appear on the Start menu and/or the desktop. You can also specify a subfolder under which the icon will reside within Program Neighborhood. For example, if I entered \Office 2000 as the neighborhood folder, when a client ran PN, the Office folder would appear as shown in Figure 19.16.

This was created by specifying "\Office
2000" for the PN subfolder when configuring the Outlook 2000 published application.

Figure 19.16   *Subfolders in Program Neighborhood.*

7. If your application has been published as Explicit, the next dialog box
   prompts you to select the domain from which to retrieve user and
   group information. Security on a published application in a server farm
   must be set through domain groups. It can't be based on local security
   groups. After you select the appropriate domain, the groups and users
   are listed in the Available list on the left side of the dialog box. Select
   the desired groups and add them to the configured list. In this example,
   I'll select my domain Outlook group NOISYRIVER\TSE_App_
   Outlook. When you're finished, click Next.

8. After access to the application has been defined (if necessary), you can
   publish this application on additional servers in addition to the current
   one (see Figure 19.17). This dialog box looks very similar to the previous one and functions in much the same way. To publish an application
   on multiple servers, you must have the Load Balancing option pack
   installed on each of the machines that will publish the application. The
   desired application must also be installed on these servers.

Tip

*All the servers that are publishing this application may not have the path and file-
name for the application in the same location. To update the file and working
directory information on a remote server, highlight that server in the Configured
column and click the Edit Configuration button. This brings up a dialog box with
Command Line and Working Directory fields containing the initial information
you entered for the published application. You can make any changes here for the
specific server. You don't have the option of browsing for the file from this dialog
box. You must know the explicit path of the command line and working directory
if you need to make a change.* ◆

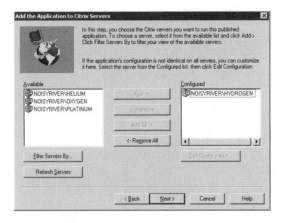

Figure 19.17   *Selecting the MetaFrame servers to publish the application.*

9. After you have selected all the servers that will publish this application and made any necessary configuration changes, the final dialog box just notifies you that the publication was successful. After you click Finish, the new application that has just been published appears in the main Application Configuration window.

You should now log onto Program Neighborhood as a client that belongs to a group with access to your published application to ensure that it's visible in PN. You can then test to make sure that the application is working properly. Figure 19.18 shows the published Microsoft Outlook application in Program Neighborhood.

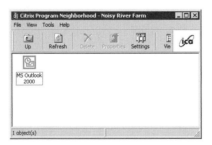

Figure 19.18   *Program Neighborhood with the published Microsoft Outlook.*

Application Installation Examples

To finish this chapter, I'll walk through the installation of a few applications on Terminal Server. The installation is for a fictitious client who requires the following applications to be installed:

- Microsoft Office 2000
- Internet Explorer 5.01
- Adobe Acrobat 3.01
- A custom Visual Basic application accessing a Microsoft SQL Server via ODBC
- Symantec Norton AntiVirus 2000
- Hummingbird Exceed 6.2

I will perform the installation on both a Windows 2000 Advanced Server running Terminal Services and Citrix MetaFrame 1.8 and a Windows NT 4.0 Terminal Server (SP5) with Citrix MetaFrame 1.8 (SP1). The server drives have been remapped to X: for the system, Y: for applications, and Z: for the CD-ROM.

Full user restrictions have been implemented on the server, and it has been configured and tuned as suggested in Chapter 12.

Author's Note

Unless otherwise stated, the application installation steps are identical for both TS 2000 and TSE 4.0.

Although I've selected these applications as examples of installation on Terminal Server, please don't take this as an endorsement or recommendation as to products you should select to run in your Terminal Server environment. Most of the competing products of those listed also run on Terminal Server. For example, although I have chosen to install Norton AntiVirus, I could just as easily have selected McAfee's or Trend Micro's products.

The actual product list was based on a question from a colleague who wanted more information on how to install these particular applications. ◆

Installation Order

The first step is to identify the core components for the application installation and then establish an installation order so that I have a checklist to follow. I find that this helps in creating a timeline for when certain applications can expect to be installed on the server.

Based on the list just shown, I have created the installation checklist shown in Table 19.6. I've also noted whether the component needs to be installed on TS 2000, TSE 4.0, or both. TS 2000 ships with many of the most current core Microsoft tools, so they don't need to be updated.

Table 19.6   Application Installation Order

Application	TS 2000 or TSE 4.0?
Microsoft Data Access Components (MDAC) 2.5	Only required on TSE 4.0. MDAC 2.5 is installed by Windows 2000.
ODBC Connection Configuration	Both
Internet Explorer 5.01	Only required on TSE 4.0. Windows 2000 ships with IE 5.01.
Norton Anti-Virus 2000	Both
Adobe Acrobat 3.01	Both
Microsoft Office 2000	Both
Hummingbird Exceed 6.2	Both
Custom VB Application	Both

MDAC 2.5

Windows 2000 ships with MDAC 2.5, so you don't need to install this component on a TS 2000 server. The installation files can be retrieved from the Microsoft Web site at http://www.microsoft.com/data/default.htm.

Additional Components

No additional components are required.

Installation Steps (TSE 4.0 Only)

There is nothing tricky about the MDAC installation. Simply place the server into installation mode (CHANGE USER /INSTALL) and run the downloaded file. This is typically called MDAC_25.EXE.

When the installation is complete, don't let the MDAC installation reboot the server. Perform the post-installation steps in the following section prior to restarting the server.

Post-Installation Steps (TSE 4.0)

After the MDAC installation is complete, you can run the application-compatibility script for ODBC. This script simply updates the trace log location to point to a user's home directory. Normally trace logs are used only when you're troubleshooting an application issue. After the ACS has run, return the server to execute mode and then reboot.

ODBC Connection Configuration

The custom Visual Basic application requires an ODBC data source definition. Even though the VB application won't be installed until later, the data source can be created and tested now that the MDAC has been installed.

Additional Components

No additional components are required.

Installation Steps (TSE 4.0 and TS 2000)

Whenever you're creating an ODBC data source name (DSN), you should always put the server into installation mode (CHANGE USER /INSTALL). This ensures that users will pick up any DSNs you create. I suggest that you always create system DSNs. Per-user DSNs are not normally required on a Terminal Server. Figure 19.19 shows the first dialog box displayed when creating a new DSN.

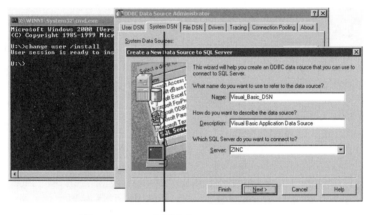

When setting up ODBC data sources to
be accessed by users, use system DSNs.

Figure 19.19   *ODBC DSN creation dialog box.*

Once the DSN has been created, simply switch the server back to execute mode (CHANGE USER /EXECUTE).

Post-Installation Steps (TSE 4.0 and TS 2000)

No further configuration is required.

Internet Explorer 5.01

Internet Explorer 5.01 ships as part of Windows 2000, so you don't need to worry about installing it on your TS 2000 server. You can perform some additional configuration and environment lockdown, however, as I discuss shortly. IE 5.01 will install on TSE 4.0.

> **Warning**
>
> *The active desktop component is not supported on TSE 4.0 and should not be installed because it can cause the system to fail.* ◆

Additional Components

Although it's not required, I highly recommend that you consider using the IE 5 Administrators Kit (IEAK) to customize your installation, including setting default policies and restrictions that will be applied to everyone who uses the browser. The IE Admin Kit is available from the Microsoft Web site at `http://www.microsoft.com/windows/ieak`.

The IEAK is really broken down into two main components. The first handles the configuration of the features of IE, such as any additional components that might be installed, and customization features such as the title bar text, the proxy server, or trusted zone settings. The second component involves configuring the policies and restrictions that will be applied by default as part of Internet Explorer. All of the policies and restrictions that are displayed in the IEAK Wizard are contained in policy template files (.ADM) that are located in the Policies folder under the IEAK installation directory. These template files can also be imported and used with the System Policy Editor to configure standard NT 4.0 system policies. These template files are used only with NT 4.0, not with Windows 2000. Windows 2000 includes group policies within the Active Directory that are specific to IE 5. I discuss policy configuration in the post-installation portion of the installation. For a complete discussion of system and group policies, see Chapter 16, "Group and System Policy Configuration."

If you plan to use the IEAK, consider the following comments and suggestions:

- *Do not* run the IEAK on a Terminal Server. You should run it from a desktop computer and then use the resulting custom installation set to install on Terminal Server.
- When selecting the components to download, determine those that you plan to install on Terminal Server and those you don't need. I recommend that you concentrate only on the core components that are required in order to run IE5. Typically, I select the following components to install:
  - Internet Explorer 5 Web browser
  - Internet Explorer help
  - Internet Explorer core fonts
  - Dynamic HTML data binding
  - Visual Basic scripting support
  - Additional Web fonts

I *don't* recommend installing NetMeeting on a Terminal Server.

- Selecting the hands-free installation will generate an IE5 installation program that automatically reboots the server when finished. You might want to select the interactive install so that you can control when the server is restarted.

- *Do not* include the Windows Update option on the Tools menu.

- *Do not* integrate the Windows Desktop Update into your installation package.

- Don't include channels as part of the installation. In the Channels dialog box, you should select the Delete Existing Channels option.

- Before configuring the system policy and restriction settings, take the time to consider exactly what you want to allow users to access and what you want to deny them. Any restrictions that you set here will apply to all users who run the custom IE5, including administrators. The easiest way I've found to deal with this issue is to configure the restrictions in the IEAK that should be common to all users and then use the policy template files to apply any additional security permissions along with the other policies on the Terminal Server. I find this easier to manage than auto-configuration URLs because only one instance of the browser is being installed and the policy files exist in a single location for all Terminal Server users. Table 19.7 shows the cross-reference between the policies and restrictions listed in the Wizard and the corresponding template files.

Table 19.7   *System Policies and Restrictions Cross-Referenced with Template Files*

Wizard Name	Template Filename (.ADM)
Control Management	AXAA.ADM
Microsoft NetMeeting	CONF.ADM
Corporate Settings	INETCORP.ADM
Corporate Restrictions	INETRES.ADM
Internet Settings	INETSET.ADM
Identity Manager	OE.ADM
Web Desktop	SP1SHELL.ADM
Offline Pages	SUBS.ADM
Microsoft Windows Media Player	WMP.ADM

- One potential "gotcha" is located under Corporate Settings/Temporary Internet Files (Machine): the setting Disable Roaming Cache. You should not enable this option, because it will disable per-user IE cache settings and configure all users to share a single cache location located by default under %systemroot%. In a restricted Terminal Server environment, this will cause cache write attempts by a regular user to fail.

Tip

If you haven't already done so, take a few minutes to review Chapter 16 so that you have a clear understanding of how policies are managed in both the NT and Windows 2000 environments. ✦

Installation Steps (TSE 4.0 Only)

The actual installation of IE5 is straightforward, particularly if you've created your own installation files using IEAK. To install IE on TSE 4.0, simply do the following:

- Place the server into install mode (CHANGE USER /INSTALL) and start the IE installation by running IE5SETUP.EXE.

- When the installation has finished, reboot the server to complete the installation.

Post-Installation Steps (TSE 4.0 and TS 2000)

Once the server has finished rebooting (for TSE 4.0), you have some final post-installation configuration steps to perform:

1. Make sure that there are no unnecessary dependencies on the Protected Storage service. This is usually not the case on Windows 2000, but on TS 4.0 there may be a problem. To determine this, simply open a command prompt and issue this command:

   ```
   net stop "protected storage"
   ```

   If any other services are configured to be dependent on Protected Storage, you'll receive a message asking whether they should be stopped. If you receive this request, record the names of these services and then cancel by saying No. If you have any dependencies such as the Terminal Server or ICA Browser service, you need to edit these dependencies, or they'll prevent you from being able to log on if the Protected Storage service ever fails to start. To remove these dependencies, you need to find the appropriate registry key for the service under this key:

   ```
   HKLM\SYSTEM\CurrentControlSet\Services
   ```

Edit the `DependOnService` value to remove *only* the `ProtectedStorage` text. *Do not* remove any other dependencies.

The Protected Storage service is intended to provide additional protection for sensitive data against unauthorized users, processes, or services. Applications that use the Microsoft CryptoAPI require the Protected Storage service.

2. The next step in the IE post-installation configuration is to simply implement any IE policies you want. On Windows 2000, this is done through group policies using Active Directory Users and Computers, and on NT 4.0 this is done using the System Policy Editor. Figure 19.20 shows some of the IE group policy settings in Windows 2000. For complete information on how to configure policies for both TSE 4.0 and TS 2000, see Chapter 16.

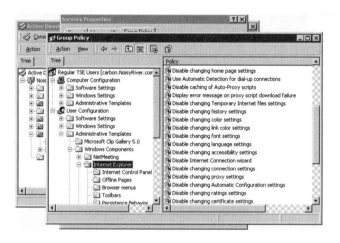

Figure 19.20   *IE settings in group policies.*

Norton AntiVirus 2000 6.0

Unfortunately, a component that has become almost mandatory on every computer is some form of antivirus software. Attempting to run a system without some form of protection is almost a certain invitation for trouble. Although Terminal Server is no exception, the much more restrictive nature of the environment and the fact that few users with full administrative privileges will be running applications on the server (at least in an ideal world) means that it's less likely to become infected. This doesn't mean that a user's Word documents might not become infected, however, because they'll be stored on a separate file server that may or may not have its own virus protection in place.

In this example I've selected the Norton AntiVirus (NAV) 2000 (version 6.0) software, not because it's superior to other competitive products, but simply because it provides a nice demonstration of some of the configuration changes you can make to an application after it has been installed. Many antivirus software packages are available, and most of them function fairly well in a Terminal Server environment.

Additional Components
No additional components are required.

Installation Steps (TSE 4.0 and TS 2000)
NAV is installed simply by placing the server into install mode (CHANGE USER /INSTALL) and running SETUP.EXE. When prompted, deselect the options Perform Live Update After Installation and Scan For Viruses After Installation. Both of these tasks will be performed manually during the post-installation steps.

After NAV has finished installing, it doesn't require a system reboot, so remember to place the server back into execute mode (CHANGE USER /EXECUTE).

Post-Installation Steps (TSE 4.0 and TS 2000)
The first thing you need to do is secure the NAV configuration features so that regular users won't be able to disable auto-protect or change any of the other settings. This is configured as follows:

1. Launch NAV 2000 and select Options from the toolbar. Then select the General option and click the Enable Password Protection check box. Enter a "strong" password that won't be guessed easily (see Figure 19.21).

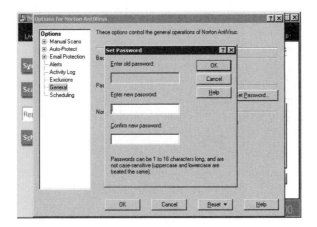

Figure 19.21   *Password-protecting NAV 2000.*

2. Click the Auto-Protect option in the left tree view and deselect the option Show the Auto-Protect Icon in the Tray. This removes the temptation for the user to launch the application to see what it is.

3. Next you need to update the file system security permissions on the executable that launches the Norton AntiVirus System Status application. The executable is called Nmain.exe and is usually located under this path:

    %systemdrive%\Program Files\Shared Files\SymantecShared

    You should update the permissions and remove the local user's group completely. You may need to break the file's inheritance with its parent. The users don't need access to this file in order to have NAV protection.

4. Move the Norton AntiVirus Start menu folder to a location accessible only by administrators and then update its permissions to include only SYSTEM and local administrators. This will prevent curious users from seeing what options are available for the application.

5. Now that NAV has been secured, the next step is to perform the other general configuration. Under the Activity Log option, change the log filename and path to point to a location on the server where you want to maintain virus logs. The log should be kept local to improve performance. I suggest creating a log folder under the NAV application installation directory.

6. Under the Auto-Protect option, select Program Files and Documents Only for the file types you want to scan. This will help reduce the amount of unnecessary scanning by NAV.

7. On the Alerts tab, deselect both Sound on Audible Alert and Alert Me on Startup If My Virus Definitions Are Out of Date.

8. On the General tab, disable the Display the Logo Screen... option. This turns off the large splash screen that typically launches when you start the program.

9. You might want to configure the LiveUpdate option so that virus definition files remain current. Although I typically don't advise automating software updates on Terminal Server, this can be a valuable feature for virus protection. If possible, you should try to schedule this during off-peak hours so as not to affect users.

Adobe Acrobat Reader 3.01

The Acrobat Reader has become a very popular Internet tool as more and more people start to deliver their documentation in this format. The following sections provide details on the setup of Acrobat Reader for this example.

Additional Components

No additional components are required.

Installation Steps (TSE 4.0 and TS 2000)

To install Acrobat Reader 3.01, simply place the server into install mode (CHANGE USER /INSTALL) and then run SETUP.EXE. After the installation finishes, remember to return to execute mode (CHANGE USER /EXECUTE).

Post-Installation Steps (TSE 4.0 and TS 2000)

No further configuration is required.

Microsoft Office 2000

The latest release of Microsoft's Office productivity suite works very well under Terminal Server, but it requires some additional work up front in order to install.

Additional Components

To install Microsoft Office 2000 on Terminal Server, you must download the Microsoft Office 2000 Resource Kit (ORK 2000), which can be found at this address:

```
http://www.microsoft.com/office/ork
```

ORK 2000 contains three components that you need in order to install Office 2000 (O2K):

- **Custom Installation Wizard.** This allows you to customize the O2K installation, specifying which components will be installed and which won't. Because users are running in a restricted environment on Terminal Server, you can't use the Install on First Use option. If users may need a component of O2K, you must install it up front. This tool creates an MST file to transform the standard Office installation.

- **Microsoft Installer Transformation File for Terminal Server.** This .MST file is required in order to transform the default .MSI installation file for O2K so that you can install it on Terminal Server. O2K won't install on Terminal Server without it.

- **The stationary Office Assistant.** O2K requires that you have at least one Office Assistant installed. Otherwise, the user will receive an error message the first time he or she runs any Office application. Normally you don't want to install any Office Assistants on Terminal Server because of the high animation and extra processing requirements. The stationary Office Assistant works well on Terminal Server, since it has no animated components.

- **An updated Policy Editor and policy templates for all Office 2000 products.** Just as with other policy templates, you can load these templates into the Policy Editor and restrict certain features in the applications to prevent users from changing them. This version of Policy Editor also ships with Windows 2000 (for NT 4.0 support). It includes some new features, such as allowing the use of environment variables for most of the field entries. It also reads Windows 2000 Group Policy .ADM files. All of the Office 2000 policy templates are automatically installed into the INF directory under %systemroot%. These template files *are* compatible with Windows 2000 group policy.

Tip

Don't install the Office 2000 Resource Kit on Terminal Server. Instead, install it on your local desktop. From there, you can perform the necessary configuration, including creating any custom transformation files for your installation. ✦

If you decide to use the Custom Installation Wizard to create your own transformation file to use when installing O2K on Terminal Server, you must do the following in order for it to work properly:

- When prompted to provide an MSI file to open, specify the DATA1.MSI file located on the Office 2000 CD. The settings are read from this file to build the list of available options.

- When prompted to open an MST file, you must specify the TERMSRV.MST file provided with ORK 2000. This file contains special settings that allow O2K to be installed on Terminal Server. If you build your own custom MST without loading these settings, it won't work on Terminal Server. You have the option of saving the changes to a different file on the next screen.

- Select a different file to save your changes to. Don't modify the TERMSRV.MST file. This is not a strict requirement but more of a suggestion, since you want to be able to switch back to a standard transform if yours doesn't work for some reason. The remainder of the wizard simply asks you to select the features you want to customize.

After you have the desired MST file, you're ready to install Office 2000 on Terminal Server.

Two of the components that typically caused issues on Terminal Server in previous versions of Microsoft Office are disabled by default in the TERMSRV.MST transformation file for Office 2000. The Find Fast tool and the System Information Tool are both not installed as part of Office. Find Fast is known to cause performance issues on Terminal Server; SysInfo allowed users to view information about the Terminal Server as well as easily gain access to a command prompt. ◆

Installation Steps (TSE 4.0 and TS 2000)

When installing Office 2000, I suggest that you log onto the console and have the O2K media available if possible. If not, ensure that you have the full UNC path to the installation files. As I mentioned earlier, there's currently an issue with Windows 2000 when you try to run a Microsoft Installer package from a mapped network drive. If you run it with a UNC path, however, it will work.

To install, you need the following:

* Your transformation file (MST), either the default TermSrv.MST or your own custom file

* The O2K installation media

Make sure that the server is in install mode (CHANGE USER /INSTALL), and execute the following command from a command prompt:

```
Z:\setup TRANSFORMS="Y:\<full path>\TermSrv.MST"
```

Z: is the CD-ROM or UNC path to where the install files are located, and Y: is the location where the desired MST file is located.

Post-Installation Steps (TSE 4.0 and TS 2000)

After the installation has completed, you have three tasks (possibly four) to perform before you're done:

* Add the stationary Office Assistant to your administrator's profile. On the machine where you installed ORK 2000, you'll find the STILLOGO.ACS file in the %systemroot%\Program Files\Microsoft Office\Office directory. Copy this file into a directory on your Terminal Server where users will have Read access (I suggest the directory where you installed Office). Create a folder called Actors in the following location under your profile:

%userprofile%\Application Data\Microsoft\Office

Copy the STILLOGO.ACS file to this location. Now you're ready to standardize the default settings for the users.

● Standardize the settings that you want users to have when they first run Office 2000. Although you can create an Office Profile file (.OPS) using the Profile Wizard in the ORK, an easier way is to put the server into install mode (CHANGE USER /INSTALL) and run each of the Office applications and configure the settings as desired. These settings will be picked up automatically by other Terminal Server users when they launch an Office application. One important task is to make sure that the Office Assistant will launch. Select Help, Show the Office Assistant. If you see a message asking whether you want to reinstall the assistant, select Yes. You won't be prompted again. The stationary Assistant should now load. When configuring the applications, select View, Options and then disable all sound and animation options. When you're finished, be sure to put the server back into execute mode (CHANGE USER /EXECUTE). Before the users can run the program, you need to create a simple compatibility script that will copy the STILLOGO.ACS file to their profile.

• Create a compatibility script to deliver the stationary Office Assistant to each user who doesn't already have it. Start by creating the script O2KUSR.CMD in the %systemroot%\Application Compatibility Scripts\Logon directory, with the following information:

```
@ECHO OFF
if exist "%USERPROFILE%\Application Data\Microsoft\Office\Actors\
➥stillogo.acs" goto done
xcopy "Y:\Program Files\Microsoft Office\stillogo.*" "%USERPROFILE%\
➥Application Data\Microsoft\Office\Actors" /s /q /i
:DONE
```

Of course, you should replace the path that I used in this example with the path to where you have O2K installed. If the script USRLOGN1.CMD doesn't exist in the %systemroot%\System32 directory, you can create it. Otherwise, simply add the following code to the end of the script:

```
Call O2Kusr.cmd
```

That's it. Now whenever someone logs onto the Terminal Server, if he doesn't have the stationary Office assistant, it will automatically be added to his profile. Log on as a regular user to ensure that this is working properly.

• The final step in configuring Office 2000 is to apply any desired policies. The policy template files, along with an updated System Policy Editor, are available in the ORK. If you're running on an NT 4.0 Terminal Server, you can copy the desired template files from the INF directory on your local computer to the INF directory on the Terminal

Server and add the policies to the System Policy Editor. Before you can use these template files in Windows 2000 group policies, however, you need to add them to the list of administrative templates. To do this, open a group policy for the Terminal Server environment (see Chapter 16 for more information), right-click Administrative Templates and select the desired Office 2000 templates to load. After they're loaded,

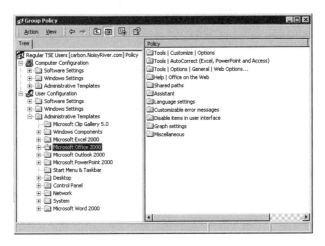

they'll appear in the group policy tree, as shown in Figure 19.22.

Figure 19.22 *Office 2000 administrative templates in Group Policy.*

Hummingbird Exceed 6.2

Hummingbird's Exceed is one of the most popular PC to X Windows connectivity products on the market. Version 6.2 now includes support for Terminal Server. Particular attention must be paid during the installation to ensure that the Terminal Server support is properly enabled for Exceed. The release notes on the Exceed 6.2 installation CD provide complete details on the Terminal Server support available in version 6.2.

Additional Components

No additional components are required.

Installation Steps (TSE 4.0 and TS 2000)

The installation of the Exceed software on Terminal Server is performed as follows:

1. Place the server into installation mode (CHANGE USER /INSTALL) and run SETUP from the CD.

2. Proceed through the installation until you're prompted to select the

type of installation to perform. Choose the Administrative install and
then click Next.

3. On the next screen, select Custom. This places the Exceed binaries into
   a single location where all users will share them, which is what you
   want on a Terminal Server.

4. Select the installation directory for the binaries; for example,
   y:\Program Files\Exceed.nt.

5. Select the components that you want to install, followed by the desired
   fonts on the next screen.

6. The final screen presents a summary of the options you've selected.
   Clicking Finish begins the installation of the software.

7. Depending on the options that you selected, you may need to reboot
   the server. If not, make sure that the server is placed back into execute
   mode (CHANGE USER /EXECUTE) after the installation is complete.

After the binaries have been installed, there is one more procedure. You
must install the user components, which "triggers" Exceed to recognize that
this is a Terminal Server installation, at which point it will automatically
configure Exceed users to run the product. To install the user components,
simply run SETUP from within the USERINS directory under the Exceed
installation directory. (The server *must* remain in execute mode (CHANGE
USER /EXECUTE) during this setup; otherwise, the Terminal Server support
for Exceed won't be configured properly.)

> **Tip**
>
> *On a TS 2000 server, if you try to launch a SETUP.EXE program when the server
> is not in installation mode, you'll receive a warning, and Terminal Server won't
> allow the installation to continue. You can circumvent this problem on a TS 2000
> server by placing it into installation mode (CHANGE USER /INSTALL) prior to
> launching SETUP; after the introduction dialog box appears, place the server back
> into execute mode (CHANGE USER /EXECUTE). The user components will
> continue to install properly after switching the server back into execute mode.* ◆

Follow these steps to complete the Exceed installation:

1. When prompted for the Exceed home directory, enter the path
   where the binaries have been installed; for example, y:\Program
   Files\Exceed.nt.

2. When the user home directory is requested, leave the default setting,
   which will create a directory called User under Exceed.nt. From here,
   the files will be copied for each user who runs Exceed.

3. The final screen simply gives you a summary. Click Finish to complete the copying of the necessary files.

4. Before the install finishes, you're prompted to select the appropriate keyboard file.

5. Next you're asked to provide a password for Xconfig. Normally you can leave this option blank.

6. The last screen asks whether you want a shortcut created on the desktop. After you make the desired selection, the installation finally completes.

At this point, the necessary Exceed files have been installed on the Terminal Server, but users won't yet be able to run the application. There are still some things that need to be configured during the post-installation phase before the installation is complete.

Post-Installation Steps (TSE 4.0 and TS 2000)
After the Exceed binaries and the initial user files have been installed, the following steps still need to be done before Exceed can be used by your users:

1. Decide whether all users or only a subset will access Exceed. By default, Exceed is automatically configured for every user who logs onto the Terminal Server, unless a local (or global) group exists called EXCEED_USERS. I recommend that you create the group locally on the server and then assign the appropriate domain groups as required, even if all users will be running Exceed.

2. After the appropriate access has been configured, modify the location where the per-user Exceed files will be stored. Otherwise, the default local will be used, which is the User directory under the Exceed.nt application directory. This per-user location is important for two reasons:

   • So that each user can maintain his or her own unique display number. This is used by Exceed to determine which X Windows display belongs to which user. If two users have the same display number assigned, all applications launched by either user show up in one user's X session.

   • So that users can maintain their own personal settings. The default location is updateable only by an administrator. Regular users receive an error message if they try to modify the information.

   The location for the per-user information is entered into the OVERRIDE.INI file in the Exceed.nt\USERINS directory. The single entry is added to the bottom of this file and should contain text similar to the following:

```
[*]
DestinationPath=w:\Exceed
```

The first entry ([*]) signals that this information applies to all Exceed users. The second line simply specifies the location of the destination path, which is where the per-user information is maintained. In this example, I used the W: drive, which happens to be my root drive. You can specify any location, even a UNC path, but remember that users must have write access to this location, and it shouldn't be shared by multiple users. Environment variables can't be used, but you can use the %<PERSONAL> Exceed macro, which is automatically expanded to the user's profile directory. I *don't* recommend using this, however, particularly with roaming profiles, since the total size of the per-user information is approximately 775KB. This data would be copied with the profile back and forth between the local server and the remote p rofile server every time a user logged on or off.

Custom Visual Basic Application

Typically, a Visual Basic application will be delivered as a prepackaged installation that you need to run while in install mode. Usually ODBC DSNs need to be validated, but unless the application is attempting to write data into its application directory (which I've seen some apps do), there should be no problems with getting a VB application to run.

Additional Components

Typically, no additional components are required, although the VB application install usually adds custom controls that are required by the application to run.

Installation Steps (TSE 4.0 and TS 2000)

Perform your standard installation. Put the server into install mode (CHANGE USER /INSTALL), install the application, and reset the server to execute mode (CHANGE USER /EXECUTE).

During the installation, you might want to monitor registry and file changes so that you are aware of exactly what's being changed. This can be helpful if there are issues with the application or if it introduces any system problems or conflicts.

Post-Installation Steps (TSE 4.0 and TS 2000)

If you haven't already done so, you might need to create an ODBC data source entry before the application will run.

Part IV

Appendixes

A Terminal Server/MetaFrame Command Reference

B Network Primer

C File and Folder Security Primer

D Terminal Server System and Application Volume Security Permissions

E Registry Security Primer

F Terminal Server Registry Security Permissions

Terminal Server/MetaFrame Command Reference

Tip

For almost all Terminal Server or MetaFrame commands, the /? parameter displays the usage for that command.

For each of the listed commands, I have included in parentheses the operating system version on which it is included, and whether MetaFrame is required to support the tool. Certain commands that are only available through MetaFrame with TSE 4.0 are included with TS 2000. ◆

ACLCHECK (TSE 4.0/MetaFrame)

ACLCHECK is a security and audit utility used to perform a file and registry audit. This command performs the same function as the QUERY ACL command. ACLCHECK is only available on a TSE 4.0/MetaFrame server. On a TS 2000/MetaFrame server you must use the QUERY ACL command.

ACLCHECK performs the following functions:

- Reports on any file access allowed by accounts other than Administrator, the Administrators group, or SYSTEM.

- Reports on any registry keys that have Write, Delete, Add, Link, Change Permissions, or Take Ownership permissions granted to accounts other than Administrator, the Administrators group, or SYSTEM.

- Checks the execute list created by the Application Security utility to ensure that no executables in the list are writable by non–Administrator accounts.

- Returns the system security level: Low, Medium, or High.

Usage:

```
aclcheck [path] [/registry_only ¦ /files_only [/ignore_execute]]
```

Option	Function
path	The name of the drive or directory path to audit. If no path or drive is given, ACLCHECK checks all drives unless /registry_only is specified.
/ignore_execute	ACLCHECK won't report on files with user Execute permissions.
/registry_only	Checks only the system registry.
/files_only	Checks only disk files.

ACLSET (TSE 4.0/MetaFrame)

> **Warning**
>
> *Unlike many commands,* ACLSET *without any parameters proceeds to secure all local drives on the MetaFrame server. The changes applied will prevent the regular user from accessing any applications on the Terminal Server.* ♦

The counterpart to the ACLCHECK command, ACLSET automatically secures all files on the local file system of the MetaFrame server, ensuring that there are no holes in the file security. ACLSET sets all file and directory permissions to grant Full Control to Administrators and SYSTEM groups only. The User group is granted no access.

This utility is only available with TSE 4.0/MetaFrame.

Usage:

```
aclset [drive ¦ directory]
```

Option	Function
None	ACLSET with no parameters secures the file system of all local hard drives.
drive	Secures all files and directories on the specified drive.
directory	Secures all files and subdirectories under the specified directory.

ALTADDR (TSE 4.0/MetaFrame)(TS 2000/MetaFrame)

The ALTADDR command is used to manage the alternate IP address on a MetaFrame server that's returned to a client accessing a published application located on the internal side of a firewall, which is performing network address translation (NAT). This is required because normally the master ICA browser returns the "true" IP address of a MetaFrame server to a client. But because the client is located on the external interface of the firewall, and because NAT is being performed, the client is unable to connect if it's given the "true" IP address of the MetaFrame server. Instead it must receive the external IP address of the MetaFrame server. ALTADDR allows you to define the external address of the MetaFrame server that's then returned by the master ICA browser if requested by the ICA client. The client must be configured to request the alternate address in order to receive it. See Chapter 15, "Web Computing with MetaFrame," for a complete discussion on accessing a MetaFrame server through a firewall.

Usage:

```
altaddr [Common Options] [[/set AlternateAddress]
altaddr [Common Options] [/delete [AdapterAddress]]
altaddr [Common Options] [AdapterAddress AlternateAddress]
```

Option	Function
Common Options	[/V] For verbose display mode
	[/?] Displays the usage for ALTADDR
	[/SERVER:Name] Applies the configuration to the specified server instead of the current server.
/set	Sets the alternate TCP/IP address specified.
/delete	Deletes all alternate addresses on the server unless a specific adapter address is given.
AlternateAddress	The alternate IP address to set or delete.
AdapterAddress	Assigns the alternate address to the adapter specified by this IP address.

APP (TSE 4.0/MetaFrame)(TS 2000/MetaFrame)

APP is a scripting tool aid for application integrators to assist them in getting applications to run on MetaFrame. It's often used to improve application security by allowing you to perform specific actions before and after the execution of an application.

Tip

APP *provides only limited functionality. Very often I use* APP *to control calling other scripts written using languages such as KiXtart, which provide more robust functionality such as registry updates. After the application terminates, I can use* APP *to call other scripts to perform additional cleanup.* ◆

Usage:

```
app scriptfile
```

Option	Function
`scriptfile`	The name of the script file containing the APP commands. The commands are listed in the following table. If `scriptfile` is omitted, APP terminates with an error. The script file *must* reside in %systemroot%\Scripts.

APP Command	Description
`copy source target`	Copies files from `source` to `target`. Wildcards (* or ?) are supported.
`delete file`	Deletes the specified file if permissions allow. Wildcards are supported.
`deleteall directory`	Deletes all files in the specified directory. Wildcards are supported.
`path file`	Sets `<file>` to be executed by the `execute` command.
`workdir directory`	Sets the working directory for the `execute` command.
`execute`	Executes the file specified by the path command. The working directory is set with the workdir command.

For example, the following commands will execute Notepad, setting the working directory to u:\temp:

```
path c:\wtsrv\notepad.exe
workdir u:\temp
execute
```

You can execute multiple executables in a single script, like this:

```
path x:\wtsrv\foo.exe
workdir u:\temp
execute
path y:\winword\boo.exe
workdir u:\temp
execute
```

This executes foo.exe, waits until it completes, and then executes boo.exe. It won't spawn the foo.exe process and then continue.

APPSEC (TSE 4.0)(TS 2000)

Running this utility launches the GUI application shown in Figure A.1. Although the interface for the application is slightly different between the 4.0 and 2000 versions, the utility performs the same function. When the Enabled radio button has been selected, all non-administrators on the server will be able to access only the applications listed in the authorized application list. Attempts to execute any other applications will fail.

There are two main restrictions in the functionality of this tool:

- 16-bit applications can't be secured using APPSEC. Since they run within a virtual DOS session (NTVDM), APPSEC is not able to distinguish a valid 16-bit application from another invalid 16-bit application.

- Valid applications must be located on one of the server's physical disks. When enabled, APPSEC won't allow any non-administrator to run any application that's located on a network drive.

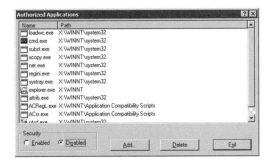

Figure A.1   *The Authorized Applications dialog box for the* APPSEC *utility.*

AUDITLOG (TSE 4.0/MetaFrame)(TS 2000/MetaFrame)

The AUDITLOG utility is made available to simplify the review of logon/logoff activity on a MetaFrame server. AUDITLOG generates a report based on the Security portion of the event log.

Author's Note

Logon/logoff auditing must be enabled to use AUDITLOG. *Otherwise, you get the following message:*

```
Unable to open security event log, make sure logon/logoff auditing is
enabled.
```

See Chapter 12, " Terminal Server Configuration and Tuning," for information on enabling auditing on your Terminal Server. ◆

Usage:

```
auditlog [username ¦ session] [/before:mm/dd/yy] [/after:mm/dd/yy]
➥ [/write:filename ¦[/time ¦ /fail ¦ /all ¦ /detail]] [/eventlog:filename]
auditlog /clear[:backup_log_filename]
```

Option	Function
username	Generates the report for the specified user.
session	Generates a report for the specified connection session. This will be the name assigned to the connection type, such as RDP-tcp#1, or CONSOLE for logons at the console. This option is most useful when reporting on the console usage.
/before:mm/dd/yy	Generates the report only for dates before the one entered.
/after:mm/dd/yy	Generates the report only for dates after the one entered.
/write:filename	Writes the output of AUDITLOG to the specified file. The data is comma-delimited so that it can be imported easily into other applications, such as a spreadsheet or database, to produce reports or statistics. If the file already exists, the new data is appended to the end of the file.
/time	Generates a report that displays the logon/logoff times and total times for each user. The output of this report differs from the standard report. It will list the username and the logon computer, followed by a list of logon dates and times and finally the totals.
/fail	Generates a report for failed logon attempts only.
/all	Generates a report of all logon/logoff activity. This includes noninteractive logons such as drive mappings or the "logon" of system processes at startup.
/detail	Creates a detailed report of logon/logoff activity. This report reproduces the complete information displayed for each event in the security log pertaining to logon/logoff.
/eventlog:filename	Allows you to run AUDITLOG against a file containing a backup of the security event log. The backup file can be created using the /clear option or from within the event viewer.
/clear[:backup_log_filename]	Clears the event log and saves the current contents to the backup file, if specified. If the file already exists, this command fails.

CHANGE CLIENT (TSE 4.0/MetaFrame) (TS 2000/MetaFrame)

CHANGE CLIENT is used to manage the settings for the current ICA client device mappings.

Usage:

```
change client [/view | /flush | /current]
change client [host_device client_device] [{/default | [/default_drives]
➥[/default_printers]} [/ascending]] [/noremap] [/persistent]
➥[/force_prt_todef] [/delete host_device] [/delete_client_printers]
```

Option	Function
host_device client_device	This is general usage of CHANGE CLIENT. host_device represents the mapped client device and client_device is the device on the client to be mapped to host_device. For example, CHANGE CLIENT P: C: maps the P: drive on the server to the C: drive on the client computer.
/view	Displays the list of all connected client devices.
/flush	Forces the MetaFrame server and the client to resynchronize disk data.
/current	Displays the current ICA client device mappings. Equivalent to typing CHANGE CLIENT only.
/default	Resets the drive and printer mappings to their defaults.
/default_drives	Resets the host drive mappings to their defaults.
/default_printers	Resets the host printer mappings to their defaults.
/ascending	Changes the drive order from descending to ascending when searching for available drivers and printers to map. This option is valid only with /default, /default_drives, or /default_printers.
/noremap	Prevents any client drives that conflict with MetaFrame drives from being mapped.
/persistent	Makes the current client drive mappings persistent by saving them into the user's profile. These settings are lost if the user has a mandatory profile.

continues ▶

▶ *continued*

/force_prt_todef	Forces the default printer for the MetaFrame client to map to the default printer on the client's local desktop.
/delete *host_device*	Deletes the client device that's mapped to the device specified by *host_device*.
/delete_client_printers	Deletes all the client printers from the session.

CHANGE LOGON (TSE 4.0)(TS 2000)

Used mainly for system maintenance, this utility will enable or disable logons for all client sessions on the Terminal Server. This command will *not* disable logons from the Terminal Server console.

> **Warning**
>
> *Using the* CHANGE LOGON *command is equivalent to disabling logons from within the Citrix Server Administration utility. When logons are disabled, there is a delay between when you execute the command and when the information is sent to the ICA master browser (if MetaFrame is also installed). This delay can mean that the master browser will continue to attempt to send users to the server, even though they won't be able to log on. For complete information on tuning the master browser to accommodate this situation, see Chapter 12.*◆

Usage:

```
change logon {/enable | /disable | /query}
```

Option	Function
/enable	Allows clients to log onto the Terminal Server.
/disable	Prevents users from logging onto the Terminal Server. Users who are currently logged on are unaffected by this command. After the user logs off, however, he or she can't log on again until logons are enabled.
/query	Displays the current state of logons.

CHANGE PORT (TSE 4.0)(TS 2000)

This command allows the mapping of COM ports to other port numbers. This is available for applications compatible with DOS. Because many DOS applications support only COM ports 1 through 4, this command allows higher-numbered COM ports to be mapped to lower numbers.

Usage:

```
change port [portx=porty ¦ /d portx]
```

Options	Function
portx=porty	Maps COM port *x* to port *y*.
/d portx	Deletes the mapping for COM port *x*.

CHANGE USER (TSE 4.0)(TS 2000)

This command switches the .INI mapping settings back and forth from execute mode to installation mode and is used when installing applications onto a Terminal Server.

When in install mode, the following happens:

- Any INI files located in the system root (usually WTSRV on TSE 4.0 and WINNT on TS 2000) that are updated/created by the installation and that use the standard APIs for INI file manipulation will be "flagged" by Terminal Server as being changed. When back in execute mode, when a user logs onto the server and executes the updated program, the system compares the last update time for the necessary INI file with the new one. If the file hasn't been updated, the system automatically provides the user with a new file in his or her personal system directory. Installation mode is used to create these master INI files that reside in the Terminal Server system root directory. User-specific INI files are maintained to provide compatibility with applications that use INI files to retain configuration information and that don't function properly in a multiuser system.

- The local registry on the server is monitored, and changes are recorded under the following key:

```
HKEY_LOCAL_MACHINE\SOFTWARE\Microsoft\Windows
↪NT\CurrentVersion\TerminalServer\Install
```

Changes made in HKEY_CURRENT_USER are copied under the \Software key in the above registry location. HKEY_LOCAL_MACHINE changes go under \MACHINE.

When placed back into execute mode, the following happens:

- When an application attempts to access an INI file that doesn't exist in the user's personal SYSTEM directory, Terminal Server looks in the system root of the server and then copies that file to the Windows directory under the user's home directory. If a file on the server is newer, it's either recopied or the changes are merged.

- When an application attempts to access the HKEY_CURRENT_USER key for a user and the requested registry entry doesn't exist, TSE copies the existing key from the \Install key mentioned earlier and places it into the user's personal profile. Of course, if the user is using a mandatory profile, these changes won't be saved when he or she exits.

For examples on the use of this command, see Chapter 19, "Application Integration."

Usage:

```
change user {/install ¦ /execute ¦ /query}
```

Option	Function
/install	Switches the server from execution mode to installation mode.
/execute	Switches the server back to execution mode.
/query	Displays the current state of the file mapping, either install or execute.

CLTPRINT (TSE 4.0/MetaFrame)(TS 2000/MetaFrame)

This command sets the number of available printer pipes to the client print spooler. This setting has no effect on print jobs that are spooled on the Terminal Server itself. A *printer pipe* is used to send data from an application to the client print spooler. The number of available pipes represents the number of print jobs that can be simultaneously sent to a client printer. The default number of printer pipes is 10.

> *Tip*
>
> *If you change the number of available printer pipes, you must stop and restart the spooler service for the changes to take effect.*◆

Usage:

```
cltprint [/q] [/pipes:nn]
```

Option	Function
/q	Displays the current number of printer pipes.
/pipes:nn	Sets the number of available printer pipes. *nn* must be between 10 and 63.

CNVRTUC (TSE 4.0)

CNVRTUC is used to convert the registry-based user information to SAM-based. This utility is required only when upgrading from a WinFrame 1.6 server that doesn't already have the SAM-based changes applied. This command is not required if upgrading from WinFrame 1.7 or performing a clean installation. This command is only valid on TSE 4.0, which supports an upgrade from WinFrame. Windows 2000 Terminal Services doesn't support such an upgrade.

> **Warning**
>
> *Because information is being written to the SAM, the user running this command must have administrator privileges.*
>
> *You should also ensure that the registry where the SAM is located has been set sufficiently large to accommodate the user information. This registry will grow approximately 1KB in size for each user account that's converted.*◆

Usage:

```
cnvrtuc {/all ¦ /user username} /domain domainname
```

Option	Function
/all	Converts all registry-based users.
/user *username*	Converts only the specified user's registry-based configuration.
/domain *domainname*	The target domain where the converted user's information will be moved.

CONNECT (TSE 4.0)

The equivalent command in TS 2000 is TSCON. Aside from the name, the syntax is identical.

This command enables you to attach a user session to a Terminal Server session. You can only connect user sessions that have an active connection on the Terminal Server. You can't connect a user to a session that's not his or hers unless you specify the password for the owner of that session. If a user is currently connected to the target session, he or she will be disconnected. You also can't connect a user on one server with a session on another.

A session can't be connected at the console and an active session on the console can't be disconnected using this command. To connect to a session that you don't own, you must have the Connect permission set in the Terminal Server Connection Configuration utility.◆

Usage:

```
connect {sessionid ¦ sessionname} [/server:servername]
⇒[/dest:sessionname] [/password:password] [/v]
```

Option	Function
sessionid ¦ sessionname	Specifies either the ID or the name of the session. If the destination session name is included, this specifies the session that will connect to the destination. If no destination is specified, this is the target session that the current session will connect to. You can see the session ID or name using either Terminal Server Administration or the QUERY SESSION command.
/server:servername	Specifies the Terminal Server on which the sessions reside. If omitted, the current server is used.
/dest:sessionname	The target session used when you're establishing a connection for another user. If the target session is currently connected, it will be disconnected.
/password:password	The password of the user who owns the target session. It's required only if the connecting user doesn't own the target session.
/v	Runs the command in verbose mode.

CPROFILE (TSE 4.0)(TS 2000)

The CPROFILE command cleans one or more user profiles of wasted space, including removing user-specific file associations. User-specific file associations are removed only if they were enabled using the PERUSER command. If disabled, CPROFILE clears only the wasted space from the profile. If the profile is currently in use, it won't be modified.

The file that's modified by CPROFILE is NTUSER.DAT.◆

Usage:

```
cprofile [/l] [/i] [/v] [filelist]
```

Option	Function
/l	Cleans all local profiles in %systemroot%\Profiles. Additional profiles can be specified with this command (see the *filelist* parameter).
/i	Prompts for confirmation for each profile to be cleaned.
/v	Runs the command in verbose mode.
filelist	A list of files (separated by spaces) to be cleaned. You can also use wildcard characters.

DISCONN (TSE 4.0)

The equivalent command in TS 2000 is TSDISCON. Aside from the name, the syntax is identical.

DISCONN is used to disconnect any non-console Terminal Server session in your environment.

Warning

If you run DISCONN *without any parameters, it immediately disconnects your session.*◆

Usage:

```
disconn [sessionid ¦ sessionname] [/server:servername] [/v]
```

Option	Function
sessionid	The ID of the session to disconnect. You can determine the ID by running Terminal Server Administration or the QUERY USER command. The default setting is the ID of the person running the command.
sessionname	The name of the session to disconnect, determined the same way you would find the session ID. The default setting is the session name of the person running the command.
/server:*servername*	*servername* is the name of the Terminal Server on which you want to run the command. The default setting is the current Terminal Server.
/v	Runs the command in verbose mode.

DOSKBD (TSE 4.0)

DOSKBD is only supported on a TSE 4.0 server, and no equivalent exists for Windows 2000. If you need to run DOS-based applications in your environment, you must use TSE 4.0.

This command is used to tune the DOS polling detection algorithm for a specific virtual DOS session. Different DOS sessions can have different algorithm configurations. DOSKBD is most often used in a batch script to configure an environment before running a DOS-based application.

Usage:

```
doskbd [[/defaults] ¦ [[/detectprobationcount:nnn] [/inprobationcount:nnn]
➥[/msallowed:nnn] [/mssleep:nnn] [/busymsallowed:nnn]
➥[/msprobationtrial:nnn] [/msgoodprobationend:nnn] [/detectioninterval:nnn]
➥[/startmonitor [appname] ¦ /stopmonitor]]] [/q]
```

Author's Note

The valid range for nnn is 0 to 32767.◆

Option	Function
/defaults	Resets all parameters back to the system default.
/detectprobationcount:*nnn*	The number of peeks per system tick required to force the application into the probation state. The default is 80.
/inprobationcount:*nnn*	The number of peeks per system tick required to put the application to sleep when in the probation state. This should be less than or equal to the detectprobationcount value. The default is 35.
/msallowed:*nnn*	Number of milliseconds that the application is allowed to be in the probation state before automatically being put to sleep. The default is 0.
/mssleep:*nnn*	Number of milliseconds that an application is put to sleep. The default is 100.
/busymsallowed:*nnn*	Number of milliseconds to wait before an application can be put in the probation state when it has been detected as "busy." The default is 60.
/msprobationtrial:*nnn*	When in the probation state, the detectprobationcount is substituted for the inprobationcount once every msprobationtrial interval. This allows for a check to see if the application is now better behaved. The default interval is 2500.
/msgoodprobationend:*nnn*	Number of milliseconds that a probationary application must not be put to sleep before it can be removed from probation. The default is 2500.

Option	Function
/detectioninterval:*nnn*	Number of timer ticks used to count the number of polling events. The default is 1.
/startmonitor [*appname*]	Executes *appname* and gathers polling statistics for it.
/stopmonitor	Stops gathering polling statistics.
/q	Runs DOSKBD in quiet mode. Information is not displayed about the actions being performed.

Author's Note

The term peek here is actually an old assembly language term used to describe the inspection of a register or section of memory. In this case, it refers to the number of times that the DOS application peeks at the keyboard to see if there has been any input. ✦

FLATTEMP (TSE 4.0)(TS 2000)

This command controls whether all users on a Terminal Server by default will share the same TEMP directory. By default, FLATTEMP is disabled, so Terminal Server automatically manages a user's TEMP directory (TEMP and TMP environment variables) by assigning it to a unique directory located under the directory pointed to by the system environment variable TEMP. The user's directory is not assigned the user's user ID but instead the session ID (sometimes referred to as logon ID) on that Terminal Server.

For example, on a TSE 4.0 server, if TEMP=X:\TEMP is the definition for the system environment variable, and a user logged onto the Terminal Server has session ID 17, Terminal Server will automatically set his or her TEMP and TMP environment variables to point at X:\TEMP\17. This way, temporary variables used during a user's session are kept separate from those of other users on the server. When the user logs off, the contents of the temporary directory are automatically deleted.

If FLATTEMP is enabled, all users by default will have TEMP and TMP points at X:\TEMP, unless they have redefined it in the user environment settings in the System applet under the Control Panel.

On a TS 2000 server, the FLATTEMP option is also disabled by default, even though each user has his own temp directory located within his profile in the Local Settings\Temp directory. If FLATTEMP is enabled on a TS 2000 server, each user still has his own temporary directory in his profile, but Terminal Server no longer automatically deletes it when he logs off.

> **Warning**
>
> *If you have enabled* FLATTEMP *and are assigning TEMP directories in each user's environment settings, I recommended that the TEMP location* not *be on a network share. Even short interruptions in communication could result in problems if an application doesn't have access to its temporary files.*
>
> *I recommend that you leave* FLATTEMP *disabled and allow Terminal Server to manage the user TEMP locations.* ◆

Usage:

```
flattemp {/query ¦ /enable ¦ /disable}
```

Option	Function
/query	Displays the current setting for FLATTEMP.
/enable	Configures all users to share the same TEMP directory by default.
/disable	Configures all users to have a unique TEMP directory by default.

The FLATTEMP option can also be managed on a TS 2000 server through the Terminal Services Configuration application. It's the Use Temporary Folders Per Session option shown in Figure A.2.

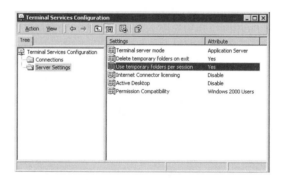

Figure A.2 *Managing the* FLATTEMP *setting using Terminal Services Configuration on TS 2000.*

ICAPORT (TSE 4.0/MetaFrame)(TS 2000/MetaFrame)

ICAPORT is used to set the TCP/IP listening port number used by a MetaFrame server for ICA connections. By default, MetaFrame will listen for TCP/IP client connections on port 1494. You can use ICAPORT to change this port to any number in the range 0–65535. If you change the port number, you have to restart the server for the changes to take effect.

Warning

When assigning an alternate port number, make sure that it's not already in use. Avoid well known TCP and UPD port numbers such as 80 (for HTTP) or 23 (for Telnet). These are standard port numbers that have been assigned to particular TCP/UDP services.

While ports 1 through 1024 are reserved for this purpose, some ports above this are also commonly used, such as many in the 6000 range that are used for X11 (a graphical UNIX interface). The following list shows some commonly assigned ports:

21	*FTP*
67	*BOOTP/DHCP*
110	*POP3*
177	*X11 logons*
2049	*NFS*
6667	*IRC* ◆

After the port number has been changed, all clients that want to connect to the MetaFrame server will need their client updated as well. To assign an alternate port on the client, you simply use the standard TCP/IP convention of assigning a port number by appending :*port number* immediately after the IP address or DNS name. For example, entering ORCA:7832 as the MetaFrame server name would tell the client to attempt to establish an ICA connection with ORCA on port 7832. If you define the wrong port or attempt to connect to a server that has had the default port changed, you get a message stating that the MetaFrame server is not accepting connections.

Tip

You can also specify the port number by adding ICAPortNumber=nnn to the APPSRV.INI file on the client. This file contains the configuration information that's normally set using the Citrix ICA client. You can add this entry in one of two places. If you add it to the [WFCLIENT] section of the file, the defined port number will be used by all MetaFrame client entries. If you add this value to an individual server key, shown as [servername] in the file, the alternate port will be used only for that server entry. ◆

Usage:

```
icaport {query ¦ /port:nnn ¦ /reset}
```

Option	Function
/query	Displays the current setting for ICAPORT.
/port:nnn	Reassigns the listening TCP/IP port number.
/reset	Resets the port number to the default of 1494.

KILL (TSE 4.0)

The equivalent command in TS 2000 is TSKILL. Aside from the name, the syntax is identical.

KILL is used to terminate processes on a Terminal Server. You can kill only your own processes unless you have administrative privileges, in which case you can kill any process on the Terminal Server.

Usage:

```
kill {processid ¦ processname} [/server:servername] [/id:sessionid ¦ /a] [/v]
```

Option	Function
processid	ID of the process to terminate.
processname	Name of the process to terminate. You can use wildcards when specifying the name.
/server:servername	The Terminal Server on which the process to terminate resides. The default is the current server.
/id:sessionid	The Terminal Server session where the process to terminate resides.
/a	Specifies that the process should be killed under all sessions on the Terminal Server. This is normally used with the processname parameter.
/v	Runs the command in verbose mode.

LOGOFF (TSE 4.0)(TS 2000)

This command enables you to log off a Terminal Server session.

Warning

If you don't specify any parameters when running LOGOFF, it immediately logs you off your current session. ✦

Usage:

```
logoff [sessionid ¦ sessionname] [/server:servername] [/v]
```

Option	Function
sessionid	ID of the session to log off.
sessionname	Name of the session to log off.
/server:servername	The Terminal Server on which the session to log off resides. The default is the current server.
/v	Runs the command in verbose mode.

MSG (TSE 4.0)(TS 2000)

Use MSG to send messages to one or more Terminal Server users in your environment.

Tip

To send a message to other users, the sender must have the Message permission set for his or her connection. Connection permissions are discussed in Chapter 12. ◆

Usage:

```
msg {username ¦ sessionname ¦ sessionid ¦ @filename ¦ *} [/server:servername]
➥[/time:seconds] [/v] [/w] [message]
```

Option	Function
username	Name of the user who will receive the message.
sessionname	Name of the session that will receive the message.
sessionid	ID of the session that will receive the message.
@filename	A file that can contain a mixture of usernames, session names, and session IDs to which you want to send the message. One entry should appear per line, separated by a carriage return and linefeed.
*	Sends the message to all users on the server.
/server:servername	The Terminal Server where the message will be displayed.
/time:seconds	Length of time that the message will display on the user's screen before automatically closing. The default is 60.
/v	Runs the command in verbose mode.
/w	Forces the dialog box to remain on the user's display until acknowledged. If the /time parameter is also used, this setting is ignored.
message	The message you want to send. If you specify no message, input is read from standard input (Stdin).

NDSPSVR (TSE 4.0/MetaFrame)(TS 2000/MetaFrame)

NDSPSVR is used to enable or disable a preferred server for NDS logons. When disabled (the default), MetaFrame uses the first NetWare directory server listed in the bindery of the preferred NetWare server for NDS logons. If no preferred server is set, the first NetWare server to respond to the Query Nearest Server broadcast is used. This can result in a server located across a WAN link being used. To avoid this problem, use NDSPSVR to specify a NetWare directory server on the local network.

> **Tip**
>
> *Changes that you make in this setting don't take effect until after you reboot the MetaFrame server.* ◆

Usage:

```
ndspsvr [/query ¦ /enable:fileservername ¦ /disable]
```

Option	Function
/query	Displays the current setting for NDSPSVR.
/enable:*fileservername*	Sets the listed server as the preferred NDS server.
/disable	Disables the currently set preferred server.

PERUSER (TSE 4.0)

> **Author's Note**
>
> *This utility is only available on TSE 4.0. On TS 2000, users have the special registry key HKEY_CURRENT_USER\SOFTWARE\Classes, in which they can maintain their own personal file associations. This key contains only those associations set for the user. The Classes key under HKEY_LOCAL_MACHINE still maintains the global list of associations, and those are used unless one exists in the personal Classes key.* ◆

This command enables or disables per-user file associations. By default, all file associations in Terminal Server are global and apply to all users. The file association information is maintained in the HKEY_CLASSES_ROOT key of the Terminal Server registry. When per-user file associations are enabled, each user maintains his or her own list of associations, which resides in the HKEY_CURRENT_USER key when he or she is logged on, and is stored in the NTUSER.DAT file (the user's profile) when he or she logs out. Users with mandatory profiles can't save any file association changes to their profiles when they log out.

> **Warning**
>
> *Enabling per-user file associations can cause each user's profile to grow more than 1MB. I recommend that you don't enable per-user file associations unless absolutely necessary. When enabled, this setting affects all Terminal Server users.* ✦

Usage:

```
peruser {/query ¦ /enable ¦ /disable}
```

Option	Function
/query	Displays the current setting for PERUSER.
/enable	Enables per-user file associations.
/disable	Disables per-user file associations.

QUERY ACL (TSE 4.0/MetaFrame) (TS 2000/MetaFrame)

Same function and syntax as the ACLCHECK command.

QUERY LICENSE (TSE 4.0/MetaFrame) (TS 2000/MetaFrame)

QUERY LICENSE is a MetaFrame tool that displays information about the Citrix licenses in the environment. This command tells you how many licenses are available and how many are in use on both the network and the local server.

Usage:

```
query license [/server:servername ¦ /all]
```

Option	Function
/server:servername	The server whose license information you want to display. The default is the current server.
/all	Displays information about all licenses on the network.

QUERY PROCESS (TSE 4.0)(TS 2000)

This command displays the following information on processes running on a Terminal Server:

- The owner of the process
- The session name and ID that own the process
- The state of the process

- The process ID
- The image (executable) name of the process

> ### Tip
> *Unless a user has the Query Process right, the user can view only his or her own processes.* ◆

Usage:

```
query process [processid ¦ username ¦ sessionname ¦ /id:sessionid
➥¦ programname ¦ *] [/server:servername] [/system]
```

Option	Function
processid	ID of the process you want to display.
username	Name of the user whose processes you want to display.
sessionname	Name of the session containing the processes to display.
/id:sessionid	ID of the session containing the processes to display.
programname	Name of the executable for which you want to display all processes. You must include the .EXE extension.
*	Shows information for all processes.
/server:servername	Name of the Terminal Server containing the processes to display. The default is the current server.
/system	Displays system process information.

QUERY SERVER (TSE 4.0/MetaFrame) (TS 2000/MetaFrame)

An extremely useful administration tool, QUERY SERVER displays information about all available Citrix servers in your environment. QUERY SERVER uses information from the ICA master browser to gather the statistics that are displayed. For information on ICA and the master browser, see Chapter 3, "Citrix MetaFrame." This tool provides a quick way to view much of the information that's available through the MetaFrame Administration tool.

Troubleshooting Tip

QUERY SERVER *queries the MetaFrame servers on only one network card at a time. If you have two or more network cards on your server, to access the MetaFrame servers on the other card's network you must specify the proper address of any MetaFrame server on that subnet.* ◆

Usage:

```
query server [[servername] [[/ping] [/count:n] [/size:n]]¦
➡[/stats ¦ /reset ¦ /load ¦ /addr ¦ /debugnhwatch]] [/tcp]
➡[/ipx] [/netbios][/tcpserver:x] [/ipxserver:x] [/netbiosserver:x]
➡[/license ¦ /app ¦ /gateway ¦ /serial ¦ /disc ¦ /update ¦
➡ /election ¦ /delete] [/continue] [/DEBUG:n]
```

Option	Function
servername	Name of the server to query. The name is entered *without* the double backslash (\\) characters.
/ping	Pings the named server.
/count:n	Number of times to ping. The default is 5.
/size:n	Byte size of the ping packet. The default is 256.
/stats	Displays the browser statistics.
/reset	Resets the browser statistics.
/load	Displays load-balancing data (valid only when the server has load balancing installed).
/addr	Displays network address data.
/debugnhwatch	Displays Program Neighborhood debugging information for the specified server. You must include the MetaFrame server name for this parameter to work properly. When run, it displays diagnostic information about what the server "knows" about the farm it belongs to and the applications available.
/tcp	Shows TCP/IP information.
/ipx	Shows IPX information.
/netbios	Shows NetBIOS information.
/tcpserver:x	Sets the default TCP/IP server address to x.
/ipxserver:x	Sets the default IPX server address to x.
/netbiosserver:x	Sets the default NetBIOS server address to x.
/license	Displays the user licenses.
/app	Displays published application names and corresponding servers.
/gateway	Shows the configured ICA gateway addresses.
/serial	Shows license serial numbers.
/disc	Displays information on disconnected sessions.

continues ▶

Option	Function
/update	Forces the ICA browser update information to be sent to the master ICA browser immediately. If a server name exists in the *servername* parameter, only that server will send updated information; otherwise, all Citrix servers send their update information.
/election	Forces an ICA browser election.
/delete	Forces the deletion of the ICA master browser data. The master browser eventually reconstructs its database as update information comes in from the other Citrix servers on the network.
/continue	Suppresses pausing after each page of output.
/DEBUG:*n*	Displays debug messages. After the *n*th message, the application halts automatically.

QUERY SESSION (TSE 4.0)(TS 2000)

QUERY SESSION allows you to view detailed information about sessions on any Terminal Server in your environment. Executing QUERY SESSION without any parameters lists all sessions configured on the Terminal Server. The following information is normally displayed:

- **Session name.** The name assigned when the connections were created.
- **Username.** If a user is connected to a session, his or her name will be displayed.
- **Session ID.** ID assigned to the session by the system.
- **State.** The state of the session, which is one of the following:

active	A user is currently logged onto the session.
conn	The session is connected but no user is currently logged on.
connq	The session is currently in the process of connecting.
shadow	The session is shadowing another session.
listen	The session is waiting to accept a client connection.
disc	The session has been disconnected.
idle	The session has been initialized.
down	The session has failed to initialize and is unavailable.
init	The session is currently initializing.

- **Type.** The session type, which is wdcon (console), wdica (ICA), or rdpwd (RDP).

- **Device.** The device name assigned to the session. It appears blank for console or network connections.

Usage:

```
query session [sessionname | username | sessionid] [/server:servername]
⮡ [/address] [/mode] [/flow] [/connect] [/counter] [/sm] [/vm]
```

Option	Function
sessionname	Name of the session you want to query.
username	Name of the user whose session information you want to query.
sessionid	ID of the session you want to query.
/server:servername	Name of the Terminal Server containing the sessions to query. The default is the current server.
/address	Provides an alternate listing showing the session name, the client name, the network transport used, and the network address of the client. This parameter functions properly only on a TSE 4.0 server.
/mode	Displays the current asynchronous line settings.
/flow	Displays the flow control settings.
/connect	Displays the connect settings.
/counter	Displays the total sessions created, disconnected, and reconnected. This parameter is valid only on TS 2000.
/sm	Lists only the session name and the session's current state.
/vm	Lists the virtual memory information for each session, including such things as the PagedPoolCommit and AllocatedPagedPool counters. This parameter is valid only on a TSE 4.0 server.

QUERY TERMSERVER (TSE 4.0)(TS 2000)

This command lists the available Terminal Servers and provides some basic information about them. It returns the server name and the network and node address (if requested). This command should not be confused with the QUERY SERVER command, which displays information specific to ICA.

> **Tip**
>
> *An asterisk (*) appears in the output beside the name of the Terminal Server from which the command was run.* ◆

Usage:

```
query termserver [servername] [/domain:domainname] [/address] [/continue]
```

Option	Function
servername	The specific Terminal Server to query.
/domain:domainname	Provides Terminal Server information for the specified NT domain. The default is the current domain.
/address	Displays the network and node address for each server.
/continue	Suppresses stopping after each screen of data.

QUERY USER (TSE 4.0)(TS 2000)

QUERY USER displays information about the users who are currently logged onto a Terminal Server. It returns the following information:

- The username. A greater-than (>) character appears beside the name of the current user.
- The session name.
- The session ID.
- The session state, either active or disconnected.
- The amount of idle time since the last keyboard or mouse input was received. If the idle time is less than one minute, it appears as a dot (.)
- The logon time.

Usage:

```
query user [username ¦ sessionname ¦ sessionid] [/server:servername]
```

Option	Function
username	Name of the user you want to query.
sessionname	Name of the session you want to query.
sessionid	ID of the session you want to query.
/server:servername	Name of the Terminal Server on which to perform the query. The default is the current server.

QUERY WINSTA (TSE 4.0) (TS 2000)

Same function and syntax as the QUERY SESSION command.

REGISTER (TSE 4.0)(TS 2000)

The REGISTER program assigns special execution settings to an application on a Terminal Server. Most often the REGISTER program is used to assign "system global" characteristics to an executable or one of its components, usually a DLL. By default, objects and resources run in a "user global" state on a Terminal Server. This is how multiple instances of the same application can execute on the same Terminal Server without affecting each other.

At the simplest level, it works as follows. Assume you have an object called X running on your Windows NT workstation. An application accesses this information by the name X and everything is fine. Now put this same object on a Terminal Server. When the object is referenced in the environment, it's no longer simply X, but is now X:*n*, where *n* is the session ID belonging to the user who initiated the application. This way, two instances of the same object can exist on the server but are uniquely named and maintained independently of each other. X:9 and X:13 are considered distinct.

The most common purpose of the REGISTER command is to modify this behavior so that an object is referenced by the same name for all users in the environment, thereby making the object globally available on the server. If you apply REGISTER to X, it would simply be X on the Terminal Server and not X:9 or X:13.

Tip

For changes using REGISTER *to take effect, you must restart the Terminal Server.* ◆

Usage:

```
register filename [/system ¦ /user] [/v]
```

Option	Function
filename	Name of the file to register.
/system	Registers *filename* as a system global resource.
/user	Registers *filename* as a user global resource.
/v	Runs the application in verbose mode.

RESET SESSION (TSE 4.0)(TS 2000)

This command performs a reset of a given Terminal Server session, causing the device to close and reopen, resetting the session to its startup state. If a session fails to reset properly, it will usually end in a down state.

Usage:

```
reset session {sessionname ¦ sessionid} [/server:servername] [/v]
```

Option	Function
sessionname	The name of the session you want to reset.
sessionid	The ID of the session you want to reset.
/server:*servername*	The Terminal Server where you intend to reset the connection.
/v	Runs the application in verbose mode.

RESET WINSTA (TSE 4.0)(TS 2000)

Same function and syntax as the RESET SESSION command.

RMVICA (TSE 4.0/MetaFrame)(TS 2000/MetaFrame)

Uninstalls MetaFrame 1.8 from the Terminal Server.

Usage:

```
rmvica [/u]
```

Option	Function
/u	Uninstall MetaFrame in unattended mode.

SHADOW (TSE 4.0/MetaFrame)(TS 2000)

> **Author's Note**
>
> While the SHADOW command is included with TSE 4.0, it's only useful if you're also using MetaFrame, since RDP 4.0 doesn't support session shadowing.
>
> Shadowing is also called remote control when referring to RDP 5.0 shadow sessions, or when using the Terminal Services management tools.
>
> Finally, in order to successfully shadow a user who is running a seamless published application on a TSE 4.0 server with MetaFrame 1.8, Service Pack 1 for MetaFrame 1.8 must be installed. ◆

SHADOW enables you to establish a connection with another user's active session so that you can view and interact with the other user's activities. In order to shadow a user, the following criteria must be met:

- The shadower's monitor resolution must be equal to or greater than that of the person to be shadowed.

- The shadower's session must have the same color depth as the person to be shadowed.

When using the ICA client, multiple people can shadow the same user session simultaneously, but you can't shadow a session that's currently busy shadowing someone else. With the RDP client, only one person can shadow a user at a time.

> **Warning**
>
> *To be able to shadow, you must have the Shadow/Remote Control access permission. When notification is enabled, the user will be warned and prompted for confirmation before you can establish the shadow session with that user.*
>
> *The console can't be shadowed, nor can it directly shadow other sessions.* ◆

Usage:

```
shadow {sessionname ¦ sessionid} [/server:servername] [/v]
```

Option	Function
sessionname	The name of the session you want to shadow.
sessionid	The ID of the session you want to shadow.
/server:servername	The Terminal Server where the user you want to shadow is currently located.
/v	Runs the application in verbose mode.

SHUTDOWN (TSE 4.0)

The equivalent command in TS 2000 is TSSHUTDN. Aside from the name, the syntax is identical.

SHUTDOWN allows an administrator to safely shut down a Terminal Server from the command prompt.

Usage:

```
shutdown [waittime] [/server:servername] [/reboot] [/powerdown]
➥[/delay:logoffdelay] [/v]
```

Option	Function
waittime	Time (in seconds) that SHUTDOWN will wait for users to log off the server. The default is 60 seconds.
/server:servername	Terminal Server to be shut down.
/reboot	Terminal Server will shut down and restart.
/powerdown	Terminal Server will shut down and then initiate the actual power down, if possible.
/delay:logoffdelay	Amount of time that SHUTDOWN will wait after all user sessions have been terminated before terminating all processes. The default is 30 seconds.
/v	Runs the application in verbose mode.

TSCON (TS 2000)

Same function and syntax as the CONNECT command.

TSDISCON (TS 2000)

Same function and syntax as the DISCONN command.

TSKILL (TS 2000)

Same function and syntax as the KILL command.

TSPROF (TSE 4.0)(TS 2000)

TSPROF allows you to view and copy the Terminal Server user configuration information from one user to another and to update the Terminal Server profile path for a user. Typically this utility is used to script the migration or setup of user accounts for Terminal Server.

> ### Tip
>
> TSPROF *doesn't let you edit the contents of the Terminal Server Home Directory field, although it copies this information from one user's configuration to another when using the* /copy *command.*
>
> TSPROF *performs environment variable expansion; for example, if you have used %username% in the home directory or Terminal Server profile path for a user account, these variables will be properly converted as the information in that profile is copied to the new account.* ◆

Usage:

```
tsprof /update {/domain:domainname ¦ /local} /profile:profilepath username
tsprof /copy {/domain:domainname ¦ /local}[/profile:profilepath] srcusername
➥destusername
tsprof /q {/domain:domainname ¦ /local} username
```

Option	Function
/update	Updates the profile path for the named user.
/domain:domainname	The name of the domain in which you will perform the operation. The current domain is the default.
/local	Applies the profile change to the local user accounts only.
/profile:profilepath	The path to the profiles on the Terminal Server.

Option	Function
/copy	Copies the user's configuration from *srcusername* to *destusername*. Also updates the profile path on the destination.
srcusername	Name of the user from whom you will copy the configuration information (source).
destusername	Name of the user to whom you will copy information (destination).
/q	Displays the user's profile path, ensuring that it's valid.
username	Name of the person whose profile you want to update.

Tip

If the user who is being queried doesn't have a profile path defined or the user ID doesn't exist, you receive this message:

```
Failed getting User Configuration, Error = 2 (0x2) ◆
```

TSSHUTDN (TS 2000)

Same function and syntax as the SHUTDOWN command.

Network Primer

The OSI Model

The sometimes complicated interrelationship of components in a network can quickly become overwhelming without an understanding of the basic underlying theory that defines most networks. The most widely recognized model for understanding network communications is the OSI model. The *Open Systems Interconnection (OSI) reference model* was defined in 1978 by the International Standards Organization (ISO) to help define (and understand) how the different devices on a network interact with each other.

The OSI model consists of seven independent functional layers, each providing and utilizing the services of the adjacent layers. The model represents a peer-to-peer communication relationship in which equivalent layers on different computers communicate with each other through a common protocol.

Figure B.1 demonstrates this peer-to-peer relationship between two computers. Although the information travels down the layers on one computer and then up the layers on the other, conceptually, equivalent layers are talking directly to each other. This allows layers to work functionally independently of each other with a change in one layer not requiring subsequent changes in the others. The only requirement is that each layer be able to communicate with the adjacent layers immediately above and below. The figure also shows where RDP and ICA conceptually fit into the OSI model, at the session layer.

Author's Note

The System Network Architecture (SNA) model, developed by IBM, was the basis for the OSI reference model. ♦

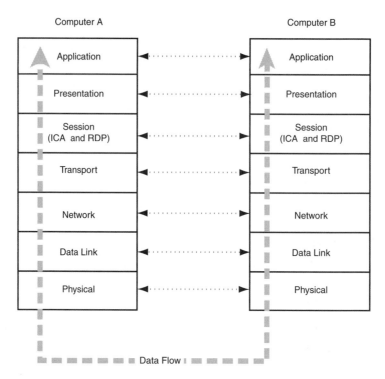

Figure B.1 *RDP and ICA within the OSI reference model.*

Following is a brief description of each of the OSI layers. Layers 5 through 7 are application-related; layers 1 through 4 are network-related:

- **Application layer (layer 7).** The uppermost layer provides services to user applications, allowing them to communicate with other applications that reside on other computers as if those applications were local. Examples include file copying and database access.

- **Presentation layer (layer 6).** This layer translates data into a standard format agreed upon by the computers involved in the data exchange.

- **Session layer (layer 5).** This layer provides synchronization between applications on different computers. RDP and ICA function at this layer, converting presentation information into the appropriate protocol data, which is then sent to the appropriate layer on the client machine to be decoded and displayed.

- **Transport layer (layer 4).** This layer provides for flow control and reliable data transfer between end nodes. This layer breaks up messages from the session layer into deliverable packets and reassembles these packets into messages to send to the session layer. *Transmission Control Protocol (TCP)* and *User Datagram Protocol (UDP)* exist at this layer.

- **Network layer (layer 3).** This layer handles the routing of data packets through the network. It handles the conversion of data from the transport layer into acceptable data packets if they're too large for the data link layer (layer 2). Of course, it also handles reassembling the packets for the transport layer at the receiving end. *Internet Protocol (IP)* is a layer 3 protocol.

- **Data Link layer (layer 2).** The data link layer formats the packets from the network layer into groupings called *frames,* which are passed to the physical layer (layer 1) for transmission. Error detection and recovery from physical errors are detected here. This layer also determines whether a broadcast is targeted for the current computer. Both switches and bridges are found at layer 2.

- **Physical layer (layer 1).** The physical layer handles the encoding and decoding of data for the data link layer and is also responsible for sending bits to and receiving bits from the physical network. Repeaters function at this layer.

Figure B.2 shows the association of internetworking equipment (repeaters, switches, and so on) and the OSI layers within which they reside.

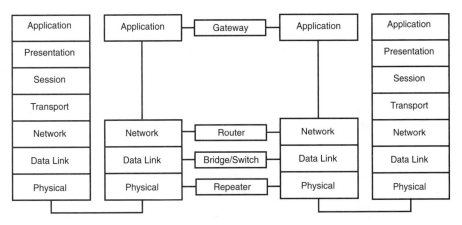

Figure B.2 *Internetworking equipment and the OSI layers where they reside.*

Author's Note

Internetworking vendors are blurring the traditional boundaries of the OSI reference model with current product offerings and virtual LAN (VLAN) technology. Some layer 3 switches now perform routing functions (found at layer 3) as well as the switching/bridging functions of layer 2. In general, the first packet is routed for path determination, and all subsequent packets are switched along the same path. ◆

Communications Protocols

Terminal Server clients (and applications in general) require a means to navigate through the network and locate the intended destination. Similarly, the destination server must be able to recognize that the data on the wire is intended for it and be able to act on the packet accordingly. For two nodes to communicate, they must use the same set of well-defined rules. These rules are known as a *protocol*, and they govern the conversations between the nodes. Hosts that share a common protocol can communicate directly, whereas hosts that use different protocols for communication require an intermediary device, a *gateway*, to perform the necessary mapping and protocol conversions. For example, Microsoft's SNA Server performs the gateway function that enables IP devices to communicate to SNA mainframes.

> **Author's Note**
>
> *Citrix's ICA gateway functionality (discussed in Chapter 3) doesn't correspond to this literal definition because the ICA gateway is created between two MetaFrame servers that are communicating with the same protocol. In this case, the gateway exists to allow ICA information on one network segment to traverse a router to another segment. An ICA gateway doesn't allow ICA data to be shared between MetaFrame servers running different communications protocols.* ♦

Three protocols are used by RDP/ICA clients to communicate with a Terminal Server. Out of these, RDP currently supports only TCP/IP, while ICA supports NetBIOS, IPX/SPX, and TCP/IP.

- **NetBEUI.** The *NetBIOS Extended User Interface* (*NetBEUI*) is a non-routable layer 2 protocol best suited for small LANs of between 2 and 200 workstations. Developed originally by IBM for OS/2 and LAN Manager networks, it's certainly the fastest protocol for small networks that don't require routing to other networks. NetBEUI is often chosen for MetaFrame dial-up connections instead of TCP/IP, for the simple reason of performance.

- **IPX/SPX.** *Internetwork Packet Exchange/Sequenced Packet Exchange* (*IPX/SPX*) was developed by Novell for the NetWare operating system in the early 80s and is based on an early Xerox network called *Xerox Network System (XNS)*. IPX is actually the protocol used to transport packets and resides in the network and transport layers (layers 3 and 4) of the OSI model. SPX operates at the transport layer and provides connection-oriented services to IPX, offering additional reliability. NWLink is Microsoft's implementation of IPX/SPX.

- **TCP/IP.** *Transmission Control Protocol/Internet Protocol* offers the most widely accepted means for interconnecting dissimilar network components. TCP/IP was born in conjunction with the Internet's predecessor, *ARPANET* (*Advanced Research Projects Agency network*) in the early 70s. IP is the protocol and is located at the network layer. TCP is the main transport layer protocol used in conjunction with IP and is connection-oriented, utilizing a connection ID, also known as a *port*, for each connection that's established. Another common transport layer protocol is User Datagram Protocol (UDP). This protocol is connectionless and doesn't attempt to acknowledge packet receipt. Although UDP may be more efficient than TCP, it's not as reliable.

Author's Note

The ICA client by default uses UDP broadcasts to determine the master browser in a MetaFrame environment. The ICA master browser is discussed in Chapter 3. ◆

Physical and Logical Networks

For most users, a *local area network* (*LAN*) and a *wide area network* (*WAN*) are nothing more than abstract terms used to describe how computers are connected to allow the transfer of data. The graphical interface of Windows hides a well-structured cable plant and selection of networking components that interconnect heterogeneous systems using a set of predefined rules such as those discussed earlier. Although LANs and WANs both service the interconnection of networking devices, they're most often differentiated for geographical reasons.

LANs

A LAN is almost always confined to a single building. Typically, LANs use higher-speed connections to link network segments together. Technologies such as *Ethernet, Fast Ethernet, Fibre Distributed Data Interface* (*FDDI*), and *Token Ring* dominate today's corporate LANs. Routers, bridges, and switches are devices used most often to link different LAN segments, technologies, and services together. Figure B.3 demonstrates a typical LAN configuration with multiple *subnets*. Subnets can be thought of as miniature LANS separated by a router. Traditionally, subnets have been created to isolate certain networks from others. A common example would be the creation of a development subnet where application and server testing could be performed without fear of affecting a production environment.

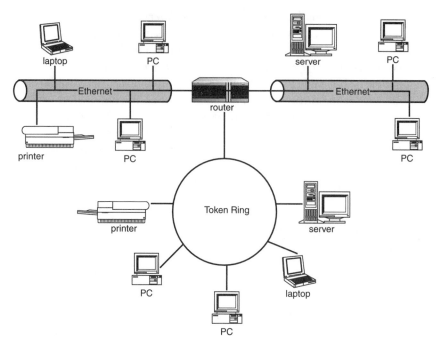

Figure B.3   *Typical LAN configuration with multiple subnets.*

Author's Note

Occasionally, you'll hear of a LAN that has been extended to multiple buildings in close proximity, most often connected using private facilities. This is commonly known as a campus. University networks are a prime example. ◆

WANs

A *WAN* is the interconnection of geographically dispersed LANs extending beyond a single metropolitan area. This usually means reliance on an outside source or vendor to provide the necessary bandwidth required to support your WAN. Service offerings range from regular analog dial-in modems (connecting anywhere between 15.4Kbps and 56Kbps) all the way up to *asynchronous transfer mode (ATM)*, reaching speeds of OC48 (2.4Gbps). The most common WAN service offerings are 56Kbps, T1/E1 (1.54Mbps/2.048Mbps), fractional T1/E1 and OC3 (155Mbps) with protocols such as X.25, Frame Relay, PPP, and ATM. The primary interconnection device for the WAN is the router. Figure B.4 illustrates the interconnection of three LANs located in different cities.

Author's Note

If an interconnection for a WAN is within a single metropolitan area, this network can also be referred to as a metropolitan area network (MAN). MANs are differentiated from campuses by the fact that they don't use private connectivity facilities. ◆

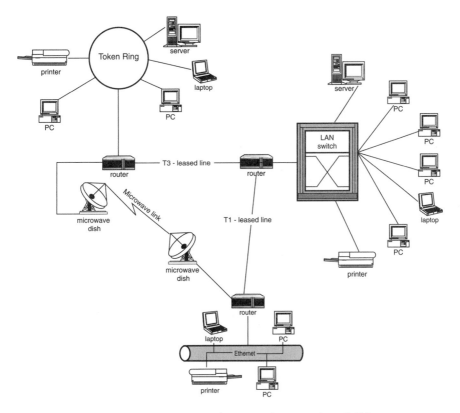

Figure B.4   *A WAN configuration between three LANs.*

C

File and Folder Security Primer

To successfully implement a secure Terminal Server, you must have a clear understanding of Windows NTFS file security. File and folder security is built around the basic permission attribute. The permission attribute defines a specific permission that can be applied to a file or folder. Permission attributes are normally grouped together into what are called *permission sets*, which make up the common security settings such as READ or WRITE.

Windows NT 4.0 and Windows 2000 define different basic security attributes and attribute sets for file security; this appendix looks at each of them in turn.

> **Author's Note**
>
> *In Windows 2000, the term folder is used to describe what's called a directory in Windows NT. I use both terms interchangeably, although folder is more common.* ◆

Windows NT 4.0 File System Security

The following list shows the six permission attributes that exist in Windows NT 4.0, the abbreviation for each that's used in attribute sets (described shortly), and a description of the rights that each permission grants:

- **Read (R).** Allows reading a file's contents or the names of files and subdirectories within a directory. This attribute also allows viewing the security permissions or other non-security file attributes assigned to a file or directory. Non-security file attributes can include the standard Read-Only, Hidden, System, and Archive settings that have existed since the days of DOS, or can include special attributes created by a software application. Microsoft Word documents contain additional attributes containing information such as author, number of revisions, and so on. The Read attribute *does not* grant access to drill into a subdirectory. To do this, you need the Execute permission (described later in this list).

- **Write (W).** Allows you to create new files or subdirectories within a directory or to modify its non-security attributes. The Write attribute on a file lets you modify its non-security attributes or append data to the file. To edit the contents of the file, you also need the Read attribute, because you need to be able to read the file's contents in order to edit them.

- **Execute (X).** Allows you to run an executable file (.EXE, .COM, and so on) or to traverse into a directory.

- **Delete (D).** Allows you to delete a file or directory. The directory must be empty to be deleted. If it contains one or more files or subdirectories, you must also have the Delete attribute on those objects so that they can be deleted.

- **Change Permissions (P).** Allows changing the security attributes of a file or directory. If you're the owner of an object, you have the inherent right to change permissions on that object.

- **Take Ownership (O).** Allows you to take ownership of a file or directory. As the owner of an object you can change permissions even if you have no other access to the object. By default, only the Administrators group has the right to take ownership of a file or folder. Taking ownership doesn't automatically grant you any rights to the object, but once you're the owner you can assign yourself the necessary rights.

Any combination of these security attributes can be assigned to both files and directories, granting or restricting access to individual users and/or groups of users. Although being able to assign each of these individual rights provides a large amount of flexibility, Microsoft also provides default permission sets that can be used to grant common permissions to files or directories. The exact permissions that are granted when these attributes are applied differ slightly between files and directories.

Windows NT 4.0 File Permissions

Table C.1 shows the five default NT 4.0 permission sets for files. The associated permission attributes that make up the permission set are listed in parentheses. This is the typical notation used when describing the individual permissions. For example, the permissions for Change are shown as (RWXD) rather than R, W, X, and D.

Table C.1   Windows NT 4.0 Default File Permission Sets

Permission Set	Permission Attributes	Description
No Access	(None)	Specifically assigns no access to the selected file. This overrides any other permissions that a user may have as a result of group or personal assignment. No Access is used to ensure that a user or group doesn't have access to the file.
Read	(RX)	Provides access to both read and execute a valid application file.
Change	(RWXD)	Allows reading, writing, execution, or deletion of a file.
Full Control	(All)	All permission attributes are assigned to the specified user or group.
Special Access	(Variable)	Allows you to assign specific permission attributes instead of using one of the predefined permission sets listed.

When viewing the permission set for a file or directory (by right-clicking, selecting Properties, and then selecting the Permissions tab), double-clicking the entry will bring up its special access dialog box. In Figure C.1, the Server Operators group has the Read and Execute attributes set for the file WRITE.EXE. This is equivalent to the Read permission set listed in Table C.1.

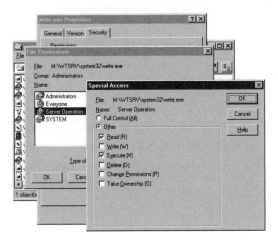

Figure C.1   *Special Access properties.*

Windows NT 4.0 Directory Permissions

Although it's not difficult to assign permissions to files, it wouldn't be practical to set the permissions manually on every file on your Terminal Server. In reality, you'll assign permissions to individual files only in certain situations, and in most cases, you'll assign permissions at the directory level. Windows NT (and henceTerminal Server) uses *permission inheritance* to assign rights to new files or subdirectories created in a directory. What this means is that after you've set permissions on a directory and the files it contains, any new file or subdirectory created in this directory will automatically inherit the rights that you assigned to the parent directory.

Even though directory permissions are built on the same permission attributes as file permissions, the permission sets for directories differ slightly from those for files. The permission sets for directories are described as a pair of attribute sets contained in parentheses, for example (RX)(RX). The first set of parentheses lists the permission attributes for that directory and any subdirectories within it. The second set of parentheses lists the file permission attributes that are set for *existing* files in the directory and automatically assigned to any files that are created within the directory or *copied* into it. If a file is *moved* into this directory, it doesn't inherit these file attributes, but retains any permissions that it had prior to being moved into this directory.

Author's Note

When a file or directory is copied into a directory, it inherits both the file permission set and owner of the target directory. When copying, you're essentially creating a new file that's a duplicate of the original file. This new file will be created with the default file permissions for the target directory.

When moving a file or directory, NT doesn't actually move the physical data on the hard drive, but instead simply moves the file pointer to the target directory. The existing file permissions and ownership remain unchanged.

How permissions are handled when moving a file or directory depends on whether the data will remain on the same disk partition or move to another partition. If it remains on the same partition, NT doesn't actually move the physical data on the hard drive, but instead simply moves the file pointer to the target directory. The existing permissions and ownership remain unchanged.

If the data moves to a different partition, it's treated as a "copy and delete" operation and the permissions are inherited as described above. ♦

There are situations when the file access is defined as (Not Specified). This means that when the permissions are set on the directory, the user or group with this permission doesn't have access to the files in the subdirectory unless the user or group has been granted explicit access to the file(s) afterward. If a file or directory is *copied* into this directory, the user or group won't be assigned any permissions on that object. If a user had access to a file that's *moved* into this directory, he or she will retain that access.

Table C.2 shows the nine permission sets for Windows NT 4.0 directories.

Table C.2   Windows NT 4.0 Default Directory Permission Sets

Permission Sets	Permission Attributes	Description
No Access	(None)	Completely restricts access to the directory and the files contained within it.
List	(RX) (Not Specified)	Provides the rights to list the file and subdirectory names within the directory and to traverse into any of the subdirectories. List does not grant users access to read the *contents* of any file, only the *name* of the file. Access to any of the files is based on existing permissions on those files.
Read	(RX)(RX)	Provides List privileges on the directory as well as Read permissions on files.
Add	(WX) (Not Specified)	Allows the creation or placement of files or subdirectories under the specified directory. Users can traverse into a directory with this permission set but can't list any of the files or subdirectories that it may contain. If a user has sufficient privileges to a file or subdirectory within this directory, the user can access it by knowing its exact filename.
Add & Read	(RWX)(RX)	Combination of the Add and Read permission sets described above.
Change	(RWXD)(RWXD)	Allows the creation, deletion, and updating of files or subdirectories. Also allows the deletion of the directory and all its files. If a user has Delete privileges for a directory but not for a file within that directory, the user can't delete the directory until that file has been deleted by someone with sufficient privileges.
Full Control	(All)(All)	Grants full access to all files and subdirectories.
Special Directory Access	(Variable)	Allows you to assign specific directory permission attributes.
Special File Access	(Variable)	Allows you to assign specific file permission attributes.

Under most circumstances, you'll use the predefined permission sets to establish your file and directory security, although the use of special file and directory access can be helpful in certain situations. The later section "Calculating Permissions" discusses how to determine what permissions a user has when he or she belongs to multiple groups with different permission settings.

The difficult part of file security isn't understanding the permissions, but understanding how to configure these permissions to create a more secure Terminal Server environment. A common problem with Terminal Server stability is the issue of users having too much access to the file system. Appendix D, "Recommended System and Application Volume Security Permissions," provides my suggestions on the security settings you should implement for system and application volumes on your Terminal Server.

Windows 2000 File System Security

Windows 2000 provides thirteen permission attributes, in comparison to the six provided with Windows NT 4.0. Figure C.2 shows some of these permission attributes for a folder called Clients.

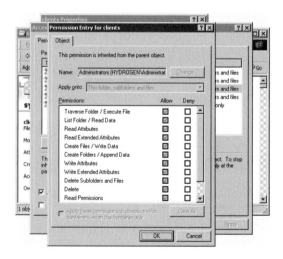

Figure C.2 *Windows 2000 permission attributes.*

Following is a list of descriptions for the thirteen permission attributes. Notice that, by comparison with the NT 4.0 permission attributes, the Windows 2000 attributes have more descriptive names that clearly state what permissions each attribute grants when applied to a folder (directory) or a file.

Author's Note

The abbreviations listed after the descriptions are my convention and not a Microsoft standard. This is simply so that I can more easily describe which permission attributes make up the permission sets that I discuss shortly. When the functionality is the same, only a single description is used. ◆

- **Traverse Folder/Execute File (TFEF).** Equivalent to the Execute permission on NT 4.0, allows you to run an executable file (.EXE, .COM, etc.) or to traverse into a folder.

- **List Folder/Read Data (LFRD).** Allows viewing a folder's contents (file or subfolder names) or a file's contents. This is similar to the NT 4.0 Read permission attribute except that it doesn't grant access to view an object's permissions or its non-security attributes.

- **Read Attributes (RA).** Allows viewing the basic non-security attributes of a file or directory. Some of the most common attributes are Read-Only, Hidden, System, and Archive.

- **Read Extended Attributes (REA).** Allows viewing extended non-security attributes. Extended attributes are usually specific to the type of file and the application that created it. For example, Microsoft Word stores information such as the author, title, subject, and keywords for a document.

- **Create Files/Write Data (CFWD).** Allows you to create files within a folder and to write data to a new file or change data within an existing file. Doesn't allow you to append data to an existing file.

- **Create Folders/Append Data (CFAD).** Allows the creation of new folders within a folder and appending of data to the end of an existing file. Doesn't allow changing data within an existing file.

- **Write Attributes (WA).** Allows writing basic non-security attribute information to a file or folder.

- **Write Extended Attributes (WEA).** Allows writing extended non-security attribute information to a file or folder.

- **Delete Subfolders and Files (DSF).** This permission will undoubtedly introduce a fair amount of confusion to many administrators. Basically, it provides someone with the ability to delete all the files and subfolders within a folder—even if that person doesn't have explicit Delete permissions on any of the objects contained within that folder. This permission can be thought of as applying to a container (the folder) and allowing for the deletion of all objects within that container regardless of individual permissions. This permission is normally granted only to users that have Full Control.

- **Delete (D).** Allows you to delete a file or folder. If you also have the Delete Subfolders and Files permission (described above) on a folder, you can simply delete the folder. If you only have the Delete permission, the folder must be empty or you must also have Delete permission on all objects within the folder; otherwise, the delete operation will fail.

- **Read Permissions (RP).** Allows you to view the security attributes of a file or folder.

- **Change Permissions (CP).** Allows changing the security attributes of a file or folder. If you're the owner of a file or folder, you have the inherent right to change permissions on that object.

- **Take Ownership (O).** Allows you to take ownership of a file or folder. As the owner of one of these objects, you can change permissions even if you have no other access to the object. By default, only the Administrators group has the right to take ownership of a file or folder. Taking ownership doesn't automatically grant you any rights to the object, but once you're the owner you can assign yourself the necessary rights.

Allow and Deny Permissions

The earlier section "Windows NT File Permissions" described the behavior of security permissions for Windows NT 4.0. The permission called No Access explicitly denies access to the assigned user or group from either a file or directory. While certainly useful if you're interested in ensuring that a particular set of users cannot access an area, this permission isn't granular enough for some situations—for example, if you want to explicitly deny write access, but allow read. With Windows 2000, this functionality is available using the Allow and Deny permission check boxes in the Permission Entry list (refer to Figure C.2).

Normally you'll select the appropriate Allow check box next to the attribute that you want to assign to the user or group, but there may be situations where you'll want to select the Deny check box to ensure that, no matter what, the particular user or group will never have access to the corresponding security attribute. This ensures that when the specific permissions for a user are calculated, the user will never have that security attribute. The later section "Calculating Permissions" describes the process used by Windows 2000 to determine the final permissions that a user has on a file or folder.

Windows 2000 File Permissions

Just as with NT 4.0, Windows 2000 provides default permission sets that can be used to grant common security permissions to both files and folders. Windows 2000 also includes five default permission sets for files. Table C.3 shows the permission sets, with the permission attributes that compose each set.

Table C.3   Windows 2000 File Permission Sets

Permission Sets	Permission Attributes	Description
Full Control	(All)	Provides full access to the file, including the ability to change security permissions and take ownership.
Modify	D + (Read & Execute set) + (Write set)	Combines the Read & Execute and the Write permission sets described below, in addition to the Delete permission.
Read & Execute	TFEF + (Read set)	Identical to the Read permission described below, but also includes the ability to launch executable files.
Read	LFRD, RA, REA, RP	Provides the basic ability to read the contents of a file, including data, security, and non-security attributes. This permission set doesn't grant access to launch an executable file.
Write	CFWD, CFAD, WA, WEA	Provides the basic ability to write data to a file. Note that you can't change a file unless you also have the Read permission set.

Just as with NT 4.0 security, Windows 2000 provides the ability to manipulate individual security attributes to fine-tune the privileges available to a user or group. Figure C.3 shows the security properties for a file that has had specific security attributes assigned to it. Notice the text beside the Advanced button in the figure (Additional permissions are present...). This signals that the specified user or group has been assigned special access that can't be defined by all the existing security sets. Only the Write attribute set is selected, which means that all the attributes that make up the Write set have been assigned to the Everyone group. Because the Read set is not selected, we can deduce that whatever other security attributes have been selected, they don't form the complete Read set.

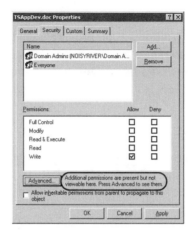

Figure C.3   *Handling special security access in Windows 2000.*

Windows 2000 Folder Permissions

Just as with Windows NT 4.0, Windows 2000 supports the assignment of permissions at the folder level, which are then automatically assigned to any files or subfolders created in that folder. Folder permissions are built on the same permission attributes as file permissions, and have nearly identical attribute sets.

Just as in NT 4.0, when a file or folder is copied into another folder, it inherits both the file permission set and owner of the target folder. When copying, you're essentially creating a new file that's a duplicate of the original file. This new file will be created with the default file permissions for the target folder.

How are permissions handled when a file or directory is moved? When the data remains on the same partition, only the data pointer is updated, so the permissions and ownership remain unchanged. When the data is moved to a different partition, it's treated as a "copy and delete" operation and the permissions *are* inherited as described.

Author's Note

Unlike NT 4.0, Windows 2000 doesn't explicitly have the (Not Specified) file access property for folders. Instead, you use the special folder security set List Folder Contents. The details of this attribute set are discussed below. ◆

Table C.4 shows the six permission sets for Windows 2000 folders.

Table C.4   Windows 2000 Folder Permission Sets

Permission Set	Permission Attributes	Description
Full Control	(All)	Provides full access to all files and folders, including the ability to change security permissions, take ownership, and delete subfolders and files.
Modify	D + (Read & Execute set) + (Write set)	Combines the Read & Execute and the Write permission sets described below, in addition to the Delete permission.
Read & Execute	TFEF + (Read set)	Identical to the Read permission described below, but also includes the ability to traverse into subfolders.
List Folder Contents	Same as Read & Execute.	This security permission set enables you to perform the same operations as the Read & Execute permission set. The only difference between the two is in how the permission set is inherited when applied to a folder. A file can inherit only the Read & Execute permission, while a folder can inherit both.
		For example, suppose a folder has the List Folder Contents (LFC) permission assigned to the Users group. If you copied a file into that folder, the Users group would be able to see it in the folder list, but wouldn't be able to view its contents or execute it. If a subfolder is copied into this folder, the Users group *would* be able to list the contents of that subfolder. If the Users group had Read & Execute permissions on the parent folder instead of List Folder Contents, they would be able to list all subfolders and read or execute the contents of all files in those folders, since the files would also inherit the Read & Execute permission.

continues ▶

Table C.4   *continued*

Permission Set	Permission Attributes	Description
Read	LFRD, RA, REA, RP	Provides the basic ability to read the contents of a folder, as well as security and non-security attributes. This permission set doesn't grant access to traverse into a folder—in other words, you can read what's in the folder but you can't actually get to that folder. For example, dir c:\dir1 would work, but not cd dir1.
Write	CFWD, CFAD, WA, WEA	Provides the basic ability to create a file or folder within a folder.

In most circumstances, you'll use the predefined permission sets to establish your file and folder security, although the use of special file and folder access can be helpful in certain situations. The later section "Calculating Permissions," discusses how to determine what permissions a user has when he or she belongs to multiple groups with different permission settings.

As mentioned earlier, the difficult part of file security is not understanding the permissions, but understanding how to configure them for more security in your Terminal Server environment. See Appendix D for suggestions on security settings for Terminal Server system and application volumes.

Calculating Permissions

A critical part of manipulating file and folder permissions is understanding how Terminal Server collects and reviews these permissions to determine the effective permissions for a user.

Author's Note

Although the examples in this section are based on Windows 2000 security attributes, the process of calculating permissions is identical for Windows NT 4.0. ◆

Consider this simple scenario. Joe User is a member of the groups Senior and Junior. These groups have the following permissions on the file README.TXT:

Senior: Deny (Read & Execute)

Junior: Allow Read

If Joe User tries to access the file README.TXT, will he be able to read the file? The answer to this question depends on how Terminal Server handles the calculation of Joe's permissions.

Terminal Server calculates file and directory permissions using the simple union ($\cup$) of all permission sets assigned to the user as follows.

If a user is assigned to the groups G1, G2, ..., Gn with permission sets S1, S2, ..., Sn (not necessarily different) on a file or folder, the user's permissions on that object will be the permission set resulting from the following calculation:

$$S1 \cup S2 \cup ... \cup Sn$$

The union of two or more permission sets is a new set consisting of all permission attributes that are in at least one of the sets being "unioned." This is made clear by the following simple example.

Sue User is a member of two groups, Marketing and Sales, and they have the permissions Read and Modify, respectively, on the file PROFITS. Sue's final permissions on the PROFITS file are calculated by taking the permission attributes for Read and Modify and calculating the union of those attributes:

```
Read = {LFRD, RA, REA, RP}
Modify = {Read & Execute, Write, D}
       = {LFRD, RA, REA, RP, TFEF, CFWD, CFAD, WA, WEA, D}

Read ∪ Modify
   = {LFRD, RA, REA, RP} ∪ {LFRD, RA, REA, RP, TFEF, CFWD, CFAD, WA, WEA, D}
   = {LFRD, RA, REA, RP, TFEF, CFWD, CFAD, WA, WEA, D}
   = Modify
```

Therefore, Sue will have Modify permissions on the file PROFITS.

After reviewing this somewhat trivial example, you may wonder why I have bothered to go into such detail regarding the union of the permission sets when it appears that permissions are based on the group with the "greater" permissions. Taking the union of Read and Full Control would seem to back up this argument because

```
Read ∪ Full Control = Full Control
```

If you're not convinced of this, simply work through the set union exercise as I did in the example.

The problem is that this simple view of "greater" permissions doesn't work when a user is assigned to multiple groups that may have special permissions assigned to them. Consider another example. We have Sue User, a member of Marketing and Sales. Marketing now has Read & Execute, while Sales has Read + Write + Delete (but not Execute). We take the union of these permission sets to calculate Sue's final permissions for the PROFITS file:

```
{Read & Execute} ∪ {Read, Write, D}
   = {Read & Execute, Read, Write, D}
   = {Read & Execute, Write, D}
   = Modify
```

Therefore, Sue will have Modify permissions.

Notice this time that neither Marketing's nor Sales' group permissions could be considered "greater" when determining final access to the PROFITS file.

Until now, I've purposely avoided the situation where a user is explicitly assigned Deny for a security set or attribute. Let's return to the example mentioned at the beginning of this section: Joe User and the two groups Senior and Junior, with respective permissions Deny (Read & Execute), and Allow Read.

The logical solution is to apply the union of these two sets and determine the resulting values. In my calculation I use the "not" symbol (a solid line) over an attribute to signify that it's a Deny permission instead of an Allow permission. For example, Deny Read appears as shown in Figure C.4.

$$\overline{\text{Read}}$$

Figure C.4   *A solid line over the Read attribute indicates that Read permission is denied.*

Before performing the calculation, we need to add one new rule to the union operation. You have both a Deny and an Allow permission in the same result set in this example. In these situations, the Deny permission *always* cancels out the Allow permission, as shown in Figure C.5.

$$\text{Read} \cup \overline{\text{Read}} = \overline{\text{Read}}$$

Figure C.5   *Deny cancels out Allow.*

We can now easily determine Joe User's permissions, as shown in Figure C.6. The Deny Read overrides the Allow Read and results in the Deny (Read & Execute) remaining in effect on the README.TXT file. Of course, this is a trivial example, and the result is as expected.

Deny (Read & Execute) $\vee$ Read

$= \overline{\text{(Read \& Execute)}} \vee \text{Read}$

$= \overline{\text{Read} \vee \text{TFEF}} \vee \text{Read}$

$= \overline{\text{Read} \vee \text{TFEF}} = \overline{\text{Read \& Execute}}$

$= \text{Deny (Read \& Execute)}$

Figure C.6   *Deny Read overrides Allow Read, resulting in Deny (Read & Execute).*

The use of the Deny permission ensures that the user or group won't be able to exercise the denied permission, regardless of the other permissions assigned to that user or group. This is a very powerful security feature that ensures that users cannot "accidentally" acquire more security rights than they should have.

Author's Note

Under Windows NT 4.0, the Deny option for security attributes doesn't exist, but the No Access attribute is available. Like Deny, No Access takes precedence over any other permissions a user or group may have, denying access to the specified object (file or directory). Granular access to denying only certain security attributes is not available under NT 4.0. ◆

To summarize, permissions on a file or folder are determined for a user by taking the union of all permission attributes assigned to that user, with Deny permissions automatically overriding any equivalent Allow permissions the user may have.

D

Terminal Server System and Application Volume Security Permissions

In this appendix:

- **Windows NT 4.0, Terminal Server Edition**
  This section describes my suggested file security modifications for both
  the system and application volumes.

- **Windows 2000 Terminal Services**
  The file security modifications required for TS 2000 are much simpler
  than those for TSE 4.0. With the more secure application-compatibility
  option in TS 2000, only a couple of permission changes are required.

Windows NT 4.0, Terminal Server Edition

Chapter 8, "Server Management Planning," discusses the default file-
security configuration of TSE 4.0 and how the permissions reflect the
default configuration for Windows NT Workstation 4.0. Unfortunately, this
configuration provides the Everyone group with much more access to the
file system than is required. In order to provide any level of confidence in
the configuration of the server, these permissions must be modified; otherwise, it's only a matter of time before a user inadvertently makes a change
to the system that negatively affects all other users.

This section describes my suggested security modifications for both the
system and application volumes, and provides CACLS scripts that can be
used to implement these changes. Use these suggestions as a starting point
for developing your own security configuration, tailored to meet the
requirements of your Terminal Server installation. In most cases, you'll need

to make modifications to allow your users' applications to function properly in the environment. For more information on security modifications for applications, see Chapter 19, "Application Integration."

> **Tip**
>
> *These base security scripts should be run prior to the installation of any . applications.* ◆

System Volume Permissions

Table D.1 summarizes the suggested security permissions for the directories on your system volume. This list assumes that the Terminal Server system root is X:\WTSRV. Also, instead of explicitly listing all directories, if a directory inherits the permissions set in its parent, I have omitted it from this list. It should also be assumed that, unless otherwise stated, the permissions on a subdirectory *are not* replicated to all child subdirectories. The listed access groups are local Terminal Server security groups.

> **Author's Note**
>
> *I highly recommend taking the time to review all these settings in detail. Although it may be easy to simply apply these permissions, it's important to understand exactly which files they affect. This can be extremely valuable in troubleshooting any application or system-related problems that may arise.* ◆

By default, I've configured permissions only for the local Administrators and Users groups. If you're going to implement additional local groups such as Server Operators, consider defining additional privileges in specific areas where these groups may require more access. Usually, I won't assign additional Server Operator privileges unless a situation explicitly requires it. This helps to keep the initial file system configuration simple.

Table D.1   Suggested System-Volume File Permissions

Directory	Suggested Permissions	Comments
Root (\)	Full Control: Administrators, System Read: Users	These permissions should be replicated down from the root into all sub-directories. You then update the specific permissions on the subdirectories as required.
\boot.ini \ntdetect.com \ntldr	Full Control: Administrators, System	These files contain system boot options and should not be accessible by regular users.

Directory	Suggested Permissions	Comments
\WTSRV\Config	Full Control: Administrators, System	Only required by admins.
\WTSRV\Ctxundo	Full Control: Administrators, System	Only required by admins. Contains MetaFrame uninstall information.
\WTSRV\ICA	Full Control: Administrators, System	Only required by admins. Contains the client database for the ICA Automatic Client Update (ACU) utility.
\WTSRV\INF	Full Control: Administrators, System	Configuration files for Terminal Server installation components, including policy template files. Users don't need access to this directory.
\WTSRV\Profiles\ Administrators	Full Control: Administrators, System	Users should not have access to the administrator's profile.
\WTSRV\Repair	Full Control: Administrators, System	Only administrators need access to this directory.
\WTSRV\System32\ Clients	Full Control: Administrators, System	Contains the files used to create both RDP and ICA client disks. Users typically don't need access to this directory.
\WTSRV\System32\ Drivers	Full Control: Administrators, System	Terminal Server device drivers.
\WTSRV\System 32\ICA PassThrough	Full Control: Administrators, System	Contains a copy of the ICA client that's used by the Shadow Taskbar application to connect and shadow users on remote computers. Regular users normally don't need access to this directory unless you provide access to published applications from within a Terminal Server session (ICA from within ICA).
\WTSRV\System32\ lserver	Full Control: Administrators, System	Contains the Terminal Server license database.
\WTSRV\System 32\ras	Full Control: Administrators, System	Contains the RAS configuration information.

When installing administrative or support software such as Citrix's Resource Management Services (RMS), consider updating your security script or creating additional scripts that ensure that the proper permissions are set on these application directories.

Author's Note

When setting permissions on any additional directories, a good rule is to be as restrictive as possible and then adjust the rights only when required to ensure that the application will function properly for a user. ✦

The following script file sets the security permissions on the system volume as described in Table D.1. You can download this script from the following Web location:

```
http://www.newriders.com/1578702399
```

```
@ECHO OFF

ECHO Setting security permissions on system volume.  Please wait...

REM ** Grant local Administrators and SYSTEM full control
REM ** Grant local Users Read access to the entire volume
REM ** Permissions will then be revoked if necessary.
Cacls X:\ /c /g Administrators:F SYSTEM:F Users:R

Echo y¦Cacls X:\* /T /c /g Administrators:F SYSTEM:F Users:R

REM ** Users do not need access to the system boot files
Cacls X:\boot.ini /e /c /r Users
Cacls X:\ntdetect.com /e /c /r Users
Cacls X:\ntldr /e /c /r Users

REM *** Revoke user access as required ***
Cacls X:\WTSRV\Config /e /c /T /r Users
Cacls X:\WTSRV\Ctxundo /e /c /T /r Users
Cacls X:\WTSRV\ICA /e /c /T /r Users
Cacls X:\WTSRV\INF /e /c /T /r Users

Cacls X:\WTSRV\Profiles\Administrator /e /c /T /r Users
Cacls X:\WTSRV\Repair /e /c /T /r Users
Cacls X:\WTSRV\System32\Clients /e /c /T /r Users
Cacls X:\WTSRV\System32\Drivers /e /c /T /r Users
Cacls "X:\WTSRV\System32\ICA PassThrough" /e /c /T /r Users
Cacls X:\WTSRV\System32\lserver /e /c /T /r Users
Cacls X:\WTSRV\System32\ras /e /c /T /r Users
```

Application Volume Permissions

Configuring the initial application-volume security permissions is much easier than configuring the system volume. In general, you can assign the permissions listed in Table D.2.

Table D.2   Suggested Application-Volume File Permissions

Directory	Suggested Permissions	Comments
Root (\)	Full Control: Administrators, System Read: Users	These permissions should be replicated down from the root into all subdirectories. You then update the specific permissions on the subdirectories as required.

Of course, you need to treat this as the starting point when installing the applications into your Terminal Server. In some situations, you may be required to grant permissions other than Read to certain files or folders for an application to function properly. I always recommend that you start out as restrictive as possible and then loosen up only when required. Make sure that you clearly document these exceptions and place them into a script so that the changes can be reapplied if necessary.

Restricted access to an application can be based on additional security groups if necessary. For example, if you want to restrict access to Microsoft Project, you might create a group called TSE_MSProject_Users and define security on the MS Project directory to allow only that group Read access to the executables.

Author's Note

If you're implementing Citrix's application publishing, you can also manage access to the application through user groups. See Chapter 19, "Application Integration" for implementation instructions on how to publish an application. ♦

The following script file sets the security permissions on the system volume as described in Table D.2. You can download this script file from the following Web location:

```
http://www.newriders.com/1578702399

@ECHO OFF

ECHO Setting security permissions on application volume.  Please wait...

REM ** Grant local administrators and SYSTEM full control
REM ** Grant local users read access to the entire volume.
REM ** Permissions can be adjusted on specific applications if necessary.
Cacls Y:\ /T /c /g Administrators:F SYSTEM:F Users:R
echo y¦Cacls Y:\* /T /c /g Administrators:F SYSTEM:F Users:R
```

Windows 2000 Terminal Services

When installing Terminal Services on a Windows 2000 server, one of the decisions that you had to make was how to set the application-compatibility security permissions. Two choices were available:

- **Permissions Compatible with Windows 2000 Users.** With this option, users have much more restrictive access to both the file system and the registry, requiring more work in order to get applications to run properly in the environment. I always recommend that you select this option and then adjust permissions only as required to get a program to work properly.

- **Permissions Compatible with Terminal Server 4.0 Users.** This option grants users full control to many portions of the registry and file system to be able to run most applications. I *do not* recommend choosing this option.

If you selected the TSE 4.0–compatible option, you can change this setting by starting Terminal Services Configuration, found under Administrative Tools on the Start menu. Click the Server Settings folder and then double-click the Permission Compatibility setting as shown in Figure D.1.

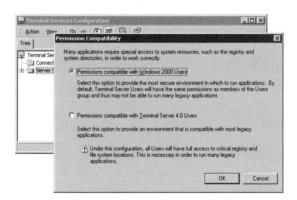

Figure D.1   *The Permission Compatibility dialog box.*

Even after you've enabled the Windows 2000 user permissions, some file-system security changes must be implemented, as summarized in Table D.3.

Table D.3   Suggested Windows 2000 System-Volume Permission Changes

Directory	Suggested Permissions	Comments
Root (\)	Full Control: Administrators, System Read: Users	*Do not* replicate these permissions. They should be applied only to the root folder. This change must be made because, by default, the Everyone group has full control to the root. This is because of a permission requirement set during the installation of Windows 2000.
\boot.ini \config.sys \io.sys \msdos.sys \ntdetect.com \ntldr	Full Control: Administrators, System	These files contain system boot options and should not be accessible by regular users.
\Documents and Settings	Revoke the Everyone group.	The Everyone group's access to this directory should be revoked. Do not replicate the changes into the subfolders.
\Documents and Settings\All Users	Revoke Everyone.	This change should be propagated down through all subfolders.
\Documents and Settings\ Default User	Revoke Everyone.	This change should be propagated down through all subfolders.
\WINNT	Revoke Everyone.	The Everyone group's access to this directory should also be revoked. You *should not* apply this to subfolders, but simply to the WINNT folder.

The following script file sets the security permissions on the system volume as described in Table D.3. You can download this script file from the following Web location:

```
http://www.newriders.com/157 8702399

@ECHO OFF

ECHO Setting security permissions on system volume.  Please wait...

REM ** Grant local Administrators and SYSTEM full control
REM ** Grant local Users Read access to the root of the system volume.
Cacls X:\ /c /g Administrators:F SYSTEM:F Users:R

REM ** Users do not need access to the system boot files
Cacls X:\boot.ini /e /c /r Users
Cacls X:\config.sys /e /c /r Users
```

```
Cacls X:\io.sys /e /c /r Users
Cacls X:\msdos.sys /e /c /r Users
Cacls X:\ntdetect.com /e /c /r Users
Cacls X:\ntldr /e /c /r Users

REM ** Revoke Everyone access to Documents and Settings
Cacls "X:\Documents and Settings" /e /c /r Everyone
Cacls "X:\Documents and Settings\All Users" /e /c /r Everyone
Cacls "X:\Documents and Settings\All Users\*" /e /c /r Everyone
Cacls "X:\Documents and Settings\Default User" /e /c /r Everyone
Cacls "X:\Documents and Settings\Default User\*" /e /c /r Everyone

REM ** Revoke Everyone access to WinNT folder
Cacls X:\WINNT /e /c /r Everyone
```

Author's Note

The application volume permissions on a TS 2000 server can be configured identically to those on a TSE 4.0 server. See the earlier section "Application Volume Permissions" for details. ◆

E

Registry Security Primer

Since its initial release, Windows NT has maintained operating system, user account, and application information in a central repository known as the *registry*. The registry is a special database of information that is a critical component of the operating system, and as such requires the proper protection, particularly in a Terminal Server environment where users have local access not only to the registry, but also to the tools used to manipulate the registry.

The Need for Registry Security

Very often the security of the registry is overlooked on a typical Windows server because it's interactively accessible only from the server's console (when the proper network security is in place). It's of little concern to many people that the Everyone group has full access to many portions of the registry, since only authorized administrators have access to the server room where the hardware resides and sufficient privileges to access the server from the console.

This appendix provides a brief overview of the security of the registry, the security attributes that are available, and the privileges they grant. Appendix F, "Terminal Server Registry Security Permissions," summarizes my suggestions for the base security that should be implemented on a Terminal Server.

Registry Components

Under Windows 2000, the layout, security attributes, and manipulation tools are nearly identical to those used in Windows NT 4.0. The major difference between the two registries is in the user interface for updating the registry key permissions. Figure E.1 shows the REGEDT32 tool under Windows 2000, along with the advanced permissions dialog box for registry security.

Figure E.2 shows the same REGEDT32 tool under Windows NT 4.0 with the equivalent permissions dialog box open.

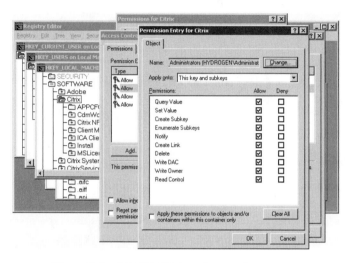

Figure E.1   *REGEDT32 under Windows 2000.*

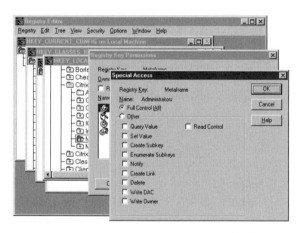

Figure E.2   *REGEDT32 under Windows NT 4.0.*

The registry consists of the following five components, commonly called *subtrees* or *hives*:

- HKEY_LOCAL_MACHINE (HKLM). Contains all the information pertaining to the configuration of the Terminal Server. This includes the hardware, software, and system configuration, as well as the local security account information.

- HKEY_USERS (HKU). This registry hive contains profile data for all users who are currently logged onto the Terminal Server, listed by SID. In addition to USERS, the DEFAULT subkey is also always present. When a user logs off the server, his or her profile information is unloaded from this hive. When a user logs on, his or her profile information (either from a roaming profile or a local profile) is loaded into this hive. Figure E.3 shows an example of the HKEY_USERS hive with six active user sessions.

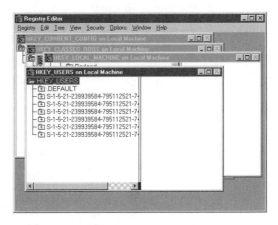

Figure E.3   HKEY_USERS *hive.*

- HKEY_CURRENT_USER (HKCU). This is simply a pointer into the HKEY_USERS hive for each individual user. Within your Terminal Server session, HKEY_CURRENT_USER will point directly to your profile information subkey within the HKEY_USERS hive.

- HKEY_CLASSES_ROOT (HKCR). This is a pointer into the HKEY_LOCAL_MACHINE\SOFTWARE\Classes subkey and contains all of the file-association information as well as OLE class configurations.

- HKEY_CURRENT_CONFIG (HKCC). This is also a pointer, this time to the subkey HKEY_LOCAL_MACHINE\SYSTEM\CurrentControlSet \Hardware Profiles\Current. This subkey contains the server's current hardware configuration information.

Registry Security Permissions

Much like file security, registry security consists of permission attributes and standard permission sets. This section starts by examining the 10 permission attributes for the registry as shown in Table E.1. These permission attributes are the same for both NT 4.0 and Windows 2000.

Table E.1   *Registry Permission Attributes*

Permission Attribute	Abbreviation	Description
Query Value	(Q)	Grants access to read the value of a key. If you don't have this permission, the key will appear grayed out and you won't be able to view either the key values or any subkeys under that key, even if you have the Enumerate Subkeys permission.
Set Value	(S)	Allows access to set or modify the value of a key. This doesn't grant permission to add or delete keys.
Create Subkey	(C)	Allows the creation of a new subkey under the selected key.
Enumerate Subkeys	(E)	Allows the generation of a list of all subkeys under the selected key. To view subkeys under a given key, you must also have the Query Value permission.
Notify	(N)	Grants the right to monitor notification events from the key. This means that if a change occurs in the key, the user with this right will automatically receive notification of the change.
Create Link	(L)	Allows the creation of a symbolic link from one key to another.
Delete Key	(D)	Grants access to delete the selected key. You can't delete a registry key unless you also have the Delete Key permission on all subkeys that it may contain, since these subkeys must first be deleted before the parent key can be deleted.
Write DAC	(W)	Allows the modification of the Access Control List (ACL) for the key. (DAC stands for *discretionary access control*.)
Write Owner	(O)	Grants the right to take ownership of a key. If you're the owner of a key, you have the inherent permission to modify the Access Control List (Write DAC permission).
Read Control	(R)	Grants the right to view the security data associated with the key.

Just as with the file system, permission sets exist for the registry. These permission sets are a predefined group of security attributes that are grouped together to provide a certain level of permissions. But unlike the file system, which has a robust list of permission sets, the registry provides only two, as listed in Table E.2.

Table E.2   Default Registry Permission Sets

Permission Set	Set Attributes	Description
Read	(QENR)	This set defines the basic read access to keys and values, including viewing the existing security permissions.
Full Control	(All)	As the name suggests, this permission set provides full control over subkeys and values.

Unfortunately, no permission set exists that would grant only a "Change" permission. You have only the option of granting Read or Full Control. If you want to grant a user or group anything other than Read permission, you have to assign individual permissions.

You should never grant a non-administrator group full control to any registry key (with the exception of the group's HKEY_CURRENT_USER key) unless absolutely necessary. In many situations, the Read permission set is appropriate.

Author's Note

For example, Chapter 19, "Application Integration," talks about the installation of Office 2000 on Terminal Server; one of the requirements is granting users the ability to write to the HKEY_CLASSES_ROOT\CLSID key. The users in that example were not given Full Control, but instead were assigned the individual permissions Query Value, Set Value, and Create Subkey. ◆

Windows 2000 Allow and Deny

Just as with the file system, Windows 2000 provides the ability to explicitly allow or deny a permission attribute or set. This has an advantage over the Windows NT registry security in that you can ensure that a user or group won't have access to a certain privilege—regardless of the other groups to which they belong. As long as they've been explicitly denied access, this will override any other attributes. Figure E.4 demonstrates the use of the Deny permission. In this example, the Power Users group has explicitly been denied access to create links, write security settings, or take ownership of a registry object. Someone who belongs to the Power Users group—even if he or she also belongs to a group with the Full Control permission set—would be prevented from performing the denied actions.

Figure E.4   *The Deny permission setting.*

Windows 2000 Permission Inheritance

Another feature that has carried over from the file system to the registry is the capacity of an object (in this case a registry key) to automatically inherit security permission changes made to the parent key. Just as with the file system, in many situations the listed permissions are grayed out and can't be edited (see Figure E.5).

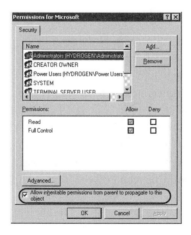

Figure E.5   *Inherited permissions.*

Notice that the check box labeled "Allow Inheritable Permissions from Parent to Propagate to This Object" is also selected. This means that the permissions are being inherited by the parent object and can't be edited here. You can override the assigned behavior by selecting the opposite state for the permission (Allow or Deny). You can also grant privileges in addition to those that are being inherited, but you can't modify or change inherited permissions unless you deselect the inherit permissions check box. When you do so, the dialog box shown in Figure E.6 appears. Here you have the option to specify how you want security on the object configured now that you're breaking its inheritance with the parent object. You can make a copy of the inherited permissions, which you can then edit; or you can choose to remove all inherited permissions, keeping only those permissions that have been explicitly defined on the object. In most cases, this will result in an empty authentication list unless you have explicitly added additional permissions.

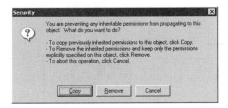

Figure E.6   *Preventing the propagation of inherited permissions.*

Figure E.7 shows a simple example of how inherited permissions work. In the first picture you see the parent key Software with its two subkeys Citrix and Microsoft and their respective subkeys. The gray folders signify inherited permissions, so right now all subkeys would have these permissions:

Administrators   Full Control

Users   Read

In the second picture, the inheritance in the Citrix key was broken and the Users group permissions were removed. At this point, a change in the permissions of the Software key would automatically update only the Microsoft and RDP subkeys. The Citrix key would not be affected. An interesting point to note is that the inheritance for the ICA subkey was never changed, even though the Citrix inheritance was broken. So when the Users group was removed from the Citrix DAC (discretionary access control) list, the permissions would also be reflected in the ICA subkey.

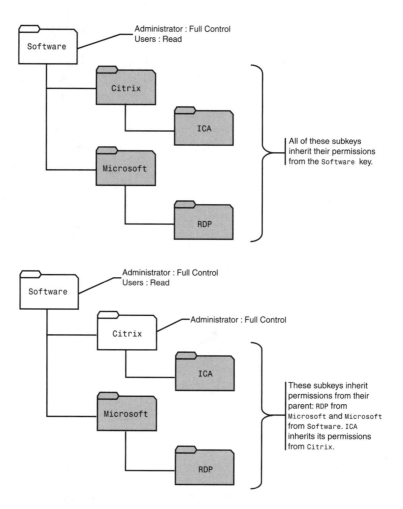

Figure E.7   *Inherited permission example for registry keys.*

Warning

*After deselecting the Allow Inheritable Permissions... option, you're free to rese-
lect it, but inheriting from the parent is not automatically re-enabled. If you want
to reinstate inheritance, you need to select the Advanced option from the parent
key and select the check box for the option Reset Permissions on All Child
Objects and Enable Propagation of Inheritable Permissions. Doing so will remove
any explicitly defined permissions that you or anyone else may have set on all subkeys, as well as automatically selecting the Allow Inheritable Permissions option
on these keys.* ◆

Calculating Permissions

Registry permissions are calculated the same way as file permissions, through the union of all permission attributes. Remember that any attributes set to Deny automatically take precedence over those set to Allow.

For more information, see the "Calculating Permissions" section of Appendix C, "File and Folder Security Primer."

Registry Hive Files

The registry hives are stored in a set of files located in the folder %systemroot%\System32\Config. Table E.3 lists the registry hives and associated files. All the listed files have an associated file with the same name and the extension LOG. Each file is essentially a backup of its associated registry hive and provides a means of recovering the registry in case of a system failure during a write operation.

Table E.3   Registry Hive Files

Registry Hive	Hive Filename
HKEY_LOCAL_MACHINE\SAM	SAM and SAM.LOG.
HKEY_LOCAL_MACHINE\SECURITY	SECURITY and SECURITY.LOG.
HKEY_LOCAL_MACHINE\SOFTWARE	SOFTWARE and SOFTWARE.LOG.
HKEY_LOCAL_MACHINE\SYSTEM	SYSTEM and SYSTEM.LOG.
HKEY_USERS\DEFAULT	DEFAULT and DEFAULT.LOG.
HKEY_CURRENT_USER	NTUSER.DAT. This file is not stored in the Config folder with the other files, but instead resides wherever the user's profile is retained. User profiles are discussed in Chapter 17, "User Profile and Account Configuration."

REGEDT32 and REGEDIT

Both Windows 2000 and Windows NT 4.0 ship with two registry-manipulation tools, REGEDT32 and REGEDIT. Either tool can be used for performing most general registry updates, but there are certain situations where one tool provides a functional advantage over the other. Following are the two main differences in the tools:

- **REGEDT32.** Allows you to manage the security configuration of the registry. REGEDIT doesn't provide any security functionality, so if you need to set permissions on a key or configure auditing you have to use REGEDT32.

- **REGEDIT.** One of REGEDIT's biggest advantages is the ability to perform a full-text search of keys, values, and data. REGEDT32 allows only the searching of the registry keys.

F

Terminal Server Registry Security Permissions

In this appendix:

- **Windows NT 4.0, Terminal Server Edition**
  This section describes my suggested registry security modifications for TSE 4.0.
- **Windows 2000 Terminal Services**
  Unlike TSE 4.0, a Windows 2000 Terminal Server's registry is much more secure when the server has been configured for Windows 2000 application compatibility.

Warning

Although I have had success with implementing security modifications to the registry, it doesn't guarantee that these changes will work under all circumstances. Whenever editing the registry, please use caution and ensure that you have a backup of the registry and a current Emergency Repair Disk. Incorrect changes to the registry could render your system inoperable. ◆

Windows NT 4.0, Terminal Server Edition

Chapter 8, "Server Management Planning," discusses the importance of registry security and how the default configuration for TSE 4.0 was too lax, allowing the Everyone group to have Full Control access to large portions of the registry.

Author's Note

Microsoft has issued a security bulletin (#MS00-008) with regard to an area of the registry containing lax security that could be exploited to allow a person to gain elevated privileges on the server. The bulletin includes a simple utility that updates the permissions on the potentially exploited areas. Even if you're not considering applying registry security to your Terminal Server, I recommend that you apply this security patch. This issue applies only to TSE 4.0, not TS 2000. For more information, see this address:

`http://www.microsoft.com/technet/security/bulletin/fq00-008.asp` ✦

This section describes my suggested security modifications to the registry, along with suggestions on how these changes can be implemented. Just as with the security suggestions covered in the earlier appendixes, these changes should be taken as a starting point for developing your own complete security configuration for your environment. Security changes may be necessary to accommodate the requirements of an application. For more information on security modifications for applications, see Chapter 19, "Application Integration."

Tip

The base registry security should be set prior to the installation of any applications. ✦

Although the registry's security requirements are similar to those of the file system, the overall assignment of security in the registry is much more difficult. The problem is that in certain situations, applications may have a legitimate reason for writing to the registry. Fortunately, more and more applications are adhering to the standard of writing machine-specific information to HKEY_LOCAL_MACHINE while maintaining user-specific information in the user's personal profile (HKEY_CURRENT_USER).

To accommodate these special security requirements, much of the security in the registry must be handled on a key-by-key basis. Table F.1 summarizes the most common registry security changes that I make. As mentioned in Chapter 8, the security changes are concentrated in the keys under the HKEY_LOCAL_MACHINE\Software key. The other root keys (HARDWARE, SAM, SYSTEM) are configured during the Terminal Server installation to grant only Read access to non-administrator accounts. The HKEY_USERS keys are handled by the user's profile.

Author's Note

Due to a limitation in the current implementation of REGINI, the local Users group cannot be scripted as part of the security update. If you plan to use REGINI to script security, you'll have to settle for using the Everyone group. This is why the permissions in Table F.1 contain references to the Everyone group. If you plan to update security manually or are using an alternate tool that supports the Users group, you can replace Everyone with User.

Although I use REGINI in this example, it's certainly not the only tool that could be used to perform this task. A number of commercial and shareware registry-management and administration tools are available. One example is Aelita's MultiReg (www.aelita.com). Regardless of the tool that you use, you should still exercise caution and be sure to test your script prior to running it on any production server. ✦

Table F.1   Suggested Registry Security Changes for the SOFTWARE *Key*

Key (SOFTWARE)	Suggested Permissions	Comments
\	Full Control: Administrators, System	These permissions should not be replicated.
	Read: Everyone	
\Citrix	Full Control: Administrators, System	This key contains MetaFrame configuration information. Users don't need access to this key. The permissions should be replicated to the subkeys.
\Classes	Full Control: Administrators, System	This key contains all the information on file associations as well as installed classes (such as ActiveX). By default, users can't edit this key using a registry editing tool, but they can update options through other means such as updating associations through the Options menu in NT Explorer. This is because of the privileges granted the INTERACTIVE group. I suggest removing access for this group and replicating the changes to all subkeys.
	Read: Everyone	

continues ▶

Table F.1   continued

Key (SOFTWARE)	Suggested Permissions	Comments
\Description	Full Control: Administrators, System	Users don't need access to this key. Replicate to all subkeys.
\Microsoft	Full Control: Administrators, System Read: Everyone	These changes are applied to the Microsoft key and all subkeys except NetDDE, which by default provides no access to the Everyone group.
\ODBC	Full Control: Administrators, System Read: Everyone	Replace permissions on subkeys.
\Policies	Full Control: Administrators, System Read: Everyone	These permissions are already set appropriately and don't need to be adjusted.
\Program Groups	Full Control: Administrators, System Read: Everyone	
\Secure	Full Control: Administrators, System Read: Everyone	
\Windows 3.1 Migration Status	Full Control: Administrators, System Read: Everyone	Replace permissions on subkeys.

When installing additional applications or administrative support tools, be sure to review any Software keys that may be added during the installation and ensure that the appropriate security has been set. Monitoring registry changes is discussed in Chapter 19.

In general, there are two options available for making security updates to the registry. The first option is to manually update the security on the appropriate keys. While this option is somewhat tedious, the fact that the majority of the permission changes are cascaded down into the subkeys does help to speed things up. If you look at the directories located under the SOFTWARE key immediately after installation, between 10 and 15 would need to be updated. In general, each has its appropriate permissions set and then cascades down into all subkeys. In situations where I have implemented these security changes, they haven't prevented a user from being able to log onto a Terminal Server, although they need some updating during the application-integration phase to ensure that users can run their applications.

Author's Note

If you attempt to manually update the permissions on the HKLM\SOFTWARE\Microsoft\Windows NT *key and replace permissions on subkeys, you may receive the error shown in Figure F.1. Even though the error appears, if you select any of the subkeys under this key you'll notice that the security permissions have been updated as requested.* ◆

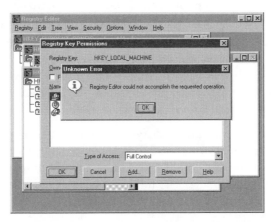

Figure F.1   *Error when manually updating permissions on all subkeys under the* Windows NT *key.*

The other option, instead of manually updating the registry key, is to use the REGINI tool to script the necessary permission changes. The following script is a sample file that could be processed by REGINI to update the permissions on the Citrix key. The numbers within the square brackets represent the security permissions to be set. The numbers correspond as follows:

1	Administrators, Full Control
17	SYSTEM, Full Control
8	Everyone (World), Read

For a complete list of the available permissions, refer to the REGINI.DOC file that accompanies the utility.

```
HKEY_LOCAL_MACHINE\Software [17 1 8]
        Citrix [1 17]
            APPCFG [1 17]
            CdmWorkStation [1 17]
                CurrentVersion [1 17]
            Client Management [1 17]
                ICA Client Update [1 17]
                    CurrentUpdates [1 17]
            ICA Client [1 17]
                4.0 [1 17]
                    WFCMGR32 [1 17]
                PASS THROUGH [1 17]
            Install [1 17]
                Software [1 17]
                    Citrix [1 17]
        MSLicensing [1 17]
            Store [1 17]
```

Unfortunately, much of the registry is unique to the installation, and currently no option is available that would tell REGINI to cascade permission changes down to all of the subkeys. If you want to develop a script to update the permissions for your SOFTWARE key, you need to do the following:

1. Use the REGDMP utility to get a dump of your current SOFTWARE contents. The output contains a list of all keys and values within this key and most likely will be around 2MB in size. The follow command dumps the information to the file called SOFTWARE.TXT:

   ```
   regdmp HKEY_LOCAL_MACHINE\Software > Software.txt
   ```

2. After you have the output file, you need to update it so that the necessary permission information is contained within the square brackets. To do this manually would take a large amount of time, probably between 2 and 3 hours. The following is an example of the contents of the ODBC key as captured in the output file:

   ```
   ODBC [17 1 8]
       ODBC.INI [17 1 8]
           Hydra License [17 1 8]
               Driver = X:\WTSRV\System32\odbcjt32.dll
               DBQ = X:\WTSRV\System32\lserver\Hydra.mdb
               DriverId = REG_DWORD 0x00000019
               SafeTransactions = REG_DWORD 0x00000000
               UID = sa
               Engines [17 1 8]
                   Jet [17 1 8]
                       ImplicitCommitSync = Yes
                       Threads = REG_DWORD 0x00000003
                       UserCommitSync = Yes
           ODBC Data Sources [17 1 8]
   ```

```
            Hydra License = Microsoft Access Driver (*.mdb)
ODBCINST.INI [17 1 8]
    Microsoft Access Driver (*.mdb) [17 1 8]
        UsageCount = REG_DWORD 0x00000001
        Driver = X:\WTSRV\System32\odbcjt32.dll
        Setup = X:\WTSRV\System32\odbcjt32.dll
        Name = Microsoft Access Driver (*.mdb)
        APILevel = 1
        ConnectFunctions = YYN
        DriverODBCVer = 02.50
        FileUsage = 2
        FileExtns = *.mdb
        SQLLevel = 0
    ODBC Drivers [17 1 8]
        Microsoft Access Driver (*.mdb) = Installed
```

Unfortunately, two additional situations complicate this problem:

- First, if REGINI detects a permission that it can't evaluate to one of its known types, it won't display the [ ] permission information at all. This means that you may have key names with no preexisting security information. This makes it much more difficult to perform a search-and-replace action to update the security information.

- Second, permissions are not set on any key values, so all lines that contain an equal (=) sign can actually be ignored.

3. To ease the process of creating a scripted registry security update file to use with REGINI, I have created a simple KixTart script called ConfigRegFile.kix that parses the output of REGDMP, removes all value entries, and assigns a standard security permission of [17 1 8] to each registry key under SOFTWARE. This script looks for the input file called SOFTWARE.TXT and creates an output file called SOFTWARE_SEC_UPDATE.TXT. To use this script, simply run it from the same directory where you have the REGDMP output file called SOFTWARE.TXT by executing the command:

```
kix32 ConfigRegFile.kix
```

The generated file can then be used with REGINI by simply executing this command:

```
REGINI software_sec_update.txt
```

4. If you want, you can modify the security on specific keys directly in the SOFTWARE_SEC_UPDATE.TXT file prior to running REGINI against it. For example, you might remove the Users Read access from the Citrix key.

For more information on KixTart, see Chapter 19.

The contents of ConfigRegFile.kix are shown below. You can download this script file from the following Web location:

```
http://www.newriders.com/1578702399
```

```
; This script will take an output file from REGDMP as input,
; then remove all value entries (contain = sign), including those
; that extend across multiple lines using the '/' continuation
; character. At the same time, all valid registry keys are
; updated with the standard permissions [17 1 8] and written to
; the output file called 'software_sec_update.txt'. This file can
; then be used as input for REGINI to update the security on the
; registry.
; The assigned permissions are:
; Administrators = Full Control
; System         = Full Control
; Everyone       = Read
;
; Author: Todd Mathers, Copyright (c) 2000
;
; You may freely modify and use this script as required within
; your Terminal Server environment. If you have any
; suggestions or comments please feel free to contact me at
; TSEBook@NoisyRiver.com

BREAK ON

$Continued = 0

; open the output file for reading
if Open(5, "software.txt", 2)  = 0

   ; now open the output file
   if Open(6, "software_sec_update.txt", 5) = 0

      "Processing the output file. Please wait"
      $x = ReadLine(5)
      while @ERROR = 0
            ; process the line
            ; if it contains an '=' ignore it and any continuations
            if (InStr($x, "=") = 0)
               ; now check for an existing '['
               $y = InStr($x, "[")
               if $y > 0
                  ; replace the existing security with the
                  ; desired permissions
                  $x = SubStr($x, 1, $y - 1) + "[17 1 8]"
               else
                  ; it didn't have a security setting, so
                  ; simply append one
                  $x = $x + " [17 1 8]"
               endif
```

```
            ; now write it out to the output file
            $z = WriteLine(6, $x + Chr(13) + Chr(10))
            if $z <> 0
                "The write operation failed." ?
                exit
            endif
        else
            ; ignore any continuation lines

            while (SubStr('$x', Len($x), 1) = "\")
                ; signals the next line is a continuation of the current line
                ; so we can pull it now
                $x = ReadLine(5)
            loop
        endif
        $x = ReadLine(5)
    loop
  endif
endif
```

Windows 2000 Terminal Services

When installing Terminal Services on a Windows 2000 server, one of the decisions that you had to make was how to set the application-compatibility security permissions. Two choices were available:

- **Permissions Compatible with Windows 2000 Users.** With this option, users have much more restrictive access to both the file system and the registry, requiring more work in order to get applications to run properly in the environment. I always recommend that you select this option and then adjust permissions only as required to get a program to work properly.

- **Permissions Compatible with Terminal Server 4.0 Users.** This option grants users full control to many portions of the registry and file system in order to be able to run most applications. I *do not* recommend choosing this option.

If you selected the TSE 4.0-compatible option, you can change this setting by starting Terminal Services Configuration, found under Administrative Tools on the Start menu. Click the Server Settings folder and then double-click the Permission Compatibility setting as shown in Figure F.2.

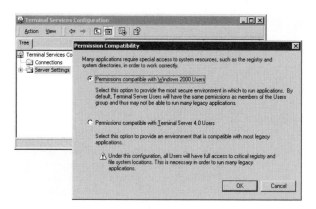

Figure F.2   *The Permission Compatibility dialog box.*

Fortunately, once the Windows 2000 user permissions have been enabled on your Terminal Server, the server's registry is much more secure than the default registry configuration for a TSE 4.0 server.

One possible area of concern is the permissions granted to the Power Users group. This group is maintained to allow a means of granting users access to run certain legacy applications. Instead of adding users to this group, I recommend instead that you modify the required file or registry permissions to support a user's access to a particular application. The Power Users group grants too much access for any regular user on a Terminal Server. Luckily, after a clean install of Windows 2000 and Terminal Services, no users by default are made members of the Power Users group.

As long as users are never added to the Power Users group, the Windows 2000 registry security permissions, coupled with additional group policy restrictions, such as limiting access to the registry editing tools, should provide a secure registry environment. For more information on implementing group policies, see Chapter 16, "Group and System Policy Configuration."

Tip

One trick I use is to configure user rights so that if someone is a member of the local Power Users group, he or she won't have sufficient privileges to log locally onto the Terminal Server or to access the computer from the network. ◆

User rights can either by managed through the Local Security Settings tool on the Terminal Server or via the domain using group policies. Figure F.3 shows one of the settings from within Local Security Settings. I discuss the basic security configuration of a Terminal Server in Chapter 12, "Terminal Server Configuration and Tuning."

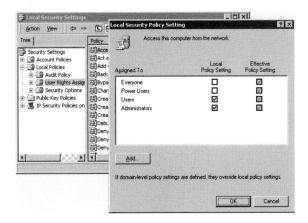

Figure F.3   *Configuring user rights to deny Power Users access to a Terminal Server.*

Index

Symbols

A

E

G

H

M

Q-R

Selected Titles from the
New Riders Professional Library

Sandra Osborne:

Windows NT Registry
ISBN: 1-56205-941-6

Mark T. Edmead and Paul Hinsberg:

Windows NT Performance: Monitoring, Benchmarking, and Tuning
ISBN: 1-56205-942-4

Karanjit Siyan:

Windows 2000 TCP/IP
ISBN: 0-7357-0992-0

Ted Harwood:

Windows NT Terminal Server and Citrix MetaFrame
ISBN: 1-56205-944-0

Eric K. Cone, Jon Boggs,
and Sergio Perez:

Planning for Windows 2000
ISBN: 0-7357-0048-6

Sean Baird and Chris Miller:

SQL Server System Administration
ISBN: 1-56205-955-6

Stu Sjouwerman and Ed Tittel:

Windows 2000 Power Toolkit
ISBN: 0-7357-1061-9

Roger Abell, Herman Knief,
Andrew Daniels, Jeffrey Graham:

Windows 2000 DNS
ISBN: 0-7357-0973-4

Lori Sanders:

Windows 2000 User Management
ISBN: 1-56205-886-X

Jeffrey A. Ferris:

Windows 2000 Deployment & Desktop Management
ISBN: 0-7357-0975-0

Doug and Beth Sheresh:

Understanding Directory Services
ISBN: 0-7357-0910-6

Michael J. Martin:

Understanding the Network
ISBN: 0-7357-0977-7

Gilbert Held:

Understanding Data Communications, Sixth Edition
ISBN: 0-7357-0036-2

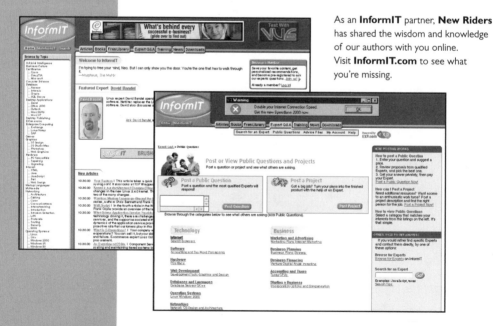
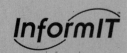